# 1981 YEARBOOK

## EVENTS OF 1980

Symbol of a turbulent year: the eruption of Mount St. Helens, the first active
volcano in the continental U.S. since 1915.

# FUNK & WAGNALLS NEW ENCYCLOPEDIA 1981 YEARBOOK

LEON L. BRAM
Vice-President and
Editorial Director

NORMA H. DICKEY
Editor in Chief
Yearbooks and
Special Projects

ROBERT HALASZ
Editor

**Funk & Wagnalls**

a company of
The Dun & Bradstreet Corporation

ISBN 0-8343-0036-2

# TABLE OF CONTENTS

# MEMBERS OF THE STAFF

**EDITOR**                        Robert Halasz

**MANAGING EDITOR**               Irna Gadd

**SUPERVISING EDITORS**           William Golightly
                                  Marjorie Joyce
                                  John Milward
                                  Steven Moll
                                  Peter K. Reinhart

**PRODUCTION CHIEF**              Frank A. Petruzalek

**PICTURE EDITOR**                John Schultz

**DESIGNERS**                     Maggie Jarvis
                                  Erla Sigurdardottir

**COPY EDITORS**                  Charlotte R. Gross
                                  Judith K. Johnson
                                  Stephan O. Parnes

**INDEXERS**                      Charles Paul May
                                  Gerard Wallace

**PICTURE RESEARCHERS**           Donna Dennis
                                  Leonora Morgan

**EDITORIAL ASSISTANTS**          Susan Edwards
                                  Jane Knutila
                                  Dorian Kreindler

**PRODUCTION EXECUTIVE**          Edward Haas

# FOREWORD TO THE EVENTS OF 1980 YEARBOOK

Recession and double-digit inflation dogged the United States in 1980, provoking discontent that culminated in the ouster of Jimmy Carter and the election of Ronald Reagan as the fortieth President. All over the world, slow economic growth, and often actual economic decline, were registered under the impact of inflation, high oil prices, and uncertain food supplies. War between Iraq and Iran threatened the Western world's oil supplies and was expected to lead, once more, to higher prices. Cold war tensions revived as the U.S., alarmed by the Soviet invasion of Afghanistan, sent naval forces to the Indian Ocean and adopted draft registration. The Soviet Union could take little pleasure in the West's problems, with its forces bogged down in Afghanistan, unrest in neighboring Poland, and another poor grain harvest that would mean lower meat supplies.

Some political figures, among them Indira Gandhi in India and Pierre Elliott Trudeau in Canada, returned to power in 1980; others, including President Tito of Yugoslavia and the deposed former shah of Iran, passed from the scene permanently. Zimbabwe, formerly Rhodesia, became an independent nation during the year.

The earth itself was restless, as deadly earthquakes struck Algeria and Italy and Mount St. Helens erupted in the state of Washington. Awesome views of the planet Saturn, its rings, and its satellites were provided by the Voyager I spacecraft. Major advances in gene splicing were reported by researchers. All this, plus the Olympic Games, a new congressional scandal, the flight of Cuban refugees, the hostage drama, and much more occurred in 1980.

THE EDITORS

# Looking into the Eighties

by JOSEPH C. HARSCH

*A veteran news correspondent both at home and abroad, Joseph C. Harsch has written for the* Christian Science Monitor *since 1929. He has also been a commentator for all three major networks.*

At the beginning of the 1980's, the American people find themselves moving into a phase in their national experience for which they are poorly prepared. The times ahead will test their adaptability to a changing environment.

Most Americans were born and grew up in a country of expanding wealth and power. Now they are hemmed in by limitations on that power and wealth. Their enjoyment of prosperity has been curbed by a near-doubling of the price of gasoline in one year. Their proudest and most typical industry—automobiles—is staggering under a flood of foreign imports. Their President attempts to lead the Atlantic allies as his predecessors were accustomed to do, but he finds himself having to let the allies rewrite the policies of the alliance to their taste.

The change in what America and an American President can and cannot do is illustrated by the contrast between what President Dwight D. Eisenhower could do during the Middle East crisis of 1956 and what President Jimmy Carter could not do during the Middle East crisis of 1980.

In October, 1956, three of America's friends—Great Britain, France, and Israel—invaded Egypt against the wishes of the U.S. government and in defiance of warnings from Washington. Publicly, President Eisenhower took the case to the United Nations.

Privately, he told the three associates that there would be no Western Hemisphere oil and no financial or economic aid until they had broken off the assault on Egypt and withdrawn from Egyptian territory.

The troops of the three stopped shooting at Egyptians on Nov. 6. The British and French withdrew from Egyptian territory on Dec. 22. The Israelis withdrew on March 1, 1957, from the whole of the Sinai Peninsula. They had stalled as long as they could. President Eisenhower was insistent.

In other words, in 1956 an American President could order the country's closest ally, Britain, its then strongest continental ally, France, and its client, Israel, to cease and desist from purposes of their own. And he was obeyed.

During the first five months of 1980 the current President attempted to marshal the allies for a policy of strong sanctions against Iran over the American hostages in Tehran, and stronger sanctions against the Soviet Union over the invasion of Afghanistan. At the same time he tried to persuade Israel to cease and desist from establishing new settlements on occupied Arab territory and to proceed toward negotiating self-government for the Arabs of the West Bank and Gaza Strip who have been under Israeli military occupation since the 1967 war.

*Computer-programmed robots at a Chrysler Corp. plant perform sheet welding for Chrysler's new K cars, the Plymouth Reliant and Dodge Aries. Increasing automation will be needed if American automobiles are to compete successfully against foreign imports.*

*A cartoon expresses the disarray in the Western alliance resulting from Washington's inability to obtain agreement on strong sanctions against Iran in retaliation for the imprisonment of American hostages.*

*Despite international censure and perceived damage to U.S. Mideast peace efforts, Israelis march in support of establishing further settlements on Arab territory occupied since the 1967 war.*

*Soviet troops and equipment in Afghanistan. Unable to gain effective sanctions against Iran, President Jimmy Carter was equally unsuccessful in seeking meaningful measures to punish Moscow for invading Afghanistan.*

Left: The building of the Verrazano-Narrows Bridge, in New York City, linking Staten Island with Brooklyn. This project epitomized U.S. engineering skill during the early 1960's.

In all three purposes President Carter was frustrated. The West European allies watered down the policy of sanctions against Iran until the subject was dropped in alliance discussions. They paid lip service only to sanctions against Moscow. And the Israeli parliament responded to pleas for a resumption of talks with Egypt aimed at Arab autonomy on the West Bank by passing a law reaffirming that all of Jerusalem (including East Jerusalem, occupied since 1967) is the nation's capital.

The Truman-Eisenhower-Kennedy era was a high point in American wealth, prestige, power, and influence. During that era the United States probably was closer to being able to dominate the world than any single country ever had been before. Its industry, modernized and expanded to meet the needs of the grand alliance in World War II, was buoyant and productive. Its products were the most advanced. Its factories were the latest. Its work force was the most experienced. Everyone wanted the products of that industrial fabric. It provided them, bountifully.

During those years Germany and Japan were still recovering from defeat and war damage. The Soviet Union had yet to repair the terrible toll to its main industrial centers from enemy occupation and bombing. France had stagnated under the German occupation. Britain was triumphant but weary. All but the Soviet Union needed to draw on American resources for recovery. So long as they needed American help, and the proceeds of American industry, they had to be respectful of American wishes.

American aid in the form of the Marshall Plan helped put Western Europe back on its feet after World War II. Top: The Cologne Cathedral, damaged by blasts and shells, rises above the rubble of other historic structures in this West German city. Bottom: The restored cathedral and its rebuilt environs.

For two decades following World War II, the U.S. was the only superpower with global reach.

Jubilant residents of West Berlin greet an American airlift plane bringing supplies to the embattled city in 1949. Soviet authorities blockaded all land traffic between West Berlin and West Germany for 11 months but failed to wrest control of West Berlin from the three Western Allied powers.

U.S. Army troops patrol the demarcation line separating North Korea and South Korea following the end of the conflict there in 1953. At a cost of 33,629 American lives, U.S. intervention kept North Korea from annexing the South.

President John F. Kennedy addresses Americans on TV following the announcement that U.S. spy planes had photographed secret Soviet missile bases in Cuba. The subsequent U.S. limited naval blockade resulted in Soviet removal of the missiles and a major cold war victory for Washington.

During that era the U.S. saved Berlin from the Soviet blockade, made good the independence of South Korea, put an abrupt end to Communist infiltration in Lebanon, stopped the invasion of Egypt by America's own allies, and made possible the economic recovery of its allies and of its former enemies, Germany and Japan.

It was a golden age of American power during which a surging American economy could sustain armies and fleets of sea and air that could and did dominate the world. America was not only a superpower but also the only superpower with global reach. The Soviets had decisive regional power but little capacity to project that power beyond their own frontiers. In the test of strength and will of the Cuban missile crisis, the Soviets backed down and took their missiles home. This was one of the prime humiliations of history. Moscow resolved that the Soviet Union would not again be so humbled in the eyes of the world.

Americans have tended to assume that the conditions of the golden age were ordained from above and intended by the Deity to last forever. Yet those conditions were unusual, not normal. The exhaustion of other industrial nations due to war was temporary. Their financial and economic weakness was temporary. Their military weakness was bound also to be temporary. And the Soviet Union had the industrial capacity and skill also to become a global power.

In 1980 Americans bumped up against the results of change. The temporary and abnormal conditions that had made the U.S. the single and dominant

*While other nations rebuilt their factories, the facilities of many American industries gradually became obsolete. Top: Steelworkers protest the loss of jobs resulting from sales lost to cheaper foreign steel. Bottom: An antiquated steel plant in Dearborn, Mich.*

great power had disappeared. The other powers had recovered from exhaustion, had rebuilt their factories, had regained economic and financial health, and had again developed respectable and significant military power.

The most important single manifestation of the change is the fact that the U.S. has ceased to be a net exporting country. By 1980 Americans were buying from the outside world more than the outside world wanted or needed from America. An annual trade deficit had become normal.

From World War II down almost to 1980, the world needed and wanted the products of American industry. But American industry did not keep in step with modern technology. The U.S. is still in the lead in some of the new industries; computers are a prime example. But in the older industries— automobiles and steel—U.S. companies lived off accumulated fat and became obsolete. Japan, West Germany, Sweden, France, and Italy are all producing vehicles competitive with the major automobile companies of Detroit.

The trade deficit meant a declining dollar. A declining dollar meant reduced leverage for Washington in the rest of the world. Guns are not the only means to power and influence. A surplus of goods wanted by others and a sound currency are just as important—some would say more so.

*An assembly line at a California factory is shown producing computer parts for both domestic use and export. Computer business thrives as one of the major export industries in the U.S.*

Economic health is the foundation of military power and diplomatic influence. By 1980 the U.S. was sinking toward the condition that characterizes the Soviet position in today's world. The Kremlin resorts to military power for extending its influence because it has few other means of leverage.

American industry has fallen behind in many of the older branches, but Soviet industry never caught up. Moscow has little to offer that others want except guns, gold, and oil. And the oil is beginning to run low. By the end of the 1980's the Soviets may well be needing, and insisting on getting, some of the Middle Eastern oil that still flows so copiously toward the West.

Soviet backwardness in consumer goods and the basic inefficiency of the Soviet economic system have not kept Moscow from making steady progress in weapons. There is ample military power at the disposal of the Kremlin. But there will be a fascinating competition during the 1980's between a Soviet effort to regain economic momentum and an American effort to get back into the industrial forefront.

As 1980 opened, both the Soviet and U.S. economies were in a condition of semistagnation. Soviet national income growth for 1979 was only 0.7 percent, one of the poorest annual performances since World War II. The U.S. growth rate for 1979 was a mediocre 2.7 percent.

Two reasons lie behind the slowdown in the Soviet economy, and both will be particularly difficult for Moscow to overcome. Energy production has slowed

*While many U.S. industries have fallen behind foreign competitors, Soviet industry has never caught up. Its auto production owes much to imported technology. Energy production has slowed well below plan, with an actual decline in coal production during 1979.*

*A sign at the occupied U.S. Embassy in Tehran expresses the opinion of much of the world. U.S. dependence on foreign oil is a major reason why America is seen as weak.*

well below plan. In 1979 there was an actual decline in coal production. Natural gas continued to increase, as did oil, but the rate of increase in oil was down to 2.4 percent. Most projections for Soviet oil production anticipate an early leveling off and a probable beginning of a decline by the end of the decade. Natural gas production will probably parallel the decline in oil production.

Accompanying this decline in the prospective supply of energy is the growing likelihood of labor shortage. The average expansion of the work force dropped to 1 percent annually in the 1970's, with no compensating increase in productivity. Inefficient agricultural and industrial methods and the heavy demands of the armed services for manpower mean that the Soviet economy is approaching a labor shortage. Soviet methods are wasteful of labor by Western standards, but there is no sign that the government is willing to consider any easing of the rigid central control of the economy.

If during the 1980's Moscow could learn to use its existing work force more efficiently and could at the same time find new sources of energy, a resumption of rapid economic growth would be possible. But since neither of those changes is in sight, the prospect is for a continued slow growth rate right through the decade.

In the U.S. there is no inherent reason comparable to those two in the Soviet condition to prevent a quicker American recovery. It would take considerable optimism to think that by 1990 the U.S. will have gained full independence from imported oil. But already the release of domestic oil from unrealistically low price levels, plus the rapid rise in prices of imported oil, have reduced imports to the point where oil is, at least temporarily, a glut on world markets. And progress toward energy self-sufficiency could come from increased coal production, a start at producing synthetic fuels, and a rapid expansion of solar technology.

No labor shortage exists in the U.S. now and none is in prospect; indeed, modernization of obsolete sectors of the economy calls for increasing automation. As the old automobile assembly lines are scrapped and replaced, the auto work force should decline by at least half. Some Japanese plants are said to use one twentieth of a U.S. factory work force to produce the same number of vehicles.

The chances are that by the end of the decade the

U.S. economy will be moving ahead comfortably while the Soviet economy will still be hobbled by both energy and labor shortages and by the general inefficiency of the centralized state system.

But no amount of economic recovery is likely to restore to the U.S. the position it occupied during the Truman-Eisenhower-Kennedy golden era. The conditions that created, or permitted, that position were unique. American predominance in most of the world was due to the weakness and exhaustion of others. The rest of the world is no longer weak or exhausted.

Vast areas of poverty and misery still remain in the world. Most of Latin America and Africa and much of Asia await some accident or formula or leader to lift

*The Third World seeks advanced technology to lift itself out of poverty. Above: Philippine farmers learn efficient, scientific rice-farming techniques. Below: An Indian farmer employs camel power, an age-old technique for harvesting sugarcane.*

*Afghan rebels pose atop a downed Soviet helicopter. Even Moscow's satellites and clients are showing signs of restiveness under Soviet "leadership."*

them across that vital line that separates stagnation from economic advancement.

But there are also countries in the so-called Third World that have crossed that line and are now generating jobs faster than people. They have tasted the joys of a rising standard of living. At the same time has come political independence, which can appear in the eyes of others as assertiveness.

The "first" and "second" worlds are also becoming increasingly restive. Western Europe values its alliance with the U.S. but demands a fair share in the policies of the alliance, as witness its refusal to follow Washington's lead with regard to the Iran and Afghan crises.

This new assertiveness plagues Moscow even more than Washington. Rumania has refused to applaud or even condone the invasion of Afghanistan. Poland would obviously break out of the Soviet orbit were it not for 20 Soviet divisions on one side of it in East Germany, 5 to the south in Czechoslovakia, 2 in Poland itself, and another 66 in western Russia. Iraq, not long ago seemingly a client of the Kremlin, is seeking new ties with the West. Angola, Ethiopia, and even South Yemen show signs of restiveness under Soviet "leadership." And Afghanistan is far from pacified.

Moscow's troubles with its satellites and clients spring largely from the fact that it has so little other than weapons to offer them. If they want help in improving their industries or in obtaining consumer goods, they must largely look outside the Soviet orbit. In contrast, the U.S. is the keystone of a vast, worldwide trading community held together more by mutual economic interest than by power.

Guns are the main and often the only cement of the Soviet empire. And Afghanistan is providing an interesting example of the price to be paid for using them.

Since the Soviet resort to guns in Afghanistan, the U.S. has tabled SALT II, put détente into the deep freeze, and given serious thought to closer relations with China. Communist parties around the world have indicated their dismay. Several of them have become less amenable to Soviet influence. The whole world has been made uneasy and less likely than before to want to traffic with Moscow. Continuing Afghan resistance makes it likely that, as in the case of the U.S. in Vietnam, Moscow must either send in a much larger force or be satisfied to occupy only the main cities and highways.

Probably there will be other times and places where Moscow will be tempted to expand its empire either by employing its own troops or through proxies such as the Cubans in Angola and Ethiopia. However, each such action is likely to cause the rest of the world to tend to draw together for mutual protection.

The U.S. and the Soviet Union are still the most powerful countries in the world, but no longer in the sense that prevailed during the first 25 years after

*A Soviet patrol surveys some of the vast area bordering on China. Fearful of its neighbor, the Soviet Union deploys nearly a third of its land, air, and strategic forces along the Chinese frontier.*

*Numbering more than 4,000,000 men, the Chinese army is the world's largest. A combination of North America, Western Europe, Japan, and China can outgun and outnumber the Soviet Union in every category.*

World War II. Western Europe has not only recovered its economic vitality but collectively is again a formidable military power. China has the world's largest armed forces. Although the equipment is mostly out-of-date, the sheer numbers, approximately 4,360,000, are enough to command respect. The Soviets respect them sufficiently to deploy nearly a third of their land, air, and strategic forces along their Chinese frontier—46 army divisions compared to 31 in Central and Eastern Europe on the NATO front.

It seems reasonable to expect that throughout the decade of the 1980's the Soviet Union will continue to do its utmost to expand its influence chiefly by military means, because it will be lacking in other, more lasting instruments of influence. Barring some radical change in leadership, when Leonid Brezhnev drops the helm the Soviet economy is likely to continue to stagnate and hence be unable to satisfy other than the military needs of its clients.

It is equally reasonable to think that the U.S. will continue at the center of the non-Communist world, because it is the strongest among those who do not wish to be controlled from Moscow. But U.S. interests must depend on improving cooperation on a mutual basis with like-minded countries, rather than by relying only on its own military power. A combination of North America, Western Europe, Japan, and China can outgun and outnumber the Soviet Union in every category. But keeping this potential coalition in sound condition will require more emphasis on diplomacy than was necessary during the period when others had no choice but to follow where Washington led. Washington will have to cultivate allies, instead of taking them for granted. No longer will there be an automatic Western alliance.

The condition of the world ten years from now will depend heavily on how well Washington reads the realities of today and learns to cultivate friends. It will depend also in important part on how successful the U.S. is in modernizing the obsolete segments of its economy.

If the U.S. does a good job in both departments— cultivating friends and modernizing its industry—it will be in a safer and stronger position than it is today. But if it should fail in either or both of these departments, and if at the same time the Soviet economy manages to break out of its stagnation— then we would all be living in another and different world in which Moscow would be the influential center of events.

Arms will play a role, yes, but Moscow's use of guns also makes enemies for Moscow. Other nations must keep up their defenses to the point where Moscow's guns do not become decisive and dominant. But the race between the U.S. and Soviet economies will probably play a more important role in determining the relative influence of Washington versus Moscow at the end of the decade.

*A Grumman Corp. aerospace design engineer is shown using a recently developed computer graphics system to visualize and develop the configuration for a new military aircraft. Such sophisticated scientific techniques are needed to enable the U.S. to maintain industrial and military world leadership.*

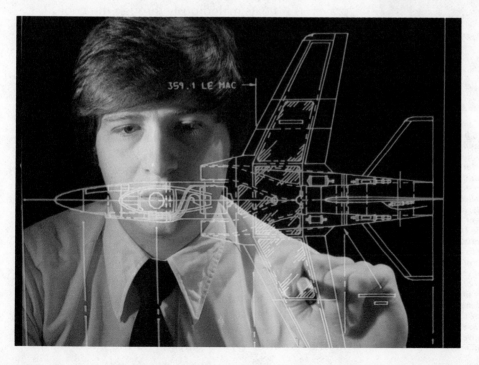

21

# Understanding ISLAM

by WILFRED CANTWELL SMITH

*Wilfred Cantwell Smith, a Canadian, has been professor of comparative religion at McGill University in Montréal and director of the Institute of Islamic Studies there; director of the Center for the Study of World Religions at Harvard University; and chairman of the department of religion at Dalhousie University in Halifax, Nova Scotia. In 1978 he returned to Harvard as professor of comparative history of religion and chairman of the Committee on the Study of Religion. He is an ordained minister of the United Church of Canada and the author of several books on comparative religion and Islamic affairs.*

**A**gainst the still background of the first streaks of dawn, in any city or hamlet of the Islamic world, one hears, if awake in time to listen, the *adhan* call to prayer as it floats melodiously through the cool morning air; a splendid recitative, voiced from some nearby mosque, full of artistic beauty and for the Muslims themselves, of course, full of rich meaning. For them it is no small matter that the same call, at the same times of day, in the same sonorous Arabic, is heard throughout the Muslim world: from the southern Philippines and parts of China, throughout Indonesia, in many parts of India and throughout Bangladesh and Pakistan, Central Asia and Iran, to the eastern and southern Mediterranean and down into Africa. It is a large world; its participants form a large community; Islam is in every sense a great affair. The Muslim, in Singapore, Cairo, or Timbuktu, does not feel isolated, but is vividly conscious of belonging to a living community spread across the globe.

He is conscious also of that community stretching back in time, to a past glory of which he is aware and proud. The same call to prayer, with its serene dignity, has been repeated five times each day now for 14 centuries. By his prayer, and the faith that it

*One of the great achievements of Islamic art is the Persian miniature, exemplified in this photograph of a 16th-century painting depicting Muhammad. Note that the face of the Prophet has been removed, because of an Islamic tradition of frowning upon the representation of living beings.*

23

*The Dome of the Rock in East Jerusalem, built upon the site where, according to Muslim tradition, Muhammad ascended to heaven. It was erected over the rocky outcrop believed to be the altar place of the Temple built by Solomon.*

expresses, the Muslim is firmly related to a past that stands imposingly behind him, bequeathing him traditions and institutions that made his ancestors great.

A thousand years ago his civilization was in the forefront of world affairs. Fables of its magnificence have been preserved for our children in the *Arabian Nights*. Before the West had emerged from the Dark Ages to build its Gothic cathedrals or to elaborate its scholastic theologies or to organize its feudal system, it was Muslim centers that were writing the poetry and the letters of credit, deploying the navies and developing medicine and natural science, carrying forward Greek philosophy and playing with crossword puzzles. (Things are different now; yet, a modern Muslim may speculate, who knows how things will once again stand a thousand years hence?)

Above all, the call relates the worshiper to God. Essentially, it is a personal call, to each Muslim, to pray. The call to prayer, and the many other symbols and rites and habits through which his faith is expressed and mediated, lift the individual out of his humdrum workaday world into a setting not only of time and place but one that centers on God.

No religious movement is a matter simply of ideas; it is carried forward both in individual lives and in institutions. Nonetheless, Islam, perhaps more than any other religion, has constructed a highly systematic outlook—a framework of ideas through which its adherents have looked out upon the universe and have interpreted all the details of their lives. This view of the world differs from the corresponding Western world view, especially that of the modern West. Islam has been a civilization as well as what the West calls a religion. Thus, to understand it in relation to the West it must be compared not only to Christianity and Judaism but to Western civilization at large. This is a critical point, and a source of much mutual misunderstanding.

For the Westerner, there seem to be two realms, a secular and a religious; and most Westerners think of the first as perhaps more basic. Some, even while calling themselves Christian or Jewish, may ascribe little importance to religious matters; others, even when taking these seriously, may hold them apart from their everyday activities. In any case, especially regarding religious positions other than their own, they think of them as added on to a basically secular existence. Not so for the Muslim: his framework integrates all of life into a complex whole—government, politics, and art, as well as his devotional practices. This contrast is the situation today. It was not always so in Christendom. Church and state were linked more closely in medieval times, as were culture and faith. (And again today there is a surge in the United States of conservative religious groups back to the political arena.) There is, too, a minority among Muslims, converts to the Western position, who are seeking a secular understanding of much of their lives. Yet most Islamic and Western peoples are separated by their radically divergent views of the universe—religious on the one hand, and secular plus perhaps some religion on the other.

The Western outlook derives from the fact that Western civilization has two sources: Greece and Rome on the one hand, and Palestine on the other. From the latter come Christian and Jewish religion, from the former come philosophy, government, law, grammar, and science. The two traditions have sometimes been in harmony, sometimes in conflict, sometimes have interpenetrated, but have never fused. Islamic civilization, and the Islamic world view, have in contrast been unitary. Whereas the Christian Church developed during its formative

*Ritual flagellation by Shi'ite Muslims commemorating the martyrdom of Husain, a grandson of Muhammad killed in 680 A.D. Under persecution the Shi'ites developed a tradition of suffering in a righteous cause. The Shi'ite form of Islam later became the national religion of Persia, which was renamed Iran in 1935.*

This time exposure shows Muslim pilgrims, clad in white, circling the Kaaba—the main shrine of Islam—in Mecca, Saudi Arabia. Every Muslim physically and economically able to do so is required at least once in his lifetime to make a pilgrimage to Mecca, where Muhammad was born and first preached the Muslim faith.

centuries as a somewhat peripheral or persecuted minority (like the Jewish community later) in a society that other people were responsible for running—in economic, political, military ways—Muslims from the beginning were responsible for ordering their own society: organizing its administration, collecting its taxes, leading its armies, establishing its culture. Their world view was appropriate to this task. The Islamic enterprise was from the start a venture to construct on earth a right or just social order.

## The View from Islam

The faith of Muslims, as of Jews and Christians, is monotheistic—a development from the same Near Eastern tradition. God is utterly central, and He is one—this is constantly recited, written, sung, chanted. While some Westerners share a similar vision, others have to some degree forgotten how the world looks and feels to those who take God seriously and perceive everyday things and all human life as held together in divine power. Furthermore, Christians, for instance, speak much of mystery, and for them God as Trinity is finally incomprehensible; for Muslims revelation is clear (*mubin*), straightforward, dependable. (In the complexities of the 20th century, this may be Islam's principal problem, as well as its continuing strength.)

Alongside God's oneness and awesome supremacy is His primary attribute of mercy. The interpretation of this mercy, over against His power, has fluctuated historically. Both are deeply embedded in Muslim consciousness.

Fundamental to the Islamic perception both of God and of humankind is the matter of will. The universe came into being and is sustained (and will some day vanish) through God's will. The Koran is the revelation of God's will. The primary quality of human life, accordingly, is the moral.

*Indian girls study the Koran at a Muslim school. More than 200,000,000 Muslims live on the Indian subcontinent, in India, Pakistan, or Bangladesh.*

From the Supreme Reality all other realities are sensed as derivative, and to it they remain secondary. Human beings too are seen and felt as subordinate to God, and yet as being in very special, very close, relation ("He is nearer to us than our jugular vein," says the Koran). For they have been given not only existence but also freedom. They are therefore responsible. (The freedom is not absolute; but the moral responsibility is the fundamental theme of Islamic doctrines of man.)

When God created the universe, He made it orderly, prescribing behavior that nature must observe. Men and women, however, were created conscious and free. For them too there is an ordained pattern, which they ought to follow: there is a right way for human beings to live, in relation to God and to one another. Unlike the stars and the palm trees, however, people may choose whether to conform or not. To undertake to live in accord with the enjoined norms is to be *Muslim* (this is what the word means: "he who surrenders to God's will"). The alternative is to reject in principle the claims of morality on humankind (or anyway, on oneself)—to be a rebellious "infidel."

This view presupposes that right and wrong are known. This is the second great element in the Islamic outlook, again contrasting with modern Western ideas. Muslims hold that God in His mercy has not left humankind without guidance in these matters. As soon as He created man and woman, He told them what they should do and what they should refrain from doing. Adam, that is, was the first "prophet." The last is Muhammad, whom God chose as His messenger to convey His final, perfect revelation to humanity. This is the Koran, and the authoritative commentary on it that Muhammad's sayings and deeds have been interpreted as providing. Now that this revelation is available, two things are clear: what is the right way to live, both individually and corporately, and the enormous importance of so living. On earth, society structured in accord with these cosmic principles will of course be sound, will flourish, will endure. For eternity, also, the stakes are high indeed: Heaven and Hell. Accordingly, the followers of Muhammad have faithfully undertaken two mighty missions: to construct on earth a society in accord with the ordained Muslim norms, and to invite all humanity to join in this supreme endeavor.

*Islamic architecture often makes use of older building traditions. This mud brick spiral minaret in Samarra, Iraq, displays the ziggurat form characteristic of temples in ancient Babylonia.*

In principle, the responsibility for implementing the vision rests with the community as a whole and each of its members. They have in fact entrusted the task of interpreting the various details of the revealed moral system to a learned class (not an ordained clergy). The task of organizing and administering the community politically was formerly given to a caliph, but this system of government endured only for a time. In any case, it remains the duty of all Muslims, individually and collectively, to see to it that the vision is carried out.

For a thousand years or so the enterprise on the whole worked well—impressively well. Islamic history was marked by such a striking measure of both worldly and spiritual success as to confirm Muslims in their conviction not only of the rightness of their cause but also of the rightness of their understanding of the universe. Other factors were at work in their "success," in addition to this grand world view—political, economic, technological, even climatic. Of crucial importance was the piety, the moral commitment, the personal faith of the individual participants.

No ideal works out ideally in concrete situations,

*A Muslim wedding in oil-rich Kuwait illustrates the impact of the West on contemporary Islam.*

of course. Many of the world's religious groups have ways of dealing with this tendency to failure—the doctrine of "original sin," for example. Some claim that earthly matters are less important than "otherworldly" concerns. Some feel that religion must be involved only in private, personal affairs, leaving public and social matters to other groups. The West's tendency, especially in modern times, has been to relegate to the religious sphere these otherworldly and personal matters, retaining in its secular grasp all the rest of life. Some Westerners even imagine that this pattern is "natural." In the Islamic instance this has not been the case; here the explicit assignment has been to establish and maintain a good society on earth.

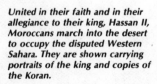

*United in their faith and in their allegiance to their king, Hassan II, Moroccans march into the desert to occupy the disputed Western Sahara. They are shown carrying portraits of the king and copies of the Koran.*

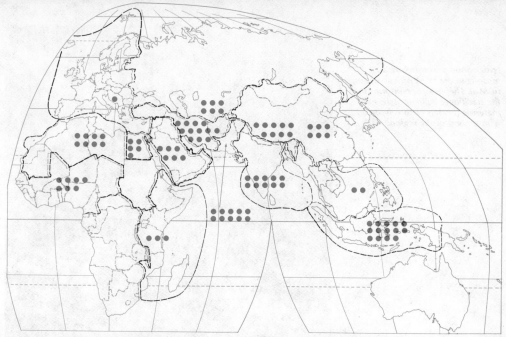

*World population of Muslims, by major regions. Each dot represents 1 percent of the world Muslim population, which totals perhaps 600,000,000.*

### The Historical Experience

Islamic history so far may be seen as falling roughly into three major periods, which one may call the classical, the medieval, and the modern. (The first corresponds in time to much of the West's medieval period.) The classical period was Arabic-speaking. It saw prodigious expansion of Arab empires centered at Damascus (Syria), later Baghdad (modern Iraq), and still later also Córdoba (Spain). It was marked by brilliant achievements in economics, science, and culture. The destruction of Baghdad (and of the caliphate) by the Mongols in 1258 may be taken as marking the end of this age.

After a short phase of difficult readjustment, a medieval period followed, of still greater expansion and further brilliance. Arabic continued to be spoken in what are today the Arab countries, and as a learned classical tongue elsewhere, but Persian, and presently also Turkish, Urdu, Malay, and many other local languages, flourished strongly, and some great literatures were produced (especially in Persian, its poetry among the world's most impressive). In the 16th century A.D., the Ottoman Empire ruled the eastern Mediterranean world (and the Balkans almost to Vienna). The Safawid empire in Iran and the

31

*Friday noon prayer before a mosque in the West African nation of Mali. The mosque conforms to the traditional building style and materials (beaten earth reinforced with timber) of the region.*

Mogul empire in India were also majestic, powerful, and still expanding. The spread of Islam in Central Asia, in what is now Indonesia, in sub-Saharan Africa, and elsewhere, showed continued vitality, success, and confidence.

During this period three new religious developments may be noted. All have to do with the historical fact that while from the 14th century Muslim "success" in mundane terms continued often brilliantly, yet the political and religious aspects were at this point somewhat less closely integrated with each other than in classical times. The first of the three is the development and expansion of the Sufi movement—perhaps one of the richest, deepest, and certainly most widespread mystic movements in human history. Second is the crystallization of the shari'a ("Islamic Law"), a systematizing of the moral demands into a somewhat abstract code, a fixed pattern of rules.

Thirdly, and of interest to Westerners at the present time, is the coming to power, in Iran, later spreading to most of the population there, of what had earlier been a rather small dissident minority, the Shi'ah group or sect. The Shi'ites had felt that "the establishment" in the Islamic world had "betrayed the revolution," failing to implement the pure theory of the Islamic ideal. (Most Muslims—more than 85 percent today—are Sunni, who by and large went along with the official or standard development of Muslim thought and practice.) At first, the Shi'ah movement mounted an active opposition, but unsuccessfully; and under persecution it developed a tradition of martyrdom and of suffering in a righteous cause. Presently, it shelved its activist resistance and adopted a different form of social idealism, a futuristic hope for a divinely guided leader (imam), to come in God's good time. Separate community loyalties for Sunnis and Shi'ites have been fairly strong, and at times hostility between them has continued sporadically. Nonetheless, in overall perspective the differences between them have not been great.

One difference became important: In Iran, the clergy were financially and otherwise quite independent of the government and therefore had closer ties to the populace than was the case in most Sunni countries.

*Iranians pray during an antigovernment rally in Tehran shortly before the fall of the shah. The Shi'ite clergy has historically been quite independent of the government and therefore has close ties to the populace.*

Black inmates exchange greetings at the entrance to a mosque in a Pennsylvania prison. The World Community of Islam in the West (popularly known as Black Muslims) has gained many adherents among U.S. blacks.

Modern Islamic history, of the 19th century and on into most of the 20th, has been marked by a reversal of fortune. The Islamic movement has suffered a major setback to its history of mundane success. There has been an inner loss of creativity and also the onslaught of a rival and mightier force, the West, which during the modern period has asserted—almost as suddenly as did Islam before—military dominance, scientific prowess, and cultural creativity. Materially and spiritually aggressive, it has challenged Islam at every level.

By 1900, most Muslims were subjects of a European power. No proud and sensitive people accustomed to supremacy adjust easily to being pushed around by outsiders. In the Islamic case, this was especially poignant because of the link between worldly success and personal piety. A profound malaise set in. Some intellectuals developed modernized, Westernized outlooks advocating "liberal" or "modern" patterns of government, morality, and culture. Yet in certain cases (for example, Iran) these patterns soon proved not merely alien but corrupt, tyrannical, and destructive. In other cases some sort of synthesis or compromise between Islamic-derived and Western-derived ways has seemed possible or even necessary; yet the needed loyalty to achieve or to maintain it has not always been available. The question of morale is never unimportant in a society; and the Islamic world has few sources for any morale other than Islamic. (In the West, the Greco-Roman source has been available, to supplement the Judeo-

Christian—though some Westerners are beginning to doubt whether a nonreligious source will suffice even there.)

But the tide may be turning. Muslims have been struck by increasing signs that Western civilization may in its turn be now declining. And in very recent years many Muslims have begun to feel that the recent era of Islamic weakness and subjection may perhaps be drawing to a close. The increase in the world price of oil in the 1970's was religiously important. Some Muslims began to feel that perhaps God was not letting Islamic history down after all. It was exhilarating for some to sense that the Islamic world, with its oil deposits (placed in Muslim lands by divine providence?), might no longer be victim of the powerful but now vulnerable West.

Both in the West and in the Islamic world there are some who are searching for mutual understanding, for cultural and even religious collaboration, for avenues to a truly world civilization. It is not clear, however, that either side as a whole has the inner power to rise to this. Both in the West and in the Islamic world there are also those who see the two systems as radical alternatives. Among these, disdain of the other, and hostility and bitterness, reign. If these sentiments prevail, both Islam and the West may lose. For one thing, there are other movements on the world stage, such as Communism, to be reckoned with. Beyond that, it is possible that the two are in fact linked by another haunting question, on which their future, separately and jointly, depends: whether the West itself will in coming decades advance or collapse.

*Wealthy Arabs in Kuwait stand beside their Mercedes while inspecting properties in the oil-rich emirate. The increase in the world price of oil is religiously important; many Muslims feel oil deposits have been placed in their hands by divine providence.*

# America, What's Cooking?

by ORSON BEAN

*The versatile Orson Bean has appeared on the stage in dramas, comedies, and musicals; in nightclubs as a stand-up comedian; and on TV as a host of variety shows. His eating habits are equally variable.*

America is a country that was founded, populated, and made great by people who got up and left where it was bad to come to where it might be good. The Jews who left Russia, the Italians who left Sicily, the Irish who left the potato famine waved good-bye to countless friends and relations who chose to remain where they were. There were no Freddie Laker flights in those days for a quick trip home to see mom; good-bye was good-bye. So they took what they could of their culture with them—and what they held onto most strongly was the way they ate. Nothin' says lovin' like something from the oven—or the wok or the skewer. America is called the great melting pot, and the culinary nature of the metaphor is no coincidence. Within one generation, new Americans dress, talk, and act differently. Almost everything about them changes—but the way they eat stays the same. And they share it and we become family.

My mother's people were longtime Yankees, but my paternal grandparents emigrated from Scotland and Ireland. I grew up in Cambridge, Mass., during the 1930's. There was a depression, and I remember

Illustrations by John Faulkner

*"At breakfast time it was my job to 'watch the toast'.
. . . If my mind wandered . . . the burning smell reached
my mother's nostrils first."*

the day my father lost his job and walked home from
Boston to save the nickel on the subway. The
preparation and consumption of food became the
most important daily event in my life. I recall only
four or five kinds of breakfast cereal in my
childhood. Shredded Wheat came packaged nine
biscuits to a box, three rows of three. Between the
rows were pieces of cardboard on which were
printed, in blue ink, pictures of famous American
Indians. Wheaties featured sports stars on its
package, and Checked Rice had the Lone Ranger.

Kellogg's Corn Flakes boxes held no interest for
me. Old man Kellogg had invented his product for
adults as a substitute for spicier foods which, he
claimed, promoted an unnatural interest in sex. My
grandfather turned me on to Grape-Nuts, which I ate
only to please him. They were, in those days, tougher
in consistency than they are today, and getting
through a bowl of them was like trying to consume a
handful of BB's—it could kill half the morning.

At breakfast time it was my job to "watch the
toast." In the beginning we made our toast on a
small metal frame that rested over the gas burner on
our stove. Then we graduated to an electric toaster.
It had two little doors and the bread was toasted on

one side at a time. If my mind wandered while toast watching, as it frequently did, the burning smell reached my mother's nostrils first and her yells reached my ears. I hated the taste of scraped toast, but we couldn't afford to waste a slice of bread. Much later in my life an ad appeared in the Boston *Globe* announcing a miraculous new invention: the automatic toaster. "The toast pops up to let you know it's ready," the ad read. Many years later still, after I'd grown up and left Boston, I picked up a copy of the New York *Times*. Macy's had yet another toaster for sale: "The toast glides up noiselessly," the ad read. "No annoying pop-up."

Margarine, which was then called oleomargarine, was sold uncolored, like a bar of lard. A little envelope of orange powder, packaged separately inside the box, would be sprinkled over the bar in a bowl and then the whole thing squished through the fingers until the color was spread fairly uniformly through it. One day a great advance appeared on the market. The oleo came sealed in a transparent plastic pouch with a bright orange dot that looked like an M&M candy inside it. The squishing was now nonmessy—a boon to my life. The reason that margarine, for so long, could not be sold precolored was that the powerful dairy industry wanted it that way. They finally solved the problem by buying the margarine companies.

In this time of cereals like FrankenBerry, Cap'n Crunch, and Count Chocula, when I am appalled to see my children polish off two-thirds of a box, I force myself to remember the days when I would spread Hershey's syrup on a slice of white bread and then top it off with Marshmallow Fluff. I am here to tell the tale today, and they will be here tomorrow.

Fruits and vegetables in the 1930's were available only when locally in season. Strawberries, unspeakably delicious, appeared in the spring and after three weeks or so were gone for another year. Ditto melons, asparagus, and the oh-so-anticipated sweet corn of late August.

In our family, as in other depression families, food was stretched over a period of several days. Sunday chicken (dinner at noon—the evening meal was cornflakes) would produce chicken croquettes on Monday and soup on Tuesday. Yesterday's mashed potatoes were formed into patties and panfried to be served as a main course. Food wasn't purchased and stored for the week as it is today. We had a wooden icebox in the kitchen, and it was my job after school each day to empty the pan of water from underneath where the drippings from the ice collected. I never remember being able to do so without sloshing it down the front of my pants, to my habitual embarrassment. Our icebox, unlike the giant two-door, juice-dispensing refrigerators of today, held relatively little. When I was sent to the store to buy provisions, they were usually for a meal to be cooked within the hour.

A loaf of bread at the A&P cost 4¢. Hamburger was 15¢ a pound for regular grind, 17¢ for premium. Since our usual purchase was a quarter of a pound, my mother always reminded me to ask the butcher for premium. For some reason this embarrassed me. Cookies, on the rare occasions that we bought them, were sold in bulk and the grocer would put on a white cloth glove before reaching into the carton to dispense them. "Untouched by human hands," the sign above them read.

Turkey was enjoyed twice a year, at Thanksgiving and Christmas. Several days before the holiday, I'd be sent to purchase day-old bread, which would then be allowed to become stale before being crumbled up to make stuffing. The packaged stuffing turned out

*". . . a grilled cheese sandwich cost a nickel. Fried on
the grill, it was squashed flat with an iron weight. . . ."*

today by Pepperidge Farm had to be invented, I
suppose, since, with the addition of preservatives,
bread hardly goes stale anymore. I don't think eating
is better or worse now than it was during my
childhood, but I do miss the ten months of
anticipation that preceded turkey time.

The grammar school I attended in Cambridge was
only a few blocks from where I lived, in the top half
of a two-family house in an upper-middle-class
neighborhood. I'd come home for lunch each day at
noon, but that changed when my mother went to
work. From that time on, a dime was left for me on
the oilcloth-covered kitchen table that my father
called the catchall. I'd take the money and walk
another couple of blocks to a drugstore lunch
counter where a grilled cheese sandwich cost a
nickel. Fried on the grill, it was squashed flat with an
iron weight until it had the look and consistency of

an old washcloth. It was delicious. A glass of milk or Coke was a nickel, and so I dined for a dime, perusing the comic books that were displayed on the magazine rack behind me until the proprietor kicked me out and I made my way back to school.

Mixes and convenience foods didn't exist then. The preparation of the meal was the heart of the event. When grandpa sent maple syrup from Vermont, we celebrated the occasion by serving waffles and flapjacks. They were made the only way they could be: from scratch. Watching the ingredients turn into batter was a genuine thrill. The anticipation affected the taste. One day I opened the front door of my house and discovered a sample box that had been left there. It was a new product called Instant Waffle Mix. Unable to resist a bargain and being (like all children) greedy, I followed the man distributing the samples. I collected (stole) seventeen boxes of this new miracle product from my neighbors' doorsteps and presented them proudly to my mother. God punished me; waffles were never the same in my house.

The life of a child in the depression years of the 1930's revolved around certain specific events: Saturday-morning movies at the local theater (a cartoon, a Dick Tracy serial, and a feature), the 5 P.M. to 6 P.M. radio shows (*Captain Midnight, Jack Armstrong,* and *Little Orphan Annie*), and, most important of all, penny candy. A penny in those days was genuine coin of the realm. It could buy foot-long strips of paper with dots of brightly colored sugar impregnated on them, long strands of licorice, or packs of bubble gum with trading cards—baseball players, Indians, and, in the early days, war cards: the Rape of Nanking. There were small wax bottles with sweet syrupy liquid inside them and red wax lips to wear and, finally, to chew until the sweetness was gone and we were left with a mouthful of candle wax. A nickel, hard to come by, would purchase a cup of ice cream with pictures of movie stars on the inside cover—one Bonita Granville was worth five Ida Lupinos. Jingles the snow-cone vendor, a friendly white-haired man, would, for 2¢, shave ice into a cone-shaped paper cup and pour raspberry syrup over it. Nothing in my life has ever tasted as good as these sweet, succulent treats.

In the summer my mother and I would go to visit grandpa and grandma in Vermont. My father would remain in Cambridge at his new job as supervisor for

*"A penny in those days . . . could buy foot-long strips of paper with dots of brightly colored sugar . . . long strands of licorice . . . packs of bubble gum with trading cards. . . ."*

the WPA. During one week in August he would visit us. Life in Vermont was very different. My grandfather was a solid New England oak tree, indifferent to the vicissitudes of the economy, Republican to his soul (his mother and Calvin Coolidge's mother were sisters), and contemptuous of my father's New Deal Democratic political views. "Anybody who wants to work can make a living," he'd say. Food was important to him, and the preparation of it in his house was inherently theatrical. When the corn in his garden was ready for picking, he would place a large pot of water on his wood-burning stove. When the water was boiling, he would turn to me and say: "Run down to the garden and pick eighteen of the best ears you can find. If you don't have the corn husked and in the pot within five minutes of picking, it's not worth eating." Racing for my life, I'd run to the garden. Back at the house I'd husk like a fiend. "Thirty seconds to go,"

*" 'If you don't have the corn husked and in the pot within five minutes of picking, it's not worth eating,' . . . my grandfather would announce. In retrospect, I realize he must have stretched the clock. . . ."*

my grandfather would announce. In retrospect, I realize he must have stretched the clock, but back then, with my heart beating, time had stopped and I was living in an existential moment. The corn was plunged in, with a second to spare; I waited, proud, ecstatic, part of the continuum of life, and when my teeth sank into the sweet, succulent kernels, I experienced total connection with the cosmos.

Preserving fruits and vegetables in Ball canning jars took up a major portion of the summer. My grandparents had a fairly large garden that provided produce to last most of the winter. Corn and stewed tomatoes are what I remember most. Pickled beets were canned, too, and rhubarb and other forgotten staples. Bread was baked weekly; its delicious odor filled the house on Tuesdays. Once a summer, grandpa would take me by the hand and we'd walk to the general store and buy a bottle of Hires Root Beer extract. Preparing and bottling the root beer was man's work. Siphoning the liquid into pint-sized bottles and then capping them was exciting and dangerous. The bottles would be stored in the cool, damp cellar under my grandparents' house, and a wait of several weeks would then ensue. Every third or fourth day a minor explosion would be heard

from downstairs; a bottle of root beer had exploded. Finally the wait was over, and we were able to sample the fruits of our labor. No Dom Pérignon 1937 ever tasted as good.

On Sundays, after church, where we'd hear a lecture on love and tolerance (Once I remember a sermon on the need to accept all human beings: "We must find love in our hearts for everyone," preached the pastor, "including the summer people"), dinner would consist of chicken pie, with a dessert of strawberry shortcake, both made with huge quantities of baking-powder biscuits. Yet my grandparents never got fat. They ingested energy and passed it on, part of the universal life flow.

A French snob—forgive the redundancy—once wrote that America's sole contribution to world cuisine is catsup. But even he, if dropped through the Golden Arches, would add to his list the computerized McDonald's French fry. It is quite simply the finest French fried potato in the world, searingly hot, instantly fresh, and cooked by space-age technology to perfection. Vast portions of the U.S. were, until not long ago, a culinary waste-land, at least as far as restaurants go. The driver going from New York to Florida ate grease and grits.

The advent of the fast-food chains at least provided consistency and predictability. If the food was mediocre, at least it wasn't poison. Junk food is not an American invention; the English meat pie preceded it. But the phrase and the packaging of it as an event are American. McDonald's and Col. Sanders have become worldwide phenomena, parts of what the French disdainfully call "Le Coca-Cola-ization du monde." But of course, as they do with all things American, from our blue jeans to our blockbuster movies, they love/hate our fast food, and Parisians line up on the Champs Elysées for a "hamburger Américain."

Junk food is fun food—and fun is good for you. McDonald's is the supreme packager of the event of eating, with prizes, balloons, music, throwaway plastic boxes, and contests. My 12-year-old son came home all excited one day, carrying a booklet with Ronald the Clown's picture on it. He'd been pasting McDonald's stamps onto it for a month. "Only one more stamp," he announced, "and I win either $25,000 or an Egg McMuffin!"

Making the consumption of food an event—presenting the food itself in ways that please the eye—is something that rich people have done for centuries. The Japanese developed it to a high art. Now it's the poor people's turn. Junk food is to cuisine what comic strips are to literature—not better, not worse, just different. The comics, like junk food, are for fun. There are good ones and bad ones, depending on your taste.

The restaurant business, in the past year, has apparently been hit hard by the economic crunch and inflation. Fifteen years ago, when I was working in the theater, my wife and I were living in New York City. I had a week off once, and we decided that instead of going away, we'd stay home and play tourist. People came from all over the country to eat in the famous restaurants of Manhattan. Why, we reasoned, shouldn't we? Let's throw caution to the winds, we thought, and spend $50 a night for dinner. So we dined high off the hog at the finest restaurants in New York.

Times change. A few months ago, Gael Greene, the restaurant editor at *New York* magazine, wrote a cover story entitled "Nineteen Restaurants Where You Can Still Dine for $50 a Couple."

*". . . Parisians line up on the Champs Elysées for a 'hamburger Américain.'"*

One of the things I enjoy when eating out is reading menus. "Mile-high stack of pancakes drenched in syrup with a generous portion of rich creamery butter," etc. Once in a truckers' diner, where the menu consisted of press-in white plastic letters on a lined black felt sign, I read on the dessert list "Jello du jour." In a fancier restaurant, another time, the roast prime rib of beef "with au jus" was accompanied by "baked potato en foil."

California, where I live now, has lots of little specialty restaurants, such as *sushi* bars. I don't like raw fish—never tried it, don't like it—as in skydiving. I dined at an omelet parlor recently where each selection on the menu had a descriptive line underneath it. One of the delicacies offered was a chicken omelet. The description read: "Mother and child reunion."

The luxury of eating out takes many forms. In the 1950's I used to hang out at a place in New York called the Village Vanguard. Lenny Bruce was performing there, and I would go to worship at his shrine. I got to know the chef in the kitchen, an old guy named Sherm. Once a week, Sherm would go somewhere and buy a bird to cook. I say a bird because no one ever knew what it was, only that it was immense—a condor, perhaps. He'd boil it in a huge caldron and then, in the ensuing week, he'd carve from it chicken sandwiches, turkey sandwiches, and, to order, a veal cutlet. Once, one of the waiters dashed into the kitchen and ordered a hot turkey sandwich. "Ain't got it," said Sherm. "OK," said the waiter, "make it a hot chicken sandwich." "Dummy," said Sherm, "would I refuse you a hot turkey sandwich if I had chicken?"

**O**nce, in Miami, I wandered into a juice bar/natural-food shop. "A large glass of orange juice, please," I said to the sweet old lady behind the counter. "I've got some just squeezed," she answered, "but it's not cold. Or I've got some I squeezed an hour ago that's been in the refrigerator. Which would you like?" "Is there any difference?" I asked. "Not unless you're a health-food nut," she said.

The cult of natural food has reached epidemic proportions in certain parts of the country, notably California. People giving dinner parties often have to prepare a vegetarian and a nonvegetarian meal. Eccentric subdivisions within the world of "vegies" include those who will not only refuse to eat meat sauce on their spaghetti but will demand to be served spinach noodles. Some of them go so far as to bring their own cooking utensils and prepare special meals for themselves. They usually eat in sullen silence, their eyes reproaching their fellow diners. They stir unpasteurized honey into their herb tea and refrain from salt, coffee, and anything processed. Many of them take no wine and, in general, I find them a pain in the neck.

Neither do they appear to me to be particularly healthy. Some of the worst-looking people I've ever seen are the customers in health-food stores. "Gimme a pound of them prunes," they'll mutter, "and a package of Miller's bran." The only people who look worse than they do are the ones who are waiting on them. "We've got a special on figs," they'll say. "Here, try one." And so the joyless

*"Once a week, Sherm would go somewhere and buy a
bird to cook. . . . a condor, perhaps. He'd boil it in a
huge caldron. . . ."*

exchange continues until the customer shuffles out
of the store and goes home to consume his
purchase. Meat is bad for them, sugar is bad for
them, starch and booze are bad for them—
sometimes it seems that pleasure itself is bad for
them. I'll bet Cotton Mather would have been a
health-food nut if he were around today. My
grandfather spent ninety-nine years in near-perfect
health, and the main staple of his diet, as far as I
could see, was doughnuts, which he and my
grandmother fried in a huge vat of grease on their
wood-burning stove. A negative attitude is bad for
people, of that I'm sure. Food should, among other
things, be fun to eat; it needn't be a problem.

   In 1970 cyclamates were taken off the market for
causing cancer in mice, and diet soft drinks stopped
tasting good. They were replaced by saccharin,
which in turn was also found to cause cancer in

mice. Nitrites, which preserve bacon, were put on the no-no list. Later it was announced that Americans were consuming twenty times more nitrites in beer than in bacon. Then, after people had had a chance to get good and worried, it was announced that nitrites might not be harmful after all. One day "they" (the same "they" who don't fix the potholes and brought us Vietnam) put out a statement that broiled hamburgers cause cancer. That scare quietly went away too. Cholesterol was a hassle; people struck all sorts of tasties off their diets. Then the news recently came out that we could quit worrying, and eggs went back on the in list.

What we eat is not a problem; worrying about it is. A Twinky a day keeps the doctor away; the daily ingestion of a little BHT preserves freshness. H. G. Wells's Martians died from lack of immunity to the common cold. I shall dance on the graves of my health-food friends and sip a Diet Pepsi in their memory.

# 1981 YEARBOOK

## EVENTS OF 1980

# CHRONOLOGY FOR 1980

**JAN. 6**

**JAN. 23**

**4** ● President Jimmy Carter, responding to the Soviet military invasion of Afghanistan, stops U.S. deliveries of 17,000,000 metric tons of grain and of computers and oil-drilling equipment ordered by the U.S.S.R., curtails Soviet fishing in American waters, and defers new cultural and economic exchanges between the two nations.

**6** ● Indira Gandhi and her Congress-I Party faction win a sweeping victory in India's parliamentary elections. She became prime minister on Jan. 14.

**7** ● The Soviet Union vetoes a United Nations Security Council resolution demanding that Soviet troops withdraw from Afghanistan.
● Vice-President Walter F. Mondale announces that the federal government will buy all grain previously contracted to the U.S.S.R. in order to stabilize the grain futures market.

**13** ● The U.N. Security Council votes 10 to 2 to cut off all shipments to Iran except for food and medicine in an effort to obtain the release of 53 Americans held hostage in Iran, but the Soviet Union casts one of the negative votes, thus vetoing the resolution.

**23** ● In the annual State of the Union address to Congress, President Carter says the United States would use military force if necessary to repel an attack on the Persian Gulf and asks authority to resume registration for a possible future military draft.

**24** ● In a major policy shift, the U.S. announces it is willing to sell military equipment to China for the first time, although the sales will not yet include weapons.

**28** ● President Carter sends to Congress a budget for fiscal 1981 that foresees approximately $616 billion in outlays, $600 billion in revenues, and a deficit of $16 billion. It holds the line on most nonmilitary programs, raises military spending, and forecasts a mild recession and increased unemployment in 1980.

- Six U.S. embassy employees not among the 53 known American hostages in Tehran are flown out of Iran, posing as Canadian diplomats and carrying forged visas.

**29** • A conference of Islamic states denounces the Soviet invasion of Afghanistan and demands the "immediate withdrawal" of Soviet troops.

### FEBRUARY

**3** • New Mexico state police and National Guardsmen occupy the state penitentiary at Santa Fe after a 36-hr. rampage in which 33 inmates were killed.

**18** • Pierre Elliott Trudeau emerges as Canada's leader again as his Liberal Party defeats Prime Minister Joe Clark's Progressive Conservatives in national parliamentary elections.

**24** • The U.S. hockey team wins a gold medal as the two-week-long, thirteenth Winter Olympic Games, held in Lake Placid, N.Y., comes to an end. Earlier, Eric Heiden of Madison, Wis., won five gold medals in speed-skating competition.

**26** • Egypt and Israel exchange ambassadors as part of the process toward normalization of relations between the two countries.

**FEB. 18**

**FEB. 24**

**FEB. 3**

**MARCH 23**

**APRIL 12**

## MARCH

**4** • The party headed by guerrilla leader Robert Mugabe sweeps to victory in Rhodesia, official results show, taking 63 percent of the 2,700,000 black votes in parliamentary elections held Feb. 27-29.

**10** • A U.N. inquiry commission leaves Iran after Ayatollah Ruhollah Khomeini sides with the captors of the American hostages in Tehran, who had refused to allow the panel to meet the hostages.

**14** • President Carter announces, as an anti-inflation measure, that he will cut federal spending by $13 billion and impose a fee on imported oil aimed at raising gasoline prices 10¢ a gallon; simultaneously, the Federal Reserve Board raises loan costs for banks.

**23** • The former shah of Iran, Mohammed Riza Pahlavi, flies to Egypt, just 24 hr. before Iran is due to present Panamanian authorities with a formal request for his extradition.

**27** • Congress approves the windfall profits tax on domestic oil companies that had been urged by President Carter, thus giving him one of his biggest legislative victories since taking office.

## APRIL

**7** • President Carter announces that the U.S. is breaking diplomatic relations with Iran and is imposing an embargo on American exports to Iran.

**12** • Army enlisted men, led by a 28-year-old sergeant, Samuel K. Doe, overthrow the government of the African nation of Liberia and kill its president, William R. Tolbert, Jr.
 • The U.S. Olympic Committee votes to endorse President Carter's call for a boycott of the Olympic Games to be held in Moscow.

**17** • President Carter announces further steps against Iran, including a ban on imports and a request for legislation to allow seizure of frozen Iranian assets to pay for U.S. claims. He also foresees "some sort of military action" if economic and political sanctions fail to produce the early release of the 53 American hostages.

**APRIL 18**

18 • Rhodesia becomes the independent African nation of Zimbabwe, ending the struggle by the country's blacks for majority rule.

22 • Foreign ministers of the European Community vote unanimously to impose full economic sanctions against Iran on May 17 unless "decisive progress" is made to free the American hostages in Tehran.
 • Consumer prices in the U.S. are found to have increased at an annual rate of about 18 percent during the first three months of 1980, the Labor Department reports.

**APRIL 24**

24 • Rep. John Anderson drops out of his candidacy for the Republican Party Presidential nomination and declares he will run as an independent.
 • Eight Americans die as a U.S. strike team lands in Iran but fails in its mission to rescue the American hostages.

**APRIL 24**

26 • Cyrus R. Vance resigns as secretary of state in protest against the raid on Iran; three days later, Sen. Edmund S. Muskie of Maine is appointed to succeed him.

## MAY

2 • The U.S. Department of Labor reports that unemployment jumped to its highest level in three years in April as hundreds of thousands of blue-collar workers were laid off because of declining economic activity.

4 • President Tito of Yugoslavia, the last survivor of the major World War II leaders, dies at the age of 87.

8 • Egyptian President Anwar el-Sadat calls for an indefinite delay in talks with Israel concerning Palestinian autonomy, citing a "formidable gap" between the Israeli and Egyptian positions. The deadline for completing the negotiations was May 26.

9 • Thirty-five persons are killed when a ship strikes the Sunshine Skyway Bridge spanning Tampa Bay in Florida. The collision tears away a section of the bridge, dropping a bus, three cars, and a pickup truck into the bay.

12 • Pope John Paul II concludes an 11-day pilgrimage to six African nations.

14 • A week after promising that refugees fleeing Cuba would be received with "an open heart and open arms," President Carter orders the Coast Guard to stop the influx. About 800 vessels had carried more than 40,000 Cubans to Florida by this date; more than 125,000 eventually entered.

15 • Maxie L. Anderson and his son Kris set a record by accomplishing the first nonstop balloon flight across North America.

MAY 9

MAY 14

56

17 • A weekend of racial rioting breaks out in Miami, Fla., taking 18 lives and causing an estimated $100,000,000 in damages.

18 • Mount St. Helens, a volcano in the state of Washington, erupts, devastating a 150-sq.mi. area and leaving 34 persons dead; 28 are missing and presumed dead.
   • Limited sanctions against Iran are imposed by the European Community, but rather than halting all sales except for food and medicine, as requested by President Carter, it cancels only those covered by contracts signed since Nov. 4, 1979, when the U.S. embassy was seized. Moreover, Great Britain later limits the ban to new contracts only.

20 • Voters in Québec reject a proposal to allow the provincial government to negotiate independence from Canada.

27 • South Korean troops regain full control of the city of Kwangju, seized six days earlier by students and other antigovernment elements; earlier, the government had imposed total martial law in an effort to quell widespread demonstrations.

**MAY 17**

**MAY 18**

## JUNE

2 • Great Britain accepts a plan offered by the other members of the European Community by which its budget contribution to the EC would be lowered from about $2.6 billion annually to about $900,000,000.

3 • The National Bureau of Economic Research, the widely recognized arbiter of business cycles, declares that the U.S. is in a recession that began in January.

6 • The Department of Labor reports that the nation's unemployment rate rose to 7.8 percent in May—an increase from 6.2 percent in March and the biggest two-month increase since such records first were kept.

16 • The U.S. Supreme Court rules that new forms of life created in the laboratory are eligible for patents, thus encouraging the development of genetic engineering.

19 • A preliminary Department of Commerce report disclosed by Administration sources estimates that the U.S. gross national product

**JUNE 23**

**JULY 2**

plunged at an annual rate of 8.5 percent during the year's second quarter. The figure was later set at 9.6 percent, making the quarterly decline the largest since the Great Depression.

**22** • Japan's governing Liberal-Democratic Party wins firm majorities in both houses of the parliament in general elections.

**23** • Concluding a two-day conference in Venice, President Carter and the leaders of six other major non-Communist industrial nations pledge that their governments will seek to cut oil consumption sharply by 1990.

**26** • French President Valéry Giscard d'Estaing announces that France has developed and tested a prototype of a neutron bomb warhead. These devices destroy living beings with powerful radiation emissions but avoid major structural damage from blast and heat.

• Congress approves legislation sought by the Carter administration creating a $20 billion federal program to speed distillation of crude-oil substitutes from tar sands, oil shale, and coal.

**30** • The Supreme Court rules, 5-4, that Congress has not acted unconstitutionally in refusing to finance most abortions for poor women. The Court said Congress may refuse to finance even those that are medically required.

# JULY

**2** ● President Carter signs a proclamation requiring 4,000,000 young men to register for possible military conscription.

● In a 6-3 decision, the Supreme Court explicitly endorses for the first time the awarding of federal benefits based on the race of the recipients by upholding the constitutionality of a public-works program in which 10 percent of spending was reserved for minority contractors.

**3** ● Reacting to moderating inflation and the worsening recession, the Federal Reserve Board announces that it will remove the remaining credit controls imposed in March.

**16** ● Ronald Reagan is nominated as the Republican Party's candidate for President by the party's National Convention in Detroit; hours later, Reagan chooses George Bush to be his running mate.

**17** ● Zenko Suzuki is elected prime minister of Japan and forms a cabinet carefully balanced among rival factions of the ruling Liberal-Democratic Party; the previous prime minister, Masayoshi Ohira, died on June 12.

**JULY 17**

**JULY 16**

**AUG. 14**

**AUG. 19**

**27** ● Mohammed Riza Pahlavi, exiled shah of Iran, dies in Cairo; Iranian officials, who had demanded his return, say his death will not change the disposition of the American hostages.

**30** ● Israel's parliament enacts into law a bill affirming Jerusalem as the capital of Israel.

### AUGUST

**2** ● Eighty-four people are killed in the worst terrorist incident in Italian history—the bombing of the railroad station in Bologna.

**3** ● The twenty-second Summer Olympic Games, held in Moscow, close with Soviet athletes winning 80 of the 205 gold medals and East Germans winning 47. The U.S., Canada, West Germany, and Japan were among many nations boycotting the Games because of the Soviet invasion of Afghanistan.

**5** ● Government officials announce that the Carter administration has adopted a new strategy for nuclear war that gives priority to attacking military targets in the Soviet Union, rather than to destroying cities and industrial complexes.

**13** ● The Interstate Commerce Commission orders a halt to the practice of setting freight rates collectively by the nation's railways, arguing that such action stifles competition.

**14** ● Jimmy Carter is renominated in New York City by the Democratic Party's National Convention to run for a second term as President of the U.S.; later that day, Walter Mondale is nominated for a second term as Vice-President.
 ● Seventeen thousand Polish workers seize the Lenin shipyard in Gdańsk and issue economic and political demands, touching off a widespread strike movement.

**19** ● An Israeli force estimated at 500 men, backed by artillery and air attacks, conducts the biggest raid against Palestinian bases in Lebanon since 1978.

**24** ● In an effort to stem the national crisis caused by the walkout of about 300,000 workers, Poland's prime minister and three other full members of the ruling Politburo are dismissed from office.

**AUG. 31**

28 • President Carter outlines a "revitalization" plan for the economy that emphasizes federal financial aid for business investment, especially in the old industrial cities that have been losing jobs.

31 • Leaders of more than 300,000 striking Polish workers declare an end to the 17-day strike after winning the right to form independent self-governing unions and to strike, a pledge to restrain censorship and open the state-controlled media to a wide variety of opinion, and the release of jailed dissidents. Three days later, about 200,000 coal miners go back to work under a similar accord.

## SEPTEMBER

**SEPT. 7**

7 • Hua Kuo-feng (Hua Guofeng) announces his resignation as premier of China and asks the National People's Congress to replace him with Chao Chi-yang (Zhao Ziyang).

11 • A military coup by the Turkish armed forces ousts the government of Prime Minister Süleyman Demirel, dissolves the parliament, and suspends the constitution.

• An attaché with the Cuban mission to the U.N. is assassinated in New York City—the first U.N. official ever killed in the city.

**13** ● A six-day conference between Canadian Prime Minister Pierre Trudeau and the ten provincial prime ministers ends without an agreement on efforts to devise a constitution for Canada.

**17** ● Iraqi President Saddam Hussein cancels his country's 1975 border agreement with Iran. Two days later, Arab diplomats report that Iraq has seized 90 sq.mi. of Iranian territory.

**18** ● Members of the Organization of Petroleum Exporting Countries (OPEC) agree to freeze their base oil prices at existing levels, which average $32 a barrel, in return for an agreement that Saudi Arabia—the world's leading oil exporter—would raise its price to that level.

**19** ● A fuel explosion rocks an underground Titan II nuclear missile silo near Damascus, Ark., killing one airman and injuring 21 persons.

**21** ● In the first debate of the 1980 Presidential campaign since the primaries, Ronald Reagan and John Anderson present their views, but President Carter is absent, having declined to participate.

**24** ● Iraq and Iran strike at each other's oil refineries, inspiring fears of a new shortage of the world's oil supplies.

**26** ● A terrorist bomb believed planted by a neo-Nazi kills 13 persons in Munich; a week later, a bomb explodes outside a Paris synagogue, killing four.

**SEPT. 18**

**SEPT. 24**

## OCTOBER

**1** • Iran announces that it will make every effort to maintain freedom of international shipping through the Strait of Hormuz, the sea route through which passes oil from Persian Gulf countries. The statement follows reports that the U.S. is considering sending a naval force to the area to keep the waterway open.

**5** • The West German governing coalition headed by Chancellor Helmut Schmidt retains power, increasing its majority in the *Bundestag* (lower house of the parliament) to 45 seats.

**10** • At least 6000 people are killed in an earthquake that destroys El Asnam, Algeria.

**17** • The U.S. Department of Commerce reports that the gross national product rose at an annual rate of 1 percent during the third quarter of 1980, indicating that the recession might be over.

**18** • Australia's governing coalition, headed by Prime Minister Malcolm Fraser, retains power in parliamentary elections, but by a reduced margin.

**22** • The U.S. and China sign an agreement committing China to buy 6,000,000 to 8,000,000 metric tons of U.S. wheat and corn each year for the next four years.

**28** • Jimmy Carter and Ronald Reagan debate the issues in Cleveland for 95 min. John Anderson is excluded from the televised debate.

**30** • Edward Seaga's Labour Party wins a landslide victory in Jamaica's parliamentary elections, ousting the government headed by Prime Minister Michael Manley.

## NOVEMBER

**2** • Iran's parliament approves four conditions set earlier by Ayatollah Ruhollah Khomeini for the release of 52 American hostages who had been held for a year.

**4** • Ronald Reagan is elected President of the U.S., defeating Jimmy Carter by a landslide margin. Democrats retain control of the House of Representatives, but Republicans win a majority in the Senate for the first time since 1952.

**OCT. 18**

**OCT. 30**

63

**NOV. 20**

**NOV. 23**

**DEC. 5**

**17** ● Six present or former members of the Ku Klux Klan are acquitted of charges of murdering five members of the Communist Workers Party in 1979 at an anti-Klan rally in Greensboro, N.C.

**20** ● The Dow Jones industrial average of 30 leading stocks on the New York Stock Exchange closes above 1000 for the first time since Dec. 31, 1976.

**21** ● A fire sweeps through the MGM Grand Hotel in Las Vegas, Nev., killing more than 80 persons and injuring hundreds.

**23** ● An earthquake strikes southern Italy, leaving about 4500 people either dead or missing and presumed dead.

### DECEMBER

**5** ● The U.S. suspends new military and economic aid to El Salvador pending clarification of the regime's role in the murder of three U.S. nuns and a lay missionary.

**7** ● Three days after the death of Premier Francisco Sá Carneiro, his longtime political rival, Gen. António Ramalho Eanes, is reelected to a second term as president of Portugal.

**8** ● John Lennon, one of the four Beatles, is shot to death outside his apartment house in New York City.

**12** ● The North Atlantic Treaty Organization warns the U.S.S.R. that armed intervention in Poland would end détente.

**16** ● Ministers of OPEC agree in Indonesia to allow 12 of its members to raise their oil prices by up to $4 a barrel.

**21** ● Iran demands the deposit of $24 billion from the U.S. in "guarantees" for the recovery of its frozen assets and the wealth of the late shah in exchange for the release of the hostages.

# A

**ACCIDENTS AND DISASTERS.** The following were among the notable accidents and disasters of 1980.

Jan. 1, Azores: An earthquake kills at least 52 people and injures more than 300.

Jan. 1, Canada: Fire in a crowded social club during a New Year's Eve celebration in Chapais, Québec, causes 44 deaths.

Jan. 20, Colombia: At least 222 people are killed and more than 500 injured when overcrowded bleachers collapse in the bullring in Sincelejo.

Jan. 21, Iran: All 128 people aboard an Iranian airliner are killed when the plane crashes in the Elburz Mountains northeast of Tehran.

Jan. 28, Florida: Twenty-three crewmen of the U.S. Coast Guard buoy tender *Blackthorn* are drowned when their vessel collides with the oil tanker *Texas Capricorn* and sinks in Tampa Bay.

Feb. 13–22, Southern California and Arizona: Pacific Ocean storms, gales, and floods cause at least 36 deaths, destroy many homes, and force thousands to flee in six California counties.

March 14, Poland: A Polish airliner crashes attempting an emergency landing at Warsaw's domestic airport; all 87 people aboard are killed, including 14 amateur U.S. boxers and 8 officials of their team.

March 27, North Sea: One hundred twenty-three offshore oil workers on a floating platform are drowned when the structure capsizes in stormy seas in Norway's Ekofisk undersea oilfield.

April 12, Brazil: A Transbrasil Airlines jet, attempting to land in a tropical rainstorm at Florianópolis, crashes two minutes from the airport, killing 54 of the 58 persons on board.

April 22, Philippines: About 200 people drown when the passenger vessel *Don Juan* sinks 130 mi. southeast of Manila after a collision with an oil tanker.

April 25, Canary Islands: All 146 people aboard a British-operated airliner are killed when the plane crashes into Teide peak.

May 9, Florida: Thirty-five people die when a bus and several other vehicles fall 140 ft. from the Sunshine Skyway Bridge into Tampa Bay after the Liberian-registered freighter *Summit Venture* knocks out a bridge support during a thunderstorm.

May 18, Washington State: A huge eruption of volcanic Mount St. Helens in southwestern Washington leaves 34 people dead and 28 presumed dead and spreads volcanic ash over large areas of Washington and Oregon, destroying homes, farms, timberland, wildlife, roads, bridges, and other property. Smaller eruptions preceded and followed the main blast that blew the top off the mountain. *See* EARTH SCIENCES.

May 20, Jamaica: At least 144 women die in a fire in the Eventide Home for poor and elderly women in Kingston.

June 3, Nebraska: Seven tornadoes tear through Grand Island, destroy more than 550 buildings, and kill five people.

Mid-June–early September, southern, midwestern, and eastern U.S.: Drought and a merciless heat wave leave 1265 persons dead in Missouri,

*The Sunshine Skyway Bridge across Tampa Bay, Fla., after it was struck by the freighter* Summit Venture *on May 9. A bus and several cars plunged into the water, leaving 35 dead; another car braked to a stop only 2 ft. from the broken span's edge.*

A Texas rancher inspects the dried-out bed of a pond, normally 40 ft. deep, during a summer drought that was the worst in the U.S. since the 1930's. The toll to crops and livestock in 26 states was estimated at nearly $20 billion.

Texas, and 24 other states, according to the National Oceanic and Atmospheric Administration. The worst drought since the 1930's killed millions of chickens and caused nearly $20 billion damage, including widespread harm to range grass, wheat, corn, cotton, and other crops. See AGRICULTURE.

July 26, New Jersey: Twenty-three people die in a fire in the Brinley Inn, a Bradley Beach hotel for the aged and mentally retarded.

Aug. 4–11, Caribbean Sea and Gulf of Mexico: Hurricane Allen causes at least 272 deaths as it rips through 1200 mi. of island and coastal territory in Barbados, St. Lucia, Haiti, Jamaica, Mexico's Yucatán, and southern Texas.

Aug. 16, England: Fire in two adjoining Soho social clubs in London kills 37 people.

Aug. 18, Iran: At least 90 people are killed and 38 injured by the accidental explosion of road-building dynamite in a village 150 mi. east of Abadan.

Aug. 19, Poland: At least 62 people are killed and 50 injured when a freight train, on the wrong track, collides head-on with a crowded passenger train near the city of Toruń.

Aug. 19, Saudi Arabia: In aviation history's third worst disaster (the second worst single-plane accident), all 301 people aboard a Saudi Arabian airliner are killed by toxic smoke when it burns after landing at Riyadh airport.

Sept. 8, India: At least 250 people are killed by monsoon-caused landslides in Darjeeling.

Sept. 14, Saudi Arabia: All 89 servicemen aboard a Saudi Arabian air force transport plane are killed when the aircraft catches fire and crashes in the desert near Medina.

Oct. 10, Algeria: A double earthquake strikes El Asnam, Algeria, killing at least 6000 people. See ALGERIA.

Oct. 23, Spain: A blast from a boiler or propane gas tank kills 64 persons at a school in Ortuella, Spain.

Oct. 24, Mexico: At least 40 persons die when an earthquake, with its epicenter in the state of Oaxaca, strikes southern Mexico.

Nov. 1, Poland: Fifty persons die when a fire sweeps through a mental hospital in Warsaw.

Nov. 15–28, California: Brush and timber fires covering more than 125 sq.mi. of southern California kill several persons and cause nearly $82,000,000 worth of property damage.

Nov. 20, Japan: Japan's worst hotel fire since World War II takes at least 44 lives in Kawaji.

Nov. 21, Nevada: A fire sweeps through the MGM Grand Hotel in Las Vegas, Nev., killing more than 80 people.

Nov. 23, Italy: Europe's worst earthquake disaster since 1915 kills 3105 in southern Italy, with another 1575 missing and presumed dead. Estimates of those homeless range from 200,000 to 300,000.

Dec. 4, New York: Twenty-six persons, most of them corporate executives, die in a flash fire that races through a hotel in Harrison, New York.

Dec. 21, Colombia: All 70 persons aboard a Colombian jetliner on a domestic flight die in a crash ascribed to a bomb explosion.    L.A.S.

**ADVERTISING.** External factors seemed to intrude on the world of advertising in 1980 to a greater degree than ever before. In January, following the Soviet intervention in Afghanistan, President Jimmy Carter called for a boycott of the Summer Olympics in Moscow—a move that caused NBC-

TV to lose millions of dollars in advertising long planned by some 20 major sponsors. Late in the year, a ten-week strike by performers in prime-time television series brought on a frantic reshuffling of program schedules as the networks offered mostly reruns to advertisers at greatly reduced prices; *see* TELEVISION AND RADIO BROADCASTING. (NBC, however, took advantage of the program drought on its competitors' networks to present *Shogun,* a 12-hr. miniseries that was sold to advertisers at a bargain price of about $40,000 per half-minute spot—and which surprised everyone by drawing an audience second only to that of the original telecast of *Roots.*) To its dismay, giant Procter & Gamble Co., the nation's largest advertiser, found one of its products—Rely tampons—linked to a fatal disease, toxic shock syndrome; *see* HEALTH AND MEDICINE. The company promptly discontinued the product along with a multimillion-dollar advertising budget designated for its promotion.

Perhaps the most significant factor affecting advertising was the onset of the U.S. recession. After several years in which ad spending climbed at an annual rate of 12 to 18 percent, the growth rate slowed to 9 percent in the first half of the year, according to Leading National Advertisers, which measures spending by some 10,000 companies advertising about 20,000 different products. Anticipating a pickup in the latter half of the year, Robert Coen of McCann-Erickson Inc. estimated that expenditures for all advertisers in all media in 1980 would reach $55.5 billion, up 11.5 percent from $49.8 billion in 1979.

**Trends.** Procter & Gamble, which spends some $475,000,000 a year for regular television advertising, helped establish an entire new ad medium—commercial cable television—when it joined American Express, Holiday Inns, and two dozen other companies supporting Cable News Network, a 24-hr. news service for cable-television systems that began operating at midyear. Searching for new ways to reach the public, Anheuser-Busch became the first advertiser to run commercials in a closed-circuit telecast of a prizefight (Sugar Ray Leonard versus Roberto Durán) beamed to movie theaters in midsummer, and it repeated the venture in October (Muhammad Ali versus Larry Holmes).

A second trend involved the discovery—led by

*Jeans were as popular as ever in 1980. A controversial television commercial for Calvin Klein jeans showed 15-year-old actress Brooke Shields posing provocatively while voicing suggestive lines such as "What comes between me and my Calvins? Nothing!"*

Stephen O. Frankfurt, director of creative planning and development at Kenyon & Eckhardt Inc.—of an entire new market, "the maturity market." Long accustomed to aiming their messages at 18-to-34-year-old consumers (who supposedly buy the most products for their growing families), advertisers noted the rapid growth of a large body of customers age 45 to 64. To reach the new target, they turned to a handful of publications that appeared on the scene, including magazines with names such as *Prime Time* and *50 Plus* and a projected cable-television programming service that was to feature only programs geared to the older market.

Chastened last year by a Congress that thought the Federal Trade Commission (FTC) frequently overstepped its bounds in dealing with "unfair" advertising, the commission in 1980 adopted a friendlier posture toward the ad industry, going so far as to call in leading agency executives for discussions on ways to help regulate their business. The meetings led to proposals that in suggesting rules in the future the FTC would spell out in detail why the rules are needed, what the alternatives might be, and what costs and benefits would result. As an indication of its new attitude, the FTC offered to drop two of three regulations that would restrict food advertisers.

The trend of ad agencies acquiring large public-relations companies reached a high point in July when J. Walter Thompson Co., the biggest advertising agency in the United States, and Hill & Knowlton, the largest public-relations firm in the world, were united in a merger. BBDO International announced plans to acquire Doremus & Co.

The most closely watched campaigns of 1980 were those for new small automobile lines of Chrysler and Ford, which the manufacturers hoped would combat growing sales of foreign models and pull the U.S. auto industry—and perhaps the entire U.S. economy—out of the recessionary doldrums. Beleaguered Chrysler put a red-white-and-blue "buy American" push behind its new cars. Ford promoted its new Escort as a true "World Car."

Three television stations owned by the Washington *Post–Newsweek* broadcasting group rejected Mobil Corp. commercials defending the high profits of oil companies. The stations judged the spots to be editorial in nature and argued that airing the ads would obligate them to give free time to opposing viewpoints. The three major networks also turned down a Mobil commercial that maintained its profits were actually lower, in terms of return of invested capital, than those of the networks.                    D.H.D.

**AFGHANISTAN.** Civil war raged in Afghanistan in 1980. A Marxist regime led by Babrak Karmal, who was installed when Soviet military forces invaded in late 1979, fought to put down resistance by Muslim rebels headquartered in the countryside. Karmal's troops and the Soviet troops backing him could boast superior weaponry, but the insurgents, inadequately equipped with captured weaponry and a small amount of arms from Arab countries, waged a dogged resistance.

As the year began the Soviets moved to consolidate their control of Kabul, the Afghan capital. Karmal held the title of president, but he had little independent authority over his country; he was the third head of government since the Marxists came to power in April, 1978. Soviet officers and security forces took command of defense and even the civilian ministries; Afghan officials became mere figureheads. The newspapers and institutions of higher learning were also heavily controlled by Soviet advisers.

Within several weeks after the invasion, the Soviets began spreading out across all of Afghanistan. Mechanized Soviet ground divisions seized strategic points such as airfields and provincial cities. One motorized division pushed south from Soviet Uzbekistan through northeast Afghanistan to Bagram Air Base near Kabul. Another crossed from Soviet Turkmenistan toward Herat and Kandahar. Muslim rebels put up stiff opposition as the Soviets positioned themselves in remote regions of the land.

Most of the world community was outraged by the Soviet intervention. U.S. President Jimmy Carter moved to boycott the 1980 Summer Olympic Games in Moscow and postponed further consideration of the strategic arms limitation treaty (SALT II). At the United Nations on Jan. 14, the General Assembly, by a vote of 104–18, called for the "immediate, unconditional, and total withdrawal" of Soviet forces. On Jan. 29 foreign ministers of Islamic nations condemned Soviet action as a "flagrant violation" of international law.

Although Soviet power in Kabul was overwhelming, Afghan citizens gave vent to their anger. In late February, Kabul merchants closed their shops to protest the Soviet presence. Citizens waved green Islamic banners, shouted anti-Soviet slogans, and chanted "God is Great." In a powerful display of force, Soviet jet fighters and helicopters flew warningly overhead; the Afghan army and civilian militia rushed reinforcements to the city center. Fighting between the government and civilians took the lives of several hundred people, and order was not restored in the capital for several days.

It became increasingly difficult for Western intelligence sources to assess the progress of the war, since Soviet and Afghan government officials did not permit foreigners freedom of travel. By early April, however, U.S. government analysts said that Soviet troops and insurgent forces had reached a standoff, with major cities, towns, and lines of communication under Soviet control, but with the bulk of the countryside held by the rebels. Soviet casualty figures were reported as ranging anywhere from 2000 to 5000 dead in 1980. Moreover, Afghan army units were said to be suffering widespread desertions, so that their overall size was reduced by 50 percent.

In Kabul public hostility toward the Soviets persisted. In a remarkable demonstration in late April, teenage girls left their schools and marched through the streets shouting "Death to Karmal; death to the Soviets." Security forces fired on the marches, which took place intermittently for two weeks, and an estimated 56 young people were killed. According to diplomatic sources, the mood in the capital turned more sullen than ever.

The Soviets continued their military buildup. At the end of June, when Soviet President Leonid I. Brezhnev declared that a Soviet division and 108 tanks were being removed from Afghanistan, Western sources discounted the news, saying it had been preceded by a large shift of troops *into* Afghanistan, bringing the Soviet total to above 80,000 men. At the same time, there were reports of fighting between two Afghan Marxist factions in the ruling People's Democratic Party, Karmal's Parcham (Banner) and the Khalq (Masses). In July many members of the Khalq were purged from government and army positions. The infighting further weakened the government's ability to suppress rebel activity.

The Muslim insurgents made significant gains in several provincial cities. At Herat during August, armed bands of rebels were seen cruising the streets in broad daylight, while Soviet troops confined their activities to controlling the airport outside town. Similarly, Kandahar, another major city, was said to be largely in rebel hands. By late summer, insurgents began stepping up guerrilla activity in Kabul. In response, the government extended the overnight curfew by two additional hours.

The Afghan economy, meanwhile, was in ruins. Western experts believed that the gross national product had fallen 70 to 80 percent during the year. Hundreds of thousands of refugees fled from the war to neighboring Pakistan, many taking their sheep and goats with them. Widespread strikes were instigated by rebels. The fighting, and Soviet scorched-earth tactics intended to deprive the insurgents of supplies, cut crop yields. As

*Afghan rebels resisting Soviet intervention in their country are shown in a mountain area near the Pakistan border. More than 80,000 Soviet troops occupied Afghanistan in 1980.*

winter approached, the Afghan regime faced the prospect of widespread hunger across the nation, but famine threatened also to deprive the rebels of their capacity to continue resistance.

Although Babrak Karmal could point to no particular success at home, the Soviets accorded him an effusive welcome when he visited Moscow in October, his first trip abroad since his installation as president. Soviet President Brezhnev pledged unswerving support for "revolutionary Afghanistan" and indicated that Soviet forces would not be withdrawn from the country any time soon. Indeed, Soviet forces were reported to be repeatedly violating Pakistani airspace in hot pursuit of fleeing insurgents.

As 1980 closed, the outlook for peace seemed bleak. The Soviets were apparently determined to maintain a Marxist government in power in Kabul. The Muslim insurgents, although ill-armed and disunited, were adamant in their opposition to any such regime, particularly one controlled by the Kremlin. The rebel spirit was perhaps best expressed early in the year by one elderly Kabul resident who told a Western newsman: "Please tell people in the West that we will go on killing the Russians as long as a single one remains here."

*See* STATISTICS OF THE WORLD.          F.W.

# AFRICA

The year 1980 was troubled for a continent tormented by drought and faced with famine. Amid this despair was also political strife. But a major source of conflict ended as Zimbabwe became an independent nation.

Drought, refugees, food shortages, and famine bedeviled Africa in 1980. It was estimated that 26 African nations faced severe food shortages; 7 faced famine. Other estimates indicated that 1,000,000 Africans died from starvation or diseases related to lack of food in 1980. In the 1960's, African states were able to produce some 98 percent of the continent's food needs; in contrast, estimates suggested that by 1985, only 80 percent of its requirements would be met by African production.

**Food Shortages.** One reason for the food problem arose from a dramatic increase in the continent's birth rate. While food production had increased by 1 percent a year during the 1970's, the birth rate had increased by 3 percent a year. More and better medicines, and government programs to eradicate diseases and dangerous parasites, had improved the chances for Africans to live longer. Migrations from farm areas to the towns, factories, and mines of Africa were a second reason for the continent's food problem; a third was shifts in production from food crops to cash export crops. A fourth was the lack of adequate storage and transportation systems.

Finally, desertification had become another serious, long-term problem. The Sahara has been moving southward some 3.5 mi. each year. According to United Nations estimates, Mauritania, which is about four-fifths desert, will be completely desert in less than 20 years. As the desert moves south, farmers and herdspeople are displaced; they, in turn, put increased pressure on the remaining water resources, vegetation, and arable land, and in turn the cycle of desertification continues its movement southward.

In addition to these long-term problems, in the late 1970's Africa experienced two severe, unexpected problems that fueled the famine of 1980. Rainfall in much of Africa decreased, affecting food output in 1979 and setting the stage for the drought of 1980. East Africa was the most affected, with Kenya, Tanzania, and Uganda needing to import 1,000,000 tons of corn in 1980. The drought extended through Zambia, Zaire,

Mozambique, and Zimbabwe to Botswana and the northern frontier of South Africa. Throughout the region cattle and crops were severely reduced, and in some areas famine was averted only by emergency food relief and donations.

An increasing flow of refugees exacerbated the food shortage caused by drought and other problems. The guerrilla wars in Ethiopia's Ogaden and Eritrea regions, the civil war in Chad, the collapse of Idi Amin's regime in Uganda, and fighting in Angola, South-West Africa, Zimbabwe, and the Western Sahara all created refugees and placed severe burdens on the food reserves of countries receiving the migrants. In 1980 it was estimated that 40 percent of the world's refugees were Africans. Every fourth inhabitant in Somalia was a refugee. About 500,000 Eritreans fleeing the war in Ethiopia's northwest settled in the Sudan; countless thousands of people fled from Uganda. Cameroon was believed to host some 200,000 refugees from fighting in Chad. Given their own problems, none of the host countries was able to absorb the stream of refugees. Somalia had received some $132,000,000 in food and supplies from international relief agencies; the Sudan some $280,000,-000. Unfortunately, the aid was believed to be too little and, perhaps, too late. In East Africa (including the Horn of Africa) alone, some 12,000,000 people were believed by United Nations Children's Fund estimates to be facing starvation in late 1980.

The world did not begin to focus its attention on Africa's famine conditions until early in the year, and the magnitude of the problem was not clear until the fall. Many of those most affected by famine conditions lived far from effective government oversight; others were members of minority groups. Some African states were reluctant, for reasons of pride, politics, or ideology, to call attention to their food shortages. Effective relief efforts were slow to be mobilized. Somalia, which had experienced a severe refugee and food problem for more than three years, did not declare a national emergency or seek U.N. help until September, 1979. The U.N., in its turn, took six

*Africa was tormented by famine in 1980. This starving child, standing in a cornfield in Uganda, was unlikely to benefit from the harvest, much of which was being confiscated by armed factions engaged in an ongoing struggle for power.*

months to assess the Somali situation, and it was not until February, 1980, that U.N. Secretary-General Kurt Waldheim issued a global plea for aid. Coming on the heels of the relief campaigns for the Cambodian refugees and the Vietnamese boat people—and coming during difficult times for the industrialized world—pleas for aid to Africa seemed, for the most part, to be ignored or to meet with indifference.

**Strife and Political Instability.** Fighting continued throughout the year in the Western Sahara, where Morocco was faced with the increasingly effective Polisario nationalist movement. Composed of indigenous tribesmen and initially aided only by Algeria, the Polisario had become effective in gaining widespread African support. At the 1980 annual meeting of the Organization of African Unity (OAU), held in Freetown, Sierra Leone, July 1-4, it appeared likely that 26 member states would support the admission of the Polisario regime as the Saharan Arab Democratic Republic, giving the OAU its fifty-first member. Only the threat of a walkout by Morocco and its supporters prevented this circumstance. The war in the Sahara continued to be a severe burden on Morocco's economy and political stability. Mauritania, which had joined Morocco in the occupation of the Western Sahara but had withdrawn in 1979,

continued to be racked by the experience. In January, Lt. Col. Mohammed Khouna Ould Haidala staged a coup, removing the figures who had engineered Mauritania's earlier participation in the Western Sahara adventure.

Also in January, Libyan-supported guerrillas attacked military and police installations in Gafsa, Tunisia. Although the attack was repulsed, tensions between the two countries continued throughout the year. In Chad, the long civil war between various religious and tribal factions continued. A cease-fire had been agreed upon in September, 1979; however, the lack of OAU monitoring forces and the maneuvering of the factions led to a renewal of fighting in February. Libyan forces were taking part in the war in exchange for privileges in Chad's mineral-rich north. In December, Libyan troops occupied Chad's capital, N'Djamena.

In Ethiopia, the guerrilla war in Eritrea continued unabated, as did the fighting in the Ogaden. Somali guerrillas, aided by regular troops, appeared once more to be in control of the countryside, with Ethiopian forces confined to the garrison towns. The United States agreed to supply Somalia with defensive military equipment in exchange for the use of Somali naval and air facilities. Border raids and internal dissidence led So-

After a military coup in Liberia, soldiers on April 22 shoot 13 top officials
of the former regime, after tying them to posts placed on a beach site.

malia's President Muhammad Siad Barre to declare a state of emergency in late October.

In Liberia, a military coup in April, staged by indigenous African enlisted men, overthrew the government of William Tolbert, who was killed, and seemingly marked the end of Americo-Liberian dominance in the country. President Luis de Almeida Cabral of Guinea-Bissau was overthrown on Nov. 14. The coup, staged by Prime Minister João Bernardo Vieira, appeared to end earlier prospects of uniting Cape Verde with Guinea-Bissau. On Nov. 25, Sangoulé Lamizana, who had been president of Upper Volta since 1966, was overthrown in a bloodless coup. Col. Saye Zerbo, who led the coup, cited the country's poor economic conditions as the prime cause of Lamizana's overthrow.

**Continuity and Peaceful Transition.** In February, Gaafar al-Nimeiry was reelected as head of the ruling Sudanese Socialist Union, and, in accordance with the constitution, was to serve as president of the Sudan for another six years. Félix Houphouët-Boigny, who had been president of the Ivory Coast since 1960, easily won reelection in December. Robert Mugabe, regarded by many as the most radical of the Rhodesian guerrilla leaders, became prime minister after his party won an electoral victory. On April 18, Rhodesia,

renamed Zimbabwe, achieved independence under a black African majority government. With Zimbabwe's independence, South-West Africa, or Namibia, remained the last sizable white-controlled territory in continental Africa, other than South Africa. While continuing to resist nationalist guerrilla attacks on South-West Africa, South Africa appeared to be moving toward acceptance of some form of black rule in the territory.

**Papal Visit.** In early May, Pope John Paul II paid an 11-day visit to six African countries. It was the second visit by a Roman Catholic pontiff to a continent where there were about 50,000,000 Catholics and where Christianity was growing at a faster rate than on any other continent. Among the controversial issues facing the pope was the tendency in Africa to adapt traditional folk religious practices to Catholicism. This tendency often included deviation from such Catholic doctrines as monogamy and clerical celibacy. Marriage among African priests and nuns was said to be widespread, and polygamy was said to be common among priests and bishops. John Paul, while paying tribute to indigenous African social and religious traditions, firmly condemned such practices.

See also individual articles on many of the countries mentioned. J.T.S.

**AGRICULTURE.** In response to the Soviet invasion of Afghanistan, the Carter administration on Jan. 4, 1980, imposed an embargo on grain shipments to the U.S.S.R. About 13,000,000 metric tons of corn and 4,000,000 of wheat were withheld from shipment to the Soviet Union. In order to lessen the impact on the farm economy and to avoid possible bankruptcy for grain-exporting companies, the federal government agreed to buy excess grain on the U.S. market at a cost of $2.5 to $3 billion.

U.S. farmers objected to the embargo, fearing economic hardship. The major grain-exporting nations cooperated with the embargo, although Argentina increased its grain shipments to the U.S.S.R., which experienced another bad harvest; see UNION OF SOVIET SOCIALIST REPUBLICS. On July 24, Canada announced it was withdrawing from the embargo.

Meat shortages and food production failures helped trigger an industrial workers' strike in Poland in August; see POLAND. In September the U.S. government agreed to extend to Poland $670,000,-000 in agricultural credits, the largest amount ever granted to a foreign country.

**U.S. Farm Production.** Wheat production in the United States increased slightly to a record 64,300,000 metric tons, but a disastrous drought in the nation's midsection, including much of the corn belt, reduced corn production by about 17 percent. The soybean crop was down 22 percent from 1979 levels. As a result, corn prices jumped from $2.98 a bushel in early April to $3.49 at the end of October; soybeans soared from $5.68 to $8.57; and wheat, in demand because of poor harvests abroad, rose from $3.98 to $4.90. The peanut crop fell about 42 percent and the cotton crop about 23 percent because of the drought.

Pork production in 1980 reached record levels, forcing prices below the production cost for most of the year. At one point, pork producers were losing $47,000,000 a week as hog numbers reached 55,600,000. After several years of declining beef production, the U.S. cattle herd grew to 123,000,000 head.

Net farm income fell about 25 percent in 1980. Production costs skyrocketed, and record high interest rates and higher fuel bills added to farmers' woes. U.S. consumers spent $287 billion for food in 1980, but retail prices rose more slowly than the general rate of inflation—just below 10 percent. Enrollment in the government's food stamp program climbed almost 20 percent from the 1979 level to 20,800,000 people.

**Legislation.** The Energy Security Act of 1980 made available $1.45 billion for the development of alcohol fuels processed from crops and forest products (gasohol). Public support for gasohol continued to grow, and about 4000 service stations were selling the product, a blend of 10 percent alcohol and 90 percent gasoline.

In July, President Jimmy Carter signed into law the Motor Carrier Act of 1980, deregulating much of trucking. A provision of the new law exempted many agricultural truckers from Interstate Commerce Commission regulations.

In September a House-Senate conference committee gave final approval to legislation creating a new all-crop, all-risk federal crop insurance program. The legislation provides farmers and ranchers with federally subsidized, voluntary crop in-

*Although corn and soybeans suffered from the drought that gripped much of the U.S., a bumper apple crop was produced.*

The summer heat wave that brought temperatures of 100° F. or more for 33 consecutive days in Texas wreaked havoc on agriculture throughout the central part of the U.S. This farmer displays the undersized ears and dried kernels of corn common in much of the Midwest.

surance. It was forecast that premium income would reach $1.2 billion by 1985, with crops worth $15 billion insured.

While the debate continued over future directions in agriculture, new data showed that the number of farms continued to decline while farm size continued to grow. Farms in the U.S. numbered about 2,430,000 in 1980. More than 1,200,000 of these were classified as small family farms yielding average net incomes below the nonmetropolitan average. The 500,000 largest farms produced the overwhelming portion of farm commodities.

**Government Actions.** In August the Food and Drug Administration and the Department of Agriculture (USDA) dropped plans to phase out the use of nitrites in processed foods. A 1978 study at the Massachusetts Institute of Technology (MIT) found that nitrites, used to preserve meats such as ham, hot dogs, and luncheon meats, caused lymphatic cancer in test rats. A subsequent review of the MIT study cast doubts on the original findings. Although the government agencies canceled moves to ban the preservative, they planned more research.

The USDA reported to Congress that foreign nationals owned less than 1 percent of U.S. farmland, or about 5,600,000 acres. The majority of these foreign nationals were citizens of Canada, the United Kingdom, the Netherlands, West Germany, and Luxembourg. Owners from oil-rich Arab countries were few in number, despite reports that Arabs were investing heavily in U.S. farmland. A 1979 law required that non-U.S. citizens reveal their U.S. farmland holdings. Federal officials, however, believed that some foreign nationals, fearful of retaliation in their own countries, did not report their holdings.

In a controversial decision, the U.S. Department of Commerce ruled that Mexican farmers were not dumping winter vegetables in the U.S. at unfair prices. Florida growers had brought suit against the Mexicans under antidumping laws. The Florida producers appealed, charging that Carter administration officials intervened in the case in order to get an outcome favorable to Mexico. U.S. officials admitted that a decision in favor of the Florida growers would hamper negotiations on Mexican oil purchases, illegal immigration of Mexicans to the U.S., and drug control.

**Agricultural Trade.** U.S. agricultural exports climbed to a record $40 billion in 1980, an increase of $10 billion over 1979. The agricultural trade surplus also grew to $22 billion. The U.S. remained the world's largest producer of soybeans and feed grains. It was the largest exporter of wheat and soybeans, and the only major exporter of corn and other feed grains.

Japan remained the best customer, purchasing food and food products worth $5.1 billion. Following the January embargo, Mexico agreed to buy large quantities of U.S. grain formerly earmarked for the Soviet Union. The value of food exports to Mexico doubled in 1980 to $2 billion.

U.S. agricultural shipments to China exceeded $1.6 billion in 1980. In October the U.S. agreed to sell as much as 8,000,000 metric tons of grain to the People's Republic during each of the following four years.

**World Food Production.** The worldwide grain supply and outlook was tighter in 1980 than in recent years. World wheat production increased 7 percent from 1979 figures to a record 448,000,000 metric tons. International trade in wheat was projected to reach 88,000,000 metric tons, a 3 percent increase over 1979. World rice production fell from 384,000,000 metric tons in 1979 to 374,000,000 metric tons in 1980. World production of coarse or feed grains declined slightly to 721,000,000 metric tons.                     L.W.W.

**ALABAMA.** See STATISTICS OF THE WORLD.

**ALASKA.** See STATISTICS OF THE WORLD.

**ALBANIA.** Albania slowly emerged from isolation in 1980. Its actions were prompted by economic need and fear of Soviet interference in the Balkan region, particularly after the Soviet invasion of Afghanistan in 1979.

The Albanian government began preparation of its 1981–85 economic plan early in the year. Since Albania had broken with its only ally, the People's Republic of China, in 1978, the new plan envisioned development entirely without credits or economic aid from abroad. Increased trade with such countries as Italy and Greece was considered vital for the country's advancement, however. In July, Albania signed a commercial accord with neighboring Yugoslavia that called for $270,000,000 in trade between the two countries during 1981–85. Trade between the two totaled $80,000,000 in 1980.

After years of hostility, relations between Albania and Yugoslavia improved on the political front as well. In January, shortly after the Soviet strike into Afghanistan, Albania announced that it would consider itself attacked if the Soviets moved against Yugoslavia. Upon the death of President Tito in May, Albania published an un-

critical obituary of the Yugoslav leader, long considered an enemy by Albanian Communist leader Enver Hoxha.

A cabinet reshuffle took place in April. It marked the first major internal change since the mid-1970's. Prime Minister Mehmet Shehu gave up the post of minister of defense to Kadri Hazbiu, formerly minister of the interior, and several other ministries changed hands. The reorganization appeared to leave Hoxha fully in command, as he had been for three decades.

*See* STATISTICS OF THE WORLD.                     F.W.

**ALBERTA.** *See* STATISTICS OF THE WORLD. *See also* CANADA.

**ALGERIA.** Two massive earthquakes struck the Algerian city of El Asnam on Oct. 10, 1980, killing at least 6000 people. Some estimates of the dead were far higher, but it was doubtful that the actual toll would ever be known. The number of homeless in the devastated region surrounding the city was estimated at 250,000.

*A search for survivors is conducted in El Asnam, Algeria, after two earthquakes on Oct. 10 left at least 6000 dead and an estimated 250,000 homeless.*

**Domestic Affairs.** Chadli Benjedid, the career soldier who became president in early 1979, consolidated his position by reshuffling both the cabinet and the country's only legal political party, the National Liberation Front. A new five-year plan allocated increased spending, amounting to $33 billion, for housing, education, and health and promised a larger role for the private sector. Huge, state-run enterprises such as the oil and gas monopoly were broken up into smaller units. Many sectors of the economy, such as textiles, food processing, and light engineering, were to be opened to "nonexploitative" private industry. Farmers were given the right to sell their produce directly to customers, in an effort to halt a long slide in agricultural productivity. (In 1979 Algeria had to import $3 billion worth of food.) The most fertile farmland, however, remained state-owned.

Arabic-speaking university students demanded the immediate Arabization of all studies because top government posts still go to French speakers, a legacy of Algeria's former rule by France. But in April, members of the non-Arab Berber minority, who prefer French to Arabic, rioted in the Kabylia region against the government's commitment to increase the use of Arabic.

Because of sharply higher prices, Algeria earned about $13 billion for its oil in 1980, but production peaked in 1978, and it was believed that the oilfields could be depleted within 25 years if no major new discoveries were made. Algeria tried unsuccessfully to extract sharply higher prices for its natural gas from other countries. In the fall, it said it would not renew a major ten-year oil contract with France unless the French accepted gas prices roughly double what they had been paying.

**Foreign Policy.** Algeria softened its image as a militant anti-Western country. In November it acted as a go-between in negotiations between the United States and Iran aimed at freeing the American hostages in Tehran. There was no change, however, in Algeria's military support for the Polisario guerrillas, who had been fighting to expel Morocco from the Western Sahara since 1975. Algeria tilted toward Iran in the Iran-Iraq conflict, since Iraq supported Morocco.

See STATISTICS OF THE WORLD. See also AFRICA; MOROCCO.                                                    R.H.

**ANGOLA.** In mid-September, 1980, the Angolan government of José Eduardo dos Santos celebrated its first anniversary amid the difficulties that had plagued the country since its independence in 1975.

Foremost among these was the continuing civil war that pitted the forces of the ruling Popular Movement for the Liberation of Angola–Party of Labor (MPLA-PT) and its Cuban–Soviet allies against several rebel groups, notably the National Union for the Total Liberation of Angola (Unita). A major Unita guerrilla campaign was launched in late 1979 against MPLA-PT and Cuban forces in southern Angola. Dos Santos was forced to draw closer to the Soviet Union, and, after a visit by a Russian military delegation, he visited Moscow in January. Economic and technical agreements were reached, as was a protocol on cultural and scientific cooperation. MPLA-PT military officers continued to receive training in the Soviet Union, including Minister of Defense Henrique ("Iko") Carreira, who, in February, was relieved so he could follow a course of study to attain the rank of general. (He was replaced in a July cabinet shuffle.)

Guerrilla activity continued unabated throughout the year. Much of the fighting was concentrated in southern Angola where, independently, South African forces continued to harass nationalists seeking to liberate South-West Africa, also known as Namibia, from South African control. In air-ground assaults beginning in May and extending through late June, South African units killed at least 360 Namibian guerrillas and reportedly destroyed bases, supplies, and the command structure of Namibian nationalists operating in southern Angola. Angola claimed that hundreds of Angolan civilians were also killed, but South Africa denied it. Again in October South Africans raided Angola, killing 28 persons.

In foreign affairs Angola continued to collaborate with the Western powers to convince South Africa to relinquish control of Namibia. Angolan officials met with representatives of eight other black southern African states to devise ways to reduce their economic dependence on South Africa. After meetings in Lusaka, Zambia, in April, Angola pledged with the others to create a regional economic plan and to coordinate agricultural, mining, transport, and communications development.

See STATISTICS OF THE WORLD. See also AFRICA; SOUTH-WEST AFRICA.                                    J.T.S.

**ANTHROPOLOGY.** In 1980 anthropologists worked on a variety of fossil finds, including the remains of *Aegyptopithecus zeuxis,* a small ape that has been identified as a forerunner of humans. Mary Leakey, who in 1979 reported new evidence of humans walking upright 3,600,000 years ago in what is now Tanzania, announced new information about this important link in human evolution.

**Human Ancestor Found.** Interest in a small, cat-sized ape called *Aegyptopithecus zeuxis* intensified in anthropological circles when more evidence was announced on Feb. 6 that the animal,

*In this artist's sketch,* Aegyptopithecus zeuxis *crouches with fangs bared. This early primate, a social animal and a vegetarian regarded by anthropologists as the oldest known common ancestor of humans and apes, lived 30,000,000 years ago in what is now Egypt.*

which roamed the trees of Egypt 30,000,000 years ago, was in fact an ancestor of both apes and humans. Previously, *Propliopithecus,* a contemporary of *Aegyptopithecus,* was considered the forerunner of humans because both males and females of this group possessed small canine and front premolar teeth, a characteristic that distinguishes humans from apes.

A dozen or so lower jaw *Aegyptopithecus* fossils were previously uncovered in the Faiyûm area of Egypt near the edge of the Sahara, 60 km (40 mi.) southwest of Cairo. The discovery of another six to eight jaw fragments just about clinched the case that *Aegyptopithecus* and not *Propliopithecus* should be regarded as a member of the evolutionary chain that eventually led to humankind. In fact, *Aegyptopithecus* is similar to *Dryopithecus,* a precursor of humans that appeared about 20,000,000 years ago.

*Aegyptopithecus* males weighed no more than 5.5 kg (12 lb.) and the females about four fifths of that. Evidence indicated that they were members of a complex society, according to paleontologist Elwyn Simons of Duke University, who worked on the project with paleontologist John Fleagle of the State University of New York at Stony Brook and Duke University anatomist Richard Kay.

Kay said that *Aegyptopithecus*'s teeth were the key element in determining its evolutionary importance. "The males had large, fanglike canine teeth," he said, "whereas females had comparatively small canines." Fleagle explained that the difference in tooth size indicated that the males had developed large fangs in order to fight one another for mates and to defend their dependents from outside aggressors—a characteristic of many primates.

Examination of its eye sockets indicated that *Aegyptopithecus* was most active during the daytime, like today's apes and monkeys. This fact convinced the researchers that there was probably extensive visual and vocal communication between members of the species. Such socialization, they said, required *Aegyptopithecus* to be more aggressive, courageous, inventive, and intelligent than other species that lived in monogamous, or pair-group, societies with relatively simple needs. The more complex social life of *Aegyptopithecus* may have fostered brain growth. *Aegyptopithecus* was the most advanced form of life on earth in its time, according to the researchers, with a cranial capacity of about 30 cc (1.8 cu. in.)—larger, relative to its body size, than that of any other mammal of the period.

Studies by Kay showed that the animal's teeth were equipped for a vegetarian diet, with fruit the staple. Studies of the arm and leg bones by Fleagle indicated that it was a tree dweller that ran along the limbs rather than swinging from branch to branch.

**Tanzania Footprints.** Mary Leakey reported that the fossilized footprints she discovered in 1979 in the Laetolil region of northern Tanzania depict a carefree episode in the lives of humanlike creatures who lived 3,600,000 years ago. In addition to the two side-by-side trails that indicated an adult and a child walking upright, a third set of adult prints was discovered within the prints of the first adult. Such playful behavior, three individuals strolling along with one of them following the pair, may have represented an outing by a family—a male, a female, and their child. These ancestors of humans probably had only recently developed the ability to walk upright and were enjoying this newly found pleasure with companions, according to Leakey.

**New Facts about Animal Domestication.** The discovery of bones of domesticated cattle at three sites in the Lukenya Hill District of the Kenya highlands led to a major breakthrough in ancient pastoral-nomadic studies. Based on radiocarbon dating results released in 1980, the bones were dated to 15,000 years ago. This was a startling find when compared to the standard view that the domestication of cattle, a true indication of social organization and culture, originated in the Middle East only 8000 years ago. Anthropologist Charles M. Nelson of the University of Massachusetts felt that the discovery by his team should force a reassessment of hunting and gathering so-

cieties and the development of domestication, a crucial factor in prehistory.

In an interview, Nelson also said that other researchers had recently discovered domesticated grain 18,000 years old in Africa. Such findings, along with his own, suggest that many of the elements necessary for the development of civilization, such as agriculture and animal husbandry, may have originated in Africa and been exported to the Middle East. B.R.

**ARAB LEAGUE.** In 1980 the Arab League's annual summit conference, held Nov. 25–27 in Amman, Jordan, was boycotted by Algeria, Lebanon, Libya, the Palestine Liberation Organization (PLO), Syria, and the People's Democratic Republic of Yemen (South Yemen). These members were sympathetic to Iran in its war with Iraq. In the cases of Lebanon and the PLO, their dependence on Syria forced them to abandon their neutrality and adopt Syria's position. Iraq and the other 14 countries present were backing, at least verbally, Iraq's position. Iraq is an Arab nation while Iran is not. *See also* MIDDLE EAST.

One of the major goals of the conference was to agree on a fresh diplomatic initiative for resolving the Palestinian issue. As expected, the participants reiterated their previous rejection of the Camp David accords between Egypt (which had been suspended from league membership) and Israel. Israel, the conferees reemphasized, must withdraw from all Arab territories occupied since the 1967 war, and there must be full recognition by the international community of the Palestinian right to self-determination and a homeland. The

**Carrying on the Tradition**

Mary Nicol, daughter of the British landscape artist Erskine Nicol, was just 20 when she attended the London gathering of scientists at which she heard a lecture by a charismatic anthropologist from Kenya, Louis Leakey. Three years later they were married, and they embarked on a collaboration that produced three sons and many of the important anthropological finds of the century. After the flamboyant Leakey died in 1972, his reclusive wife continued to live in remote Olduvai Gorge in northern Tanzania, where their discoveries and those of son Richard have pushed back the origins of early humans more than 1,000,000 years. Mary Leakey continues to produce astonishing new finds virtually every year, including the 1980 discovery of a clear set of humanlike footprints 3,600,000 years old.

*Mary Leakey.*

*The remains of this fortress in Iraq, built of mud brick around 3000 B.C., include the earliest known intact vaulted roof. Teams from the universities of Chicago and Copenhagen excavated the structure.*

participants said that United Nations Security Council Resolution 242, adopted in 1967, "did not constitute a sound basis for the settlement of the Middle East crisis." This resolution did not establish the right of Palestinians to a homeland. The communiqué issued by the Arab League at the end of the conference also restated the league's position, first adopted in 1974, that the PLO is the sole legitimate representative of the Palestinian people.

With regard to the Iran-Iraq war, the conference supported the "legitimate rights" of Iraq, thereby implicitly endorsing Iraq's demand for full control of the disputed Shatt-al-Arab waterway at the head of the Persian Gulf. It urged Iraq and Iran to agree to a cease-fire.

A $5 billion fund was established to provide poorer Arab countries such as Jordan and Tunisia with long-term, low-interest loans for development projects.

Earlier, a Feb. 28 emergency meeting of the league ended without agreement on a resolution condemning Libya for abetting an attack by Tunisian exiles in Gafsa, Tunisia. A commission was created on Feb. 29 to defuse the confrontation between the two north African countries.

See also articles on individual countries and PALESTINE LIBERATION ORGANIZATION.        R.H.

**ARCHEOLOGY.** In 1980 archeologists recovered both Old and New World material from a variety of sites including forests, the seabed, and the desert.

**Mayan Canals.** A major question puzzling archeologists about the Mayan civilization was answered in 1980 through the interpretation by Mayan experts of a fortuitous radar scanning mission conducted as a test by the Jet Propulsion Laboratory of Pasadena, Calif., over the tropical forests of Belize (British Honduras) and Guatemala. Searching for Mayan sites, Richard E.W. Adams of the University of Texas at San Antonio discovered from the radar survey data a remarkable network of drainage canals that led to larger waterways, including the Pasión River in northern Guatemala. Built sometime between 250 B.C. and 900 A.D. when the Maya flourished there, these canals represent the first real evidence of how the Mayan population of 2,000,000 to 3,000,000 was supported in generally uncultivable waste regions. Raised cultivation sites located near the man-made canals indicate that agricultural techniques during this time were much more sophisticated than the slash-and-burn method (in which trees are felled and burned to enrich the land, which is abandoned after a year or two) that most archeologists attribute to the Maya.

Adams and T. Patrick Culbert of the University of Arizona traveled through thick forests in February using the radar evidence, which made it easy for them to locate the identified canals. Mayan specialists next need to link these canal networks to major Mayan sites in order to piece together the whole story. The discovery of the canals, 3 m wide by 61 cm deep (10 ft. by 2 ft.), and what eventually happened to them may in fact provide the key to the sudden collapse of the mighty Mayan civilization in Guatemala about 900 A.D.

**The First Vaulted Building.** An important Iraqi site located on a major ancient Mesopotamian trade route was soon to be destroyed with the completion of a modern dam under construction on the Diyala River in the Hamrin Basin northeast of Baghdad. A team of archeologists from the University of Chicago and the University of Copenhagen managed to salvage some of the most important artifacts and recorded a massive round mud-brick structure there. A landmark in architectural history, according to project director McGuire Gibson of Chicago's Oriental Institute, the unbaked-clay structure is unusual both for its size and the fact that it is vaulted, an architectural element usually missing in prehistory.

The excavations at Tell Razuk (near the modern village of Uç Tepe, the location of this discovery) also proved that fortified settlements existed much earlier than suspected, at least as early as 3000 B.C., the approximate date of the vaulted-roof structure. The building, which is 27 m (86 ft.) in diameter, had buttresses on the outer wall at 5-m (16-ft.) intervals. Archeologists found evidence of many meals in the fortress, which had evidently housed a garrison. The international salvage operations conducted around the Hamrin Basin were sponsored by the Iraqi Organization of Antiquities.

**Oldest Peruvian Site Unearthed.** What has been hailed as the oldest major civilized site in Peru yielded many surprises in 1980, including material with radiocarbon dates of between 2400 and 1800 B.C. The earliest date for culture in Peru had previously been estimated at 1500 B.C. Terence Grieder of the University of Texas at Austin confirmed that the remote site at La Galgada in the Andean highlands was a "metropolis" with a population of about 500, an immense figure for that early time.

The ancient pre-ceramic culture that inhabited the site did not produce pottery but rather used carved gourds as vessels. But the people were by no means primitive. Two sophisticated temples and three houses were unearthed. The temples display spectacular stonework, and one of them,

the largest known for this period, measures about 100 m (305 ft.) in width and 50 m (152 ft.) in height. Other finds included samples of what Grieder claimed are the oldest handmade colored textiles in the world.

**An American Shipwreck near Australia.** A shipwreck found by skin divers off the treacherous western coast of Australia in 1978 was the focus of underwater excavations during 1979 and 1980. In 1980 Graeme Henderson, curator at the Department of Maritime Archeology at the Western Australian Museum, announced that the trading vessel, an East Indiaman dating from the early 19th century, may have originated in the United States, perhaps sailing from Boston or Salem, Mass. The route across the Atlantic, around the Cape of Good Hope at the southern tip of Africa, and from there to the Indian Ocean and the southern Pacific eventually led these traders to East Asia in search of luxury goods.

The vessel, found in the region of Point Cloates, was the first American ship recovered by archeologists in these waters and yielded much information about American trade and shipbuilding during an era of expansion. Among the most convincing evidence found at the wreck site was a small collection of American copper coins; a barrel lid that had the words Boston, Mass., burnt on it; and the insignia of J. Davis on a copper dovetail fitting, which could be traced to a ship merchant of Boston.                                    B.R.

**ARCHITECTURE AND CITY PLANNING.** The search for energy efficiency and the move toward less impersonal architecture concerned architects at the beginning of the 1980's. Despite this trend, taller, shinier, modern high rises continued to go up in most major cities. At the same time, however, the recycling of existing structures was a popular solution in older communities.

**Energy-Efficient Architecture.** In February the U.S. Department of Energy (DOE) proposed national building energy performance standards that would specify the amount of energy a building could consume at the design, rather than the construction, stage. Leaving energy considerations, in effect, to the architects has met with strong approval from the American Institute of Architects (AIA), but builders, engineers, and other groups foresaw problems if the standards became law. In September the U.S. Congress delayed implementing BEPS but authorized several pilot projects.

Whereas many architects were focusing on designs for energy-conserving multiple-family housing, the DOE built a demonstration "solar" house in Brookhaven, N.Y. The clapboard, conventionally styled house can be heated for less than one third the cost of similar buildings with fuel-oper-

The new Corning (N.Y.) Museum of Glass, which opened on June 1, is a glass-sheathed undulating structure on stilts. Designed by Gunnar Birkerts, it housed a collection of about 20,000 pieces.

ated systems. Created by the Total Environmental Action Group of New Hampshire, the structure uses passive solar techniques such as a glass-enclosed porch that, with the help of interior brick walls, can store heat naturally in the winter and be shaded to retain overnight coolness in the summer. Prefabricated dome houses have also become available, their manufacturers promoting the energy efficiency of such structures.

**New U.S. Buildings and Commissions.** An architecture full of color and allusions to other times and places existed until 1980 mainly in drawings and interior design. One breakthrough is the 13-story Public Services Building in Portland, Oreg., which was commissioned in May. The controversial design by Princeton, N.J., architect Michael Graves, dubbed an "oversized jukebox" by one critic, contains fanciful references to the past. Two terra-cotta-colored inset columns form the center of the art deco facade and support an enormous keystone that fronts the top four stories. The $22,500,000 poured concrete building was to be tiled in muted green, blue, and beige.

A medical complex in a late modernist mode but with postmodernist touches was completed near Detroit during the year. An AIA Honor Award was given in May to its designers, William Kessler Associates, the Zeidler Partnership, and Giffels Associates. The large complex, arranged in a simple cruciform design, is sheathed in alumi-

num panels that are rounded at the corners. Several boldly colored panels highlight the exterior. The Medical Center Concourse, an underground tunnel that ties the new structure to older units, is lighted at intersections by mirrored periscopes that reflect the surrounding landscape when viewed aboveground.

A spectacular late modernist "Crystal Cathedral" was completed in Garden Grove, Calif., in September. Philip Johnson of Johnson-Burgee in New York City designed the church for television preacher Robert Schuller. Measuring 415 by 207 ft., the $18,000,000 one-room building has a ceiling height of more than 120 ft. In plan, it resembles an elongated four-pointed star and is constructed of slender steel pipes framing 10,661 panels of silver-coated mirrored glass. Air circulation is achieved by opening strategic windows at the bottom and top.

Honoring the ancient art of glassmaking, the Corning (N.Y.) Museum of Glass opened on June 1. Architect Gunnar Birkerts designed a glass-sheathed undulating structure poised on stilts to house the museum's collection of about 20,000 pieces. The building replaced the original museum, which was flooded in 1972 during a hurricane.

**Urban Development and Restoration.** In a competition for downtown Los Angeles's $700,000,000, 11.2-acre Bunker Hill development project, mod-

81

*California Center, the redevelopment project in the Bunker Hill section of Los Angeles, was designed to include residential, commercial, and cultural facilities within an area devoid of vehicular traffic. The three prominent office towers (center) border the residential buildings to the left. As many as 800 housing units were planned.*

ernist monumentality won over the smaller scale favored by postmodernists. Canadian Arthur Erickson's design was chosen over the team entry of such noted postmodernists as Charles Moore, Cesar Pelli, and Frank Gehry. Erickson's elegant plan consists of 6.2 acres of park and glass-skinned boxes of varying heights and shapes. The structures were to house a performing arts center, an office complex, apartments, a hotel, and a plaza with several shops and restaurants.

A new U.S. courthouse and office building is giving Fort Lauderdale, Fla., a focus. Again monumentality in design helped to define the area, for architect William Morgan created a simple rectangular structure enclosing a city block. A large, shady entrance and a multilevel plaza that has been scooped out of the middle of the concrete building provide open spaces.

A triumph in the renovation of existing buildings was the $7,500,000 Civic and Arts Center in Madison, Wis. The New York City firm of Hardy Holzman Pfeiffer, which leads the profession in "recycling," refurbished the facades of a baroque movie palace and a nearby Montgomery Ward store that dated from 1941. A beige brick wall filled in the old storefronts between the two. Behind the wall the movie theater was restored, another theater was built, and an art gallery and several small performing areas were installed.

The 1884 Villard Houses, built by McKim, Mead, and White on Madison Avenue in New York City, were refurbished by the owners of the $100,000,-000 Helmsley Palace Hotel, which rises 51 stories above them. The hotel, designed by Emery Roth and Sons, uses the center section of the neo-renaissance houses as its main entrance. One wing, restored to its former marble and gold-leafed

### A Palace Unfit for a King

When real-estate magnate Harry Helmsley opened the plush Palace Hotel in New York City in September, it meant nothing but trouble for the operators of the Palace Hotel on the Bowery, where a distinctly seedy clientele rents rooms for $2.85 a night. (By contrast, rents at Helmsley's Palace begin at $120 a night.) The Bowery locale was deluged with phone calls for reservations coming from as far away as Japan, Germany, and Hawaii, and as near as the Citibank Corp., which requested a conference room. Said the Bowery Palace's manager: "Taking into consideration the price and all, they might have decided to stay here."

opulence, houses meeting rooms and a bar and restaurant. The large, light-colored rooms of the second wing are the result of renovations by James Stewart Polshek for the Urban Center, the headquarters of five urban art and architecture organizations.

**International Architectural Events.** The nearly completed Haj airport terminal in Jidda, Saudi Arabia, is composed of ½-acre fiberglass tents, suspended 65 ft. aboveground by cables attached to pylon supports. Designed by Skidmore Owings and Merrill for Muslims traveling to Mecca, the structure was expected to shelter as many as 80,000 pilgrims on 105 acres of land. It is believed to be the largest area ever covered.

A competition was held among 329 firms from 28 nations to select a design for Australia's legislative complex in Canberra, which is the capital city. The commission was awarded to the New York–Philadelphia firm of Mitchell-Giurgola. The plans included headquarters for both legislative houses, quarters for the prime minister, and a forum for official functions. The circular site is located on top of a large hill overlooking the city, and the winning design set the buildings snugly into the hillsides. The 1,500,000-sq.ft. project was to be constructed of precast concrete panels faced with granite.

**Prizes.** The second annual $100,000 Pritzker Prize, sponsored by the Hyatt Foundation, was awarded in July to the 78-year-old Mexican architect Luis Barragán. The reclusive yet influential architect is famous for a small body of minimalist buildings, gardens, and courtyards, all of which feature simple, brightly colored concrete walls.

On Oct. 23, architects from 12 countries shared $500,000 from the first Aga Khan Prize. The sole purpose for awarding the prize was to "encourage architecture that is in keeping with traditional Islamic character and current Islamic aspirations." The 15 winning projects ranged from a summer residence created from two 100-year-old houses in Turkey to a drainage and road system in Indonesia. M.M.

*Mexican architect Luis Barragán, winner of the 1980 Pritzker Prize, designed strikingly simple, visually arresting structures. This home and riding academy is representative of his work.*

**ARGENTINA.** Gen. Roberto Eduardo Viola, former commander in chief of the Argentine army, was named the country's president on Oct. 3, 1980, ending a long squabble among army, navy, and air force officers. He was to succeed Gen. Jorge Rafael Videla as president in March, 1981. Gen. Viola, regarded as a shrewd politician, had the support of the army generals, many of whom he promoted before retiring as army commander in chief in December, 1979.

The navy, however, made no secret of its opposition to giving Viola the wide-ranging powers that Videla exercised in the years following the military coup of March, 1976, that toppled the government of President Isabel Martínez de Perón. Both Videla and Viola had said publicly that they wanted to return the country to civilian rule as soon as possible. But neither gave a timetable.

Meanwhile, the Argentine government continued to face strong criticism from human rights activists at home and abroad who claimed that more than 7000 persons had disappeared since the military came into power in 1976. The Inter-American Human Rights Commission charged the government on April 18 with killing and torturing many people held in detention. Its report accused the government's security agents of "systematic torture and other cruel, inhuman, and degrading practices."

Argentine journalists were particularly singled out for detention, several groups charged. Robert Cox, the former editor of the Buenos Aires *Herald* who fled the country in late 1979 after his family had been threatened, listed 63 journalists who disappeared in the four years 1976–79. In remarks to the General Assembly of the International Press Institute on May 6 in Switzerland, he said that the only improvement came when international groups put pressure on the military government.

Although widely criticized on the human rights front, the junta was praised for its economic policies. Under Economy Minister José Alfredo Martínez de Hoz, the annual inflation rate was cut between 1976 and 1980 from 970 percent to 80 percent. Martínez de Hoz reported on Sept. 23 that the 1980 figure would represent "the first time in four years [inflation would] be under 100 percent." Unemployment, he said in a May report, was virtually at zero. In July he opened the country's capital market to unrestricted inflows of short-term foreign capital in an attempt to reduce interest rates and thus keep inflation at bay.

Earlier, in January, Argentina announced it would not follow the U.S. lead by embargoing grain to the Soviet Union because of the Soviet invasion of Afghanistan in December, 1979. Indeed, Soviet-Argentine trade was stepped up.

More than 16,000,000 metric tons of wheat, corn, sorghum, and other grains had been sent to Soviet markets by mid-September, and future sales were being planned by Argentine grain dealers. The United States sought through diplomatic channels to prevent the Argentine sales, but the Videla government turned a deaf ear.

*See* STATISTICS OF THE WORLD. J.N.G.

**ARIZONA.** *See* STATISTICS OF THE WORLD.

**ARKANSAS.** *See* STATISTICS OF THE WORLD.

**ART.** The art news of 1980 was once more dominated by the buying and selling of major works of art and the activity in the major U.S. art auction houses, where all previous sales records were exceeded by a significant margin.

**Sales.** During a single week in early May each of ten paintings surpassed the million-dollar mark at auction. First among these was "Juliet and Her Nurse," painted in 1836 by the English artist J.M.W. Turner. It was sold for $6,400,000. The price of the painting, purchased anonymously, broke all records for any work of art ever auctioned.

The Turner painting was consigned to Sotheby Parke Bernet in New York City by Flora Whitney Miller with the request that part of the proceeds be donated to New York's Whitney Museum of American Art. The museum was founded by Flora Miller's mother, Gertrude Vanderbilt Whitney, and it was from her mother that Miller inherited the Turner. The oil, in the family since 1901, had been auctioned twice before. In 1836 it sold for $27,000, and in 1893 it sold for $42,000.

A sale of ten paintings from the collection of Henry Ford 2nd at Christie's in New York City on May 13 garnered a total of $18,390,000. Vincent van Gogh's "Le Jardin du Poète, Arles" ("Garden of a Poet in Arles") went for $5,200,000, Paul Cézanne's "Peasant in a Blue Blouse" sold for $3,900,000, and Paul Gauguin's "The Beach at Pouldu" fetched $2,900,000. Another Van Gogh, "The Public Garden," went for $1,900,000, and a Pierre Auguste Renoir painting sold for $1,200,000.

On May 12 a sale of the collection of Edgar William and Bernice Chrysler Garbisch at Sotheby's accounted for four additional sales of $1,000,000 or more. Fetching the highest price of $3,000,000 was Pablo Picasso's "Saltimbanque, Seated with Arms Crossed," followed by "Tahitian Woman under the Palms" by Gauguin for $1,800,000, Van Gogh's "Portrait of Adeline Ravoux" for the same price, and Renoir's "Woman in an Oriental Costume," which sold for $1,000,000.

On Sept. 30 it was announced that four trustees of the Whitney Museum had purchased Jasper Johns's painting "Three Flags" for $1,000,000, the largest sum ever paid for a work by a living American artist. During October at Sotheby's, six paintings sold for more than $1,000,000 each, to set a new record for impressionist pieces. On Nov. 13 it was announced that London's National Gallery had bought a painting by Albrecht Altdorfer, "Christ Taking Leave of His Mother Before the Passion," for about $5,000,000.

**Major Exhibitions.** A number of well-presented shows of 20th-century art highlighted the 1980 season. The major exhibition of the year was "Pablo Picasso: A Retrospective," staged at New York City's Museum of Modern Art from May 22 through Sept. 30, with the help of the Museé Picasso in Paris. Called the largest one-person show ever presented, it included almost 1000 paintings, drawings, sculptures, and prints borrowed from many private collectors and 53 museums. In a rare move the important permanent collection of the museum was taken from display and all three floors were given over to the Picasso works.

A $4.50 admission fee, the highest ever charged at a U.S. museum, did not deter visitors. Advance-purchase tickets were sold out several weeks before the exhibition's closing, which was extended two weeks to accommodate the crowds.

The high bid of $3,900,000 took Paul Cézanne's "Paysan en Blouse Bleue" ("Peasant in a Blue Blouse") during an auction at Christie's New York City gallery. The impressionist painting, part of the collection of Henry Ford 2nd, went to the Kimbell Museum in Fort Worth, Texas.

At the door and stretching around the corner, a line of ticket holders waits to gain entrance to the Museum of Modern Art's Picasso exhibit. Such queues were a daily sight during the show. The official attendance figure for "Pablo Picasso: A Retrospective" was 1,021,404.

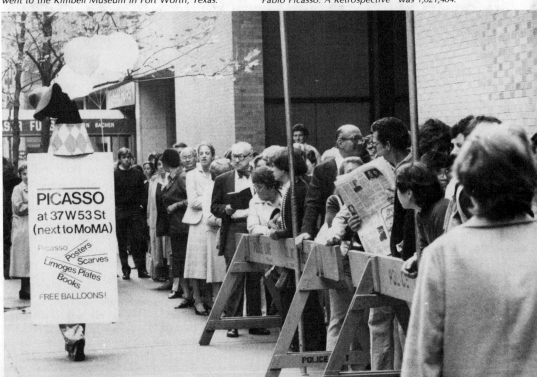

PICASSO
at 37 W 53 St
(next to MoMA)

Picasso Posters
Scarves
Limoges Plates
Books

FREE BALLOONS!

An architectural treasure at the Metropolitan Museum of Art in New York City was saved from obscurity with the June opening of the Met's new American Wing. The long-ignored facade of the 1822–24 Branch Bank of the U.S. was incorporated into the rear wall.

"The Avant-Garde in Russia, 1910–1930: New Perspectives" premiered at the Los Angeles County Museum of Art from July 8 to Sept. 28. This was the first major museum presentation of avant-garde Russian painting from the early decades of the 20th century. Included were more than 400 paintings, sculptures, drawings, prints, photographs, books, and textiles. The exhibition and the catalog offered new insights into this highly regarded but rarely seen movement.

On Sept. 23 the Whitney Museum opened "Edward Hopper, the Art and the Artist," a tribute to one of the most admired of American realist painters. The exhibition consisted of nearly 400 paintings and drawings, many of which had been willed to the Whitney by Hopper's widow.

New York City's Solomon R. Guggenheim Mu-

seum and the San Francisco Museum of Modern Art cosponsored the most comprehensive collection of German expressionist painting and graphics ever assembled. Most of the 350 works came from West German museums, and many had never been seen before in the United States. The West German government was a major benefactor of the exhibition, entitled "Expressionism: A German Intuition, 1905–1920," which opened at the Guggenheim on Nov. 15.

Two shows of major American abstract expressionist painters were presented in 1980. "Philip Guston," a retrospective view from 1930 to the present, was developed by the San Francisco Museum of Modern Art and contained 80 paintings and 25 drawings. The exhibition opened on May 15, shortly before Guston's death on June 7.

The Metropolitan Museum of Art in New York City presented 75 paintings from the holdings of Clyfford Still during May and June. This showing was to be the last in Still's lifetime; he succumbed to cancer on June 23.

A collection of 105 pieces dating from the 18th to the 2nd century B.C. comprised "The Great Bronze Age of China: An Exhibit from the People's Republic of China." Included were bronze vessels, jade and stone objects, and life-size terracotta soldiers and horses found near the tomb of the first emperor of China. The exhibit, which opened at the Metropolitan Museum in New York in April, was to be shown in five U.S. cities before being returned to China in September, 1981.

**New Museum Construction.** Because of rising costs, little art museum expansion or building took place during 1980. But New York's Metropolitan Museum opened two new wings. One, the André Meyer Galleries, is devoted to the presentation of 19th-century European art, and the other to the Met's collection of American art. Included in the latter is the full neoclassical facade of the 1822–24 Branch Bank of the U.S., originally located on Wall Street.

In Los Angeles it was announced that a new museum of contemporary art would be developed as part of a $700,000,000 redevelopment project; *see* ARCHITECTURE AND CITY PLANNING. The 100,000-sq.ft. building was to house international art from the post–World War II period. The museum would be administered by a private-sector board of trustees. As a first official act, the board appointed Pontus Hulten the director. Hulten, highly regarded in international art circles, was to continue to head the Georges Pompidou Art and Cultural Center (Beaubourg) in Paris until his contract expired in September, 1981.          H.T.H.

**ASTRONOMY.** Astronomers in 1980 were nearly swamped by new and surprising information on the solar system as Voyager I flew past Saturn, Pioneer-Venus mapped the cloud-hidden surface of Venus, and an international team of scientists studied the sun at the peak of its 11-year cycle of activity. The 27-antenna Very Large Array radio telescope was officially dedicated at Socorro, N.Mex., in October.

**Saturn.** The U.S. space probe Voyager I swung by Saturn on Nov. 12, approaching within 124,000 km (78,000 mi.) of the planet's cloud tops as it relayed photographic images and physical data back to earth, 1.5 billion km (nearly 1 billion mi.) away. Voyager I then continued on a trajectory out of the solar system and into deep space.

Most spectacular were Voyager's findings about Saturn's rings, previously thought to consist of a few almost homogeneous rings with two major gaps. Voyager revealed that the rings actually are made up of perhaps as many as 1000 thin ringlets, some of them even within the supposed gaps. Two newly discovered phenomena, in particular, intrigued scientists. One was that the so-called B ring, the brightest as seen from earth, showed spokelike features extending across its many ringlets. Each spoke was observed for several hours before fading from sight. The phenomenon may be the result of the shifting of smaller particles above the ring plane by Saturn's magnetic field. The other odd discovery was that the faint, outer F ring consists of ringlets intertwined in a braided structure. This may also be the result of electrostatic forces, but an adequate hypothesis remained to be developed.

Of equal interest was Voyager's flight past Saturn's largest moon, Titan, at a distance of about 4000 km (2500 mi.); Titan is the only moon in the solar system known to have an atmosphere. Data from the fly-by downgraded Titan's size to slightly less than Jupiter's Ganymede, the largest known satellite in the solar system. The atmosphere, previously thought to be mainly methane, was found to consist of 99 percent nitrogen with only 1 percent methane and traces of acetylene and ethane.

*Spectacular findings concerning Saturn's rings were among the various highlights from Voyager I's flight past the planet. The rings were found to be made of perhaps as many as 1000 thin ringlets, often with unexpected structures and features.*

*As Voyager 1 neared Saturn, the cloud surface of the giant planet began to reveal subtly shaded yellow and brown bands. The winds of the planet's upper atmosphere reach speeds of up to 1600 km (1000 mi.) per hr. In this view from a distance of 51,000,000 km (32,000,000 mi.), one of Saturn's 15 known moons can also be seen.*

Atmospheric pressure at Titan's hidden surface is about 50 percent greater than that of the earth's atmosphere. The cold surface temperatures, estimated at −294° F., virtually preclude any possibility of life on Titan.

Saturn's other moons, viewed at various distances, were revealed as mainly icy bodies with light to heavy cratering. One of them, Mimas, has a giant crater nearly a third as wide as Mimas itself. Another, Rhea, shows an unequal patterning of craters, which aroused speculation that the early solar system underwent two periods of intense meteor bombardment rather than one. Moons 10 and 11 were found to share nearly the same orbit. Voyager also discovered three more moons, bringing the known total to 15. The 13th and 14th moons lie just outside and inside the major rings, respectively, and their gravitational effects may help to keep the ring particles from escaping or falling in toward Saturn.

The planet itself turned out to have a banded cloud surface like its neighboring gas giant, Jupi-

ter. The subtly shaded yellow and brown bands do not show the major turbulences of the Jovian atmosphere, but smaller versions of Jupiter's famous Great Red Spot were observed on Saturn. The winds of the planet's upper atmosphere, on the other hand, move about four times more rapidly than those on Jupiter, reaching speeds of up to 1600 km (1000 mi.) per hr. The planet as a whole was found to spin more rapidly than previously thought; the Saturnian day is 10 hr. 39 min. long. Still more was expected to be learned from the Voyager II fly-by of Saturn, scheduled for August, 1981.

**Venus.** A map of 93 percent of the cloud-covered surface of Venus was produced in 1980 from radar observations by the U.S. space probe Pioneer-Venus, in orbit around the planet. The newly unveiled surface was shown to be mainly a rolling plain, with few mountains or valleys. The largest highland, Aphrodite Terra, is about the size of the continental United States. Another highland, Ishtar Terra, is higher and more jagged, with Maxwell

Montes, the highest point on Venus, rising 11.8 km (7.3 mi.) high. Other major features include Beta Region, with two very large shield volcanoes (state of activity unknown); Alpha Region, made up of old, rough terrain; and several rift valleys. The Soviet Union was making use of the map to select landing sites for the four probes that it planned to send to the planet by 1985.

**Other Solar System News.** Maps were also released in 1980 of the Jovian moons Io, Ganymede, Callisto, and Europa. Built up from images returned by Voyagers I and II, the maps contained no new finds but enhanced studies of the moons by providing a standard reference frame. Further analysis of Voyager data also added two tiny moons to Jupiter's retinue, bringing the known total to 16. One of the moons travels at the fastest known speed in the solar system, about 113,600 km (70,400 mi.) per hr.

Data from Mars all but ended when the power system aboard the Viking II lander finally failed and the Viking I orbiter ran out of altitude-control gas. Only the Viking I lander remained in operation, possibly until 1994. Final pictures from the Viking I orbiter showed unexpected surface activity on Mars, including a front or shock wave moving through the atmosphere and clouds apparently caused by volcanic venting. Earth-based radar studies of Mars indicated two regions of

subsurface moistness, and analyses of Viking data suggested that such subsurface water, rather than ancient rains, produced the erosion features that are seen on the planet.

One major disappointment in 1980 was the denial of funding for a 1986 fly-by of Halley's comet and a rendezvous with comet Tempel 2, long sought by the National Aeronautics and Space Administration (NASA). When the European Space Agency announced plans for a high-speed ballistic fly-by of Halley's comet, however, NASA studied the possibility of helping with that mission or launching a similar one.

**The Active Sun.** The International Solar Maximum year, lasting from August, 1979, to February, 1981, was highlighted in 1980 by the February launch of NASA's Solar Maximum Mission Satellite, carrying seven telescopes that operate at wavelengths ranging from visible light to gamma rays. The satellite observed an apparent variation of 0.1 percent in the solar constant, a measure of the sun's energy output. Such a variation is of keen interest, because a drop of only 6 percent could cover the earth with ice. Further observations are needed to establish whether the 0.1 percent drop is a real trend or a normal fluctuation caused by the solar cycle. The satellite also observed several major solar flares. The data, combined with ground observations, led to the preliminary conclusion that

An artist's rendition of the northern highlands region of Venus, Ishtar Terra, as revealed by 1980 radar observations, shows how the land would look if the planet's clouds were rolled away. On the right, or east, is Venus's highest mountain, Maxwell Montes.

The 27-antenna Very Large Array radio telescope was dedicated in New Mexico in October. These huge dishes, each 82 ft. in diameter and spread out in a Y shape along 38 mi. of railroad track, should enable astronomers to make detailed radio maps of distant galaxies.

flares occur when strong magnetic fields on the sun collide.

Earth-based solar studies yielded evidence of large gas "rivers" on the sun. A fast and a slow current exist in both the southern and northern solar hemispheres, varying from the average motion of the sun by only 3 m (10 ft.) per sec. Believed to be caused by subsurface magnetic fields, they form near the poles and migrate toward the equator during the 11-year cycle of sunspot activity. Sunspots were found to form along the boundary between the fast and slow currents.

**Cygnus Superbubble.** Analysis of X-ray data from orbiting observatory HEAO-1 revealed a "superbubble" of extremely hot gases about 6000 light-years away in the direction of the constellation Cygnus. The bubble, 1200 light-years wide and containing as much mass as 10,000 stars, may have been formed by a chain reaction of 30 to 100 supernovas. The shock wave of the bubble has 10 to 20 times as much energy as our sun has released in its entire lifetime. Some astronomers suggested that about 200 superbubbles may exist in our galaxy and that such chain reactions of

giant supernovas early in the history of the universe initiated the collapse of gas and dust into clusters of galaxies.

**Other Astrophysical Developments.** One 1980 result from HEAO-2 was the confirmation of a spectral line from the center of our galaxy that is believed to be caused by the mutual annihilation of electrons and positrons formed in energetic processes by massive stars. The orbiting observatory also showed that many distant quasars are the sources of X rays. Some astronomers suggested that much of the overall X-ray glow in the sky comes from quasars rather than from hot gases theorized to be spread throughout the universe. If such gases existed, they could help to provide the mass needed to halt the expansion of the universe, but the argument is greatly weakened if the X-ray glow actually derives from quasars. Developments in physics that suggest the elementary particle called the neutrino may have mass also have profound implications for cosmological theory.

*See also* Physics; Space Science and Exploration.

D.D.

**AUSTRALIA.** A national election was held in Australia in October, 1980. Voters returned to power the coalition of the Liberal and National Country parties led by Prime Minister Malcolm Fraser, but with a greatly reduced majority. The result shook Fraser, who admitted it was a clear sign of public dissatisfaction. And the closeness of the race bolstered the long-term hopes of the opposition Labour Party, which had now lost three consecutive elections.

**Domestic Affairs.** With an election approaching, Fraser began the year on a note of optimism. In speeches, he emphasized the theme "Australia—the lucky country," pointing out that the nation had entered the decade with abundant resources, 70 percent self-sufficiency in oil, a lower annual inflation rate (10 percent) than many industrial states, and rising exports.

The Soviet invasion of Afghanistan worked to Fraser's political advantage. Since taking office in 1975, he had been warning of the potential threat of Soviet expansionism—to the derision of the parliamentary opposition and the skepticism of much of the electorate. With the Soviet strike into Afghanistan, Fraser's stance appeared vindicated.

Fraser acted early in the year to strengthen Australian defenses. He ordered increased patrolling and surveillance in the Indian Ocean, and in February he announced a higher expenditure for the military. Among other projects, his government planned to acquire a new guided missile frigate and 75 new tactical fighters, modernize armaments mills, upgrade existing weapons systems, and establish a "ready reaction force."

When the prime minister moved to punish the Soviets for their Afghan action by cutting back on Australian-Soviet contacts, he achieved mixed results. His effort to halt Australian participation in the Moscow Summer Olympics did not win overwhelming public approval, and the Australian Olympic Federation voted to allow athletes to compete. Fraser limited cultural and scientific exchanges with the Soviets and pledged to make no new grain-sales agreements with the U.S.S.R., but economic considerations forced him to permit sales of wool and other products.

Opposition leader William Hayden's attacks on the Fraser administration dealt primarily with economic issues. Hayden charged that foreign investment, which was growing at a rate of $2.3 billion a year, was being allowed in Australia without adequate provision for domestic control of the enterprises involved. He also made political capital out of the issue of unemployment, which, in September, stood at 330,000, or 5.9 percent of the work force.

*Former Labour Prime Minister Gough Whitlam speaks for the land rights of Australian aborigines at a demonstration. Aborigines from Western Australia were protesting oil drilling at a site they regarded as sacred.*

*In Melbourne, Premier Dick Hamer of Victoria displays a $1,000,000, 60-lb. gold nugget found near Wedderburn. Skyrocketing gold prices brought on a gold rush in mineral-rich Australia during 1980.*

The Fraser government budget, announced in August, gave priority, as usual, to the control of inflation. But it also sought to attract potential Labour voters in the upcoming election by raising spending on social welfare, health, and education.

The issue of fair treatment of aborigines caused concern for Fraser in the late summer. Aborigines living at Noonkanbah in Western Australia greatly objected to oil drilling on a site they regarded as sacred. Neither their protests nor a labor-union boycott stopped development of the area by an oil firm operating with state-government backing, and the aborigines took their complaint to a United Nations body in Geneva during September. Even so, Fraser refused to intervene in the affair with federal authority—a decision that came in for criticism in liberal circles.

In September the prime minister set Oct. 18 as election day. As the official campaign got under way, his Liberal–National Country coalition was given the edge. Within weeks, however, polls showed Labour ahead. When the votes were finally cast, Fraser emerged with a slimmed-down majority in the House of Representatives. The final tally was coalition 71, Labour 54. In the Senate neither the coalition nor Labour won a majority,

leaving the balance of power with the Democrats. Experts said Fraser's weak showing was the result of economic issues and public dislike of his personal style, which many considered arrogant.

On Nov. 2 Fraser reshuffled his cabinet, dropping five ministers. Foreign Minister Andrew Peacock exchanged posts with Industrial Relations Minister Tony Street.

**Foreign Affairs.** Always friendly to the United States, the Fraser administration drew even closer in 1980. The prime minister flew to Washington in January to declare his firm support of President Jimmy Carter's criticism of the Soviet invasion of Afghanistan. In addition to enhancing Australia's own defenses and cooling relations with the U.S.S.R., he indicated he was prepared to permit American B-52 bombers to use Australian air bases and to allow the U.S. Navy to set up a base at Cockburn Sound, near Perth.

Australia backed the U.S. on the issue of Iran's seizure of American hostages. Except for food and medical supplies, Australia embargoed exports to Iran beginning in May. Only one 1980 issue seriously troubled Australian-American ties. In October, when Washington announced a major sale of grain to China, Australian officials charged that the U.S. was poaching on their nation's traditional market.

*See* STATISTICS OF THE WORLD.                F.W.

**AUSTRIA.** In May, 1980, Austria celebrated the 25th anniversary of its "State Treaty," the 1955 document that marked the end of occupation by the victorious World War II Allies and the beginning of Austria's neutrality and postwar sovereignty. There was much to celebrate: democracy, stability, and prosperity.

Austria continued to weather international economic storms better than most developed nations. Real economic growth for 1980 was expected to be 4 percent or better. As of October, unemployment stood at less than 1 percent, and inflation was expected to average 6.5 percent for the year. The dark spot in the generally bright picture was a balance of trade deficit.

An election for the largely ceremonial presidency was held in May. Rudolf Kirchschläger, 65, was chosen for a second six-year term. Not a member of any political party, Kirchschläger ran as a candidate of the ruling Socialists. The main opposition party, the conservative People's Party, nominated no candidate, indicating basic agreement with Kirchschläger's handling of the office.

A political corruption scandal shook the capital during the summer. Ten businessmen and officials were alleged to have been involved in kickbacks that were paid in connection with construction of a huge $3 billion hospital. The affair focused at-

Chrysler Corp. rolls out its first front-wheel-drive compact, the fuel-efficient K car.

tention on controversial Socialist Finance Minister Hannes Androsch, 42, who was ultimately responsible for the project. Androsch had clashed in the past with 69-year-old Chancellor Bruno Kreisky, leader of the Socialists, and Kreisky took the occasion of the scandal to reduce Androsch's official powers.

In foreign policy, Kreisky decided in March to grant de facto diplomatic recognition to the Palestine Liberation Organization. The move greatly disturbed the Israeli government.

*See* STATISTICS OF THE WORLD.                     F.W.

**AUTOMOBILES.** Hard hit by the recession and the switch by consumers to gasoline-efficient imports, sales of domestic automakers plummeted to 6,787,848 new units from 8,620,461 cars in 1979, a drop of 21.2 percent. Import sales rose to about 2,400,000 units, up 100,000 cars from 1979, and took about 26 percent of U.S. deliveries, up from 22 percent in 1979. On July 7 the Japanese automotive industry announced Japan had overtaken the United States as the leading producer of cars in the world.

U.S. companies permanently closed some plants, cut back production sharply, and put 250,000 blue-collar workers on indefinite layoff at the business low point. All four U.S. producers had net losses for the first three quarters of 1980, a combined total of $3.6 billion. General Motors Corp. (GM) and Ford Motor Co. slashed dividend payments. A record 1643 domestic auto dealers

went out of business during the 1980 model year, compared to 468 for 1979 and 89 for 1978.

**Chrysler Rescue.** The administration of U.S. President Jimmy Carter used legislation authorizing $1.5 billion in loan guarantees to Chrysler Corp. to keep the financially strapped firm afloat. In June the government nervously approved $500,000,000 in loan guarantees, and Chrysler quickly sold that amount in notes. A month later, the federal loan-guarantee board doled out $300,000,000 more.

But the aid did not come easily. Short of funds, Chrysler ran out of cash entirely in mid-June and stopped paying suppliers. Some banks balked at helping out. Infusions of money from states (including Michigan) and labor concessions were needed. Chairman Lee Iacocca said Chrysler came "within a whisker of bankruptcy" before federal help arrived. Federal officials, worried about the long-term financial outlook for the company, imposed various controls over the way it ran its business.

Severe cost cutting was deemed necessary. More factory closings were planned as the company prepared to pull out of full-size car output. Chrysler also saw a need to trim future development in order to hoard cash. Iacocca was relying heavily on the new, more fuel-efficient 1981-model K cars, the Plymouth Reliant and Dodge Aries compacts, for Chrysler's salvation. Chrysler also began speeding up development of other less fuel-thirsty front-wheel-drive cars and trucks.

**Aiding the Auto Industry.** The Carter administration responded to industry pleas for help with a promise to work more closely and abandon the previous "confrontationist" relationship. A package of modest assistance was assembled by a task force headed by Transportation Secretary Neil Goldschmidt and announced by President Carter during a quick Detroit stopover in July. Carter offered some financial help for hard-hit car dealers and auto-oriented areas, faster study of certain industry-favoring tax changes, and minor easing or delay of some government exhaust-emission and safety rules. A government-industry-labor committee was formed to develop more ways to handle auto industry difficulties.

The Administration took some limited steps aimed at discouraging an unbridled rise in imports, especially from Japan, but stopped short of endorsing specific restrictions. Carter asked the International Trade Commission (ITC) to speed up a review of Japanese import practices that could result in restraints on auto imports, but on Nov. 10 the ITC, by a 3–2 vote, rejected any such action. The issue was opened on complaints by the United Automobile Workers (UAW) and Ford, both of which had abandoned their traditional free-trade stances. The UAW urged Japanese producers to build cars in the U.S.

**Cooperation from Abroad.** Foreign automakers began showing interest in building some U.S. plants. Ford and Toyota Motor Co. met in September to discuss a joint production agreement that could make it easier and cheaper for Ford to make small cars in the U.S., using a Toyota design.

Nissan Motor Co. planned a U.S. truck plant, and Honda Motor Co. said it would build a $200,000,000 car-assembly plant in Ohio. Volkswagen tentatively planned a second U.S. car plant, in the Detroit area. Chrysler and Peugeot, the French auto company, agreed to negotiate joint car production in the U.S. Japanese trade delegations journeyed to the U.S. to talk about buying auto parts and establishing joint ventures to make components.

Signs indicated that Japanese automakers might moderate exports to the U.S. The Japanese trade ministry urged the country's auto producers to show export restraint, and Toyota and Nissan pledged to UAW President Douglas Fraser to be "prudent." In September, Renault, the French government-owned automaker, agreed to increase its investment to at least 46 percent of American Motors Corp. (AMC) and could later exercise options to make its share more than 55 percent of the U.S. firm. The deal would provide more than $200,000,000 to keep AMC alive.

**New U.S.-Made Small Cars.** Domestic manufacturers went all out to challenge foreign small cars. Chrysler began producing its K cars in August, preparing to compete head-on with GM's own weight-reducing front-wheel-drive compact X cars, offered since April, 1979. Chrysler expected its new cars to get 25 to 40 mpg. At the same time, Ford brought out its new fuel-thrifty Ford Escort and Mercury Lynx subcompacts, and GM planned its own new subcompact J cars for the spring of 1981. The Chrysler and Ford cars went on sale in early October.

Small cars for the 1981 model year included the new front-wheel-drive AMC Eagle (opposite page). Ford Motor Co.'s 1981 Mustang models (right) were little changed, but among its new subcompacts was the front-wheel-drive Ford Escort (below).

*A Detroit radio station cosponsors a rally against imported cars, which total more than a quarter of all U.S. auto sales. "Pay a dollar," said the station, "and whack an import with a sledgehammer, and we will donate the money to Chrysler Corp."*

### Going Topless

The operation takes 25 hours, can cost as much as $50,000, and is not covered by any medical insurance plan. So why are thousands of U.S. motorists bent on having this operation performed? Because they live in southern California and Florida and want to enjoy as much sunshine as possible—and because the last convertible rolled off the Detroit assembly lines in 1976. Throughout the sunbelt, companies specializing in cutting the hardtops off new cars have sprung up. There are drawbacks, however. The new polyvinyl tops, unlike the automatic ones of the 1940's through the 1970's, have to be raised by hand. And the customizers must add a lot of structural steel, so the newly glamorized but unbalanced machines won't, as one owner complained, "flop like noodles" when they hit the highways.

Giant GM had other ambitious car-development ideas, planning to spend half of the industry's projected $80 billion investment in small-car projects over the next five years. GM said its worldwide front-wheel-drive capacity by 1983 would top 6,000,000 cars a year, five times the 1980 figure, and that by 1985 its new-car fleet would average 31 mpg.

**Auto Safety.** Ford faced what would be by far the biggest auto recall in history, after the National Highway Traffic Safety Administration tentatively found in June that 1970–79 Ford car and light-truck transmissions had a safety defect. The problem involved a tendency for the transmissions to shift suddenly from park to reverse, often resulting in death or injury, the agency said. It was preparing to order a recall of 16,000,000 Ford vehicles. Ford insisted that its transmissions were no worse than its competitors' designs and that the fault lay with sloppy shifting by drivers.

In March, Ford was acquitted of reckless homicide charges by a Winamac, Ind., jury, in a trial involving the death in 1978 of three teenage girls whose 1973 Ford Pinto burst into flames when struck from behind by a speeding van.     A.R.K.

# B

**BAHAMAS.** *See* STATISTICS OF THE WORLD.

**BAHRAIN.** *See* STATISTICS OF THE WORLD. *See also* PERSIAN GULF STATES.

**BANGLADESH.** In 1980 military strongman Ziaur Rahman intensified his efforts to achieve a "peaceful revolution" in Bangladesh, the poorest large country in Asia.

**Politics.** The opposition, though a small minority in the elected, 330-member parliament, proved troublesome. As a show of strength, it engineered a dawn-to-noon general strike on Feb. 9, and a week later it boycotted the opening of the winter session of parliament. Fellow military men counseled President Zia (as he is commonly known) to deal harshly with the opposition. Instead, Zia promised its leaders that parliamentary sessions would be longer and more frequent and that political prisoners would be released. The boycott was called off, and on March 24 Zia announced an amnesty for political prisoners, including five prominent opposition figures.

At the same time, the 43-year-old president took his case to the people, particularly in the countryside, where he hammered away at the "four points" of his "peaceful revolution": a doubling of food production within five years, the spread of literacy, mass indoctrination in family planning, and the establishment of village militias.

The militia idea was the most controversial, because the opposition saw it as an attempt to form a quasi-military arm for Zia's Bangladesh Nationalist Party. In May the president launched yet another ambitious program that was intended to transfer local power in the country's 64,000 villages from the traditional elders and headmen to elected groups charged with carrying out his four points.

**The Economy.** As part of his plan to double food production, Zia pushed ahead with a pet project: canal-building by volunteer village labor. More than 100 canals were dug in 1980, and many more were planned; and 600,000 acres were irrigated and made suitable for year-round planting. The objective was to irrigate millions of acres of arid land and convert them to cropland over the next few years.

Since independence in 1971, all financial institutions in the country had been state-controlled. In August, however, Zia announced that, in order

*The second year of better-than-average crops brought Bangladesh near to self-sufficiency in agriculture. Many irrigation canals were dug in 1980 in order to make arid land suitable for growing food.*

to attract foreign investment, a number of private banks would be allowed to function.

**Foreign Affairs.** Bangladesh continued to take a neutralist path in world affairs and to cultivate its subcontinental neighbors, Pakistan and India. Its ties with the latter were strained, however, by disputes over borders and the rights to water from the Ganges River system. In August, President Zia met with President Jimmy Carter in Washington and made a plea for increased economic aid to his struggling country.

*See* STATISTICS OF THE WORLD.          R.J.C.

97

**BANKING AND FINANCE.** The major event in U.S. banking and finance during 1980 was the Federal Reserve Board's adoption in March of tighter credit measures. This policy worked all too well, effectively increasing the severity of a recession that had already begun; *see also* ECONOMY AND BUSINESS. The board began lifting the restrictions in May. By autumn, however, the money supply was found to be growing too rapidly again, and in late fall the board imposed a second tightening of credit.

International financiers were trying to find ways of recycling the enormous monetary surpluses of the oil-exporting nations following 1979's sharp petroleum price increases. Hardest hit by high oil prices were the oil-importing developing countries.

### U.S. BANKING AND FINANCE

**Credit Controls.** As part of his anti-inflation program announced on March 14, President Jimmy Carter, invoking the emergency powers of the 1969 Credit Control Act, gave the Federal Reserve System (FRS) the authority to regulate the credit activities of all U.S. lenders—department stores, gasoline companies, and finance companies, as well as member banks—to restrain spending by individuals. Simultaneously, the Federal Reserve Board announced that, for the first time in history, large commercial banks borrowing from the system would pay a 3 percent surcharge on the current 13 percent discount rate. The discount rate, which is the interest rate charged by the system on short-term loans to member commercial banks, was already at a record level before the surcharge was added.

As concern over the recession began to overtake worries about inflation, the Federal Reserve Board revoked the surcharge on May 6. The discount rate was cut three times, falling to 10 percent on July 25. On May 21 the credit controls adopted in March were eased roughly by half. Finally, on July 3 the board announced that it was removing the remaining credit controls imposed in March.

**The Money Supply.** During 1980 the Federal Reserve Board was closely watching M-1B—its new measure of cash, checking accounts, and deposits that behave like checking accounts. The target rate for 1980 was an increase in M-1B of 4 to 6.5 percent. By late September, M-1B had increased in 1980 at an annual rate of 6.2 percent, but during the summer it had risen at an annual rate of 16 percent.

New powers to control the money supply were made available to the FRS by the Depository Institutions Deregulation and Monetary Control Act, passed on March 28. The law stipulated that, after a phase-in period of eight years, all financial institutions taking deposits from the public would be required to keep cash reserves with the system. Previously, only FRS member banks had been required to do so, and the number of banks withdrawing from FRS membership had reached nearly 9000. This large number of nonmembers made the system's control of the money supply more difficult.

**Interest Rates.** In October, 1979, the Federal Reserve Board decided to let interest rates rise and fall with market pressures while focusing on more direct controls of the money supply. As a result, interest rates fluctuated considerably in 1980. As the board tightened credit, the prime rate—the rate banks charge their most creditworthy corporate customers—shot up to a record 20 percent on April 3. This action made the cost of loans to businesses more expensive than it had been since the nation's early years. Three-month Treasury bills were auctioned at a record annual rate of 15.7 percent on March 24. By mid-June, however, the

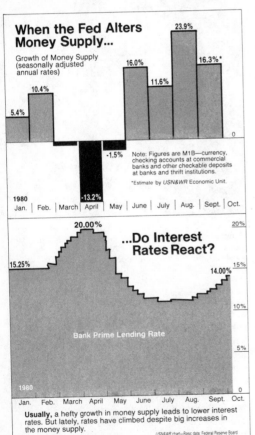

**When the Fed Alters Money Supply...**

Growth of Money Supply (seasonally adjusted annual rates)

5.4% · 10.4% · 16.0% · 11.6% · 23.9% · 16.3%* · -1.5% · -13.2%

Note: Figures are M1B—currency, checking accounts at commercial banks and other checkable deposits at banks and thrift institutions.

*Estimate by USN&WR Economic Unit.

1980 Jan. | Feb. | March | April | May | June | July | Aug. | Sept. | Oct.

**...Do Interest Rates React?**

20.00% · 20% · 15.25% · 14.00% · 15% · 10% · 5%

Bank Prime Lending Rate

1980 Jan. | Feb. | March | April | May | June | July | Aug. | Sept. | Oct.

**Usually,** a hefty growth in money supply leads to lower interest rates. But lately, rates have climbed despite big increases in the money supply.

USN&WR chart—Basic data: Federal Reserve Board

same bills had dropped to an annual rate of 6.4 percent. In July the prime rate fell as low as 10.75 percent, but it began climbing again the following month, reaching 21.5 percent on Dec. 20.

**Stocks and Bonds.** The Dow Jones industrial average of 30 blue-chip stocks traded on the New York Stock Exchange (NYSE) began the year at 824.57. Amidst fears of recession, it sank to 759.13 on April 21, its lowest level in two years. From that point the Dow rose until, on Sept. 22, it closed at 974.57, its highest level since early 1977. On the same day, the broadest measures of the NYSE, the American Stock Exchange, and the over-the-counter market each rose to record highs. Following the election of Ronald Reagan there was another surge, with all three markets several times setting new records in late November. The Dow Jones closed above 1000 on Nov. 20.

Bonds, however, tended to do poorly because of high interest rates. Whenever the cost of money climbs, bonds that earlier sold at lower interest rates become less valuable than newer offerings paying higher returns. Even new bond offerings do not sell well, because under inflationary conditions investors hesitate to lock themselves into long-term fixed-income securities. In March the investment banking house of Morgan Stanley & Co. estimated that bond values had plunged more than $500 billion, or 20 percent, in the previous six months.

On Aug. 7 official trading began on the NYSE's New York Futures Exchange. Since their creation in 1972, most financial futures had been traded in Chicago. Businesspeople use the financial-futures markets to protect themselves against sudden shifts in interest rates and dramatic fluctuations in the value of national currencies.

**Precious Metals.** Under the impact of international crises, gold bullion prices soared above $800 in January, peaking at $875 an ounce on Jan. 21; during 1979 gold prices had climbed from $219 an ounce to $524. By March 17, the price had dropped below $500, but from that point it began rising again.

Silver prices were erratic. On Jan. 21, New York's Commodity Exchange briefly curbed futures trading in the metal, restricting it to the liquidation of contracts. The action was taken to counter wealthy hoarders' buying of large futures contracts on margin—paying only part of the current price and using a broker's credit for the balance—with every indication of taking actual delivery of the metal and thus cornering the market.

The biggest speculators were Texas billionaires Nelson Bunker Hunt and W. Herbert Hunt who, along with Arab partners, built up silver holdings to more than 200,000,000 oz. between mid-1979

When the bell rang at 9:00 A.M. on Aug. 7, action began for 200 commodities traders at the first session of the New York Futures Exchange. A subsidiary of the New York Stock Exchange, the NYFE initially began trading in 20-year Treasury bonds and five foreign currencies. Treasury bill futures were added to the offerings on Aug. 14.

and early 1980. (By comparison, U.S. silver consumption in 1979, mostly by industry, was only 165,000,000 oz.) Their widely publicized purchases helped raise the price from $6 an ounce in early 1979 to a high of $50 an ounce just before the suspension of trading.

By March 27, silver had fallen to $10.80 an ounce, and the Hunt brothers, who had bought on credit, were forced to either put up more collateral or sell their contracts. Rumors spread that the Hunts' principal broker, Bache Halsey Stuart Shields, Inc., had been unable to obtain collateral of $100,000,000 from its clients; other brokers reportedly were owed $200,000,000. The news

### The Silver Bulls

Nelson Bunker Hunt is 54 years old, weighs 275 lb., does not smoke or drink, is a board member of the ultraconservative John Birch Society, owns an unrivaled string of racehorses, and is quite possibly the richest man in the Western world—even after having nearly cornered the U.S. silver futures market along with his less flamboyant brother Herbert. The two are among the 14 children of the legendary late Texas billionaire H. L. Hunt, and they manage a Dallas-based family empire that includes oil wells, coal mines, millions of acres of farmland and urban real estate, and 400 pizza parlors. Bunker is still bullish on silver, but he likes other colors, too. His jockeys wear light green and dark green—the colors of money.

*Nelson Bunker Hunt (right) and W. Herbert Hunt.*

caused the worst financial panic in 20 years. In less than 10 minutes, the Dow Jones average plunged to a five-year low before recovering, amid fears that some Wall Street brokerage firms and large banks might collapse.

On May 27, 13 major banks loaned $1.1 billion to the Placid Oil Co., which is owned in trust for members of the Hunt family, so that Placid could pay off debts owed by the Hunt brothers. The brothers also agreed to turn over 63,000,000 oz. of silver, mineral-rich property leases, and other assets to a partnership with Placid in order to pay their debts, which had reached approximately $1.7 billion.

**Banks and S&Ls.** The new banking law provided for an expansion of services that savings and loan associations (S&Ls) may offer in competition with banks. It authorized all financial institutions that provide federal insurance on deposits to issue negotiable orders of withdrawal, or so-called NOW, accounts which pay interest directly on checking balances. Savings-to-checking transfers, share drafts at credit unions, and electronic payments at S&Ls were also approved.

The law called for a gradual end to federally set interest ceilings on all types of deposits. S&Ls were given the right to offer a range of new activities, including consumer, construction, and commercial real-estate loans; credit cards and lines of credit; and trust services. Lending for

housing was to be liberalized. State limits on interest rates were set aside for a variety of loans.

Despite a three-month moratorium imposed by Congress, foreign-owned banks continued acquiring U.S. financial institutions and toward the end of the year controlled 12 percent of U.S. banking assets. Large American banks, unlike U.S. offices of foreign banks, are subject to antitrust laws and geographic restrictions that prohibit operations across state lines. Foreign-owned banks can also escape the reserve requirements imposed by the FRS.

**Consumer Credit.** A major factor in the recession was that individuals were paying off their debts at a faster rate than they were contracting new ones. From March to July, consumer installment debt dropped by $6 billion; in June alone, it fell by a record $3.46 billion. Credit-card issuers were hurt by rising costs for obtaining their own credit while operating under state ceilings on what rates they could charge the cardholders. U.S. banks were said to have lost at least $250,000,000 on credit-card operations during the first half of 1980.

**Chrysler.** Nearly a year of financial brinkmanship ended on June 24 with an immediate $500,000,000 federal loan guarantee to the troubled Chrysler Corp. It was the largest and most complex effort ever by the federal government to assist a private corporation. *See also* AUTOMOBILES.

## INTERNATIONAL FINANCE

**Debts.** On Sept. 29 the International Monetary Fund (IMF) approved a plan virtually tripling the amount of credit available to its 141 member nations. To supplement the IMF's resources, the members approved direct borrowing by the IMF from wealthy countries as well as from private capital markets. The World Bank proposed to double its loan-to-capital ratio; earlier, a capital increase from $40 billion to $85 billion for the World Bank had been approved.

This easing of terms for loans was made necessary by the prospect that 12 oil-exporting countries would earn a surplus of $115 billion in 1980, compared with only $5 billion in 1978. Conversely, the annual deficit for the oil-importing developing countries was estimated to have climbed from $36 billion in 1978 to $76 billion in 1980. In 1979 the IMF borrowed $10 billion from oil-exporting countries and other rich nations to help deficit nations pay their oil bills and maintain economic growth. The loan was expected to be exhausted by early 1981.

The debt burden of the less developed countries had tripled to an estimated $325 billion. Many private banks, backed by their governments, were reportedly unwilling, or even unable, to extend further credit. It was thought that developing countries might spend as much as 30 percent of their 1980 export earnings on oil, while much of the balance would go for debt-service payments.

On Nov. 25, A. W. Clausen, president of the Bank of America, was chosen president of the World Bank, effective July 1, 1981, to succeed Robert S. McNamara, who was retiring.

**National Currencies.** Supported by interest rates as high as 20 percent, the dollar showed increasing strength in early 1980. Paradoxically, Western nations that had seen the dollar's weakness as a threat to international finance regarded the dollar's rise as jeopardizing their own attempts to curb inflation. For countries that pay in U.S. currency for oil and other imported minerals, the stronger dollar meant a higher import bill. But as U.S. interest rates dipped, the dollar began to fall, too. On July 7 it fell to its lowest level in five years against the British pound, the lowest against the Swiss franc since Jan. 14, and the lowest against the West German mark since Feb. 18.

West German, Swiss, and Japanese central bankers moved to stem the strengthened dollar by selling U.S. currency from their reserves and by increasing interest rates. All three countries overcame their past reluctance to see their currencies either widely used in international trade or held in other countries' reserves. The three asked oil-exporting nations to invest in their currencies to increase the values of these monetary units and thus combat inflation. The British pound traded Oct. 24 at a seven-year high against the dollar and gained against other European currencies. This strength could be attributed to a minimum lending rate of 16 percent and Great Britain's self-sufficiency in oil. R.H.

**BARBADOS.** *See* STATISTICS OF THE WORLD.

*President Jimmy Carter shakes hands with Chrysler Corp. Chairman Lee Iacocca (left) during signing ceremonies for federal legislation. Federal loan guarantees rescued Chrysler from probable bankruptcy.*

*In this experiment by B. F. Skinner and two Harvard University associates, two pigeons communicate by pecking disks in order to transmit information that earns snacks as rewards. Skinner called this interaction "sustained and natural conversation."*

**BEHAVIORAL SCIENCES.** Behavioral research in 1980 indicated a link between the viewing of sexually violent films and aggressive behavior toward women. Controversy continued over the language abilities of apes and whether alcoholics can safely return to moderate drinking. Further strides were made in the new field of behavioral medicine.

**Effects of Filmed Violence.** Two research reports at the September meeting of the American Psychological Association in Montréal suggested that sexually violent films, including so-called aggressive-erotic pornography, can cause male viewers to behave more aggressively toward women. This finding might seem to contradict the 1970 report of the Presidential Commission on Obscenity and Pornography, which found no such linkage, but researchers pointed out that filmed violence and pornography have become much more graphic since that time.

One 1980 report was of an experiment conducted at the University of Wisconsin by Edward Donnerstein, in which 120 male students were paired with male and female students who were secret confederates in the project. Mild electric shocks were administered by the latter as part of a test procedure, in a way that would anger some of the subjects. The subjects were then selectively shown films that were either nonsexual, nonviolently sexual, or aggressively sexual. Afterward, when the subjects in turn were asked to administer shocks in a further test, the angered males who had seen the violent film were found to have administered the most shocks, especially when their partners were women.

The other 1980 report involved a study of 271 male and female students at the University of Manitoba. Some were shown a nonviolent film and others a sexually violent film. One week later all subjects answered a lengthy questionnaire about sexual attitudes, and the results indicated that the male subjects who saw the violent film were more accepting of interpersonal violence, including sexual violence against women.

**Animal Language.** Experiments with chimpanzees and a gorilla over the past several years have led some researchers to believe that apes can use the abstract concepts of true human language. A 1979 report from Herbert Terrace of Columbia University cast doubt on these results, and in 1980 a further attack came from the behavioral psychologist B. F. Skinner. He and two assistants conducted an experiment in which two pigeons, named Jack and Jill, were taught two complex and interrelated procedures involving colored lights and coded disks. After training, Jack, for example, could peck a disk to ask what color was being hidden from him, but not from her; Jill would then peck the appropriate disk. Jack would then peck the disk rewarding Jill with a snack and the disk coded for color that would reward him with his own snack.

The end result, in Skinner's opinion, was both a put-down of the ape experiments and a support for his own views that "verbal" behavior—in humans as well as other animals—is simply a learned response to a "verbal" environment. Others who do not take the extreme behaviorist positions of Skinner saw the experiment as a further indication that the ape behavior in question is only conditioning, not true communication through sign language. Researchers involved in the ape experiments felt that their work included variables that the apes could not have handled through mere rote learning.

**Alcoholics and Drinking Behavior.** Controversy was aroused in January when the National Institute on Alcohol Abuse and Alcoholism (NIAAA) released a report on a comprehensive four-year study of alcoholism conducted for the NIAAA by the Rand Corp. The results could be taken to suggest that alcoholics younger than 40 and with relatively few symptoms of alcohol dependence are more likely to relapse into alcoholism if they try to abstain completely than if they resume low-level social drinking. John DeLuca, the NIAAA director, praised the report as a whole but could not accept the possibility of a safe return to moderate drinking (which the report in no way recommended).

Two 1980 research reports indicated that alcohol abusers with a biological-family background of alcoholism showed more severe symptoms and had greater social problems than abusers with a background of adoptive-family alcoholism or other disruptive childhood experiences. The results suggested that heredity plays an important role in the development of alcoholic behavior. Two other reports indicated that although in the long term alcohol is a depressant, in the short term it can act as an antidepressant or an antianxiety drug such as Valium. This finding indicates that alcohol abusers continue to drink, although futilely, to regain the immediate effects.

**Behavioral Medicine.** Only in recent years have scientists begun to explore in detail the countless ways in which mind and body interact. In 1980 a new field known as behavioral medicine was, among other activities, attempting to track down the neurochemical mechanisms related to stress that can lead to disease. Stress-related diseases include hypertension and heart disease, gastrointestinal disorders, migraine headaches, and certain maladaptive behavior, such as bed-wetting, over which patients have no voluntary control. Treatment in behavioral medicine consists primarily of conditioning techniques.

In 1980 a panel convened by the National Heart, Lung, and Brain Institute concluded that the so-called type A pattern of stressful behavior—aggressive, impatient, overcontrolling—is indeed a significant risk factor for heart disease. Preliminary results from ongoing studies also indicated that by changing this behavior pattern, type A persons can significantly lower their susceptibility to heart attacks. Early results of another project, conducted by researchers at New York City's Mount Sinai School of Medicine and the University of Vermont School of Medicine, showed that the stress of a loved one's death can lead to deficiencies in a person's immune system, which defends against disease.                S.M.

**BELGIUM.** Inflation, unemployment, the energy crisis, and a trade deficit posed serious problems for Belgium in 1980 and caused a government crisis in October. Earlier, in April, the language dispute had brought about a government crisis.

The language problem had opened a split in Premier Wilfried Martens's six-party coalition in December, 1979. The premier's Flemish-speaking Social Christian Party had protested a decision to give self-governing status to French-speaking Brussels, which is located in Flemish-speaking Flanders. French-speaking parties threatened to quit the coalition if the proposal for Brussels were canceled. Martens kept his cabinet together briefly by a Jan. 10 postponement of the Brussels plan, yet the three members of the French-speaking Democratic Front resigned on Jan. 16. Their replacement by three other French-speaking ministers was approved on Jan. 23.

The Martens government then resigned on April 9, a week after the defeat of the plan to divide Belgium into three autonomous regions. On May 11, Martens succeeded in forming a fresh six-party coalition. The new government, inducted on May 18, was committed to regional autonomy but postponement of action on Brussels. Parliament on Aug. 5 and 7 approved the autonomy program, which mandated regional assemblies and executives for Wallonia and Flanders but deferred decision on Brussels. On Oct. 15 the first Walloon parliament was officially installed in Namur.

On Oct. 4, Martens offered his resignation again, this time because of a split over economic policies. The Liberals wanted social security spending cut, but the Socialists were opposed. On Oct. 22 a four-party coalition (including the French and Flemish wings of both the Social Christian and Socialist parties) took office, the fourth government under Martens in 18 months.

Belgium was unable to avoid involvement in the Arab-Israeli confrontation. In Antwerp on July 27, a Palestinian threw grenades into a group that included Jewish youths from other countries. A boy was killed and 13 people injured. Belgian parliamentarians visited Yasir Arafat, leader of the Palestine Liberation Organization (PLO), in Beirut, Lebanon. Arafat told a newsman he was satisfied with Belgium's attitude and support of the PLO.

A $560,800,000 cut in government spending for 1980 was announced in March in an effort to support the currency and defray the rising costs of borrowing. New energy conservation measures were instituted to reduce the deficit in the balance of payments.

*See* STATISTICS OF THE WORLD.                L.A.S.

**BENIN.** *See* STATISTICS OF THE WORLD.

**BHUTAN.** *See* STATISTICS OF THE WORLD.

**BOLIVIA.** The military pushed aside the interim government of Lydia Gueiler Tejada on July 17, 1980, and imposed a tough-fisted regime on Bolivia.

The move came after a June 29 presidential election in which Hernán Siles Zuazo, a former president, emerged as the top vote-getter. His leftist views were anathema to the military, which had already done what it could to postpone the vote. Only the strong determination of Gueiler prevented the postponement and also staved off a threatened coup in the week before the voting. But as Siles's less-than-majority victory became apparent, the military decided to act in order to prevent his accession. Leader of the coup was the army chief of staff, Gen. Luis García Meza, who declared himself president.

García and his fellow military immediately ran into stiff opposition. The country's tin miners, along with other workers, refused to return to work and, for brief periods at the end of July, seized and held various cities in the mining sectors of the country until dislodged by army forces. The Roman Catholic council of bishops condemned the military for the violence of the takeover. Military men in civilian dress, for example, entered a number of public buildings and killed or kidnapped many government and labor officials. Gueiler took refuge in the papal nuncio's home, while Siles and other Bolivian politicians went into hiding.

The United States condemned the coup, but García declared: "We will not be terrorized by clowns in Washington." The Organization of American States, for its part, passed a resolution on July 25 expressing "serious concern about grave violations of human rights" in the aftermath of the coup. Meanwhile, charges of drug running by leading officers involved in the coup were alleged though roundly denied by the military. In August the U.S. announced the termination of its narcotics-related assistance to Bolivia, and the withdrawal of personnel working to control drug traffic.

The turmoil left the economy in a shambles. While under Gueiler there had been some growth in the gross national product and improvement in cutting unemployment, the takeover reversed both—and indicated that Bolivia might well have a zero growth rate in 1980. Unemployment rose between mid-July and mid-September to 23 percent, a 4 percentage point increase.

*See* STATISTICS OF THE WORLD. *See also* ORGANIZATION OF AMERICAN STATES. J.N.G.

**BOTSWANA.** *See* STATISTICS OF THE WORLD.

**BRAZIL.** The chief event in Brazil during 1980 was a 12-day visit by Pope John Paul II, June 30–July 11, to the world's most populous Catholic country. Although John Paul had declared that his mission to Brazil was "purely religious and pastoral," his remarks spotlighted the vast social and economic divisions among the country's nearly 120,000,000 people.

On the one hand, he identified himself with the progressives who dominate the Brazilian clergy and speak out on behalf of human rights, land reforms, labor unions, and the poor. He pointedly embraced Archbishop Hélder Câmara of Recife, the church's best-known radical and opponent of the military regime. Before an audience of business and civic leaders in Salvador, he declared: "The achievement of justice on this continent is confronted by a clear choice. Either it is to be carried out by means of profound and courageous reform or it is carried out by the forces of violence."

On the other hand, he warned activist clergymen to eschew "the class struggle" and leave politics to public men. At an eight-hour meeting with 200 Brazilian bishops, he told them "your principal job is evangelizing." He repeated many times the church's commitment to nonviolence.

The pope's endorsement of the Brazilian church's social mission was not to the taste of the military government of President João Baptista de Figueiredo; many priests and even some bishops had been jailed, tortured, or beaten since 1968 for criticism of the government's policies. But the pope and the president spent 43 minutes alone and then appeared on the balcony of the presidential palace to acknowledge cheers from the throngs below with apparent warmth.

No sooner had the pope left Brazil than a wave of rightist terrorism sprang up in most Brazilian cities. The campaign, which actually began earlier, was seen as a last stand by backers of the right-wing philosophy that had dominated Brazil during 16 years of military rule. Firebombings, sniper attacks, vandalism, and death threats were part of the terrorist onslaught. A Jewish nursery school in São Paulo was hit by a firebomb in August, raising fears of an anti-Semitic campaign on the part of some of the terrorists. Newsstands were bombed in Rio de Janeiro, São Paulo, Belo Horizonte, and Curitiba—the targets apparently being some of the politically and sexually liberal publications freely available on the newsracks as part of the gradual liberalization of government that began under Gen. Ernesto Geisel and continued under his successor, Figueiredo.

In a Belo Horizonte speech on Sept. 11, Figueiredo pledged to pursue the "redemocratization"

*Beneath the statue of Christ the Redeemer overlooking Rio de Janeiro, Pope John Paul II blesses his audience. He pleaded for social justice during a 12-day, 9000-mi. tour of Brazil—the world's most populous predominantly Roman Catholic country.*

of Brazil "even if they [the terrorists] rain four, twenty, or a thousand bombs down on our heads." He added: "If these thugs insist on disrupting the peace and dignity of our people, let them come after me with their bloody hands, but enough of this killing of innocent people." He indicated he would deal firmly with those involved—even if they were military men, as many in Brazil suspected. At the same time, Figueiredo, as part of the liberalization campaign, freed all remaining political prisoners from earlier military governments.

Figueiredo had reason for concern. Between Jan. 1 and Sept. 1, more than 1000 Brazilians had disappeared; nearly 300 corpses had turned up along roadsides, in garbage dumps, and elsewhere in Rio de Janeiro by May 15, according to police statistics. Not all were victims of rightist terrorists, but police estimated that fully half were.

Brazil's strong economic showing through the 1960's and 1970's ran into difficult times in 1980. Inflation, which had been cut from more than 100 percent in 1964 to an annual rate of 20 percent in the early 1970's, was running at more than 100 percent in 1980. Planning Minister Antônio Delfim Netto, who was responsible for curbing

inflation, admitted in a September speech that he had made little progress. Moreover, the nation's foreign debt reached a staggering $50 billion, requiring interest payments of $7.3 billion in 1980.

*See* STATISTICS OF THE WORLD.　　　　J.N.G.

**BRITISH COLUMBIA.** *See* STATISTICS OF THE WORLD.

**BULGARIA.** Unlike some of its East European neighbors, Bulgaria appeared to escape reverberations from the historic 1980 workers' revolt in Poland. Its internal climate remained calm, and its foreign policy faithfully reflected that of the Soviet Union.

The Communist Party, led by 69-year-old Todor Zhivkov, prepared for the 12th party congress, which was scheduled to be held in March, 1981. No major political reshuffles occurred during 1980, and Zhivkov took evident satisfaction in announcing, in a February speech, that the national income had grown by 6.5 percent in 1979 and foreign trade by 11.4 percent. To encourage domestic development, the government passed legislation easing restrictions on joint economic ventures on Bulgarian territory. Under a decree issued in March, foreign firms were permitted to repatriate their profits after taxes and to own the major share in any joint enterprise. A key stipulation, however, was that the chairman of a joint enterprise must be Bulgarian.

The Soviet Union's closest Warsaw Pact ally, Bulgaria was the first East European country to support the widely criticized Soviet invasion of Afghanistan. In 1980 Bulgarian spokesmen argued the Soviet case for the invasion during visits to Third World countries. Zhivkov himself visited Libya and Malta in March, and Foreign Minister Peter Mladenov journeyed to India and Kuwait that same month. In April Zhivkov visited Syria, and in May, Iraq. Ethiopian leader Mengistu Haile Mariam was received by Zhivkov in Sofia in July. They signed a treaty of friendship and coopera-tion, including military collaboration, between their two countries. Zhivkov held meetings with Soviet President Leonid I. Brezhnev in the Crimea in August. The official Soviet news agency Tass reported that Brezhnev and Zhivkov had achieved a complete identity of views on all subjects dis-cussed.

*See* STATISTICS OF THE WORLD.                       F.W.

**BURMA.** Burma remained firmly under the au-thoritarian, one-man rule of President Ne Win in 1980. The unpredictable 70-year-old former gen-eral, however, showed signs of mellowing.

**Politics.** In an unexpected move on May 28, Ne Win pardoned all political prisoners and invited exiles to return without fear of punishment. Among the returnees was former Prime Minister U Nu, Burma's leading political figure from in-dependence in 1948 until his overthrow by Ne Win in 1962. On his arrival in Rangoon on July 29, U Nu, 73, a devout Buddhist, promised to devote himself to religious pursuits.

On Aug. 13 the New York *Times* reported that the Burmese government had proposed a new law that would create two types of citizenship: one for members of Burma's indigenous ethnic groups and one for "naturalized" citizens, con-sisting of about 3,000,000 people, mostly Chinese, Pakistanis, and Bangladeshis. The new law would bar naturalized citizens from military and political posts and the leadership of economic organiza-tions engaged in production and distribution. Ac-cording to the *Times,* the law was proposed to prevent Chinese and Indians from profiting dis-proportionately from Burma's economy and to deter immigration from Bangladesh and China.

The country continued to be plagued by insur-gencies, both ethnic and political. In May, Ne Win offered an amnesty to those who surren-dered, and in August, the government announced that more than 1000 had laid down their arms. Nevertheless, the long-standing Kachin, Shan, and Karen rebellions remained very much alive, and a Chinese-backed Communist insurgency grew in strength despite a government military offensive.

**The Economy.** Burma's per capita income re-mained one of the world's lowest. The govern-ment pursued fiscal reforms recommended by the International Monetary Fund, but the economy, hobbled by bureaucratic bottlenecks and a lack of managerial skill, remained largely stagnant.

**Foreign Affairs.** Burma adhered to its longtime policy of neutrality in 1980, but Ne Win, wary of both China and Soviet-backed Vietnam, contin-ued to relax his country's rigid isolationism and strengthen ties with its non-Communist neigh-bors and the West. On Aug. 29, Burma and the United States signed a two-year, $5,000,000 aid package intended to help improve the country's health care. It was the first U.S. economic assist-ance program for Burma in 17 years.

*See* STATISTICS OF THE WORLD.                       R.J.C.

**BURUNDI.** *See* STATISTICS OF THE WORLD.

# C

**CABINET, UNITED STATES.** Cyrus R. Vance re-signed as secretary of state on April 26 in dis-agreement over the Carter administration's at-tempt to rescue Americans held hostage in Iran; *see* MILITARY AND NAVAL AFFAIRS. Vance told Pres-ident Jimmy Carter that he could not give him "public backing" on the decision.

The President nominated Sen. Edmund S. Mus-kie (D, Maine; see biography at PEOPLE IN THE NEWS) on April 29 to succeed Vance as secretary of state. Carter denied "erroneous" reports that his national security adviser, Zbigniew Brzezinski, was growing in influence at the expense of the secretary of state. Muskie's nomination was con-firmed on May 7 by a 94-2 vote of his former col-leagues in the Senate.

Secretary of the Treasury G. William Miller, the former chairman of the board of Textron, Inc., came under attack but kept his cabinet post after the Securities and Exchange Commission (SEC) accused his former company of having concealed questionable payments to foreign officials in or-der to get military contracts. According to the SEC charges, filed in federal court in Washington,

## A Professional Departs

Many observers of the political scene in Washington, D.C., were not surprised by the resignation of Secretary of State Cyrus R. Vance in late April. Ostensibly provoked by the attempted rescue of the American hostages in Iran, a move Vance reportedly considered both provocative and risky, the resignation seemed the inevitable outcome of a steady decline in Vance's prestige and a parallel rise in the influence of National Security Adviser Zbigniew Brzezinski. The two foreign policy experts disagreed fundamentally on U.S.-Soviet relations, with Vance favoring a softer line. The West Virginia-born Vance, who turned 63 in March, nevertheless retained the respect of his colleagues both in Washington and abroad. As one aide said: "You've got to admit the man's a real professional."

*Cyrus R. Vance.*

D.C., on Jan. 31, the alleged bribes totaled $5,400,-000. The complaint said Miller had made "erroneous and misleading" statements to shareholders in denying these payments. It also said he had sought to conceal the allegedly improper expenditure of $600,000 in Textron money to entertain Department of Defense officials while he headed the company.

Miller denied on Feb. 1 that he had known of questionable overseas payments. The spending on Defense personnel, he said, was "normal courtesy and hospitality." President Carter told newsmen on Feb. 2 that he would not demand Miller's resignation, and Attorney General Benjamin R. Civiletti told a Senate subcommittee on Feb. 5 that there was no evidence that warranted the appointment of a special prosecutor.

Civiletti was himself the subject of a Justice Department probe of his conduct in the Billy Carter affair. Civiletti had withheld information on the case for national security reasons, he said, raising a possible question of obstruction of justice. He also first denied, then admitted, that he had a brief conversation with the President on June 17 concerning Billy Carter's failure to register as a Libyan agent. On Oct. 2 a special Senate subcommittee issued a report of its investigation of the "Billygate" affair, criticizing both Civiletti and Brzezinski for acting "to protect the President from taking personal responsibility."

**Membership.** In addition to Brzezinski, other cabinet-level officers—officials of cabinet rank but without holding cabinet positions—included Donald F. McHenry, ambassador to the United Nations; James T. McIntyre, director of the Office of Management and Budget; and Charles L. Schultze, chairman of the Council of Economic Advisers.

The executive departments, the years of their establishment, and their heads during 1980 follow:

Department of State, 1789: Secretary, Cyrus R. Vance, replaced by Edmund S. Muskie.

Department of the Treasury, 1789: Secretary, G. William Miller.

Department of the Interior, 1849: Secretary, Cecil D. Andrus.

Department of Agriculture, 1862: Secretary, Bob Bergland.

Department of Justice, 1870: Attorney General, Benjamin R. Civiletti.

Department of Commerce, 1913: Secretary, Philip M. Klutznick.

Department of Labor, 1913: Secretary, F. Ray Marshall.

Department of Defense, 1949: Secretary, Harold Brown.

Department of Health and Human Services, 1953: Secretary, Patricia Roberts Harris.

Department of Housing and Urban Development, 1965: Secretary, Moon Landrieu.

Department of Transportation, 1966: Secretary, Neil E. Goldschmidt.

Department of Energy, 1977: Secretary, Charles W. Duncan, Jr.

Department of Education, 1979: Secretary, Shirley M. Hufstedler.                                        L.A.S.

**CALIFORNIA.** See STATISTICS OF THE WORLD.

This refugee camp in Thailand, near the Cambodian frontier, holds thousands of Cambodians who fled their Vietnamese-occupied homeland. They, and the people in Cambodia, were receiving food supplies from international aid organizations in 1980.

**CAMBODIA,** officially known as the PEOPLE'S RE-PUBLIC OF KAMPUCHEA. For Cambodia—a country shattered by war, brutality, and deprivation—1980 was yet another year of anguish.

**Politics.** It was the second year in power for the Vietnam-installed Communist regime of President Heng Samrin. Western correspondents permitted to visit the country reported considerable unhappiness with the Vietnamese military presence. At the same time, the average Cambodian had no desire to return to the despotic Khmer Rouge government of former Premier Pol Pot and its extreme brand of communism.

As the year progressed, Cambodians sifted back into cities from which they had been herded by Pol Pot's soldiers. Families, forcibly separated, were reunited and allowed to acquire such minor items of property as farm animals and bicycles. Schools were reopened, and religion, if not encouraged, was tolerated. A new constitution was in preparation, and in September the Heng Samrin government announced that carefully selected candidates would take part in elections for a Na-

tional Assembly to be held in early 1981.

In their jungle lairs along the Thai border, the ousted followers of Pol Pot remained defiant. In January, in a transparent attempt to gloss over their bloodstained image, the Khmer Rouge removed Pol Pot as their nominal leader (he remained as commander of their guerrilla forces). In his place they installed as premier the more ingratiating Khieu Samphan, 49, a French-educated intellectual with a doctorate in economics.

In the months that followed, Khieu Samphan and Deputy Premier Ieng Sary conceded that the Khmer Rouge government had erred in introducing radical measures after its victory in 1975. Pleading for international support, the two insisted that they no longer wished to impose their brand of socialism on Cambodia but wanted simply to drive out the Vietnamese. Under prodding from their ally China, the Khmer Rouge leaders even hinted that they might find a place in their resistance movement for Prince Norodom Sihanouk, the popular former ruler of Cambodia in exile in North Korea.

**The Battleground.** Despite overwhelming superiority in manpower and Soviet-supplied equipment, Hanoi's 200,000-man occupying army was unable to eradicate resistance by the Khmer Rouge and other guerrilla groups. In late June the Vietnamese raided border villages and refugee camps in Thailand in an attempt to curtail support for the guerrillas and punish the Thais for their opposition to the Heng Samrin government in Phnom Penh.

In July the Vietnamese intensified their attacks on Khmer Rouge strongholds near Thailand, and in August and September they concentrated large numbers of troops in western Cambodia. The Khmer Rouge were said to control only enclaves in formerly uninhabited areas.

**Flight and Famine.** Hundreds of thousands of Cambodian refugees continued to pack camps along the Thai border and in Thailand itself. Some fled their homeland because of politics, many more because of the scarcity of food caused by poor weather and political disruption.

In March the United Nations called an emergency conference to raise $100,000,000 for food aid to Cambodia. But Western nations, which had responded generously in 1979, were outraged by reports that Vietnamese troops were siphoning off the food relief, and they substantially decreased their donations. (The Khmer Rouge, with Thai cooperation, were also diverting food to their 60,000 supporters in Cambodian enclaves.) The specter of famine receded in the latter part of the year, however, and relief organizations took the guardedly optimistic position that the worst of the Cambodian food crisis might be over.

The refugee problem remained critical. In March Thailand closed its border to new refugees, and the prospect for those inside Thailand was not a happy one. The Thais were anxious to see them resettle in other countries or return to Cambodia of their own volition. Few countries were willing to take them, however, and few Cambodians wished to return home.

**Foreign Affairs.** The puppet government of Heng Samrin continued to have difficulty gaining diplomatic recognition abroad. India recognized it in July, but most of the world, outside the Soviet bloc, withheld judgment. On Oct. 13 the U.N. General Assembly voted once again to seat the Khmer Rouge delegation as the official representatives of Cambodia, a setback for the Vietnamese and their Soviet sponsors; the General Assembly also approved on Oct. 22 a resolution requesting Vietnam to withdraw its military forces from Cambodia.

*See* STATISTICS OF THE WORLD.          R.J.C.

**CAMEROON.** *See* STATISTICS OF THE WORLD.

**CANADA.** Nine months after suffering a humiliating rejection by the voters of Canada, Pierre Elliott Trudeau and the Liberal Party were swept back into office in February, 1980. Later in the year a series of conflicts arose between the federal and provincial governments that threatened the country with a full-fledged constitutional crisis.

**Politics.** Trudeau, 60, won his fourth term as prime minister with little trouble. Canadians considered Joe Clark, the 40-year-old Progressive Conservative leader, to be a lackluster prime minister. In addition, they were incensed by his proposals to allow oil producers substantial price increases and to increase the excise tax on gasoline by 18¢ (U.S. 15¢) a gallon, thereby raising the price of gas to consumers by 34¢ over the year. (Clark had lost a confidence vote in parliament in December, 1979, forcing the election.) Trudeau, who reluctantly came out of retirement to lead the Liberals once again, made political capital by promising to hold the line on gasoline prices.

In the voting on Feb. 18, Trudeau and the Liberals rolled to a landslide victory, gaining 44 percent of the popular vote to 33 percent for the Conservatives and 20 percent for the New Democrats. The Liberals gained an outright majority in the House of Commons by taking 146 seats. The Conservatives won 103, the New Democrats 32.

*Pierre Elliott Trudeau takes the oath of office as Canadian prime minister. The Liberal Party leader resumed power on March 3 after nine months of Progressive Conservative rule.*

**Québec Referendum.** The most immediate problem facing Trudeau was the threat by the huge, French-speaking province of Québec to reshape the map of Canada by seceding from the 113-year-old federation. The separatists, led by Québec Premier René Lévesque and his Parti Québécois, had committed themselves to a provincial referendum on the issue before pressing for independence. Confident of victory, Lévesque set May 20 as the day of the balloting. The voters were asked whether or not to give him authority to negotiate an agreement with the federal government that would transform Québec into a sovereign state in "economic association" with Canada.

Strong federalist Trudeau, himself a Québecer, campaigned strenuously in favor of a no vote. If Québec rejected separatism, the prime minister promised, he would make every effort to bring about constitutional reform that presumably would enhance the province's position within the Canadian federation. Polls pointed to a strong separatist showing, but when the ballots were counted a surprisingly impressive majority (59.5 percent) went on record to keep Québec a part of Canada.

**Regional Strains.** Québec was not the only region to give Trudeau trouble. In the frigid Northwest Territories, Indians and Inuit (Eskimos) clamored for a degree of autonomy, while the Newfoundland government hotly contested the federal government's claim to ownership of the rich Hibernia offshore oilfields. In the resource-rich western provinces, more and more voices were raised against the power wielded over them by the government in Ottawa.

Alberta, the country's leading oil producer, presented Trudeau with a challenge on a question of enormous significance to the country: Who should control oil prices and revenues? The usual practice had been for prices to be set by agreement between the oil-producing state and the federal government. At government insistence, the price had been held down to $14.75 (U.S. $12.80) a barrel at the wellhead, less than half the world price. Joe Clark's Conservatives promised

Non *bested* oui *by a margin of 3-2 as Québec voters on May 20 turned back an effort to negotiate political sovereignty for the province in economic association with Canada.*

## Canada's "Blue-Eyed Arab"

During 1980 the leading spokesman for the increasingly powerful—and vocal—oil- and agriculture-rich provinces of western Canada was Premier Peter Lougheed (pronounced *La*-heed) of Alberta, which produces 86 percent of Canada's oil. The 52-year-old conservative was born in Calgary in 1928 and attended the University of Alberta. He earned a law degree and played professional football briefly (for the Edmonton Eskimos) before settling down in Calgary as an attorney. When he assumed the leadership of the Conservative Party in 1965, it held not one seat in the Alberta legislature. In 1971 it achieved a majority; by 1980 it held 75 of 79 seats. The handsome, aloof premier has frequently disclaimed any interest in national office. The cornerstone of his policy is to secure prices for his province that reflect the ever-rising oil rates of the Organization of Petroleum Exporting Countries. For this stance opponents have called him a "blue-eyed Arab," which he resents as a

slur on his Canadian patriotism. "The East is used to us Westerners coming to them on bended knees," he observed in 1975. "Now we have some leverage, and we plan to use it."

*Premier Peter Lougheed.*

the oil producers a hefty price hike; when Trudeau refused to go along with the deal, the battle was joined.

The legal situation was far from clear. In Canada the provinces have ownership rights to oil and other resources within their borders. Once the oil crosses a provincial or national border, however, the federal government claims the right to set the price. In addition to pricing, Alberta and the federal government had serious differences over sharing the oil revenue and on a government proposal (opposed by the province) to impose an export tax on natural gas sold to the United States.

In late July, Trudeau and Alberta Premier Peter Lougheed met in Ottawa, but the two leaders failed to resolve their differences. On July 31, Alberta unilaterally announced that it was raising the domestic price of oil. It was the first time a province had set oil prices without the agreement of the federal government, but the hike was a moderate $2.00 (U.S. $1.74) a barrel and the government chose not to contest it.

In late October, Trudeau announced a plan that would raise energy prices at a much slower rate than Alberta wanted and would also give the federal government an increased share of the revenues. Lougheed responded by announcing that he would cut oil and gas production by 15 percent within nine months. U.S. companies, which dominate the Canadian oil industry, were angered by new policy guidelines intended to raise Canadian ownership to 50 percent by 1990.

**Constitutional Reform.** Honoring his prereferendum pledge to the voters of Québec that he would work for a "brand new constitution," Trudeau presided over a conference of the ten provincial premiers on June 9. Provincial and federal authorities had bickered off and on for a half century over constitutional reform, and this time the premiers told Trudeau they would not be stampeded into action. At stake in the dispute was the fundamental issue of how Canada was to be governed.

Complexities abounded. The current Canadian "constitution" was a piece of British legislation, the British North America Act of 1867. The provincial leaders agreed with Trudeau on the desirability of "bringing home" this constitution and forging a Canadian document. But chasms separated them on how to amend the constitution once it was "patriated" and on how it would allocate powers between the federal and provincial governments—specifically, which level of government would exercise final authority over resources, the economy, education, family law, and a host of other areas of life. Another sticking point: Should a Canadian constitution, as Trudeau favored and some provinces opposed, contain a bill of rights?

At the June 9 meeting, the leaders agreed to negotiate over the summer and hold a formal conference from Sept. 8 to 12. That session ended in total failure, and an angry Trudeau vowed to proceed with constitutional reform without the agreement of the provinces. On Oct. 2, the government accordingly introduced a resolution in parliament that asked Great Britain to transfer the constitution and the power to amend it to Canada. Britain was also asked to amend the constitution to include the disputed bill of rights even before it transferred the charter.

Trudeau asked that the resolution be reported out of a House-Senate committee by Dec. 9. But its fate was in grave doubt, since six provincial premiers decided in October to bring suit in court to stop Trudeau from acting without their consent.

**The Economy.** Recession in the U.S. spilled over into Canada, putting many out of work in the country's industrial heartland and adding impetus to the Liberal government's attempt to lessen dependency on its southern neighbor. In September the government said it expected the country's gross national product to post a "fractional decline" in 1980, the first full-year drop in real output since 1954. Still, promising oil explorations off the east coast and new oil finds in Alberta gave Canadians hope for an expanding economy.

**Foreign Affairs.** The year began with an upsurge of good feeling between Canada and the U.S. Prime Minister Clark had taken a strongly pro-U.S. position in world affairs, particularly over Iran and Afghanistan. Americans applauded their northern neighbor when the Canadian embassy in Tehran spirited six U.S. diplomats out of Iran in late January. In April, Canada lined up behind the U.S. in boycotting the Moscow Olympics. But as the year progressed, Canada–U.S. relations became increasingly strained. Ottawa complained that the U.S. paid little heed to its complaints over environment and border questions. Canadians also charged the U.S. with foot-dragging on the proposed Alaska Highway natural gas pipeline.

The biggest single irritant concerned a treaty signed in March, 1979, establishing boundaries and quotas for the fishing fleets in Canada's Maritime Provinces and the New England states. The treaty was approved by Canada but was gathering dust in the U.S. Senate, largely because New England Senators thought it unfair to their states. Exasperated Canadians charged that election year politics in the U.S. made the Carter administration reluctant to push for Senate approval of the important pact. A similar problem arose when a U.S.-Canada tax treaty was signed in late September after seven years of negotiations. So many questions were raised about the tax provisions that observers feared that this treaty too would become stalled in the U.S. Senate.

See STATISTICS OF THE WORLD. See also FISHER-
IES.                                                      R.J.C.

**CAPE VERDE.** See STATISTICS OF THE WORLD.

**CARIBBEAN COUNTRIES.** Growing political, economic, and social turmoil were evident all over the Caribbean in 1980. Jamaica elected a new government in October, Haiti struggled to overcome the effects of a century of poverty, and the Dominican Republic sought to reconstruct its economy after disastrous 1979 hurricanes. On other islands, Cuba appeared to be making political gains; several hundred Cubans were on Grenada, helping to build an airport extension, a small port facility, and other infrastructures, with other Cubans involved in hospital work and in the training of police. It all suggested an area in transition and change.

**Jamaica Turnabout.** Edward P.G. Seaga, a Harvard University-educated sociologist, became Jamaica's prime minister on Nov. 1, succeeding Michael Manley, a socialist who had held the post for eight and a half years. Manley and his People's National Party lost the parliamentary elections of Oct. 30, which saw Seaga's Jamaica Labour Party score a massive sweep of 51 out of 60 parliamentary seats. The issues in the vote centered on Manley's performance as prime minister, with Seaga charging he had led Jamaica to the brink of economic collapse. The island nation was virtually bankrupt, the Bank of Jamaica said in late October; the economy vainly struggled to dig itself out of a foreign debt of more than $1.3 billion, and unemployment ran above 30 percent. Seaga claimed Manley's social welfare schemes were partly responsible. The issue of Jamaica's close ties with Cuba's President Fidel Castro was also brought up in the campaign, as was the growing violence, particularly in West Kingston, that left nearly 700 dead by election day. Seaga renewed talks with the International Monetary Fund (IMF), which Manley had broken off in March, in order to win immediate standby credits to pay island debts and purchase needed commodities. But he said it would be years before Jamaica could emerge from its economic tailspin, and he warned on Nov. 1 that Jamaicans faced continued "hard times in the days ahead."

**Dominican Republic.** The ravages of hurricanes David and Frederic in August and September, 1979, left the Dominican Republic's economy in a shambles. It was the hardest hit of the countries in the paths of both storms. Compounding the problem was the impact of soaring oil prices, the low price for sugar (the country's key export), and a potential $200,000,000 budget deficit. A package of new economic policies was disclosed in May. They included agro-industry tax incentives, an urban property tax, removal of the government subsidy on gasoline that kept prices low, and a tax on automobile licenses. Moreover, President Silves-

Haitian refugees, among the many thousands of Haitians who came to the U.S. in 1980, land their boat near Miami Beach, Fla. One refugee lies exhausted on the beach.

tre Antonio Guzmán Fernández announced a government austerity program; salaries of government employees were frozen and a moratorium was imposed on new hiring, except in education and health.

There were two bright points in the economy—tourism and gold mining. Tourism revenues were up $25,000,000 to an estimated $150,000,000 in 1980, with 550,000 tourists expected during the year. Earnings from gold mining were expected to reach $196,000,000 in 1980, up $20,000,000 over 1979.

**Cuban Connection.** The United States kept a wary eye on developments throughout the Caribbean, but particularly on the island of Grenada, whose prime minister, Maurice Bishop, expressed continuing friendship with Cuba's Fidel Castro and accepted Cuban aid, including a $10,000,000 loan and the presence of 350 Cuban technicians, educators, and doctors. Moreover, Bishop turned up at the July 19 ceremonies in Managua, Nicaragua, marking the first anniversary of the Sandinista guerrilla triumph in that Central American country. Other Caribbean islands watched Grenadan developments with concern, and a Trinidadian statement in April said that the training of Gre-

nadan police by Cubans was not in keeping with Caribbean needs.

**Haiti.** On Haiti, the government of President-for-life Jean-Claude Duvalier was freshly buffeted with new allegations of political repression. Moreover, the economic improvement of recent years came to a standstill in 1980 as a result of soaring oil prices and low prices for Haitian exports. The allegations of growing political repression were aired by Amnesty International, the U.S. State Department, and the human rights commission of the Organization of American States. In April Duvalier reinstated a ban on criticizing and writing uncomplimentary items either about his own role or that of his mother, Simone. The law provided for jail terms of up to three years. In late November the government rounded up an undisclosed number of journalists, politicians, and human rights activists, with the reported intention of distracting attention from Haiti's worsening economic situation. With representatives of the World Bank and the IMF scheduled to meet in Port-au-Prince on Dec. 8, it was thought that the Thanksgiving-weekend timing of the roundup was designed to lessen publicity.

An estimated 30,000 Haitians left their home-

*A chemical in a vial is shown fluorescing as it is struck by laser light from the glass tip at left. The tip, acting as a lens, collects the light of the glow and sends it back down the optical fiber that had conducted the laser light. This system, called a remote fiber fluorometer, enables chemists to identify a chemical at a distance by observing the characteristic spectrum of its glow.*

land by boat in 1980, the majority going to Florida. Haitians are traditionally a migratory people, with thousands scattered through the Caribbean islands, but the flow in 1980 was larger than ever

and was believed to be due to growing political and economic problems in Haiti. Most of those who left were from the lower middle class, people seeking a better way of life in the U.S. *See also* UNITED STATES OF AMERICA.

**Hurricane Allen.** Hurricane Allen, described as the worst storm to hit the region in a century, took more than 250 lives on Caribbean islands in August, mostly in Haiti. The storm severely damaged or destroyed crops on St. Lucia, St. Vincent, Grenada, Guadeloupe, Dominica, Haiti, Martinique, and Jamaica.

*See* STATISTICS OF THE WORLD. *See also* CUBA; PUERTO RICO. J.N.G.

**CENTRAL AFRICAN REPUBLIC.** *See* STATISTICS OF THE WORLD.

**CEYLON.** *See* SRI LANKA.

**CHAD.** *See* STATISTICS OF THE WORLD. *See also* AFRICA.

**CHEMISTRY.** Two developments of great practical potential took place in 1980 in chemical research. One was a method for breaking down PCBs in oil-based fluids. The other, on the horizon, was a method for producing oxygen and hydrogen from water by artificial photosynthesis. Even the (so far) seemingly futile attempts to create superheavy elements excited chemists by leading to a method for producing new isotopes of neutron-rich actinides.

**Breaking Down PCBs.** In August, Goodyear Tire & Rubber Co. announced the development of a chemical process that can break down polychlorinated biphenyls (PCBs), polybrominated biphenyls (PBBs), DDT, and certain other organic pesticides and herbicides. These chemicals are found as contaminants in oil-based heat-transfer, hydraulic, capacitor, and transformer fluids. Goodyear claimed that the process, which uses sodium naphthalide as a reagent, can reduce PCB levels in a large tank of oil from 200 parts per million to less than 10 parts per million within a couple of hours. Goodyear planned to patent the process and then release it to the public.

**Chemical Photoconversion.** Researchers studied how photosynthesis works in plants in order to re-create the process artificially. They were seeking a practical means of splitting water into hydrogen and oxygen for fuel and industrial uses. In July a group of scientists led by James R. Bolton of the University of Western Ontario announced that they had found a way to mimic photosynthesis. The scientists found that a molecule known as P-Q (a porphyrin linked to a quinone), when placed in a solution of frozen methanol and 2 percent chloroform (at a temperature close to its freezing point), behaves as chlorophyll does when exposed to light. When illuminated, P-Q, like chlorophyll, releases an electron that travels to an acceptor molecule. In the case of P-Q, the porphyrin end behaves like the chlorophyll and the quinone end acts as the electron acceptor.

The 1961 winner of the Nobel Prize in chemistry, Melvin Calvin of the University of California at Berkeley, reported in August, at the Third International Conference on Photochemical Conversion and Storage of Solar Energy, that he had developed a synthetic chloroplast. Unlike other artificial photosynthetic methods, which are designed solely to produce molecular hydrogen, Calvin's system was also designed to produce oxygen atoms. Light shines on molecules containing manganese, causing the manganese to lose electrons. The ionized manganese-containing molecules split water molecules into hydrogen ions and oxygen atoms and quickly bond to the oxygen atoms before molecular oxygen has a chance to form. By trapping the highly reactive oxygen atoms, Calvin's synthetic chloroplast can be used to oxidize certain chemicals. For example, propylene can be turned into propylene oxide—a chemical used in making plastics. Some problems remained to be worked out before the process became practical. The primary problem was that the catalytic chemicals needed for the reaction are not recycled; they must be added continually to the system.

Other scientists were working on water-splitting methods that do not necessarily mimic photosynthesis. In one of these methods, described in July by Michael Graetzel of the École Polytechnique Fédérale in Lausanne, Switzerland, all the catalytic chemicals needed for the reaction are recycled. Platinum and ruthenium oxide are used to collect the hydrogen molecules and oxygen molecules, respectively, that form from the water-splitting reaction. This system also has problems, in that the oxygen and hydrogen can slowly recombine, and a modification was being developed.

**Fiber Optics for Chemical Analysis.** Scientists at Lawrence Livermore National Laboratory have developed a method for using fiber optics to safely analyze corrosive, hot, or radioactive materials more than 1.5 km (about 1 mi.) away from the laboratory. The system, announced in March, consists of a tunable laser hooked up to a fiber-optics network. To analyze a sample, the scientists use the fiber optics to shine laser light on it, causing it to fluoresce. Light from the fluorescing sample is transmitted over the fiber-optics network to the laboratory where it can be analyzed. Special arrangements must be made for samples that do not normally fluoresce or do not fluoresce brightly enough to be analyzed remotely.     J.S.

**CHILE.** Voters by a margin of 2 to 1 approved a new constitution for Chile on Sept. 11, 1980, the seventh anniversary of the military seizure of power. The new constitution institutionalized military rule, allowing the regime to remain in power at least through 1989. Gen. Augusto Pinochet Ugarte, the nation's president, told the United States, which had been critical of human rights violations in Chile, in a victory statement, to "leave us alone."

The U.S., however, was not alone in its continuing criticism of human rights violations in Chile. On the eve of the Sept. 11 vote, Amnesty International, the London-based human rights organization, reported that arbitrary arrests and systematic torture in Chile had increased dramatically during July and August. More than 1000 people had been arrested between July 15 and Sept. 10, the organization said.

Opposition to military rule was low key, but Christian Democratic leader Eduardo Frei Montalva, a former president, said on Sept. 9 that the vote on the constitution was "a sham, a deceit, a fraud." The constitution was prepared over 18 months by a Pinochet-appointed group of jurists, and the document was kept under wraps until a month before the vote, which allowed the voter only to approve the document in its entirety or reject it.

During the year the military muffled many dissenters. A purge of "unreliable" teachers got under way in February, resulting in the removal of 70 professors from state-run universities. But there was violent resistance. A Chilean policeman, on duty at the Flame of Eternal Liberty, erected by the military to commemorate the Sept. 11, 1973, overthrow of President Salvador Allende Gossens, was killed on April 29. On July 15 Lt. Col. Roger Vergara Campos, director of the army intelligence school, was assassinated, an event blamed for the massive arrests noted by Amnesty International.

Economic prospects continued to brighten. Earnings from copper, Chile's major export, were up during 1980—a hopeful sign, since imports continued to soar in cost. High economic growth, averaging more than 8 percent a year, apparently had reconciled many Chileans to their authoritarian regime. Even the annual inflation rate of about 30 percent did not seem burdensome compared to the dizzy three-digit heights reached shortly before President Salvador Allende Gossens was overthrown in 1973. Despite high economic growth, however, a May report indicated that unemployment was persisting at 15 percent of the labor force, with little likelihood that it would drop during the early 1980's.

*See* STATISTICS OF THE WORLD.     J.N.G.

In China's more relaxed political climate, advertisements for foreign films as well as traditional Chinese operas and plays can be seen in the streets and markets of Peking.

**CHINA, PEOPLE'S REPUBLIC OF.** The year 1980 was a time of accelerating political change as the Chinese leadership moved farther away from the revolutionary style of the late Mao Tse-tung (Mao Zedong). In economic affairs, this was manifest by continued emphasis on agriculture, consumer goods, and technology. In foreign affairs, it meant improving relations with the United States and Japan.

**Politics.** The third session of the Fifth National People's Congress, China's parliament, convened in Peking on Aug. 30 and continued until Sept. 10. The more than 3000 delegates in attendance elected 61-year-old Chao Chi-yang (Zhao Ziyang), leader of the Szechwan (Sichuan) provincial government and its Community Party and protégé of the powerful Deputy Premier Teng Hsiao-ping (Deng Xiaoping), to replace Premier Hua Kuo-feng (Hua Guofeng), who resigned. Hua continued as chairman of the Communist Party, but Hu Yaobang was made general secretary of the party and was responsible for running it on a day-to-day basis.

Like Teng, Chao was purged by Maoist extremists during the Cultural Revolution of the late 1960's. He represented the new generation of technocrats and pragmatists who had gained influence since Mao's death in 1976.

The Panchen Lama, second highest figure in Tibetan Buddhism who had been released in 1978 after 14 years of detention, was named a deputy chairman of the Congressional Standing Committee in a move designed to woo the Tibetans. Peking had recently acknowledged that its political and economic policies in Tibet had failed to produce desired results.

Earlier in the year, on Feb. 14, Peking announced a sweeping reorganization designed to modernize China's 5,000,000-man armed forces. Hundreds of senior and middle-level officers were replaced, among them 11 regional military commanders, 4 members of the Military Affairs Commission that governed the armed forces, and the commander of the navy. On Feb. 25 it was revealed that Teng Hsiao-ping had stepped down as army chief of staff in favor of Yang Dechi, 70. Teng's power, however, was not diminished. This was affirmed by the posthumous rehabilitation, in February, of Teng's erstwhile Communist Party cohort Liu Shao-chi (Liu Shaoqi), purged as public enemy number one during the Cultural Revolution.

China announced on May 18 that it had successfully launched its first intercontinental ballistic missile. Successful launching of the 6000-mi. rocket meant that China could, for the first time, hit targets in most of the Soviet Union. During 1980 the Carter administration offered to sell China, for the first time, transport aircraft and helicopters, but China's ground and air forces, though massive, were considered largely obsolescent.

**Gang of Four Trial.** On Nov. 20 the long-awaited trial of Mao's widow, Chiang Ch'ing (Jiang Qing), and three other members of what had long been denounced as the "Gang of Four," began in Peking. Six other former high officials were also placed on trial. They were charged with alleged offenses committed during the Cultural Revolution of the 1960's. The indictment accused them of persecuting large numbers of officials, plotting to assassinate Mao, and attempting to overthrow the state.

After a week of testimony, seven of the nine accused who had appeared before the court thus far had admitted varying degrees of guilt. But Chiang Ch'ing and a colleague, Chang Ch'unch'iao (Zhang Chunqiao), had refused to confess or even to cooperate with the court.

**The Economy.** Economic reforms unveiled during the National People's Congress were aimed at stimulating the economy and raising the standard of living. Factories and firms were to pay taxes on their profits rather than surrendering everything to the state. The remainder would be available for reinvestment, higher salaries, or other workers' benefits. Local governments were also to be afforded a greater measure of fiscal autonomy. An income tax was instituted for the first time in China, although the level of taxable income ($575 a year) was so high that few Chinese citizens would be affected.

Economic figures for 1979 were released in May. Output of grain was reported at 332,100,000 metric tons (36.7 bu. of wheat or 49 bu. of rice equal 1 metric ton), up 9 percent from 1978. The 1980 target was set at 335,800,000 metric tons. Combined agricultural and industrial output grew at the rate of 8.5 percent, down from a growth rate of 12.3 percent in 1978. Industrial output was reported to grow in the first half of 1980 at a rate of 13.6 percent, resulting chiefly from a 24.2 percent growth in light industry as opposed to 6 percent in heavy industries. Salaried workers' real incomes were said to increase 7.6 percent in 1979, while those of peasants went up 11.2 percent. The rate of inflation was given as 5.8 percent.

In a move designed to increase trade, Peking decided in April to permit customs-free exports

---

### Genghis Who?

A dispatch filed from Peking during the year revealed that ceremonies had been held in the Inner Mongolian Autonomous Region in early May to honor one of the region's native sons, "an outstanding military strategist and statesman." This revered general is better known in the West as one of history's most rapacious warlords, leader of the Mongol hordes that dominated Eastern Europe for 300 years. In China, however, more than 750 years after his death, Genghis Khan was praised, admired, and rehabilitated.

---

to Taiwan. Admission to the International Monetary Fund (April 17) and the World Bank (May 15) paved the way for China to gain long-term development credit to hasten the "Four Modernizations" campaign.

Oil production increased only 2 percent and coal production 2.8 percent in 1979, however, and no growth was forecast for 1980. China's major

The "Gang of Four" trial of disgraced former Chinese officials began in November. Chiang Ch'ing, the widow of Mao Tse-tung, refused to confess guilt and called her interrogators "fascists."

### His Aim: "A Civilized Socialist State"

On Sept. 7 the rumors became fact: Chao Chi-yang, 61-year-old head of the Communist Party of Szechwan Province, was the new premier of the People's Republic of China. Described by Western observers as a pragmatist and a populist, Chao was expected to take charge of China's much needed economic modernization. He seemed to be a good choice. In three years he was credited with having led Szechwan out of starvation and economic chaos, increasing farm output by 25 percent and industrial production by 81 percent. Few details of the new premier's life are available. He was born in 1919 in Hunan Province, became a member of the Young Communist League in 1932 and a party member in 1938, and was purged during the Cultural Revolution of the 1960's. He is married and has at least one son.

*Premier Chao Chi-yang (Zhao Ziyang).*

oilfields appeared to have begun to decline unexpectedly early, threatening its industrialization goals and the volume of exports needed to help pay for expensive purchase of foreign technology and plants.

**Foreign Affairs.** The convergence of Chinese and U.S. views on certain international issues was underscored during President Jimmy Carter's meeting with Hua in Tokyo on July 10. The two leaders agreed that Chinese-American solidarity could minimize the threat to peace created by the Soviet invasion of Afghanistan and Moscow's support for the Vietnamese invasion of Cambodia. Peking, however, took bitter exception to Ronald Reagan's statements in mid-August that he favored the establishment of official relations with Taiwan. The Chinese charged Reagan with attempting to develop a two-China policy. Despite the efforts of George Bush to mollify the Chinese, Peking remained wary and U.S.-Chinese relations became mired in U.S. Presidential politics.

Economic ties grew closer. On Jan. 24 the U.S. Congress approved most-favored-nation status for China, putting into effect a bilateral trade agreement signed in 1979. On Sept. 17 the two countries signed major agreements covering textile trade, civil aviation, consular services, and shipping. Trade between the two countries was forecast at $4 billion for 1980, compared to $2.3 billion in 1979. On Oct. 22 a grain agreement committed China to buy 6,000,000 to 8,000,000 metric tons of U.S. wheat and corn each year through 1984.

During a six-day visit to Japan from May 27 to June 1, the first ever by a Chinese premier, Hua and Japanese Prime Minister Masayoshi Ohira issued a communiqué emphasizing their common outlook on international problems in Asia. On May 29, Japan and China signed a contract for the joint development of oil deposits in the Yellow Sea, beginning in 1981. In return for Japan's total investment of 49 percent, including an initial outlay of $210,000,000 for exploration, China was to supply Japan with 42.5 percent of the crude oil produced from the joint venture. In a press conference prior to leaving Japan, Hua expressed China's aim to seek further cooperation with Japan in technological development. He voiced approval of Japan's growing defense capabilities, its alliance with the U.S., and its developing relations with Western Europe. He assured the Japanese no moves were under way in North Korea to upset the status quo in the south.

Relations with the Soviet Union were strained early in 1980 by Moscow's charges that China was training and assisting the Afghan rebels. Tensions eased somewhat on April 20, when China's new ambassador to Moscow assumed his post, vacant since May, 1979. The annual trade agreement between the two nations, however, signed on June 6, showed a 15 percent drop, reflecting Moscow's declining role in the Chinese economy and Chinese disapproval of the Soviet invasion of Afghanistan.

*See* STATISTICS OF THE WORLD.     T.L.K.

**CHINA, REPUBLIC OF.** *See* TAIWAN.

**CIVIL RIGHTS AND CIVIL LIBERTIES.** During 1980 a congressionally mandated quota of public works funds for minority contractors was upheld by the U.S. Supreme Court. The attempted assassination of a prominent civil rights leader and racial disturbances in Miami, Fla., and other cities raised the specter of the serious racial violence that marked the late 1960's. Refugees from Cuba and Haiti added to the civil rights concerns of the Carter administration. Court decisions and congressional legislation laid down new guidelines affecting a number of civil liberties issues.

**Affirmative Action.** For the third year in a row, a U.S. Supreme Court ruling in a sensitive affirmative action case was one of the most important civil rights actions of the year. In a 6–3 ruling on July 2, the Court upheld the constitutionality of a provision of a 1977 act mandating that, where possible, 10 percent of the public works funds allocated under the law should go to minority contractors. The minority set-aside provision was attacked by white construction-industry and trade-union officials, but the Court found that Congress had acted within its authority to seek to alleviate past discrimination in the construction industry.

**Black Representation.** Another Supreme Court decision was adverse to the interests of blacks: The High Court ruled 6–3 on April 22 that at-large local elections are not inherently unconstitutional, even if they dilute the voting strength of blacks or other minorities. The decision upheld a prior system of electing the three-member administrative commission of Mobile, Ala., by citywide voting rather than by individual districts. Under this system, in operation between 1911 and 1978, no black had ever been elected to the commission although blacks made up more than 35 percent of Mobile's population. Civil rights groups were fearful that the decision would mark an end to 15 years of steady progress in access to electoral office for Southern blacks.

**Racial Violence.** In the worst of several racial disturbances in 1980, 18 persons were killed and $100,000,000 in property damage sustained during a riot in May in the Liberty City ghetto area of Miami. The riot began immediately after an all-white jury acquitted four Dade County police-

*A black Miami resident voices his anger to white policemen on May 18 during racial violence that took a toll of 18 dead and $100,000,000 in property damage. The riot followed the acquittal of four policemen charged with beating a black man to death.*

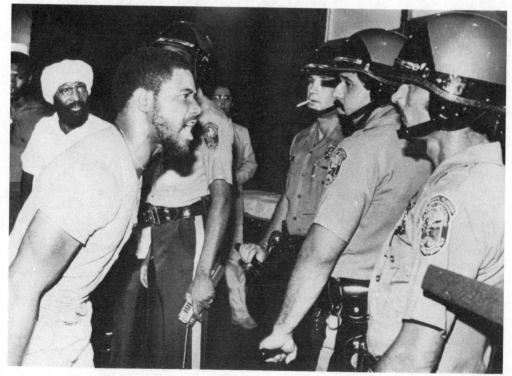

*One of the thorniest civil rights questions in 1980 involved the treatment of refugees and migrants from Latin America. In July, 13 of a party of Salvadorans who crossed the border from Mexico with inadequate water rations were found dead in the Arizona desert.*

men accused in the fatal beating of a black insurance executive, Arthur McDuffie.

On May 29, Vernon E. Jordan, Jr., president of the National Urban League, was seriously wounded by a sniper in Fort Wayne, Ind. On Nov. 17, six present or former members of the Ku Klux Klan were acquitted by an all-white jury in Greensboro, N.C., of charges of murdering radical activists, one of them black, during a 1979 incident. These developments, plus the unsolved murders of blacks in Atlanta, Buffalo, and other cities, gave rise to fears among blacks that a campaign of terror was being launched against them. *See also* NEGROES IN THE UNITED STATES.

**Refugees.** One of the thorniest civil rights problems faced by the Administration was the entrance of large numbers of refugees from Cuba and Haiti. In March, President Jimmy Carter signed the Refugee Act of 1980, which removed geographical limitations on immigration and increased the total number of refugees and immigrants allowed to enter the United States annually from 290,000 to 320,000. It was the first major overhaul of immigration law since 1965.

But the arrival of more than 125,000 Cubans and perhaps 30,000 Haitians in 1980 had serious civil rights implications for Miami and other areas where large numbers of refugees settled. In July a federal district court judge in Florida ruled that Haitians applying for asylum in the U.S. had been routinely denied due process. The Carter administration therefore pledged to treat Haitian refugees in the same manner as Cuban refugees.

**Hispanics.** In an apparent backlash against the influx of refugees in the Miami area, voters in Dade County, which includes Miami, approved a measure ending six years of bilingualism by banning mandatory county governmental use of Spanish or any language other than English.

Hispanics were disturbed by the disposal of a widely publicized criminal case. On July 29 a mistrial was declared in Tucson, Ariz., after an all-white jury was unable to reach a verdict regarding two whites accused of robbing and torturing three young Mexican aliens. The two, prominent members of a ranching family, and their late father had been acquitted of similar charges in 1977 arising from the alleged incident. The U.S. Justice Department said on Aug. 29 that it would seek a new trial.

**Illegal Break-ins.** Two former officials of the Federal Bureau of Investigation (FBI), W. Mark Felt and Edward S. Miller, were found guilty on Nov. 6 in Washington, D.C., of conspiring to violate the constitutional rights of citizens by authorizing government agents to break into homes secretly, without search warrants, in a hunt for bombing suspects in 1972 and 1973. The verdict marked the first time that the federal government had successfully concluded a trial of counterintelligence officials charged with abuses of authority. The case involved break-ins into the homes of friends and relatives of the Weather Underground, a militant radical antiwar group. Felt and Miller were sentenced to pay small fines.

**Intelligence Agencies.** Without formally hearing arguments, the Supreme Court ruled on Feb. 19 that employees of the Central Intelligence Agency (CIA) must honor their agreement not to publish any information about the agency without specific prior approval. The Court thus held that Frank W. Snepp 3rd, a former CIA officer who published an account of the fall of Saigon, South Vietnam, without the agency's permission, must turn over to the federal government all the earnings from the book.

On Oct. 14, President Carter signed into law a bill passed by Congress giving it specific authority to oversee the activities of all U.S. intelligence agencies. The act reduced from eight to two the number of congressional committees that must be informed about future covert operations and required that, except in rare circumstances, the intelligence agencies report on "any significant anticipated intelligence activities."

**Abscam.** Seven members of Congress and 13 other persons were indicted in 1980 on bribery and other charges with regard to a corruption scandal code-named Abscam; several were convicted during the year. However, the FBI's use of undercover operatives in building a case against the defendants was criticized by civil libertarians. In late November a federal judge overturned the convictions of two defendants, ruling that the government had "stretched" federal statutes and "entrapped" the defendants. *See also* CRIME AND LAW ENFORCEMENT.

**Newspapers.** The Supreme Court ruled on July 2 in a 7-1 vote that the First Amendment gives the public and the press an all but absolute right to attend criminal trials, thus reversing a Virginia court ruling that upheld the exclusion of the public and press from a murder trial. Exactly one year earlier, the High Court had held that judges could close pretrial criminal hearings to the public and press. After that decision, judges in more than 30 cases banned either the press or the public, or both, from criminal trials.

In an incident that troubled journalists, law-enforcement officials entered a Boise, Idaho, television station on July 26 in search of evidence for possible use in criminal cases arising from a prison riot. On Oct. 1, Congress passed a bill banning most such surprise searches of newsrooms and other locations engaged in activities protected by the First Amendment. Instead, authorities would have to seek a subpoena.

**Other Issues.** On June 25 the Supreme Court ruled 6-3 that private citizens may sue state officials whenever a state policy violates a federal law. The decision gave individuals a powerful legal tool with which to challenge the way states administer dozens of federal programs.

On Nov. 17 the Supreme Court struck down a Kentucky law that required the posting of the Ten Commandments in every public school classroom in the state. On Feb. 5 a new Massachusetts state law-went into effect requiring a period of voluntary prayer in public school. The action made the state the ninth to require either spoken prayer or silent meditation in public schools since the 1963 Supreme Court decision declaring unconstitutional the recitation of prayers and Bible readings in public schools.

In September a federal judge ordered the reinstatement of a former Air Force sergeant dismissed from the service after he openly declared his homosexuality. In the same month the Justice Department liberalized its guidelines to allow homosexual foreign visitors to enter the country more easily.

*See also* WOMEN.                                           D.C.

*The U.S. Treasury Department's first entries into the gold medallion market went on sale on July 15. The 1-oz. Grant Wood and ½-oz. Marian Anderson commemoratives were the first in a series on American artists.*

**COIN COLLECTING,** *or* **NUMISMATICS.** The year 1980 was possibly a turning point in coin collecting. Even as the record prices achieved by precious metals led to the removal of millions of collectable coins from circulation, the past performance of coins as a hedge against inflation contributed to record prices for rare or extremely fine coins.

Until 1964, U.S. half dollars, quarters, and dimes were struck in silver .900 fine, meaning they contained 900 parts silver per 1000 parts of total metal. Most silver currency was removed after 1965, but, because the debasement was announced in advance, millions of pre-1964 coins were hoarded. Those that had been circulated were not of great value to collectors. When silver prices rose during 1979 and peaked at more than $50 per ounce in early 1980, however, bullion and coin dealers were offering as much as 20 times face value. Only those coins whose numismatic value exceeded their intrinsic value were immune from melting. The fact that so many lower-grade coins were destroyed was expected to drive prices up even further and ultimately exclude less affluent collectors from the hobby.

Some major collections changed hands during the year. The collection of the Chase Manhattan Bank, the core of which was formed by the pioneering collector Farran Zerbe, was transferred to the Smithsonian Institution early in the year. A small part of it, including duplicates of items in the Smithsonian, was given to the American Numismatic Society in New York City.

Disposition continued on the John Work Garrett Collection, owned by Johns Hopkins University. Two of four projected auctions took place during 1980, and the prices realized were described as "stratospheric." Proof specimens of $50 and $20 gold pieces struck by Augustus Humbert brought $500,000 and $350,000, respectively, and the first 1804 silver dollar for sale in a decade fetched $400,000.

On the national scene the government continued to stockpile Susan B. Anthony dollars, which were still meeting with public resistance. The General Services Administration also concluded its sales of Carson City silver dollars, more than 3,000,000 of which were discovered in U.S. Treasury vaults during the late 1960's. Prices ranged from $200 to $220 in the final round of bidding.

The U.S. government also ventured into the production of bullion "coins," not struck for circulation but—like South Africa's Krugerrand and Canada's Maple Leaf—intended to be a convenient way of holding gold. A ½-oz. medallion portraying singer Marian Anderson and a 1-oz. piece portraying painter Grant Wood, issued during the summer, were the first in a projected set of ten pieces to be issued through 1984. The price varied according to the spot price of gold on the New York Commodities Exchange.     W.E.M.

**COLOMBIA.** Urban guerrillas occupied the Dominican Republic embassy in Bogotá, the Colombian capital, for two months in 1980 in an effort to secure the release of fellow guerrillas from Colombian jails.

The effort failed, although the embassy occupation attracted worldwide attention. The incident led to fears for the safety of the diplomats from 17 nations, who were taken hostage while attending an embassy reception on Feb. 27. Among the more than 50 persons seized was U.S. Ambassador Diego C. Asencio. Through long and arduous negotiations between the guerrillas, who were members of the M-19 (Movimiento de 19 Abril) organization, and the Colombian government, a number of the diplomats and other persons seized were released. At least one escaped. When it became evident to the guerrillas that the Colombian government was not going to yield to any of their demands, which included $50,000,000 in ransom, they accepted the offer of Cuban President Fidel Castro for asylum in Cuba and on April 27 left Colombia on board a Cuban jetliner—61 days after they began their occupation of the Dominican embassy. They took 12 of the remaining hostages, including Asencio, to Cuba, where they were released.

The M-19 organization, many of whose members had family connections with the government, the local business community, and foreign diplomats, lost many of its members during a 1979 crackdown following the movement's most audacious coup—the construction of a 250-ft. tunnel into a military armory just north of Bogotá that facilitated the theft of 5300 weapons. Seizing the Dominican embassy during the Feb. 27 reception in honor of Dominican independence day was seen by the M-19 strategists as perhaps the most dramatic incident they could devise to win the release of 311 persons (described by M-19 as political prisoners) held in Colombian jails. Not all the persons whose release they were demanding were from the M-19 movement, which was thought to be less radical than most urban guerrilla groups in Latin America. Many were members of other leftist, anarchist, and Marxist groups—all described by the government as terrorists.

During the negotiations, the Colombian government did agree to speed up the trials of the accused terrorists under detention and reportedly paid $2,500,000 ransom, but that was a far cry from what the M-19 wanted. Colombian observers estimated the M-19 organization's strength at between 500 and 1000 persons.

Colombian President Julio César Turbay Ayala was beset with fresh charges in February that he was somehow linked to drug smuggling efforts, but the chief executive denied the allegations in a broadcast to the nation. The incident was quickly forgotten as he and his government struggled with the embassy occupation.

Later in the year, Colombia's economic problems were outlined in a Turbay Ayala message to the nation. He admitted on Aug. 20 that unemployment was at an all-time high of 19 percent and that inflation for the year would total 40 percent or more. Coffee sales were up in volume but down in earnings, as were other exports. These factors, he concluded, coupled with the high price of imports, meant that the nation "will have to tighten its belt."

*See* STATISTICS OF THE WORLD. J.N.G.

**COLORADO.** *See* STATISTICS OF THE WORLD.

*Some of the hostages seized by the M-19 guerrillas at the Dominican Republic embassy in Bogotá are shown in this picture. The guerrillas held many of the hostages for two months in an effort to secure the release of their comrades from Colombian jails.*

*A Commonwealth conference was held in New Delhi, Sept. 3–8, with the leaders of 16 Asian and Pacific nations attending. The conference was critical of the Soviet invasion of Afghanistan and the Vietnamese occupation of Cambodia.*

**COMMONWEALTH OF NATIONS.** In 1980 the Commonwealth of Nations was often concerned with such external issues as the Soviet presence in Afghanistan and the rise in oil prices. Its membership increased to 44 with the addition to its ranks of Zimbabwe and Vanuatu.

**Asia-Pacific Meeting.** The most important Commonwealth conference of the year took place in early September, when the heads of government of 16 members located in Asia and the Pacific gathered in New Delhi. The main issue confronting the conferees was whether to take a stand on events in Afghanistan and Cambodia.

India's Prime Minister Indira Gandhi, whose government had close ties with the Soviet Union, was criticized openly. Alone among the participants, her government had not issued a forthright condemnation of the Soviet intervention in Afghanistan. Moreover, India was the only country outside the Soviet bloc to have recognized the Moscow-backed, Vietnam-installed government of Heng Samrin in Cambodia.

Singapore's Prime Minister Lee Kuan Yew, an outspoken critic of Moscow, reflected the sentiments of most conferees when he demanded that the group condemn Soviet actions in Afghanistan and Vietnam's continued occupation of Cambodia. A minority of one, Gandhi eventually yielded to pressure and accepted a final communiqué containing a veiled condemnation of the Soviet Union and a call for the withdrawal of foreign troops from Cambodia.

**Other Conferences.** The Commonwealth law ministers met from April 29 to May 2 at Sam Lord's Castle, Barbados. The ministers recommended Commonwealth arrangements whereby legal judgments could be enforced across national boundaries, and whereby prisoners convicted in one member country might serve their sentences in their home countries if they so desired.

The eighth Commonwealth Education Conference was held in Colombo, Sri Lanka, from Aug. 5 to 13. The conferees recommended greater efforts to educate the illiterate, the handicapped, and women and girls. They also hoped that developed Commonwealth members would try to keep tuition fees at a reasonable level for students from developing countries.

The Commonwealth finance ministers met in Hamilton, Bermuda, on Sept. 24 and 25. The ministers took note of the damage being done to developing economies by rising world oil prices and called on the industrialized countries and oil-exporting countries to step up the volume of their assistance to oil-importing developing states. The ministers agreed that the World Bank should increase its lending capacity by a substantial amount.

**New Members.** On April 18 the Commonwealth welcomed Zimbabwe as a member. On that date, the resource-rich country, formerly known as Rhodesia, became fully independent under black majority rule.

The Anglo-French condominium of the New Hebrides became the independent Republic of Vanuatu on July 30 and elected to join the Commonwealth. An island chain situated in the southwest Pacific, Vanuatu has a land area of 5700 sq.mi. and a chiefly Melanesian population of more than 112,000. The country's export crops include copra, cocoa, and coffee.

*See also* PACIFIC ISLANDS; ZIMBABWE.      R.J.C.

**COMMUNICATIONS.** In 1980 a major step toward deregulation of the telecommunications industry was taken by the Federal Communications Commission (FCC) when it gave the American Telephone and Telegraph Co. (AT&T) the green light to enter the data communications field. Distinctions between telecommunications, data processing, and information services were blurred as telephone, television, computer, and publishing industries both vied and cooperated in providing offices and homes with an increasingly wide range of services.

AT&T continued to develop optical systems for transmitting messages through long glass fibers in the form of modulated light waves. Worldwide, work in this area turned from the basic studies of previous years to planning and building operating optical-fiber systems.

At the World Administrative Radio Conference, participating nations agreed to disagree as to how to allocate orbital positions for future communications satellites.

**Deregulation.** In April, AT&T gained FCC approval to set up an unregulated subsidiary that would compete in the lucrative market of data processing and information services. The subsidiary was to operate without the financial and technical support of AT&T's other, regulated divisions. This long-anticipated move became the focus of a swarm of lawsuits, conflicts, and consent agreements. AT&T faced many challenges, from federal agencies as well as its competitors, as to how the research, development, marketing, manufacturing, and financing for its new subsidiary were to be carried out. The subsidiary was also expected to have a major effect on current congressional efforts to rewrite the 1934 Communications Act.

As a direct extension of present operations, AT&T's Bell System planned to provide a computer-stored yellow-pages service to homes through small video terminals. In another move, Pennsylvania Bell made it possible for its subscribers to transmit delayed voice messages. This was, in effect, a form of electronic mail in which the sender specified phone number, message, and delivery time. A comparable system was to be offered by Bell's Advanced Communications Service (ACS), eventually including digital transmission of the outputs of almost every kind of office communications equipment. This placed Bell in direct competition with General Telephone & Electronics Corp.'s Telenet and with International Business Machines Corp. (IBM). In 1980, however, software and organizational problems continued to plague ACS. Xerox Corp.'s XTEN, a system with similar goals but with microwave transmission facilities, was also troubled by such problems.

**Home Terminals.** AT&T and a host of other businesses were also taking part in tests of systems that provide news and other data to terminals in

*Engineers at Bell Telephone of Pennsylvania make test calls to check out the 1A Voice Storage System, an advanced communications service that enables network subscribers to send and receive delayed messages.*

private homes. For example, a system called Viewtron was tested in 1980 in Coral Gables, Fla. AT&T provided telephone linkage and modified home terminals for Knight-Ridder newspapers, whose central computer sent news, advertising, and other consumer services into homes. In this two-way system users were able to transmit orders for goods to the central computer through the terminals. Cable systems were also tested. In Dallas, for example, Dow Jones & Co., in conjunction with the Dallas *Morning News*, sent information into home terminals through cable linkage provided by Sammons Communications. And in Columbus, Ohio, a computer time-sharing company called CompuServe might eventually provide both offices and homes with data from a wide range of newspapers and news agencies.

The overall picture was of a field whose possibilities were only beginning to be explored. One projection was that by the end of the decade, one out of four homes would be using some form of computer or modified television terminal.

**Telephone Competitors.** While exploring new fields, Bell Systems was being threatened in an old one: long-distance telephony. In June a federal court awarded MCI Communications Corp. $1.8 billion in damages against AT&T, on the charge that AT&T had denied MCI the telephone

*A new microprocessor from Bell Laboratories, although small enough to rest on a telephone pushbutton, holds more than 45,000 transistors and can perform more than 1,000,000 additions and multiplications in a second. Future digital switching, data processing, and voice recognition systems will make heavy use of such circuits.*

connections needed to complete its long-distance microwave communications network. This setback, and the possibility of other suits and increasing competition, might greatly affect AT&T's price-averaging practice of compensating for the higher costs of its local services by overcharging for long-distance calls. Another source of competition was Satellite Business Systems (SBS), a joint venture of Communications Satellite Corp. (Comsat), IBM, and Aetna Life and Casualty Co. SBS started as a data transfer service for large corporations but then ventured into the field of voice transmissions.

**Fiber Optics.** In its drive to develop practical optical-fiber telephony, AT&T in 1980 started work on a 611-mi. linkup of Boston, New York City, Philadelphia, and Washington, D.C. By 1985 the system was expected to connect 19 of Bell's electronic digital switches. A cable no thicker than a finger but consisting of thousands of optical fibers would be able to transmit as many as 80,000 phone calls at a time. The all-digital system permitted Bell to carry voice, video, and data while utilizing large-scale integrated circuitry.

Bell also tested optical-fiber equipment that eventually would enable it to lay a cable between the United States and Europe. Cheaper than alternative systems, it was to be powered by lasers operating at a 1.3-micrometer wavelength rather than the current 0.8 micrometers. This change would lessen weakening of the light signal as it travels along the fiber, greatly reducing the need for costly amplifiers.

**Satellite and Radio Problems.** For communications satellites, allocations of orbital position and radio frequencies were still a problem. A communications satellite is best placed in a geosynchronous orbit that keeps it stationed above a desired point on the earth's surface. If two such satellites use the same frequencies, they must remain at least 200 mi. apart, in terms of ground distance, to avoid interference. With 80 satellites already in such orbits, the crowding problem is real.

As 1979 ended, the World Administrative Radio Conference (WARC) had just concluded its session. WARC, a United Nations-sponsored meeting, takes place once every 20 years to try to reach international accord on communications questions. Specialized meetings are held more often. The 1979 conference left unsettled many questions as to how to allocate unassigned frequencies, as well as how to guarantee access to satellites of developing nations. The question was left to be dealt with by a smaller WARC in 1984, by which time the space shuttle might make possible the assembly of larger, more efficient communications platforms in space. H.H.

**COMMUNISM.** The Communist world presented a turbulent picture in 1980. Poland experienced a workers' revolt that ultimately brought about the dismissal of both the prime minister and the head of the Communist Party. Two Communist countries, Afghanistan and Cambodia, suffered civil war and occupation by their Communist neighbors. China installed a new premier and moved ahead with its plans to try the so-called Gang of Four, which included Mao Tse-tung's widow.

**Strikes in Poland.** A workers' revolt shook Poland. Beginning in July, Poles laid down their tools to protest a meat price increase. As the strikes gained momentum, worker demands turned to political as well as economic issues; a key demand was for independent trade unions.

The unrest brought about the dismissal of Prime Minister Edward Babiuch and ultimately of Communist Party leader Edward Gierek. But the regime pledged to accept the formation of free trade unions. That concession, which could undermine the Communist Party's monopoly of power, gravely worried the Soviet Union and Poland's other Communist neighbors, and it remained unclear how far the Kremlin was prepared to allow Polish liberalization to go.

**Military Action.** The Soviet Union, which invaded Afghanistan in December, 1979, to replace one Communist leader with another, was maintaining more than 80,000 troops in that country by the end of 1980. Resistance continued from Afghan Muslim tribesmen, however, and Soviet involvement in Afghanistan heightened international tensions.

Moscow's ally, Vietnam, which marched into Cambodia in December, 1978, to install a puppet government, had 200,000 troops stationed around the Cambodian countryside. They also kept 40,000 troops in neighboring Laos. Even so, ousted Cambodian Communist dictator Pol Pot and the remnants of his forces continued to hold out against the Vietnamese.

**An Extended Brezhnev Doctrine.** In 1968 the Soviets used the so-called Brezhnev Doctrine to justify their invasion of Czechoslovakia. The doctrine, named for Soviet leader Leonid I. Brezhnev, asserted the Soviet right to intervene in a traditionally Communist country if the interests of the Communist bloc seemed threatened.

To defend their invasion of Afghanistan, the Soviets, in January, 1980, expanded the doctrine to apply to countries *outside* the established Communist bloc. They said that intervention could be undertaken in the name of the "internationalist solidarity of revolutionaries." Western analysts believed the Soviets were laying the ideological groundwork to justify future action, if

Coal miners were among the Polish workers who demanded, and won, the right to form independent trade unions. Other Soviet-bloc countries feared that this concession could undermine the Communist Party's monopoly of power.

they chose to move, in any developing country beset by political unrest.

**Succession.** Lacking democratic elections to provide for orderly political succession, a number of Communist states struggled with the problem of transferring power to a new generation.

In China, 76-year-old strongman Deputy Premier Teng Hsiao-ping (Deng Xiaoping) pushed through plans to reform the economy by introducing decentralization and market forces and to install like-minded leaders for the nation when he retired or died. The Peking government also placed on trial the so-called Gang of Four—Mao Tse-tung's widow and three other ousted Communist leaders—for political crimes.

President Tito, founder of Communist Yugoslavia and its leader since World War II, died in May at the age of 87. An elaborate plan formulated by Tito that provided for rotating party and government leadership took effect with relative ease, although the country faced potentially serious difficulties.

Vietnam's leadership underwent a shake-up in February that aimed at revitalizing the government with younger men. In North Korea, 68-year-old dictator Kim Il Sung took steps to make his son, Kim Chong Il, his political heir.

Seventy-six-year-old Aleksei Kosygin, the Soviet Union's prime minister for 16 years, retired because of ill health in October; he was succeeded by Nikolai A. Tikhonov, a 75-year-old Ukrainian economic planner and longtime Brezhnev associate. Kosygin's departure pointed up the fact that many Kremlin leaders—including his successor—were in their seventies, and that political succession would soon become a major problem in Moscow.

**Sino-Soviet Split.** Relations did not improve between the chief Communist powers, the U.S.S.R. and China, in 1980. The two rival states vied for influence in the Communist camp, in the West, and in the Third World. Chinese leaders regularly denounced Soviet expansionism and particularly the Soviet intervention in Afghanistan. Soviet leaders worried about the widening contacts between China and the United States.

**Eurocommunism.** A pan-European conference of Communist parties was held in Paris, April 28–29. Convened by the French and Polish Communists at the encouragement of the Soviet Union, the summit was envisioned by its organizers as a propaganda exercise against North Atlantic Treaty Organization (NATO) plans to install several hundred U.S. medium-range nuclear missiles in Europe and as a means of increasing Soviet leverage in the Communist movement. Neither the independent-minded, ruling Rumanian and Yugoslav Communist parties nor the important, but nonruling, Italian and Spanish parties attended. In the end, the conference, with 22 parties participating, achieved little except a call for a European conference on disarmament.

For several years the major "Eurocommunist" parties—those of Italy, France, and Spain—maintained a loose alliance based on independence of the Soviet Union and on allegiance to policies of reform. In 1980 that alliance lay in tatters. During a January visit to Moscow, French Communist leader Georges Marchais enthusiastically backed the Soviet move into Afghanistan. Italian and Spanish Communists deplored the invasion, and they both supported liberalization of the Polish system. Not surprisingly, Soviet theoreticians roundly criticized the Italian and Spanish parties and their leaders.

**Warsaw Pact.** At a two-day summit held in Poland in May, leaders of the Warsaw Pact nations celebrated the 25th anniversary of their Soviet-dominated military alliance. They proposed an immediate gathering of leaders "of all regions of the world" to discuss "removing the hotbeds of international tension and preventing war," but the suggestion was too vague to elicit a definitive Western response.

NATO officials remained concerned about the burgeoning strength of Warsaw Pact armed forces. In its 1980 assessment of East–West military preparedness, the London International Institute for Strategic Studies said the balance in Europe was moving steadily in favor of the Warsaw Pact.

The pact countries held widely publicized maneuvers in East Germany during September. They were planned long before Polish labor unrest developed into a full-scale emergency, but taking place at such a sensitive time for Poland, the exercises served to warn Poles about the considerable military muscle the Kremlin possessed to enforce its will.

The same countries held an unpublicized summit meeting in Moscow on Dec. 5. They reportedly decided to allow the Polish authorities to deal with unrest in that country rather than authorizing an invasion.

**Comecon.** The Soviet-dominated Communist trading community, Comecon (Council for Mutual Economic Assistance), faced a deepening economic crisis in 1980. Growth rates in the ten Comecon countries were falling. The Soviet Union was unable to fill the community's mounting oil needs, forcing member nations to dip into their limited foreign currency reserves to buy oil on the world market. The U.S. Central Intelligence Agency (CIA) estimated that at the end of 1979 Comecon countries owed more than $50 billion they had borrowed in the West in recent years. Comecon prime ministers held a summit in Prague in June to discuss their mutual problems but apparently found no long-term solutions.

See articles on individual countries mentioned.

F.W.

**COMOROS.** See STATISTICS OF THE WORLD.

**CONGO.** *See* STATISTICS OF THE WORLD.

**CONGRESS OF THE UNITED STATES.** The second session of the 96th Congress recessed on Oct. 4, 1980, to enable members to campaign for reelection, with a postelection session beginning on Nov. 12. Before the recess Congress passed major energy legislation, approved a draft registration act, and cleared other important legislation, including trucking, rail, and banking bills. Seven members of Congress were indicted in an influence-peddling and bribery scandal called Abscam.

**Energy.** President Jimmy Carter won one of his biggest legislative victories since taking office when Congress approved, on March 27, the proposed windfall profits tax on the domestic oil industry. The tax was the centerpiece of the energy program that the President had announced in April, 1979. The tax was to raise $227.3 billion in revenue over the next ten years to offset the increased earnings that oil producers were expected to realize from decontrol of prices. *See also* PETROLEUM AND NATURAL GAS.

On June 26, Congress passed another segment of the President's energy program, a bill to create a federal corporation to develop synthetic fuels as an alternative to imported oil; *see also* ENERGY. It provided $20 billion through loan, purchase, and price guarantees to assist private industry in the building by 1987 of ten synthetic fuels plants, each capable of producing 50,000 bbl of oil a day. The legislation also directed the President to resume filling the Strategic Petroleum Reserve, held in underground salt domes along the Gulf Coast.

On June 4, however, both houses of Congress voted overwhelmingly to reject a fee of $4.62 per barrel of imported oil that the President had imposed in March as an energy-conservation and budget-balancing measure. After Carter vetoed the bill, Congress overrode the veto. On June 27 the House of Representatives killed the proposed Energy Mobilization Board, a key element in Carter's program to cut oil imports. But on July 30 the President's standby gasoline rationing plan was allowed to become law.

**National Security.** Congress on June 25 approved the President's proposal for a resumption of draft registration. Men born in 1960 and 1961 were required to register at their post offices in late July and early August.

On Sept. 30, Congress completed approval of a bill reducing from eight to two the number of congressional committees to be informed of covert actions by the Central Intelligence Agency. It required, except in rare circumstances, that Congress be notified before covert operations could begin and gave Congress, for the first time, statu-

## Shape of the House In 1981

| | Democrats | Republicans | Net Gain |
|---|---|---|---|
| Alabama | 4 | 3 | — |
| Alaska | 0 | 1 | — |
| Arizona | 2 | 2 | — |
| Arkansas | 2 | 2 | — |
| California | 22 | 21 | 3R |
| Colorado | 3 | 2 | — |
| Connecticut | 4 | 2 | 1R |
| Delaware | 0 | 1 | — |
| Florida | 11 | 4 | 1R |
| Georgia | 9 | 1 | — |
| Hawaii | 2 | 0 | — |
| Idaho | 0 | 2 | — |
| Illinois | 10 | 14 | — |
| Indiana | 6 | 5 | 1R |
| Iowa | 3 | 3 | — |
| Kansas | 1 | 4 | — |
| Kentucky | 4 | 3 | — |
| Louisiana | 6 | 2 | — |
| Maine | 0 | 2 | — |
| Maryland | 7 | 1 | 1D |
| Massachusetts | 10 | 2 | — |
| Michigan | 12 | 7 | 1R |
| Minnesota | 3 | 5 | 1R |
| Mississippi | 3 | 2 | — |
| Missouri | 6 | 4 | 2R |
| Montana | 1 | 1 | — |
| Nebraska | 0 | 3 | 1R |
| Nevada | 1 | 0 | — |
| New Hampshire | 1 | 1 | — |
| New Jersey | 8 | 7 | 2R |
| New Mexico | 0 | 2 | 1R |
| New York | 22 | 17 | 4R |
| North Carolina | 7 | 4 | 2R |
| North Dakota | 1 | 0 | 1D |
| Ohio | 10 | 13 | — |
| Oklahoma | 5 | 1 | — |
| Oregon | 3 | 1 | 1R |
| Pennsylvania | 13 | 12 | 2R |
| Rhode Island | 1 | 1 | 1R |
| South Carolina | 2 | 4 | 2R |
| South Dakota | 1 | 1 | — |
| Tennessee | 5 | 3 | — |
| Texas | 19 | 5 | 1R |
| Utah | 0 | 2 | 1R |
| Vermont | 0 | 1 | — |
| Virginia | 1 | 9 | 3R |
| Washington | 5 | 2 | 1R |
| West Virginia | 2 | 2 | 2R |
| Wisconsin | 5 | 4 | 1R |
| Wyoming | 0 | 1 | — |
| **Totals** | **243** | **192** | **35R, 2D** |

| | |
|---|---|
| Net gain by Republicans | 33 |
| Seats needed for control | 218 |
| Democratic margin of control before election | 58 |
| Democratic margin of control after election | 25 |

Seven members of Congress were indicted during 1980, and four were convicted, on charges arising from an investigation into official corruption called Abscam. Here, in a videotape played at an Abscam trial, U.S. Rep. Michael Myers (second from left) holds an envelope containing $50,000 that he has just received from an undercover FBI agent.

tory authority to oversee the activities of all U.S. intelligence agencies.

**Budget.** Congress on June 12 approved a final fiscal-1980 budget of $572.6 billion, with a forecast deficit of $47 billion, which was $24 billion more than originally projected. (The final deficit was $59 billion.) At the same time, it approved a preliminary fiscal-1981 budget of $613.6 billion with a surplus of $200 million that did not, however, take into account lower tax revenues because of the recession.

The second and final budget resolution was due on Sept. 15, but Congress recessed without acting. Instead, a stopgap financing resolution was adopted to keep the federal government going even though only 3 of the 13 regular appropriations bills had been passed. On its return the lame-duck session approved an overall spending ceiling of $632.4 billion, although Congress had already approved spending bills totaling more than that sum, thereby leaving it to the 97th Congress to reconcile the discrepancy.

**Other Legislation.** The most important banking legislation since the Great Depression was approved on March 28; see BANKING AND FINANCE. It gave small savers a break on interest rates, provided more competition between commercial banks and thrift institutions, and gave the Federal Reserve System new tools to control the money supply.

A measure cutting back government regulation of the interstate trucking industry was adopted on June 19. Similarly, on Oct. 1, Congress passed a bill giving railroads more flexibility to set their own rates. See TRANSPORTATION.

President Carter signed into law on March 17 a bill increasing from 17,400 to 50,000 the number of refugees admitted annually to the United States, and the total number of immigrants, including refugees, was increased to 320,000 from 290,000 annually. The law also allowed the President to admit more than the "normal flow" of 50,000 refugees in emergency situations, thus allowing admission of more Cuban refugees in 1980. See also CUBA; UNITED STATES OF AMERICA.

By a vote of 48 to 46 the Senate approved the sale of 38 tons of enriched uranium fuel to India on Sept. 24. President Carter had authorized the shipments in June, but the House of Representatives had voted to block the sale. Disapproval, however, was required by both houses of Congress to block it. India had exploded a nuclear device and had refused to say it would not produce nuclear weapons.

**Abscam.** Six members of the House of Representatives and a Senator were indicted during 1980 on charges arising from Abscam, the most sweeping inquiry ever by the Federal Bureau of Investigation into official corruption. On Aug. 31, Rep. Michael O. Myers (D, Pa.) and three codefendants were convicted of bribery and conspiracy in the first of the Abscam trials. The House of Representatives expelled Myers on Oct. 2; he was the first House member expelled since three joined the Confederate Army during the Civil War. By early December three other House members had been convicted in Abscam trials. Only one of the indicted members, Raymond Lederer (D, Pa.), won reelection on Nov. 4.

(Daniel Flood [D, Pa.] resigned his House seat on Jan. 31 and pleaded guilty on Feb. 26 to conspiracy to violate federal campaign laws by soliciting "campaign contributions" from persons seeking federal contracts. He was placed on probation for a year. Charles C. Diggs, Jr. [D, Mich.], who had been convicted in 1979 of mail fraud and salary kickbacks, resigned his seat on June 3 and soon thereafter began serving a three-year jail sentence.)

**Postelection Session.** The lame-duck session convened on Nov. 12 with 18 Senators and 77 House members who would not be members of the 97th Congress. Some did not seek reelection, but many others were Democrats swept out of office on Nov. 4 as Republicans gained a net total of 12 Senate and 33 House seats, winning control of the Senate in 1981. *See also* ELECTIONS.

On Nov. 12, Congress approved a bill designating more than 104,000,000 acres of federal land in Alaska as national parks, wildlife refuges, and national conservation areas. On Dec. 3 it established a $1.6 billion fund to clean up dangerous toxic waste dumps and chemical spills. *See* ENVIRONMENT. On Dec. 16, Congress adjourned with action on five major appropriations bills still uncompleted. R.H.

**CONNECTICUT.** *See* STATISTICS OF THE WORLD.

**CONSTRUCTION.** Inflation remained the key deterrent to new construction during 1980. The decline in real value growth was expected to continue into 1984, when a five-year surge was predicted.

While construction starts were down in 1980 because of the recession and higher interest rates, the construction industry had a more profitable year than did many other fields. Of the ten largest U.S. construction firms, seven reported increased financial returns. Among this group profits rose from 12 to 59 percent, according to nine-month statements. Increased profits came primarily from specialty construction, such as electrical and me-

High, west-facing rooms at the 51-story Helmsley Palace Hotel in New York City offer guests a birds-eye view of St. Patrick's Cathedral (lower left). In the foreground are the landmark Villard Houses, built by McKim, Mead, and White in 1884.

chanical contracting, and from overseas projects. Another major growth area was new hotel building, spurred by an influx of foreign visitors. Current construction was expected to increase the capacity of major hotel chains by 20 percent.

**Labor Costs.** Recessionary pressures did little to control construction labor costs. Common laborers on heavy construction sites earned from $8.42 per hour in Atlanta to $16.44 per hour in San Francisco. Hourly wages for carpenters ranged from $11.36 in Birmingham, Ala., to $20.65 in San Francisco. Skilled wage rates increased about 9 percent in 1980, whereas common labor rates rose more than 12 percent. Overall building costs increased about 7 percent. In response to industry complaints regarding increasing labor prices, the American Federation of Labor and Congress of Industrial Organizations proposed a reindustrialization plan that would entail labor-management-

# CONSTRUCTION

government cooperation and would include private and public financing as well as union pension-fund financing.

**Building-Material Costs.** The cost of building materials remained relatively stable, increasing from 6 to 9 percent above that in 1979. This was in contrast to the 9 to 12 percent increase in labor costs. Cement supplies remained tight in some parts of the country, but shortages were considerably fewer than in preceding years.

**Housing Starts Fall.** Predictably, housing starts plummeted during the first half of the year; see HOUSING. This drop was caused primarily by higher interest rates and tighter supplies of mortgage funds. By July and August the number of building permits and housing starts had increased sharply. The bidding volume was also up in multiunit housing construction, accelerating rapidly after the midyear easing of mortgage funds and rates.

**Nonresidential Construction Falls.** Nonresidential construction declined as a result of recessionary pressures. Stores and warehouses were the main areas of lowered building activity. The construction volume of the nation's factories was also low due to the economic pressures. Office construction was strong, however, a reflection of low vacancy rates and higher rentals. Only financing constraints held back this area during 1980.

The building of institutions such as schools and hospitals was mixed. In general, hospital construction was off sharply, but school construction showed some recovery trends. Even with the low-er number of starts, inflation forced contract values for nonresidential construction to new highs.

**Nonbuilding Construction Grows.** Heavy construction in areas other than buildings was the industry's growth segment. Dam and reservoir construction as well as harbor development started the year on a strong note, but such projects were cut back during the second half of 1980. Environmental and electrical utility construction continued to be strong early in the year; the real pinch brought on by spending cuts was expected to be felt in 1981. Public works spending was expected to increase by about 8 percent for 1980, with utility construction cuts bringing down otherwise higher figures.

**Proposed Legislation.** Factory building was heralded as the major hope for the future in the lagging construction industry, and firms hoped for the passage of the proposed reindustrialization plan, which would step up plant construction by at least 11 percent. Proposed building energy performance standards were tabled by Congress until "at least" 1982, however. These regulations would require energy-saving measures on new construction for as many as 22 classes of buildings. At the same time, the country's new Energy Mobilization Board obtained the waiver of some federal laws that had prevented use of some energy-saving construction methods.

**Nuclear Construction Ups and Downs.** Nuclear power plant construction slowed or halted in most countries, including the United States; see NUCLEAR POWER. A notable exception was Japan, which authorized the start of construction on six new reactors. Great Britain approved construction starts for two gas-cooled reactors at an initial cost of about $3,000,000 each.

**Prospects for 1981.** Government programs to aid the construction industry in 1981 were to include about $600,000,000 for highway rehabilitation. The same amount was earmarked for retraining and relocating workers displaced by imports or technological changes within the industry. Government financing for coal port expansion was also expected to add to total 1981 income and to improve the industry's overall performance in 1981.                                                        R.W.S.

**COSTA RICA.** With unemployment rising and the value of its currency declining, Costa Rica faced difficult political and economic crises in 1980. Exports of coffee and bananas brought in 9 percent less revenue during 1980 than in 1979, despite higher world market prices for bananas. Poor weather limited the banana crop; although coffee production increased slightly, the world price was down, and Costa Rica export earnings were similarly down.

These conditions brought political problems for President Rodrigo Carazo Odio, who, in a May speech by former President José Figueres Ferrer, was called a "lackluster" president. Moreover, several defections from Carazo's cabinet led to growing criticism of the president by labor and educational groups ("impotent" was the characterization of Carazo employed by a spokesman for the educators). These attacks, together with increasingly shrill opposition in the media, were unusual in a country that prides itself on gentlemanly politics. Carazo continued to receive criticism for his support of the successful Sandinista guerrillas' 1979 struggle against the Somoza family dynasty in Nicaragua. The new Nicaraguan regime was considered dangerously left wing by many Costa Ricans. Relations with Cuba were also strained as Costa Rica championed the rights of Cubans seeking to leave their country. As a result, a columnist in Costa Rica's *La República* asked in September: "Are we beginning to drift into the political quagmires of our Central American neighbors? Quagmires that we have remained aloof from for decades?"

*See* STATISTICS OF THE WORLD.                J.N.G.

**COUNCIL FOR MUTUAL ECONOMIC ASSISTANCE.** *See* COMMUNISM.

**CRIME AND LAW ENFORCEMENT.** The year 1980 was marked by a continued rise in the crime rate. Serious crimes reported in the Federal Bureau of Investigation (FBI) crime index during the first six months of the year increased 10 percent over the same period in 1979. All regions of the country reported increases in violent crimes such as robbery and forcible rape and in property crimes such as burglary and larceny. The continued increase in reported crimes surprised many criminologists who thought that the decrease in the number of 15- to 24-year-olds (the most likely age group for committing crimes) would result in a corresponding decrease in crime. In a survey, four out of ten Americans said they were "highly fearful" that they would be victims of murder, robbery, rape, or assault.

**White-Collar Crime.** In 1980 former federal appeals court Judge William H. Webster completed his second full year as FBI director. Fully one quarter of the bureau's $600,000,000 budget was spent fighting white-collar and organized crime, with a de-emphasis on automobile thefts and bank robberies. A report found that for those convicted of various types of embezzlement the incarceration rate was 29 percent in 1979, compared with 18 percent in 1975; for bribery, the rate rose to 41 percent from 29 percent. For embezzlement the average prison sentence rose from 22 months to 30 months; for mail fraud, from 20 months to 29 months. According to Justice Department data, 74 persons were sentenced to prison between 1977 and 1979 for price-fixing and other antitrust violations, compared with 43 from 1969 through 1976. High-technology criminals, however, engaged in activities such as computer fraud and pirating of movies, records, and tapes, were said to be cheating Americans of a minimum estimated $2 billion a year.

**Abscam.** The most highly publicized and controversial of several FBI undercover operations was code-named Abscam—a contraction of Abdul Enterprises, a phony company, and scam. During the yearlong probe, FBI agents posed as representatives of wealthy Arab businessmen offering large sums of money to public officials in exchange for political favors. The undercover agents held meetings, secretly videotaped, with several officials on the pretext of needing special legislation that would allow the bogus Arabs to reside in the United States and other favors. A number of officials were ultimately indicted, including several members of Congress. Four U.S. Representatives had been convicted by early December, with trials for the others pending. The operation was marred, however, by charges that investigators entrapped or induced the officials into committing crimes and then leaked their names to the media. In November a federal judge overturned the convictions of two defendants on grounds that included entrapment.

**Other FBI Activities.** Two other undercover operations received less national attention but were equally indicative of the FBI's new priorities and tactics. In an investigation of organized crime, labor racketeering, and public corruption in the

**Next Case**

In the Des Moines Polk County District Court on a March morning, a judge, a defendant, the defendant's attorney, and an amused crowd of onlookers watched and waited as the courthouse janitor attempted to unlock the door to the judge's chambers. Nothing the janitor tried seemed to work. The attorney made a suggestion, and the defendant took over. Within three seconds he had opened the door, using a pipe wrench and a paper clip. It didn't take much longer for the judge to put on his robes, take his seat, thank the defendant, and sentence him to prison for ten years. His crime? Burglarizing a laundry.

Southwest, FBI operatives posed as insurance agents offering kickbacks to willing public officials in return for insurance contracts with city and state governments. The so-called Brilab (for bribery-labor) probe resulted in June indictments for fraud, conspiracy, and racketeering against alleged organized crime leader Carlos Marcello and Texas political and labor figures, among others.

In February the FBI wound up a two-and-a-half-year investigation of Miami (Fla.) pornography (called Operation Miporn) with a massive St. Valentine's Day arrest of many of the alleged major producers and distributors of pornography and pirated films in the country. And on Sept. 2, Joe Bonanno, the once-powerful boss of one of New York's crime families, was convicted of obstruction of justice.

**Police and Minorities.** Racial violence in Miami, following the May 17 acquittal of four county policemen charged with fatally beating a black insurance executive, pointed up the worsening of relations between police and minorities in 1980. A New York *Times* report shortly after the Miami incident found that in almost every city examined there was renewed belief among members of minorities that the police had different standards for them than for whites. The Community Relations Service, a part of the U.S. Justice Department, found that in the six-month period ended in April incidents in which minority groups charged excessive use of police force rose 142 percent over the same period a year earlier.

At the same time, many blacks felt that police were not doing enough to bring to justice perpetrators of crimes suspected of being racially motivated, such as the shooting of National Urban League President Vernon E. Jordan, Jr., on May 29 and the murder of blacks in Atlanta, Buffalo, and other cities; *see* NEGROES IN THE UNITED STATES.

**Terrorists.** Eight suspected members of the Puerto Rican terrorist organization FALN (Armed Forces of [Puerto Rican] National Liberation) were convicted in Chicago on July 30 of conspiracy to commit armed robbery and of illegal possession

*Thirty-three inmates of the New Mexico State Penitentiary were killed in a February prison riot. This was the scene in a cellblock after the 36 hr. of rioting ended.*

of weapons. According to the FBI, the FALN, a supporter of Puerto Rican independence, was suspected of more than 100 bombings since 1974 that caused 5 deaths, 80 injuries, and more than $3,500,000 in damage. The eight were among 11 suspected FALN members apprehended on April 4 in Evanston, Ill., near a van in which a large cache of weapons was found. Each of the eight was sentenced to eight years in prison on Aug. 26.

Omega 7, an anti-Castro terrorist group, took responsibility for the fatal shooting on Sept. 11 in New York City of Félix García Rodríguez, an attaché with the Cuban mission to the United Nations. He was believed to be the first U.N. official ever assassinated in New York. According to the FBI, Omega 7 had begun its terrorist campaign in 1975 and since then had been responsible for 2 murders and 20 bombings. In 1979, three men identified as Omega 7 members were convicted of the 1976 murder of Orlando Letelier, a former Chilean diplomat, in Washington, D.C. Their conviction was overturned on Sept. 15, 1980.

**Prison Riot.** Thirty-three inmates of the New Mexico State Penitentiary at Santa Fe were killed Feb. 2–3. All the dead were killed by inmates; police and National Guardsmen retook the prison without firing a shot. On Sept. 25 an official report concluded that the 36-hr. riot probably resulted from a hard-line corrections policy, adopted in 1975, that eliminated most incentives and diminished inmates' self-esteem.

For court decisions relating to crime and law enforcement, see SUPREME COURT OF THE UNITED STATES. See also CIVIL RIGHTS AND CIVIL LIBERTIES.                                          D.C.

*More than 125,000 Cubans came to the U.S. in boats arriving in Florida from the port of Mariel. The mass exodus was testimony to dissatisfaction with life in Cuba, where even Fidel Castro described economic conditions as "intolerable."*

---

### Real-Life Melodrama

Everett Clarke, the voice of *The Whistler* in radio mystery programs, was no stranger to murder. But he himself was the victim of an actual crime saga. On the night of Sept. 9, he was found stabbed to death in his Chicago acting studio, several hours after cries of "No, Paul, no!" were heard there. Paul DeWitt, a student of Clarke's, confessed the crime after being identified as the man seen crouching on a window ledge outside Clarke's office shortly after the murder. Prior to the identification, police said they did not know if the cries witnesses heard meant Clarke was pleading with his killer or giving DeWitt a drama lesson.

---

**CUBA.** A massive flow of more than 125,000 refugees from Cuba came to the United States from mid-April through Sept. 26, 1980, after Cuban President Fidel Castro opened the gates to those who wanted to flee their island homeland. Ever since Castro came to power in 1959, large numbers of Cubans had clamored to leave. Close to 1,000,000 actually left Cuba between 1959 and 1979, some 650,000 coming to the U.S. But the tide surged dramatically in 1980.

It all started over a relatively minor dispute between the Castro government and the embassies of Peru and Venezuela in Havana in early 1980, resulting in the removal of Cuban security guards on April 4 from the two diplomatic missions. In the next two days, more than 10,000 Cubans surged into the Peruvian embassy, seeking asylum and hoping to leave the island. In the next two weeks, close to 800 left the island for Costa Rica and then for Peru; others accepted safe-conduct passes to return to their homes and await flights.

The incident was clearly an embarrassment to Castro, symbolizing the rather large numbers of Cubans so dissatisfied with his rule that they wanted to flee. As it became clear that many more than the 10,000 or so wanted to leave, Castro halted the airlift to Costa Rica. Simultaneously, Cuban-Americans in Florida took matters into their own hands, launching a Dunkirk-like evacuation flotilla of boats from Key West, Florida, to the Cuban port of Mariel, west of Havana. Castro then announced that Cubans who wanted to leave could, in fact, do so. The flotilla of small boats began shuttling back and forth between Cuba and Florida with their human cargo of refugees. President Jimmy Carter, who at first welcomed the Cuban refugee exodus, on May 5, began to vacillate and on May 14 sought to stop the traffic. But it was too late. The boatlift continued until Cuba officially put a stop to it on Sept. 26. *See also* UNITED STATES OF AMERICA.

Castro in effect rid Cuba of those most disaffected against his government. Perhaps 1500 were people in prison or in mental institutions. Castro also sought to improve relations with the U.S. by returning skyjackers who had commandeered planes in August and September to fly to Cuba, and by allowing 33 U.S. citizens in Cuban jails on a variety of charges to return to their homeland. Although 3 chose to remain in Cuba, the other 30 returned to U.S. soil on Oct. 27.

The Cuban economy was clearly in bad shape. In early May, a speech delivered by Castro at the end of December, 1979, but kept secret for four months, became available. It painted a picture of "intolerable" economic conditions—to use Castro's own word. The speech was a broad admission that 21 years after coming to power, the Castro government was unable to adequately feed, clothe, house, or provide sufficient employment for the island's 10,000,000 people. The speech recited a litany of woes: chronic shortages of foodstuffs such as bread, repeated shortfalls in sugar and tobacco production, staggering unemployment, mounting crime, and government inefficiency and corruption. "This year, 1979," Castro concluded, "was one of the worst years." The same could have been said for 1980. The sugar and tobacco harvests were way down, due to plant diseases and weather conditions. In an ironic twist, Cuba even imported 40,000 tons of sugar in August from the neighboring Dominican Republic to meet previous export commitments and domestic requirements.

*See* STATISTICS OF THE WORLD. J.N.G.

**CYPRUS.** Despite deeply rooted mistrust on both sides, fresh movement was made in Cyprus during 1980 to lessen the long-standing antagonism between the island's Greek and Turkish communities. Intercommunal talks were resumed in mid-year after a 14-month hiatus. Turkish Cypriot leaders, heads of a self-proclaimed state that controls 38 percent of the island, asserted in a statement made public on Jan. 13 that "a step toward rapprochement . . . can be taken if the Greek Cypriot administration states that it has no authority over the Turkish Cypriot authority."

In an announcement scheduled by the Greek leadership before the Turkish overture, President Spyros Kyprianou on Jan. 14 disclosed "the first of a series of measures" by his Greek-run regime to benefit Turkish Cypriots. It provided for pensions and other social benefits, jobs in government-controlled fields, and schooling for Turkish students in Greek institutions. An affirmative Turkish response, Kyprianou said, would help "create the right climate for the restoration of peace."

Attempts to revive negotiations between the two communities were initially unsuccessful. Kurt Waldheim, secretary-general of the United Nations, reported on April 3 that he had offered to send a representative to help start new talks. Since he found no "indications of sufficient flexibility to make such a visit worthwhile," Waldheim wrote, "I decided not to pursue the matter."

Four months later, however, leaders of the two communities agreed to resume negotiations, and the talks were renewed in Nicosia on Aug. 9 under U.N. sponsorship. Waldheim said he understood that both sides favored "a federal solution of the constitutional aspect and a bizonal solution of the territorial aspect." Kyprianou added that the Greek community still rejected the term "bizonal" if the Turks interpreted it to mean partition.

*See* STATISTICS OF THE WORLD. L.A.S.

**CZECHOSLOVAKIA.** As a result of the Soviet invasion 12 years earlier, Czechoslovakia in 1980 remained the most Stalinist nation in the Soviet bloc. The government, led by 67-year-old President Gustáv Husák, kept up constant pressure on reform-minded Czechoslovak citizens, such as the signers of the human rights document Charter 77. It refused to sanction even needed economic reforms for fear such a move would lead to pressure for political liberalization as well.

One target of official wrath was the informal study groups held for young people by academics who had been dismissed from their teaching posts in the purges that followed the 1968 invasion. In March and April the Czechoslovak government deported two Oxford University philosophers who were visiting Prague as tourists to deliver guest lectures to such groups. The noted Czechoslovak philosopher Julius Tomin was regularly harassed by police for organizing the seminars. Czech journalist Jiri Lederer, a cofounder of Charter 77, arrived in West Germany on Sept. 2 after being expelled from his country.

Officials dealt sternly with other human rights activists as well. In September police detained 11 people, including former Foreign Minister Jiří Hájek, for sending a letter of support to Polish strikers in Gdańsk. Czechoslovakia's government-controlled newspapers joined those of the Soviet Union and other Soviet-bloc countries in charging that "anti-Socialist elements" were among the leaders of the Polish strikes.

Within the Czechoslovak Communist Party itself, there was debate about how to deal with the country's shabby economic performance. The industrial plant was largely outdated, workers turned in lackluster performances, and the quality of products was often too poor for them to compete favorably in the international marketplace. Western experts believed that Czechoslovakia needed reforms that would put market forces into play, along the lines of those adopted in Hungary in recent years. Presidium member Vasil Bilak, the Czechoslovak party's principal hard-liner, opposed such change, but technocrats led by Premier Lubomír Štrougal appeared to be more open-minded. The Štrougal faction won party approval for only a limited attack on the economic crisis. In March the government announced a series of new measures for the 1981–85 economic plan, with the government retaining strong central control but tying incentives to more efficient work and better-quality production.

In terms of foreign policy, Husák toured Vietnam, Laos, and Cambodia in February as part of the Soviet effort to maintain close Warsaw Pact links with the area. In July Foreign Minister Bohuslav Chňoupek visited Afghanistan as a show of support for the Soviet-installed government there.

*See* STATISTICS OF THE WORLD.

# D

**DAHOMEY.** *See* BENIN.

**DANCE.** The eyes of the dance world during 1980 focused on the American Ballet Theatre (ABT) as it set precedents in labor relations and administration. Although no fresh ground was broken, several new dances provoked animated reaction. Historically significant dance styles found an increasingly wide audience, reflecting a growing sophistication toward the art form.

For the first time the ensemble of a ballet company demanded significant increases in salary. A lockout by ABT management, which had begun on Oct. 29, 1979, continued into the new year. A settlement was reached just before the scheduled start of the troupe's transcontinental tour on Feb. 4.

This labor dispute occurred on the eve of a major upheaval in artistic directorship. Lucia Chase, one of the founders of ABT in 1939, was replaced by Mikhail Baryshnikov on Sept. 1. Baryshnikov's staff maintained some continuity with the past, particularly in Antony Tudor as choreographer emeritus and Nora Kaye as associate director. Major changes in artistic profile were, of course, expected.

A trend toward an international repertory of proven quality was anticipated during ABT's inaugural season under Baryshnikov, which began on Dec. 10 at the John F. Kennedy Center for the Performing Arts in Washington, D.C. Included were new productions of George Balanchine's *The Prodigal Son* and *La Sonnambula,* Paul Taylor's *Airs,* Frederick Ashton's *Les Rendezvous,* and Waslaw Nijinsky's *Afternoon of a Faun.*

Amid milestones of change, ABT celebrated its 40th anniversary. The May 4 opening of its ten-week season at the Metropolitan Opera House in New York City became a gala featuring many alumni, including Alicia Alonso and Ivan Nagy. Its most illustrious star, Natalia Makarova, became a full-fledged choreographer, reviving Marius Petipa's classic *La Bayadère* with the addition of some new choreography. Premiered on May 21, the work stimulated serious discussion on the feasibility of choreographic modernization. The only element of the ballet to receive unanimous praise, however, was the spectacular decor by Pierluigi Samaritini. Makarova's own ballet company debuted in New York City's Uris Theater in October.

Two major figures in dance returned to work in 1980: George Balanchine, chief choreographer of the New York City Ballet; and Robert Joffrey, artistic director of the Joffrey Ballet. Following an eight-month layoff resulting from financial difficulties, the Joffrey Ballet re-formed in May with a virtually new roster and new productions. Joffrey himself created a new ballet, *Postcards,* to music

Above: After an eight-month layoff because of financial difficulties, the Joffrey Ballet was re-formed in May. Cynthia Anderson and Michael Bjerknes are shown in Robert Joffrey's new ballet, Postcards, which was set to the music of Erik Satie. Right: The ancient art of Chinese acrobatics dazzled American audiences in 1980. Here members of the Acrobats of Canton perform at Radio City Music Hall in New York City. Below: Le Sacre du Printemps (Rehearsal) was a new work, with choreography by Paul Taylor. It presents both a rehearsal of a dance and the dance itself.

by Erik Satie, which premiered on June 10 in Seattle. Laura Dean created her first work for the troupe, *Night,* which premiered on Oct. 29 during the Joffrey's season at New York's City Center. Joffrey's talent for selecting revivals was again evidenced in Ashton's *Illuminations.*

The New York City Ballet's season at the New York State Theater, from April 29 to June 29, featured Balanchine's first new works for that company since 1978. *Ballade,* set to music by Gabriel Fauré, was especially noteworthy for the lyricism it demanded of Merrill Ashley and for the prominence it gave to newcomer Ib Andersen, formerly of the Royal Danish Ballet. *Robert Schumann's Davidsbundlertanze* was carefully scrutinized by critics and audiences alike. Some thought it a masterpiece, and all remarked on Balanchine's ability to explore yet another avenue of expression at this point in his career.

Another intriguing new dance came from Paul Taylor. His *Le Sacre du Printemps (Rehearsal),* first performed in February at the Lisner Auditorium in Washington, D.C., contains plots within plots and ironies piled on ironies. It presents both a rehearsal of a dance and the dance itself. Aware of historical precedent, Taylor also comments on the famous Nijinsky choreography of the first *Sacre* in 1913, reducing its two-dimensional style to cartoonlike drawings.

**International Dance News.** The ancient art of Chinese acrobatics soared to dizzying heights of virtuosity under the Shanghai Acrobatic Theater. Between March 25 and June 22, the troupe performed in New York City, Philadelphia, Chicago, Minneapolis, and San Francisco. Chicago's International Dance Festival welcomed the entire Royal Danish Ballet in June. The troupe presented a week of full-length ballets by the 19th-century Danish master August Bournonville. The Paris Opera Ballet's spring tour to New York City, Washington, D.C., and Chicago was canceled because the dancers objected to guest appearances by Rudolf Nureyev and Peter Schaufuss. Instead, Nureyev presented under his own aegis in November the U.S. premiere of *La Sylphide* with the original French choreography. His backup ensemble at New York's Uris Theater was the Boston Ballet, which, under the direction of Violette Verdy, became the first American ballet company to perform in China. The tour took place in June.

**Broadway.** The Broadway stage continued to offer works in the tradition of *A Chorus Line* and *Dancin'.* New productions such as *Barnum, A Day in Hollywood/A Night in the Ukraine,* and *42nd Street,* as well as revivals of *Brigadoon* and *West Side Story,* featured dance numbers. *See also* THEATER.                          N.T.G.

**DELAWARE.** *See* STATISTICS OF THE WORLD.

**DEMOCRATIC PARTY.** A divisive struggle for the Presidential nomination, the political unpopularity of President Jimmy Carter and his inability to come to grips with the nation's economic problems, and a rising conservative tide combined to make 1980 a debacle for the Democratic Party. Carter was demolished by Republican challenger Ronald Reagan in the November election, winning only six states and the District of Columbia. Moreover, the Democrats lost control of the U.S. Senate for the first time in 28 years, with several of the party's most prominent national figures ousted in the GOP landslide. Although the Democrats retained control of the U.S. House of Representatives, the Republicans narrowed the margin to the point where conservative Democrats joining with the Republicans might provide a working majority for the new Republican President. *See* ELECTIONS.

**Campaign for the Nomination.** As the 1980 primary election season commenced, Jimmy Carter seemed a certain loser. He was challenged for renomination as the Democratic standard-bearer by the party's most popular elected official, Sen. Edward M. Kennedy of Massachusetts. While all the public opinion polls showed that Kennedy would handily defeat Carter in the primaries, Carter was quietly assembling the same sort of grass-roots organization that had propelled him from obscurity to the Democratic Presidential nomination in 1976.

Carter was also helped politically by the taking of U.S. hostages in Iran in November, 1979. As the crisis continued, the country rallied around its President, and Carter was able to use the crisis as an excuse to cancel political travel and avoid participating in a debate with Kennedy before the Jan. 21 Iowa precinct caucuses. The result was that Carter defeated Kennedy by a 2-to-1 margin in Iowa and followed with an unexpected win in New Hampshire on Feb. 26. After Kennedy won his home state primary on March 4, Carter ran off five wins in a row, including the critical March 18 primary in Illinois. Kennedy countered with victories in New York and Connecticut, but Carter began pulling away with wins in several Southern and Midwestern primaries. By mid-May, Carter virtually had the nomination sewn up, but Kennedy's repeated attacks on Carter's refusal to leave the White House and debate and the President's use of awards of federal grants, appointments, and other favors to local party officials began drawing blood.

In May, Carter declared the Iranian crisis "manageable" and began actively campaigning to deny Kennedy a strong finish in the primaries. But, in what was viewed as more of a protest against Carter's economic policies than an endorsement of Kennedy's doomed candidacy, Kennedy won five of the final eight contests on June 3, including the vital California primary. Despite Kennedy's strong showing, Carter finished the day with more than 300 delegates above the 1666 required to win the nomination.

Kennedy remained in the race despite intense pressure by party leaders to persuade him to withdraw. A meeting with Carter in early June failed to resolve their differences, and the Senator remained an active candidate, hoping Carter's fortunes would sour by the convention. By mid-summer, Kennedy was given an opening when polls showed approval of Carter's performance as low as 22 percent, and a scandal erupted involving Carter's brother Billy; see PRESIDENT OF THE UNITED STATES. After a Louis Harris survey in July showed Republican Ronald Reagan running well ahead of Carter, dissident Democrats launched a drive to deny Carter the nomination by challenging a convention rule requiring all delegates to remain bound to the candidate for whom they were pledged on the first ballot.

**The Convention.** The Democratic National Convention was convened on Aug. 11 in New York City's Madison Square Garden. The keynote address by U.S. Rep. Morris Udall of Arizona was, however, overshadowed by the climactic vote on the proposed rules change, which was won by the Carter forces by a comfortable margin. With Carter's nomination assured, Kennedy withdrew from the race. He won a moral victory the next night, however, when the delegates adopted his platform plank urging a $12 billion economic stimulus program to combat unemployment. Another Kennedy-sponsored plank pledged the party not to support any program that would increase unemployment. Carter was renominated on Aug. 14 and, after his acceptance speech, was joined on the podium by Kennedy in a restrained if symbolically important show of party unity. Vice-President Walter F. Mondale was renominated without challenge.

**The Campaign.** With the polls showing widespread dissatisfaction with Carter's record as President, his campaign strategists sought to make Ronald Reagan's fitness for the Presidency the central issue of the campaign. Carter aimed to depict Reagan as an aging archconservative whose views were not only outside the American mainstream but were also dangerously naive. He attacked Reagan's opposition to the strategic arms

*President Jimmy Carter applauds as his rival for the Democratic Party Presidential nomination, Sen. Edward M. Kennedy of Massachusetts (right), joins other Democrats on Aug. 14 in celebrating Carter's nomination for a second term by the party's national convention.*

limitation treaty as an invitation to nuclear catastrophe and his opposition to Democratic social programs as heartless. Time and again, he insinuated that Reagan's election might well result in a war with the Soviet Union. The strategy was successful in raising doubts about Reagan, but a backlash developed when the President suggested in September that Reagan's candidacy had created "stirrings of hate" and claimed in October that a Reagan victory would separate "black from white, Jew from Christian, North from South."

With the President having gained in polls to the point where the election was rated a toss-up, Reagan agreed on Oct. 21 to debate Carter, vindicating the prior Carter strategy decision of boycotting a proposed three-way debate, including independent John Anderson, on the ground that any exposure given Anderson would be at Carter's expense. In the Oct. 28 debate, Carter scored points by portraying himself as a competent, stable chief executive, but his strategy of painting Reagan as reckless and dangerous backfired when Reagan came across to television viewers as a knowledgeable and amiable contender. In the view of many political analysts, Carter's inability to destroy Reagan's credibility in the debate was the final blow to his reelection.

**Election Results.** Carter won only 49 electoral votes to 489 for Reagan and carried only his home state of Georgia in the South, which had solidly supported him in 1976. Carter carried so many Democrats down with him that the Republicans gained control of the U.S. Senate, narrowed the Democratic majority in the House, and picked up four governorships.

The Democratic Party was left in shambles, searching for a leader to pick up the pieces and facing the need for an intensive effort to match a Republican Party that was better organized and financed at the local, state, and national levels.

See also biographies of Edward M. Kennedy, Walter F. Mondale, and Edmund Muskie in the biography section of People in the News.          T.D.

**DENMARK.** Economic reverses caused increasing political stress in Denmark during 1980. The minority Social Democratic government of Anker Jørgensen faced opposition from both the Right and the Left as economic pressures influenced action in such areas as foreign relations, military policy, nuclear power, and social benefits.

A new word, "Denmarkization," was coined by Western European journalists critical of Denmark for allegedly expecting military protection from the United States and other Western nations while refusing to do its own share. Jørgensen's military-spending policy provided for increasing

Taking a break from politics, President Jimmy Carter wears a cowboy hat as he relaxes during a summer party on the White House lawn.

the defense budget only enough to account for inflation. This policy was derided as "the zero solution," as opposed to the call by the North Atlantic Treaty Organization for a 3 percent annual increase in real terms by its members. Denmark's military expenditures were scheduled to rise from $1.3 billion in 1980 to $1.5 billion in 1981.

The government indefinitely postponed its decision on the controversial question of whether to build nuclear power plants. The need for adequate energy sources was growing critical for Denmark, which has no coal or hydroelectric resources and only a small share of North Sea oil, and was suffering economic distress from recession and inflation, both traceable at least partly to the rising prices of imported oil.

The postponement of the nuclear decision, announced on Jan. 26, was said to mean that Denmark could not have a nuclear plant in operation during the 20th century. The Jørgensen government was unwilling to go ahead with nuclear power construction until it found satisfactory ways to dispose of radioactive wastes and safe sites for nuclear plants in its densely populated country.

According to data reported on Jan. 29, Denmark's trade deficit had increased from $2.85 billion in 1978 to $3.87 billion in 1979. In an effort to lessen the deficit's effect on the economy, Jørgensen proposed an economic austerity program on April 10. Initially, the plan included $1.33 billion in higher taxes and reductions of $830,000,000 in government spending; most of the spending cuts were to be in pensions and unemployment benefits. After attacks on the plan from both the Right and the Left, Jørgensen negotiated changes. He announced on May 5 that he had achieved a narrow parliamentary majority for the program by persuading three small centrist parties—Social

Liberal, Center-Democrat, and Christian—to support the revised plan. The program, to be in effect through 1981, would increase taxes by about $1 billion and cut government spending by some $1.4 billion.

See STATISTICS OF THE WORLD.            L.A.S.

**DISTRICT OF COLUMBIA.** See STATISTICS OF THE WORLD.

**DJIBOUTI.** See STATISTICS OF THE WORLD.

**DOMINICA.** See STATISTICS OF THE WORLD.

**DOMINICAN REPUBLIC.** See STATISTICS OF THE WORLD. See also CARIBBEAN COUNTRIES.

# E

**EARTH SCIENCES.** Events relating to the earth sciences grabbed the headlines repeatedly in 1980. In May, Mount St. Helens erupted violently in Washington State. Throughout the summer, an unusual meteorological pattern brought a devastating heat wave and drought to the central and southern United States as well as cold and rain to most of Europe. A rare earthquake startled residents of Kentucky and surrounding states. Tremors also rattled Californians with increasing frequency. In October a massive earthquake struck an Algerian city, and in November the deadliest earthquake in Europe since 1915 struck southern Italy.

## GEOLOGY AND GEOPHYSICS

The eruption of Mount St. Helens allowed U.S. scientists a unique opportunity to scrutinize each move of an active volcano. Geologists learned more about earthquakes that are not associated with obvious geologic faults. New methods of analysis led to revised theories about the structure of the earth's interior. Finally, scientists found new evidence for theories on the cause of the extinctions of the dinosaurs and many other organisms 65,000,000 years ago.

**Volcanology.** Mount St. Helens reawakened with a flourish. Dormant since 1857, the 2950-m (9677-ft.) volcano announced itself on March 20 with an earthquake of Richter magnitude 4.0. Seismic activity increased rapidly the following week as scientists scrambled to install monitoring instruments on the mountain. Their haste paid off. Mount St. Helens erupted moderately at 12:36 P.M. local time on March 27, becoming the first active volcano in the continental U.S. since 1915.

On April 1 geologists recorded the first burst of harmonic tremors, the continuous, rhythmic activity that volcanologists associate with the movement of magma underground. By the end of April, geologists confirmed the existence of an enormous bulge on the north side of the volcano that was swelling outward at the astounding rate of 1.5 m (5 ft.) per day. On May 18 at 8:32 A.M., with a force estimated at that of a 5.6-megaton bomb, the volcano blasted away about 400 m (1300 ft.) of its north slope, flinging hot gases and ash more than 18,300 m (60,000 ft.) in the air, killing 34 persons (with 28 others missing and presumed dead) and obliterating 400 sq.km (150 sq.mi.) of land.

Researchers monitored earthquake activity and the changes in the shape of the volcano as it filled with molten rock. They analyzed the amounts and kinds of gases it gave off and the content of the ash it spread across the countryside. By picking out a certain pattern of seismic signals, they were able to warn workers and scientists off the mountain just before other major eruptions on July 22 and Aug. 7.

**Seismology.** Beginning in 1979 and continuing in 1980, northern Californians experienced an increased number of moderate-sized earthquakes, from Livermore to the Mammoth Lakes area near the California–Nevada border. Seismologists also detected an increase in the number of small earthquakes in southern California and changes in the amount of the gas radon released from the ground, which is usually taken as a signal of rocks cracking beneath the surface. Some seismologists said the activity represented only an apparent increase when compared with the sparse historical data. William Ellsworth of the U.S. Geological Survey noted, however, that the stepped-up activity near San Francisco appeared to mirror that of the 50 years preceding the 1906 quake.

Vast stretches of forest in the vicinity of Washington's Mount St. Helens lie flattened after the volcano's May 18 eruption, indicating both the fury and the direction of the blast.

On July 27 a 5.1 magnitude earthquake, the first in the area since 1933, struck near Maysville, Ky., and was felt throughout 14 surrounding states. The Kentucky event was an example of the "intraplate" quakes that occur within a tectonic plate, instead of—like those in California—along a well-defined fault where two tectonic plates meet. This characteristic makes intraplate quakes very difficult to predict, but Mary Lou Zoback and Mark D. Zoback of the U.S. Geological Survey reported an important step toward this goal by determining the direction and type of stress in various places in the continental U.S. Theoretically, earthquakes are most likely to occur along the path of maximum stress. The Zobacks found that in the mid-continent the stress is east-west, apparently along an ancient rifting zone. In the eastern U.S. the maximum stress lies perpendicular to the coast. The next step, they said, is to find the weak spots in the crust that are most likely to give way under the stress.

**Earth's Interior.** Three researchers from the California Institute of Technology developed a new view of the earth's interior. Traditionally, the earth's mantle, between the crust and the core, has been thought to be well mixed and nearly molten. But Gerald J. Wasserburg, Don J. De-Paolo, and Stein B. Jacobsen told the meeting in May of the American Geophysical Union that, based on comparisons of the ratios of two radioisotopes in various rocks, the mantle appeared to consist of two layers: an upper layer that supplies molten rock to volcanoes, and a lower layer that has remained unmelted and untouched since the earth formed.

Taking a deeper look at the earth, researchers at the Carnegie Institution of Washington, D.C., found that the earth's core may not be composed of iron and nickel, as assumed from previous studies, but of iron and oxygen. When Peter M. Bell and Ho-Kwang Mao subjected a synthetic rock sample to extremely high pressures and temperatures like those near the earth's core, they found that a complex chemical transformation occurs in which oxygen-carrying iron separates from other elements and sinks.

**Dinosaur Extinction.** Scientists know that 65,000,-000 years ago dinosaurs suddenly became extinct, along with about 50 to 75 percent of all the earth's plant and animal species. No satisfactory explana-

At a depth of more than 400 m (1250 ft.) off the coast of Hawaii, botanist Sylvia Earle tests the first scientific use of a flexible armored suit. The deepest solo dive in the open sea was also the first made without a tether to the surface. Linked only to the submarine that brought her down, her suit contained a 48-hr. supply of continually processed air at a one-atmosphere pressure that made lengthy decompression processes unnecessary.

tion for this has yet been found. But at the meeting in January of the American Association for the Advancement of Science, scientists proposed new solutions to the mystery.

Based on the fossils found in sediments from the North Sea, Stefan Gartner of Texas A. & M. University suggested that the Arctic Ocean was once isolated and contained fresh water. About 65,000,000 years ago, he said, the ocean opened and spilled its fresh water. This spillover, he believed, reduced the salt content of the rest of the oceans, killing marine life, and altered the global climate, killing land life.

Scientists from the Lawrence Berkeley Laboratory in California suggested an extraterrestrial cause for the extinctions. In a variety of rock samples, Walter Alvarez, Luis Alvarez, Frank Asaro, and Helen Michel found high concentrations of certain elements that are not usually found on earth but are found in asteroids and comets. They suggested that a huge asteroid struck the earth 65,000,000 years ago and threw up a dust cloud that blocked out sunlight long enough to cause the extinctions.

### OCEANOGRAPHY

Researchers using deep-sea instrumentation off the coast of Nova Scotia in 1980 found that cold, dense, and very swift currents—as fast as 50 cm (19 in.) per second—scour the bottom of the western Atlantic Ocean. Such currents may carry

sediments long distances and transfer heat energy in the ocean, the researchers said.

By using a specially adapted research submarine and camera, scientists for the first time saw some of the fundamental processes that take place at a center of sea-floor spreading—one of the many "seams" in the ocean bottom where molten rock oozes forth to form new ocean crust. In a series of dives that began in 1979 and continued in 1980 off the coast of Ecuador, the researchers found chimneylike vents that spew out a mixture of hot water and dissolved metals. The composition of the water-metal solution has important and as yet incompletely assessed implications for the composition of sea water and for ore formation.

### CLIMATOLOGY

A major goal for climatologists and meteorologists is prediction. Meteorologists have reasonable accuracy on the scale of days to weeks, and climatologists feel fairly confident that the geologic record of ancient climates tells them the probable range of what to expect hundreds and thousands of years from now. The challenge lies where climatology and meteorology overlap: predicting weather for several months or a few years ahead.

The importance of prediction on that time scale came clearly into focus in 1980. Unrelenting heat and drought scorched the central and southern

U.S. from June to September while Europeans shivered through a summer of unusual damp and cold. Had scientists been able to predict the persistent meteorological pattern that produced these conditions, world agriculture might have benefited. Before the summer was half over, scientists were feeding into their computers data on the conditions preceding the event, in the hope that something would emerge that would help them predict the next such incident. One theory, suggested by Jerome Namias of the Scripps Institution of Oceanography's Climate Research Group, held that the Pacific Ocean, cooled by strong winds the previous year, fed energy into a susceptible air circulation pattern, which in turn triggered the development of the circulation patterns responsible for the unusual weather.

*See also* ACCIDENTS AND DISASTERS; AGRICULTURE.                                                   S.W.

**ECONOMY AND BUSINESS.** Recession and inflation were 1980's twin economic problems—hitting businesses as well as individuals in the United States. By fall the recession appeared to be easing or ending, but the inflation rate was climbing again. The federal deficit for fiscal 1980 was $59 billion—far above the original estimate of $12.9 billion.

The long-predicted recession struck in early 1980, but the Carter administration was at that point more concerned with an annual inflation rate of 18 percent. On March 14, President Jimmy Carter unveiled an anti-inflation program that placed severe restraints on consumer credit and loans by banks; *see* BANKING AND FINANCE. The result was a 9.9 percent drop in the gross national product (GNP) during the second quarter, the worst quarterly decline on record. But in the third quarter, the GNP advanced 2.4 percent, and in the final quarter, 5 percent.

Most Western nations shared some or all of the U.S. economic problems. A *Business Week* forecast in August predicted that Western industrial nations would post only a 0.5 percent growth rate in 1980, compared to 3.3 percent in 1979.

World economic activity was expected to increase by 2 percent in 1980, according to the *Business Week* forecast. The major beneficiaries were the oil-exporting countries, which were expected to earn a surplus of $115 billion. The prospects for oil-importing developing countries were bleak.

**Inflation and Recession.** The consumer price index rose during the first half of 1980 in the U.S. at an average annual rate of 14.3 percent. Among major Western European nations, West Germany had the lowest inflation during that period, at an annual rate of 5.7 percent. Great Britain had the highest, at an annual rate of 20.3 percent.

The second-quarter downturn in the U.S. was in large part due to a slide in consumer spending. Consumer installment debt fell by nearly $2 billion in April as Americans paid off more than they borrowed for the first time since May, 1975. Inflation dropped to an annual rate of 11.6 percent during the second quarter as reflected in the consumer price index, compared to 18.2 percent during the first quarter. In July and August inflation slowed appreciably, but it returned to a double-digit rate in September.

By midyear, credit restrictions had been revoked to soften the recession. Consumers started buying again, with a 1.5 percent spending jump in August—the largest monthly increase since the end of the last recession in 1975.

Economic indicators were favorable during the third quarter, suggesting that the end of the recession might be near, but higher interest rates in September seemed to dampen hopes of a quick recovery. The back-and-forth seesawing of stimulative-dampening economic policies confused businesspeople as well as the larger public.

**Profits and Productivity.** After-tax profits of U.S. corporations rose 5.9 percent in dollar terms from the final quarter of 1979 to the first quarter of 1980, but, after accounting for inflation, there was an actual drop of 12.7 percent. During the recession-ridden second quarter, profits dropped by 18.2 percent from the first quarter, the worst quarterly decline in more than 25 years. Profits rose by 7.9 percent during the third quarter.

U.S. nonfarm productivity dropped by 1.6 per-

---

**Have You Ever Been to Lima?**

Business International, a consulting firm with headquarters in New York City, released a detailed survey of travel expenses around the world just before the 1980 summer vacation period began. Among the interesting results: London, the most expensive city in the world for a visiting business executive, had the most expensive hotel rooms (average $192); dinner for four at a leading restaurant in Paris ran $525; a week's car rental in Lagos, Nigeria (the world's fourth most expensive city to visit), cost $603, plus 83¢ per mile. Some cities in the United States ranked fairly low. New York City was eighth, Chicago fifteenth, and San Francisco sixteenth. The cheapest city, according to the survey? Lima, the capital city of Peru.

cent during 1979, and the 1980 decline was expected to be more than 4 percent. U.S. output per man-hour in manufacturing thus had become lower than that in Japan, West Germany, Italy, France, Canada, and Great Britain. Among the reasons cited were high taxes and excessive government regulations. Interest rates that at one point in 1980 reached a minimum of 21.5 percent discouraged new business investment that could lead to significant productivity and profits improvement.

Mining, oil, electronics, trading, and shipping companies generally performed the best, if they operated globally. Japanese companies showed higher profit increases than the firms of many other countries. Automotive, trading, electronics, and photographic suppliers were among key industries with higher 1980 profits in Japan.

**Unemployment.** In April and May, as the U.S. recession hit hardest, unemployment jumped from 6.2 percent to 7.8 percent, then dropped slightly. In automobile-manufacturing cities, and areas with related industries, such as steel, the unemployment rate sometimes surpassed 20 percent.

But production workers of all kinds felt the economic pinch, with an average jobless rate of 16.5 percent. *See also* AUTOMOBILES; LABOR; MANUFACTURING INDUSTRIES.

In July the unemployment rate in the nine-nation European Community (EC) rose to 6.1 percent, the highest since the EC was created in 1957. The jobless rate during that month was 3.4 percent in West Germany, 5.5 percent in the Netherlands, 6.6 percent in France, 7 percent in Italy, and 7.8 percent in Great Britain.

**Wage-Price Guidelines.** The voluntary pay and price guidelines were to expire at the end of September, but the Council on Wage and Price Stability extended them. Standards called for holding pay increases in an annual range of 7.5 percent to 9.5 percent, and price increases to no more than those of 1976–77, with adjustments. The Ford Motor Co.'s 1979 labor contract with the United Automobile Workers exceeded the guidelines, according to the council, which reacted by declaring Ford's automotive operations possibly ineligible for any new major government contract. The same action was threatened against the Mobil Oil

A padlocked U.S. Steel plant in Youngstown, Ohio, symbolizes the problems facing the nation's older industries, which need new investment to meet foreign competition. Steelworkers unsuccessfully sought to buy the plant and keep it going.

*Heads of government of seven leading non-Communist nations gather in Venice for an economic summit meeting with outgoing European Commission head Roy Jenkins (right). Inflation was the primary topic, with special concern for continual increases in oil prices.*

Corp. by President Carter for allegedly violating the price guidelines. A compromise agreement with Mobil was announced on April 24.

**Revitalization Plan.** On Aug. 28 the President offered an economic revitalization plan and announced the creation of a 15-member Economic Revitalization Board headed by American Federation of Labor and Congress of Industrial Organizations President Lane Kirkland and Irving Shapiro, chairman of E. I. du Pont de Nemours & Co. The plan called for the board, beginning in 1981, to offer federal loans, grants, subsidies, and tax incentives to attract investment to regions hard hit by unemployment and recession. It also called for increased federal investment in the nation's transportation network. Republican Party Presidential candidate Ronald Reagan offered a similar plan to revitalize the lagging U.S. economy, leaving business executives hopeful, though wary, of prospects for tax relief in 1981.

**International Trade.** The U.S. merchandise trade deficit seemed likely to be about the same in 1980 as the total of $24.7 billion in 1979. Decreased U.S. industrial productivity, higher oil costs, and a weak U.S. export-incentive policy were blamed for the deficit. The General Agreement on Tariffs and Trade predicted world trade would expand in volume only by 2 to 3 percent in 1980, compared to 6 percent in 1979. The deflationary effect of 1979 oil price increases seemed to be responsible.

The President lifted quotas on imports of Japanese color television sets on June 30 and an-

nounced liberalization of existing restraints on shipments from South Korea and Taiwan. On March 21 the Department of Commerce suspended a mechanism under which prices of steel imports could not fall below a certain level without risking a federal investigation, but on Sept. 30 President Carter revived the system. *See also* MANUFACTURING INDUSTRIES.

**Comecon Countries.** Poland, which was racked by labor unrest, and Czechoslovakia seemed to be

---

**First the Iran Raid . . . Then This**

The economic summit meeting held in Venice in June had its lighter moments. For example, U.S. President Jimmy Carter was the only world leader who refused to travel about the city's omnipresent lagoons in the sleek, efficient Venetian motor launches. Carter preferred to use an admiral's barge, borrowed from the U.S. Sixth Fleet. The American crew of the barge, which is similar in size and shape to a cabin cruiser, had to make several passes on the first day of the conference before they finally managed to dock it. As hundreds of Italians lined the shore, cheering and jeering, the President, a former naval officer, merely stood on the deck in silent contemplation.

turning in the poorest economic performances of 1980 among Soviet-bloc East European members of Comecon (Council for Mutual Economic Assistance). The Soviet and East German economies were the strongest. Soviet industrial productivity was up 4.2 percent, and labor productivity jumped 3.2 percent. East Germany had a 5.7 percent labor productivity hike and a 16 percent increase in exports for the same period.

Economic sanctions against the U.S.S.R. by the U.S. following the Soviet invasion of Afghanistan halved U.S.-Soviet trade in the first six months of 1980. The U.S. trade surplus of $529,000,000 with the U.S.S.R. for this period was down from $1.2 billion for the same period in 1979.

**Developing Countries.** Developing Latin American nations received an economic shot in the arm on Aug. 4. Mexico and Venezuela pledged to return to Central American and Caribbean nations 30 percent of the money they spent on Mexican and Venezuelan oil in the form of loans to carry 4 percent interest annually for a five-year period. Interest would be reduced to 2 percent annually over 20 years if the money were used to develop alternative energy resources.

Developing countries faced more stringent European tariffs and trade quotas, however, as the European Commission's new import plan went into effect. The complex system set stricter limits on more developed Third World nations while continuing to grant concessions to the poorer ones.

Western control of international finance was challenged in late September, when developing nations asked the United Nations for a committee to oversee lending policies by the International Monetary Fund (IMF). The IMF, facing depletion of its $10 billion fund to aid developing nations, nevertheless agreed on Sept. 29 to lend them more money. It was not immediately clear whether the IMF would turn to the private capital markets for new funds, as advocated by the U.S., or secure new funding from Arab oil states in return for greater Arab control over fund management, as advocated by the Europeans.

**OPEC's Impact.** Price increases in 1979 by the Organization of Petroleum Exporting Countries (OPEC) were blamed for worldwide slow growth and recession in 1980. By midsummer, light oil from the Persian Gulf had a $32-a-barrel theoretical base price, while the ceiling for North African crudes was pegged at $37 a barrel. Oil supplies were ample until the war between Iran and Iraq that broke out in September cut off exports from the two countries. *See also* ORGANIZATION OF PETROLEUM EXPORTING COUNTRIES; PETROLEUM AND NATURAL GAS. For the U.S., high prices had the

effect of encouraging conservation. U.S. oil imports for the first nine months of 1980 totaled only 1.88 billion bbl, compared to 2.28 billion bbl during the same period of 1979, a decline of 17.5 percent. Because of price increases, however, the value of oil imports rose from $41.5 billion to $58.9 billion during this period.

**Economic Summit.** The economic summit held in Venice on June 22 and 23 brought together the heads of the U.S., West German, Japanese, British, French, Canadian, and Italian governments. Inflation was the primary question addressed, with concern over the continual increases in OPEC oil prices. The seven leaders ratified a number of goals set by the 21-nation International Energy Agency (IEA), including cutting oil's share in total IEA member-nation energy consumption to 40 percent from the present level of 53 percent by 1990. A pledge was made to double coal production and use by early 1990, build no new oil-fired power plants except in exceptional circumstances, and press conservation efforts for autos, buildings, and industry.

See also articles on individual countries, and the various sectors of the U.S. economy in UNITED STATES OF AMERICA.                                R.W.S.

**ECUADOR.** Ecuadoran President Jaime Roldós Aguilera won the first round of a bitter and mushrooming feud between himself and his former mentor, Assad Bucaram, in 1980. Bucaram, the uncle of Roldós's wife, had been unable to run for the presidency because his parents were born abroad (in Lebanon).

In early June, Roldós outmaneuvered the politically powerful Bucaram, president of Ecuador's single-chamber legislature. Bucaram sought to have Interior Minister Carlos Feraud dismissed on charges of corruption. The Bucaram effort failed, 33 to 27, even though many of the legislators were Bucaram supporters. Roldós's backers immediately claimed that the June 10 vote marked a shift in the balance of power away from old-time politicians toward the populist philosophy of Roldós's supporters. (Roldós had won the presidency handily in 1979, becoming at 38 the youngest chief executive in Ecuador's history.) But Bucaram, in an Aug. 18 speech, promised to "avenge our defeat," making it clear that the political feud was far from over.

Roldós's problems were compounded by a September economic report that showed the economy growing by only 2 percent over the previous year despite massive government spending efforts that lowered unemployment from 9 percent to 7 percent. Declining oil and banana production cut into export earnings.

*See* STATISTICS OF THE WORLD.                        J.N.G.

**EDUCATION.** In 1980 falling enrollments and increasing costs at all levels resulted in an unstable, grim outlook for the field of education. At the same time, federal power in educational matters expanded, chiefly in the operations of the new Department of Education. During the year's Presidential campaign, teachers demonstrated the power of their political lobby, and parents voiced their concern over educational quality.

**Department of Education.** On May 4 the Department of Education achieved full status as the nation's 13th cabinet-level agency. The department consolidated more than 150 federal education programs, most of which had been part of the Department of Health, Education, and Welfare. The first secretary, former Federal Judge Shirley M. Hufstedler, stressed that the new department would assist states and localities in their attempt to "strive unceasingly for the very highest possible quality at every level of the educational process." She reiterated, however, the department's view that "the homes and communities of the nation will continue to be the front line of education."

**Bilingual Education.** For the fledgling department, setting federal codes for bilingual education was a pressing policy issue. In September it issued regulations whereby all schools with an appreciable number of students whose native language is not English were required to install bilingual programs.

The value and impact of bilingual education remained unclear. Advocates said that introducing English gradually into elementary school subjects has resulted in more effective learning and fewer discipline problems among non-English-speaking students. Opponents charged that special bilin-

To underscore the importance of a strong public school system, the Atlanta Chamber of Commerce and local parent groups turned to mass media. Broadcast and print advertisements, as well as school open houses and neighborhood information booths, promoted the city's public education offerings.

gual courses have separated children from classes taught in English and have retarded the youngsters' mastery of English.

The debate over the efficacy of bilingual education was particularly sharp in California, Texas, and other southwestern states where Hispanics form a large part of the student body.

**Teacher and Faculty Unions.** The Democratic Party's convention in August highlighted the increasing force of teachers' unions in national politics. The National Education Association (NEA) was instrumental in the creation of the new Department of Education as well as President Jimmy Carter's victories in many state primaries. The 1,300,000-member NEA and 500,000-member American Federation of Teachers (AFT) exerted broad power in shaping federal and local policies in elementary and secondary education.

Because teachers' contracts had emerged as the supreme standard of teacher rights and responsibility, collective bargaining assumed great importance to local school boards. Failed negotiations resulted in more than 400 teachers' strikes in the 1979–80 academic year—a record number.

Educational leaders differed over the impact of

---

**Growing Up Is the Best Revenge**

Back in the turbulent 1960's, John Mount was expelled from high school in Plainfield, N.J., for refusing to cut his shoulder-length hair. Now 31—and still sporting long locks—Mount is getting a say in how things are run at Plainfield High. In September he was appointed to the local board of education. Interviewed in Trenton, where he was legislative director of a public interest group, Mount explained that he entered Rutgers University on a probationary basis and finally got his degree in 1979. "I'll hold no grudges against the school system," he promised.

*In September the U.S. Department of Education issued regulations requiring many schools to install bilingual programs. At this Miami, Fla., school, attended by many children of Cuban immigrants, students spend half the day speaking English and half speaking Spanish.*

the teachers' union movement. Unionization helped to improve faculty salaries and increase job security, but some critics maintained that teachers' unions had become too powerful. In an era of declining enrollments and fiscal pressures,

---

**From Sit-ins to Tuck-ins**

It was reported in *Time* magazine as well as on network television: During the spring, 1980, term, three male students at the University of Maryland were responsible for the presleep tucking-in of more than 100 female students—for a fee of 99¢ per tuck-in. The Maryland women, not to be outdone, began their own service. Five of them, for a nickel apiece, offered a group lullaby-and-motherly-kiss service. Among the women's customers was the university's vice-chancellor for student affairs, William L. Thomas. Nodding his approval, rubbing his freshly kissed cheek, and remembering the student riots of the 1960's, the vice-chancellor said: "It's a very gentle custom."

---

they said, unions protected the interests of teachers at the expense of educational quality. Unlike the NEA, the AFT endorsed the testing of prospective teachers in their respective fields. Most educational authorities felt, however, that teacher testing could not predict classroom performance.

A U.S. Supreme Court decision in February dealt a serious blow to faculty unions in private colleges and universities. The Court ruled that professors in private institutions were managers, not subordinate employees. Thus, it upheld the right of New York City's Yeshiva University to refuse to bargain with a faculty union.

**Academic Scandals.** Extension courses came under increasing scrutiny and criticism in the wake of scandals that wrenched major western colleges, including the University of Southern California and the University of Arizona. Investigations revealed that many athletes maintained their eligibility by taking questionable or nonexistent courses.

These probes, however, also indicated that the abuse of adult-education courses was most widespread among teachers. Since many school districts tied salary advances to in-service education, thousands of teachers resorted to undemanding correspondence courses to increase their income. Many educational leaders called for more stringent accreditation standards, closer monitoring of in-service education by school districts, and even federal controls in accreditation.

**Private Schools.** Because of the lower birthrate in the 1960's and 1970's, school enrollments continued to decline, and local school boards reluctantly took steps to shut down surplus institutions. At the same time, private schools experienced total enrollment increases for the first time in more than ten years.

The greater popularity of private schools disturbed many educational leaders, because their growth appeared to reflect the declining faith of parents in the academic or moral character of public education. "White flight" into private schools to avoid racial integration left some public school districts overwhelmingly black or Hispanic. As a result, acceptable desegregation standards seemed impossible to effect.

The most rapid growth in private education took place in evangelical Christian schools. By the end of 1980 at least 12,000 Christian schools served as many as 1,800,000 students. Although concentrated in the Southeast, Christian schools gained power across the nation, often reflecting hostility to what Pentecostal families called "secular humanism" in public schools.

**Testing and Intelligence.** The simmering controversy over the value of testing grew more intense during the year. In February consumer activist Ralph Nader released a study of the Educational Testing Service, the designer of the Scholastic Aptitude Test. He called it a "private regulator of the human mind" that "served as a formidable barrier to millions of students." The NEA began campaigning to abolish standardized testing in public schools, and at least 14 states and the federal government considered bills requiring test makers to offer the contents of exams for public inspection.

The most striking rebuke to test critics came from Berkeley, Calif., psychologist Arthur R. Jensen. In his book *Bias in Mental Testing,* Jensen concluded that IQ tests are not culturally biased in favor of middle-class whites. Because blacks score an average of 15 points lower on IQ tests than whites, the Jensen study implied that blacks are less intelligent than whites. During the resulting national debate over the extent to which intelligence is inherited, many eminent scholars attacked Jensen's position.

**Mastery Learning.** A promising new technique for improving student performance was "mastery learning." Developed by University of Chicago professor Benjamin Bloom, the system assumed that all children can learn basic subjects—but with varying speed. The mastery learning method entails frequent testing of students to find out how much material has been learned. Slower learners are presented the lesson in a second, alternative way while faster learners receive enrichment lessons. Adopted by more than 3000 school systems, the mastery learning technique seemed to produce higher levels of achievement for most students, including those previously thought unteachable.                                          G.S.

**EGYPT.** President Anwar el-Sadat consolidated his rule over Egypt in 1980. On May 15 he centralized all executive authority in his hands by assuming the post of prime minister in addition to the presidency; Prime Minister Mustafa Khalil had resigned three days earlier.

**Politics and Religion.** A nationwide referendum on May 22 approved six amendments to the 1971 constitution. Of the six, the two most important were the provision allowing the president more than two successive six-year terms of office, meaning that Sadat would not have to step down in 1982, and the one making the Islamic religious code—the *shari'a*—"the" principal source of legislation in Egypt, instead of, as before, "a" principal source of legislation. According to the government, the referendum was approved by 98.96 percent of the voters, but the two small official opposition parties opposed the amendments, and some persons said they thought that the balloting had been rigged.

The provision regarding the *shari'a* was intended to lay greater stress on Islam and thereby undercut Muslim fundamentalists opposed to Sadat's rule. But the stress on Islam alienated Egypt's Copts, who number anywhere from 3,000,000 to

**A Desert Mystery**

To the nomadic Bedouin smugglers of the area, the gradual withdrawal of Israel from the Sinai has provided a financial windfall. It works like this: First, they steal a luxury automobile, such as a Mercedes-Benz or a Volvo; then they bury it in the sand in Israeli territory. When Israel moves on and the dunes become Egyptian, the smugglers dig out the cars and sell them at marked-down prices to wealthy Egyptians. Hundreds of the stolen cars were dug up by Israeli officials during the year; no one knows how many hundreds more were successfully buried and sold. For, as it is written, the empty, windswept wastes of the vast desert will keep their secrets as long as Allah reigns.

An Israeli worker fastens a plaque to the gate of the new Israeli embassy in Egypt. The stucco house in a Cairo suburb was the first Israeli embassy in an Arab land.

7,000,000. In April the church's highest authority, the Coptic Synod, curtailed Easter celebrations in an unprecedented move because of harassment by Muslim extremists. It refused to accept the customary practice of receiving senior government officials at Easter services. The Coptic Synod complained of violence by Muslim extremists, including attacks on churches and the abduction of Christian girls.

**The Economy.** Two years earlier Sadat had promised that 1980 would be "the year of prosperity." There was a consumer boom in clothing, television sets, and transistor radios, but it was only reaching the relatively small middle class. Visitors reported that Cairo had more buses and telephones, but housing remained scarce.

On assuming the post of prime minister, Sadat announced a general increase in wages and a reduction of 10 to 20 percent in the price of basic foods, textiles, and other commodities. Government subsidies for those commodities, already very high, were increased. The minimum wage was increased from $22 to $30 a month. Social security was to be extended to all workers by the end of 1980, some taxes were to be reduced or abolished, and bonuses and welfare benefits were to be increased.

These announcements left observers wondering where the money for these benefits would

come from. The government previously had been spending about $1.5 billion a year, about 10 percent of the gross national product, just to subsidize food staples. On the other hand, Egypt was earning increased income from exporting oil previously in Israeli-occupied territory. Revenue from the Suez Canal and earnings sent home by Egyptians working overseas was expected to come to about $3 billion in 1980.

**Relations with Israel.** The normalization of relations with Israel arising from the Camp David agreements continued. On Jan. 25, Israel completed two thirds of its withdrawal from the Sinai Peninsula, handing over 5500 sq.mi., including the strategic Mitla and Gidi mountain passes and a major supply base. The border between the two countries was declared open; Egypt formally ended its economic boycott of Israel; and telex, postal, and telephone links began. The two countries exchanged ambassadors in February, with Israel's embassy in Cairo formally opening on Feb. 18. Nefertiti, a new airline, began flights to Tel Aviv in March, while El Al started flights to Cairo. Israeli President Yitzhak Navon made a five-day visit to Egypt in October, the first ever by an Israeli head of state to an Arab country. On Oct. 29, Israel and Egypt agreed to open a land trade route across the Sinai to augment air and sea routes.

These measures were somewhat misleading,

however, for few Egyptians came to Israel and trade was minor, except for the Sinai oil that Egypt had previously pledged to Israel. Negotiations on Palestinian autonomy, a central part of the peace process, had stalled even before Sadat decided on May 15 not to resume them because of Israel's impending decision to reaffirm its annexation of East Jerusalem. Each side accused the other of bad faith. *See* ISRAEL; MIDDLE EAST.

**Other Foreign Relations.** Egypt continued to align itself ever closer with the United States. A major arms deal, including tanks and F-16 fighters, was announced in February. The aborted attempt to rescue the American hostages in Iran was routed through an air base in Egypt. Sadat ruled out permanent U.S. bases on Egyptian territory, but he gave the green light for joint exercises, such as the one that the newly created Rapid Deployment Force held with Egyptian paratroopers in the desert in November.

Sadat also indicated his contempt for Iran's regime by giving refuge to Mohammed Riza Pahlavi, the exiled former shah of Iran, who arrived from Panama on March 24. He died in Cairo on July 27 and was buried there.

*See* STATISTICS OF THE WORLD.                    R.H.

**ELECTIONS.** In the most resounding political triumph for the Republican Party since Dwight D. Eisenhower captured the White House in 1952, former Gov. Ronald Reagan of California demolished Democratic incumbent President Jimmy Carter of Georgia in the Presidential election of Nov. 4, 1980. Reagan's victory was accompanied by the totally unexpected seizure of the U.S. Sen-

*Last respects are paid to deposed Iranian Shah Mohammed Riza Pahlavi in Cairo on July 29. At center is Egyptian President Anwar el-Sadat, who gave the shah his last refuge, with Empress Farah, the shah's widow, on his right and Crown Prince Riza on his left.*

*Republican Presidential candidate Ronald Reagan campaigns at a Chester, Pa., shipyard on Aug. 19. Reagan cut deeply into the normally Democratic blue-collar vote in his successful bid for election.*

ate by the Republicans and a better-than-expected showing by the GOP in the House of Representatives. The ideological shift from liberal to conservative in both houses of Congress was so pronounced, moreover, that the new President was expected to enjoy a working majority in both chambers despite continued Democratic control of the House. (For a biography of the President-elect, see biography at PEOPLE IN THE NEWS.)

**Presidential Election.** Ronald Reagan was elected the 40th President of the United States by a surprising margin considering that final polls indicated him to be only narrowly ahead. Reagan won the popular vote by a comfortable cushion, 51 percent to 41 percent, with independent candidate U.S. Rep. John Anderson (R, Ill.) drawing 7 percent and Libertarian Party candidate Ed Clark taking most of the remaining 1 percent. Reagan and his running mate, George Bush of Texas, won 43,899,248 votes to 35,481,435 votes for the Democratic ticket of President Carter and Vice-President Walter F. Mondale and 5,719,437 for John Anderson and Patrick Lucey, former governor of Wisconsin. In the Electoral College the Reagan-Bush ticket scored a landslide, winning 44 states

and a whopping 489 electoral votes—219 more than needed. The Carter-Mondale ticket won only six states and the District of Columbia for a total of 49 electoral votes. Carter thus became the first Democrat in nearly a century to be denied a second term as President.

The East-West geographical split so evident in the 1976 Presidential election was obliterated by the Reagan landslide. The Republican candidate maintained his party's traditional base in the western states but also swept the heavily populated and nominally Democratic states of the industrial Northeast and Midwest, including New York, Massachusetts, Pennsylvania, New Jersey, Ohio, Illinois, Wisconsin, and Michigan. And, in the ultimate humiliation for Carter, Reagan carried every state in the Old Confederacy except Carter's home state of Georgia. Reagan's margin was so overwhelming that Anderson, whose candidacy was widely expected to hold the balance of power by siphoning liberal and independent votes away from Carter, proved no factor in the election.

For Reagan, the successful bid for the White House was the culmination of a 12-year effort and

*President Jimmy Carter and his chief challenger for the office, Ronald Reagan, during their debate in Cleveland on Oct. 28. Many political analysts thought the nationally televised debate was the deciding factor in the contest for the Presidency.*

partially erased the bitter memories of his narrow loss in the 1976 Republican primaries to former President Gerald R. Ford, who campaigned enthusiastically for Reagan this time. After his 1976 defeat, Reagan set about preparing for 1980, creating a political action committee and maintaining high visibility within Republican circles. The odds-on favorite from the start of the primary season, Reagan lost the first contest in Iowa but reeled off an impressive string of victories beginning in New Hampshire in February. His winning streak eliminated rivals one by one, and in May his last remaining challenger, George Bush—who would later become his Vice-Presidential running mate—conceded the obvious. The Republican National Convention in Detroit in July was a total Reagan victory and left the party united and well-financed for the fall campaign. *See* REPUBLICAN PARTY.

Carter's defeat by Reagan was a bitter climax to a year in which the incumbent President experienced the peaks and valleys of public sentiment. Unhappiness with his failure to solve the country's economic problems caused Carter's approval ratings to plummet in late 1979, prompting Sen. Edward M. Kennedy of Massachusetts to challenge him in the Democratic primaries. But Carter confounded the conventional wisdom by trouncing Kennedy in the primaries. After an eleventh-hour stop-Carter effort by party liberals failed, Carter was renominated on the first ballot at the New York City convention in August. *See* DEMOCRATIC PARTY; PRESIDENT OF THE UNITED STATES.

Whether the Reagan victory represented the final disintegration of Franklin D. Roosevelt's New Deal coalition of Democrats at the hands of an electorate that had turned increasingly conservative in recent years was the topic of lively debate among political scientists and politicians. Reagan's victory reflected at least a temporary repudiation by the voters of the Democratic Party's philosophy of greater involvement by the federal government in people's lives. Nevertheless, it seemed to suggest less a fundamental ideological shift than a referendum on the stewardship of the Carter administration. One national poll taken on Election Day revealed that four of five Reagan voters supported the Republican candidate because of Carter's weak performance in office rather than an ideological affinity for Reagan. The conventional political wisdom was that public dissatisfaction with inflation, unemployment, double-digit interest rates, and the inability of the Carter administration to free the American hostages held in Iran had combined to crystallize voters' negative attitudes about the President.

Reagan's support was broadly based and even cut deeply into voter groups normally in the Democratic column. Reagan did well among all age groups, independents, women, union voters, and Catholics, and he showed surprising strength with Jewish voters. Only blacks and Hispanics remained solidly for Carter although they voted in fewer numbers than in 1976. Southern voters, who had backed Carter out of regional pride four years before, deserted the President in droves.

For the second consecutive Presidential election, the campaign was enlivened by debates between the major contenders. The League of Women Voters, which had sponsored four debates in 1976, sought to repeat that formula in 1980, but Carter refused to appear when the league invited Anderson to participate at the first debate in Baltimore on Sept. 21. Anderson's support, as reflected in polls, steadily dropped following that debate with Reagan, however, and the league excluded him from its next invitation. Both Carter and Reagan then accepted, and the climactic debate was held in Cleveland on Oct. 28. Political analysts generally agreed that Carter may have won the debate on substance but that Reagan was the clear victor on style; Carter failed to destroy Reagan's credibility as a Presidential contender, and Reagan was judged to have benefited by his reasonable, amiable presence. The Carter-Reagan debate seemed to have solidified and expanded Reagan's narrow lead only a week before the election.

A continuing disenchantment with the political process was reflected in the percentage of voting-age citizens actually casting ballots, which dropped to 53.9, the lowest in 32 years and 0.5 percent below the 1976 figure.

**Congressional Elections.** With 12 Democratic seats falling to Republican challengers, the Senate in 1981 would be controlled by the Republicans for the first time since the Eisenhower landslide of 1952. The party lineup changed overnight from 59 Democrats and 41 Republicans to 53 Republicans and 47 Democrats. And, although Democrats remained in control of the House of Representatives, Republicans gained 33 seats for a total of 192 to 243 Democrats. But the ideological transformation was even more profound than the numerical change; both chambers would be far more right-leaning than before, since conservative Republicans would replace liberal Democrats in most cases.

Eighteen new faces were added to the Senate roster, the largest turnover in a quarter-century. Four incumbent Republican Senators were replaced by Republicans, while two retiring Democrats were succeeded by Democrats. But 12 incumbent Democratic Senators lost their seats,

Independent Presidential candidate John Anderson (R, Ill.) listens to the Carter-Reagan debate on a Cable News Network setup arranged so that he could respond to questions posed in the debate. Anderson polled almost 7 percent of the ballots cast for the Presidency on Nov. 4.

including several of the party's best-known national figures.

Among the more prominent Democratic casualties were Foreign Relations Committee Chairman Frank Church of Idaho, beaten by U.S. Rep. Steven Symms; Appropriations Committee Chairman Warren Magnuson of Washington, defeated by state Attorney General Slade Gorton after 36 years in the Senate; Judiciary Committee Chairman Birch Bayh of Indiana, defeated by U.S. Rep. Dan Quayle; John Culver of Iowa, who lost to U.S. Rep. Charles Grassley; Gaylord Nelson of Wisconsin, defeated by a former congressman, Robert Kasten; and George McGovern of South Dakota, the party's 1972 Presidential nominee, defeated by U.S. Rep. James Abdnor.

Agriculture Committee Chairman Herman Talmadge of Georgia, who survived a tough primary challenge after allegations of financial improprieties, was upset by Mack Mattingly; John Durkin of New Hampshire lost to Warren Rudman; and Robert Morgan of North Carolina was defeated by college professor John East.

Republicans also captured three seats vacated

by Democratic incumbents who lost primary elections. In Alabama, a former Vietnam prisoner of war, retired Adm. Jeremiah Denton, took the seat held by Donald Stewart; Florida consumer advocate Paula Hawkins became the Senate's second woman member, replacing Richard Stone; and Alaska banker Frank Murkowski won the seat previously occupied by Mike Gravel.

The only Republican denied reelection was 76-year-old Jacob Javits of New York, who was seeking a fourth term. Javits lost to Long Island local government official Alfonse D'Amato in the Republican Party primary but ran in the general election as the Liberal Party candidate, trailing D'Amato and U.S. Rep. Elizabeth Holtzman.

Republicans held on to three seats vacated by retiring Republicans. U.S. Rep. Mark Andrews succeeded Milton Young in North Dakota, former Philadelphia District Attorney Arlen Specter won Richard Schweiker's seat in Pennsylvania, and Oklahoma State Senator Don Nickles won Henry Bellmon's seat.

Democrats succeeded retiring Democrats in two races, with Illinois Secretary of State Alan

*Opposite page: Republicans wrested control of the Senate by winning 12 seats from Democrats on Nov. 4. Among the Republicans who ousted Democrats (clockwise from upper left): Rep. James Abdnor, S.Dak.; Jeremiah Denton, Ala.; Robert Kasten, Jr., Wis.; Rep. Charles Grassley, Iowa; Rep. Steven Symms, Idaho; and Paula Hawkins, Fla. Above: Rep. Dan Quayle, Ind.*

Dixon taking the seat of Adlai Stevenson 3rd and U.S. Rep. Christopher Dodd, son of former Sen. Thomas Dodd, holding on to the Connecticut seat vacated by Abraham Ribicoff.

The only Democratic liberals to survive stiff challenges were Patrick Leahy of Vermont and Gary Hart of Colorado. Republican elder statesman Barry Goldwater of Arizona narrowly won reelection to a fifth term after the 71-year-old Senator's age and health became an issue.

The Reagan steamroller helped propel Republicans to their strongest showing in the House of Representatives in nearly three decades. A host of prominent Democratic incumbents were swept away, notably Majority Whip John Brademas of Indiana, the third-ranking House Democrat, and Al Ullman of Oregon, chairman of the powerful Ways and Means Committee. Other major Democratic casualties included Harold Johnson of California, chairman of the Public Works Committee; Thomas (Lud) Ashley of Ohio, a leading expert on energy legislation; James Corman of California; Bob Eckhardt of Texas; Lester Wolff of New York; Lionel Van Deerlin of California; Richardson Prey-

er of North Carolina; and Gunn McKay of Utah. Two endangered senior Democrats, Morris Udall of Arizona and Thomas Foley of Washington, survived major challenges. The only major Republican casualty was 11-term veteran Samuel Devine of Ohio.

Four of the five Democratic congressmen implicated in the Abscam investigation of white-collar crime were turned out by the voters. Raymond Lederer of Pennsylvania was reelected, but John Murphy of New York, Frank Thompson of New Jersey, John Jenrette of South Carolina, and Michael Myers of Pennsylvania were defeated. All five had been indicted on corruption charges, and Jenrette and Myers had been convicted before standing for reelection.

The composition of the new House, with 77 new faces, was decidedly more conservative. The number of black members increased by 2 to 16, and the women members increased by a net of 4 to 19. The Democratic "Watergate babies" elected in 1974 continued to show amazing resilience. Of the 56 incumbent Democrats first elected to the House in 1974, 47 of them were

159

reelected to fourth terms despite running, in many cases, from traditionally Republican districts.

**Governors and Legislatures.** With 13 statehouses at stake, Republicans won 7 of them for a net gain of 4, reducing the Democratic margin from 31-19 to 27-23. The major gubernatorial upset was in Arkansas, where Bill Clinton (D), at 34 the youngest of the nation's governors, was defeated for reelection. Republican Christopher ("Kit") Bond of Missouri, defeated for reelection in 1976 by Joseph Teasdale, turned the tables by ousting Teasdale. Hugh Gallen of New Hampshire, a staunch Carter supporter, withstood a challenge from former governor and archconservative Meldrim Thompson to win reelection despite the strong conservative tide nationwide. Two other incumbent governors with national reputations, John D. Rockefeller 4th (D) of West Virginia and Pierre S. du Pont 4th (R) of Delaware, won reelection. Dixy Lee Ray (D) of Washington, one of two women governors, lost her bid for renomination in a primary election.

Nationwide, Republicans gained more than 200 seats in state legislatures. They won control of a number of legislative chambers, including ones in Illinois, Ohio, Pennsylvania, and Washington.

**State Propositions.** Voters in 42 states were confronted with various referendums, initiatives, and propositions, and in general they showed a disposition to resist change. Michigan voters rejected a lowering of the legal drinking age from 21 to 19, Iowa defeated a state equal rights amendment, and California turned back a proposal for no-smoking sections in most public buildings. Voters in the District of Columbia decided to seek statehood for the nation's capital, while five counties voted to secede from New Jersey. Arizona, Colorado, and the District of Columbia approved government-operated lotteries, and Illinois voters decided to reduce the size of the state legislature. Property tax cut proposals were rejected in six states, but tax relief measures were approved in six states. In Massachusetts, a controversial proposition limiting property taxes to 2.5 percent of assessed valuation was approved. The measure was expected to cut tax revenues drastically, forcing possible reductions in government services. In a backlash to the massive influx of Cuban refugees into southern Florida, voters in Dade County voted to repeal a law making Spanish the official second language in Miami and surrounding areas. *See also* STATE GOVERNMENT REVIEW.

See also biographies of John B. Anderson, George Bush, Edward M. Kennedy, and Walter F. Mondale in the biography section of PEOPLE IN THE NEWS. **T.D.**

## The Senators-Elect

Alabama—*Jeremiah Denton*, R
Alaska—*Frank Murkowski*, R
Arizona—*Barry Goldwater, R
Arkansas—*Dale Bumpers, D
California—*Alan Cranston, D
Colorado—*Gary Hart, D
Connecticut—Christopher Dodd, D
Florida—*Paula Hawkins*, R
Georgia—*Mack Mattingly*, R
Hawaii—*Daniel Inouye, D
Idaho—*Steven Symms*, R
Illinois—Alan Dixon, D
Indiana—*Dan Quayle*, R
Iowa—*Charles Grassley*, R
Kansas—*Robert Dole, R
Kentucky—*Wendell Ford, D
Louisiana—*Russell Long, D
Maryland—*Charles McC. Mathias, R
Missouri—*Thomas Eagleton, D
Nevada—*Paul Laxalt, R
New Hampshire—*Warren Rudman*, R
New York—Alfonse D'Amato, R
North Carolina—*John East*, R
North Dakota—Mark Andrews, R
Ohio—*John Glenn, D
Oklahoma—Don Nickles, R
Oregon—*Robert Packwood, R
Pennsylvania—Arlen Specter, R
South Carolina—*Ernest Hollings, D
South Dakota—*James Abdnor*, R
Utah—*Jake Garn, R
Vermont—*Patrick Leahy, D
Washington—*Slade Gorton*, R
Wisconsin—*Robert Kasten, Jr.*, R

* Denotes incumbent
R—Republican
D—Democrat
Name is in italics in cases
where a seat changed parties

## The Governors-Elect

Arkansas—*Frank White*, R
Delaware—*Pierre S. du Pont 4th, R
Indiana—Robert Orr, R
Missouri—*Christopher Bond*, R
Montana—Ted Schwinden, D
New Hampshire—*Hugh Gallen, D
North Carolina—*James B. Hunt, Jr., D
North Dakota—*Allen Olson*, R
Rhode Island—*J. Joseph Garrahy, D
Utah—*Scott Matheson, D
Vermont—*Richard Snelling, R
Washington—*John Spellman*, R
West Virginia—*John D. Rockefeller 4th, D

* Denotes incumbent
R—Republican
D—Democrat
Name is in italics in cases
where a seat changed parties

**EL SALVADOR.** Central America's flash spot during 1980 was El Salvador, the region's smallest country. A virtual civil war engulfed the nation, as leftist guerrillas battled both the moderate civilian-military junta and rightist paramilitary groups, and the right-wing forces fought the government and leftists alike. The United States extended economic and military aid to the junta after naming a new ambassador, Robert White, to the embassy in San Salvador. White was directed to try to bring the warring sides into agreement around the junta.

In the first ten months of 1980 more than 8000 persons died. Some were killed at the hands of the military, which, supporting the junta, pursued the guerrillas and in an estimated 300 major engagements killed more than 2000 suspected leftists. Hundreds of soldiers lost their lives. The other dead included rightists (some killed in battles with leftists, others in encounters with the military) and a large number of Salvadoran citizens who favored neither side but got caught up in the struggle.

Archbishop Oscar Arnulfo Romero, primate of San Salvador, was gunned down in a chapel while saying Mass, becoming the eighth Roman Catholic churchman to die in the violence since 1975. In the wake of his assassination on March 24 a new wave of violence erupted, with the Left and the Right accusing each other of murdering the prelate.

**The Junta's Policies.** The military-civilian junta, after replacing two civilians in the group in January, began a political offensive against both the Left and the Right. First, it expropriated 60 percent of the country's best farmland in a massive land reform program that took the spotlight from leftist terrorists and rightist death squads. A day later, on March 7, the junta partially nationalized the country's banking system, placing 51 percent of it in the public sector, with the remaining 49 percent left in private hands. Along with later decrees, the land reform program was the most sweeping in Latin America since the Mexican revolution of 1910 and brought about a major reversal of the landholding pattern, set in colonial times, of huge tracts controlled by relatively few persons.

The junta's dramatic reform programs appeared to lessen leftist influence. Military clashes and internal bickering further weakened the Left, but its presence was nonetheless evident. Two offensives were mounted against the military in August that left 120 soldiers dead, with only half a dozen reported leftist casualties. Yet a leftist spokesman admitted on Sept. 6 that "we are beset with prob-

Minutes after undetermined gunmen fired on a crowd of thousands of mourners at the funeral for assassinated Archbishop Oscar Arnulfo Romero in San Salvador on March 30, stretcher-bearers pick up victims. More than 8000 people died in violence during 1980.

lems we did not face two months ago." In October government forces mounted one of their biggest offensives in the three-year battle against leftist guerrillas.

**Consolidation of Power.** But if the Left had problems, so did the junta, whose two military men appeared to squabble. Col. Jaime Abdul Gutiérrez, the more conservative, emerged the stronger in a mid-May struggle with Col. Adolfo Arnoldo Majano to become sole commander in chief. An announcement that all future military appointments would be approved by the entire junta was seen to reaffirm the group's growing right-wing orientation rather than to give the civilians more influence. However, the government announced plans to hold elections for a constituent assembly in 1982, with presidential elections to follow a year later.

On Nov. 27, the bodies of six opposition leaders were found outside the capital, apparently the work of right-wing death squads encouraged by elements within the junta. The killings were a blow to the Left, but the slain men were political figures rather than guerrilla leaders.

Reacting angrily to the killing of three American nuns and a lay missionary, allegedly with the help of security forces, the U.S. suspended new military and economic aid to El Salvador on Dec. 5. Some economic aid was restored on Dec. 17. On Dec. 13 a junta member, José Napoleón Duarte, was named El Salvador's first civilian president in 49 years. But Col. Majano, the junta's most liberal member, was ousted in an action taken Dec. 7.

El Salvador's economy endured serious losses due to the war. A decline of 3 percent in the gross national product was forecast for 1980. Strikes in many industries, a decline in agricultural production, and the general civil strife were blamed.

*See* STATISTICS OF THE WORLD.                    J.N.G.

**ENERGY.** Oil continued to dominate the energy scene throughout 1980. No single issue affected international energy policy more than the evolving political turmoil in the Middle East. Aside from grabbing headlines daily, it forced the world's developed nations to rivet their attention on programs that offered hope of liberating them from their costly and debilitating dependence on imported oil.

Major action in the United States concerning energy included passage of legislation to create a synthetic fuels industry and a windfall profits tax on the oil industry; *see* PETROLEUM AND NATURAL GAS.

A study released in January stressed conservation as a means of reducing dependence on imported oil. The study by the National Academy of

This picture shows a Tenneco Inc. facility in North Dakota where oil-shale deposits were being mined. In 1980, Congress passed an act intended to encourage large-scale conversion of coal and oil shale into synthetic petroleum and natural gas.

Sciences said that major savings in energy consumption were possible without appreciably affecting either the nation's way of life or standard of living. Another report showed electricity consumption rising only 2.8 percent in 1979, compared to the 7 percent annual rate of growth in the early 1970's. By April electricity consumption in 1980 was actually at a lower level than in 1979.

---

**Reveille for Sleepy Scholars**

In an effort to conserve energy, Yale University is offering popular courses early in the morning, with the number meeting at 8:30 A.M. increased from 1 to 4 percent. "We want to move the Yale schedule back to a normal daylight rhythm," said Professor Howard R. Lamar, a Yale dean. "Yale students usually stay up very late at night and sleep in. Studies show that changing this habit will cut energy consumption significantly." The reaction of students was not given, but the faculty rejected Lamar's proposal that 8 percent of the courses be offered in the early morning.

# The "Windfall" Tax

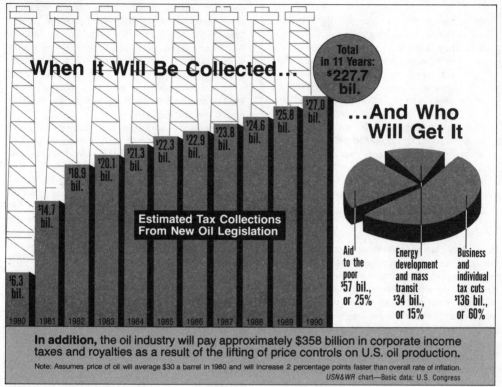

## When It Will Be Collected...

**Estimated Tax Collections From New Oil Legislation**

| | | | | | | | | | | |
|$6.3 bil.|$14.7 bil.|$18.9 bil.|$20.1 bil.|$21.3 bil.|$22.3 bil.|$22.9 bil.|$23.8 bil.|$24.6 bil.|$25.8 bil.|$27.0 bil.|
|1980|1981|1982|1983|1984|1985|1986|1987|1988|1989|1990|

Total in 11 Years: $227.7 bil.

## ...And Who Will Get It

Aid to the poor $57 bil., or 25%

Energy development and mass transit $34 bil., or 15%

Business and individual tax cuts $136 bil., or 60%

**In addition,** the oil industry will pay approximately $358 billion in corporate income taxes and royalties as a result of the lifting of price controls on U.S. oil production.

Note: Assumes price of oil will average $30 a barrel in 1980 and will increase 2 percentage points faster than overall rate of inflation.

USN&WR chart—Basic data: U.S. Congress

**Synfuels.** The most ambitious new energy program was initiated on June 30, when President Jimmy Carter signed into law the Energy Security Act of 1980. Its mission was to launch a commercially viable industry for converting coal and oil shale into synthetic petroleum and natural gas. To direct the massive undertaking, the act established the U.S. Synthetic Fuels Corp. (SFC), a quasi-governmental investment bank financed by the U.S. Department of the Treasury.

The SFC was authorized to spend $20 billion in fiscal 1981 and to seek as much as $68 billion in additional funds in future years. Its task was to finance the production of 500,000 bbl daily of synthetic fuels by 1987 and 2,000,000 bbl daily by 1992. The corporation's spending would be primarily in the form of loans, loan guarantees, purchase and price guarantees, and joint ventures, but it would have the authority to build three government-owned plants.

Not one commercial U.S. synthetic fuels plant existed in 1980. Several experimental facilities, however, were in operation. On July 31 an agreement was signed to build the world's first commercial-size plant near Morgantown, W.Va., to produce liquid fuel directly from coal. The $1.4 billion facility, designed to produce the equivalent of 20,000 bbl of oil a day by 1984, would be financed by the U.S. Department of Energy and the governments of West Germany and Japan. And on Nov. 19 the Energy Department gave a conditional $1.5 billion loan guarantee for the construction of a commercial coal gasification plant in Beulah, N.Dak.

**Coal.** Leaders of the world's wealthiest non-Communist countries agreed in Venice on June 23 to double their production and consumption of coal by 1990 in order to reduce dependence on imported oil. The U.S. has the largest reserves of coal in the world, and on March 6, President Carter outlined to Congress a ten-year program intended to induce public utilities to use more coal in the place of oil.

The coal industry, however, was faced with many problems in 1980 that were hampering production, including labor trouble, low productiv-

163

## It's Not a Joke, Son

Jokes about the changing of light bulbs were everywhere during the year. So in the fall, when a story appeared about a Jackson, Mich., woman who had changed the light bulb on her front porch, readers naturally expected a gag line to follow. But the story went on to report quite seriously that the light bulb was newsworthy because it had lasted 50 years. The company that manufactured the bulb did provide a little levity, however, with its explanation that the bulb must have been defective—otherwise it would have burned out like any other bulb, many, many years before.

ity, and decaying facilities for transporting coal. Pollutants emitted from the burning of coal had been linked to a growing acid rain problem in the Northeast. Finally, most utilities were maintaining that they could not afford the expense of converting to coal. A report issued by the Massachusetts Institute of Technology in May, however, predicted growing demand for U.S. coal from other countries. The study concluded that even with its high environmental and transportation costs, U.S. coal had become roughly 60 percent cheaper than imported oil.

**Gasohol.** The global automobile fleet consumes about one fifth of all oil produced. In the U.S., home to 41 percent of the world's autos, cars consumed more than 6,000,000 bbl of oil daily. In 1980 gasohol, a mix of nine parts unleaded gasoline to one part ethyl alcohol, was growing in popularity, with more than 4000 service stations retailing the product. The measure establishing the SFC also authorized a $1.45 billion alcohol fuel production program.

But U.S. gasohol, which is produced from cereal grains, is expensive. According to one study, in 1980 it was costing more than $2.60 a gallon, counting various federal and state subsidies, to displace a gallon of gasoline worth $1 at the refinery. Researchers were experimenting with alcohol made from fodder beets in order to reduce costs. Meanwhile, Brazil was exporting large amounts of alcohol made from sugarcane to the U.S. for about $1.40 a gallon.

Methanol was also widely tested. Distilled from wood starches, it powered several test fleets in the U.S. and Brazil. Mobil Oil Corp. announced in March the development of a one-step methanol-to-gasoline process whose product gave perfor-

mances equal to or better than most commercial unleaded gasolines. Both the New Zealand government and W. R. Grace Co. signed licensing agreements to employ the Mobil process.

**Solar.** Signed on Sept. 8, the Wind Energy Systems Act pledged government support—beginning with $100,000,000 in 1981—for an eight-year program aimed at developing both large and small wind-power plants. Its goal was installation by 1988 of at least 800 Mw (megawatts) of wind-generated electric capacity.

Congress passed a research, development, and demonstration act for ocean-thermal energy conversion (OTEC) in 1980. OTEC power systems exploit small temperature differences between surface and deep waters to power chemical cycles that in turn drive electric turbines. The act's ambitious goals included production of competitively priced electric power via OTEC systems by the mid-1990's, and installation of enough OTEC systems by 1999 to produce 10,000 Mw of power or its equivalent. The first trial OTEC system, producing a mere 50 kw of electric power, completed sea trials near Hawaii in 1979.

**Geothermal.** The world's first hot, dry rock geothermal power station began generating 60 kw of electricity in April from a pair of experimental wells at Fenton Hill, N.Mex. Geothermal developers normally hunt underground reservoirs of hot water or steam in permeable rock, but Los Alamos Scientific Laboratory scientists created an artificial reservoir from hot, impermeable rock. Pressurized water pumped down one drill hole made a series of fractures in the buried rock that migrated toward a second hole. Once the fractures linked the holes, water pumped down either well flushed through the system, acquiring heat along the way.

*See also* NUCLEAR POWER. J.A.R.

**ENVIRONMENT.** Landmark environmental legislation was passed in 1980, in particular an act to deal with the disposal of toxic chemicals, an increasingly recognized environmental problem. Several major new global studies pointed out in graphic detail that the earth is being ravaged by continuing environmental plunder.

**Alaska Lands.** On Nov. 12, Congress passed legislation to protect 104,000,000 acres of virgin Alaskan wilderness from development. The Alaska Lands Act represented a compromise between the interests of wildlife conservationists and businesses bent on developing the state's natural resources.

Mineral and resource exploitation was banned from at least 56,000,000 acres of mountain wilderness and wildlife sanctuaries. Another 49,000,000 acres received more qualified protection; limited mining and logging would be permitted within national parks and wildlife refuges.

Included in the protected acreage were vital habitats for 10 percent of the ducks, 20 percent of the geese, and 45 percent of the swans in North America. Most of the rookeries for Alaska's sea lions, sea otters, and harbor seals were also protected by the legislation. One plot alone, the Alaska Marine Resources Refuge, provided nesting grounds for an estimated 40,000,000 seabirds, including several marine species breeding nowhere else in North America.

**Toxic Waste Cleanup Bill.** A $1.6 billion emergency fund for cleaning up dangerous chemical spills and abandoned chemical-waste dumps won congressional passage on Dec. 3 after three years of intense dispute between members of the many committees that helped draft it. Originally envisioned as a revolving fund to finance emergency chemical cleanups and to compensate injured parties, the legislation eventually approved virtually ignored the liability issue. It covered neither damages to individuals nor to personal property, and it also excluded oil spills from coverage.

Those who produce, transport, or dispose of hazardous wastes were made liable for all cleanup costs assumed by the fund. A small excise tax levied against producers of petrochemicals and their feedstocks was to provide 87.5 percent of the fund's financing; the remainder would come from the federal government.

**Hazardous Wastes.** Every day, 50 billion gal. of liquid wastes are being poured into U.S. industrial surface water impoundments—pits, ponds, and lagoons. A survey published by Congress in September indicated that more than 90 percent of the 26,000 industrial sites across the nation identified as containing liquid wastes went "virtually unmonitored," and hence may be contaminating groundwater below. The study, prepared by the Environmental Protection Agency (EPA), identified 251 sites where unlined impoundments contained potentially hazardous wastes above groundwater. No barriers protected the water from those wastes, and potential drinking water supply wells were within a mile of each.

The suspected human health effects from exposure to air and groundwater contaminated by chemical-waste dumps brought global attention to a small neighborhood in Niagara Falls, N.Y. Between 1947 and 1952 the Hooker Chemicals and Plastics Corp. buried an estimated 21,800 tons of toxic wastes at the site known as Love Canal. In 1953, Hooker sold the site to the Niagara Falls School Board for $1. The city erected a school atop the site and sold adjacent land to housing developers. Hundreds of families lived there.

A young resident of the contaminated Love Canal area in Niagara Falls, N.Y., makes her position known at a public hearing. A contested study indicated that 30 percent of the residents in the immediate area had suffered chromosomal damage, presumably as a result of chemicals dumped on the site.

Over a period of time, area homeowners began noticing noxious sludge bubbling up through their yards and basements. By 1977, 82 industrial chemicals had been identified in the air, water, and soil around Love Canal, including 11 known or suspected carcinogens. In August of that year, the state of New York recommended that pregnant women and small children be evacuated. Eventually the state relocated 239 families living nearest the site and bought their homes.

On May 21, 1980, following announcements of a preliminary study finding chromosomal abnormalities in the blood of 11 of 36 people still living at Love Canal, President Jimmy Carter issued an executive order designating Love Canal a federal emergency. More than 700 families remaining in the area were offered federal aid for temporary relocation pending completion of a comprehensive battery of health tests by the government. The final tab for relocation expenses and evidence-gathering health-effects studies was to be

An Arizona rancher holds one Grand Canyon wild burro while another is lifted out of the canyon by helicopter. During 1980, hundreds of the animals—not indigenous to the canyon—were rounded up and transported to a Texas ranch. The National Park Service had previously announced plans to slaughter the canyon burros because they were destroying vegetation needed by native wildlife.

added to restitution claims against Hooker in four suits filed by the U.S. Justice Department in December, 1979.

On June 23 a report by the state of New York was released detailing a high miscarriage rate among women living adjacent to the buried waste dump. Although elevated rates of miscarriage and birth defects were reported elsewhere in the community, the rate was highest—50 percent, not the 15 percent that is normal—along

99th St., immediately adjacent to the dump.

The EPA estimated that as many as 1,600,000 Americans might be exposed to highly or moderately serious health hazards from toxic-waste dumps. Proper waste burial was expensive, so dumping into streams, abandoned yards, and along roadsides was not uncommon. Douglas M. Costle, administrator of the agency, said on Feb. 26 that there were more than 750,000 generators of chemical wastes in the United States and that they annually produced some 57,000,000 tons of hazardous wastes. He estimated that 90 percent of those wastes were "disposed of by environmentally unsound methods."

During 1980 the EPA issued rules requiring large companies that handle, store, or dispose of hazardous wastes to obtain federal permits, keep records, and report to the agency on the status and whereabouts of the material. It listed 416 chemicals covered by the rules.

**Resource Conservation.** The World Conservation Strategy, unveiled in 33 national capitals during March, was one of the first major documents to establish how and why resource conservation and economic development of the world's poorer nations are two sides of the same coin. Drafted by the International Union for Conservation and Natural Resources together with several United Nations agencies, it won the tacit endorsement of most of the world's nations together with the explicit endorsement of most leading international environmental organizations.

In grim detail, it outlined a rapid and accelerating degradation of the environment. For example, excluding Antarctica, 89 percent of the world's land suffered from drought, nutritional deficiencies or toxicities, shallow soil, excess water, or permafrost. But if current rates of soil degradation

### Alive and Well

For three years the snail darter was the little fish that could—could halt the completion of a $130,000,000 dam, that is. The site of the Tellico Dam in Tennessee was the only known habitat of the 3-in.-long fish, an endangered species protected by federal law. The dam was only completed after Congress granted an exemption to the law in 1979. In November came the sequel to the story: Another population of snail darters was discovered in a previously unknown habitat 80 mi. from the dam.

were to continue, close to one third of the world's arable land would be destroyed during the next 20 years.

Much of the problem resulted from timber cutting to house and heat the world's poor. One billion people were already malnourished and living in abject poverty. Yet even if every couple adopted zero-population-growth policies—had no more than two children—there would still be 50 percent more people to feed in the year 2000.

It was expected that 90 percent of the growth in world population over the next 20 years would occur in the tropics. For the poorest and hungriest, often there were no places to turn for food but to the forests. And lowland tropical forests, the richest in species, had been most exploited. An area the size of Delaware was being permanently converted to other forms each week; an area the size of Great Britain was lost annually. And these conversions, the document said, would likely account for the extinction of up to 1,000,000 species of life by 1999.

A 766-page companion tome issued by the U.S. State Department in July quantified the strategy's assessments of global environmental havoc. The purpose of the report was to "galvanize" action. Ambassadors of every nation maintaining diplomatic ties with the U.S. were briefed on its findings and copies of the entire report were presented to world leaders because, said Assistant Secretary of State Thomas Pickering, "governments inevitably will have to get involved."

**Earth Day, 1980.** The festive 1970 Earth Day "teach-in" to clean up America and the rest of the planet as well highlighted the rising of a strong and growing political force. On April 22 people gathered throughout the nation to celebrate Earth Day's 10th anniversary and the decade of environmental changes it fostered.

There was much to rally behind. Earth Day's legacy included such landmark legislation as the Clean Air Act, Toxic Substances Control Act, Endangered Species Act, Safe Drinking Water Act, Resource Conservation and Recovery Act, Water Quality Improvement Act, and Environmental Pesticide Control Act. Though many critics charged that regulations to put these acts in force were both needless and inflationary, government officials and environmental advocates argued that they represented a net benefit to society.

A report prepared for the President's Council on Environmental Quality in April supported that contention. It said that about 14,000 lives were saved in 1978 (the last year for which figures were available) as a result of air quality improvements made since 1970. And its estimate of the annual benefit in 1978 from air pollution control was

$21.4 billion, $4.8 billion more than the council's estimate of the costs for complying with the Clean Air Act that year and $2 billion more than its estimate of all spending on air pollution control in 1978 (including voluntary expenditures). The report said that these assessments probably undervalued society's gain, "if, as many believe, the Clean Air Act has not only resulted in improved air quality . . . but has also helped prevent further degradation."

**Acid Rain.** The Council on Environmental Quality said on Feb. 19 that acid rain, created when rain falls through atmosphere polluted by fossil fuel wastes, had increased fiftyfold in the last 25 years in the eastern half of the U.S. "As a result of this increased acidity," the report said, "many lakes in the northeastern part of the U.S. and Canada now can no longer support fish and other life." EPA administrator Costle predicted on April 21 that President Carter's proposed program to convert the oil-burning power plants of electric utilities to coal could result in a 10 to 15 percent increase in the amount of acid rain falling on the Northeast. Present air quality standards were set to protect human health, which is not directly affected by acid rain.

On Aug. 5 the U.S. and Canada signed an agreement to curb acid rain by preparing a new air quality treaty. At least half of the acid rain that fell in Canada was thought to have originated in the U.S.

**Agent Orange.** The potent herbicide known as Agent Orange, used to strip the Vietnamese countryside of protective coverage, remained in the news in 1980. Veterans' groups had previously

---

**Look Out: Here Comes Olivia!**

On July 29 a group of ornithologists installed four peregrine falcon chicks in their new home, a box high atop the Manhattan Life Insurance Co.'s building adjoining Central Park in New York City. The installation was part of an elaborate plan to save the endangered species of predatory bird. Within less than six weeks, Olivia, the oldest of the four chicks, had made her first kill. On Sept. 5 she returned to her penthouse after an excursion to the park; she brought with her a freshly killed pigeon. No more supermarket chickens for the falcons, predicted the delighted ornithologists. There were, however, no quotes from the pigeon lovers of New York City.

filed suits against the five chemical companies that manufactured the product, charging that it led to birth defects in their children, cancer, loss of libido, and various neurological problems. In January the companies charged that the federal government was responsible for negligent misuse of the product. The main ingredient of Agent Orange is a chemical called 2,4,5-T, which contains traces of an extraordinarily toxic substance called dioxin.

Five research studies released by members of Congress on April 4 found a higher than normal incidence of some forms of cancer among workers who had been exposed to components of Agent Orange overseas. The Veterans Administration declined to concede such a link. A federal study released in August indicated no significant effects on mating, fertility, or health of offspring in male mice fed the components of Agent Orange.                                                                J.A.R.

**EQUATORIAL GUINEA.** See STATISTICS OF THE WORLD.

**ETHIOPIA.** In 1980 Ethiopia again appeared on its way to dismemberment. Its Marxist central government seemed powerless to halt the process, despite the assistance of 3000 Soviet advisers and 13,500 Cuban soldiers. Through assassination, execution, or imprisonment, however, Ethiopia's Marxist leader, Lt. Col. Mengistu Haile Mariam, reportedly had made his authority unchallenged. In December, 1979, government forces again had laid siege to Nakfa, the stronghold of the Eritrean People's Liberation Front (EPLF). More than 5000 Ethiopian troops were reported killed before they were routed and forced to abandon much of the Eritrean coast. Soviet ships were employed in the evacuation. Disturbed by the heavy losses, the Soviets appeared to have urged the government to make a peace offer to the Eritrean Liberation Front (ELF). The Eritreans, however, who had been fighting for self-determination for 19 years, flatly rejected the offer. After Sudan closed its borders to Eritrean secessionists in April, in a move to improve relations with the Mengistu government, the EPLF declared itself ready to enter into negotiations on self-determination on condition that the United Nations, the Arab League, and the Organization of African Unity supervise the talks. The Mengistu government rejected this idea, and the guerrilla war continued.

Efforts to resettle the drought-stricken populations in Wallo and Tigre provinces began in 1979. The resulting tightening of central government control met with growing resistance in 1980. By late in the year secessionist groups had intensified hit-and-run attacks on government garrisons. The military retaliated with bombings and helicopter attacks on villages in the region. More than 80,000 people were reported to have been displaced in the attacks.

In the Ogaden, fighting continued throughout the year, pitting Ethiopian forces against ethnic Somali guerrillas supplied by the Somali government. On Aug. 21 the United States agreed to provide Somalia with military aid in exchange for the use of port facilities. (The U.S. ambassador to Ethiopia had already been expelled.) Clashes along the Somali border soon intensified. In September Ethiopian air attacks were reported against several Somali border towns and the Somalis claimed to have repelled ground attacks. The Soviet Union had reportedly sent sophisticated attack helicopters to Ethiopia. In the Ogaden, however, as in Eritrea and the outlying provinces, the Mengistu government was unable to dislodge its enemies or force them to abandon their commitment to dismember the Ethiopian state.

See STATISTICS OF THE WORLD. See also AFRICA; SOMALIA.                                                J.T.S.

**EUROPEAN COMMUNITIES,** a supranational organization comprising the European Economic Community, the European Atomic Energy Community, and the European Coal and Steel Community. Because the communities share the same institutional framework, they are frequently referred to as the European Community (EC), or Common Market. In 1980 the nine member countries were Belgium, Denmark, France, Great Britain, Ireland, Italy, Luxembourg, the Netherlands, and West Germany.

**Internal Affairs.** Two major internal struggles challenged the EC in 1980. The first involved an unprecedented vote by the European Parliament in the closing days in 1979 to reject the proposed 1980 EC budget, primarily to protest the amount of money the Council of Ministers proposed to spend on agriculture—more than 70 percent of the budget. A budget was finally approved in July with only minor revisions.

The second confrontation was over Britain's contribution to EC finances. By 1980, Britain was providing one fifth of the EC's financial resources but getting back substantially less. The lion's share of the EC budget was allocated to agricultural subsidies, yet only 2 percent of Britain's population was employed in agriculture. Thus, Britain was "losing money" on the EC (an estimated $2.5 billion each year) and demanded that something be done about reducing its contribution, using its veto power to force concessions. A compromise was finally reached on May 30, although Britain would remain a net contributor of about $900,000,000 a year.

European Community Commission President Roy Jenkins, Italian Premier Francesco Cossiga, and Italian Foreign Minister Emilio Colombo (left to right) are shown at an April meeting of leaders of the nine EC nations. A later meeting was needed to settle a controversy over Great Britain's contribution to the EC's finances.

On Oct. 30 the EC foreign and industry ministers declared the steel industry "in manifest crisis" and voted to set up a mandatory steel cartel to cut back production and drive up prices. The West Germans agreed to the plan reluctantly, feeling that it would help inefficient plants in other countries and penalize their own more competitive mills.

Final preparations for EC enlargement to include Greece were completed during 1980, with formal entry scheduled for Jan. 1, 1981. President Valéry Giscard d'Estaing of France, however, called for a slowdown in progress toward Spanish and Portuguese membership. European Commission President Roy Jenkins served out his four-year term in 1980. The new commission president beginning in January, 1981, was to be Gaston Thorn, Luxembourg's foreign minister.

**External Affairs.** A meeting of EC heads of government in Venice on June 13 backed full self-determination for the Palestinian people and declared that the Palestine Liberation Organization should be associated with negotiations for a peace settlement in the Middle East. It called for an end to Israel's occupation of the West Bank and Gaza Strip and opposed Jewish settlements in the occupied territories.

EC relations with the United States were generally good during 1980, the worst strain coming over steel antidumping suits filed by U.S. Steel Corp. in March (and later withdrawn). The EC did not join the American embargo on grain sales to the Soviet Union after the invasion of Afghanistan but did promise not to make up any shortfall caused by the U.S. action. On May 18 the EC foreign ministers agreed to impose limited sanctions against Iran for its seizure of the U.S. embassy in Tehran and holding of American hostages. The restrictions affected only contracts signed after Nov. 4, 1979.

See also articles on individual countries mentioned. W.M.

Fashion was characterized by variety in 1980. "Fake furs" were popular, both in traditional and innovative styles. Sweaters were shorter and softer. Blouses in sheer fabrics made an important impact, especially in georgette.

# F

**FASHION.** Variety characterized fashion in 1980. Inflation demanded emphasis on wearable, more traditional, and functional styling. Higher quality fabrics and better workmanship were prerequisites for the average customer, who wanted clothes that would look as right in 1981 as they did in 1980. But the uncertainties of the times created a need for an occasional escape as well. What better way to escape than in the more daring avant-garde look or in fantasy dressing? For the "good old times" advocates, the frilly, feminine, almost Victorian look was available. For the first time since the mid-1970's, the customer was able to find clothes that suited her wants and her need to express her individuality.

Among the new influences of 1980, the Western look, from head to toe, was far in the lead. But behind the Far West garb came camouflage outfits, safari looks, ethnic looks, and cross-cultural influences, just to mention a few. Naturally, this influenced fabrics and colors. Natural fibers—cotton, wool, silk, and linen—in woven fabrics as well as in knits were the most used. Sheers made an important impact, especially in georgette. Knits, in all types of ready-to-wear, made the headlines in fashion news; lacy open-work crochet and handmade looks predominated. Mixtures of fibers and fabrics added excitement to even the most basic styles. The color palate included brights and softened brights such as purples, reds, blues, greens, and pinks. Neutrals continued to be popular and winter white emerged as a fashion extra. The mixing of colors gained as the year progressed, appearing in unusual stripings and bold unsymmetrical patterns. Trimmings and detailing included appliqués, embroideries, laces, fringes, and beading. Shirring, pleating, and ruffles or smocking added softness.

Pants were back for day and night. From jodhpurs to bloomers, from diaper shorts to Bermuda walking shorts, lengths ranged from ankle to "short short." Jump suits, especially for the young, were a fashion must. From tweeds to camouflage patterns to parachute cloth, they sported zipper, rib, and rope trims. The more pockets they had, the better they sold. In 1980 well-known and lesser-known designers added jeans to their collections. Tight and sexy jeans were worn by both sexes and every age group.

Sportswear was still most popular in ready-to-wear lines. New soft blouses, many with the trims and detailing already mentioned, gave a great boost to the sportswear industry. New diversified silhouettes appeared in sweaters. Shorter, softer, and more feminine, in a multitude of textures, stitches, and fiber mixtures, they became an integral part of the wardrobe of the customer of any age. Skirts were softer and wider. Jackets were easy, soft, and elegant, either short and close to the waist or long and straight.

Dress styles ranged from strictly business for day to frilly and feminine for evening. Sleeves were dolman, raglan, short and puffed, and even "leg of mutton." Draped necklines, collars, and the wide use of trimmings changed the mood from severe to soft. Waistlines were less apparent and emphasis moved toward the hips. The disco influence continued to encourage more fluid and seductive late-day clothing. The newest silhouettes were tied at the bottom, whatever the length of the garment. In skirts and dresses, lengths were shorter and varied from several inches below the knee to several inches above; perhaps most important, length was no longer an issue. The wearer suited herself.

Coats played an unimportant role in 1980 fashion. Quilted coats, introduced in 1978, and quilted jackets and vests were widely sold to both the young and the more mature. Narrow cloth coats, reefers, and capes rounded out the picture. Toward the end of the year, the fashion "fake fur" coat was introduced. No longer replicas of the traditional luxury furs, these were presented in new exciting silhouettes in make-believe fun fur imitations.

**Accessories.** The shoe industry revised the boot. The Western boot in leather or vinyl was available at all prices. Other boots ranged in height from ankle to knee. Heels started to get lower. Pumps

---

### The (Wet) End Justifies the Jeans

Everyone knows designer jeans are chic, with almost 200 different labels being put out. But no one has gone further than Calvin Klein, who offered cradle-to-grave denim coverage, starting with a denim diaper cover selling for $15. Tom Shwartz, treasurer of the Childrenswear Manufacturers Association, was not amused, however. "I think the idea is absolutely ridiculous," he said. "The designer deserves to be hit by a speeding car."

took some of the emphasis away from sandals, and espadrilles and ballerina slippers complemented sporty as well as dressy looks. By late spring, the jazz shoe, a flat-heeled laced shoe, was introduced and well accepted. Stockings were textured or opaque, and 1980 brought the handmade look in knit panty hose. Colored hosiery was popular, in soft pastels for summer, rich darks for fall. Handbags were smaller and appeared soft. Shoulder, clutch, and disco bags were the favorites, but the multiple-sized and -shaped parachute-cloth bags were frequently seen. Belts were soft and buckled. Newest among them was the web belt, worn with anything from jeans to dresses. Hats, worn mainly by the young, gained in acceptance. The Western hat covered many heads. Small disco hats, often feather trimmed, were worn not only for dancing but to complement many an outfit. As winter reappeared, sets of mohair or angora hats, gloves, and scarves became popular. Jewelry ran the gamut from beautifully tailored gold or silver necklaces, bracelets, and earrings to heavy cord necklaces and ethnic feathered earrings. Chains in metals or in mixed media continued to be featured, but pearls made a strong comeback for the neck as well as the ears. To enhance the longer hair styles, hair ornaments, particularly combs, were again popular. Many variations of beads were used with cornrow and cornbraid hairdos, the hair news of the year.

**Menswear.** Men, too, were taken with the Western fad. Boots, belt buckles, and hats pointed up the cowboy influence. Plaid shirts with Western yokes and press fasteners instead of buttons were widely sold early in the year. The distinguishing logo—alligator, fox, horsehead—multiplied, on knit shirts, sweaters, belts, socks, and robes. As traditional business suits increased in price, more jacket and slacks outfits were worn. The "preppy look"—tweed jackets, chino pants, sweaters, and "penny" loafers—was everywhere in the fall. But jeans held on, in traditional denim, brushed cotton, and corduroy. The jazz shoe appeared in male as well as female sizes. Sports clothing was again popular, and running shoes, shorts, and shirts were staple wardrobe items. Down jackets, vests, and coats were as popular with men as with women.                                                                    M.H.

**FIJI.** See Statistics of the World.

**FINLAND.** Finland's economy appeared to retain its relative health during 1980 despite troubles caused by inflation, unemployment, and other recessionary trends. Under an agreement that ran out in February, the coalition government of Premier Mauno Koivisto had held increases in labor costs to no more than 11 percent a year, but a

*Braided hair came into fashion in 1980 as some women underwent the long, expensive process needed to emulate Bo Derek in the 1979 film "10." The Western hat covered many heads, both male and female. Hats gained in popularity among the young, and men took to the Western look.*

During the summer of 1980, French fishers blocked water accesses to French ports in order to publicize their economic grievances. Here a naval vessel uses water cannons to clear out two fishing boats.

ship strike in the spring forced employers to grant raises considerably above this level.

The maritime walkout halted Finnish shipping from late March to late May and cost shipowners an estimated $80,000,000. The only important Finnish industry seriously damaged by the strike, however, was the pulp industry, which lost heavily in Western Europe, its major market. The first settlement in the strike provided increases of 14 to 16 percent in wages and fringe benefits for seamen and maritime officers. The final settlement was even higher, with increases of 18 to 20 percent for marine engineers and telegraph operators.

Despite the strong influence of the Soviet Union on Finland, an influence that inspired the disparagement "Finlandization," the U.S.S.R. apparently continued to use spies and native traitors to ensure the success of its policy in Finland. The supposedly subservient Finnish government, however, resented and resisted Soviet espionage. Eila Helin, a Finn who once headed the data library of the Finnish government's Kemira chemical company, was convicted by a Finnish court and sentenced to a four-year prison term for passing classified information to a foreign nation from 1974 to early 1979. The Helsinki Court of Appeals, which announced the sentence on March 18, did not identify the power that employed Helin, but it was known to be the Soviet Union. Helin was also fined about $8600, said to be the total sum the Soviets paid her for five years of spying.

*See* STATISTICS OF THE WORLD. L.A.S.

**FISHERIES.** Commercial landings of edible and industrial fish by U.S. fishers at ports in the 50 states totaled a record 6.3 billion lb. and were valued at a record $2.2 billion in 1979, the latest year for which data were available. This amounted to an increase of 4 percent in quantity and 20 percent in value compared with the 1978 record year. The greatest bulk consisted of menhaden and anchovies caught for reduction to animal feed and for industrial uses. The food finfish catch amounted to nearly 1.4 billion lb. The National Marine Fisheries Service indicated that the annual catch of marine species by recreational anglers approached that figure.

**Foreign Fishing in U.S. Waters.** The 1977 act establishing the U.S. 200-mi. fisheries jurisdiction provided that stocks surplus to American needs could be harvested by licensed foreign vessels for fees based on the ex-vessel value of the fish in the United States. The foreign catch in 1979 (excluding tuna) was 3.6 billion lb., 6 percent below 1978 and 29 percent less than the average for the five preceding years. Japan was the leading harvester in the U.S. zone, with the Soviet Union ranking second. The U.S.S.R. lost its fishing privileges within the U.S. 200-mi. zone in early 1980, in retaliation for the Soviet invasion of Afghanistan.

Alaskan waters provided 89 percent of the foreign catch; one species, the Alaskan pollack, accounted for 65 percent of the total foreign catch. Foreign fleets seeking higher-value species such as squid and butterfish on the East Coast complained about U.S. regulations that made it difficult for them to fill their quotas.

On Dec. 22 President Carter signed into law a bill phasing out foreign fishing within the U.S. 200-mi. zone in five years.

**U.S. Fisheries Trade.** Exports set a new value record of $1.08 billion for 1979, exceeding the $905,500,000 of 1978. Imports, however, increased at a much faster rate, from $3.08 billion in 1978 to a record-setting $3.8 billion in 1979.

**Tuna Problems.** The U.S. 200-mi.-limit law was unique in that it excluded tuna, a migratory species, from its provisions. This exclusion had led to problems in both foreign and domestic waters. Because the U.S. State Department did not recognize the jurisdiction of other countries over tuna within their 200-mi. limits, some U.S. tuna seiners continued to fish in those waters without licenses. After repeated warnings, Mexico seized six U.S. tuna seiners in July, and Ecuador seized nine in October and early November. In retaliation, the U.S. State Department banned importation of all tuna products from Mexico and Ecuador (and also from Costa Rica and Peru), as required by law. U.S. negotiators continued to try to reach accords with Latin American countries so that U.S. fishing boats would have access to tuna waters. But Mexico announced on Dec. 29 that it would terminate its two fishing agreements with the U.S.

On the East Coast, Japanese long-liners, using fishing lines with bait and hooks attached at intervals, were catching more than 8000 giant bluefin tuna each spring from spawning grounds in the Gulf of Mexico, while U.S. fishers were restricted to less than half the Japanese catch. A strong effort in Congress to add tuna to the 200-mi. limit resulted in a compromise calling for observers on all foreign long-liners.

**U.S.-Canadian Fisheries Treaties.** Disputes over boundaries on Georges Bank, off the New England and Nova Scotia coasts, and the division of the scallop catch made U.S. Senate ratification of the East Coast fishing treaty, signed in early 1979, highly unlikely. The dispute over albacore tuna in Canada's Pacific waters, however, was eased, and fishers from both nations were expected to be able to fish each other's waters for that species.

**French Fishing Protests.** In July, French fishers blocked water accesses to France's ports. Their protests culminated growing dissatisfaction arising from high fuel costs, cuts in the size of crews, and low prices for fish. The blockade was finally broken on Aug. 27 by naval tugboats near Marseilles.                                                          A.J.R.

**FLORIDA.** *See* STATISTICS OF THE WORLD.

**FRANCE.** Political stability and a lagging, mildly depressed economy were characteristic of France in 1980. More dramatic events occurred in foreign affairs.

**Political Calm.** Calm prevailed in French politics in 1980. President Valéry Giscard d'Estaing and his centrist coalition easily surmounted minor objections from the Left and the Right. In September polls forecasting the April–May, 1981, presidential elections, he was running well ahead of his rivals. Giscard's lead was largely due to the disarray of the former Union of the Left. Within the Communist Party, leading intellectuals and some rank and file were questioning party principles and chieftains, and the Socialist Party was split over policy and leadership.

Scandals, terrorism, and regional disturbances

---

**At Last, an *Immortelle*!**

The French Academy, founded in 1635 by Cardinal Richelieu, has 40 members, known as "The Immortals." Mostly writers, they are elected for life. When an obscure author named Roger Caillois died, editor-writer Jean d'Ormesson nominated Marguerite Yourcenar, a highly qualified historical novelist, to assume his seat. After much wrangling, the vote was taken: 20 to 12 in favor of the first woman ever admitted to the academy. The new *immortelle* was born in Belgium on June 8, 1903. Her French father was a firm believer in the intellectual equality of the sexes; he would have been delighted by her election. There is one more surprising fact to report: Yourcenar, a resident of Mount Desert Island, Maine, has been a U.S. citizen for 30 years.

*Marguerite Yourcenar.*

did nevertheless provide occasion for political sniping at the administration. Former minister Michel Poniatowski was accused of improper handling of the four-year hunt for the assassin of Jean de Broglie. More serious were the frequent terrorist episodes in Paris resulting in the death of a former premier of Syria; attacks on Turkish envoys; and an alarming rise in anti-Semitic incidents, including an Oct. 3 attack on a Paris synagogue that resulted in the deaths of four persons. Giscard expressed support for the French Jewish community, and 100,000 people of many political persuasions took part in a rally protesting the bombing, but fears of an upsurge in right-wing extremism were not completely assuaged. Violence was no stranger to the outlying regions of France where autonomist groups of Corsicans, Bretons, and Basques protested and attacked French authority.

**Economic Doldrums.** With one eye on the stagnant economy and the other on the forthcoming elections, the cabinet under Premier Raymond Barre in September proposed a 1981 budget with items to attract a wide range of interests. To combat low-level production, continuing unemployment, and persistent double-digit inflation, $2 billion was provided to offer tax advantages to business as well as bonuses for creating new jobs. An 18 percent rise in the military budget was viewed as a stimulant to the economy, too. Increases in social security benefits and family allocations were also scheduled. In October the cabinet approved a five-year plan stressing advanced technology and allotting $23 billion for research and development.

Labor unrest in transportation and communications was sporadic but not massive. Fishermen struck because of mounting fuel costs, diminishing markets, and lack of governmental protection. Blockading mostly English Channel and some Mediterranean ports, the fishermen disrupted tourist and commercial activity during the summer. An official policy of carrot-and-stick, using the navy and offering minor concessions, produced an indecisive outcome in September. French farmers in the southwest took to violence in June to prevent the influx of less expensive produce from Spain.

Energy remained basic to the economic problems of France. To satisfy national needs with less dependence on oil from the volatile Middle East, the government extended its construction of nuclear power plants. Resistance of a regional and antinuclear nature was overcome in Brittany, and throughout the country residents near nuclear plants were wooed by a 15 percent discount of their electricity bills until 1990.

This rabbi was presiding over a service in a Paris synagogue on Oct. 3 when a bomb exploded outside, killing four persons. The incident followed a number of earlier attacks on Jewish targets.

In part to meet the high cost of petroleum and the outflow of payments, the French sought and secured numerous contracts abroad to supply billions of francs worth of armaments and technology to the Soviet Union, Iraq, and other states. In October, China agreed in principle to buy two nuclear power plants from France, and in the same month Saudi Arabia agreed to pay $3.4 billion for French ships and helicopters. The French government-owned Renault gained a controlling interest in the American Motors Corp. at a cost of $200,000,000.

**Foreign Crises.** In facing the international crises involving the Iranian holding of American hostages, the Soviets' intervention in Afghanistan, the Palestine Liberation Organization's (PLO) demands for recognition and support, and the Iraq-Iran war, France pursued policies often at variance with those of the U.S. At semiannual meetings in February and July with West German

175

Chancellor Helmut Schmidt and at the economic summit sessions in Venice in June, Giscard spoke for a "strong independent Europe" that would take no dictation from either the U.S. or the Soviet Union. Underscoring his rhetoric of independence from Washington, Giscard conferred with Soviet President Leonid I. Brezhnev in Warsaw in May without prior consultation with the U.S. Giscard also refused to apply full sanctions against Iran, boycott the Olympics in Moscow, or refrain from endorsing the PLO's quest for a self-determined Palestinian state. When Giscard visited China in October, he received a polite but cool reception, because the Chinese did not favor the French emphasis on détente with Moscow.

While Western Europe and the U.S. pondered possible revisions of their military strategy, the French announced their development of a neutron bomb, which possesses advantages for the defense of the West against possible aggression by the U.S.S.R. The weapon was tested, but no decision on production was to be made for two or three years. French military power was exerted in Africa—in Chad (early in the year) and in support of Tunisia against Libyan attacks. French troops also appeared briefly in the New Hebrides in July when the Pacific island chain became the new nation of Vanuatu.

Within the European Community, the French stubbornly protected their agricultural interests. France rankled Spain and Portugal by delaying consideration of their admission to the Common Market.

See STATISTICS OF THE WORLD.          D.J.H.

# G

**GABON.** See STATISTICS OF THE WORLD.
**GAMBIA.** See STATISTICS OF THE WORLD.
**GEORGIA.** See STATISTICS OF THE WORLD.
**GERMAN DEMOCRATIC REPUBLIC, or EAST GERMANY.** The East German government watched apprehensively in 1980 as workers' strikes shook neighboring Poland. Leaders were aware that although East German living standards were relatively high, citizens were far from satisfied with Communist rule. Moreover, the East German public was well informed about what was taking place in Poland, since it could watch West German television coverage of events.

**Domestic Affairs.** Communist Party leader and head of state Erich Honecker continued to govern the country with a firm hand. Security police kept track of potential dissidents, and trade unions were closely supervised by the party. Western reporters visiting East Germany observed widespread public discussion about the Polish strikes. But for the most part, East German workers made no move to emulate the Poles.

The only major work stoppage was a strike by West German employees of the East German state railway, which serves West Berlin as well as East Germany. For a few days in September, strikers demanding pay increases and democratic unions halted deliveries to West Berlin and transit inside the city. American, British, and French officials who nominally administer West Berlin under postwar accords made no move to intervene. When East German authorities refused to compromise with the protesters, the work stoppage fizzled.

As the Polish crisis deepened, the government announced on Oct. 28 that the joint border with Poland would only be open for private trips if officially certified invitations from friends or relatives could be produced. This action effectively ended eight years of free travel between the two countries. In November the government threatened East Germany's Protestant Church, which had a membership of nearly half the population, with a crackdown unless its leaders refrained from all political criticism and it separated itself from special ties with the West German Church. The warning also threatened to revoke an agreement that gave the church broadcast time on radio and television.

The economy remained relatively strong, despite the impact of soaring oil-import costs. In a semiannual report in July the government announced that the economy was growing at a yearly rate of 5 percent. Western analysts believed that a low rate of capital investment was proving to be a long-term hindrance to more rapid economic development.

**Foreign Affairs.** East Germany closely adhered to the Soviet foreign policy line, maintaining thousands of advisers in several African, Asian, and Latin American countries to further Russian interests. In September the U.S.S.R. and its Warsaw Pact allies conducted a large-scale military exercise on East German soil.

*Soviet President Leonid I. Brezhnev (left) receives West German Chancellor Helmut Schmidt in Moscow on June 30. Schmidt made clear his displeasure over Soviet intervention in Afghanistan but signed a long-term economic agreement with the U.S.S.R.*

Relations between East Germany and West Germany cooled in 1980. At East German request, a scheduled meeting between Honecker and West German Chancellor Helmut Schmidt was postponed in January, evidently as a show of Communist displeasure over Western condemnation of the Soviet invasion of Afghanistan.

On April 30 the two Germanys reached an accord under which East Germany was to receive $282,000,000 over a five-year period from Bonn for improvement of rail, water, and road links between West Berlin and West Germany. A planned Schmidt visit to East Germany, however, was again postponed on Aug. 22 due to the unsettled state of affairs in Poland. And, in October, East Germany almost doubled the amount of money Western visitors must exchange when they enter the country, from $7.20 to $13.90 for each day spent there. For the thousands of visitors who were entering East Berlin every day from the West, often for only an hour or two to see relatives or friends, the fee was almost quadrupled, from $3.60 to $13.90. Since 8,000,000 West Germans and West Berliners have been visiting East Germany each year, the action was a particular blow, and Bonn protested vigorously, but in vain. Western analysts believed Honecker was attempting to isolate his people from Western contacts to lessen the possibility of Polish-style unrest.

See STATISTICS OF THE WORLD.　　　　F.W.

**GERMANY, FEDERAL REPUBLIC OF,** *or* **WEST GERMANY.** The German Federal Republic held a national election in 1980. Voters returned to power the two-party alliance led by Chancellor Helmut Schmidt. The Christian Democratic parties took their worst drubbing since 1949.

**National Election.** The election was held on Oct. 5. Voters gave a clear victory to Schmidt's Social Democrats and his coalition partners, the Free Democrats, who made surprising gains. After ballots were counted, the Social Democrats held 218 seats (up from 214) in the *Bundestag,* the Free Democrats 53 seats (up from 39), and the Christian Democratic Union–Christian Social Union (CDU-CSU) 226 seats (down from 243). The election not only gave Schmidt a healthy majority but also strengthened the hand of the Free Democrats, who were expected to make greater policy demands on their national coalition partner.

The result was a triumph for both Schmidt, who was widely credited with increasing West Germany's influence in the world, and Free Democratic leader Hans-Dietrich Genscher. It was a severe blow to Franz Josef Strauss, leader of the CDU-CSU, whose controversial personality apparently drove voters from the conservative banner.

During the campaign both Schmidt and Strauss lowered the general level of their appeals to acrimony not ordinarily heard in postwar Germany. Genscher received praise for running a more dignified campaign. With regard to issues, Strauss painted himself as a better friend of the United States than Schmidt who, he said, was steering West Germany toward neutrality. And Strauss, a vigorous anti-Communist, seemed to have been given fresh ammunition late in the race when unrest in Poland led East European leaders to harden their stance toward West Germany. In addition, Strauss attempted to make capital out of economic issues. But in the end, his arguments failed to catch fire. Opinion polls showed that voters approved of Schmidt's handling of East-West issues and that the economy was still sound enough to satisfy the electorate.

**State Elections.** Three state elections that preceded the national vote resulted in a confusing political picture. In the first, in Baden-Württemberg in March, a new environmentalist party, the Greens, made an unexpectedly strong showing, garnering 5.3 percent of the vote. The Christian Democrats remained in power, but both they and the Social Democrats lost votes, while the Free Democrats gained marginally.

In April, in Saarland, the Social Democrats gained. The Christian Democrats lost significantly but retained state control in coalition with the local Free Democrats.

In North Rhine–Westphalia in May, the Social Democrats won a clear majority, and the Christian Democrats lost heavily. The Free Democrats fell short of the 5 percent vote necessary to take a state parliamentary seat.

**The Economy.** The economy, which remained basically prosperous and stable, took something of a downturn in 1980. Growth was strong in the first quarter but decreased in the second. In August, West Germany registered the first monthly deficit on visible trade in 15 years. Unemployment in early August hit 3.7 percent, or about 850,000 workers, and was expected to increase further. In January experts predicted that the gross national product would increase by 2.5 percent for the year, but by October the prediction had sunk to 1 percent. Government hopes that the inflation rate could be held to 4.5 percent also appeared certain to be dashed. In a gloomy forecast issued in October, the nation's five leading economic institutes said growth would halt in 1981 because of the effects of oil price rises and the tight-money policy of the central bank.

**Terrorism.** A bomb exploded at the Munich Oktoberfest on Sept. 26, killing 13 people and injuring many others. The incident was thought to have been the work of a 21-year-old member of a neo-Nazi paramilitary group who was himself killed in the explosion.

In October, after a two-and-one-half-year trial, a West Berlin court jailed six terrorists for terms of between 5 and 15 years on charges that included the kidnapping, in 1975, of Peter Lorenz, Christian Democratic leader in West Berlin. All six defendants belonged to an extreme left-wing offshoot of the Red Army Faction, or Baader-Meinhof gang.

**The Loser in "Dirtiest Ever" Campaign**

It was the nastiest political campaign in West Germany's history. The conservative challenger, Franz Josef Strauss, minister-president of Bavaria and leader of the combined opposition of Christian Democrats and Christian Socialists, was the target of much scurrilous invective—as was his opponent, Chancellor Helmut Schmidt. Strauss, 65, short and stocky with a round face and bull neck, campaigned against the expanding federal bureaucracy and the growing national debt. Although labeled by his opponents a "warmonger," "unstable," "unfit to be entrusted with the nation's future," and even compared to Adolf Hitler, Strauss had long been beloved in his native Bavaria. But he had aroused equally strong negative passions in much of the rest of West Germany during his 31-year-long political career.

*Franz Josef Strauss.*

*Rescue workers remove a victim after the Sept. 26 Munich bomb explosion that killed 13 persons. A member of a neo-Nazi group was believed responsible for the terrorist blast.*

**Defense.** In a statement made in February, Chancellor Schmidt declared he would increase defense spending by 3 percent in 1980, in line with the target established by the North Atlantic Treaty Organization (NATO). After the national election, however, the West German government decided to cut the rate of increase, and decrease planned purchases of new tanks and fighter aircraft. The stagnating economy was cited as the reason for this decision.

**Papal Visit.** In mid-November, Pope John Paul II became the first pontiff to visit Germany since 1782. Besides his goal of strengthening the Roman Catholic Church, which had become the largest religious group in West Germany, the pope hoped to bring Catholics and Protestants closer together and spoke of German reunification.

**Foreign Affairs.** Relations between West Germany and the U.S. were troubled in 1980. Although Schmidt was a firm supporter of NATO and was, like President Jimmy Carter, greatly disturbed by the Soviet invasion of Afghanistan, he was caught on the horns of a dilemma. On the one hand, he

believed that Western-Soviet relations should not be "business as usual"; on the other, he thought the German national interest required the preservation of East-West détente as much as possible, particularly in view of his country's ethnic and even family links with East Germany. Moreover, Schmidt's personal relationship with Carter was uneasy.

As the year began, Schmidt, in a statement to the parliament, promised West German support for Carter's proposed sanctions against Iran and the Soviet Union. In private discussions with U.S. officials, however, he urged that lines of communication with Moscow be kept open, and he criticized Carter for inadequate consultation with the Western allies. In early March, Schmidt flew to Washington for a summit with Carter, at which he made the same points.

The West German leader backed Carter's boycott of the Moscow Summer Olympics, but he accepted an invitation to meet in Moscow with Soviet President Leonid I. Brezhnev at the end of June. When the West German–Soviet summit took place, Schmidt made clear his displeasure over Soviet intervention in Afghanistan but signed a long-term economic cooperation agreement with the U.S.S.R. He counted it as an achievement of his visit that the Soviets agreed to future East-West negotiations on the control of nuclear weapons in Europe.

Schmidt made it a priority to develop friendly relations with East Germany. The Afghan and Polish crises complicated his efforts in 1980. In January, East German leader Erich Honecker called off a scheduled East-West German summit; an August meeting was also postponed. In October, Honecker raised minimum costs of Western visits to East Germany, and in November many East German performing artists and clergymen were ordered to cancel tours of West Germany.

Workers' strikes in Poland affected Bonn's ties with Warsaw. In August, Polish Communist Party leader Edward Gierek canceled a proposed meeting with Schmidt in order to deal with Polish internal problems. Schmidt, however, helped arrange a $674,000,000 loan from a consortium of banks to help revive the faltering Polish economy. The Polish hierarchy subsequently ousted Gierek; until that time he had been the Communist spokesman with whom Schmidt felt most comfortable.

*See* STATISTICS OF THE WORLD.　　　　F.W.

**GHANA.** During 1980 the civilian government of President Hilla Limann concentrated on asserting itself as the legitimate government of Ghana.

Limann, Ghana's first civilian ruler since 1972, took office in September, 1979, after a coup by junior military officers and a general "housecleaning" of corrupt senior officers and officials. Among Limann's first moves was the forced retirement of Flight Lt. Jerry Rawlings, who had led the military junta, and his main supporters. After his retirement in late 1979, Rawlings continued to serve as a vocal watchdog over government activity. While denouncing government "incompetency" throughout 1980, Rawlings's personal attacks on Limann decreased by year's end. By mid-1980, the government had withstood three abortive, bloodless coup attempts, each thwarted by the president's intelligence service. To check military hostility, Limann established an armed forces review commission designed to examine grievances coming from the lower ranks over pay, living conditions, and advancement opportunities.

With the military quieted, at least temporarily, Limann was able to turn to the economy, which was riddled with low productivity and inflation in excess of 50 percent. An austerity budget issued in December, 1979, sparked a wave of strikes in early 1980. Limann withstood them, asserting that

the economy could not afford continual wage hikes and establishing industrial courts to settle legitimate worker disputes. At the same time, in late May, Limann announced a crash two-year program for agricultural development intended to make Ghana self-sufficient in food production and ultimately to make it a food exporter.

*See* STATISTICS OF THE WORLD.　　　　J.T.S.

**GREAT BRITAIN.** Economic storms lashed Great Britain in 1980. Criticism of Conservative Prime Minister Margaret Thatcher mounted, but she refused to alter controversial economic policies designed to restructure the British economy.

**Politics and the Economy.** Thatcher, who took office in a 1979 national election, believed that waste, inefficiency, and deadwood must be eliminated from the economy by means of survival-of-the-fittest economic policies. As a result, she took tough decisions to slash government spending, dismantle welfare programs, and curb the influence of unions. High interest rates choked investment, causing business bankruptcies and keeping the pound so high in value against other currencies as to hurt British exports. Inflation persisted, running in 1980 at an annual rate of 15.5 percent, and unemployment rose sharply. Even the North Sea oil bonanza, which was expected to make Britain self-sufficient in oil by 1981, hurt industrial exports by pushing up the value of the pound. But at each new development, Thatcher reiterated that if her policies were maintained, the economy would prosper in the long run.

The first test of Thatcher's determination came in January, when more than 100,000 steelworkers struck, demanding a pay increase of 20 percent. The prime minister was eager to see the walkout ended before it damaged the economy and her own prestige; even so, she refused to let the government join the negotiations and bail out the debt-ridden state-owned British Steel Corp. After 13 weeks a compromise was reached on March 31. The settlement included a pay increase of 15.5 percent (17 percent with benefits), but the Thatcher government was able to claim it had not given in to union demands. It was the longest national walkout since 1945.

Unemployment hit nearly 1,400,000 in April, the highest level since the Great Depression. By July, the figure was 1,900,000. The opposition Labour Party mounted a challenge in Parliament in July. Addressing the House of Commons, Thatcher firmly declared there would be no "U-turns" in economic policy. With a parliamentary majority of 43 at her command, she beat down Labour's no-confidence motion 333 to 274.

In August unemployment officially passed the 2,000,000 mark. For the first time, senior minis-

A caricature of the "Iron Lady"—British Prime Minister Margaret Thatcher—complete with axes instead of hands, takes part in a March 9 London rally protesting cuts in government spending. Although Thatcher maintained that her policies would reduce the rate of inflation, the cost of living continued to soar in 1980.

### Left Foot Forward

The 1980 national convention of the British Labour Party was tumultuous, but on Nov. 10 the party's members in the House of Commons, with less fuss, elected a new leader. They chose Michael Foot, 67, a member of Parliament for 30 years, to succeed former Prime Minister James Callaghan, who had resigned. Described as rumpled, bookish, and a peacemaker, the white-haired former journalist offers the British public a clear choice between the conservative policies of Prime Minister Margaret Thatcher and his own left-wing stance. Foot, staunchly allied with the British labor unions, favors increasing both state ownership of industry and public expenditures. But he has long given top priority to nuclear disarmament, which he considers "essential to the salvation of the world."

*Michael Foot.*

*Iranians rally in London on May 1 to protest the storming of Iran's embassy there by armed ethnic Arabs who held the occupants hostage for five days and killed at least one. British commandos counterattacked, rescuing 19 hostages.*

ters in the government expressed doubts about Conservative economic plans, and British industrialists demanded lower interest rates. At the Conservative Party conference in Brighton in October, Thatcher called unemployment a "human tragedy." But she maintained that time would prove her decisions on the economy to have been correct.

Meanwhile, the Labour Party suffered a serious schism. Throughout the year the radical left wing worked to take control of the party from former Prime Minister James Callaghan and moderate elements. The Labour Party's conference in Blackpool, Sept. 29 to Oct. 3, became a battleground between the two factions. Led by Tony Benn, the Left pushed through a plank urging withdrawal from the European Community (EC), or Common Market. It also won on the issue of requiring all candidates for Parliament to be rechosen by their local party branch before each election. Infighting left the matter of how to choose a party leader up in the air, but it was agreed that the choice would not, as in the past, be left solely to the party members in the House of Commons.

In the wake of the party conference, the 68-year-old Callaghan resigned as leader. His move appeared to benefit moderates, who hoped to select a younger moderate leader before new rule changes could be put into effect that would aid the left wing. Former Chancellor of the Exchequer Denis Healey appeared to be the front-runner, but on Nov. 10, Michael Foot, the left-wing candidate, was chosen. Foot had long been an advocate of unilateral nuclear disarmament.

**Defense.** Details of Britain's defense policy were issued in a white paper in April, 1980. The government pointed to Soviet intervention in Afghanistan as one reason why Great Britain's defenses must be upgraded. It announced an increase of 3.5 percent in real terms in the military budget for 1980–81 and said that while overall public expenditures would fall in the coming three years, military spending would continue to rise. (The military increase was later cut to 2.5 percent.)

In June, Britain became the first member of the North Atlantic Treaty Organization to announce its chosen locations for placement of American cruise missiles capable of hitting Soviet targets.

"Queen Mum," the mother of Queen Elizabeth II, prepares to ride to London's St. Paul's Cathedral with her eldest grandson, Prince Charles, for a thanksgiving service marking her 80th birthday. Hundreds of thousands of viewers hailed the procession.

Defense spokesmen said 160 cruise missiles would be placed at two bases within 60 mi. of London. In July the Thatcher government decided to modernize Britain's nuclear force with Trident missiles purchased from the United States. The Tridents would arm four or five new British-built submarines.

**Terrorism.** In May six armed ethnic Arabs from Iran seized the Iranian embassy in London and held its occupants hostage for five days. The attackers released several hostages, but after they killed one and threw his body into the street, British authorities ordered a commando attack on the building. Five gunmen were killed and 19 hostages were saved; another hostage was found dead inside the building.

**Northern Ireland.** On July 2 the British government proposed a new plan to provide home rule for Northern Ireland, but it did not appear to generate greater enthusiasm among Catholics or Protestants than earlier proposals. Nevertheless, Humphrey Atkins, the secretary of state for Northern Ireland, began a series of meetings with political leaders in September to discuss the proposals.

At least 1000 British soldiers were withdrawn from Northern Ireland during 1980, but terrorism continued in sporadic bombings and shootings perpetrated by both sides. The Community of Peace People, founded by Betty Williams and Mairead Corrigan, who shared a Nobel Peace Prize in 1977, was torn by disagreements during 1980 to such an extent that Williams resigned. The Peace People's director supported the movement to have convicted terrorists treated as political prisoners. Hundreds of men convicted without juries by special antiterrorist courts were refusing to wear prison uniforms, wrapping themselves in blankets instead. In October seven of them began a hunger strike to back their demands, and the largest demonstration in years was held in Belfast in their support.

**Foreign Affairs.** A February election in war-torn Zimbabwe (Rhodesia) represented a major achievement of the Thatcher government. It was supervised by British governor Lord Soames, and 94 percent of the country's eligible voters, black and white, took part. Robert Mugabe, a black whose party won 57 of the 80 assembly seats available to blacks, became prime minister, and Britain granted Zimbabwe independence in April. See ZIMBABWE.

In foreign policy as well as defense, the Thatcher government considered the U.S. its closest ally. The prime minister backed President Jimmy Carter in his opposition to Soviet intervention in Afghanistan. She agreed in May to economic sanctions against Iran, but under pressure at home, she had to settle for restrictions that were severely watered down.

Britain's relations with Saudi Arabia suffered a chill. The Saudis were deeply offended by a film, *Death of a Princess,* that appeared on British television in April and related the true story of a Saudi princess executed in 1977 for taking a lover. The Saudis asked Britain to withdraw its ambassador, and not until late July did relations between the two nations return to normal.

Thatcher took a tough approach toward other EC members. At a May meeting of foreign ministers in Brussels, Britain demanded, and got, concessions from other market members on the amount of Britain's contribution to the EC budget.

The Anglo-French condominium of the New Hebrides became the independent republic of Vanuatu on July 30. Several weeks before that date, dissident elements on the island of Espiritu Santo declared their secession. A joint British-French force was called in to keep order; *see also* COMMONWEALTH OF NATIONS; EUROPEAN COMMUNITIES; PACIFIC ISLANDS.

*See* STATISTICS OF THE WORLD.                F.W.

**GREECE.** Inflation remained the major economic problem in Greece during 1980, but the business community seemed unwilling to accept any strong measures to solve the problem. A new president took office during the year. Greece rejoined the North Atlantic Treaty Organization (NATO), and hopeful steps were taken to end the disputes with Turkey.

---

**Alexander the Inebriate**

Greek scholars reacted angrily to a paper by Maxwell O'Brien of Queens College in New York City, published in October, that claimed Alexander the Great had been an alcoholic. O'Brien concluded that Alexander, whose conquests introduced Greek civilization to much of Asia, died at the age of 32 from acute alcohol withdrawal complicated by malaria. One Greek scholar replied that "civilizations only develop where there are vineyards, and common sense [says] that you can't achieve much under the influence of Coca-Cola." More philosophically, a French academic concluded: "After so many victories the man deserved a drink."

---

**Domestic Affairs.** The rate of inflation had increased to 25 percent during 1979, but government action to reduce the rate to 15 percent in 1980 was opposed by a majority of the nation's merchants. Most Greek stores were closed on Jan. 21 in a protest by shopowners against anti-inflation rules that curbed profits and imports. Storekeepers complained that import controls would decrease their sales volume and that the profit limits made them absorb a 25 percent luxury consumption tax and other costs.

The government yielded partially in early

---

**New Leader, Same Policy**
Constantine Karamanlis, twice premier of Greece and the nation's dominant political figure since the military junta was overthrown in 1974, stepped down as head of government and was elected to the largely ceremonial office of president on May 5. Three days later, the parliamentary caucus of the governing New Democracy Party elected as his successor Foreign Minister George Rallis, 62. The normally aloof and soft-spoken Rallis acknowledged that stepping into his predecessor's shoes would be no easy role. "Mr. Karamanlis is a great statesman," he said. "For the time being, I just hope to be a good politician."

*Constantine Karamanlis (left) and George Rallis.*

*Greece rejoined the military wing of NATO on Oct. 20 after a six-year absence. Here Greek Orthodox priests take part in one of many demonstrations against NATO membership.*

March and suspended the import curbs for a two-month trial period. Businessmen agreed to keep imports down to 85 percent of the 1978 total. It was agreed that the suspension would be made permanent if the voluntary measures reduced imports sufficiently. The retail prices of imports were frozen for three months; price increases for most industrial consumer goods were limited to 15 percent throughout 1980, and profit margins were to be held to the November, 1979, levels.

More than 30,000 Greek bank employees went on strike on Jan. 17 but settled on Feb. 23 for an 11 percent wage increase. The strikers also won government agreement to drop plans to align the Greek bank working hours with the schedules observed in Western European banks. The Greek unions insisted that the Greek climate was unsuited to the proposed afternoon working hours.

Prime Minister Constantine Karamanlis was elected by the parliament on May 5 to a five-year term as president, succeeding Constantine Tsatsos. The ruling New Democracy Party on May 8 elected George Rallis to replace Karamanlis as prime minister. Evangelos Averoff-Tossizza, who barely lost to Rallis in the 88–84 vote, agreed to serve as deputy prime minister in addition to his former post as minister of defense.

**Foreign Affairs.** Civilian air traffic had been banned by Greece and Turkey over the eastern Aegean Sea since the invasion of Cyprus by Tur-

key in 1974. The curbs were ended by Turkey on Feb. 22 and by Greece on Feb. 23.

The foreign ministers of Greece and Turkey met in Ankara (Turkey) on June 28 in what was described as a "warm-up meeting to establish a general understanding." They agreed to regular meetings to seek solutions to Greek-Turkish disputes.

Greece rejoined the military wing of NATO on Oct. 20, six years after leaving it to protest the Turkish invasion of Cyprus in 1974. Greece's earlier attempts to reenter the alliance had been vetoed by Turkey, which had demanded more control over the Aegean. In 1980 the new military regime in Turkey accepted a plan under which Greece could rejoin NATO first and the two nations could work out the details later. The agreement also made it possible for the United States to continue operating its four bases in Greece, a right which it would have lost if the NATO question had remained unsettled.

*See* STATISTICS OF THE WORLD. L.A.S.

**GRENADA.** *See* STATISTICS OF THE WORLD. *See also* CARIBBEAN COUNTRIES.

**GUAM.** *See* STATISTICS OF THE WORLD.

**GUATEMALA.** A return to the civil savagery that tore Guatemala apart during the mid-1960's was seen as the likely result of the escalating violence evident throughout 1980.

The seizure of the Spanish embassy on Jan. 31 by angry peasants led by leftist guerrillas and other agitators, together with the bomb blast and fire that followed the seizure, began the year on a note of violence—and hardly a month followed that did not produce similar incidents. Clashes between government forces and terrorists left hundreds dead. By Oct. 1 the toll had risen to 1200 fatalities, according to a government source. At San Carlos University, 15 professors were killed by unidentified gunmen between Feb. 1 and June 15. Moderates and leftists claimed the deaths were carried out by rightist guerrillas with the tacit support of the government. All the murdered professors were politically left-of-center.

The government of Gen. Romeo Lucas García, which came to power in 1978 elections, seemed powerless to stop the violence. When he took office, he promised a variety of social reforms and a return to civilian government, but the reforms were not enacted and civilian rule appeared a long way off. Vice-President Francisco Villagrán Kramer resigned on Sept. 1, protesting the government's "policy of violation of human rights." Villagrán had repeatedly protested what he termed the government's identification with right-wing terrorists.

To many observers, Guatemala seemed to be slipping toward civil war throughout 1980. The respected columnist Alvaro Contreras Véliz, writing in Guatemala City's *Prensa Libre*, asked: "Are we heading back toward another era like the 1960's?" Later he wrote: "We are at the abyss, looking down." Clearly, next to El Salvador, Guatemala was 1980's most volatile Central American country.

The political disintegration caught the United States by surprise. In May the U.S. rushed Deputy Assistant Secretary of State for Inter-American Affairs James R. Cheek to Guatemala City to confer with the government about rightist violence. Lucas refused to receive him. Washington recalled Ambassador Frank V. Ortiz in July, but failed to obtain Guatemalan approval for his replacement, George W. Landau, until recently ambassador to Chile and a reputed advocate of human rights. The result was a vacancy in the Guatemalan capital that left the U.S. unrepresented at a critical juncture. With the election of Ronald Reagan,

however, the government was hoping for a more sympathetic attitude from Washington.

*See* STATISTICS OF THE WORLD. J.N.G.

**GUINEA.** *See* STATISTICS OF THE WORLD.

**GUINEA-BISSAU.** *See* STATISTICS OF THE WORLD. *See also* AFRICA.

**GUYANA.** Prime Minister Forbes Burnham, in power since 1964, shed his office to become president on Oct. 6, 1980, as a new constitution went into effect. As president under the new constitution, Burnham had the power to appoint and dismiss the prime minister and vice-president, as well as to veto bills approved by the parliament. He also became the commander in chief of the army. Burnham appointed his longtime deputy, Ptolemy Reid, to be prime minister.

Parliamentary elections were scheduled for Jan. 26, 1981. Members of the Working People's Alliance (WPA) and the People's Progressive Party (PPP) threatened to boycott the elections. Both the WPA and the PPP, which was headed by former Prime Minister Cheddi B. Jagan, had charged the Burnham government with rigging a referendum on the proposed constitution in 1979.

On Dec. 17 Burnham was declared the winner of a presidential election in which he reportedly received 76 percent of the vote. According to the leader of a team of international observers, the election was "fraudulent in every possible respect."

On June 13 Walter Rodney, a 38-year-old historian who was a leader of the WPA, was killed when a bomb exploded in his car. The government claimed that Rodney had planned to plant the bomb at the prison where WPA members were being held on charges of plotting to overthrow the government. Members of the WPA, a small but active group of intellectuals and young people, said the bomb had been given to Rodney by an undercover government agent who told him it was a radio transmitter that needed to be tested.

Bad weather, rising oil prices, and sabotage of crops were blamed by the government in a Sept. 15 report on the economy that suggested 1980 would see no growth in the nation's economy.

*See* STATISTICS OF THE WORLD. J.N.G.

**H**

**HAITI.** *See* STATISTICS OF THE WORLD. *See also* CARIBBEAN COUNTRIES; UNITED STATES OF AMERICA.

186

**HAWAII.** *See* STATISTICS OF THE WORLD. *See also* STATE GOVERNMENT REVIEW.

# HEALTH AND MEDICINE

Among the major medical news stories in 1980 were some highly encouraging advances. A better rabies vaccine was developed, and tests indicated that a new vaccine might greatly reduce the occurrence of hepatitis. There was progress in the development of gene cloning techniques and in new methods of preventive care for children's teeth.

Headline events in the field of health and medicine in 1980 included an outbreak of a disease linked with the use of tampons, a controversial reassessment of the dangers of cholesterol, a report on confusing worldwide trends in heart disease, and an alarming rise in lung cancer among women. The medical profession also revised its code of ethics, permitting doctors to advertise their fees.

## MEDICINE

Of great concern in 1980 to the approximately 50,000,000 U.S. women who use tampons regularly was toxic shock syndrome, a recently identified disease linked predominantly with tampon use. The disease begins with a high fever, followed by severe vomiting and diarrhea, a rash on the palms and soles, and a rapid drop in blood pressure. Of the more than 650 cases of toxic shock syndrome that had been reported by the end of 1980, nearly 10 percent ended in death.

Epidemiological detective work by physicians at the Center for Disease Control, in Atlanta, quicky associated toxic shock syndrome with the use of superabsorbent tampons, which had appeared on the market back in 1976. (The syndrome itself was first recognized in 1978.) Since that time, 90 percent of the victims had been menstruating females, mainly under the age of 30. The other 10 percent had been nonmenstruating females and, rarely, children of both sexes.

Toxic shock syndrome appeared to be caused by a toxic agent produced by a bacterium, *Staphylococcus aureus*, which also causes other human diseases. Although there were some indications that the syndrome had been around for many years, its occurrence apparently was accelerated by the use of superabsorbent tampons, which can be worn longer and provide a breeding ground for the bacterium. One tampon brand, Procter & Gamble Co.'s Rely, was voluntarily withdrawn from the market in September, and all tampon manufacturers agreed to place a warning label henceforth that tells women to change tampons three or four times a day and to use sanitary napkins, rather than tampons, at night and when their periods are lightest. The manufacturers, however, did not judge the evidence certain enough to require a change in their products.

**Cholesterol and Diet.** Two conflicting sets of dietary recommendations in 1980 sparked controversy among experts. In February the Department of Health and Human Services, along with the Department of Agriculture, issued a report containing their long-standing advice that Americans should restrict their intake of cholesterol and saturated fats. In May, however, the Food and Nutrition Board of the National Research Council issued the statement that no good evidence exists linking reduced intake of these substances with a decreased risk of heart attacks.

As is usual in these controversies, the difference revolved around what constitutes good evidence. A link between higher rates of heart disease and high per capita consumption of cholesterol and saturated fats had been found by many international studies. On the other hand, people in scientific studies who had ingested reduced amounts of these substances had not shown a substantial reduction in death from heart disease. The 1980 controversy was further clouded by economic issues, because both the chairman of the Food and Nutrition Board and the board member who wrote the report admitted that they were consultants to commercial organizations that promote or sell food containing high levels of cholesterol or fats.

Robert Levy, director of the National Heart, Lung, and Blood Institute, recommended that Americans continue to seek a low-cholesterol diet until more evidence was available. His institute also announced results of a study linking reduced chances of heart attack with high levels of a certain protein in the blood. According to the report, high-density lipoprotein (HDL), which binds to and transports cholesterol in the blood, appears to help keep the substance from accumulating in deposits on artery walls. A high level of HDL in the blood may be in part hereditary but is

187

Supermarket meats commonly contain nitrites to keep them from spoiling before they reach the consumer. Research has shown that nitrites in quantity can cause cancer in animals, but opponents of a ban on nitrites in human food say that such an action would be a gross overreaction. In 1980 the Food and Drug Administration agreed, but it recommended a reduction in nitrite use.

also aided by exercise and even by moderate drinking. (Adverse effects of alcohol consumption, it should be added, easily outweigh any such benefit.) No clear linkage between diet and HDL levels was found by the study, but smoking and obesity were clearly shown to have adverse effects.

**Cancer Tests and Treatment.** Cancer screening tests came under attack in 1980 as the result of an evaluation sponsored by the American Cancer Society (ACS). The report stated that chest X rays and examinations of cells in sputum had not been shown to lengthen survival for persons found to have lung cancer, that a Pap test and examination for cervical cancer need not be conducted every year, and that an annual sigmoidoscopy and testing for blood in the stool did not improve detection of colon and rectal cancer. The report also concluded that an examination for breast cancer once every three years is as effective as an annual examination. Not all physicians concurred. The American College of Obstetrics and Gynecology, for example, still endorsed an annual Pap test.

According to a report from the National Institutes of Health, chemotherapy substantially prolonged the lives of premenopausal women whose tumors had spread beyond the breast itself. Its

recommendation that anticancer drugs be used following surgery for breast cancer in these cases would affect about one fourth of the 109,000 women found to have breast cancer each year. The panel also recommended further study of chemotherapy for breast-cancer patients who have reached menopause.

Controversy surrounded the use of tetrahydrocannabinol (THC)—the principal active ingredient in marijuana—to reduce nausea and vomiting among cancer patients receiving antitumor drugs. Because vomiting decreases the amount of drug that reaches a cancer, THC could make the difference between effective and ineffective therapy. Therefore the National Cancer Institute (NCI) approved the release of laboratory-made THC to cancer specialists in 1980, although some doctors disputed its value. But one detriment of the use of THC appeared to be that some older patients find the mild euphoria induced by the substance to be very upsetting.

Researchers at Johns Hopkins University developed a technique to help fight liver cancer. Such cancers produce large amounts of the protein ferritin. The researchers injected ferritin into rabbits, whose immune systems made antibodies to the protein. The antibodies were then extracted, dosed with radioactive iodine, and injected into cancer patients. The antibodies sought out the ferritin in the patients' liver cancers, and the radioactive iodine helped to reduce tumor growth. The technique was not a cure, but it did increase patient survival rates. It was thought that it might also prove useful in treating other ferritin-producing cancers such as lung cancer and multiple myeloma.

**Cancer Research.** Hopes that the protein interferon (one of the body's natural defenses against viral infections) might be a significant anticancer agent met with some disappointment in 1980. In a test conducted by the ACS, 50 patients with cancers of the bone marrow, breast, or lung received interferon. In no case was a tumor completely destroyed, and specialists judged the results inferior to those obtained by conventional treatments. Even so, the ACS committed another $3,400,000 to clinical trials of interferon, and the NCI budgeted $10,000,000 for similar research. In the meantime, scientists in Boston and in Switzerland announced that they had made interferon by gene cloning, injecting human interferon into bacteria that then produced more of the scarce protein; *see* LIFE SCIENCES. A company named Biogen funded the work and was to support its further development.

Three separate research papers in 1980 linked liver cancer with hepatitis B. The researchers found genetic material of the virus inserted into the chromosomes of liver cancer cells, strong evidence that the hepatitis virus can produce liver cancer. It was not yet, however, positive proof.

**Carcinogens.** Governmental restrictions on the use of known carcinogens in food and cosmetic products were not extended in 1980. As with the diet controversy, the question revolved around what constitutes adequate proof. Opponents of complete bans on such products as artificial sweeteners and nitrite preservatives contended that the extension of the results of animal tests to humans could be carried to meaningless extremes. At any rate, in August the Food and Drug Administration (FDA) and the Department of Agriculture decided not to ban the use of nitrites in food but simply to try to reduce that use. In November the FDA also held back from banning the use of lead acetate in cosmetics, deciding that the amount of the carcinogen involved in such products as hair darkeners was too minimal to be significant.

**Heart Disease and Treatment.** Heart disease remained a major killer, but reports in 1980 showed confusing trends in the United States and worldwide. A statistical report from the World Health Organization (WHO) in November indicated that

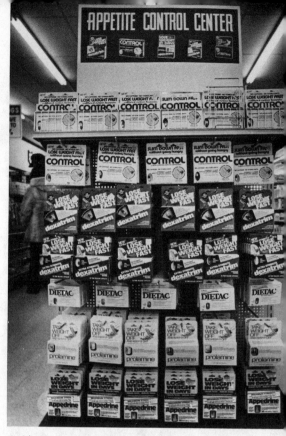

Amid 1980 controversies over proper dietary standards, the great American battle against obesity continued. Drugstores were clogged with nonprescription diet drugs whose appetite-suppressing, weight-loss claims the Food and Drug Administration must monitor. It must also check into their side effects and interactions with other drugs.

deaths from heart attack decreased notably in the U.S. and several other nations from 1966 to 1977, increased in central Europe and elsewhere, and did not change significantly in nations such as Canada. No clear pattern of environmental or other changes could be found in these figures. Some researchers saw a general trend toward a reduction of heart disease and other chronic diseases and toward a healthier, but perhaps not longer, old age.

In 1980 a revolutionary view of heart disease gained wide acceptance among specialists. For several decades, heart attacks were thought to be caused by fatty deposits in coronary arteries, even though some victims had little or no such blockage. In 1979 Italian cardiologists reported new studies on patients who had chest pains typical of heart disease but whose coronary arteries had minimal deposits. Direct viewing of the arteries in many of the patients revealed spontaneous contractions that could shut off blood flow to the

189

*Severe financial problems plagued U.S. inner-city hospitals in 1980 because those least able to pay for medical care have become increasingly dependent on such hospitals for emergency care. Here demonstrators protest plans by New York City to close Harlem's Sydenham Hospital.*

heart. These findings were confirmed in 1980 by other researchers, raising the possibility that such spasms could be a contributing factor to heart disease. Because calcium takes part in the natural processes that cause arterial muscles to contract, physicians began to seek to reduce arterial spasms by giving patients drugs to block the action of calcium. Two of them, nifedipine and verapamil, proved effective in early tests and may offer hope to persons with a heart disease that is not relieved by conventional drugs or surgery.

A drug called sulfinpyrazone (Anturane), available as a treatment for gout, was shown to prevent death from heart malfunction among persons who had recently survived a heart attack. The FDA was reviewing the study.

A small electronic device to help avert heart attacks was designed and tested by Michel Mirowski and colleagues at Johns Hopkins Univer-

sity. Attacks usually result from ventricular fibrillation, an extremely rapid but ineffective beating of the heart's ventricles. Mirowski's device, called an automatic implantable defibrillator, is placed in a patient's body. It senses when the heart begins to fibrillate and delivers up to four large electric shocks to restore normal heart function. In six patients tested, the device successfully reversed seven instances of cardiac arrest. It was expensive, however, and was intended for use only in patients not helped by drugs or surgery.

**Drugs and Vaccines.** Years of work on the development of nonaddictive pain relievers began to bear fruit in 1980. Two chemically modified forms of morphine, butorphanol tartrate (Stadol) and nalbuphine hydrochloride (Nubain), were approved for marketing. They were as effective as morphine but much less likely to induce mental changes such as hallucinations. Under consideration was a third chemical, zomepirac, which was expected to be just as unlikely to cause dependence.

In July makers of Valium, Librium, and other minor tranquilizers agreed to warn physicians that the drugs were not meant to relieve the stress of everyday life. Doctors were still free to prescribe such drugs as they wished. Legal sales of the drugs were found to be declining, however, along with sales of sedatives and painkillers such as Darvon.

The FDA held hearings on the possibility that a morning-sickness drug, Bendectin, might be a low-level cause of birth defects. Thus far studies had not proved a causal connection but had not been sufficient to clear the drug entirely. Research studies associated oral contraceptive use with adverse metabolic effects such as higher blood pressure and higher insulin level. These effects were found to be reversible, however, when use of the oral contraceptives was discontinued.

An old-fashioned general "remedy," sweet spirits of nitre (ethyl nitrite), was banned by the FDA not only because of its unproved effectiveness but also because of its possible fatal effect on children. A caution on aspirin use by children suffering from viral illnesses was also issued in 1980 because studies had implied a relationship between such use and the development of the rare Reye's syndrome, a disease that is sometimes fatal.

Large-scale tests showed that a new vaccine could greatly reduce the occurrence of hepatitis. If the vaccine proved equally effective in two ongoing tests, it might be licensed by 1982. In 1980 a safer, more effective, and less painful rabies vaccine that can also be taken preventively made its appearance as well. Produced from viruses in human cell cultures (present vaccines are derived from duck eggs), the vaccine can be injected into the arm instead of the stomach.

**Smoking and Health.** A 1980 report from the U.S. surgeon general helped to demolish the idea that women are less subject to lung cancer from smoking than are men. The report indicated that lung cancer among women was increasing rapidly and could surpass breast cancer as a killer in three years. It also stated that pregnant women who

*A carpenter nails down the first planks of a nature trail for the handicapped at the Fire Island National Seashore, N.Y. The trail, completed in 1980, was the first such facility for the handicapped anywhere in the National Park System.*

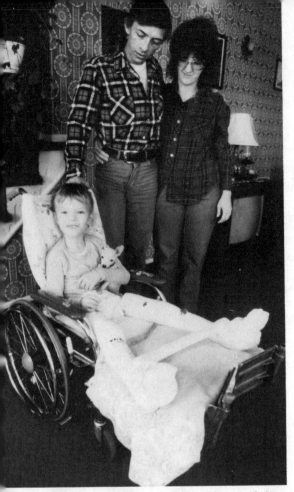

Paul Schmoyer and his wife Rose stand next to their son Brian, who Schmoyer says is a victim of Agent Orange. Schmoyer was subjected to the potent herbicide during his service in Vietnam. He and other veterans have filed damage suits against the chemical companies that produced Agent Orange. A 1980 federal study indicated no significant effect on the health of offspring of male mice fed the components of the herbicide.

smoke run an increased risk of problems in pregnancy and childbirth. The Tobacco Institute disputed the report and called its findings simplistic.

According to a National Institute of Education survey, the 1968–74 rise in teenage cigarette smoking appeared to have come to a halt, along with marijuana smoking. This good news was countered by bad news from researchers at the University of California at San Diego, who found evidence that nonsmokers can suffer lung damage from regular proximity to smokers. The respiratory impairments that showed up were small but significant, comparable to those suffered by light smokers.

**Gene Cloning.** A research team in London reported in September that no ill effects had been found in 17 human volunteers who had received insulin made by bacteria into which the human insulin gene had been inserted. Another recombinant DNA technique was reported by a group of University of California at Los Angeles scientists led by Martin Cline. The group introduced a new gene into the blood cells of mice and obtained evidence that the altered genes were functioning properly. Later it was learned that Cline had used the same approach in an attempt to correct a blood disease in two young women, one in Italy and one in Israel. The women had a serious condition called beta thalassemia major, in which hemoglobin undergoes alterations, and Cline tried to introduce genes for normal hemoglobin into the women. Results were still pending.

**Medical Ethics.** To the surprise of many observers, the American Medical Association (AMA) moved quickly, at its annual meeting in July in Chicago, to scrap its old code of medical ethics and adopt a shorter, looser one. The new code permitted doctors to advertise their fees and to refer patients to chiropractors, proclaimed that physicians should not take part in prisoner executions, and placed greater emphasis on patient rights.

An excess of physicians in the U.S. by 1990 was predicted by the Congressional Office of Technology Assessment and the General Medical Education National Advisory Council. Both groups agreed that physicians would by then be concentrated in subspecialties rather than in family medicine and in cities rather than small towns. The groups urged immediate steps to reduce the number of physicians in training and to stimulate redistribution.

Severe financial problems continued to plague inner-city hospitals in 1980. The difficulty was that the segments of the population least able to pay for medical care had come largely to depend upon emergency-care treatment in inner-city hospitals, placing a great financial burden on them. Another troublesome aspect of the problem was that such hospitals traditionally have been a leading training ground for interns. W.A.C.

## MENTAL HEALTH

Mental health experts in 1980 were surprised by the results of a seven-year WHO study that covered nine countries and focused on schizophrenia. Although the symptoms of schizophrenia are the same worldwide, the WHO found that recovery rates varied dramatically from country to country. In industrialized countries such as the U.S., recovery rates were low. Almost half of all those who experienced psychotic breakdowns never recovered. In developing nations, however, recovery rates were high. In Nigeria, for example, 51 percent of the mental patients recovered after a single psychotic episode, and in India 58 percent recovered after a single episode.

Although these facts need to be analyzed and interpreted before trying to draw lessons from them, certain differences in treatment between developing and industrialized nations were clear. In developing nations, mental illness tends to be blamed on external forces rather than on parents, biochemical malfunctions, or internal feelings and pressures. And instead of institutionalizing or isolating patients, villagers and faith healers are called in, along with family members, to provide a network of support and sympathy.

**Neuroleptics.** For the treatment of schizophrenia in industrialized nations, many U.S. psychiatrists still considered the drugs called neuroleptics, introduced into the U.S. in 1954, the most important advance in such treatment. Neuroleptics can calm and control psychotic patients, making further

treatment possible and enabling many to be treated on an outpatient basis.

Neuroleptics, of course, cannot cure schizophrenia. They merely relieve some of the symptoms. They do more, however, than simply sedate the patient. Research on schizophrenia has revealed that the mechanism by which neuroleptics relieve symptoms is actually very specific. It is known that a sudden burst of the chemical messenger dopamine precipitates psychotic episodes. Neuroleptics act by attaching themselves to cell membranes in the brain and blocking off dopamine receptors.

That same blockade of dopamine receptors, however, can lead to a very serious hyperkinetic disease known as tardive dyskinesia. Furthermore, the exact relationships between period of use, dosage, and tardive dyskinesia have yet to be determined. Thus tardive dyskinesia was seen as an-

*Behavioral medicine, a growing field, uses conditioning techniques such as biofeedback to treat stress-related illness. Here volunteers are trained in the use of biofeedback to avoid motion sickness.*

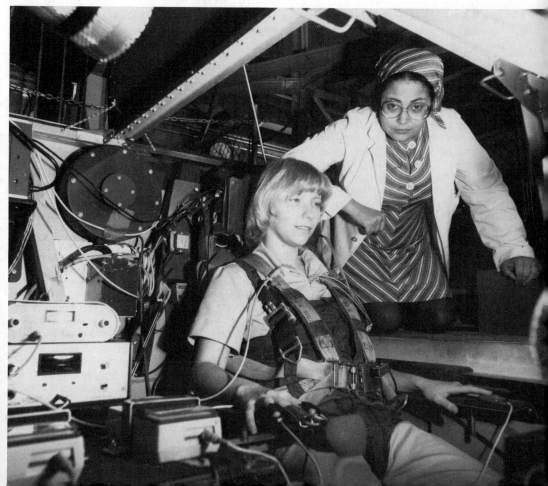

other in the list of serious and sometimes permanent side effects from neuroleptics, including blurred vision, fainting, and muscle spasms.

This led to a problem. Because there are not enough psychiatrists to care for the estimated 5,000,000 chronically ill mental patients in the U.S., general practitioners are routinely asked to treat and prescribe drugs for patients with emotional problems and complaints. General practitioners, however, may be uninformed concerning the dangers involved in prescribing neuroleptics. The AMA, well aware of the problem, planned to sponsor its first symposium on the treatment of chronically ill mental patients in January, 1981.

**Psychiatrists and Bias.** Researchers Charles Ford and Robert Sbordone of the University of California have estimated that psychiatrists give the elderly only 2 to 4 percent of their professional time, even though older people represent 10 percent of the total patient population. To Ford and Sbordone it appeared that psychiatrists share in certain widespread negative attitudes toward the elderly. Results in 1980 of a survey aimed at psychiatrists tended to confirm their opinion. The survey questionnaire described four cases of mental illness and asked psychiatrists to give their prognosis for each one. In the 179 questionnaires that were completed and returned, the prognosis varied according to whether the psychiatrists were told that a hypothetical patient was young or old. In general, young patients received much more favorable ratings.

"Older patients," Ford and Sbordone concluded, "are regarded as less ideal because they are viewed as having a poorer prognosis. Why psychiatrists should regard younger patients as having a better prognosis than older patients is unclear." It was hoped, however, that as psychiatrists working in general hospitals became increasingly involved with the problems of the elderly, these biases would disappear.

Another aspect of this problem was explored by researchers Joseph A. Flaherty and Robert Meagher of the University of Illinois. In a study of 66 black and 36 white male schizophrenic inpatients, they found evidence of continuing racial bias among psychiatrists. According to Flaherty and Meagher, black patients were given more antipsychotic drugs, fewer privileges, less recreational and occupational therapy, and more time in seclusion or under restraints. Black inpatients spent almost eight out of every ten hospital days in seclusion or restraints, whereas white inpatients spent less than five such days. Black patients also spent far less time in the hospital and were inclined to leave although advised they should not.                                               J.O.

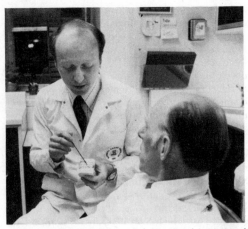

*Using a model, a member of the National Institute of Dental Research shows how a fluoride-holding capsule can be attached to a tooth to help prevent decay. The capsule, which was tested in 1980, releases fluoride through a plastic membrane for as long as six months.*

## DENTISTRY

In 1980 the National Institute of Dental Research continued testing a new method of coating children's teeth with fluoride. The treatment consists of attaching a fluoride-containing capsule to one of the child's molars. The device, developed by researchers at the Southern Research Institute in Birmingham, Ala., slowly releases fluoride over a period of months, gradually depositing a protective coating on the child's teeth. Fluoride coating of teeth decreases cavities in children by at least 50 percent and reduces loss of permanent molars to an even greater extent. For people in areas with nonfluoridated water who want fluoride protection for their children's teeth, the new device provides a less expensive alternative to application of the substance to each tooth individually.

A team of bioengineers at the University of Washington in Seattle developed a specially designed dental chair for people with cerebral palsy. Because the uncontrolled head movements found in many persons with this disease make close dental work nearly impossible, cerebral palsy victims are prone to tooth and gum disease. The problem is especially serious in children. In the mechanism, designed by Fredric Harris and colleagues, movements of the patient's head are detected by a set of pressure-sensitive instruments. These signals activate hydraulic motors that apply gentle pressure to keep the patient's head in a fixed position. The chair was still under development in 1980 but had already been successfully used many times.                                      W.A.C.

**HONDURAS.** The Central American country of Honduras inched toward civilian rule in 1980 after eight years of military government. Elections for a 71-seat Constituent Assembly were held on April 20, with the Liberal Party winning a 7-seat majority over the expected winner, the National Party, which had links with the military. The Liberal Party victory propelled its leader, Roberto Suazo Córdova, a 53-year-old country doctor, into national prominence.

Then, in July, the assembly met to name an interim president—and the incumbent, Gen. Policarpo Paz García, was tapped to fill the role pending the election of a civilian president in 1981. On Aug. 15 he named a new 16-member cabinet with only one military official: Col. César Elvir Sierra, the foreign minister. The government raised minimum wages in 1980 and sought to avoid unrest by beginning a land redistribution program.

Honduran leftists seized 13 persons in the offices of the Organization of American States (OAS) in Tegucigalpa, the Honduran capital, on Aug. 15, demanding a halt to alleged collaboration between Paz García's government and the joint military-civilian junta in El Salvador. Under an amnesty, they left the OAS site two days later. On Oct. 17 it was announced that under the auspices of the OAS, Honduras and El Salvador had settled a long-standing border dispute and had agreed to restore diplomatic relations.

*See* Statistics of the World.    J.N.G.

**HOUSING.** New U.S. housing starts declined sharply in 1980 to about 1,300,000, or approximately 28 percent lower than during 1979. High mortgage rates, inflation, and the recession were all blamed. Housing starts and sales picked up in midyear as mortgage rates declined temporarily, but in late summer and fall interest rates again moved into the 12.5 to 13 percent range, causing another dip in activity. Edwin B. Brooks, Jr., president of the U.S. League of Savings Associations, cited difficulty in obtaining mortgage money as an additional problem in the housing field.

**Single-Family Housing.** Single-family home sales were down about 14 percent from 1979, and the volume of building new single-family units dropped about 28 percent nationwide. Construction starts were strongest in the South, where new one-family homes valued at about $15 billion were built and sold.

**Multifamily Housing.** Housing structures for more than one family took on a new direction. Many owners of apartment buildings located in large cities sought state government permission to turn their buildings into cooperatives. The apartment stock in Manhattan (New York City), for example, was expected to be as much as 90 percent con-

verted by 1985, according to a government survey that was released at midyear. About 80 percent of the owners who sought to convert Manhattan rental buildings into cooperatives were successful.

This trend toward cooperatives, combined with high finance costs, constricted the rental housing market in many urban areas. The outlook for rental apartments improved, however, with a proposed $40.5 billion governmental subsidy plan to build 40,000 rental units for low- and middle-income families. Approval by the U.S. House of Representatives was the first step in an overall plan to provide 352,000 new housing units, but it was rejected by the Senate.

Another attempt to furnish low-cost housing during the year came from congressional outlays channeled through the General National Mortgage Association to local community agencies. A $250,000,000 expenditure was used for 7600 new and rehabilitated housing units.

**Financing Availability.** Even for those willing to pay high mortgage rates, money was sometimes not available. Savings and loan associations acquired increased deposits early in the year, following President Jimmy Carter's call for tighter credit measures. Those early deposits were primarily six-month certificates of deposit offering high yields. Once interest rates began to fall, the savings and loan institutions lost many of these deposits to other investments paying higher returns. By June, withdrawals began to exceed deposits, constricting the supply of money available for home mortgages and sharply curbing sales of both new and existing housing units.

In April the Federal Home Loan Bank Board approved the offering of renegotiated-rate mortgages by federally chartered savings and loans. The interest on these mortgages could be raised or lowered every three to five years to reflect prevailing money availability.

**Housing Worldwide.** Although housing costs were high in the United States in 1980, they were about 156 percent higher in the Middle East, according to a worldwide study of home building costs. This difference could be attributed to higher-priced construction materials that had to be imported into the Middle Eastern countries. Paris had the lowest urban housing construction costs in 1980, about 10 percent lower than those for similar housing units built in the U.S.

Throughout the world, steel-framed multifamily dwellings were generally less costly to build than those with concrete frames. This situation was partly a result of shortages in cement.

**Energy Laws.** Federal energy legislation was passed that could further cut housing starts. The

laws were protested by contractors and home buyers alike, although homeowners would eventually recover the additional construction costs through increased energy efficiency. Regulations limited the amount of energy that could be consumed by a new building. Housing construction costs were expected to increase by as much as $1 per square foot if the laws were not modified before taking effect.

**Housing Plans.** Housing construction was expected to pick up by mid-1981. New housing bidding volume, an index of activity among contractors seeking work, showed an increase of 14 percent in 1980 and led the way in planning by firms connected with the industry. A survey by the economists at the brokerage firm of Goldman, Sachs, however, indicated that only about 45 percent of those statistically most likely to be purchasing their first home could afford prevailing mortgage costs. In 1971 the figure stood at 83.5 percent; by 1975 it had dropped to 79.8 percent. The resolution of this discrepancy would depend on the future trends of interest rates, government funding for middle-class as well as low-income families, and the industry's ability to find new construction methods that would lower building and financing costs. R.W.S.

*Despite a generally depressed real estate market, the conversion of existing buildings into condominiums or cooperatives continued unabated in 1980. Many of the conversions were taking place in or near the heart of major cities, where older housing stock was being renovated for the "urban gentry," upper- or upper-middle-class professionals choosing a city residence rather than a suburban one. The two town houses in the photograph were carved out of an old mansion on Chicago's near north side.*

*Architect Frank Gehry won a 1980 American Institute of Architects award for his design to remodel his Santa Monica, Calif., home. The design was intended to interact sculpturally with the existing wooden structure. Shown below is the new kitchen area.*

**HUNGARY.** The Hungarian government, led by Communist Party First Secretary János Kádár, 68, showed considerable flexibility in dealing with the nation's economic shortcomings in 1980. Its policies reflected Kádár's conviction that "we cannot be independent of world trends"—an allusion to slow growth worldwide and increased oil prices.

Kádár made his declaration at the 12th Communist Party Congress, March 24–28. During that gathering, party leaders openly acknowledged economic problems, including a lower-than-planned growth rate, a large trade deficit, and inflation. They announced that growth targets for the 1981–85 economic plan would be scaled down, as would government subsidies for industrial and consumer goods.

To carry these measures through, the top party leadership was reshuffled during the congress. Five of 15 Politburo members and 2 party secretaries were removed, and membership in the Politburo was reduced from 15 to 13. Following parliamentary elections in June, in which only 15 of 352 seats were contested, the cabinet was also reorganized. Western analysts believed the moves marked a victory for advocates of a cautious economic reform policy.

Kádár devoted keen attention to the widespread workers' strikes that broke out in nearby Poland during the summer. On the whole, his re-

gime enjoyed a better relationship with the work force than did the Polish regime. To head off any Hungarian pressure for the kind of independent trade unions Polish workers demanded, Kádár took steps in September to give greater autonomy to existing, Communist-led trade unions.

The Hungarian government continued to follow closely the Soviet foreign policy line. At the party congress, officials attacked China and backed the Soviet invasion of Afghanistan. They refrained from any direct verbal attack on the United States, however. Western diplomats interpreted this to mean that Budapest wanted to maintain the relatively friendly bilateral ties that had developed with Washington in recent years.

*See* STATISTICS OF THE WORLD.                      F.W.

# I

**ICELAND.** The Icelandic economy continued to struggle under the heavy burden of inflation during 1980. Another economic problem was settled, however, by agreement with Norway over fishing rights around a small Arctic island. Early in the year a new government was sworn in after months of political uncertainty.

The government crisis was resolved by compromise when Gunnar Thoroddsen succeeded in forming a coalition. A majority of his right-of-center Independence Party, however, refused to support his new cabinet, which was installed on Feb. 8 with a slim majority of the Althing's (parliament's) 60 votes. Thoroddsen's coalition partners were the centrist Progressive Party and the leftwing People's Alliance, which opposed Iceland's membership in the North Atlantic Treaty Organization (NATO). Iceland had been ruled by a minority caretaker government since the overthrow of the Olafur Jóhannesson coalition cabinet in October, 1979. After the inconclusive election of December, 1979, it took two months for a new cabinet to win acceptance from the Althing.

Vigdis Finnbogadóttir was elected on June 30 to the largely ceremonial post of president of Iceland. A leftist and an opponent of Iceland's membership in NATO, she was the first woman to win the post. She defeated three men in the polling.

The bitter fishing dispute with Norway was settled on May 10 with concessions by Norway. The dispute involved economic rights in the neighborhood of volcanic Jan Mayen Island, a Norwegian possession. The Arctic island, in whose vicinity Icelanders traditionally fish, is 360 mi. northeast of Iceland. A Norwegian decision in 1979 to impose a 200-mi. economic zone around the island meant that the economic zones around Iceland and Jan Mayen Island overlapped. In mid-1979 Iceland had sent out a coast guard vessel to keep Norwegian fishermen out of the disputed area. The agreement of May 10 gave Iceland full control of the area of overlap, and Norway accepted for its fishermen only 15 percent of the total permissible catch of capelin, the area's main fish resource. In response to criticism by Norwegian fishermen, the Norwegian government said it had made these concessions because of the Icelandic economy's great dependence on fishing and because it wanted to continue good relations with a country maintaining one of the important NATO bases.

*See* STATISTICS OF THE WORLD.                      L.A.S.

**IDAHO.** *See* STATISTICS OF THE WORLD.

**ILLINOIS.** *See* STATISTICS OF THE WORLD.

**INDIA.** For India, 1980 unquestionably was the year of Indira Gandhi. It also was a year of considerable turmoil in the country at large.

**Politics.** In the general elections held Jan. 3 and 6, Gandhi and her Indian National Congress (I), or Congress-I Party ("I" for Indira), which was crushed at the polls in 1977, soundly trounced her badly divided opponents. It was, said Indian commentators, less an endorsement of Gandhi's authoritarian tendencies than a rebuke to the factionalism and ineptitude that characterized two years of rule by the Janata Party coalition under Morarji Desai and Charan Singh. The vote gave Gandhi an overwhelming 350 of the 542 seats in the House of the People, the lower house of parliament. Janata won only 32 seats.

In the months that followed, the defeated Janata Party all but disintegrated, while Prime Minister Gandhi consolidated her power. In February she dissolved nine state assemblies controlled by opposition parties on the ground that they no longer represented the will of the people. (The Janata Party had done the same to her state-level officeholders three years earlier.) Gandhi ordered new state elections, and in the voting in late May, her supporters gained control of eight out of the nine contested states.

As she tightened her grip on power, Gandhi and her controversial 33-year-old son Sanjay were cleared by the courts of charges leveled against

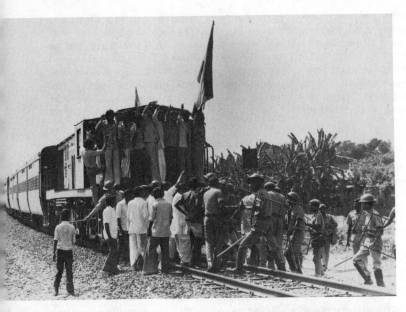

Strikes and demonstrations in Assam during 1980 halted a significant supply of petroleum to the rest of India. Here angry demonstrators seek to block an Assam-bound train in April as part of their threatened retaliatory economic blockade against the state.

Indira Gandhi (left) receives congratulations after elections returned her to power with an overwhelming parliamentary majority. She was sworn in for another term as prime minister of India on Jan. 14.

them by the Janata government. Sanjay, who won a seat in parliament in the January sweep, controlled a sizable bloc in parliament and was considered the heir apparent to the prime ministership. On June 23, however, he died in a plane crash.

**Law and Order.** The strategic northeast region was the scene of violent ethnic unrest. In the key oil-producing state of Assam, students, furious at the continuing influx of Bengalis (most of them Hindus who had left Muslim Bangladesh), demanded their expulsion. With strikes and demonstrations, the students (backed by most native Assamese) closed down government offices, disrupted transportation, and, most importantly, halted the flow of petroleum to the rest of India.

The Gandhi government called out the army in April to disperse the pickets and arrest the student leaders, but when hundreds of thousands of Assamese took to the streets in support of the students, it released most of the prisoners and sent the soldiers back to the barracks. Strikes and picketing resumed. Assam's oil tap remained turned off until November, when troops arrested the pickets and turned on the pumps. An estimated $900,000,000 in oil production had been lost.

The trouble in Assam spilled over into other areas, including Mizoram, Nagaland, and Meghalaya. In Tripura the ethnic turmoil took its ugliest turn in early June when tribesmen descended on a Bengali village and massacred at least 350 people.

Dreaded sectarian riots also erupted during the summer. On Aug. 13, Muslims rioted in Moradabad, Uttar Pradesh, after a report that pigs, considered "unclean," had entered a Muslim prayer area. The Muslims clashed with police, and then with Hindus in other parts of the country. More than 140 were killed in Uttar Pradesh alone.

**Detention Law.** Faced with appalling violence, Gandhi's government in late September announced an ordinance that would permit the government to jail anyone for a year without trial. Opposition leaders, recalling that Gandhi imprisoned more than 150,000 people for political reasons during her emergency rule of 1975–77, feared that the new law would be used against them and not against lawbreakers.

**Satellites and A-Bombs.** On July 18, India became the seventh nation to launch an earth satellite when it blasted off an Indian-built, four-stage rocket from a range north of Madras. The successful launch meant that India had the means to send up spy satellites and develop intermediate-range ballistic missiles able to deliver nuclear warheads. Moreover, Gandhi made it clear that she would not hesitate to authorize additional nuclear blasts. (India exploded its first nuclear device in 1974.)

**The Economy.** India continued to be more than self-sufficient in food, but industrial growth fell sharply and exports declined in an economic slide that caused the government to reduce taxes and introduce new incentives for the private sector. In July the government announced that it would allow private enterprise to play a larger role in the economy.

**Foreign Affairs.** As in the past, Gandhi maintained close ties with the Soviet Union. India refused to condemn the Soviet intervention in Afghanistan publicly (though it did complain to Moscow privately), and in July it became the only country outside of the Soviet bloc to recognize the Soviet-backed, Vietnam-installed government of Heng

Samrin in Cambodia. Soviet President Leonid Brezhnev visited India in December; new Soviet-Indian technological and trade agreements were announced.

India had been moving toward better relations with Pakistan, but the Soviet invasion of Afghanistan drove another wedge between the two countries. Pakistan, uneasy at having Soviet troops on its border, sought military aid from the United States and elsewhere. India strenuously opposed such aid but at the same time concluded a new $1.6 billion arms purchase deal of its own with the Soviet Union in May.

India and the U.S. had a row over uranium shipments. In 1963 the U.S. reached agreement with India to supply its Tarapur atomic power station with fuel until 1993. But in 1978 the U.S. Congress passed the Nuclear Nonproliferation Act prohibiting the shipment of such fuels unless the recipient country accepted internationally supervised safeguards that would prevent the fuel from being used to make nuclear weapons. India refused to accept such safeguards. In June, nevertheless, President Jimmy Carter authorized a 38-ton shipment of uranium. A majority vote in both houses would have blocked the shipment, and indeed the House of Representatives did vote to do so. The Senate, however, declined to reject the sale by a narrow margin, and shipments of uranium were resumed.

*See* STATISTICS OF THE WORLD. R.J.C.

**INDIANA.** *See* STATISTICS OF THE WORLD.

**INDIANS, AMERICAN.** In 1980 the Sioux Indians won a ruling in their favor, and the Passamaquoddy and Penobscot tribes of Maine settled their claim to two thirds of the state. Northwest Indians won the first round of a fishing rights case, the Crow and Northern Cheyenne landed huge energy development contracts for their reservations, and ten Arizona tribes received controversially large allocations of Central Arizona Project water from Interior Secretary Cecil D. Andrus.

**Black Hills Decision.** In June the U.S. Supreme Court ruled in favor of a claim by eight Sioux Indian tribes, ending 58 years of litigation and granting them $122,500,000 as compensation for the 1877 seizure of 7,000,000 acres of land in the Black Hills of South Dakota. It was the largest sum ever granted for Indian land. But the Oglala Sioux announced that the ruling did not settle their claim, and they filed suit for $11 billion in damages and the return of the land. Many Sioux individuals and some tribal leaders considered the ruling unacceptable and proposed that the tribes reject the money if acceptance extinguished claims to the land itself. (The Sioux lost the Black Hills, which includes Mt. Rushmore, after gold prospectors invaded the area, provoking an Indian reaction culminating in Lt. Col. George A. Custer's massacre at Little Bighorn. Congress then revoked the treaty rights extended to the Sioux only nine years earlier.)

**Eastern Land Claims.** Using an eagle feather pen, President Jimmy Carter on Oct. 10 signed a bill awarding the Passamaquoddy and Penobscot Indians of Maine a $27,000,000 trust fund and a $54,500,000 fund for the purchase of 300,000 acres of timberland. The Indians, on their part, relinquished all claims to their aboriginal territory of some 12,500,000 acres, or about two thirds of the state. The Maine Indians' claim, which had become the precedent for more than a dozen other eastern Indian land claims, was based on the violation of a little-known law, passed in 1790, requiring all sales and cessions of Indian land to be approved by Congress. The law was frequently disregarded in the East in early land transfers between Indian tribes and the states.

An effort to settle a similar claim by the Cayuga tribe of New York was rejected by the House of Representatives in March; the proposed settlement would have given the tribe about 3600 acres of federal forestland, an 1800-acre state park, and an $8,000,000 trust fund. The tribe subsequently said it would sue for the return of its claimed 64,000 acres, in addition to damages. Some of the other larger claims included those of the Oneida, who claimed 5,750,000 acres in New York; the Catawba, who claimed 140,000 acres in South Carolina; and the St. Regis Mohawk, who sought 14,000 acres in New York.

**Fishing Rights.** A federal judge in San Francisco ruled on Sept. 29 that treaty Indians of western Washington had a guaranteed right to the protection of the environment surrounding the waters in which they fished. The decision by Judge William Orrick, Jr., ended the first round of phase two of the long-running fishing rights controversy. In phase one, Judge George Boldt ruled that the Indians were entitled to half the harvest of salmon and steelhead returning to waters in the treaty area. Judge Orrick's decision, according to Washington State Fisheries Director Gordon Sandison, meant that the state and federal governments must be responsible for environmental conditions that could harm fish. The decision was expected to have an impact on logging, housing, nuclear power plants, dams, and any other development that would affect the waters and the fish.

**Energy Resource Developments.** The Council of Energy Resources Tribes (CERT), composed of 26 tribes rich in coal, oil, gas, and uranium resources, met in Washington, D.C., in September. The CERT tribes owned about one third of the low-sulfur exploitable coal deposits west of the Mississippi River, one half of the uranium on lands held in private ownership, and large reserves of oil and gas. U.S. Energy Secretary Charles W. Duncan, Jr., said, in his talk to the group, that the CERT tribes were now producing from their lands more than 1,000,000 bbl of oil each day—about 12 percent of the total imported daily from members of the Organization of Petroleum Exporting Countries.

In April the Crow tribe of Montana sold the Shell Oil Co. the rights to mine 210,000,000 tons of

---

### Lily of the Mohawks

On June 22 several hundred Indians from the United States and Canada, in full tribal regalia, knelt before Pope John Paul II in Rome's Saint Peter's Basilica. The occasion? The beatification of five candidates for sainthood, including Kateri Tekakwitha, the first American Indian—and the first American layperson—to be thus honored. "The Lily of the Mohawks," as she is known, converted to Christianity during the 17th century. Although stoned and persecuted by her tribe, she became the central figure in a cult that grew in upstate New York after her death at the age of 24. In 1884 her canonization was proposed; the examination of her cause did not begin until 1932. In 1943 she was declared "venerable" by Pope Pius XII. And 37 years later the Roman Catholic Church took the final step before granting full sainthood.

*Kateri Tekakwitha.*

*This 1868 picture shows the signing of a treaty between the U.S. and the Sioux nation, setting aside a reservation for the Sioux in South Dakota. But gold was soon discovered, the area was invaded by prospectors, and Congress abrogated the treaty in 1877. On June 30 the Supreme Court ruled that the Sioux were entitled to $122,500,000 as compensation.*

coal on 2560 acres of reservation land. The 6000-member tribe received a $6,200,000 signing bonus and was to start receiving a guaranteed income in 1986 of $3,000,000 a year, increasing in steps to $6,000,000 annually by 1994. A neighboring tribe, the Northern Cheyenne, approved in September an oil and gas exploration agreement with the Atlantic Richfield Co. This agreement also had a $6,000,000 signing bonus, with a 25 percent royalty on all oil and gas produced.

The Jicarilla Apache tribe of New Mexico in June became the first Indian tribe to acquire 100 percent ownership of producing oil and natural gas wells on its land. The tribe bought out a joint venture partner, the Palmer Oil and Gas Co.

Pueblo Indians were fighting in 1980 the proposed development of a $125,000,000 geothermal power plant in the Jemez Mts. of New Mexico. The Indians asserted that the plant would infringe on their religious rights because the Jemez range is sacred to them.                                          V.L.

**INDONESIA.** In 1980 Indonesia's President Suharto remained firmly in control of the world's fifth most populous nation. But discontent with his rule became more widespread and more vocal.

**Politics.** On Feb. 11 truckloads of students from schools all over Indonesia descended on the Indonesian parliament, where they demonstrated in support of members backing strong student councils instead of weak, faculty-dominated groups favored by the government. An antigovernment motion on the issue was defeated 279 to 101, but the rare vote served notice that the normally docile body no longer regarded itself as merely a rubber stamp for Suharto's policies.

A more important protest came on May 13, when a "Group of 50," including some of the country's most respected elder statesmen and retired soldiers, presented a petition to the parliament. In it, they accused the president of improperly expanding his powers and using the army for his own political ends. Angry at the direct challenge, the government imposed a news blackout on the petition and accused unnamed opponents of plotting to overthrow Suharto and assassinate him, an allegation that few Indonesians took seriously.

East Timor, which Indonesia invaded and annexed in 1975, remained ravaged by war and threatened by starvation and disease as small groups of armed guerrillas continued to resist the occupation. The United Nations annually called for Indonesia's withdrawal from this former Portuguese colony.

**The Economy.** As the largest exporter of crude oil in the Far East, Indonesia was enabled by rising oil prices to finance a strongly expansionary budget for the fiscal year beginning on April 1. Some of its growing treasury of petroleum dollars was channeled into agriculture, education, health, housing, and public works. A healthy economic growth of 7.5 percent was forecast for the year.

**Foreign Affairs.** Acting jointly with the four other members of the Association of Southeast Asian Nations (Thailand, Malaysia, Singapore, and the Philippines), staunchly anti-Communist Indonesia condemned the Soviet invasion of Afghanistan and the Vietnamese occupation of Cambodia. In June Vietnamese Foreign Minister Nguyen Co Thach visited Djakarta, but his talks with Indonesian officials failed to resolve their differences over Cambodia or any other issue. During 1980 Indonesia and China, after a freeze in relations following Peking's alleged role in the Communist coup attempt of 1965, moved cautiously in the direction of friendlier ties.

*See* STATISTICS OF THE WORLD.                                    R.J.C.

**INTERNATIONAL CONFERENCES.** Many important international conferences were held in 1980. Some of them can be found under the following entries: AFRICA; ARAB LEAGUE; BANKING AND FINANCE; COMMONWEALTH OF NATIONS; COMMUNISM; ECONOMY AND BUSINESS; EUROPEAN COMMUNITIES; MIDDLE EAST; NORTH ATLANTIC TREATY ORGANIZATION; ORGANIZATION OF AMERICAN STATES; ORGANIZATION OF PETROLEUM EXPORTING COUNTRIES; UNITED NATIONS. See also articles on individual countries.

**Conference of Islamic States.** In January, 36 foreign ministers of countries representing 500,000,-000 Muslims met in Islamabad, Pakistan, and vigorously condemned "Soviet military aggression against the Afghan people." They demanded the "immediate and unconditional withdrawal of all Soviet troops." It was the strongest criticism ever leveled at Moscow by a nonaligned group. The Islamic foreign ministers met in Islamabad again in May and reaffirmed their earlier resolution. In September they met again in Fez, Morocco, and agreed on a holy war against Israel for annexing East Jerusalem. During the year the conference also criticized Iran's holding of American hostages, condemned the abortive American attempt to rescue them, and sponsored an unsuccessful peace mission to Iran and Iraq.

**European Security Conference.** After months of procedural haggling, the representatives of the United States, Canada, and all European countries except Albania met in Madrid in November. Called to review compliance with the 1975 Helsinki accord on East-West security problems and human rights, the conference got off to an uncertain start as Western delegates sharply rebuked the Soviet Union for its intervention in Afghanistan and its record on human rights.

**Nuclear Arms Talks.** In October a new round of talks opened in Geneva between the U.S. and U.S.S.R., aimed at curbing the deployment of medium-range nuclear missiles and bombers in Europe. As in previous talks on limiting strategic nuclear weapons, the issues were complex. It was believed the talks would last for many months, perhaps for years.

**ASEAN Conferences.** During 1980 the foreign ministers of the Association of Southeast Asian Nations (ASEAN) conferred periodically. The five members of ASEAN—Indonesia, Malaysia, the Philippines, Singapore, and Thailand—took strong exception to the Soviet intervention in Afghanistan and Vietnam's continued occupation of Cambodia. In an unusual meeting in March, the ASEAN ministers met in Kuala Lumpur, Malaysia, with their counterparts from Western Europe.

**Socialist International Congress.** The democratic socialist parties of the world convened in Madrid in November. In a bleak final resolution, they portrayed the world of the 1980's as one characterized by an accelerated arms race, a widening gap between rich nations and poor, and increasing violations of human rights.                                    R.J.C.

**IOWA.** *See* STATISTICS OF THE WORLD.

**IRAN.** Militant Muslim clerics consolidated their hold on Iran, as the country experienced almost constant tumult during 1980. Americans taken hostage at the U.S. embassy in late 1979 remained imprisoned. War with Iraq broke out in September, with Iran getting the worst of it but defiantly determined to reject Iraq's demands and keep fighting.

**Struggle for Power.** Abolhassan Bani-Sadr (see biography at PEOPLE IN THE NEWS) was elected president of Iran on Jan. 25 by a landslide margin, receiving 10,709,330 votes, or 75.7 percent of the total. Since the ballot was blank, the voters had to write in their choice, and since more than 50 percent of adult Iranians are illiterate, someone else—a local mullah (Muslim clergyman) or electoral official—often did the writing. Bani-Sadr was considered the candidate favored by the armed forces and civil service. The Islamic Republican Party (IRP), representing clerical elements and Iran's largest party, was left without a candidate after its nominee was disqualified because it was found that his father was an Afghan.

Bani-Sadr's triumph was illusory, however. The

*Turban-clad Muslim clerics dominated the Iranian parliament elected in 1980. Their supporters dominated the radio, television, and newspapers and sought to bring the army and civil service under their control.*

constitution adopted in 1979 made the president inferior to the *faqih,* or religious guide, Ayatollah Ruhollah Khomeini, who had the power to dismiss the president, to declare war, and to name the top military and judicial authorities. Although Khomeini named Bani-Sadr supreme commander of the military on Feb. 19, the president's rivals were already moving to reduce him to a figurehead.

Balloting for the parliament, held on March 14 and on May 9, resulted in the election of clerics as the dominant group. Bani-Sadr had the power to appoint the prime minister, but his choices were rejected by the clergy and the IRP, which controlled the Majlis (parliament). Finally, on Aug. 9, Bani-Sadr reluctantly appointed Mohammed Ali Rajai, primarily a doctrinaire Muslim and only secondly a politician. On Sept. 7, Bani-Sadr approved 14 candidates for the 21-member cabinet but rejected Rajai's other choices. In early November, Iran still had no ministers of commerce, economy and finance, education, or foreign affairs.

After the presidential election, Bani-Sadr's

bases of support, the army and civil service, were heavily purged. In July paramilitary revolutionary guards took over key military commands. At least 64 army officers were executed in July and August.

The radio, television, and most newspapers were run by supporters of the IRP. At least 40 people were killed in April as Muslim fundamentalists, at Khomeini's behest, sought to drive leftists from the nation's universities. The universities were closed on June 4 pending reorganization to make them thoroughly Islamic.

Persons accused of narcotics trafficking or sex crimes were being summarily executed, sometimes in public. Amnesty International reported on Aug. 28 that at least 1000 people had been executed in the 18 months since the revolution. It said persons brought before Islamic revolutionary tribunals were consistently being denied fair trials.

On July 10 the government announced it had smashed a plot by military officers who planned to restore to power Shahpur Bakhtiar, the last prime minister appointed by Shah Mohammed Riza Pahlavi (who died on July 27 in Cairo). On

July 18 an assassination attempt on Bakhtiar in Paris, reportedly by Palestinians, failed.

In May, Iranian soldiers and revolutionary guards gained control of Sanandaj and Saqqiz in Kurdistan from elements demanding autonomy. Kurdish rebels continued to hold the city of Mahabad. Kurds boycotted the presidential and parliamentary elections.

**The Hostages.** Although Bani-Sadr opposed the holding of the American hostages, the militant Muslim students refused to recognize the authority of anyone except Khomeini, who endorsed the embassy occupation. Fifty Americans were being held at the embassy at the beginning of the year; three others were being held at the Iranian foreign ministry. In January six U.S. employees of the embassy, posing as Canadian diplomats and carrying forged visas, were flown out of the country. Canadian diplomats had been hiding them since the embassy occupation. On July 11 one of the remaining 53, Richard Queen, was released because of illness; he was found to have contracted multiple sclerosis.

Iran ignored a 1979 United Nations Security Council resolution demanding the release of the hostages. It also ignored a May 24 decision by the International Court of Justice to the same effect. A U.S. raid on April 24 that attempted to release the hostages failed; see MILITARY AND NAVAL AFFAIRS. The U.S. previously had broken diplomatic relations with Iran and had cut off trade. The European Community also imposed economic sanctions against Iran for holding the hostages.

On Sept. 12, Khomeini said the hostages would be freed if the U.S. promised not to intervene in Iran's affairs, released Iran's frozen assets in the U.S. (amounting to between $8 billion and $13 billion), turned over the property of the late shah in the U.S., and canceled financial claims made by U.S. private individuals and companies against Iran. The parliament approved the four conditions on Nov. 2. The U.S. then accepted them "in principle" but pointed out that under U.S. law it would have problems fulfilling the last two conditions. On Dec. 21, Iran demanded that the U.S. deposit $24 billion in Algeria as a guarantee that its conditions for the release of the hostages would be met.

**War with Iraq.** Relations with neighboring Iraq, bad in 1979, worsened in early 1980. Khomeini frequently appealed to Shi'ite Muslims, a majority in Iraq, which is ruled by Sunni Muslims, to rise in revolt. Iraq in turn encouraged the Arabs who form a majority in Iran's Khuzistan Province, which contains most of the country's oil, to demand autonomy and sabotage oil production. In early May, Khuzistan Arabs seized the Iranian embassy in London and held it for several days before the terrorists were killed or captured by British commandos and policemen.

Almost daily clashes along the Iraq-Iran border began on Sept. 2. On Sept. 17, Iraq terminated its 1975 border agreement with the shah. This accord had given the Iranians partial sovereignty over the Shatt-al-Arab, the combined estuary of the Tigris and Euphrates rivers that forms the frontier be-

**Don't Count Him Out Yet**
Like all aging leaders of nations with controlled communications, Iran's Ayatollah Ruhollah Khomeini was the object of much speculation during 1980. As the Iran-Iraq war began, Iranian President Abolhassan Bani-Sadr appeared to gain influence as a reputed war hero. Prime Minister Mohammed Ali Rajai spoke at the United Nations early in the fall, attracting considerable attention. There was even the inevitable rumor that the ayatollah had cancer and was dying. (The Central Intelligence Agency promptly reported that Khomeini was in good shape for a sedentary 80-year-old.) Later in the year Khomeini was apparently in full charge of the American hostages debate. And when Sadegh Ghotbzadeh, a former foreign minister whom Khomeini was said to regard as a son, was imprisoned in mid-November, the ayatollah promptly had him released.

*Ayatollah Ruhollah Khomeini.*

Five of the American hostages seized at the U.S. embassy in Tehran in November, 1979, are shown reading mail. Despite diplomatic efforts and a military attempt to free them, 52 hostages were still being held at the end of 1980.

tween the two countries at the head of the Persian Gulf. Iraq also demanded Arab control of three small islands in the strategic Strait of Hormuz that Iran seized in 1971. Iraq began major hostilities on Sept. 22. By late November, Iraq had occupied much of Khuzistan Province and had cut off most of Iran's oil supply. But Iran refused to accept a cease-fire offer from Iraq and was resisting Iraq's territorial demands. *See also* IRAQ; MIDDLE EAST; MILITARY AND NAVAL AFFAIRS; RELIGION.

**Economic Conditions.** Iran earns almost all of its foreign revenue from oil exports. In April Japan, its chief customer, refused to accept a price hike and stopped buying Iranian oil. Smaller customers, including East European countries, took up the slack, but exports reportedly were only 700,000 bbl a day when the war with Iraq started. Extensive damage to the oil installations brought the total down to 100,000 bbl a day. Nevertheless, refineries farther north were producing enough oil to keep the war effort going, and Eastern Europe was providing foodstuffs and some industrial goods. In spite of Western Europe's and Japan's ban on new contracts with Iran and the freeze of assets in the U.S., Iran was reported to have $7 billion in currency reserves in Europe and $2 billion in gold. The nation's import bill had been cut in half, to about $10 billion a year.

High inflation and heavy unemployment troubled Iran during 1980. Construction had ground to a halt, and heavy industries were reported operating at only 25 to 40 percent of capacity. The government, however, was subsidizing the price of basic commodities and was granting wage increases to workers that surpassed the rising cost of living.

*See* STATISTICS OF THE WORLD.             R.H.

**IRAQ.** In 1980, President Saddam Hussein gambled on making Iraq the prime power in the Arab world and Persian Gulf by invading Iran. In the process, he jeopardized the ambitious development programs that were being financed by oil revenues that had been expected to reach $30 billion in 1980.

**War with Iran.** In February, Iraq began calling for revision of the border settlement that it had signed with Iran in 1975. At that time, Iraq, in return for an end to Iranian support for Kurdish rebels in Iraq, agreed to give Iran partial sovereignty over the Shatt-al-Arab, the channel formed by the confluence of the Tigris and Euphrates rivers. The

205

*Although Iraq maintained the upper hand in its war with Iran, several of its cities were bombed by Iranian warplanes. This picture shows a raid on Baghdad in progress. A French-built nuclear facility was one of the targets.*

Shatt-al-Arab flows into the Persian Gulf, which normally is the sea route for most of Iraq's oil exports. Iraq also demanded some land farther north along its border with Iran and the return to Arab sovereignty of three small islands in the strategic Strait of Hormuz that had been seized by Iran in 1971.

The enmity between the two countries was also fueled by Ayatollah Ruhollah Khomeini's call on Iraq's Shi'ite Muslims, who are believed to constitute about 60 percent of the nation's population, to revolt against Iraq's leaders, who are Sunni Muslims. Iraq repudiated the border agreement on Sept. 17 and began major hostilities on Sept. 22. Its troops occupied much of Khuzistan Province, Iran's chief oil-producing area; *see also* MILITARY AND NAVAL AFFAIRS. Iraq then indicated it had gained its objectives and was willing to make peace, but Iran vowed to fight on. The offer was made repeatedly and rejected just as often. Although Iraq was unable to export oil by way of the Persian Gulf because of the war, on Nov. 20 it began sending about 500,000 bbl a day to the West by means of a pipeline running through Turkey. The pipeline was, however, reportedly cut on Dec. 12, as was another one running through Syria.

**Domestic Affairs.** Since making himself president and prime minister in 1979, Hussein had begun a cult of personality; see also biography at PEOPLE IN THE NEWS. His portraits adorned buildings everywhere, and he appeared nearly nightly on television, touring villages and cuddling children. After the war began, he was shown in uniform, mingling with troops and visiting the wounded. Workers' salaries were raised in 1980, more consumer goods were made available, and housing starts increased.

Hussein continued to deal ruthlessly with potential opposition. A leader of the Shi'ite community, Imam Mohammed al-Bakr Sadr, was arrested and, according to Amnesty International, executed. As many as 30,000 Shi'ites believed to be of Iranian descent were rounded up and dumped across the border. A National Assembly was inaugurated after the first elections since 1958, held on June 20, but the Revolutionary Command Council remained the key decision-making body, with Hussein its chairman and its deliberations secret.

Iraq's oil facilities were damaged in the war but, given its estimated $35 billion in foreign reserves, it could count on foreign help in restoring production once the fighting ended. Baghdad, the capital, was reported to be without shortages of consumer goods in November.

**Foreign Relations.** Iraq, though it signed a security pact with Moscow in 1972, was moving away from the U.S.S.R., which had become only fourteenth among its providers of nonmilitary goods. It remained dependent on the Soviet Union for military equipment but bought warplanes from France and was looking to Western nations for other arms deals. It strongly denounced the Soviet invasion of Afghanistan.

In its war with Iran, Iraq had the backing of Jordan, Saudi Arabia, and other Arab countries fearful of Iran's revolutionary aspirations. Iraq severed relations with Libya, Syria, and North Korea, which were supporting Iran.

*See* STATISTICS OF THE WORLD; *see also* ARAB LEAGUE; MIDDLE EAST; RELIGION. R.H.

**IRELAND, NORTHERN.** *See* GREAT BRITAIN; IRELAND, REPUBLIC OF.

**IRELAND, REPUBLIC OF.** During 1980 the Irish economy was troubled by inflation, unemployment, strikes, and the continuing problem of Northern Ireland. Inflation was expected to exceed 18 percent for the year, and unemployment had reached 9 percent by October.

Demonstrations and strikes were mounted against the tax system early in the year as unfair to those earning wages and salaries. In actions organized by the Irish Congress of Trade Unions (ICTU), hundreds of thousands of protestors marched in Dublin and other cities on Jan. 22. Much industry was suspended for the day.

In response to the protests, the government proposed some income tax cuts—for example, in taxes on married people. The revenue loss would be recouped by increases in the value-added tax and in taxes on alcoholic beverages, cigarettes, and petroleum products. The proposals were submitted by Finance Minister Michael O'Kennedy in his budget message on Feb. 27.

A three-week strike against Aer Lingus in June put a crimp in the beginning of the tourist season, and a two-month crisis began when oil workers went on strike on the expiration of their contract with Texaco on Sept. 1. By the end of the month the walkout had closed 60 percent of the gasoline stations in Dublin and was spreading elsewhere. On Sept. 30, with the effects of the strike deepening, Prime Minister Charles J. Haughey ordered the army to start delivering gasoline to stations.

Haughey had also intervened to get the ICTU and the Federated Union of Employers to agree on a national pay package in mid-September. The agreement provided pay increases totaling about 16 percent.

Haughey met with British Prime Minister Margaret Thatcher in London on May 21. Although Haughey remained in favor of incorporating Northern Ireland into the Irish Republic and Thatcher held to her position of keeping Ulster in the United Kingdom and granting it a measure of home rule, the two leaders did agree to develop "new and closer political cooperation."

On July 27, Haughey renewed his government's opposition to the terrorism of the outlawed Irish Republican Army (IRA). Addressing workers for his Fianna Fáil Party in Cork, Haughey assailed the New York-based Northern Ireland Aid Committee and the Irish National Caucus, based in Washington, D.C., for supporting violence in Northern Ireland by aiding the IRA.

*See* STATISTICS OF THE WORLD. L.A.S.

**ISRAEL.** Disagreements over how to cope with inflation, over Israeli policy in the West Bank, and over the autonomy negotiations with Egypt threatened the unity of Prime Minister Menachem Begin's government during 1980.

**Palestinian Issues.** The year began auspiciously with Begin's visit to Egypt in January. He and

*The Israeli army on Jan. 25 completes the first phase of its withdrawal from occupied Egyptian territory under the peace treaty signed in 1979. With this withdrawal, Israel had returned two thirds of the Sinai Peninsula to Egypt.*

**The Firebrand from Tel Aviv**

When a bill affirming Jerusalem as the capital of Israel was overwhelmingly approved by the Israeli parliament in July, nobody was more elated than its sponsor, Geula Cohen. The 54-year-old legislator, a member of parliament since 1974, had come to be known as "the hardest of the hard-liners." In 1978 she was physically removed from a session for interrupting a speech in which Prime Minister Menachem Begin reported on peace talks at Camp David, Md. Her position, often stated in highly emotional language, is that peace with the Arabs is an impossibility. Geula Cohen was born in Tel Aviv in 1925. She joined the underground as a youngster, escaped from a British prison, and served as a radio announcer for the militant Stern Group until 1948 and Israeli independence.

*Geula Cohen.*

Egyptian President Anwar el-Sadat laid out procedures for normalization of relations and the autonomy negotiations. On Jan. 25 Israel completed the first phase of its withdrawal from Egyptian territory under terms of the March 26, 1979, Egyptian-Israeli peace treaty, having returned two thirds of the Sinai Peninsula to Egypt. The withdrawal was followed by establishment of direct communications between the two countries, including a telephone link, air travel, and exchange of ambassadors. Later, trade ties were established, with a land route opened.

By spring it became evident that the May 26

**Ancient Name, Modern Problem**

The prophet Jeremiah would feel comfortable with the new monetary system of his homeland. Commanded by God to buy a certain field, Jeremiah reports in the Old Testament that he paid for it "17 shekels of silver." During 1980 the Israeli pound was removed from circulation and replaced by a new currency based on a monetary unit with an ancient name: the shekel. (In March a shekel was worth approximately 25 U.S. cents.) At the time of the official switchover in the fall, Israeli accountants were busily and happily lopping lots of zeros off their ledgers, since each shekel represented 10 pounds and inflation in the land of Jeremiah had reached an annual rate of 134 percent.

deadline for agreement on Palestinian autonomy arrangements would not be met. Egypt and Israel disagreed on whether the autonomous council called for in the Camp David agreements was to have legislative or only executive powers, on qualifications for voting in elections, and on Israel's control of internal security in the autonomous region.

The tense relations caused by these disagreements were exacerbated after the Israeli Knesset (parliament) passed a law on July 30 reaffirming a 1967 decision to make Jerusalem, "complete and united," the capital of Israel. It was approved by a vote of 69 to 15 with 3 abstentions. Although it did nothing to change the status of Arab East Jerusalem, which Israel had annexed 13 years earlier, it sparked a flurry of international protest, including censure by the United Nations Security Council, criticism by the United States, a request by Sadat for delay in the autonomy talks, and the removal from Jerusalem of the 13 embassies that had been established there. Relations with Egypt were eased somewhat by the October visit of Israel's president, Yitzhak Navon, to Cairo, where he was received cordially by Sadat.

Other Security Council resolutions rebuked Israel for deporting three Arab leaders from the West Bank after a terrorist attack on Jews in Hebron in May, for bomb attacks that seriously injured two West Bank mayors in June, and for armed incursions into Lebanon in April. In August, however, Israel mounted its largest raid into Lebanon since 1978; *see* MILITARY AND NAVAL AFFAIRS.

Relations between Israel and Arab inhabitants of the occupied West Bank continued to deterio-

Construction is shown outside new offices being prepared for Israel's prime minister in predominantly Arab East Jerusalem, which was annexed after it was occupied in 1967. On July 30, Israel's parliament passed a controversial resolution reaffirming that all of Jerusalem was the capital of Israel.

rate. On May 2, six Jews were killed and 16 wounded by Arab terrorists in Hebron. Israeli military authorities charged the Muslim judge in Hebron and the mayors of Halhul and Hebron with making inflammatory statements inciting the attacks. They were immediately deported to Lebanon without any official hearing. The two mayors appealed their deportation and were permitted to return in October for a judicial appeal ordered by the Israeli Supreme Court.

In bombings on June 2, the mayor of Nablus lost both legs and the mayor of Ramallah, a foot; the mayor of Bireh escaped unscathed. The attacks sparked a general strike in the entire West Bank and in East Jerusalem against the occupa-

tion. On Nov. 2, Israeli troops fired on Palestinian students protesting against the closing of a Palestinian university north of Jerusalem. Eleven were wounded and further demonstrations followed.

**Political Affairs.** Differences in the cabinet over West Bank policy and the autonomy negotiations led to the resignation of Defense Minister Ezer Weizman in May. The appointment of Yitzhak Shamir, former Knesset speaker, to replace Moshe Dayan, who resigned as foreign minister in 1979, was criticized because Shamir had opposed the peace treaty with Egypt. The fourth resignation from Begin's cabinet in two years occurred on July 31 when the minister of justice, Shmuel Tamir, left the cabinet to end the "intolerable situ-

Arnaldo Forlani became premier of Italy's fortieth post-World War II government on Oct. 18. His Christian Democratic Party was joined by three other parties in the governing coalition.

ation" in which his party, the Democratic Movement, was left with only four Knesset members while it had three cabinet posts.

Tamir's resignation called attention to the fragmentation of Begin's coalition. When the Democratic Movement entered the government after the 1977 election, it had 15 Knesset seats, but defections brought it down to 4, helping to narrow Begin's majority in the 120-member Knesset from 78 to 63 seats. On Nov. 19 the government survived a no-confidence vote by 57 votes to 54, the narrowest margin of more than 20 no-confidence motions in 1980. Dayan and Weizman both voted against the Begin government on this challenge to its economic policies, and four days later Weizman was expelled from Begin's Herut Party, leaving the governing coalition with only 60 seats in the Knesset. The opposition Labor Party was leading in public opinion polls and was working to force an election.

**The Economy.** Inflation reached an all-time high annual rate of 138.4 percent in October and the Israeli pound declined from about 35 per U.S. dollar in December, 1979, to more than 66 in November, 1980. In an attempt to mitigate the psychological effects of inflation, the government introduced a new unit of currency in February,

the shekel. Over a period of months it replaced the Israeli pound at the rate of one shekel for ten pounds. Although budget policies stimulated exports and reduced imports, the trade deficit for the first nine months of 1980 was $2.36 billion. Stringent budgetary policies contributed to unemployment, which reached 4.1 percent, the highest since 1977. The escalating cost of oil imports was a major cause of inflation. In 1980 Israel was expected to pay $2.5 billion, more than triple the 1979 bill, for imported oil, much of it coming from Sinai wells returned to Egypt.

During October the United States and Israel signed a 14-year oil agreement, arising from the Egyptian-Israeli peace negotiations, that assured Israel's oil needs would be provided after Israel withdrew from Egyptian oilfields in Sinai. The October agreement established a formula for supply and determination of price.

See STATISTICS OF THE WORLD. See also EGYPT; MIDDLE EAST; UNITED NATIONS. D.P.

**ITALY.** Chronic terrorism, political instability, widespread strikes, and severe economic problems afflicted Italy during 1980. The deadliest earthquake in Europe since 1915 struck southern Italy Nov. 23. Authorities listed 3105 people as dead, 1571 missing and presumed dead, and 7671 injured. A total of 133 towns were listed as seriously damaged or destroyed, and the homeless were estimated at 200,000 to 300,000. The government was severely criticized because the army was slow to arrive on the scene and did not have sufficient equipment.

**Politics.** Premier Francesco Cossiga resigned on March 19, after the Socialists decided to vote against his minority Christian Democratic government rather than allow it to remain in power by abstaining, as they had been doing. The Socialist Party had demanded that the Communists be admitted to the cabinet, but the Christian Democrats refused.

Cossiga was able to form a center-left coalition government on April 4, with the Christian Democrats holding 15 ministries, the Socialists 9, and the Republicans 3. Socialist leader Bettino Craxi made the new alignment possible by abandoning support for the Communists in defiance of the left wing of his party. In mid-April the Senate approved the cabinet by a vote of 178 to 127, and the Chamber of Deputies approved it by 335 to 271.

On May 31 a special parliamentary commission narrowly rejected impeachment charges against Cossiga. It was claimed that he had permitted the son of Carlo Donat-Cattin, vice secretary of the Christian Democratic Party, to elude arrest as a terrorist suspect. The parliament in effect dismissed the case on July 27 by a vote of 507 to 416 in a joint session of the two chambers.

Earlier, the accused Cossiga had scored a personal triumph in the regional, provincial, and municipal elections held on June 8 and 9. In the voting for regional councils the Christian Democrats won 36.8 percent of the vote, a gain of 1.5 percent over similar elections in 1975. The Communists obtained 31.5 percent of the vote, a drop of 1.9 percent compared with the local elections in 1975. The Socialists made a good showing with 12.7 percent of the vote.

On Sept. 27 Cossiga's government resigned again after a one-vote defeat (297 to 298) in the Chamber of Deputies over its economic program. Some 30 of the coalition's supporters turned against it in the secret vote, which came a few minutes after it had gained a vote of confidence in an open ballot. The coalition's economic proposals aimed at strengthening the lira, fighting the 20 percent inflation rate, backing declining industries, and aiding the south.

The Communists charged the government was incompetent to deal with the acute economic and social crises and declared they would oppose any ministry that excluded them. The unemployment rate was reaching 8 percent, and petroleum shortages were threatened because of the Iraqi-Iranian war. Fiat auto workers were on strike protesting the planned dismissal of 14,000 workers, climaxing the most serious labor unrest in nearly a dozen years. (The 38-day strike ended without the dismissal, but Fiat won the right to lay off 24,000 workers for as long as 34 months.)

Former Foreign Minister Arnaldo Forlani consented on Oct. 2 to form Italy's fortieth government since World War II. His ministry was installed on Oct. 18 with 14 Christian Democrats, 7 Socialists, 3 Social Democrats, and 3 Republicans. The coalition had 360 votes in the 630-seat chamber, a larger majority than almost any government since World War II. The two rival Socialist parties had agreed to collaborate on Oct. 8.

**The Economy.** Forlani pledged to reduce Italy's unemployment rate by stressing the south, where the jobless rate was 10 percent. In September the consumer price index was 21.2 percent higher than the previous September. By October the lira seemed to be holding its own after the central bank raised its discount rate. In defiance of economic laws, Italy seemed to be leading Europe with a 3.5 percent economic growth rate.

**Terrorism.** Extremists of the Right and Left persisted in deadly assaults on judges, policemen,

Survivors of the devastating earthquake that struck southern Italy on Nov. 23 sift through rubble for possible survivors. About 4500 people were listed as dead or missing.

A terrorist bomb blast attributed to neo-Fascists exploded in the waiting room of the Bologna railway station on Aug. 2, killing 84 persons. Italian political leaders are shown attending a memorial service for the victims in Bologna's Cathedral of San Petronio.

and public officials. They also resorted to outright massacre, culminating on Aug. 2 in the bombing of the Bologna railway station, where 84 people were killed and more than 200 wounded, presumably the work of neo-Fascists. Horrified Italians demonstrated widely in protest against ineffectual official measures, although on Feb. 2 the parliament had passed an emergency law under which anyone accused of terrorism could be jailed without trial for 12 years. According to some reports, the police had succeeded in weakening the left-wing terrorist groups by year's end.

**Foreign Affairs.** Italy joined six other leading industrial nations in Venice, June 22–23, to discuss oil conservation and alternative energy sources to forestall a worldwide recession. President Jimmy Carter and Premier Cossiga both supported the North Atlantic Treaty Organization decision to seek arms control and deployment of European theater nuclear forces at the same time.

*See* STATISTICS OF THE WORLD.                    J.N.

**IVORY COAST.** *See* STATISTICS OF THE WORLD.

# J

**JAMAICA.** *See* STATISTICS OF THE WORLD. *See also* CARIBBEAN COUNTRIES.

**JAPAN.** After a tumultuous mid-1980 political struggle, the ruling Liberal-Democratic Party re-emerged in firm control of Japan's government. Signs of stability and moderate growth appeared in the economy, but the high cost of energy remained a severe problem. In foreign affairs, Tokyo showed mounting apprehension of Soviet power in the Far East.

**Politics.** The ruling Liberal-Democratic Party of Prime Minister Masayoshi Ohira was overturned

as a no-confidence motion (247–187) was adopted in the lower house of the parliament on May 16. The opposition Socialists charged the Liberal-Democrats with corruption and failure to check inflation. The defeat of the government was assured when 69 Liberal-Democratic dissidents, led by Ohira's political rivals, former prime ministers Takeo Miki and Takeo Fukuda, abstained from the voting.

New elections for the entire House of Representatives and half of the seats in the House of Councillors (upper house) were scheduled for

June 22. Before they could be held, however, on June 12, Prime Minister Ohira died of a heart attack. These events did not keep the Liberal-Democrats from waging an effective campaign; indeed it was the opposition parties that were caught off guard by the early elections, which resulted from the no-confidence vote they had not expected to carry.

Results of the balloting on June 22 gave the Liberal-Democrats a firm majority in the House of Representatives, with 284 out of 511 seats, a gain of 26. The Socialists retained their 107 seats; the Communists dropped from 41 to 29 seats, the Democratic Socialists from 36 to 32; and the Komeito, a Buddhist party, from 58 to 33. In the less important 252-member upper house, the Liberal-Democrats won 135 seats, giving them an 8-seat majority.

On July 17, 69-year-old Zenko Suzuki (see biography at PEOPLE IN THE NEWS), chairman of the executive council of the Liberal-Democratic Party, was elected prime minister by the House of Representatives. Suzuki named a new cabinet that included representatives of all the major Liberal-Democratic factions. In his first address on Aug. 18, Suzuki outlined his government's major policies. He reaffirmed Japan's commitment to its mutual defense treaty with the United States and pledged to try to reduce deficit spending, cut back the number of government employees, and diversify Japan's sources of energy imports.

**Economy.** Japan's gross national product, second largest among non-Communist nations, expanded 6.1 percent during fiscal year 1979 (April, 1979–March, 1980) after adjustment for an inflation rate of 8 percent. This growth rate was achieved with the help of a strong 1.8 percent increase during the first quarter of 1980. In foreign trade, Japan registered a deficit of $13 billion in fiscal 1979 compared with a surplus of more than $14 billion the previous year. Exports increased 8.1 percent, but imports rose at a 42.3 percent rate due primarily to a 66.4 percent increase in the cost of imported oil. A $6 billion surplus in trade with the U.S. was more than offset by a $23 billion deficit with Middle East countries.

Between April and June, economic growth slowed to a 2.5 percent annual rate, compared to a 7.6 percent annual rate for the January to March period. After the Suzuki cabinet took office in July, the emphasis in economic policy shifted noticeably from maintaining price stability to stimulating moderate growth. Bank credit was eased on Aug. 20. On Sept. 5 the government implemented an eight-point antirecession program, including greater public works spending and increased aid to small businesses. Japan's economic planning agency forecast economic growth at 4.8 percent in fiscal 1980 and inflation at 6.4 percent. These statistics compared favorably to those of the other leading non-Communist countries. Another piece of good news was that in September, Japan posted a trade surplus of $950,000,000, its first monthly trade surplus since July, 1979.

**Foreign Relations.** Ohira visited President Jimmy Carter in Washington on May 1 on the first stop of a trip that took him also to Mexico and Canada. The two leaders signed a five-year agreement calling for cooperation between their nations in a broad range of scientific research projects. Al-

### In the Land of the Rising Grandson

Repeating a ceremony more than 1200 years old, the Deputy Grand Chamberlain removed the hat that denotes a juvenile from the youth's head and replaced it with a coronet. At that moment, in Tokyo on Feb. 23, Prince Hiro of Japan became the first grandson of a reigning Japanese emperor to come of age, on his 20th birthday. Hiro, second in line for the Japanese throne as the eldest son of Crown Prince Akihito, 46, and grandson of Emperor Hirohito, 78, is a history major at Gakushuin University. His hobbies are music—he is a member of the university orchestra—and mountain climbing. He has climbed more than 50 peaks in the land he will someday serve, as "the symbol of the state and the unity of the people."

*Prince Hiro.*

*Japanese workers assemble engines for Toyota autos being exported. Despite some problems, Japan's economy registered moderate growth in 1980.*

though Carter refused to give Ohira the assurances he sought that the U.S. would not employ force again to resolve the Iranian hostage crisis, he did agree to provide assistance if the loss of Iranian oil caused Japan further trouble. In Mexico, Ohira tried unsuccessfully to gain an increase

in Mexican oil exports to offset the decline in shipments from Iran following Japan's refusal to pay the higher prices demanded by Tehran in April.

On May 24 the Japanese Olympic Committee voted to join the U.S.-led boycott of the Moscow Olympics protesting the Soviet invasion of Afghanistan. The vote came after a government threat that the passports of athletes who did not support the boycott would be revoked. Japan also backed the U.S., along with Western Europe, by imposing a freeze on contracts with Iran on May 22, as retaliation for the continued detention of the American hostages there. The sanctions also suspended contracts concluded since the hostage seizure.

Japan's relations with the Soviet Union deteriorated further after President Carter visited Japanese leaders and Chinese Premier Hua Kuo-feng (Hua Guofeng) in Tokyo, July 9–10, while attending memorial services for Ohira. Moscow charged that the creation of a U.S.-Japan-China tripartite alliance would seriously destabilize the situation in Asia.

At U.S. urging, the Suzuki government moved to take on a greater share of the cost of Japan's national defense. The 1981–82 budget request included a 9.7 percent increase in defense spending, 1.8 percent above the growth rate allowed for

## Finders Keepers?

In September, Japanese divers uncovered one of the richest treasures in naval history—millions of dollars worth of platinum ingots aboard the *Admiral Nakhimov,* a Russian cruiser sunk in Japanese waters during the Russo-Japanese War of 1904–05. Some estimates indicated that as much as $4 billion worth of platinum and gold might be recovered. Moscow immediately claimed the treasure, but the Japanese government rejected the claim. Ryoichi Sasagawa, the Japanese shipbuilding tycoon who financed the salvage operation, offered to return the treasure to the Soviets— but only in exchange for Soviet territory that had been seized from Japan at the end of World War II.

the general budget. This budget, if passed, would mean a post-World War II high for military spending, though still only 0.91 percent of the gross national product. The government's reasons for the spending hike were made clear in an Aug. 5 white paper issued by the Defense Agency, which urged a rapid buildup and modernization of the nation's armed forces to meet the accelerating increase of Soviet military power in the Far East. But on Dec. 22 the finance ministry announced that the actual military budget increase would be about 6.6 percent rather than the earlier announced 9.7 percent.

See STATISTICS OF THE WORLD.          T.L.K.

**JORDAN.** Jordan was the first Arab nation to side with Iraq in the 1980 Iran-Iraq war, and it continued to oppose the Israeli-Egyptian peace negotiations. In late November, Jordanian and Syrian forces were massed on their common border. And domestically, Mudar Badran returned as prime minister.

**Iran-Iraq War.** As the only Middle Eastern country actively supporting its neighbor, Iraq, in the Iran-Iraq war, Jordan reportedly permitted Soviet ammunition, military spare parts, and other supplies to pass through the Red Sea port of 'Aqaba. The fighting in Iraq had prevented foreign vessels from entering Iraqi ports. After a visit to Iraqi President Saddam Hussein (who is no relation) in Baghdad, Oct. 4–5, King Hussein ordered the commandeering of private transport vehicles to carry food and other supplies from 'Aqaba to the Iraqi border. The king also put his military forces in a state of alert and pledged military and other assistance if requested.

**Relations with Syria.** In late November, Jordan hosted the annual meeting of the Arab League. Syria, a longtime enemy of Iraq and one of the Arab countries boycotting the meeting and supporting Iran in the Iran-Iraq war, massed an estimated 35,000–50,000 troops on the Jordanian border. Hussein, in turn, alerted his forces. Syria accused Jordan of harboring and aiding terrorists from the Muslim Brotherhood who had fomented unrest in Syria for some time. Syria also demanded assurances that Jordan would not attempt to supplant the Palestine Liberation Organization as sole representative of Palestinian interests. Jordan announced on Dec. 10 that Syria had started to pull back its troops.

**U.S. Relations.** When King Hussein paid an official state visit to Washington, June 17–18, he continued to refuse to join the U.S.-sponsored Israeli-Egyptian peace negotiations on Palestinian autonomy. The king apparently believed Jordan's survival in an unstable region was at stake and that the return of East Jerusalem and the West Bank, which Jordan had lost to Israel in the 1967 Arab-Israeli war, should be the focus of any talks.

After Hussein's visit the Carter administration announced that the United States would sell 100 M-60 tanks with advanced armament to Jordan and was considering selling 100 more. Some analysts believed the reason for the sale was to prevent Jordan from concluding a major arms agreement with the Soviet Union.

**Internal Affairs.** Abdul Hamid Sharaf, 41, prime minister from December, 1979, died on July 3 of an apparent heart attack. To succeed him, Hussein initially named Kassem al-Rimawi, the agriculture minister. On Aug. 28, however, he brought back Mudar Badran, who had been prime minister from July, 1976, to December, 1979, when the king forced his resignation.

See STATISTICS OF THE WORLD. See also ARAB LEAGUE; MIDDLE EAST; SYRIA.          C.G.

# K

**KAMPUCHEA.** See CAMBODIA.
**KANSAS.** See STATISTICS OF THE WORLD.
**KENTUCKY.** See STATISTICS OF THE WORLD.
**KENYA.** Faced with the threat of famine and worsening economic conditions, Kenya's President Daniel arap Moi drew his country closer to the United States and its foreign policies in 1980.

After two years of good harvests, 1980 brought widespread drought and crop failures. Early in the year, the government reported a corn (maize) shortage, and government stockpiles were found to be inadequate. In addition, it was discovered that some 2,000,000 bags of corn had disappeared from government storehouses. Smuggling was suspected.

In February, Kenya agreed to allow U.S. naval units to visit the major east African port of Mombasa. Storage of fuel and equipment was also permitted. Soon after, Kenya agreed to boycott the Moscow Olympics. Moi visited the U.S., West Germany, and Great Britain in late February. In April, access to air and naval facilities was formally granted to U.S. forces, although Kenya remained officially nonaligned and ruled out the establishment of actual U.S. military bases. Nevertheless, these Mombasa facilities greatly enhanced American military capabilities in the Persian Gulf area. In return, American economic aid to Kenya was increased to more than $40,000,000, with additional moneys slated for improving the military facilities. Some 105,000 tons of corn, wheat, and rice were also supplied.

While the American aid and increased food imports averted a famine, the drought and the low water level in the hydroelectric power system led to the rationing of electricity and work stoppages. These, in turn, led to strikes and demonstrations. Moi responded, in midyear, with a crackdown on strike leaders and demands for loyalty from the military and civil service. These actions seemed to be successful.

In January, for the first time in ten years, leaders from the defunct East African Community (EAC) discussed ways to revive their economic ties. Meeting in Arusha, Tanzania, in January and in Mombasa in April, the heads of state, including Moi, sought to work out a formula for the allocation of the EAC's assets. Although no agreement was reached, the meetings did serve to improve Kenya's strained relations with its former partners, Tanzania and Uganda.

See STATISTICS OF THE WORLD.          J.T.S.

**KHMER REPUBLIC.** See CAMBODIA.

**KIRIBATI.** See STATISTICS OF THE WORLD.

**KOREA, DEMOCRATIC PEOPLE'S REPUBLIC OF, or NORTH KOREA.** In 1980, Kim Il Sung of North Korea became the world's longest enduring political leader, having served continuously as his country's president since September, 1948. The 68-year-old President Kim continued to groom one of his sons, Kim Chong Il, to be his eventual successor and thereby establish the first family dynasty yet to appear in the Communist world. **Politics.** One of the world's most secretive states, North Korea provided scant information in 1980 about the workings of its political hierarchy. But the major political event of the year clearly was the 6th congress of the Workers' Party of Korea, held in P'yŏngyang, Oct. 10–14, the first such congress in ten years.

The younger Kim, 39, was all but ordained as heir apparent at the congress. He was ranked fourth in both the newly formed standing committee of the policymaking Politburo and the Politburo itself. More important, he was elevated to the number two position in the ruling Workers' Party Secretariat, just behind his father.

**Foreign Policy.** P'yŏngyang's attitude toward South Korea fluctuated sharply during the year. In January the North Koreans proposed an unprecedented meeting between the prime ministers of the North and the South. But in February and March, they staged a number of provocative border incidents, sending infiltrators across the demilitarized zone into the South.

P'yŏngyang's ambivalence toward South Korea continued through the summer. In July, President Kim took a conciliatory line, telling visiting U.S. Rep. Stephen Solarz (D, N.Y.) that North Korea would no longer insist that South Korea repeal its tough anti-Communist law before family reunions and exchanges of mail could take place in the divided peninsula. The atmosphere was soured in early September, however, when North Korean loudspeakers along the demilitarized zone urged South Korean troops to overthrow the government of President Chun Doo Hwan. On Sept. 25 the North canceled the talks, accusing the South of "trying to whip up a war atmosphere." The harsh rhetoric continued at the October party congress, where President Kim declared that the destruction of the "fascist" regime in the South was a prerequisite for serious talks. At the October meeting, Kim also stated that North Korea was prepared to establish friendly ties with the United States—once the 40,000 American troops in South Korea were withdrawn.

See STATISTICS OF THE WORLD.          R.J.C.

**KOREA, REPUBLIC OF, or SOUTH KOREA.** The year 1980 was one of political turmoil and transition in South Korea with the rise to power of Lt. Gen. Chun Doo Hwan, who became president. **Politics.** In the early months of the year, Choi Kyu Hah, 61, named caretaker president after the assassination of Park Chung Hee the previous October, moved cautiously toward democratization. Most political prisoners were released, dissident professors and students were reinstated, and civil rights were restored to hundreds, among them the perennial government critic Kim Dae Jung.

But Chun, the 47-year-old officer who seized control of the army in the December, 1979, mutiny against his military superiors (see also biography at PEOPLE IN THE NEWS), waited impatiently in the wings. Chun saw his opportunity to move in early May, when some 50,000 students, whose basic demand was quicker democratization, battled with police in the streets of Seoul. On May 17 the army imposed full martial law on the country, closed the National Assembly, banned all political activity, and arrested a number of political leaders, including Kim Dae Jung. From then on, the civilian government of President Choi was largely ignored; Chun's military men were in command.

Kim Dae Jung's detention sparked a huge student demonstration in Kwangju, the country's

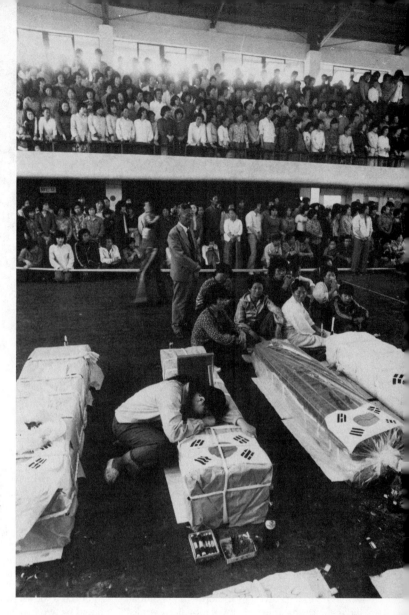

Residents of Kwangju, South Korea, mourn some of the estimated 250 victims—mostly civilians—killed in fighting that followed an antigovernment protest in May. The protesters held the city for several days before the army reestablished government control.

fifth largest city. Nonstudents joined in the antigovernment protest, and for days rioters controlled the city, occupying city hall and sacking the local tax office. Then, in the predawn hours of May 27, government troops supported by tanks moved into the city and resumed control. At least 250 people, mostly civilians, died in the Kwangju episode.

In the weeks that followed, Chun and his fellow generals tightened their grip on power. Many of Kim Dae Jung's followers were arrested, and the universities were purged of liberal professors and student leaders. More than 170 "harmful publications" were prohibited; newspapers were forced to fire journalists critical of the regime.

In the summer months, Chun undertook a major "purification campaign." More than 30,000 criminals and other "undesirables" were hauled off to military camps for rehabilitation. In a major shake-up of the bureaucracy, one out of every ten top officials was fired on charges of corruption or inefficiency. Lower-echelon officeholders by the thousands were dismissed or arrested. The purge, the largest in the country's history, also included hundreds of agents of the Korean Central Intelligence Agency.

In August, Chun was ready to complete his takeover of the government. On Aug. 16 the figurehead Choi relinquished his office. On Aug. 22, Chun resigned his army commission, and on Aug.

Riot police in Seoul fire tear gas on May 14 at students on the Korea University campus demanding an end to martial law in South Korea. The army responded to the turmoil by closing the National Assembly and banning all political activity.

27 he was chosen by the country's electoral college as South Korea's fifth president. Chun was inaugurated on Sept. 1.

In his inaugural speech, Chun promised that a draft of a new constitution would be put to a referendum and that presidential and legislative elections would be held in the first half of 1981. The new charter provided for the indirect election of the president through an electoral college chosen by popular vote. The president would be restricted to a single seven-year term and have specific limitations placed on his power. He would no longer have the authority to appoint all judges and one third of the National Assembly. His emergency powers would be restricted, and he would be able to invoke them only with the approval of the parliament. Other provisions guaranteed human rights and forbade the use of torture to extract confessions. The document would also dissolve all existing political parties and the already moribund National Assembly. In an Oct. 22 referendum, in which 95.5 percent of the country's 20,300,000 eligible voters took part, the charter received an affirmative vote of 92 percent, according to official count.

Buoyed by the overwhelming vote, Chun made it clear that he would be a candidate for the presidency in 1981. In the meantime, his military regime ruled without opposition. Press, speech, and

assembly were strictly limited. On Nov. 12 the government announced that more than 800 politicians and high-ranking officials would be banned from participation in the country's political life for nearly eight years. On Nov. 28, 1210 people were arrested in Seoul and 67 publications were banned.

After Kim Dae Jung's detention in May, the military announced that he would stand trial for complicity in the Kwangju rioting and for plotting to overthrow the government by force. He was found guilty by a military panel on Sept. 17 and sentenced to death by hanging. The sentence was upheld by two appeals courts, leaving only a possible act of clemency by Chun standing between Kim and the gallows.

**The Economy.** Due in large measure to soaring world oil prices, the once-booming South Korean economy remained sunk in the grip of "stagflation," high inflation along with a slowing growth rate. South Korea posted high annual growth rates for a decade, but the gross national product for 1980 was expected to fall by 1 or 2 percent. Unemployment was believed to be about 9 percent of the labor force.

**Foreign Affairs.** Relations with North Korea remained stalemated during the year. Both sides offered proposals for discussions that would bring the two halves of the divided country closer, but

218

a meaningful North-South dialogue was ruled out by deep mutual distrust.

South Korea's chief allies, the United States and Japan, were distressed by Chun's military takeover and by the death sentence handed down to Kim Dae Jung. Both governments considered the death sentence to be unwarranted.

*See* STATISTICS OF THE WORLD.                 R.J.C.

**KUWAIT.** The small but oil-rich emirate of Kuwait found itself caught in the cross fire of the Iran-Iraq war in 1980. The leaders of this tiny, essentially defenseless Arab country just to the south of Iraq sympathized with Arab Iraq. As the war continued, it discreetly allowed war materials and other goods to cross the border into Iraq, whose Persian Gulf ports were being blockaded. But in November a border post was twice bombed by Iranian warplanes, seemingly as a warning to Kuwait not to give Iraq too much help.

A substantial number of Kuwaitis are Shi'ite Muslims, presumed to be sympathetic to Iran's leader, Ayatollah Ruhollah Khomeini. Furthermore, Kuwait's Palestinian population was considered pro-Iran and a possible source of subversion. And even though Kuwait's leaders were pro-Iraq, they were also mindful that Iraq has long-standing territorial claims against Kuwait.

Despite the political climate, Kuwait did not shelve earlier plans to liberalize its government. Its leaders announced their intention to lift a four-year freeze on parliamentary activity in February, 1981, with the election of a new National Assembly.

In April, Kuwait, not in need of increased oil income, slashed oil production from 2,200,000 bbl a day to 1,500,000 bbl a day. At the same time, it dramatically reduced the allotment of oil going to three major oil companies from two thirds of average daily production to less than one third. The companies were also required to comply with a number of new conditions; for example, they would not in the future be allowed to sell the oil to whomever they pleased. One of Kuwait's intentions was to sell half its oil in the form of finished products by 1984; another was to have nearly half its oil transported in its own tankers by then.

*See* STATISTICS OF THE WORLD.                 R.H.

# L

**LABOR.** High unemployment was the dominant labor development in the United States during 1980. In a major union breakthrough, the Amalgamated Clothing and Textile Workers Union climaxed a 17-year-long organizing battle with J. P. Stevens & Co. by winning its first union contract from the firm. Labor leader George Meany died soon after his retirement from the presidency of the American Federation of Labor and Congress of Industrial Organizations (AFL-CIO). The AFL-CIO added a woman to its executive council for the first time in its history. Organized labor helped develop new voluntary wage guidelines to curb inflation. A three-month-long strike by television actors delayed the start of the fall season of television programs.

**Unemployment Climbs.** An economic recession during the first half of 1980 sent unemployment rising from 5.9 percent of the U.S. work force at the end of 1979 to 7.8 percent by mid-1980. It was the highest jobless rate since 1976, when the economy was recovering from its last recession. Unemployment had held steady at about 6 percent since early 1978, but it rose rapidly in the spring of 1980. By July the U.S. Department of Labor counted 8,200,000 persons out of work, 2,000,-000 more than at the start of the year. An estimated 1,000,000 jobs were lost in the automobile, steel, and home construction industries alone, which felt the strongest effects of the economic downturn.

The economy staged a very slow and uncertain recovery during the second half of the year, and unemployment ebbed slightly. In October the unemployment rate was 7.6 percent. There were 97,176,000 persons employed (compared with 97,474,000 in October, 1979) and 8,005,000 persons unemployed (compared with 6,121,000 in October, 1979). As in previous years, the unemployment rate in 1980 for blacks and other minorities remained about twice that for whites: 14.3 percent to 6.7 percent in October. Unemployment among minority teenagers remained even more severe, running at nearly 40 percent.

**Economic Policy Debate.** Leaders of organized labor urged President Jimmy Carter to seek reductions in unemployment as his chief economic priority. Labor leaders wanted the government to increase spending for job-creating programs, a traditional Democratic Party policy that the Carter

### A Sister for the Council

The 35-member executive council of the AFL-CIO waived a couple of informal rules and acquired its first woman member on Aug. 21: Joyce Dannen Miller, 52, president of the Coalition of Labor Union Women and a vice-president of the Amalgamated Clothing and Textile Workers. A union member since her college days at the University of Chicago, Joyce Miller had for many years believed that union activity could be helpful to women in achieving equal rights. Since she had continued to work while raising her three children, she was also active in developing child-care programs in her native Chicago. Associates describe the tall, dark-haired labor leader, who now has a home in Guttenberg, N.J., and an office in New York City, as "efficient but not officious."

*Joyce Dannen Miller.*

administration had pursued in 1977. In 1980, however, the President and the Congress declared that their first priority was to reduce inflation, which was persisting at a 13 percent rate for the second consecutive year. The government rejected large increases in the budget for jobs programs as inflationary. In some areas the government reduced such programs as the Comprehensive Employment and Training Act (CETA). The government decided to eliminate in 1981 at least 50,000 of the 450,000 CETA public service jobs available in 1980. To fight unemployment, the Administration proposed a traditional Republican Party economic policy: tax reductions (in 1981) that were intended to stimulate private business and lead to the creation of new private-sector jobs.

During his successful campaign for the Presidency, Republican nominee Ronald Reagan faulted Carter repeatedly for allowing unemployment to climb. The issue appeared to help Reagan win a larger share of votes from union and blue-collar households than prior Republican nominees had received—44 percent, according to one estimate.

**Other Economic Developments.** Labor leaders sat down with business leaders and public representatives to establish a new voluntary wage guideline for 1980. President Carter had set a 7 percent guideline for 1979, but labor leaders rejected it as too low. The 1980 guideline called for limiting wage and fringe benefit increases to within a range of 7.5 percent and 9.5 percent a year. The guideline contained several exceptions that allowed for larger increases, however, and many

unions either took advantage of the exceptions or ignored the guideline. The Department of Labor said that contracts covering at least 1000 workers and negotiated during the first nine months of 1980 contained first-year wage increases averaging 9.7 percent, along with other gains that pushed the added cost of the settlements to well above 10 percent per year.

Because of high unemployment in the auto industry and a large increase in U.S. sales of small, fuel-efficient imported cars from Japan, the United Automobile Workers (UAW) abandoned its long advocacy of free trade between nations. The union, which estimated that 250,000 of its 1,500,000 members were laid off indefinitely during the depth of the recession, joined the Ford Motor Co. in asking the government for temporary import quotas or higher duties until U.S. auto companies could increase their capacity to build small cars. The U.S. International Trade Commission, however, ruled that import sales had not harmed the U.S. industry sufficiently to warrant trade restrictions. UAW President Douglas A. Fraser was elected to the Chrysler Corp. board on May 13—the first time a union leader had joined the board of a major U.S. corporation.

**Stevens and Union Settle.** On Oct. 19, J. P. Stevens & Co., a symbol of corporate resistance to unionization in the South, settled with the Amalgamated Clothing and Textile Workers on its first union contract, which covered 3000 workers at mills in Roanoke Rapids, N.C. The settlement came six years after the union won a representation election at Roanoke Rapids, and 17 years after an organizing drive was launched against the company. In its fight to stay nonunion, Stevens took steps that resulted in 22 decisions by the National Labor Relations Board involving violations of federal labor laws, such as the illegal firing of workers for supporting the union. In exchange for the contract, the union agreed to halt its four-year-old consumer boycott of Stevens products and to end its "corporate isolation" campaign of pressuring other companies to sever ties with the textile manufacturer. Stevens reserved the right to resist unionization of other plants it operates around the country.

**Changes at the AFL-CIO.** George Meany, who stepped down as president of the AFL-CIO in November, 1979, because of poor health, died on Jan. 10 at the age of 85. Officials of the 13,600,000-member labor federation later disclosed that the influential labor leader, who had presided over the AFL-CIO ever since its formation in 1955, had been suffering from leukemia. Paul Hall, president of the Seafarers International Union since 1957 and the most senior vice-president of the AFL-CIO, died June 22 at the age of 65. On Aug. 21 the labor federation's policymaking executive council elected its first woman member in recognition of the huge influx of women into the work force. Joyce Dannen Miller, a vice-president of the Amalgamated Clothing and Textile Workers and president of the Coalition of Labor Union Women, joined 34 men on the council.

**Strike Activity.** The longest strike in the history of the Screen Actors Guild formally ended on Oct. 23, when the 45,000-member union ratified a new contract with television and film producers. The union had struck on July 21, when filming for the new television season was to begin, over fees for pay television and sales of home videocassettes and video disks. The strike, which forced viewers to endure two additional months of reruns, was joined by the American Federation of Television and Radio Artists and the American Federation of Musicians.

The longest major strike in the UAW's history ended on April 20, when workers at International Harvester Co. accepted a new contract. The 35,000 workers were off the job for 172 days in a strike that began on Nov. 1, 1979. The nation's oil refineries were struck for more than ten weeks by 55,000 members of the Oil, Chemical and Atomic Workers International Union, which settled in March on new contracts raising wages 10.5 percent a year.

Other strikes affected almost every human endeavor across the country: the orchestra of New York City's Metropolitan Opera, New York City transit workers, silver miners in Idaho, winery workers in northern California, tow-truck opera-

Laid-off blue-collar workers swelled the numbers of those applying for unemployment benefits in 1980. An estimated 1,000,000 jobs were lost in the automobile, steel, and home construction industries alone.

tors in Rhode Island, taxi drivers in Chicago, diaper service workers in Miami, ferry workers in Seattle, and security guards at the space center at Cape Canaveral, Fla. Numerous strikes also involved garbage workers, bus drivers, jail guards, teachers, police and fire fighters, municipal workers, and newspaper employees.

**Labor Peace.** The largest contract negotiations of the year were concluded without strikes. The Bell Telephone System settled on Aug. 9 with unions representing 700,000 workers on new contracts that raised wages 10.5 percent per year. The United Steelworkers of America and the major steel companies, bargaining again under a no-strike agreement, settled in April on contracts that raised wages for 286,000 workers by more than 30 percent over three years. Longshoremen, aluminum workers, and aerospace workers also settled on national contracts without strikes.

**Foreign and Other Developments.** American labor unions sent money and praise to striking workers in Poland for establishing the first independent trade union movement in a Communist nation; see POLAND. The U.S. rejoined the International Labor Organization (ILO) in February to end a 28-month-long boycott of the United Nations agency. The U.S. government said a pro-Soviet tilt

Members of the Screen Actors Guild were on strike against television and film producers for three months in 1980. Among those seen on a Los Angeles picket line was Telly Savalas.

in ILO policy that had prompted the U.S. withdrawal had been corrected. The International Longshoremen's Association refused to handle Iranian and Soviet ship cargo to protest the seizure of American embassy personnel in Tehran and the Soviet intervention in Afghanistan. The UAW and International Association of Machinists agreed to consider a merger that would create the nation's largest union, with 2,300,000 members. The U.S. Supreme Court ruled that workers may refuse to perform jobs they consider dangerous without being punished by employers.

**Elections.** Organized labor took a beating on Nov. 4 as President Carter, backed by most unions and the AFL-CIO, was defeated for reelection and Republicans gained control of the U.S. Senate. According to one count, the unions lost a net of 11 Senators and 30 Representatives who had been expected to look favorably on labor-backed issues in Congress. The powerful International Brotherhood of Teamsters and three other unions (the National Maritime Union, the Professional Air Traffic Controllers, and the National Association of Police Organizations) supported Ronald Reagan.                                                  O.U.

**LABRADOR.** See STATISTICS OF THE WORLD.

**LAOS.** Although it remained one of the backwaters of the Communist world, Laos in 1980 increasingly became a pawn in a complicated po-

litical game ranging Vietnam and the Soviet Union on one side and Thailand and China on the other.

**Politics.** Bolstered by a Vietnamese military force of 40,000, the government of Prime Minister Kaysone Phomvihan appeared solidly in control. It continued to suppress opposition, and in April the London-based human rights organization Amnesty International charged the Laotian government with holding tens of thousands of political prisoners for nearly five years without trial.

Resistance to the regime was not entirely eradicated among the scattered tribespeople. In the spring, Laotian and Vietnamese troops scoured the mountain areas in an attempt to crush the insurgents. In June, Hmong tribesmen (known to outsiders as the Meo) who had fled into Thailand told officials in Bangkok that the Vietnamese were using poison gas to subdue them.

In October reports reached the outside world of an attempted coup in Vientiane. If an attempt was indeed made, it failed. Spokesmen for the Laotian government claimed that pro-Chinese conspirators had plotted the overthrow of the government. About 500 people, including government officials, army officers, and students were placed under arrest.

**Economy.** Beset by appalling economic troubles, including sagging production in the socialized sectors of the economy and the continued flight of skilled people to Thailand, the government introduced a series of reforms early in the year. These included monetary incentives for higher production, higher prices to the farmers, and a more liberal attitude toward private trade.

**Foreign Affairs.** Laos remained closely aligned with Vietnam and its Soviet sponsors. For that, the poverty-stricken, landlocked country was forced to pay a price. In June, Thailand (apparently with Chinese encouragement) closed its border with Laos. The pretext for the action was the killing of a Thai marine by Laotian soldiers, but it was widely believed that the Thais acted against Laos as an indirect way of punishing the Vietnamese for an incursion they had made into Thailand. Whatever the case, the sealing of the border, which lasted for months, caused Laos grave economic hardships. International aid destined for Laos, including manufactured goods and gasoline, piled up on the Thai side of the border. In Vientiane, prices for such essential imports as rice and cooking oil soared.

*See* STATISTICS OF THE WORLD.                    R.J.C.

**LEBANON.** The political situation in Lebanon remained unstable in 1980. With no effective government, Lebanon was basically divided into districts controlled by more than 20 private Christian and Muslim armies. A Syrian peacekeeping force

of more than 20,000 also remained in Lebanon, as did Palestinian forces. Some of the armed factions continued to be subsidized by outside powers, including Iran, Iraq, Israel, Libya, and Syria.

**Infighting.** The most fundamental differences were between Christians and Muslims, but the most savage fighting was between Christians. In July Bashir Gemayel, son of Phalangist Party leader Pierre Gemayel, emerged as the dominant Christian figure. In three days of heavy fighting in and around Beirut, his 10,000–15,000-man militia, the largest Christian force, destroyed the smaller Tiger forces of the rival Christian National Liberal Party of former President Camille Chamoun. Tanks and artillery were used, and more than 300 were reportedly killed and many more wounded. Chamoun's son, Dany, who had been leader of his father's militia forces, gave up this position and renounced politics.

Sporadic heavy fighting occurred in the south between Palestinians and the Christian Lebanese army, which was led by Maj. Saad Haddad and supported by Israel. This army shelled Palestinian positions, including the Palestinian stronghold of Tyre. In April Haddad's forces engaged in a gun battle with soldiers from the United Nations Interim Force in Lebanon (UNIFIL) and also shelled UNIFIL headquarters. The Christians accused UNIFIL's 600-man Irish battalion of being partial

*With Israeli support, a Christian militia continued to control about 300 sq.mi. of territory in southern Lebanon during 1980. The militia was in frequent conflict with U.N. forces.*

to the Palestine Liberation Organization (PLO) by permitting the PLO to have bases in the area and preventing Christian militia from occupying Atiri and other villages. They took UNIFIL soldiers as hostages but later released them.

Sporadic fighting was also reported throughout the year in northern Lebanon between Phalangist militiamen and Syrian troops, and between Phalangists and supporters of former President Suleiman Franjieh, the head of another major Christian faction.

The Iran-Iraq conflict also led to fighting between their supporters in Lebanon—Shi'ite Muslims versus left-wing pro-Palestinian Muslims (the Arab Liberation Front). Clashes began in April when Shi'ites in Beirut protested the disappearance in Iraq of Imam Mohammed al-Bakr Sadr, the spiritual leader of Shi'ites in Iraq. Syrian forces put down the fighting.

**Syria.** In early February Syria announced plans to withdraw an estimated 8000 soldiers from Beirut and redeploy them in eastern Lebanon. But at the request of the Lebanese government, which maintained that its forces were too weak to keep the peace, Syria agreed to delay this move. In March some 1500 Syrian troops were shifted from Beirut to eastern Lebanon, and Lebanese government soldiers replaced them without incident.

**Israel.** In early April some 300–350 Israeli soldiers invaded southern Lebanon in reprisal for a Palestinian terrorist attack on an Israeli border kibbutz. They withdrew after a five-day occupation amid a great deal of international pressure.

On Aug. 19 Israel staged its largest raid into southern Lebanon since March, 1978. Backed by artillery and air support, about 500 Israeli soldiers attacked 18 PLO military positions that Israel said were staging areas for PLO attacks on Israel. There were other Israeli raids throughout the year on PLO targets in Lebanon and skirmishes between Syrian and Israeli planes over Lebanon.

**Government.** In June Prime Minister Selim al-Hoss resigned his position but agreed to stay on and form a caretaker government until President Elias Sarkis could find a replacement. In July Sarkis named Takieddin Solh, but Solh was unable to form a cabinet. It was not until October that Hoss was able to relinquish his post to Shafiq al-Wazam, who announced the formation of a 22-member cabinet on Oct. 26.

*See* STATISTICS OF THE WORLD.                    C.G.

**LESOTHO.** *See* STATISTICS OF THE WORLD.

**LIBERIA.** The political and economic dominance in Liberia of the Americo-Liberians came to an abrupt and bloody end in 1980 in a military coup. Descendants of those who returned to Africa from the United States as freed slaves and who

founded the republic in 1847, the Americo-Liberians controlled political and economic affairs through the True Whig Party (TWP), even though they numbered less than 5 percent of the population. In recent years efforts were made to improve economic conditions among the indigenous population and bring them into the country's political life. This was particularly true under William R. Tolbert, Jr., who had been Liberia's president since 1971. But in 1979 the country was stunned by riots over a government-proposed increase in the price of rice, the staple food. Demonstrations of workers and students were organized by the Progressive Alliance of Liberia and its leader, Gabriel Baccus Matthews.

In January the alliance won a court decision granting it official recognition as an opposition party, the Progressive People's Party (PPP). Drawing its support from the 1,700,000 indigenous Liberians, the PPP was seen as a serious challenge to TWP domination. After a speech calling for a general strike to overthrow Tolbert, Matthews was arrested on March 9, along with 33 followers. The crackdown appeared to precipitate the coup of April 12, which was carried out by indigenous enlisted men led by 28-year-old Master Sgt. Samuel K. Doe. Tolbert and at least 26 supporters were killed in the fighting. A People's Redemption Council, with Doe as head of state and Matthews as minister of foreign affairs, was quickly formed. High-ranking TWP officials were arrested, and, on April 22, 13 Tolbert officials were tied to posts on a beach and publicly executed for treason and corruption. On April 25 the 133-year-old constitution was suspended and the council took complete legislative and executive power. The initial executions brought a storm of international protests, and on April 29 the government pledged to halt future ones.

While the Doe government appeared popular among the majority population, initially it faced censure among conservative African states. Indeed, in May, Doe was barred from entering Togo for an economic conference. Ethiopia's Marxist military regime was the first to recognize the new government, and in August Doe visited the country. After receiving pledges of the new government's commitment to private enterprise and social change, the U.S., in late August, resumed its aid programs to Liberia.

*See* STATISTICS OF THE WORLD. *See also* AFRICA.                    J.T.S.

**LIBRARIES.** Libraries throughout the country continued to fight in 1980 for their economic lives as the recession threatened to further erode financial support. Despite fiscal hardships, librarians demonstrated their resilience as they were called

The Library of Congress opened its James Madison Memorial Building in 1980. A three-story-high atrium dominates the interior.

upon to provide information on coping with heat and drought, volcanic eruptions, the influx of refugees, and riots.

Oklahoma's Department of Libraries suggested that local libraries could serve their communities during the long heat wave by supplying iced tea and lemonade for patrons and by establishing a disaster hot line. The seven-county Winding Rivers Library System, based at La Crosse, Wis., provided Spanish-language materials to the Cuban refugees who were settled in the Fort McCoy area. Florida's state government extended funds for special services at five libraries in the Miami neighborhoods torn by rioting in May. French-speaking immigrants from Haiti who settled in these same neighborhoods also received special library services.

**Finance.** In a climate of budget trimming, Cleveland voters approved a second five-year tax supporting their public library's operations and its building expansion program. "Keep Libraries Alive," a campaign by the Berkeley, Calif., Public Library, helped win approval for a new tax to bolster the library's budget.

Alabama's legislators rejected their governor's recommendation of a 5 percent reduction in state aid to public libraries and instead raised the allocation by 12 percent. The Wyoming state legislature approved the disbursement of $750,000 for a statewide circulation system.

**Grants.** Columbia University received a $1,000,000 donation from the Cornelius Vander Starr Foundation to help expand and renovate its East Asian Library. The National Endowment for the Humanities awarded 101 "Challenge" grants for the expansion and renovation of various institutions. The matching grants were dominated by the $1,600,000 earmarked for the New York Public Library's four research libraries.

**New Libraries.** Plans were announced for a new $7,653,000 building to house the Kentucky Department of Library and Archives at Frankfort. A $12,000,000 project was to add 150,000 sq.ft. to the University of Oklahoma Library in Norman.

The Library of Congress opened its long-awaited James Madison Memorial Building in April. Although criticized architecturally, the structure was expected to help alleviate the burden of overuse to which the 1897-vintage main building had been subjected. The Geography and Maps Division was the first tenant in the new building, which was to come into full use in 1981.

**People.** Lee T. Handley was appointed director of SOLINET, an Atlanta-based regional organization serving libraries in ten southeastern states. Alphonse Trezza was named to head up a study on the role of federal libraries in the national library network. Until July 1, Trezza was director of the National Commission on Libraries and Information Science, the study sponsor. California state

Billy Carter (left), brother of President Jimmy Carter, is shown being greeted during his 1978 visit to Libya before a portrait of the country's leader, Muammar el-Qaddafi. According to U.S. intelligence reports, Libya's ties to Billy Carter, which included a $220,000 loan, were part of a plan to gain political influence in the U.S. through labor unions, black organizations, oil companies, and politically important individuals.

librarian Ethel Crockett retired on Aug. 14, the 8th anniversary of her appointment to this post. Elliot L. Shelkrot was appointed Pennsylvania state librarian.

An attempt by Massachusetts Gov. Edward J. King to oust state librarian A. Hunter Rineer from office and replace him with a political appointee stirred the ire of the Massachusetts library community. King proposed replacing Rineer with Gasper Caso, Jr., a library employee who had been active in the 1978 gubernatorial campaign.

**The White House Conference.** The role of libraries in the dissemination of information was discussed at the White House Conference on Libraries and Information Services. From June 7 to June 12 the librarians, information specialists, and community leaders attending the meeting focused their attention on the problems of supplying to the public the vast quantities of information available. The conferees also attempted to assess the impact of new technologies on libraries and the new services that can be offered thanks to electronically sophisticated equipment. The conference took place approximately one month after the establishment of the Office of Libraries and Learning Technologies in the new U.S. Department of Education.
R.J.S.

**LIBYA.** The erratic policies of Libyan leader Col. Muammar el-Qaddafi (see biography at PEOPLE IN THE NEWS) continued to cause havoc both at home and abroad in 1980.

**Domestic Affairs.** Qaddafi put into practice more of the concepts expressed in his Green Book, which forwarded a "Third International Theory" based on a "state of the masses" to replace traditional government forms and create a new economic system. "People's committees," which were introduced in 1979, gradually took over management of all government ministries and industries, including the oil industry. Nationalization measures included state takeover of import, export, and development functions; the replacement of private stores by government-owned supermarkets; and the introduction of state-controlled professional services. Because of the inexperience of the new managers, supermarkets had shortages of goods, and long lines of shoppers were usual.

Qaddafi vowed to "eliminate" enemies of the revolution at home and abroad. During the first half of the year some 2000 to 4000 Libyans were arrested, and many were killed. In the same period some 500 business executives and government officials appeared on televised trials to confess to corruption. Civil servants and almost two thirds of the estimated 150 skilled Libyan oilfield technicians were drafted into the army. Some foreign employees in Libya were accused of spying and arrested.

The currency system was abruptly overhauled. On May 15, bills higher than one dinar ($3.70) were no longer valid. Libyans had one week to bring their money to a bank, receive a bank receipt for their deposit, and accept a maximum cash refund of 1000 dinars.

As a result of these conditions, the economy became paralyzed. Decisions on major projects were postponed because bureaucrats were afraid to assert themselves. Foreign companies, whose presence is vital for Libya's long-term development, refused to sign new contracts.

**Foreign Affairs.** These domestic policies carried over into foreign affairs. Qaddafi repeatedly warned Libyan exiles to return home immediately or "be liquidated." Few returned. From February through June about a dozen Libyan political dissidents abroad were assassinated in Western Europe by squads sent from Libya. In May the United States and Great Britain each expelled four Libyans who had threatened Libyans in their respective countries. In the same month the U.S. closed its embassy in Tripoli as a security precaution. Also in May, ten more Libyan embassies (in Europe and Asia) were taken over by "revolutionary committees" largely made up of students and were renamed people's bureaus. In June the British embassy in Tripoli was firebombed after the expulsion from London of the head of the Libyan mission there for publicly approving the murders of Libyan exiles.

Libya continued to intervene in the affairs of its neighbors. In Chad, an estimated 3000 Libyan troops reportedly were fighting successfully on the side of President Goukouni Oueddei in that country's 16-year-old civil war. Libya was said to have introduced air attacks into this war. In late January Tunisia suspended diplomatic relations after accusing Libya of planning the Jan. 27 attack by Tunisian insurgents on the mining town of Gafsa. On Feb. 4 the French embassy in Tripoli was set on fire, and the French consulate in Benghazi, Libya's second largest city, was wrecked to protest a French naval demonstration of support for Tunisia. France recalled its diplomats.

In September Libya and Syria signed a merger agreement. In theory, the new state would have one joint congress and one executive authority, but it was not expected that the union would actually be implemented. Libya had made unsuccessful attempts to merge with Egypt in 1973 and with Tunisia in 1974.

Libya supported Iran in the Iran-Iraq war, reportedly airlifting military supplies. Iraq and Saudi Arabia severed diplomatic relations with Libya in October. After Saudi Arabia received four radar and command planes from the U.S., Qaddafi threatened to strike them. He also insulted the Saudis by declaring Muslim holy places in Saudi Arabia to be "under U.S. occupation" and by urging Muslims to forgo the annual pilgrimage to Mecca.

See STATISTICS OF THE WORLD. See also MALTA.     C.G.

**LIECHTENSTEIN.** See STATISTICS OF THE WORLD.

**LIFE SCIENCES.** Significant advances in genetic engineering and the potential conversion of plant matter to fuel dominated the life sciences in 1980, but great interest was also aroused by the identification of fossils that pushed back the known existence of life on earth by at least another 1.2 billion years.

## BIOLOGY

In 1980 a number of major advances were made in biology that could lead to a significant reduc-

tion in human suffering caused by diseases such as diabetes, cancer, numerous inherited illnesses, and, perhaps, almost all viral diseases. Most of these advances were accomplished by researchers in the rapidly expanding field of genetic engineering.

**Insulin Research.** Among the first of the devastating diseases thought likely to respond to genetic engineering was diabetes, a disease of metabolic imbalance that is linked directly to a deficiency of the pancreatic hormone insulin. For many years the treatment of diabetics with insulin derived from the pancreases of animals was considered to be a cure. Scientists later found, however, that animal-derived insulin, which varied slightly in molecular structure from that of human beings, often caused undesirable side effects and could not be produced in quantities to meet the demand. In any event, such insulin did not permanently reverse the disease, and scientists searched for a more effective treatment and possible cure.

Two important advances in 1980 brought scientists nearer to this goal. In one advance, Eli Lilly and Co. announced the first test on human beings of genetically engineered insulin. This insulin, identical to that produced by human beings, was collected from bacteria into which the human gene for producing insulin had been placed. The protein-manufacturing processes of the bacteria, in effect, had been forced to manufacture the insulin. The test on human beings began in England on July 14, when the bacteria-derived insulin was given to eight nondiabetic people to determine whether the drug would reduce blood-sugar levels (one of the functions of insulin) without generating unwanted side effects. The results were positive, and company officials were hopeful of going into full production of the insulin by 1982. Production of human insulin by bacteria should

---

**Santa Needs a Shrink**

Santa Claus take heed: A Swedish veterinarian, studying animals slaughtered in a Lapland village, found that four fifths of the reindeer had ulcers. Apparently the problem is nervous exhaustion brought on by modern technology. In former times the Lapp herders skied alongside the beasts and sang soothing songs; now they round them up aboard helicopters, snowmobiles, and motorcycles. There is concern that the resulting noise-engendered stress may be affecting the quality of the meat.

**Two Stories, Two Scientists**
One works at the University of Illinois and the other at Yale University; each figured in a major science story of the year. In June a U.S. Supreme Court decision upheld the patenting of new life forms, as a result of a discovery by Ananda Mohan Chakrabarty, 42, a Calcutta-born geneticist. In September, announcement was made of the successful injection of foreign genes into animal embryos, the work of Francis Hugh Ruddle and his colleagues at Yale. The Jersey City-born biologist, 51, is noted for his height (6'7"), making him, according to his colleagues, "the biggest name in science today."

*Ananda Mohan Chakrabarty (left) and Francis Hugh Ruddle.*

eliminate any shortage of the drug, the supply of which was otherwise expected to become critically limited during the next 20 years.

Perhaps an even more ideal approach to the treatment or cure of diabetes would be to get a diabetic's body to produce insulin normally, because it is often difficult to maintain proper insulin concentrations in the blood through injections. Normally, certain cells in the pancreas respond automatically to changes in blood-sugar level by producing or limiting the production of insulin. If cells unable to do this—the cause of diabetes—could be replaced or reinforced by the introduction of functioning cells, there would be no need for insulin injections.

One of the problems associated with such tissue transplants has been rejection by the host of the donor's cells. In July, however, researchers at Washington University in St. Louis reported an experimental success that could point the way toward alleviating this problem. The scientists, led by Paul E. Lacy, succeeded in transplanting insulin-producing pancreas cells from healthy rats into diabetic mice. The rat pancreatic cells were able to control blood-sugar levels in the mice for a few months. The reason the cells were not rejected, said Lacy, was that special techniques were used to suppress the natural immune responses in the mice. The next step would be to attempt a similar transplant between more divergent species, such as pigs and mice.

**Interferon, Viruses, and Cancer.** Viral diseases and perhaps even cancer could be next in line for attack by genetic engineers. In 1980 a human protein called interferon, a vital defender against viral infections and a possible defender against some forms of cancer, was produced from bacteria for the first time.

Interferon is manufactured by body cells in response to an invasion by viruses such as those that cause the common cold, influenza, rabies, hepatitis, and a host of other viral diseases. In a way not completely understood, the interferon manufactured by an invaded cell helps cells not yet invaded to repulse the onslaught of viruses. Scientists have sought to understand the process, but have been limited in their research by the extreme scarcity of interferon. A single experimental treatment can cost hundreds of dollars, and the interferon available is not as pure as researchers would like it to be.

These problems may have been left behind, however, as the result of a dramatic achievement in 1980 by Charles Weissmann of the University of Zurich. Through complex gene-splicing techniques, Weissmann developed a method thought likely to yield highly purified human interferon, in unlimited quantities, that probably would cost only about $10 per treatment. The method involved the transfer of a human gene for producing interferon into a strain of common bacteria. Subsequent experiments revealed that the interferon made by the bacteria protected cultured human cells from attack by viruses. Weissmann indicated, however, that a number of problems remained. For example, the bacteria produced only a few molecules of interferon per bacterium, and the interferon was not completely identical

Significant advances in genetic engineering were reported in 1980, including successful efforts to obtain suitable forms of insulin and interferon by inserting human genes into bacteria. Here a researcher extracts a culture containing bacteria into which foreign genetic materials have been inserted.

to that produced in human beings. And, at the time of Weissmann's report in January, he had not been able to discover whether the interferon would function in the human body.

By June, hints to the solution of this latter problem were uncovered at another institution. Nowell Stebbing of Genentech, a San Francisco company specializing in genetic engineering programs, reported that interferon made by bacteria had been given to squirrel monkeys before and after they had been infected with a virus that causes deadly encephalomyocarditis, a disease involving the linings of the brain, spinal cord, and heart of human beings as well as monkeys. All the animals given interferon survived, whereas those in a control group not given the substance did not survive. In addition, Stebbing reported that the Genentech method for interferon production yielded as many as 100,000 molecules of the chemical per bacterium.

For largely theoretical reasons, scientists also hoped that interferon might help to combat cancers in human beings. Hans Strander of the Karolinska Hospital in Stockholm reported that of 12 patients suffering from bone cancer who were treated with interferon, six had become free of the disease. Less impressive results were reported by two other groups of researchers. E. F. Osserman of the Columbia University College of Physicians and Surgeons revealed that of 14 patients treated with interferon for multiple myeloma (a cancer of the bone marrow), only four showed substantial improvement. In another study, sponsored by the American Cancer Society and involv-

ing breast cancer, 5 of 16 patients responded positively to interferon therapy. No positive results were found, however, in a group of 16 patients with lung cancer at the Memorial Sloan-Kettering Cancer Center in New York City. Nevertheless, the fact that some patients seemed to have benefited from taking interferon justified further long-term studies, according to researchers.

**Genetic Diseases.** Also in 1980 a number of giant steps were taken in the direction of genetically reversing heretofore uncorrectable inherited diseases. The first of these steps, according to many researchers, was clearly a significant scientific advance, whereas the second step became the focus of considerable controversy. Both achievements were the outgrowth of work done by a team of researchers led by Martin Cline at the University of California at Los Angeles.

In April, Cline and his colleagues announced that they had succeeded in transferring a gene from one kind of mouse into another kind of mouse whose cells did not possess the gene, a feat never before accomplished in complete animals. The transferred gene conferred a specific type of drug resistance to the host mice. Of particular significance was the fact that the process involved bone marrow cells, the source of red and white blood cells. Moreover, because bone marrow cells ceaselessly produce offspring throughout the life of an organism, any genetic material introduced into such cells could exert its influence for the lifetime of the individual. This would be of special significance for human beings suffering from certain inherited abnormalities of the blood-forming organs, such as sickle-cell anemia (which affects 10 percent of the black population in the United States) and thalassemia (a disease with a high incidence among Mediterranean peoples).

Presumably, more animal experiments would have to be performed before trying to treat humans, and permission to undertake human experiments would have to be obtained from appropriate sponsoring agencies. To the surprise of the scientific community, however, during the summer of 1980 Cline launched a human experiment similar to his mouse experiment. It was not performed in the U.S., where permission for the work had not been acquired. The experimental subjects were two women, both suffering from a fatal form of thalassemia, one at the Hadassah Hospital in Jerusalem and the other at the University Polyclinic in Naples. The institutions had granted Cline permission to perform his experiment.

Cline and his co-workers got bacteria to produce genes that instructed cells to manufacture normal human hemoglobin, then introduced the normal hemoglobin genes into the bone marrow of the two women. Results were still pending at year's end. In the meantime, Cline asserted that sufficient animal experimentation had been performed to justify the jump to human tests, and that the movement of the research site to Israel and Italy was not made to circumvent U.S. regulations governing human experimentation, but because of the greater likelihood of finding patients with beta thalassemia major in Mediterranean countries.

In another pioneering experiment, performed by Francis Ruddle, Jon Gordon, and George Scangos at Yale University, a different avenue to the correction of genetic defects was successfully explored. The approach might be called preventive genetic engineering, because its target was the developing embryo rather than the developed adult. The Yale scientists reported that they had succeeded in transplanting genes for the production of a specific enzyme into mouse eggs shortly after they had been fertilized. The transfer was successful in only 2 of 78 cases, however, and the researchers were not certain whether the genes were functional. They also did not yet know whether mice developed from the genetically altered eggs would perpetuate the transfer by passing the gene to their offspring. If the technique does prove to be a complete success, it can open the way to the treatment of genetically defective embryos and fetuses so that they will not be born with genetic diseases.                              C.P.

## BOTANY

Botanical research in 1980 advanced in practical areas such as the production of energy from plants, more efficient fertilizer use, and better pest control. Two significant predictions were made for the year 2000. "Global 2000," a report issued by the U.S. State Department and the Council on Environmental Quality, contained the grim prediction that by the year 2000, 40 percent of the world's forests will have disappeared, serious worldwide deterioration of agricultural soils will have occurred, and a large number of plant species will have become extinct. A concurrent report from the Office of Technology Assessment, however, optimistically stated that plants could supply up to 20 percent of human energy needs by the year 2000, although some concern was expressed about the diversion of food crops into energy production.

**Energy Production.** With the drastic increase in the price of petroleum, scientists have been searching for reasonable gasoline substitutes. One of the most promising is gasohol, a combination of gasoline and ethanol (ethyl alcohol). At the August meeting of the American Chemical Society's Chemical Congress, a number of possible ways for producing ethanol from plants were described. For example, Gerald Borglum of Miles Laboratories stated that ethanol could be produced more economically from cereal grains such as corn by using enzymes to convert their starch to sugar, followed by fermentation of the sugar. Ruxton Villet of the Solar Energy Research Institute found forage crops such as Sudan grass to be more promising than wood because they have less lignin, which slows the conversion of cellulose to sugar.

Oil-rich seeds of the jojoba plant were seen as another good possibility for biomass conversion. Werner Haag of Mobil Research and Development described a new catalyst, called Zeolite ZSM-5, which could upgrade the hydrocarbons from jojobas and other plants to a material suitable for production of premium fuel or chemicals normally made from petroleum. In order to increase the seed yield from jojoba crops, Demetrious Yermanos of the University of California at Riverside bred a strain of jojoba with both male and female flowers on one plant instead of separate male and female plants. Finally, Donald Wicklow of the U.S. Department of Agriculture found that fairy goblet fungus could digest the lignin in wheat straw, making the wheat straw more suitable for the production of ethanol.

**Fertilizer Research.** Because fertilizer production was also energy costly, research efforts to reduce fertilizer needs were under way as well. In 1980,

In August the Goodyear Tire & Rubber Co. unveiled a 5000-lb. earth-mover tire made of guayule, a rubber obtained from a shrub that grows wild in the deserts of the southwestern U.S. and Mexico. The energy crisis heightened interest in the shrub as a source of domestic rubber.

Berry Cysewski of Battelle's Pacific Northwest Laboratories found that tomatoes grown in soil treated with blue-green algae, which extract atmospheric nitrogen, could use some of the nitrogen taken in by the algae. And C. M. Farris of U.S.S. Agrichemicals, in Alabama, reported that waste products from ammonia manufacture could be used to fertilize crops.

In a related development, the Department of Agriculture completed a survey of organic farmers, who prefer to use natural rather than chemical fertilizers and pest controls. The survey concluded that organic farming was more labor-intensive but caused less pollution and consumed less energy than conventional farming.

**Pest Control.** Several interesting developments took place in pest-control research in 1980. Richard Converse of the Department of Agriculture adapted a human viral detection test to plants that increased detection sensitivity 100 times over previous techniques and made possible the detection of viruses in dormant plants. And Gary Strobel and Don Myers of Montana State University found a bacterium, *Pseudomonas,* that appears to halt the spread of Dutch elm disease (a fatal fungus carried by elm bark beetles) when it is injected into the trees.

Researchers also reported finding what appeared to be natural defense systems that some plants have against pests. A scientist at Hebrew University in Jerusalem isolated an interferon-like antiviral agent from tobacco plants, and a researcher at Washington State University described an immune system in corn and potatoes. The latter plants produce enzymes, in response to insect attacks, that seem to interfere with the insects' digestive systems.                    R.P.P.

## ZOOLOGY

Zoologists in 1980 launched an intensive effort to save the giant panda in the wild. Researchers identified fossil imprints that pushed the beginning of life on earth back to 3.5 billion years, and paleontologists found fossil bones of the world's largest flying bird.

**Panda Crisis.** According to a survey by zoologists in the People's Republic of China, more than 10 percent of the world's estimated giant panda population of 1000 have died since 1975. The rapid drop took place primarily because arrow bamboo, the pandas' main food source, came into bloom, as it does about once every century. The bamboo dies after it blooms, leaving the pandas with a severe food shortage. An international rescue mission, led by zoologist George Schaller and organized by the World Wildlife Fund, the Chinese government, and other international organizations, began a survey of the panda population in their remote mountain habitat. Scientists were to try to plan strategies to save the animals, but even if successful, the panda population would not recover for many years.

Another panda rescue effort was in progress in zoos around the world, where 35 pandas lived in captivity. Until 1980 all but one of the many attempts to breed pandas in zoos had failed. In August, Mexico City zoo officials reported the first giant panda born in captivity outside of China, but the baby was killed eight days later when its mother accidentally rolled on the cub as the mother slept. In Washington, D.C.'s National Zoo, officials tried a new ploy in May: artificial insemination. Careful monitoring revealed no later signs of pregnancy, however, and zoo officials were uncertain whether they would try it again in 1981.

**More Species Endangered.** Several other endangered species were the focus of intensive conservation efforts in 1980. The International Union for the Conservation of Nature reported that Uganda's elephants were in danger of extinction in a year or two, mostly because of illegal hunting for their prized ivory tusks. The black rhinoceros was also in danger of becoming a victim of human greed. The number of these animals, valued for their horns, plummeted in recent years. Efforts to bring India's Bengal tiger population up to survival level, on the other hand, were reported to be successful. Several projects, by various environmental groups, were initiated or under way in 1980 to determine priorities in attempts to rescue endangered species. This was thought necessary because funds and time to save all such species were simply not available.

**Oldest Known Life.** On June 19 paleobiologist J. William Schopf of the University of California at Los Angeles (UCLA) announced the discovery of bacterial cells that had created fossil imprints estimated to be 3.5 billion years old. The imprints were discovered earlier in 1980 in northwestern Australia by scientists from Australia and UCLA. The fossils, which represent at least five different types of microbial life, demonstrated that the earth was populated by multiple forms of life about 1.2 billion years earlier than had previously been confirmed.

**Big Bird.** Scientists in 1980 also discovered bones of the world's largest known flying bird, with a wingspan of 7.6 m (25 ft.), a height of 1.8 m (6 ft.), a length of 3.3 m (11 ft.), and a weight of 72 to 76 kg (160 to 170 lb.). The bird, named *Argentavis magnificens,* soared the skies from 5,000,000 to 8,000,000 years ago. Paleontologists who studied the fossil at Argentina's La Plata Museum were able to tell, from markings on the wing bones, that the bird actually flew. Records exist of larger flying reptiles and of larger nonflying birds, but

**BALD EAGLE**
*wingspan*
**8 FEET**

**GIANT TERATORN**
*wingspan*
**25 FEET**

© 1980 National Geographic Society

An artist's sketch compares the world's largest known flying bird, the extinct Argentavis magnificens (a teratorn), to a bald eagle. Fossil bones of the extinct bird indicate that it had a wingspan of 25 ft. and weighed about 165 lb.

By taking samples from this well-preserved baby mammoth found frozen in Siberia, University of California researchers proved in 1980 that the woolly mammoth, now extinct, was the ancestor of today's elephant.

this is the largest bird known to have cleared the ground.

**Other Paleontological Studies.** The 1980 discovery of fossil footprints apparently made by partially submerged carnivorous dinosaurs that touched bottom as they swam across a lake in Connecticut provided the first evidence that such dinosaurs could swim. Previously, scientists had thought that plant-eating dinosaurs were able to flee into water to escape the supposedly nonswimming carnivores.

University of California researchers proved in 1980 that the extinct woolly mammoth was the ancestor of today's elephant. They did so by taking albumin from a well-preserved baby mammoth found frozen in Siberia, injecting the protein into rabbits, and taking the antibodies produced by the rabbits and testing them against albumin from modern elephants. Such tests had previously been used only in studying relationships among living animals.                S.P.W.

**LITERATURE.** Among the major literary developments of 1980 were:

### AMERICAN

Writers in the United States began the new decade with their eyes on the past more often than on the future. Novels with historical settings, biographies, and histories dominated publishing, along with books on contemporary issues of economic and political stability. Poets demonstrated a continuing search for individual forms of expression.

**Fiction.** Several American novelists looked back to earlier periods for material. E. L. Doctorow blended history and fiction in *Loon Lake,* the story of a street urchin who rises to power within the establishment. On a more massive scale, James Michener hung the plot of *The Covenant* on virtually all of South Africa's history. Mary Lee Settle set *The Scapegoat* in West Virginia in 1912 for a story centered on a miners' strike, and in *Newsreel,* Irwin Faust's hero is a man whose life is inextricably entwined with Dwight D. Eisenhower.

Erica Jong explored contemporary perceptions of sexuality in *Fanny: Being the True History of the Adventures of Fanny Hackabout Jones,* a parody of John Cleland's classic *Fanny Hill.* The disintegration of a marriage is the subject of Herbert Gold's well-crafted *He/She.* John Gardner's *Freddy's Book* used the novel-within-a-novel technique to relate a mythic tale.

Peter DeVries's high regard for the comic possibilities of fiction is evident in *Consenting Adults; Or, The Duchess Will Be Furious,* the picaresque adventures of a college student. The posthumous publication and success of John Kennedy Toole's

Joyce Carol Oates, one of the most distinguished and prolific of American novelists, was the author in 1980 of Bellefleur, a seven-generation saga set in a castle in upstate New York.

*A Confederacy of Duncans* added an ironic footnote to the life of this author. Walker Percy offered *The Second Coming,* in which the protagonist suffers from attacks of memory.

Gilbert Sorrentino's *Aberration of Starlight* captures depression America much as James Joyce preserved early 20th-century Dublin. Southern fiction writer Barry Hannah offered *Ray,* the story of a former fighter pilot's restless search for meaning and happiness.

The *Collected Stories of Eudora Welty* presents a package of the Mississippi author's work since 1936. Other interesting collections of short stories included Stuart Dybek's *Childhood and Other Neighborhoods,* which tells of growing up in Chicago in the 1950's; Paul Theroux's *World's End and Other Stories,* a kind of travel fiction developing themes of cross-cultural conflicts and rootlessness; and Joanne Greenberg's *High Crimes and Misdemeanors,* which explores spiritual questions in tones of humor and pathos.

**Contemporary Issues.** The economy figured significantly in 1980's books on contemporary issues. Milton and Rose Friedman's *Free to Choose: A*

Personal Statement articulates the authors' laissez-faire economic theories. Lester C. Thurow, on the other hand, presents in *The Zero-Sum Society: Distribution and the Possibilities for Economic Change* his belief that the economy is no longer capable of substantial growth.

The sometimes disastrous effects of industrialization are described in Michael Brown's *Laying Waste: The Poisoning of America by Toxic Chemicals,* which focuses on the pollution of Love Canal in New York State. Life after the industrial revolution is Alvin Toffler's subject in *The Third Wave.*

Maggie Scarf headed the list of feminist writers with her *Unfinished Business: Pressure Points in the Lives of Women,* which defines the depression and suicidal tendencies resulting from the fear of being alone. Ann Jones took a more aggressive line in *Women Who Kill,* a feminist explanation of female murderers as revolutionaries against male oppression. From the male perspective, Gay Talese's *Thy Neighbor's Wife* provides a look at modern American sexual mores.

Former Yippie leader Abbie Hoffman offered *Soon to Be a Major Motion Picture,* a funny and surprisingly moving story of the 1960's and early 1970's. For his *American Dreams: Lost and Found,* Studs Terkel conducted extensive interviews with the great and not-so-great to present a variety of visions and revisions of national purpose.

**History and Biography.** Page Smith wove historical fact into a compelling narrative in *The Shaping of America: A People's History of the Young Republic, Volume 3.* The book covers the years from 1783 to 1826. In a more scholarly fashion, E. Digby Baltzell examines why Boston's upper class was so much more prominent intellectually and politically than was Philadelphia's during the early days of the U.S. in *Puritan Boston and Quaker Philadelphia.*

James H. Billington's *Fires in the Minds of Men: Origins of the Revolutionary Faith* examines revolutionaries from Paris in 1789 to Berkeley in the 1960's. Marxist historian Eugene D. Genovese's *From Rebellion to Revolution: Afro-American Slave Revolts in the Making of the Modern World* interprets slave uprisings as a challenge to a capitalistic system.

*Top: Maxine Hong Kingston followed her earlier* The Woman Warrior *with* China Men, *another account of the lives and recollections of Chinese-Americans. Center: E. L. Doctorow blended depression-era history with fiction in his novel* Loon Lake. *Bottom: In 1980, Robert Creeley came out with a new volume of highly introspective verse entitled* Later.

In what was, as far as anyone could tell, the first reception of its kind at the White House, 21 poets read selections from their works on Jan. 3, 1980. Here Stanley Kunitz reads from his poetry as Rosalynn Carter and daughter Amy listen.

The decline of patriarchy is examined in Carl N. Degler's *At Odds: Women and the Family in America from the Revolution to the Present.* He establishes the period of 1770–1820 as the most significant period of change. John Boswell's *Christianity, Social Tolerance and Homosexuality* studies homosexuals through the ages and concludes that the early Christian church was much more tolerant of homosexuality than was the church in the Middle Ages.

The rise of anti-Semitism in Vienna during the late 19th century is the subject of Carl E. Schorske's *Fin-de-Siècle Vienna: Politics and Culture.* The volume also traces the rise of socialism and nationalism. Vienna's leading intellectual figure of that period is placed in the context of 19th-century anatomical science in Frank J. Sulloway's *Freud: Biologist of the Mind: Beyond the Psychoanalytical Legend.*

Biographies of literary figures were numerous in 1980. James R. Mellow's *Nathaniel Hawthorne in His Times* is a readable, full retelling of the life of the author and his contemporaries. The mystic acceptance of death by Walt Whitman, on the other hand, provides the focus for Justin Kaplan's *Walt Whitman, A Life.* The life of poet E. E. Cummings was well told by Richard S. Kennedy in *Dreams in the Mirror.*

Townsend Ludington's *John Dos Passos: A Twentieth Century Odyssey* tells the story of one of this country's leading experimental novelists. Ronald Steel's *Walter Lippmann and the Ameri-* can Century illuminates the life of this brilliant intellectual. The powerful presence of Lyndon Johnson is captured in Merle Miller's *Lyndon: An Oral Biography.* A more private story is related in Joseph P. Lash's *Helen and Teacher: The Story of Helen Keller and Anne Sullivan Macy.*

**Poetry.** Robert Penn Warren in *Being Here: Poetry: 1977–1980* showed that he has not lost his ability to combine beautiful word music and brilliant imagery. Louis Simpson adopted a more contemporary and personal style in *Caviare at the Funeral.*

---

**First "Poetry Olympics"**

U.S. athletes were not present in Moscow for the twenty-second Summer Olympics, but some other Americans were among 400 people who gathered in London at Westminster Abbey on Sept. 26 for the first convocation of what they hope to develop into a "poetry olympics" movement. Gregory Corso, the American beat-generation poet, joined British "punk" poet John Cooper Clarke in a reading at the Abbey's Poets' Corner, and Samuel Beckett and Stephen Spender sent special poems for the occasion.

Among the more eccentric stylists were Robert Creeley, who presented *Later,* and Robert Bly, who offered *This Tree Will Be Here for a Thousand Years.*

Continuing the tale developed in *The Book of Ephraim,* James Merrill offered *Scripts for the Pageant,* a less successful work. Donald Justice's *Selected Poems,* on the other hand, proves rewarding. Galway Kinnell, a more dramatic poet, offered *Mortal Acts, Mortal Words.*

An interesting first volume of poetry was Roberta Spear's *Silks,* an unsentimental view of the endings of things. Isabella Gardner was also concerned about endings, more particularly death and loneliness, and her *That Was Then* effectively develops these themes. The literature about poetry was enriched by Helen Vendler's *Part of Nature, Part of Us: Modern American Poets,* a sensitive and sympathetic reading of 22 American poets.                                          S.C.L.

## AUSTRALIAN

In 1980 some good literary biography compensated for a generally indifferent year in imaginative literature.

**Poetry.** By far the most ambitious and almost certainly the best book of poetry was Les Murray's *The Boys Who Stole the Funeral.* The original work is a narrative composed in 140 sonnetlike poems. The story is a relatively simple one of two unemployed city boys who steal the body of an old soldier from a suburban funeral home. They drive it north for a proper burial in his home territory. The underlying theme is complex—an attempt to articulate a mythology about rural Australia.

**Drama.** A by-product of the flowering of the Australian theater during the 1970's was an explosion in play publishing. *The Man from Mukinupin* by Dorothy Hewett is a humorous celebration of country life. Barry Oakley's characters in a collection of short pieces, *The Great God Mogadon and Other Plays,* all share a desire to escape the conformism that surrounds them. The same theme dominates David Williamson's latest success, *Travelling North.* Louis Nowra's latest play, *Visions,* takes place in Paraguay in the 1860's against a background of war and civil unrest.

**Nonfiction.** The publication of Axel Clark's biography, *Christopher Brennan,* was widely praised. Brennan, one of Australia's most intellectual poets, was beset by scandal and tragedy throughout his life. A leading critic referred to the book as "that rare combination—a learned and scholarly biography interwoven with sensitive and perceptive literary criticism." W. H. Wilde and T. Inglis Moore's *Letters of Mary Gilmore,* a collection of the poet's correspondence dating from 1896 to

1962, illuminates Australian literary life during that period.

**Awards.** David Ireland won his third Miles Franklin Award, Australia's top literary honor, with the novel *A Woman of the Future.* The New South Wales Premier's Literary Award for fiction went to Peter Carey for a volume of collected stories, *War Crimes.* Journalist David Marr won the nonfiction prize with *Barwick,* a biography of Chief Justice Sir Garfield Barwick, a controversial public figure for 40 years. The Poetry Prize was given posthumously to Douglas Stewart for *The Man in the Honeysuckle.* Murray Bail won first prize in the National Book Council's Awards with his novel *Homecoming,* a stylish exploration of the human condition through the experiences of a group of Australian tourists.                                          I.K.

## CANADIAN

Laying aside the question of Québec's separation, Canadian artists in 1980 offered several outstanding novels, the second volume of an intended trilogy, some noteworthy poetry anthologies, and short stories. These literary efforts suggested a pause after the remarkable flowering of both English and French writing in the 1970's. The next evolutionary step remained to be identified.

**Works in French.** *La Grosse Femme d'à Côté est Enceinte* ("The Fat Woman Next Door Is Pregnant") by Michel Tremblay was the first novel in a trilogy called *Chroniques du Plateau Mont-Royal* ("Chronicles of Mount Royal"). His second novel, *Thérèse et Pierrete à l'École des Saints-Anges* ("Thérèse and Pierrete at the School of Saints-Anges") reflects the author's irreverence toward pompousness and hypocrisy.

**Works in English.** In his latest novel, Mordecai Richler, well known for *The Apprenticeship of Duddy Kravitz,* dealt once more with a perceived Jewish urge "to belong." *Joshua Then and Now* is a comic satire on changing morals and sexual behavior. With cheerful insouciance, the author intersperses a weak plot (Joshua Then) with set pieces on "Jewishness" in Canada (Joshua Now).

Hugh MacLennan, perhaps Canada's most internationally renowned literary figure, published his first novel in 13 years, *Voices in Time.* The book relies on the tired vehicle of time travel, a means by which a future post-apocalyptic world is able to reflect upon its self-destruction from source (the Holocaust) to termination (contemporary society).

Small English presses in British Columbia continued to support such writers as Tom Wayman, Pat Lane, and Dennis Lee; Lee, apart from his success with children's poetry, was increasingly recognized as a poet of exceptional craftsmanship.

The work of the Québec poet Gaston Miron

was translated by Marc Plourde. In his introduction to *The Agonized Life,* Plourde expresses his feeling that Miron has "brought modern poetry to ordinary people. . . ."

Perhaps more than the novel, the short story is indigenous to the Canadian psyche. Writers such as Alister MacCloud (*The Lost Salt Gift of Blood*), Beth Harbour (*Women and Children*), Joyce Harrison (*A Private Place*), and Hugh Hood (*None Genuine Without This Signature*) were well received.

Pierre Berton's first volume on the "war" between Canada and the U.S., *The Invasion of Canada, 1812–13,* could be criticized as fictionalized history. It was professionally and easily executed, however.                                    B.M.P.

## ENGLISH

Biographies and letters of novelists and poets dominated English publishing in 1980. Many major novelists produced new works, but only in a few cases were these thought among their best.

**Fiction.** The £10,000 Booker Prize went to William Golding for *Rites of Passage.* The novel tells the story of a sea voyage to Australia in the early 19th century. Its narrator is a spirited young Regency aristocrat with a witty style. The climax, however, is related in a very different tone. A lower-class clergyman, clumsy but intense and romantic minded, dies of shame because of a sexual involvement he has while on shipboard. The young narrator's view of the world is turned upside down by this event.

Anthony Burgess's novel *Earthly Powers* is an ambitious book. It tells the life story of a Catholic homosexual novelist who is caught up in all the literary, political, and religious affairs of Europe and the U.S. throughout most of the 20th century.

Graham Greene published a short, rather misanthropic novel, *Doctor Fischer of Geneva or The Bomb Party.* Angus Wilson produced his first novel in seven years, *Setting the World on Fire,* about the fate of two very different young brothers at a famous English school, Westminster. Although a rich, magisterial book, it was thought by some critics to be more fanciful than realistic. Kingsley Amis published two books, a futuristic novel about Russians in an occupied England entitled *Russian Hide-and-Seek,* and his well-received *Collected Short Stories.* Iris Murdoch's new novel, *Nuns and Soldiers,* is an elaborate disquisition on the many forms of love. Olivia Manning brought out *The Sum of Things,* to conclude her Levant Trilogy, which tells of a group of English people in World War II. Margaret Drabble offered a portrait of a modern middle-aged woman in *The Middle Ground.* John le Carré's latest spy novel, *Smiley's People,* was a great success.

**Nonfiction.** One of the most remarkable books of the year was *The Letters of Evelyn Waugh,* edited by Mark Amory. It is a further revelation of the provocative, witty, irascible, and also very unhappy life of this novelist, whose reputation grows with the years. Another outstanding collection was the sixth and last volume of the letters of Virginia Woolf. This volume, containing those letters written between 1936 and her death in 1941, shows how her brilliance and sense of fun endured until the end. The third volume of her diary, from 1925 to 1930, was also published. Another final volume in a series is that of Lord Byron's letters and journals, entitled *A Heart for Every Fate.* Covering the years 1822–27, it was edited by Leslie A. Marchand.

Graham Greene brought out his autobiographical *Ways of Escape.* The book consists of all the prefaces contained in the collected edition of his novels, in addition to further reminiscences. Anthony Powell's *Faces in My Time* is the third volume of another prominent novelist's autobiography. Bernard Crick wrote the authorized life of George Orwell. *W. H. Auden,* by Charles Osborne, is the first full-length biography of the poet. W. H. Sean Day-Lewis described his father's poetic career in *C. Day-Lewis: An English Literary Life.* Two other important biographies were Robert Bernard Martin's *Tennyson: The Unquiet Heart* and Mary Moorman's life of her father, historian *George Macaulay Trevelyan.*

**Poetry and Drama.** D. J. Enright's *Oxford Book of Contemporary Verse, 1945–1980,* furnishes the reader with a vivid impression of postwar British poetry. Two impressive plays were Ronald Harwood's *The Dresser,* about a traditional actor-manager, and Alan Bennett's *Enjoy,* concerned with an elderly lower-middle-class couple.   D.M.

## FOREIGN

Foreign literature in 1980 was highlighted by an increasing number of titles quickly translated into English and a growing appreciation for modern Oriental literary works.

**French.** In 1980 French writers had few surprises for readers, and nonfiction works again seemed to dominate. The most provocative recent works of Roland Barthes, the essayist-critic who died on March 25, were gathered in *New Critical Essays.* Philosopher André Glucksmann's *The Master Thinkers* is a denunciation of some of the most influential Western philosophers. The French film director Eric Rohmer debuted as a fiction writer. He published *Les Contes Moraux* ("Moral Tales"), which contains stories on which he based some of his best-known films, including *Claire's Knee* and *My Night at Maud's.* Julie Pavesi's novel, *La Nuit des Buchers* ("The Night of the Witchburn-

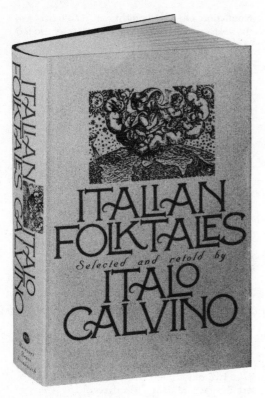

*A popular work in English translation during 1980 was Italo Calvino's* Italian Folktales.

ing"), examines the arcane world of witchcraft and satanic cults in a medieval setting. Suzanne Prou's *Les Dimanches* ("Sundays") is a more conventional story of the conflict between narrowly religious parents and freedom-loving children in contemporary provincial France.

**Italian.** Oriana Fallaci's *Un Uomo* ("A Man"), a fictionalized account of the journalist's affair with Greek activist-poet Alexander Panagoulis, was popular in Italy, but the book was judged to be overblown and cliché-ridden by foreign critics. Giorgio Manganelli's well-received *Centuria* highlights shocking, unexplainable, and often mystifying events in 100 miniature novels. *Italian Folktales* as retold by Italo Calvino became available in English translation during 1980.

**Spanish and Latin American.** Two picaresque novels by little-known writers made literary news in 1980. Gonzalo Martré, a Mexican, wrote *El Chanfalla,* the story of a little boy who leaves home and wanders through Mexico City after convincing himself that he has accidentally killed someone. Eduardo Mendoza's *El Misterio de la Cripta Embrujada* ("The Mystery of the Cursed Tomb") is

the satiric account of a hoodlum's police-sanctioned search for a missing teenager. A collection of short stories by the Argentine Julio Cortázar was published in English under the title *A Change of Light.* Cortázar displayed his literary skills in these subtle, elegiac stories. A volume of short fiction by the Mexican Carlos Fuentes also became available in English. Entitled *Burnt Water,* its pungent and often ghoulish stories center on Mexico City. A new Brazilian novel, Márcia Souza's *The Emperor of the Amazon,* stirred interest in the U.S.

**German.** The latest work of fiction by Nobel laureate Heinrich Böll, *Fursorgliche Belagerung* ("Solicitous Siege"), deals with the timely theme of terrorism. The novel tells of an influential newspaper chain owner and his family who brace themselves for an attack. *Man in the Holocene* by Swiss writer Max Frisch garnered praise on both sides of the Atlantic. A sparse novel, it chronicles the slow decline of an elderly engineer.

While Böll and Frisch concentrated on the present in their latest works, the East German Christa Wolf delved into the past in her novel, *A Model Childhood.* The heroine of this work tries to recapture her childhood, which was spent in Hitler's Germany.

**Russian and East European.** With most dissident and unorthodox intellectuals either silenced or forced into exile, literary activity inside the Soviet Union continued to be low-key. The appearance in print of a group of hitherto banned poems by Boris Pasternak, however, created a sensation in Moscow. The staging of a daring anti-Stalinist play, *The House on the Embankment,* in the Soviet Union also raised many eyebrows.

As in previous years, the most important Soviet books were published outside that country. *The Education of a True Believer* by Lev Kopelev, a leading dissident who left the U.S.S.R. in 1980, gives an account of his ultimate disillusionment with the Communist system. An absorbing novel about Boris Pasternak's last days, Yuri Krotkov's *The Nobel Prize,* was also published in English during the year. Noteworthy, too, was Vasily Belov's *The Eve,* which focuses on the forced collectivization of Russian agriculture during the 1920's.

Two of the best Eastern European novels of the year, the Polish Kazimierz Brandys's *A Question of Reality* and the Czech Milan Kundera's *The Book of Laughter and Forgetting,* were available only in translation. Both works suggest that in Eastern Europe the life of the individual and the life of the nation are intertwined, for better or worse. Yugoslavia's Milovan Djilas published an intriguing book, *Tito,* about his tortuous relationship with the late Yugoslav leader.

## A Clear-Sighted Pole in Exile

"I do not want to be famous," Czeslaw Milosz has always contended, in spite of his awesome reputation as a lecturer at the Berkeley campus of the University of California. After Oct. 9, when, cited for "uncompromising clear-sightedness," he was awarded the 1980 Nobel Prize in literature, it became increasingly difficult for the Polish exile to remain secluded. Born in Vilna (now in the Soviet Union) in 1911, he spent the World War II years in the underground, then served as cultural attaché at Polish embassies in Washington, D.C., and Paris, where he sought political asylum in 1951. He reached the United States in 1960 and became a naturalized citizen ten years later. Milosz has published much poetry, an autobiography, a novel, a history of Polish literature, and translations from the six languages of which he is a master.

*Czeslaw Milosz.*

*Swiss novelist Max Frisch, shown in his study, wrote* Man in the Holocene.

*Soviet dissident author Lev Kopelev is shown arriving in West Germany for a one-year (and probably one-way) stay. His* Education of a True Believer *describes his disillusionment with the Communist system.*

*Milan Kundera, an exiled Czech novelist and short-story writer, lives in Paris. His latest novel,* The Book of Laughter and Forgetting, *was available only in translation.*

*Nobel Prize laureate Heinrich Böll wrote* Solicitous Siege, *a novel dealing with terrorism.*

**Asian.** Important works from lesser-known literatures also made publishing news in 1980. Two novels by the Japanese writer Shusaku Endo, *Volcano* and *When I Whistle,* were issued in translation. In both, the author, a Christian, focuses on the moral dilemmas faced by Japanese who have become imbued with Western religious values.

The literary situation in China attracted a great deal of attention. For the first time in ten years works by modern Western writers became available in Chinese translation. The success of the Peking Book Fair attested to the Chinese public's hunger for Western literature and the authorities' desire to end the country's cultural isolation.

I.S. & A.E.

## BOOKS FOR CHILDREN

Among the better children's books in 1980 were those with a strong evocation of time and place. Prominent regional or historical settings make it easier to accommodate such conventions of the juvenile novel as melodramatic strains in the narrative and playful exaggeration of character flaws and virtues.

**Fiction.** For preteen children, Jane Langton created in *The Fledgling* a New England-based tale about a magical girl who flies among the geese at Walden Pond. In Larry Callen's *The Muskrat War,* a Southern backwoods settlement is menaced by swindlers, but two "Tom Sawyer" types attempt to remedy the situation.

Gene Kemp's *The Turbulent Term of Tyke Tiler* illustrates universal suburban child behavior with pranks involving pet mice and histrionic performers in a school play. The British historical novelist Leon Garfield enlivens an 18th-century setting in *Footsteps* with a cast of two-faced lawyers, noble-hearted thieves, and garrulous tenement dwellers who thwart the attempts of an intrepid 12-year-old trying to redeem his father's mysteriously tainted reputation.

For teenage readers, Erik Christian Haugaard set *Chase Me, Catch Nobody!* in the 20th century. Danish and German children are forced to outwit an omnipresent Gestapo and the ambivalent people surrounding them. Brenda Wilkinson's third novel, *Ludell's New York Time,* about a Georgia girl, is set in an urban environment.

**Picture Books.** Humorous blends of narrative and illustration distinguished a number of 1980 picture books, including *Uproar on Hollercat Hill* by Jean Marzollo (illustrated by Steven Kellogg) and *The Knight and the Dragon* by Tomie De Paola. The Marzollo-Kellogg book has 11 cats acting out a farce to satirize the traumas of family life. Tomie De Paola's narrative depicts the parallel preparations of a baggy-kneed knight and a foolish dragon as they plan for battle.

A Gathering of Days: A New England Girl's Journal, 1830-32, by Joan W. Blos, received both the Newbery Prize and an American Book Award.

*Anno's Medieval World* by Mitsumasa Anno is a factual picture book about the historical role of astrology and alchemy as tenacious systems of belief. Anno's compositions offer panoramic vistas, using parchmentlike backgrounds, earth-toned colors in architectural forms, and brilliant color accents.

**Folktales.** The German artist Ilse Plume created a whimsical picture-book version of the Grimm brothers' tale *The Bremen-Town Musicians.* A donkey, dog, cat, and rooster perform their braying, barking, yowling, and crowing concert in the midst of an unusual forest.

Alison Lurie's *Clever Gretchen and Other Forgotten Folktales* contains many examples to show the resourcefulness of heroines in traditional narratives. Ashley Bryan collected five African tales in his well-designed book *Beat the Story-Drum, Pum-Pum.*

**Poetry.** Distinguished poets were represented in handsome editions of children's books. A collection of Emily Dickinson's work, edited for young adult readers in *Acts of Light,* was embellished with illustrations by Nancy Ekholm Burkert. The Ogden Nash book of nonsense verses called *Custard and Company* contains illustrations by the popular cartoonist Quentin Blake. For the youngest child, nursery rhymes were compiled and illustrated by artists Anne Rockwell (*Gray Goose and Gander: And Other Mother Goose Rhymes*) and Marc Brown (*Finger Rhymes*).

**Nonfiction.** *Many Kinds of Courage: An Oral History of World War II* by Richard Lidz avoids the hazards of fictionalization and yet offers young readers a feeling of close identification with events. Milton Meltzer's *The Chinese Americans* is a lucid treatment of the Chinese immigration to the U.S.

In the field of science, *How the Forest Grew* by William Jaspersohn (illustrated by Chuck Eckart) is exceptional. For the child of intermediate age, Joanna Cole's *A Frog's Body* presents an informative set of photographs along with a detailed account of frog anatomy.

The theme of *Creatures of Paradise: Pictures to Grow Up With* by Bryan Holme is animals in art. Styles and media range from ancient Persian drawings to the clever animal sketches of Alexander Calder.

**People.** The 1980 Caldecott Medal winner was Barbara Cooney for her illustrations in *Ox-Cart Man.* Joan W. Blos's *A Gathering of Days: A New England Girl's Journal, 1830-32* won both the Newbery Prize and an American Book Award.

*See also* PRIZES AND AWARDS.                    D.Mac.

**LOUISIANA.** *See* STATISTICS OF THE WORLD.

**LUXEMBOURG.** Luxembourg enjoyed continued economic prosperity during 1980 despite the worsening problem of inflation and a slowdown in the growth of industrial production. Both the inflationary and the industrial growth problems were traced in a January report of the Organization for Economic Cooperation and Development to the effects of oil price increases.

Industrial production, based largely on the steel industry's operations, was maintained at a high level for the first half of 1980. A decline in operations during the second half followed American criticism of the steel industry, which had been accounting for more than half of Luxembourg's exports. The U.S. International Trade Commission issued a preliminary ruling on May 1 that the economic health of American steel manufacturers was being damaged by imports from Luxembourg and six other West European countries.

There was general recognition that steel production in Western Europe had outstripped demand. On Oct. 30 the European Community agreed to establish a steel cartel reducing output by 18 percent until June, 1981.

The long rush to establish banking offices in Luxembourg, a tax haven, appeared to end in 1980. A Luxembourg office enabled banks to raise loans for their clients without the restrictions imposed by the central banks of other Western European countries. Luxembourg also had strict bank secrecy rules.

*See* STATISTICS OF THE WORLD. *See also* EUROPEAN COMMUNITIES.                    L.A.S.

**MADAGASCAR.** *See* STATISTICS OF THE WORLD.

**MAINE.** *See* STATISTICS OF THE WORLD.

**MALAWI.** *See* STATISTICS OF THE WORLD.

**MALAYSIA.** Richly endowed Malaysia continued to prosper in 1980. But its complex society nonetheless came under increasing social strain.

**Politics.** Under Prime Minister Datuk Hussein bin Onn, the National Front coalition that had governed Malaysia since independence in 1957 provided the country with an impressive degree of stability. The security forces, working closely with Thai counterparts, were so successful in harassing Communist guerrillas that Home Affairs Minister Tan Sri Ghazali assured his people that the more than 30-year-old rebellion was less dangerous than the war against drugs.

Malaysia, however, had no intention of lowering its guard. Deeply suspicious of Vietnam's expansionist designs in the region, the government announced in January that it would significantly strengthen the air force and build a new air base on the east coast. Later in the year the finance ministry unveiled a budget that would sharply increase allocations for defense and security.

Although generally tranquil, Malaysia suffered its share of social problems. On Jan. 23 riots by 10,000 farmers in the rice bowl state of Kedah had to be put down by baton-wielding police. The farmers clearly had economic grievances, but there was evidence that they were encouraged to riot by local leaders of the Pan Malayan Islamic Party (PMIP). In late March students in the state of Perak staged demonstrations, and once again the government suspected that PMIP agitators had played a role.

In a country as racially mixed and religiously

diverse as Malaysia—it has ethnic Chinese, Indians, and other minorities as well as the Malays—the growth of Muslim fundamentalism was viewed by the government as potentially explosive. At a Southeast Asia and Pacific Regional Islamic Missionary Conference held in Kuala Lumpur in January, the country's *Yang di-Pertuan Agong* (head of state) openly denounced religious fanaticism. Throughout the year, government officials periodically warned against divisive religious zealotry, a clear reference to the Muslim militants.

**The Economy.** With a per capita annual gross national product of more than $1000, Malaysia boasted one of the strongest economies in Asia. Crude petroleum became the country's biggest single export in 1980, outstripping such traditional mainstays as rubber and tin. The economy continued to grow at approximately 8 percent annually, while the rate of inflation, up slightly from the 4 percent of recent years, was still among the world's lowest. With an embarrassment of energy riches—natural gas and coal in addition to its petroleum—the economic future of the country looked bright.

**Foreign Policy.** As in the past, Malaysia cooperated closely with its non-Communist neighbors in the Association of Southeast Asian Nations. The government strongly criticized the Soviet invasion of Afghanistan and Vietnamese occupation of Cambodia. Malaysian ties with Japan and the West remained strong.

See STATISTICS OF THE WORLD.          R.J.C.

**MALDIVES.** See STATISTICS OF THE WORLD.

**MALI.** See STATISTICS OF THE WORLD.

**MALTA.** Prime Minister Dom Mintoff announced in early 1980 that Malta had negotiated a defense agreement with Libya. Under the accord, some 50 Libyan military advisers were sent to Malta to train Maltese pilots to fly helicopters. The training program was halted abruptly in August after Malta authorized a resumption of offshore oil drilling in the Medina bank, a section of Malta's southern continental shelf in the disputed 200-mi. Mediterranean Sea area between Malta and Libya. Libya had refused for years to negotiate the rival Maltese-Libyan claims to the area.

Malta had refrained from drilling in the disputed undersea area for seven years. Earlier in 1980, however, Malta ended the suspension, and Italy's state energy authority contracted for a Texaco rig to begin exploratory drilling in the Medina Strait some 68 mi. south of the Maltese coast. Malta issued a license permitting the operation. Under orders of the Libyan government, however, a Libyan warship on Aug. 21 directed the Texaco personnel to halt drilling. On the advice of the

Italian foreign ministry, the drilling operators complied. In retaliation for Libya's move, Mintoff on Aug. 28 ordered the expulsion of the Libyan military advisers—five helicopter crews and support personnel—as security risks.

See STATISTICS OF THE WORLD.          L.A.S.

**MANITOBA.** See STATISTICS OF THE WORLD.

**MANUFACTURING INDUSTRIES.** In general, U.S. manufacturing output followed the broad trend of the economy, with sharp declines during the spring and early summer and an advance in late 1980. A surge in Defense Department orders spurred the arms and aerospace industries. Steel and rubber suffered from the slump in automobile production. The textile industry was hampered by foreign competition. The electrical equipment sector performed well, however.

Manufacturing in the Midwest was particularly hard hit by the recession, and recovery was handicapped by technological obsolescence. The term "reindustrialization" gained currency, but corporate decisions on stimulating productivity through technological advances were deferred, awaiting President-elect Ronald Reagan's promised tax cuts and shortened depreciation schedules. The end of 1980 found prognoses for 1981 clouded by scant evidence of a revival in orders for industrial machinery and by omens of even higher costs for imported oil than in 1980.

**Steel.** During the first three quarters of 1980, domestic steel production totaled 82,000,000 tons, a sharp decline from the 105,000,000 tons produced in the same 1979 period. Many large steel producers were idling at 50 percent or lower capacity through the summer. Hourly employment fell to 264,000, the lowest in the industry since 1933. In September demand rose by 10.5 percent, and with it the industry's capacity utilization rate reached 62.7 percent, according to the American Iron and Steel Institute (AISI). This figure, however, was well below the 87.5 percent annual rate for 1979. Reflecting that situation, third-quarter profits of the industry came to only $92,900,000, compared with $353,000,000 in the third quarter of 1979.

Despite these negatives, Inland Steel Co. added 13 percent to its steelmaking capacity with completion of a $1 billion blast furnace. In October a new $130,000,000 steel wire rod plant owned by Co-Steel, a Canadian company, opened in Perth Amboy, N.J.

AISI reported that competition from foreign steel imports in August represented about a 21 percent penetration of the apparent steel supply. Imports declined by about 10 percent during the first three quarters of the year, however, when compared with the same 1979 period. Some credit for holding down imports could be given to the federal government's trigger system. Instituted in 1978, it inhibited importers from dropping prices below specified levels and thus triggering the addition of a surcharge or an investigation by the Treasury Department.

American steel companies were themselves importing advances in technology. Nippon Steel helped Armco with blast furnaces and plate production, Nippon Kokan granted Inland Steel a license on a continuous annealing process, Sumitomo Metals assisted U.S. Steel Corp. in several processes, and Kawasaki Steel conferred with Bethlehem Steel Corp. and Republic Steel Corp. on a variety of items.

**Paper.** Production of paper and paperboard reflected the path of the rest of the economy in its downtrend from January to August. At 1980's nine-month mark it gained steam again. The American Paper Institute (API) reported that total output increased by 1.8 percent over the same 1979 period. The strength came from the production of newsprint and printing and writing papers. Paperboard declined by 1.6 percent from its 1979 level.

Clues to the impact of inflation were evident from the inventories-sales-earnings figures published by API. The August, 1980, dollar value of inventories held by paper merchants was only 7 percent greater than the 1979 level, signifying a decline in the physical volume of those inventories. Net sales of 23 paper companies in the first three quarters of 1980 were 24.1 billion tons, or 9 percent higher than the year before. In contrast, earnings for those companies during that same period were $1.3 billion, or 9.5 percent below the comparable 1979 figure.

The paperboard picture would have been weaker without an unexpected sale to a new customer, the People's Republic of China. The Chinese deserted their usual Japanese suppliers to place orders with U.S. companies for 275,000 tons of paperboard and 125,000 tons of paper in other forms. By fall, a 20 percent earnings decline in the second half was predicted for the major paper companies from 1979 levels and a further drop of 5 to 10 percent in 1981. In paper as in steel, signs of long-range confidence remained evident. In April, as the recession was beginning, Mead Corp. approved a $270,000,000 plant expansion at Escanaba, Mich.

*U.S. steel production dropped in 1980, but Inland Steel Co. opened the Western Hemisphere's largest blast furnace at its East Chicago, Ind., mill. The furnace was expected to increase Inland's annual raw steel capacity by 1,100,000 tons.*

*The textile industry in the South suffered layoffs and plant closings in 1980. One reason was competition from imports.*

**Textiles.** Not long after the start of the recession, textile industry worker hours dropped, beginning in May, to the 8 percent downpoint by July. Shipments fell in real volume by 1 percent from the same period in 1979, and there was a concurrent drop in apparel and textile-related home furnishings production. While domestic textile activity faltered, imports of apparel soared to levels matching the all-time high set in 1978, with new records for the months of May and June, according to the American Textile Manufacturers Institute. For the first half of 1980, imports of fabric equaled the 1979 figure. In September the United States signed a trade agreement with China permitting the entry of more Chinese textiles into the U.S. over a three-year period. The export side of the textile balance sheet was more encouraging, with exports advancing 28 percent in poundage terms from 1979 figures. Both mill earnings and capacity utilization declined as the year progressed, however, narrowing after-tax profit margins toward zero.

The most dramatic turn in the industry was the J. P. Stevens & Co. contract with the Amalgamated Clothing and Textile Workers, the culmination of a 17-year struggle. The new contract, according to President Whitney Stevens, cost his company nothing more than had already been given to the firm's nonunion workers. *See also* LABOR.

**Electrical Industry.** Performance in the electrical equipment industry was the exception to the recession-dominated U.S. economy, with most manufacturers showing better third-quarter sales and anticipating an improved fourth period. Both General Electric and Westinghouse posted third-quarter earnings increases. Technology drew headlines when Gulf & Western unveiled an electric car powered by a battery capable of 55-mph speeds for a distance of 150 mi. before recharge. Such range and speed were well beyond those of the electric cars already on the market. Although molten metal batteries under development elsewhere did offer more range and speed, the Gulf & Western model posed fewer technological problems and therefore could reach market earlier. Less spectacular but potentially more far-reaching in implications was the ultraviolet laser. Researchers at the University of Rochester said that the new laser raised efficiency from 30 percent to as high as 90 percent in controlling fusion power. It could, they said, help speed up the decades-long effort to attain fusion power, deemed by many to be the source of unlimited energy for the future.

**Rubber.** As automakers cut back production, the nation's tiremakers closed plants and laid off workers. By April, Firestone Tire & Rubber Co. had laid off 3600 indefinitely and 1500 temporarily. Five plants were slated for closing within the year. In October Firestone said it would close its Akron truck tire plant in 1981, leaving only one operating tire facility in a city once dominated by the industry. That closing idled nearly 9000 more workers. Since 1950, rubber industry employment in Akron had fallen from more than 50,000 to about 22,000.

Industry observers anticipated the closings, citing longtime overcapacity, declining demand, the trend toward longer-lasting radial tires, and the impact of tire imports, which held 9 percent of the market by 1980. The industry hit bottom in

*Oil wealth has yet to filter down to Mexico's poor. Within sight of Acapulco's luxury hotels, some 20 percent of the city's population dwell in makeshift shacks.*

August, then revived in the fourth quarter. Analysts, however, saw no possible return to higher earnings until the fourth quarter of 1981.

    *See also* AUTOMOBILES.           M.S.O.

**MARYLAND.** *See* STATISTICS OF THE WORLD.

**MASSACHUSETTS.** *See* STATISTICS OF THE WORLD. *See also* STATE GOVERNMENT REVIEW.

**MAURITANIA.** *See* STATISTICS OF THE WORLD.

**MAURITIUS.** *See* STATISTICS OF THE WORLD.

**MEXICO.** As Mexico's proven oil and natural gas reserves edged upward to 55 billion bbl, with the likelihood that the tally would continue to increase, businesspeople and government leaders from near and far beat a steady path to Mexico City in 1980. Although Mexico was exporting little more than 1,000,000 bbl of oil daily, with the bulk of it going to the United States, other nations sought to obtain increasing amounts of Mexican oil. Moreover, many countries offered to provide Mexico with technical assistance in exchange for oil. For Mexicans, it was a heady experience.

But officials of Petróleos Mexicanos, the state oil monopoly known generally as Pemex, maintained a reserved attitude, preferring instead to develop oil and natural gas resources for domestic needs—and to keep production at about 2,500,-000 bbl daily.

The steady increase in proven reserves since 1975 put Mexico in fifth place among world oil producers. President José López Portillo said in August that, although the oil revenues flowing into Mexico's treasury should help fuel industrial expansion and social programs aimed at helping Mexico's burgeoning population, the petroleum industry "is not a panacea and never will be." He pledged in his state of the nation address on Sept. 1 to keep oil and natural gas production at levels that would prevent an inflationary spiral.

**Problems of Plenty.** López Portillo was, however, sharply criticized for his handling of the oil moneys. The sudden oil affluence had led to unbalanced growth as well as rising expectations on

*Mexican President José López Portillo tours an oil refinery. Foreign business and government leaders beat a steady path to Mexico City in 1980 to seek oil supplies as Mexico's proven reserves continued to grow.*

the part of Mexico's 70,000,000 people. Government spending jumped 80 percent in 1979 and 1980, with further increases expected in 1981, much of it to subsidize the price of imported food. Labor unrest, meanwhile, was spreading, with 40 percent more industrial strikes in 1980 than 1979. At the same time, inflation was running at an annual rate of 28 percent at midyear, compared to 20 percent in 1979. Political stability was not threatened by the troubled economy, but there was little hope of improved economic conditions during the next few years. López Portillo admitted in a mid-September speech that the oil wealth was "a mixed blessing."

The problems Mexico was facing arose more from defects in the economic structure than any particular mistakes by the López Portillo government, which inherited a sagging economy when it came to office. Although 1979 saw the worst recession in 40 years, the government managed to overcome its effects by stringent economies and austerity. But in 1980 some of those restraints were lifted—and that led to the fueling of the inflationary spiral.

The population, which had long grown by 3.6 percent per year, showed some signs of slower growth, with the increase kept to below 3 percent in 1980. Yet half the population of Mexico was under the age of 14, according to a July government report. How to feed, clothe, house, educate, and find jobs for this growing legion of young people was, as López Portillo said in February, "our biggest problem."

**Political Palpitations.** Although political stability remained a hallmark of Mexico's government, there were signs of incipient crises. Clashes between the army and guerrillas took place in mountain terrain west of Mexico City. This problem refused to go away. But the region around Culiacán in Mexico's northwest was reported in March to have been fully pacified by army action, which included sweeps of the region.

The July, 1982, presidential election seemed distant to many Mexicans, but the campaign had already begun, although President López Portillo had not named his successor, and it was unlikely he would do so before mid-1981. Newspapers were full of speculation on who the candidate would be, but López Portillo gave no hints. The president evoked official ire, however, when he named his son, 27-year-old José Ramón, to the post of undersecretary in the ministry of planning. Newspapers also chided the appointment.

The first Communists ever to be elected to the Mexican Congress were more active than originally expected during 1980. Their 18-member delegation took part in debates with gusto, surprising legislative observers who had expected them to be silent for their first terms, and leading some to credit the Communists for activating debate in Mexico's Chamber of Deputies. The ruling Institutional Revolutionary Party traditionally dominated the Congress and rubber-stamped the executive branch's legislative requests.

*See* STATISTICS OF THE WORLD.　　　　J.N.G.

**MICHIGAN.** *See* STATISTICS OF THE WORLD.

# MIDDLE EAST

The war between Iraq and Iran dominated Middle Eastern affairs in the last quarter of 1980, weakening Arab solidarity, jeopardizing oil exports, and creating fears that the United States and the Soviet Union might be drawn into the fighting. Meanwhile, 52 American hostages still languished in Iran, and the Egyptian-Israeli peace process marked time.

Iraq's invasion of Iran in September started a major war between the two countries that became a focal point of Middle East tensions. It aroused international apprehensions about a global conflict, threatened the oil supplies of several European countries and Japan, and polarized the Arab world between supporters of each combatant. By November, attempts to halt the fighting had failed, including efforts by the United Nations, the Conference of Islamic States, and the Palestine Liberation Organization (PLO).

**War in the Persian Gulf.** The war began after Iraq on Sept. 17 renounced the 1975 treaty with Iran in which the two countries agreed to share sovereignty over the Shatt-al-Arab, the estuary that forms part of the border between Iraq and Iran and flows into the Persian Gulf. Iraq, on the basis of historical claims, asserted sovereignty over the whole waterway. Iraq also demanded that Iran renounce control over three tiny islands at the strategic Strait of Hormuz in the Gulf and surrender pockets of land along the Iraq-Iran land border.

During the next few days after Iraq renounced the treaty, border incidents escalated into major battles with Iraqi forces pushing deep into Khuzistan, threatening its larger cities, including Dizful; Ahwaz, the provincial capital; the port of Khorramshahr; and the huge oil complex at Abadan. Each country attacked the other's capital in air raids, and oil production and shipments from both were nearly brought to a halt. Although the Iraqi forces scored early victories in their invasion, a combination of the Iranian army and revolutionary guards made the enemy pay a heavy price, especially in sieges of the larger cities. See MILITARY AND NAVAL AFFAIRS.

Both Iraq and Iran disregarded a U.N. Security Council resolution passed unanimously on Sept. 28 calling on them to stop fighting and accept mediation or conciliation to end the war.

A good will mission headed by Pakistan's President Muhammad Zia ul-Haq and the secretary-general of the Conference of Islamic States visited Baghdad, Iraq, and Tehran in late September to assist in a settlement, but its services and those of the PLO were of no avail. During October, Iran's prime minister, Mohammed Ali Rajai, became the highest ranking official of the revolutionary regime to visit the U.S. when he participated in a meeting of the U.N. Security Council that also failed to resolve the crisis. Former Swedish Prime Minister Olof Palme served as a U.N. emissary in a mission to Iran and Iraq that ended inconclusively in November.

The war rekindled rivalries between radical and conservative Arab regimes. Libya, Syria, and the People's Democratic Republic of Yemen (South Yemen) were sympathetic to Iran, while Jordan and Saudi Arabia favored Iraq. In October, King Hussein of Jordan visited Baghdad and opened the port of 'Aqaba to supplies for his eastern neighbor. He mobilized all transport vehicles to carry supplies to the Iraqi army.

Although Saudi Arabia was officially neutral, it maintained cordial relations with Iraqi President Saddam Hussein and reportedly made its ports available for shipments to Iraq in November. Apprehensions about Iran's intentions led to Saudi requests for American military aid. On Sept. 29 the U.S. decided to send four Airborne Warning and Control Systems (AWACS) planes to Saudi Arabia to assist with air defenses in the eastern provinces. The American aid angered Libyan President Muammar el-Qaddafi, who demanded that the AWACS be evicted from Arabia. When the Saudis refused, the two countries accused each other of betraying Islam and assisting Israel. Saudi Arabia responded by breaking diplomatic relations on Oct. 28. Libya, along with Syria, South Yemen, Lebanon, Algeria, and the PLO, boycotted an Arab League summit conference held in Amman, Jordan, in late November.

The Gulf war also increased tensions between the U.S. and the Soviet Union, which were already running high because of the Soviet invasion of Afghanistan in December, 1979. Although the U.S.S.R. had been the chief supplier of military assistance to Iraq, it maintained an officially neutral position. The Soviet press, however, asserted that Iraq had "launched the offensive" and at times Soviet commentators seemed to praise Iranian resistance. Syria, one of Iran's strongest backers and long at odds with Iraq, signed a treaty with Moscow in October.

The U.S. criticized Iraq's invasion as a threat to the stability of the whole Persian Gulf. It used its influence to dissuade Arab states on the Gulf from providing Iraq with bases for air attacks on Iran. In October, Secretary of State Edmund S. Muskie stated that the U.S. was impartial, but opposed to dismemberment of Iran. President Jimmy Carter asserted: "It is to our advantage to have a strong Iran." But Muskie also urged nonintervention by countries of the region in one another's internal affairs, a comment directed at Iran's efforts to incite the Shi'ite Muslims of Iraq against their government.

Because of Western fears of a threat to Persian Gulf shipping, a flotilla of more than 60 American, British, French, and Australian warships assembled in the Arabian Sea and the Indian Ocean to prevent interference with oil shipments passing through the Strait of Hormuz. The allied fleet counterbalanced a squadron of about 30 Soviet warships deployed in the Indian Ocean. The U.S. earlier in 1980 had acquired access to air and naval facilities in Oman, as well as Kenya and Somalia, to increase its strength in the region.

Although the war cut off most oil shipments from Iraq and Iran to Western Europe and Japan, other Gulf states continued the trade. When the war began, only a little more than 10 percent of the total production of the Organization of Petroleum Exporting Countries was cut off. As relations among the states of the region deteriorated, however, there was increasing concern that there would be a serious oil shortage if the war spread.

**Iranian Hostage Crisis.** The Gulf war brought to a head the crisis in relations between the U.S. and Iran over the 52 remaining American hostages of the ones seized in Tehran on Nov. 4, 1979. An air rescue mission by American armed forces on April 24 had ended in disaster in the desert 200 mi. southeast of Tehran because of helicopter mechanical failures. On May 24 the International Court of Justice in the Hague (the Netherlands)

*War between Iran and Iraq broke out in September. Iraqi troops occupied much of Iran's oil-rich Khuzistan Province (shaded area), including Khorramshahr, or Khurramshahr (inset). Iraq demanded full control of the Shatt-al-Arab, which flows into the Persian Gulf.*

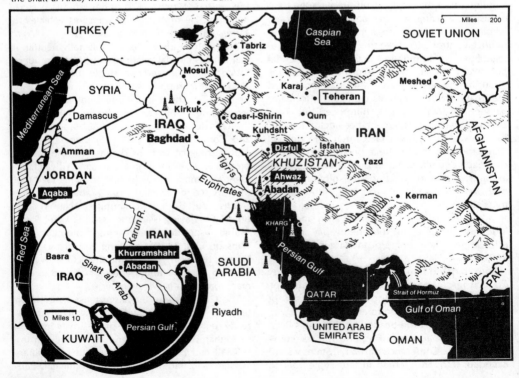

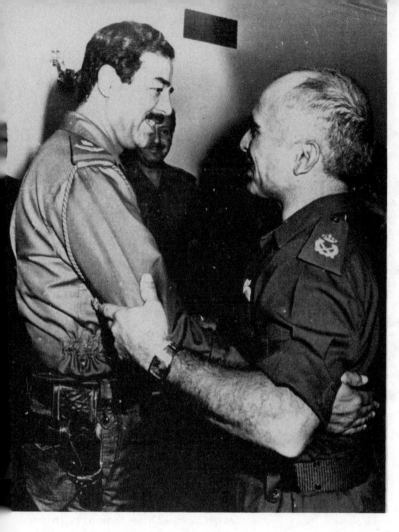

*Iraqi President Saddam Hussein (left) greets Jordan's King Hussein in Baghdad, Iraq, on Oct. 5. Jordan aligned itself with Iraq, speeding supplies to its eastern neighbor. Most other Arab nations also favored Iraq, but Libya and Syria backed Iran.*

reaffirmed its temporary ruling of December, 1979, calling for immediate release of the hostages. The court ordered Iran not to put any of them on trial and ruled that Iran was liable for reparations.

Two days before the 1980 U.S. Presidential election, Iran changed its position when the Majlis (parliament) met in Tehran to vote for conditional release of the hostages. The four conditions laid down were: the U.S. was to unfreeze all Iranian assets frozen by President Carter in 1979; abrogate and cancel all economic and financial measures taken by the U.S. against Iran; return to Iran all assets in the U.S. belonging to the deposed shah; and pledge not to interfere in any way "either directly or indirectly, politically or militarily, in the affairs of the Islamic Republic of Iran." President Carter reacted favorably to the conditions, and negotiations were initiated to implement them so that the hostages could be released. Al-

geria acted as an intermediary to carry the U.S. response to Iran and bring the Iranian reply back to Washington, but in December Iran demanded a U.S. deposit of $24 billion as a condition for releasing the hostages.

**Afghanistan.** The Soviet troops that invaded Afghanistan in December, 1979, were reinforced and settled down for a long stay in that country. Accounts regarding the effectiveness of the resistance varied. Large numbers of Afghans fled to Pakistan. A U.N. General Assembly resolution deploring the invasion and calling for the immediate withdrawal of all foreign troops from Afghanistan was overwhelmingly backed by Middle East countries in January. The Conference of Islamic States, meeting in Islamabad, Pakistan, Jan. 27–29, adopted an even stronger resolution, specifically denouncing the U.S.S.R. for aggression.

**Egypt-Israel Peace Process.** Little progress was made in the negotiations between Egypt and Is-

*Israeli Prime Minister Menachem Begin (left) confers with Egyptian President Anwar el-Sadat on Jan. 8 in Cairo during his visit to Egypt. The peace process bogged down after a May 26 deadline for arrangements on Palestinian autonomy in the occupied West Bank and Gaza Strip passed with no agreement.*

rael on the autonomy arrangements for the occupied West Bank and Gaza Strip during 1980. In January, expectations were high following Israeli Prime Minister Menachem Begin's visit to Cairo, where he had cordial meetings with Egyptian President Anwar el-Sadat. Israel completed the first phase of its withdrawal from the Egyptian Sinai on Jan. 25 in accord with terms of the March 26, 1979, Egyptian-Israeli peace treaty, leaving only a third of the peninsula to be returned by 1982. The two countries exchanged ambassadors, opened a direct telephone link, established air service, and opened a land route across the Sinai.

The May 26 deadline for the autonomy arrangements, however, passed with no agreement. Disputes between Egypt and Israel over whether the proposed autonomous council would have legislative or only administrative powers, over qualifications for voting in elections, over Israel's control of internal security in the proposed autonomous region, and over establishment of Jewish settlements in the area led to acrimonious debate. Relations between Cairo and Jerusalem were also aggravated by a law passed in the Knes-

set (Israeli parliament) on July 30 reaffirming that Jerusalem, including East Jerusalem, occupied in 1967, was the capital of Israel. Sadat replied to the legislation by calling for a delay in the autonomy talks. Only efforts by Washington to arrange for renewal of negotiations after the U.S. election prevented a breakdown in the normalization of relations between Israel and Egypt.

Israel's new Jerusalem law, its continued establishment of Jewish settlements on the West Bank, its expulsion of two Arab mayors from the West Bank following a Palestinian terrorist attack on Jews in Hebron, and Israeli attacks on Palestinian bases in Lebanon made it the focus of international protest. Resolutions in the U.N. Security Council and General Assembly censured Israel for these acts. The country's growing international isolation contrasted with increased acceptance of the PLO as the legitimate representative of the Palestinians. Austria and India extended diplomatic recognition to the PLO. Both the Council of Europe and the European Community passed resolutions calling for Palestinian self-determination.

**Political Instability.** In Turkey, long considered a stable and reliable member of the Western alliance, the deteriorating economy caused such great social turmoil that the army seized the government in a bloodless coup on Sept. 12. Authority was turned over to a six-member National Security Council; it was led by Gen. Kenan Evren and included four other generals and an admiral. After suspending the parliament, political parties, and the constitution and imposing martial law, including press censorship, the new rulers appointed a 27-man civilian cabinet, eight of whose members were retired generals. Terrorism, which according to Gen. Evren had taken some 5000 lives in the past year, declined after the coup, and the officers proceeded to draft a new constitution that they believed would bring political stability to Turkey.

Political instability continued elsewhere in the Middle East during 1980. Appointment of a new premier in Lebanon during July failed to establish the authority of the central government. The bloody fighting between the country's diverse political and religious factions continued, with the right-wing Phalangists extending their control by military conquest of a rival Maronite Christian faction. In Syria, President Hafez al-Assad's regime continued its struggle against zealots of the Muslim Brotherhood. During March, Assad was forced to send 10,000 troops to Aleppo and Hama to quell protests organized by the brotherhood. Assad attempted to break out of his growing isolation in the Arab world and to overcome deterioration of relations with Iraq and Jordan by signing an agreement in September for union with Libya. After proclamation of this "unified state" there was little further evidence of unity. Assad's chief diplomatic action during 1980 was the 20-year treaty of friendship with the Soviet Union signed in October. Similar to earlier agreements with the U.S.S.R. by Iraq and Egypt, it provided for "coordinating" positions and "cooperating in removing the threat that has arisen and restoring the peace."

See ARAB LEAGUE; PALESTINE LIBERATION ORGANIZATION; and articles on individual countries mentioned.          D.P.

**MILITARY AND NAVAL AFFAIRS.** Wars in Afghanistan and the Middle East and a dramatic though unsuccessful attempt to free the American hostages held in Iran were among the leading military events of 1980. The United States and the Soviet Union appeared on the verge of a new arms race as the 1979 arms limitation treaty between the two nations was shelved after the Soviet invasion of Afghanistan.

**Rescue Attempts.** U.S. Army and Marine comman-

*Ayatollah Sadegh Khalkhali holds his robe to his nose to ward off the stench from the body of one of the American dead put on display after the failure of a raid to rescue the American hostages in Tehran. The April 24 mission by U.S. Army and Marine commandos, supported by Air Force personnel, ended in confusion; eight servicemen were killed.*

dos secretly landed in the Iranian desert on April 24 in a bold attempt to rescue 53 Americans held hostage by Iran's revolutionary government. The mission ended in failure when mechanical difficulties forced President Jimmy Carter to terminate it, and in the ensuing withdrawal, three American Marines and five airmen died when a helicopter collided with a C-130 cargo plane. Contingency planning for the operation had been ordered in late 1979, and training for the mission was intensified after diplomatic negotiations to free the hostages failed. The plan called for about 90 counterterrorist troops to land in the desert and be driven into Tehran under cover of darkness by American intelligence agents and Iranian sympathizers for a ground assault on the U.S. embassy, where all but three of the hostages had been held since Nov. 4, 1979. The mission was scrubbed when three of the eight RH-53 helicopters that had flown from the aircraft carrier U.S.S. *Nimitz* were grounded because of mechanical problems. The assault team was left with insufficient helicopter support.

Although Carter termed the operation an "incomplete success," the failure was a source of acute embarrassment to the U.S. military and fueled the continuing controversy over the readiness of American armed forces. A special panel appointed by the Pentagon to review the operation issued an unusually critical assessment on Aug. 23. The panel, headed by former chief of naval operations Adm. James Holloway, was sharply critical of both mission planning and execution, citing deficiencies in command and control, poor communications, and such an obsession with secrecy that not even the Joint Chiefs of Staff were allowed to comment on the plans.

In an unrelated but similar operation, British commandos stormed the Iranian embassy in London on May 5 and ended a six-day siege by militant Iranian Arabs opposed to the regime of Ayatollah Ruhollah Khomeini. The Iranians had demanded release of 91 political prisoners in Iran. The Special Air Services troops attacked the embassy after a hostage was killed and his body thrown into the street; the militants threatened to kill a new hostage every half hour until their demands were met. Nineteen hostages were released unharmed, but another hostage was found dead inside the building.

**Afghanistan Invasion.** Anxious to protect its interests in a politically troubled client state on its southern border, the Soviet Union launched a massive invasion of Afghanistan on Dec. 27, 1979. Afghan troops with Soviet advisers overthrew the civilian government and assassinated President Hafizullah Amin, replacing him with a pro-Soviet puppet, Babrak Karmal. Within 24 hours of the coup, Soviet airborne troops had been airlifted into the capital, Kabul, and two Russian divisions had crossed the Afghan border. By the end of the first week of 1980, more than 50,000 Soviet troops were in Afghanistan and had occupied the major cities. The Afghan resistance proved stiffer than the Soviets had expected, however, and despite the use of such sophisticated weapons as the Mi-24 helicopter gunship and nerve gas, the Soviets continued to suffer heavy casualties in fighting reminiscent of the American experience in Vietnam. The Soviet-dominated Afghan army virtually collapsed. The invasion was condemned by most of the world community and resulted in a cooling of Soviet-American relations, but the Soviets apparently were preparing for an extended occupation of the previously neutral buffer state. By the end of 1980 more than 80,000 Soviet troops were heavily engaged in fighting against the Afghan guerrillas. *See* AFGHANISTAN.

The Iranian crisis and the Soviet invasion of Afghanistan prompted a buildup of U.S. military power in the Indian Ocean. An aerial view of the Indian Ocean naval task force shows three aircraft carriers accompanied by escort and supply ships.

**Indian Ocean Buildup.** The seizure of American hostages by Iran and the Soviet invasion of Afghanistan prompted a massive buildup of U.S. military power in the Indian Ocean and the Persian Gulf region. By May, U.S. strength in the area had climbed to a record 34,000 men and 37 warships, including two nuclear-powered aircraft carriers and 1800 marines. By October, because of the Iran-Iraq war, more than 60 U.S., British, French, and Australian warships had assembled in the region to protect tanker traffic. To underscore long-term U.S. interest in the region, the Carter administration negotiated naval and air base rights with Oman, Kenya, and Somalia. Carter declared in his State of the Union address on Jan. 23 that any attempt by other powers to gain control of the Persian Gulf region would be regarded as a threat to U.S. national security and would be resisted by "any means necessary, including military force."

Carter also asked Congress to approve a resumption of draft registration to enable the Selective Service System to mobilize rapidly in the event of a military crisis in the Persian Gulf or elsewhere. The plan was approved by Congress in June, and 19- and 20-year-old males began registering on July 21. Carter's proposal to include women in the draft registration plan was rejected by Congress.

The Iranian and Afghan crises gave fresh impetus to Pentagon plans to spend $9 billion over five years to create a Rapid Deployment Force of Marine and Army airborne troops to be airlifted on short notice to trouble spots anywhere in the world. Key elements of the plans included the development of a fleet of giant cargo jets, known as the CX, and the purchase of 15 cargo ships to be stocked with weapons and military equipment and positioned throughout the world for quick use in a crisis. The Rapid Deployment Force was officially activated in March but was not expected to be fully operational until the mid-1980's.

**Iraq and Iran Fight.** After months of sporadic border clashes between Iran and Iraq, full-scale war erupted in the Middle East in September as Iraq invaded Iran in an attempt to regain disputed territory it had been forced to give up in 1975 when Shah Mohammed Riza Pahlavi was at the peak of his military power. Capitalizing on the continuing political and revolutionary turmoil in Iran, Iraqi armor and infantry attacked across a desert front 500 mi. broad, punching into the Iranian province of Khuzistan as Soviet-built Iraqi jets bombed the Iranian capital of Tehran and attacked several key Iranian oil facilities, including the giant refinery at Abadan. The Iranian air force retaliated, sending U.S.-made Phantom jets on bombing strikes

against the Iraqi capital of Baghdad and Iraqi oil facilities. After two weeks of fighting the Iraqis had surrounded the important provincial cities of Ahwaz and Dizful and the port of Khorramshahr. Superior Iranian air power succeeded in crippling Iraqi oil production, but Iran's oil pipelines were cut in turn and its major refineries crippled by air attack. An Iraqi cease-fire offer was rejected by Iran on Oct. 5, and the next day Jordan gave open support to Iraq. Fighting continued as Iraq maintained its stranglehold on the embattled cities, and Western military analysts predicted a prolonged war of attrition.

To underscore its concern over the threat to the world's oil supply lines and to discourage Iraq's Arab neighbors from joining the war, the U.S. on Sept. 29 decided to send four Airborne Warning and Control Systems (AWACS) radar jets to Saudi Arabia to reinforce Saudi air defenses against possible attacks by Iran.

By the end of October, Iraq had occupied Khorramshahr and was advancing cautiously on Abadan, as well as objectives farther north in Khuzistan. The conflict appeared increasingly to be a war of attrition, with Iranian forces believed seriously endangered by shortages of fuel and spare parts. See IRAN; IRAQ; MIDDLE EAST.

**Lebanon.** Despite a near collapse of talks between Egypt and Israel after more than two years of negotiations, the peace treaty between the two nations continued to avert the threat of war between Israel and its more militant Arab neighbors. Fighting continued sporadically in southern Lebanon, however, between Palestinian guerrillas and Christian militiamen supported by Israel. In the most massive raids into Lebanon since 1978, at least 500 Israeli troops backed by heavy artillery fire and helicopter gunships crossed the Litani River in August to attack Palestinian strongpoints. The incursion further strained relations between the U.S. and Israel because the Israelis ignored a ban on the offensive use of their American-made weapons during the fighting.

**Arms Race.** The strategic arms limitation treaty (SALT II) signed by the U.S. and the Soviet Union in June, 1979, fell victim to the Soviet invasion of Afghanistan. President Carter asked Congress to postpone consideration of the treaty's ratification as a protest against the invasion, but he pledged to abide by the terms of the treaty if the Soviets reciprocated. Ronald Reagan, elected President in November, had promised during his campaign to renegotiate the SALT treaty to obtain better terms for the U.S.

Both superpowers continued work on a variety of new strategic weapons, and the arms race appeared to be intensifying. Construction pro-

**So They Replaced It—for 46¢**

Twice during the year, on June 3 and on June 6, a computer located in North American Defense Command headquarters at Cheyenne Mountain near Colorado Springs issued information that prompted an alert: The Soviet Union, the computer insisted, had fired intercontinental ballistic missiles at the United States. The Pentagon and Strategic Air Command headquarters in Omaha received the news first. About 100 bomber crews started the engines of their planes. Missile crews were placed in readiness. Submarines were warned. Within 3 minutes, the computer's information was found to be erroneous; within 25 minutes, normal operations had been resumed. But what caused the mistake, which was embarrassing and expensive, as well as dangerous? The failure of an electronic component no larger than a dime, worth exactly 46¢.

ceeded on the first two Trident ballistic missile submarines, and a prime contractor was chosen for the air-launched nuclear cruise missile. Congress ordered the Pentagon to develop a new strategic bomber by 1987, and development also continued on the controversial MX land-based missile system that would deploy 200 intercontinental ballistic missiles (ICBMs) shuttled among 4600 underground shelters in Nevada and Utah. In September the Administration decided to expand production of plutonium and other bomb-grade materials.

The Soviets continued testing a new generation of ICBMs, proceeded with development of two new long-range bombers, and accelerated their work on "death ray" laser weapons. They were also continuing to deploy SS-20 missiles in Europe, while the Western alliance continued with plans to deploy 108 ballistic missiles and 464 cruise missiles there. Soviet-U.S. talks on limiting intermediate-range nuclear forces in Europe began in Geneva in October.

Defense officials claimed that recent Soviet advancements were making the U.S. land-based missile force vulnerable to a Soviet first-strike attack, and in a speech in August, Secretary of Defense Harold Brown spoke of the need to close the "window of vulnerability," that is, the period during which Soviet strength was considered greater than U.S. strength.

Two unrelated incidents underscored concerns about the credibility of the U.S. strategic deterrent force. A Titan II ICBM exploded in September in its silo near Damascus, Ark., killing one serviceman and hurling its nuclear warhead 220 yd.—and raising questions about the safety and effectiveness of the aging Titan system. Two computer malfunctions in June sent false alarms to U.S. forces indicating that Soviet land-based and submarine-launched missiles had been launched against the U.S.

In a major refinement of U.S. nuclear strategy, President Carter ordered military planners to shift priority to nuclear strikes on Soviet military installations and command centers. The previous targeting policy had emphasized retaliatory strikes against Soviet population centers. The strategy shift was contained in a classified document known as Presidential Directive 59, made public on Aug. 5. The new "counterforce" strategy was prompted by the conclusion of senior U.S. strategists that the policy of massive retaliation against Soviet cities was becoming less credible and that a more flexible strategy was necessary to deter a possible Soviet first-strike attack.

Chemical and biological warfare was an issue between the U.S. and the U.S.S.R. in 1980. In August the State Department said it was "highly likely" that the Soviets had used illegal nerve gas against their enemies in Afghanistan. A controversy also arose over an anthrax epidemic in Sverdlovsk that some Western observers thought might have been accidentally caused by biological warfare agents being developed there. The Soviets vigorously denied the accusation, and it was considered quite possible that the epidemic resulted from natural causes. It was agreed, however, that the Soviets had a big lead in the ability to use and defend against chemical warfare agents. Because it was felt that the U.S. must develop the same capacity in order to deter the Soviets from using theirs, funds for a nerve gas plant in Pine Bluff, Ark., were included in the weapons authorization bill signed in September by President Carter.

Two studies released in 1980 by the Central Intelligence Agency concluded that Soviet military spending continued to outstrip U.S. defense outlays. A January report disclosed that the Russians spent nearly 50 percent more than the U.S. on military activities in 1979, and an August study revealed that the Soviets were devoting between 12 and 14 percent of gross national product to military preparedness, compared to 5.3 percent by the U.S.

The People's Republic of China joined the exclusive club of nuclear missile powers in May

Top: U.S. Marines practice making an amphibious assault during an exercise near the naval base at Subic Bay in the Philippines. The seizure of the hostages and the Soviet invasion of Afghanistan led to the creation of a Rapid Deployment Force intended to airlift U.S. troops to trouble spots anywhere in the world. Bottom: The U.S. and U.S.S.R. continued to duel for worldwide naval supremacy in 1980. Here the aircraft carrier U.S.S. Saratoga enters Philadelphia harbor for 18 months of overhaul and modernization.

when a long-range missile was fired from its Sinkiang test site and splashed down 6000 mi. away in the Pacific Ocean. The missile test demonstrated that China could reach any target in the Soviet Union.

In June, President Valéry Giscard d'Estaing of France announced the successful testing of a neutron bomb. These "enhanced radiation" nuclear weapons were designed to kill maximum numbers of enemy soldiers with limited damage to property. The U.S. had deferred production of such weapons, but if France decided to go ahead in 1982 or 1983, it would affect the balance of power in Europe by giving the West an effective counter to the Eastern bloc's three-to-one superiority in tanks.

**U.S. Military Strength.** U.S. military expenditures continued their steady rise. The Pentagon requested a fiscal year 1981 budget for the Defense Department of $147 billion, $19.6 billion more than the previous year. The Navy was to receive the largest share of the budget, $47 billion; the Air Force, $42.9 billion; and the Army, $36.1 billion. The budget sustained a military establishment of 16 Army and 3 Marine divisions, 26 Air Force tactical wings, 12 Navy and 3 Marine air wings, 17 strategic airlift squadrons, and a Navy fleet of 544 ships. Strategic forces included 1000 Minuteman missiles, 53 Titan II missiles, and 160 Polaris, 432 Poseidon, and 64 Trident I submarine-launched missiles. Troop strength stood at 2,050,357 on Sept. 30, the first annual increase in several years. More than 450,000 U.S. troops were stationed overseas in 1980, nearly half in West Germany and West Berlin.

In conventional weapons developments, the Army ordered full production of the XM-1 Abrams main battle tank in March, and defense officials confirmed in August that the U.S. had secretly developed a "stealth technology" that could make future aircraft virtually invulnerable to enemy air defenses. Secretary Brown disclosed that the Air Force had built and flown several experimental planes that had proved undetectable to existing Soviet air defense systems. The new technology, according to industry sources, reportedly involved radical changes in airframe contours and lightweight coating materials that diffuse radar waves.

**Personnel.** In 1980 the first women were graduated from U.S. military academies, and the number of women in the armed forces reached 150,000. The armed forces, however, were beset with severe personnel problems that renewed congressional demands for a resumption of the draft. The worsening economic climate in the U.S. eased the Army's manpower shortage as thousands of jobless youths streamed into recruiting centers. But the Pentagon told Congress in July that nearly one third of all recruits in 1979 were in the lowest acceptable mental category.

All three services reported severe shortages of skilled personnel, especially in the enlisted ranks, because of low pay compared with similar civilian jobs. The Army was short of drill sergeants and weapons specialists, the Air Force lacked several thousand pilots, and the Navy was short more than 21,000 petty officers.

These personnel and skill shortages, combined with increasing shortages of spare parts and equipment, led some military analysts to question the readiness of the armed forces. A confidential report revealed in September that only six of the Army's ten combat divisions in the continental U.S. were ready for combat, reinforcing the earlier assertion by the Army chief of staff, Gen. Edward C. Meyer, that the home-based units constituted a "hollow Army." Nearly half the Air Force's F-15 fighter squadrons were rated unfit for combat because of personnel shortages and a lack of spare parts. A Navy readiness report in September revealed that only 6 of 13 aircraft carriers were combat-ready.

To begin correcting these problems, the services asked Congress to approve major increases in pay and benefits for the military and began reducing the length of overseas duty tours. And Secretary Brown ordered budget planners to place spending priority on the operation and maintenance of existing equipment rather than procurement of new weapons for the fiscal year 1982 budget.

**Arms Sales.** The Carter administration's 1977 policy of reducing U.S. arms sales to other nations all but collapsed in 1980, a victim of increased Soviet military aid to Third World countries and heightened world tensions that led U.S. officials to expand their arms sales in an effort to establish new security arrangements and solidify existing relationships in various world trouble spots. In a major policy shift, the Carter administration announced in January that it was willing to sell military equipment to the Chinese for the first time, and the Pentagon disclosed in May that it would permit the Chinese to buy air-defense radar, transport aircraft, helicopters, communications equipment, and computers and would allow U.S. companies to build electronic and helicopter plants in China. A long-standing ban on sales of weapons to the Chinese remained in effect, however. The decision to sell nonlethal military equipment to the Chinese was widely interpreted as a partial retaliation against the Russians for the invasion of Afghanistan. As normalization of

Sino-American relations proceeded, however, the U.S. continued to provide defensive weapons to Taiwan, announcing in January that it would sell $280,000,000 of antiaircraft missiles and electronics gear to the Taiwanese but would continue to deny requests for advanced fighter planes and other offensive weapons. The U.S. announced a multibillion-dollar arms deal with Egypt in February, agreeing to sell the Egyptians 40 F-16 jet fighters and 250 M-60 tanks. Major arms sales were also approved for Jordan, Saudi Arabia, and Morocco, but a Saudi request for more sophisticated equipment for its U.S.-made F-15 jets was rejected by the U.S. in April. In a major reversal of policy, the Carter administration decided to permit U.S. defense contractors to design and build warplanes specifically for foreign sales.

**Military Coups.** Army enlisted men staged a coup in Liberia on April 12, assassinating President William R. Tolbert, Jr., and on July 28, Bolivian armed forces overthrew the nation's civilian government. The armed forces took control of Turkey in a bloodless coup on Sept. 11 in response to severe economic problems and growing political violence. Gen. Chun Doo Hwan was named president of the Republic of Korea, and his military colleagues retained the power in the government. A major challenge to the junta was crushed in May after students seized control of the provincial capital of Kwangju. See also the countries mentioned above.

**Naval Affairs.** The two naval superpowers, the U.S. and the U.S.S.R., continued to duel for worldwide naval supremacy in 1980, with most impartial observers believing the Soviets were maintaining a slight edge in naval power. Western naval analysts estimated Soviet fleet strength at 87 ballistic missile submarines; 257 attack and cruise missile submarines; 2 Kiev-class aircraft carriers; 2 helicopter carriers; a battle cruiser; 285 cruisers, destroyers, and frigates; and 93 amphibious warfare ships. By contrast, U.S. fleet strength included 41 ballistic missile submarines; 79 attack submarines; 13 aircraft carriers; 176 cruisers, destroyers, and frigates; and 64 amphibious warfare ships.

Western analysts reported that the Soviets had begun deploying two new classes of warships, a Kirov-class nuclear-powered battle cruiser approaching the size of a World War II battleship and an Alfa-class submarine faster than U.S. counterparts and able to dive to greater depths because of a titanium hull. They were also continuing work on their first nuclear-powered aircraft carrier. Construction proceeded on several new U.S. major combatant ships, and the third nuclear aircraft carrier, the U.S.S. *Vinson,* was launched. Ships joining the fleet in 1980 included the am-

phibious assault ship U.S.S. *Peleliu,* the nuclear attack submarine U.S.S. *Indianapolis,* and the guided missile frigate U.S.S. *Wadsworth.* Some officials urged that the fleet be beefed up by the reactivation from mothballs of the four Iowa-class battleships.

The crisis in Afghanistan and Iran gave impetus to proponents of an expanded naval force able to patrol the vital oil routes from the Persian Gulf through the Indian Ocean. The Carter administration increased its five-year shipbuilding plan by more than 40 percent and considered the creation of a permanent naval command in the Indian Ocean. The U.S. naval base at the British Indian Ocean island of Diego Garcia was scheduled for a major buildup.

The British government announced in July that it would purchase about 100 Trident nuclear ballistic missiles from the U.S. to replace its aging fleet of Polaris submarine-launched ICBMs. The Tridents would become operational with four or five new British-built nuclear submarines in the early 1990's.

*See also* NORTH ATLANTIC TREATY ORGANIZATION and articles on the individual countries mentioned. T.D.

**MINERALS AND METALS.** In 1980 the U.S. metals industry searched for mineral deposits that would help reduce dependency upon foreign imports or provide greater profits as prices for precious metals soared. Efforts were made to reopen old cobalt mineral properties, closed long ago because of poor world markets and prices. New mining areas for gold were sought and new recovery techniques were developed.

**Moves toward Self-Sufficiency.** Major steps were taken in 1980 to reopen commercial cobalt mines in the United States. Noranda Mining Inc., a U.S. subsidiary of Canada's Noranda Mines Ltd., applied for permits to operate the abandoned Blackbird mine in central Idaho. The ore contained 0.6 percent cobalt and 1.2 percent copper. Mineral production was planned at a rate of 4,000,000 lb. per year of contained cobalt by 1982. Efforts were also under way to develop a new nickel-cobalt-chromium mineral mine in the Gasquet Mts. near Del Norte, Calif. The ore contained about 0.8 percent nickel, 0.1 percent cobalt, and 2 percent chromium. The possible reopening of the Madison lead mine in Fredericktown, Mo., was also announced. The lead ore was known to contain cobalt, nickel, and copper, and it could produce 1000 tons of cobalt annually. Successful operations at these three sites would help to reduce by about 30 percent the U.S. dependency on imported cobalt, an important component of alloys for high temperature uses.

Gold mining in the U.S. was particularly active in 1980 as a result of prices that continued to exceed $600 an ounce for most of the year, following a January high of $875. The Homestake Mining Co. announced that it had found a new major deposit in California containing more than 1,000,-000 oz. The discovery took place 70 mi. north of Sacramento in a remote area where gold had not previously been mined. Because the gold particles were so finely dispersed that they could neither be panned nor be seen by the naked eye, prospectors ignored the area during the 1849 Gold Rush. Production was planned at the rate of 100,000 oz. per year. Yuba Gold Fields Inc. and St. Joe Minerals Corp. entered a joint venture for gold-dredging property near Marysville in northern California. About 20,000 oz. of gold were to be recovered annually.

In another joint effort, Freeport Gold Co. and FMC Gold Corp. broke ground 50 mi. north of Elko, Nev. Named the Jerritt Canyon Project, the mine was expected to yield about 200,000 troy oz. of gold. A chemical treatment process was to be used in conjunction with conventional mining methods to separate the microscopic gold particles from the ore, recovering 1 oz. for every 5 tons of processed materials. Elsewhere in Nevada, Carlin Gold Mining Co. began in midyear to produce gold from its new Maggie Creek project, located south of Carlin. This site and at least four other new properties were expected to help make Nevada, rather than South Dakota, the country's leading gold-producing state.

Silver also received renewed attention though prices dropped from a high of $50 per ounce in January and fluctuated between $15 and $25 through most of the year; see BANKING AND FINANCE. Sunshine Mining decided to proceed with development of its Silverpeak, Nev., property. Operations were expected to start in 1982, yielding 1,000,000 oz. of silver per year. ASARCO announced that it expected to begin production in the next few years at two new open pit mines. One project, near Barstow, Calif., was to yield 4,000,000 oz. of silver annually. Another mine, in Winnemucca, Nev., was still being evaluated.

The violent eruptions of Mount St. Helens during 1980 stirred hopes of recovering some scarce metals from the 3.3 billion cu. yd. of rock and ash materials generated. The ejecta proved to be relatively valueless, however. Samples collected throughout the Pacific Northwest were found to contain primarily aluminum and oxides of silicon, which are present in most soil samples. Other metal oxides found were iron, calcium, sodium, magnesium, potassium, titanium, and manganese. None of the metals were present in sufficient quantities for the ash to be considered useful.

*Stimulated by gold prices that exceeded $600 an ounce for most of 1980, mineral companies and private individuals stepped up searches for the metal. Here a modern prospector, clad in a wet suit, watches his partner handle containers of silt vacuumed from a riverbed.*

*Eruptions from Mount St. Helens stirred vain hopes of finding metal deposits of significant commercial value among the vast amounts of rock and ash showered on the Pacific Northwest. Here a National Guardsman leaves his helicopter, wading through ash to a camper where two persons were found dead.*

**Trade in Strategic Minerals.** Following the Soviet invasion of Afghanistan, the U.S. again faced the problem of importing scarce materials. In the case of some militarily strategic minerals, the Soviet Union had been a major supplier. On Oct. 2 the U.S. Congress passed legislation demanding that the President develop a long-term plan for obtaining minerals, especially those needed for defense purposes.

**The Law of the Sea.** The ninth session of the United Nations Law of the Sea Conference ended in August, with the final draft of the treaty expected to be completed in March, 1981. The 200-mi. territorial limit for coastal nations was affirmed, giving those countries exclusive rights to all resources within their zones. An International Seabed Authority would regulate deep-sea mining outside the 200-mi. limits.          K.B.H.

**MINNESOTA.** *See* STATISTICS OF THE WORLD.

**MISSISSIPPI.** *See* STATISTICS OF THE WORLD.

**MISSOURI.** *See* STATISTICS OF THE WORLD.

**MONACO.** *See* STATISTICS OF THE WORLD.

**MONGOLIAN PEOPLE'S REPUBLIC.** *See* STATISTICS OF THE WORLD.

**MONTANA.** *See* STATISTICS OF THE WORLD.

**MOROCCO.** Morocco remained preoccupied in 1980 with the five-year-old guerrilla war in the Western Sahara against the Algerian- and Libyan-supported Polisario Front. The war began in 1976 after Spain ceded the area to Morocco and Mauritania. Morocco took the northern two thirds and

Mauritania the poorer southern third, and they joined forces against the Polisario, which was fighting for an independent state. But Mauritania signed a peace treaty with the Polisario in 1979.

**The War.** Although both Morocco and the Polisario continued to suffer heavy casualties and the war was reportedly costing Morocco more than $1,000,000 a day, both sides seemed to harden their conditions for a settlement. King Hassan II of Morocco still claimed the entire Western Sahara for Morocco, including the part earlier claimed by Mauritania. He spoke of a war of attrition that would produce a military victory.

In March he made a symbolic first visit to the disputed territory, bringing his entourage to the main southern town of Dakhla, which Moroccan forces had taken in August, 1979, after Mauritania made peace with the Polisario. The front, on the other hand, was pushing for an independent Sahara Democratic Arab Republic (SDAR) and had secured diplomatic recognition from more than 35 countries.

The dispute threatened to split the Organization of African Unity at its annual meeting in July. Twenty-six of its 50 members, a majority, favored recognition of the SDAR. But after Morocco, Senegal, Egypt, and five other members threatened to leave the organization if such recognition was granted, a vote on the question was postponed and a committee formed to meet with both sides.

Morocco's relations with Mauritania became

strained after Moroccan jets violated Mauritanian airspace in pursuit of Polisario fighters.

**U.S. Relations.** After the overthrow of Shah Mohammed Riza Pahlavi of Iran in early 1979, the United States decided to bolster the position of King Hassan, a longtime close friend who had become diplomatically isolated because of the desert war. It concluded an arms sale worth $232,500,000 (to be paid for by Saudi Arabia) of reconnaissance planes, F-5 fighter-bombers, and helicopters. According to Assistant Secretary of State for Near Eastern and South Asian Affairs Harold H. Saunders, the weaponry would strengthen the military position of Morocco and in time produce first a stalemate and then a negotiated settlement of the dispute.

**Economic Affairs.** Meanwhile, the war continued to drain the Moroccan economy. But in October the International Monetary Fund approved a $1.1 billion loan to Morocco, to be paid over three years, one of its largest loans to a developing country. The fund attributed Morocco's economic plight to a decline in the world demand for phosphate, the country's chief export, high oil prices, and poor crop yields.

**Other Developments.** Morocco was the only Muslim country to be represented at the shah's funeral in Cairo on July 29. It gave verbal support to Iraq in the Iran-Iraq war.

See STATISTICS OF THE WORLD.           C.G.

**MOTION PICTURES.** Moviegoers paid more for their tickets in 1980. Prices averaged about $2.77 in September, with inflation driving the average price up 9.1 percent over the previous year. Although admissions dropped 6.8 percent during the first nine months, U.S. box-office receipts were expected to total more than $2.8 billion for the year, about equal to the 1979 figure.

The cost of making movies also rose, to an average of $10,000,000 per feature, up 15 percent from 1979 and 65 percent from 1978. The average marketing cost rose to $6,000,000 per film. Thus a feature in 1980 had to gross $16,000,000 to break even. Adding in other distribution costs, a $40,000,000 gross was necessary for a picture to cover all charges and show a clear profit.

Although the major studios and independent producers initiated more than 200 films during the year, patterns of production and attendance were disrupted for several months. On July 21, members of the Screen Actors Guild and the American Federation of Television and Radio Artists walked off their jobs in a labor dispute with film studios and television networks. About 20,000 nonstriking craftspeople and technicians were also idled by the walkout, which halted production of most feature films and nearly all television series in the United States. A major issue was the method of distribution for profits from home-video markets, such as pay television, video cas-

*The war between Morocco and the Polisario Front for control of the Western Sahara continued in 1980. Captured Polisario arms are shown in the foreground as Morocco holds a rally in the desert.*

The Empire Strikes Back, *sequel to* Star Wars, *was the smash box-office hit of 1980. Mark Hamill, playing Luke Skywalker, is shown riding a Tauntaun, one of the creatures on the ice planet Hoth.*

settes, and video disks. A related dispute centered on a proposed increase in the basic minimum wage for performers. The strike was not officially resolved until late October, when the performers and their employers agreed to terms, including a new formula for sharing home-video revenues and a minimum-wage raise of 32.25 percent.

**Summer Smashes.** Film attendance fell into its worst slump in four years during the summer season. Ticket sales dropped more than 10 percent from the previous summer, and box-office receipts slid nearly 11 percent, taking inflation as well as receipts into account. Many exhibitors put the blame on Hollywood for failing to produce films that would attract audiences in a period of recession. Still, *The Empire Strikes Back* grossed about $150,000,000 during the summer, earning for Twentieth Century-Fox some 16 percent of the season's entire revenue. During its first day alone, this science-fiction epic (story written by George Lucas, directed by Irvin Kershner) brought in $1,300,000. The next most successful film was *Airplane!* from Paramount Pictures, a disaster-movie spoof that earned $59,000,000 during the season. Along with just eight other films, including the

horror film *Friday the 13th,* which grossed more than $40,000,000, these blockbusters took in more than half the summer's revenue. Attendance picked up again in the autumn, helping overall box-office figures to recoup for the year.

**Studio News.** Important corporate moves and legal decisions affected the motion-picture industry during 1980. On Aug. 4 the Justice Department moved to prevent Getty Oil Co. from joining with four movie companies to provide films for pay television. Existing cable networks had opposed the new system, called Premiere, claiming it would limit their access to motion pictures. In February a federal judge ruled that a film exhibitor, Loews Corp., could produce and distribute its own pictures. The ruling, however, stipulated that these films not be shown at theaters owned by Loews. This modified but essentially upheld previous antitrust provisos that prohibited studios from exhibiting their own films in their own theaters.

Also in February, as a result of an undercover investigation by the Federal Bureau of Investigation into pornography distribution and film piracy, indictments were reported against 55 per-

### Lady Movie Mogul

Sherry Lansing, 35, was named president of 20th Century-Fox Productions on New Year's Day. On Jan. 2 she reported to Fox—a studio she had never even visited before—to begin spending approximately $100,000,000 per year making movies. Sherry Lansing had been a high school mathematics teacher, a model for hair products in TV commercials, and an actress in one film—*Rio Lobo*—before she decided to get into the business end of the film industry. In 1978, just four years later, she became senior vice-president of production at Columbia Pictures. Two enormously successful films produced under her aegis, *The China Syndrome* and *Kramer vs. Kramer,* convinced the Fox people that she was the one to be their $300,000-per-year production head.

*Sherry Lansing.*

sons in ten states. The probe represented the largest attack to date on the pornography industry and also led to indictments for alleged piracy and distribution of major films transferred illegally to video cassettes. This operation was said to cost the motion-picture industry about $700,000,000 annually. Later in the year the Justice Department took its first action to challenge motion-picture market splitting, charging that four theater companies had conspired to allocate film showings in Milwaukee.

Among the major studios, Twentieth Century-Fox made much of the year's news. On Jan. 1, Sherry Lansing was named president and head of production, making her the first woman to attain such a post. Fox also announced a plan to release films, video cassettes, and video disks for home use simultaneously with theatrical exhibition. The Rank Organization cited inflation and high interest rates as reasons for its withdrawal from film production, involving the cancellation of eight major features budgeted at a total of $57,000,000. By contrast, the president of Universal Studios and the chairman of RKO General made public a joint venture to finance and produce a series of pictures over the next three years. And Zoetrope Studios, owned by filmmaker Francis Ford Coppola, announced its plan to make six to eight films each year, with budgets of around $7,500,000.

**Films of 1980.** Some of the year's new releases sparked viewer protests. William Friedkin's *Cruising* angered homosexuals while it was still being filmed, and hostility continued after its premiere. Box-office revenues were high for a few days, then fell abruptly. Brian De Palma's *Dressed to*

*Kill* fared better financially, becoming one of the year's hits despite feminist outcries over the film's depiction of brutality toward women.

Westerns tried for a comeback in 1980, but the trail was bumpy. *Heaven's Gate,* Michael Cimino's first film since *The Deer Hunter,* became the most expensive Western ever made, with a budget estimated at $36,000,000; it was also the year's biggest movie disaster. After a couple of invitational showings in New York City, it was abruptly pulled off the market by United Artists, which feared that awesomely bad reviews would destroy the film's commercial life. The studio announced that Cimino would reedit the drama about a range war in Wyoming to something shorter than its original 3½ hr., but that did not stop the tremors that shook the big-budget movie community.

In other Westerns, Steve McQueen, who died of a heart attack on Nov. 7 following surgery for cancer, made his next-to-last film appearance in *Tom Horn.* Walter Hill reexamined Jesse James's gang in *The Long Riders.* Several more Westerns went into production during the year, including *The Legend of the Lone Ranger* and *Cattle Annie and Little Britches.*

Country-music subjects were often featured in 1980. Sissy Spacek portrayed singer Loretta Lynn in *Coal Miner's Daughter,* and music star Willie Nelson played his first major dramatic role in *Honeysuckle Rose,* a countrified remake of the Hollywood classic *Intermezzo.* Country atmosphere was also important in *Urban Cowboy* with John Travolta, about love and rivalry in a Texas honky-tonk, and in *Bronco Billy,* with Clint Eastwood running a Wild West show.

Several films dealt with characters in more affluent settings. Paul Schrader's *American Gigolo* tells of a politician's wife who gets involved with a male prostitute, played by Richard Gere. On a lighter level, *Just Tell Me What You Want* gives a comical slant to the romantic travails of well-to-do people, and *It's My Turn* explores the feminist concerns of director Claudia Weill in sophisticated surroundings.

Comedies were popular in 1980. Woody Allen wrote, directed, and played the leading role in *Stardust Memories,* the controversial story of a movie director who despises his fans. Marshall Brickman, a frequent Allen collaborator, made his directing debut with *Simon,* about an apparent visitor from another planet. *The Blues Brothers,* with television personalities John Belushi and Dan Aykroyd, was John Landis's extremely expensive follow-up to the successful *National Lampoon's Animal House.* Deliberate vulgarity was a central element in *Cheech & Chong's Next Movie, The Hollywood Knights, Up the Academy,* and *Caddyshack.* More thoughtful were *Private Benjamin,* with Goldie Hawn as an unliberated woman

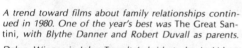

*A trend toward films about family relationships continued in 1980. One of the year's best was* The Great Santini, *with Blythe Danner and Robert Duvall as parents.*

*Debra Winger is John Travolta's bride-to-be in* Urban Cowboy, *a film about love and rivalry in a Texas honkytonk, set to country music.*

who matures after joining the U.S. Army, and *Hopscotch,* with Walter Matthau as an American spy who decides to blow the whistle on "dirty tricks" in high places. In *Rough Cut,* David Niven plays a policeman on the trail of jewel thief Burt Reynolds, and *Melvin and Howard* features Jason Robards as billionaire Howard Hughes, in a comedy focusing on Hughes's alleged will leaving much of his fortune to a man he met only once.

Several films explored family relationships, continuing a trend of recent years. Robert Redford revealed his skill as a director with *Ordinary People,* based on Judith Guest's novel about an emotionally troubled teenager and his parents. Actor James Caan made his filmmaking debut with *Hide in Plain Sight,* about a man searching for his missing wife and children. Another actor, Tony Bill, directed *My Bodyguard,* about a boy facing challenges in high school and at home. And *The Great Santini* features Robert Duvall as the macho father of a sensitive young man. *Santini* was also notable as an example of the foibles of Hollywood's new distribution options. After unsuccessful test marketing, the film was leased to home-cable and in-flight services. The film's distraught producers then put up the money to open in a small New York theater, where it did sold-out business and garnered the critical raves that made it one of 1980's minor hits.

Musical pictures remained popular. *Fame* and *Times Square* dealt with young people in New York City, punctuating the action with popular songs, while *Can't Stop the Music* put an old-fashioned success story into a disco setting. Singer Paul Simon wrote and starred in *One-Trick Pony,* about an aging rock musician. The year's concert films included *Divine Madness* with Bette Midler and *No Nukes,* which features performances from the 1979 concerts organized by MUSE—Musicians United for Safe Energy.

The most heavily promoted horror movie was *The Shining,* directed by Stanley Kubrick from Stephen King's novel. Although it earned money at the box office, many critics found it cold and lifeless. Paul Mazursky's *Willie & Phil* was also unpopular with reviewers, who were not won over by its heavy references to François Truffaut's *Jules and Jim.* A romantic film with Brooke Shields, *The*

*The Elephant Man is a motion picture about a hideously deformed man, portrayed by John Hurt, who wears a foam latex mask.*

*One of 1980's foreign-language film highlights was the epic drama* Kagemusha, *directed by Akira Kurosawa. Tatsuya Nakadai plays a petty thief who impersonates a powerful warlord in 16th-century Japan.*

The Tin Drum, *an adaptation of Günter Grass's novel, received an Academy Award in 1980 as the previous year's best foreign-language film. David Bennent plays a boy who wills himself not to grow in hopes of thereby escaping the insanity of Nazi Germany.*

*Blue Lagoon,* became a major hit despite equally poor notices, as did *Smokey and the Bandit II* with Burt Reynolds.

Veteran filmmaker Samuel Fuller made a substantial comeback with *The Big Red One,* about his own World War II experiences. John Cassavetes also returned to the fore with the gangster melodrama *Gloria,* starring Gena Rowlands. Martin Scorsese offered *Raging Bull,* with Robert De Niro as prizefighter Jake La Motta. Among newer directors, David Lynch brought to *The Elephant Man* much of the visual inventiveness that marked his cult success, *Eraserhead.* Releases near the end of 1980 included *The Stunt Man,* energetically directed by Richard Rush, and *Popeye,* a comedy by the unconventional director Robert Altman. A new fantasy epic, *Flash Gordon,* also made its bow amid much fanfare.

**Foreign Films.** Major imports from France were led by Jean-Luc Godard's *Every Man for Himself* and Maurice Pialat's *Loulou.* Ingmar Bergman directed *From the Life of the Marionettes,* a fictional investigation into the causes of a murder. Hans-Jürgen Syberberg's *Our Hitler—A Film from Germany* played several special engagements at a

running time of 7 hr. From the same country came Rainer Werner Fassbinder's *In a Year of Thirteen Moons,* about a transsexual. *Angi Vera* was a popular drama from Hungary. Italy offered *To Forget Venice,* which was well received by many critics, and Lina Wertmuller's *Blood Feud,* which was not, despite a distinguished cast including Sophia Loren, Marcello Mastroianni, and Giancarlo Giannini. Japan's Akira Kurosawa was widely praised for his epic *Kagemusha,* set in the 16th century.

**Academy Awards.** The Academy of Motion Picture Arts and Sciences presented its Oscars in Los Angeles on April 14. The family drama *Kramer vs. Kramer* was voted best picture, and Robert Benton won prizes for its adapted screenplay and direction. For their work in the same film, actor Dustin Hoffman and supporting actress Meryl Streep also earned awards. Sally Field was named best actress for *Norma Rae,* and Melvyn Douglas won an Oscar as best supporting actor in *Being There.* Steve Tesich took the prize for best original screenplay, *Breaking Away,* and *All That Jazz* won honors in four major categories. *The Tin Drum* was named best foreign-language film. An honorary Oscar went to Sir Alec Guinness.   D.S.

## MOZAMBIQUE

**MOZAMBIQUE.** Mozambique was able to turn its full attention to its many economic problems for the first time in 1980 as the war in neighboring Zimbabwe (formerly Rhodesia) came to an end. After independence in 1975, Mozambique served as a staging ground for nationalist guerrilla attacks on Rhodesia's white rulers. In retaliation, Rhodesia launched an estimated 350 air and ground attacks against Mozambique, killing 1335 Mozambicans and costing the country some $550,000,000 in lost revenues and millions in property damage, according to its government. The Rhodesians also backed an antigovernment guerrilla movement that harassed and sabotaged the administration of President Samora M. Machel. With the coming of peace and a black-African government in Zimbabwe, Machel opened Mozambique's ports and railroad to Zimbabwean commerce.

Now less dependent upon Soviet arms and support, Machel also began to court Western investors. Beginning in March, in a major reorientation of economic policy, corrupt or inefficient officials were removed or arrested. Major changes were made in the cabinet. Private enterprise was declared to have a place in the economy, and nationalized firms were urged to produce profits. Negotiations were begun to attract U.S., Brazilian, Japanese, and European firms to invest in fishing, mining, agriculture, and light industry. In August, Mozambique made an emergency appeal for food and medicine because drought was expected to cause a food deficit of 290,000 tons, according to United Nations sources, and the harried Mozambicans were already suffering from famine.

Mozambique and Zimbabwe agreed to assist one another in security matters. Zimbabwean forces quickly moved to root out anti-Machel guerrillas. In July, 272 were killed and 300 captured, according to the Mozambique army. The remnants reportedly fled to South African territory.

See STATISTICS OF THE WORLD.          J.T.S.

**MUSIC.** Among the outstanding events of 1980 in music were the following:

### CLASSICAL MUSIC
The Metropolitan Opera Company's 1980–81 season was almost aborted by a strike by the orchestra and the American Guild of Musical Artists. After a settlement was reached on Nov. 13, Met management announced a Dec. 10 opening.

The New York City Opera presented the American premiere of Kurt Weill's *Silverlake* on March 20. That same company offered premieres of three American operas on Oct. 9: Stanley Silverman's *Madame Adare*, Thomas Pasatieri's *Before Breakfast*, and Jan Bach's *The Student from Sala-*

John Williams, best known as a composer for films, was named conductor of the Boston "Pops" orchestra in 1980, succeeding the late Arthur Fiedler.

*manca.* Other operatic events of interest were the U.S. premiere of Gian-Carlo Menotti's *Chip and his Dog* in May at the Spoleto Festival U.S.A. and performances on Feb. 24 by the Encompass Theater in New York City of Jack Beeson's *Hello Out There* and Hugo Weisgall's *The Stronger.* On May 27 Kirke Mechem's *Tartuffe* received its premiere by the San Francisco Opera's American Opera Project.

International operatic activity, too, was lively in 1980. Bernard Lefort began his first season as general administrator of the Paris Opéra, replacing retiree Rolf Liebermann. In Madrid, Placido Domingo gave the lead performance at the world premiere on June 19 of Federico Moreno Torroba's *El Poeta,* and in Mannheim, West Germany, Hans Wallat conducted Giselher Klebe's *Der*

*Jüngste Tag* at the National Theater in the work's first performance on July 16. In Cardiff, Wales, on Sept. 15, the Welsh National Opera introduced William Mathias's *The Servants.*

Conductors continued to change assignments at a fast pace. John Williams, the composer of scores for films such as *Star Wars,* was named conductor of the Boston "Pops." Pinchas Zukerman opened his first season on Oct. 3 as music director of the St. Paul Chamber Orchestra. Julius Rudel said a final good-bye to the New York City Opera with his resignation as principal conductor at the end of the fall season. William H. Reese was appointed head of the Bach Choir of Bethlehem (Pa.), and David Gilbert, moving farther afield, became principal conductor of the Peking Central Philharmonic Orchestra. Closer to home, Jorge Mester was appointed conductor of the Peabody Conservatory Symphony Orchestra, and Varujan Kojian took over the podium of the Utah Symphony. In Washington, D.C., Martin Feinstein was named president of the National Symphony and retained his post as director of the Washington Opera Company. The San Francisco Symphony opened its new Louise M. Davies Symphony Hall in September, and the Boston Symphony Orchestra began a yearlong celebration of its 100th anniversary with the world premiere on Sept. 24 of Leonard Bernstein's *Diverti-*

*mento,* a work commissioned by the orchestra for its birthday festivities.

Opera companies and orchestras continued to reach for larger audiences through television and radio. The world premiere of Gottfried von Einem's *Jesu Hochzeit* was telecast live from the Theater an der Wien in Vienna on May 18. The Metropolitan Opera's taped performance of Giacomo Puccini's *Manon Lescaut* was telecast by PBS on Sept. 27, even though the Met was on strike. The San Francisco Opera announced plans to broadcast live Friday evening performances in stereo via satellite on National Public Radio, beginning on Sept. 26 with Giuseppe Verdi's *Simon Boccanegra.* NBC's new series, *Live from Studio 8H,* got off to a fine start on Jan. 9 with Zubin Mehta conducting the New York Philharmonic with Leontyne Price and Itzhak Perlman as soloists. The Jan. 14 telecast of the New York Philharmonic's Pension Concert featured tenor Luciano Pavarotti.

**Milestones.** On March 1 Roberta Peters sang for the 500th time at the Metropolitan Opera. Another Met old-timer, Risë Stevens, was appointed director of the company's National Council Auditions. Across Lincoln Center Plaza, Glenn Dicterow took up his duties as the New York Philharmonic's new concertmaster. Karlheinz Stockhausen's *Michaels Heimkehr* was first heard

*One of 1980's recording events was a new set of Ludwig van Beethoven's nine symphonies on Deutsche Grammophon, with Leonard Bernstein conducting the Vienna Philharmonic Orchestra.*

**The Most Recorded Performing Artist Ever**
When the German baritone Dietrich Fischer-Dieskau performed a series of recitals at New York City's Carnegie Hall in the spring of 1980 to celebrate the 25th anniversary of his U.S. debut, the occasion inspired one enterprising critic to review the singer's recording career. The results were astonishing. A rough tally revealed that since the late 1940's Fischer-Dieskau had recorded a total of 2780 songs, 52 operatic arias, 17 albums of opera highlights, 59 complete operas, and 117 other works, including cantatas and oratorios. Moreover, since conducting is also one of his accomplishments, he had eight recorded symphonies to his credit. Finally, it must be noted that at the age of 55, Fischer-Dieskau most likely has a long career—and many more recordings—ahead of him.

*Dietrich Fischer-Dieskau.*

in Amsterdam on June 14, in a performance in the Concertgebouw Hall with Peter Eötvös conducting. On May 1 Krzysztof Penderecki's Symphony No. 2 received its premiere by the New York Philharmonic, Mehta conducting. The Albany (N.Y.) Symphony debuted Robert Ward's Symphony No. 4, and Lukas Foss saluted the 1980 Winter Olympics with his *Round a Common Center,* a work played for the first time by the Cantilena Players at Lake Placid, N.Y.

Musical instruments, too, had their moments of fame. On Jan. 30 Benjamin Franklin's armonica, the renowned "glass harmonica" he invented, was given to the Franklin Institute science museum in Philadelphia. In New York City on March 26, the Steinway grand piano in the Martin Beck Theater was auctioned for $390,000—the highest price ever paid at auction for a musical instrument or piece of 19th-century furniture.     J.Bo.

### RECORDINGS
The end of 1980 saw the six major classical labels firmly committed to producing records from noise-free, digitally recorded tape masters. At least a dozen other labels "went digital" for part of their release programs.

Notable sonic successes in digital format during 1980 included Herbert von Karajan's production of Wolfgang Amadeus Mozart's *The Magic Flute* on Deutsche Grammophon (DG), RCA's Maurice Ravel collection with Eduardo Mata leading the Dallas Symphony, and the CBS version of Igor Stravinsky's *Petrouchka* with Zubin Mehta and the New York Philharmonic.

**Symphonic Works.** Leonard Bernstein's Vienna Philharmonic recording on DG of the nine symphonies of Ludwig van Beethoven headed the

standard repertoire issues. The three-disc album on Oiseau-Lyre of the Mozart symphonies, numbers 18–27, drew attention to Christopher Hogwood's Academy of Ancient Music in London.

Leonard Bernstein and the Israel Philharmonic recorded on DG Pëtr Ilich Tchaikovsky's *Romeo and Juliet* and *Francesca da Rimini,* and Bernard Haitink with the Amsterdam Concertgebouw offered on Philips the same composer's *Symphony No. 4.* Critics also applauded Klaus Tennstedt's interpretation of Gustav Mahler's *Symphony No. 9* with the London Philharmonic (Angel).

Concerti by Mozart and Johann Sebastian Bach fared especially well. Murray Perahia's rendition of numbers 8 and 22 and 12 and 27 of Mozart (both CBS) won critical plaudits, as did Tomas Vasáry's of numbers 14 and 26 (DG) and Emanuel Ax's numbers 20 and 22 (RCA). Angel's digital issue of Bach's *Brandenburg Concerti* by the Los Angeles Chamber Orchestra under Gerard Schwarz reaped much acclaim. Itzhak Perlman and Seiji Ozawa collaborated with the Boston Symphony on violin concerti by Alban Berg and Stravinsky (DG).

**Opera, Choral, and Solo Vocal Works.** Among the lesser-known operas, Sergei Taneyev's *Oresteia* and Zakharia Petrovich Paliashvily's *Absalom and Etery* were both issued by DG from Soviet tapes. But it was Herbert von Karajan conducting Claude Debussy's *Pelléas et Mélisande* (Angel) that won the greatest praise.

Two significant recorded opera premieres were presided over by Antal Dorati. Richard Strauss's *The Egyptian Helen* on London starred Gwyneth Jones. Dorati also led the Lausanne Chamber Orchestra and soloists on Philips in the opera buffa piece by (Franz) Joseph Haydn, *L'Incontro Improvviso.* Philips also added Verdi's *Stiffelio* to its roster of recorded operas. Carlo Maria Giulini's direction of Verdi's *Rigoletto* (DG) was well received, as was Angel's issue of a 1958 live performance of *La Traviata* with Maria Callas.

Important choral works of George Frederick Handel included Raymond Leppard's recording for RCA of *Samson,* featuring Janet Baker, Robert Tear, and Helen Watts. Christopher Hogwood's Academy of Ancient Music contributed the *Messiah,* with an "original instruments" arrangement, for Oiseau-Lyre. It was based on the 1754 London Foundling Hospital performance supervised by the composer. DG's Archive series added the Montserrat Monastery Schola recording of the *Responsoria* of Don Carlo Gesualdo.

The three collections on London of opera and Neapolitan song starring tenor Luciano Pavarotti dominated the classical best-seller lists. This success reflected both Pavarotti's vocal prowess and his personal magnetism.

**Chamber and Solo Instrumental Works.** The recording of Beethoven's string quartets by the Cleveland Quartet continued with RCA's release of Op. 18. The Boston Symphony Chamber players' series on DG added Arnold Schönberg's *Fantasy for Violin and Piano.* Alexander Zemlinsky scored belated recognition for the LaSalle Quartet's DG disc of his *String Quartet No. 2.* William Walton's *Façade,* with Edith Sitwell's text, was the subject of two new recordings and a reissue.

Solo piano recordings were plentiful. A first release was Arthur Rubinstein's playing of Robert Schumann's *Fantasia in C Major* (RCA). Ruth Laredo's recording of the solo piano music of Sergei Rachmaninoff (CBS) and Rosalyn Tureck's CBS disc of Bach's *Italian Concerto* and *Chromatic Fantasia and Fugue* were also issued. From DG came two boxed sets: a five-disc anthology with Maurizio Pollini playing major 20th-century piano works and a nine-disc reissue of Franz Schubert's piano sonatas as played by Wilhelm Kempff.

**Industry Notes.** During early 1980, major realignments affected the classical sector of the recording industry. Decca Records, marketed under the London label in the United States, became part of Polygram, the combine that includes the Philips and DG labels.

Much industry study worldwide focused on

*Perhaps the most popular classical music performer in the U.S. in 1980 was Italian tenor Luciano Pavarotti, shown leading the Columbus Day parade in New York City. Three song collections starring Pavarotti dominated sales of classical records.*

home taping of commercial discs from radio broadcasts and from records borrowed from library collections, a practice estimated to have cost the industry 20 percent of overall sales. A trade report dealt with direct mail marketing operations by such firms as Reader's Digest, Time-Life, and the Book-of-the-Month Club. Such merchandising practices accounted for about 15 percent of total record sales. D.H.

## POPULAR MUSIC

Popular music kept a relatively low profile in 1980 as no dominant musical trend emerged. And, although the record companies continued to thin their staffs and artist rosters, the bloodlettings were mild compared to those of the 1979 slump. Sales were steady. Despite worry about the relatively average earnings of hit albums, the industry did not anticipate golden eggs every year like 1978's *Saturday Night Fever*.

The charts were filled with a wide mix of rock, country, and disco-inflected rhythm-and-blues. The industry solidified its assets by streamlining the process of selling records to an older and broader-based market as it watched the effects of video disks on the record business.

**Business Trends.** Major companies increased their dominance of the market. Polygram led the way by absorbing some of its independent labels, including Mercury and Casablanca. David Geffen, retired founder of Asylum Records, formed his own self-named label in 1980. Geffen signed a distribution agreement with Warners and contracts with Donna Summer, Elton John, and John and Yoko Lennon.

The record industry was affected by two major sales-draining practices—the counterfeiting of legitimately released albums and the use of commercially sold blank tapes on which to record albums. In February two officers of Sam Goody, Inc., in New York City, one of the country's largest record retailing chains, were indicted for knowingly dealing in counterfeit cassette and eight-track tapes valued at $1,000,000. Even more alarming, however, was the increased sophistication of the pirates, reproducing albums right down to the cover art. Not only did the artist not receive royalty payments for these albums, but, in some cases, bootleg albums were returned by record stores to the legitimate manufacturer for full refunds. The most commonly circulated bootlegs were the most successful albums of the past few years, including RSO's *Saturday Night Fever* and *Grease*. Those two had officially sold a combined total of more than 42,000,000 units by the end of 1980.

The blank tape battle was fought at a lower key. Record companies discouraged the playing on radio of new albums without interruption, since this enabled listeners to make their own copies. But articles in consumer publications asserted that many "home tapers" were also the most prolific buyers of records and used their recorders to preserve rare or out-of-print works and live concerts. Too, consumers had long been critical of the often less-than-perfect, albeit official, tape releases.

**Top of the Pops.** Major albums were released in 1980 by commercially successful artists, including Pink Floyd (*The Wall*), Billy Joel (*Glass Houses*), and Bob Seeger (*Against the Wind*). The continuing success of Van Halen (*Women and Children First*), and of newer bands like AC/DC, indicated a heavy metal resurgence among rock fans. The more than 2,000,000 sales of Tom Petty's *Damn the Torpedoes* was heartening to fans of classically styled rock 'n' roll.

In evaluating 1980 releases, however, two related trends were paramount. Black soul music shed some of the overt disco stylings from the past few years, and the newly coined industry term "dance-oriented rock" began to reflect a range of music from disco to new wave.

The most significant crossover artist of 1980 was Michael Jackson, whose *Off the Wall* album, released a year earlier, continued to hover near the top of the charts with a smooth, pop-funk mixture. Michael continued to sing with his brothers, the Jacksons, who gained fame with Motown as the Jackson 5. They had a hit album in 1980 with *Triumph*. Quincy Jones, who produced the Jackson solo LP, brought the same creamy stylings to jazz guitarist George Benson, who had already sold millions to pop fans with pale, mellow vocals. The resulting *Give Me the Night* album was a dance-floor hit. The Rolling Stones' *Emotional Rescue* album drew on black styles from funk to *reggae*, and the new wave Talking Heads' *Remain in Light* LP welded the polyrhythms of African music to elements of black American funk and to their own progressive rock. Finally, Stevie Wonder surprised Motown with the first single release from his *Hotter than July* album—"Master Blaster," a *reggae* tune that climbed the charts and had pop pundits wondering whether black America was finally ready to accept the Jamaican soul music. New wavers, meanwhile, were dancing to British bands like Madness and the Specials, who based their sound on a Jamaican precursor of *reggae* called "ska."

Bands that survived the punk/new wave explosion of the late 1970's to release records in 1980 found an audience generally more open to aggressive rock styles. The Pretenders were the new wave success story of the year, although the Clash

A crowd of more than 100,000 people gathers in New York City's Central Park to pay tribute to John Lennon, who was murdered outside his Manhattan apartment house on Dec. 8.

scored significantly with *London Calling*. Even more intriguing was the appeal of danceable new wave tunes to black and disco audiences. Examples of such progressive new wave acts with hit singles in 1980 were the B-52's ("Private Idaho") and Devo ("Whip It"). Mirroring the early days of disco, these singles became popular through a growing network of rock discotheques.

Major acts continued to mount large tours. The Eagles, the Who, and Fleetwood Mac were among those that took to the road, but many promoters found themselves caught between an audience short of spending money and artists struggling to make a concert-tour profit. Tour support from record companies had become a rarity by 1980. One awesome exception to the concert doldrums was a sold-out fall tour by Bruce Springsteen and the E Street Band that promoted the singer's long-awaited double album, *The River*, a critical favorite of the year.

**Movie-Rock.** Whereas the recession hurt the live concert business, it seemed to open up the movies and television to the drawing appeal of pop musicians. Taped concertlike programs continued to be weekend staples on late-night television. At the same time, it was no longer a novelty to see rock stars on television talk shows.

In the wake of *Saturday Night Fever*, Holly-wood had gone rock happy, and 1980 saw the release of a number of music-based films, including extravaganzas like *Xanadu* (with music by the Electric Light Orchestra and Olivia Newton-John) and *Times Square* (with a new wave sound track). In Paul Simon's *One-Trick Pony*, Art Garfunkel's former partner not only composed the music but also starred in his own script. The best of the year's concert films was *No Nukes*, a documentary with performances recorded at 1979's New York City concerts sponsored by the Musicians United for Safe Energy.

Country music also found a friend in Holly-wood. Willie Nelson starred in *Honeysuckle Rose*, a rather thin story about an on-the-road country singer. The movie-music country event of the year, however, was *Urban Cowboy*, which essentially put John Travolta's disco-dancing character in cowboy duds. The sound track featured such top-five hits as Johnny Lee's "Looking for Love" and Mickey Gilley's "Stand by Me." Perhaps the country star of the year, Gilley had no less than five singles among the country top ten.

The integration of rock and video was expected to increase with growing sales of video disk players. Many believed this medium would have wide-ranging effects on the recording industry as well as on television and films.                J.M.

# N

**NAMIBIA.** *See* AFRICA; SOUTH-WEST AFRICA.

**NAURU.** *See* STATISTICS OF THE WORLD.

**NEBRASKA.** *See* STATISTICS OF THE WORLD.

**NEGROES IN THE UNITED STATES.** In 1980 the most important event relating to black Americans was the bloody rioting in Miami, Fla., May 17–19, that resulted in 18 deaths, 350 people injured, 1267 arrested, and businesses incurring at least $100,000,000 in damage. The Miami disturbance served as a grim reminder of racial strains.

**Racial Violence.** The Miami riot took place after an all-white jury in Tampa acquitted on May 17 four white former Miami police officers charged with beating to death Arthur Lee McDuffie, a black insurance company official and a former U.S. Marine. The jury's decision infuriated the Miami area's black population. A sense of outrage over alleged white police mistreatment of blacks also contributed to serious violence in Philadelphia and Wichita, Kans. Blacks marched in Jackson, Miss., on Sept. 6 to protest the slaying of a pregnant black woman by a white police officer. Civil rights groups were investigating the Nov. 8 shooting deaths of four black people by New Orleans policemen. Racial violence broke out in Chattanooga after an all-white jury on July 22 acquitted two Ku Klux Klan members charged with shooting and wounding four black women and gave a third Klan member a short sentence on a reduced charge.

Blacks also suspected law-enforcement authorities of laxity in dealing with a number of unsolved murders or intended murders in 1980 in which the victims were black. Vernon E. Jordan, Jr., president of the National Urban League, was shot and severely wounded on May 29 in Fort Wayne. Six blacks were slain in Buffalo and nearby communities in September and October, four of them allegedly by a white gunman. By late fall, 10 black Atlanta children had been murdered and four others reported missing since mid-1979. Many blacks suspected a national racist conspiracy to be at work, fears that were further fueled when an all-white jury on Nov. 17 acquitted six present or former Ku Klux Klan members of murdering five demonstrators at a 1979 anti-Klan rally in Greensboro, N.C.

**Court Cases.** In a major affirmative action ruling, the U.S. Supreme Court for the first time explicitly endorsed the power of Congress to award federal benefits on the basis of race. In its 6–3 decision on July 2, the High Court upheld a public works program that entitled minorities to 10 percent of federal construction grants. In an unwelcome ruling to blacks, however, the Court on April 22 upheld an electoral system in Mobile, Ala., that had the effect of diluting black voting strength. *See also* CIVIL RIGHTS AND CIVIL LIBERTIES.

**Economic Outlook.** In the outbreaks of racial violence a major contributing factor was the con-

## Here Comes the Judge!

One of the most interesting members of the U.S. Congress elected on Nov. 4 is Rep. George W. Crockett, Jr., from Detroit. Judge Crockett, 70, a Democrat, replaced Charles Diggs, imprisoned after a mail fraud conviction. Crockett himself was imprisoned once; he spent four months in a penitentiary on a contempt citation in 1952, the result of his impassioned defense of several Communists during a McCarthy-era trial in New York City. Previously a lawyer for the United Automobile Workers, Crockett was elected to a state criminal court in 1968; the liberal judge immediately became embroiled in new controversies, especially with Detroit police. At one point his impeachment was demanded by both houses of the state legislature. But the bar associations cleared him—and cleared the way for his eventual election to Congress.

*Rep. George W. Crockett, Jr.*

tinuing high rate of black unemployment, particularly among the young. The unemployment rate for blacks was 14.2 percent in September; for black teenagers, it was much higher. Black skilled laborers had to cope with the declining pool of jobs in the manufacturing industries, their mainstay. Blacks in government employment, the majority of them with little seniority, were adversely affected by the balance-the-budget mood and the call for a lid on government spending. Blacks seeking jobs in the service sector as waiters, hotel workers, and domestics faced competition from newly arrived groups of Vietnamese, Cubans, and Haitians, and were often impelled to accept below standard wages and working conditions.

One bright spot for blacks was the decision in early 1980 by Pittsburgh to award a contract for cable television service to Warner Amex Cable Communications Inc. Central to the award was the company's promise to give 20 percent of the operation to a coalition of 17 local groups, predominantly black. The stake was expected to bring the groups a total of $5,600,000 over the 15-year life of the contract. Blacks were also seeking to make their influence felt in cities such as Boston, Denver, Dallas, Cincinnati, Philadelphia, and St. Paul, where the process of awarding cable television franchises was still under way.

**Politics.** In the 1980 Presidential election, 82 percent of blacks voting cast ballots for President Jimmy Carter and only 14 percent for Ronald Reagan, according to one poll. Although Carter as President had not supported the social legislation that blacks considered necessary, he had named many blacks to high office, including 37 judges. Reagan was regarded as unsympathetic to blacks.

*Vernon E. Jordan, Jr., president of the National Urban League, was shot and severely wounded on May 29 in one of a number of unsolved assaults on blacks in 1980 that aroused concern among black Americans.*

*Although 1980 was a troubled year for black America, a bright spot was the growing representation of blacks in the judicial system. Here Birmingham attorney Oscar Adams (right) is sworn into office on Sept. 12 as the first black ever to sit on the Alabama Supreme Court.*

Black representation in the U.S. House of Representatives increased from 15 to 17 in the November elections. All 13 black incumbents won reelection. The new black members in the 97th Congress, all Democrats, would be Harold Washington and Gus Savage of Chicago, Mervyn Dymally of suburban Los Angeles, and George Crockett of Detroit.

The Congressional Black Caucus (CBC) continued to pursue its avowed goal "to advocate national legislative priorities for Black Americans, the poor and other underrepresented Americans throughout the nation," as stated by its chairperson, U.S. Rep. Cardiss Collins (D, Ill.). Included in these priorities was the fight against cutbacks in funds for social programs for the needy. During the spring the CBC called two news conferences to condemn the proposed fiscal 1981 federal budget as an "unmitigated disaster" for the poor. Through its Task Force on Haitian Refugees, the CBC called for the protection of these black newcomers and urged that they be provided with work permits. A consistent supporter of independence movements in southern Africa, the CBC, in common with other black Americans, rejoiced when, on April 18, the Republic of Zimbabwe was established, marking the end of 90 years of colonial rule.

**Census.** On Sept. 25 a federal district court judge, Horace W. Gilmore of Detroit, issued an order invalidating the 1980 census on the ground that it had undercounted blacks and Hispanic Americans. The court order, which was appealed, directed the federal government to adjust its totals upward for those groups. The Census Bureau conceded that it had undercounted the U.S. population in 1970 by more than 10,000,000 people, and that it had undercounted blacks in 1970 by 7.7 percent while undercounting whites by only 1.9 percent. An undercount of blacks in 1980 could have the effect of depriving black communities of a portion of badly needed federal aid and grants. B.Q.

**NEPAL.** See STATISTICS OF THE WORLD.

**NETHERLANDS, THE.** The Netherlands invested its sixth monarch in 1980 after Queen Juliana abdicated. Increasing inflation caused economic hardship, and anti-inflation moves provoked controversy. Unemployment exceeded 250,000 and was expected to rise even higher.

Juliana abdicated in a private ceremony on April 30, her 71st birthday. She was succeeded the same day by her 42-year-old daughter Beatrix. At her investiture, Queen Beatrix called for improved relations with the Third World.

The inflation rate had been 4.6 percent in the Netherlands in 1979 and was increasing in 1980. Seeking to halt this increase, the government on Jan. 10 imposed a two-month freeze on wage increases.

Frans Andriessen resigned as finance minister on Feb. 20 in opposition to a two-day-old cabinet decision to cut government spending by only about $1.56 billion. He had urged deeper cuts. Despite predictions that Andriessen's departure would topple the government, Prime Minister Andreas van Agt held his cabinet together.

Further wage controls sought by the government provoked job actions on March 4 that temporarily paralyzed much of Dutch business. Nev-

---

**Two Queens: A Full House of Orange**

In early 1980, Queen Juliana of the Netherlands announced that she would abdicate her throne, just as her mother, Queen Wilhelmina, had done in 1948. So on April 30, 1980, Juliana's daughter, Beatrix Wilhelmina Armgard, princess of the Netherlands, princess of Orange-Nassau, princess of Lippe-Biesterfeld, became the third consecutive queen of the Netherlands. The 42-year-old Beatrix, blonde, blue-eyed, dimpled, and plumpish like her mother, was reared in a somewhat informal atmosphere. In 1961 she earned a law degree from the University of Leiden. Five years later she married a German diplomat, Claus von Amsberg. The royal Dutch matriarchy will end with the reign of Beatrix, however. She and her husband have produced three sons; Prince Willem Alexander, born in 1967, is the heir apparent.

*Queen Beatrix.*

ertheless, the lower house of parliament on March 5 passed a government bill permitting curbs on pay increases. The house also accepted the proposed cuts in government spending. Union members protested the pay curbs with renewed job actions and a demonstration in Amsterdam on March 20.

The pay curbs were circumvented, however, in contracts negotiated in June by three Dutch multinationals, Royal Dutch Shell, Philips, and the Hoogovens steel group. The two-year agreements included increases averaging 2 percent, with inflation allowances expected to amount to an additional 6 percent each year.

Holland was suffering a housing shortage. An estimated 10,000 squatters were living illegally in abandoned Amsterdam buildings. Fighting broke out on Feb. 29 when about 500 squatters drove off some 200 policemen who had sought to evict illegal residents of an abandoned house. The squatters then built street barricades. More than 1000 civil and military police moved in with tanks and armored cars on March 3 and destroyed the barricades. Fighting again broke out despite assurances to the squatters that the action was directed only against barricades. The squatters demonstrated and fought police again on April 30 to mark Queen Beatrix's investiture, and another clash broke out on Sept. 8.

See STATISTICS OF THE WORLD.          L.A.S.

**NEVADA.** See STATISTICS OF THE WORLD.

**NEW BRUNSWICK.** See STATISTICS OF THE WORLD.

**NEWFOUNDLAND.** See STATISTICS OF THE WORLD.

**NEW HAMPSHIRE.** See STATISTICS OF THE WORLD.

**NEW JERSEY.** See STATISTICS OF THE WORLD.

**NEW MEXICO.** See STATISTICS OF THE WORLD.

**NEW YORK.** See STATISTICS OF THE WORLD.

**NEW ZEALAND.** In 1980 there was a serious erosion of public support for the National Party government of Prime Minister Robert D. Muldoon, and observers blamed the development on New Zealand's continuing economic woes.

**Domestic Affairs.** The country's economic problems included a lack of growth, high inflation, a severe balance of payments deficit, declining living standards, labor unrest, and the outflow of skilled workers. New Zealand was suffering from the effects of high oil import costs and the curbing of exports to Great Britain because of that nation's entry into the European Community. International economists said New Zealand's long-term prospects were bright, however, particularly in view of vast reserves of natural gas and coal.

In September the Muldoon government received a political jolt. The National Party lost a previously safe seat in a by-election, and the winner was not the Labour Party, the main opposi-

tion, but the small Social Credit Party. The swing to Social Credit suggested to some analysts that the party might be able to win enough support in the November, 1981, general election to hold the balance of power.

Prime Minister Muldoon had been out of the country during the by-election campaign, but in his typical abrasive style he sent back stinging rebukes blaming the defeat on bad party organization. A leadership crisis soon followed in which it appeared that Muldoon might be brought down by his own party. Several cabinet ministers reportedly wanted to replace Muldoon with Deputy Prime Minister and Foreign Minister Brian E. Talboys, who was also out of the country at the time. After both men had returned to New Zealand, Muldoon faced down his opponents and apparently never promised to tone down his belligerent style.

**Foreign Affairs.** New Zealand's relations with the Soviet Union cooled in 1980. In January the Muldoon government expelled Soviet Ambassador Vsevolod Sofinsky, charging that security officials had seen him handing over money to the country's Socialist Unity Party, a Communist splinter group.

Relations with the United States also went through some stress, as Muldoon made scornful remarks about President Jimmy Carter. It was felt in Washington that New Zealand should have taken stronger action against the Soviet Union for its military actions in Afghanistan and that the Muldoon government was showing too much favor toward the Arabs in the Middle East.

See STATISTICS OF THE WORLD.          F.W.

**NICARAGUA.** After one year in power, Nicaragua's leftist Sandinistas had discovered in 1980 that running the country was more difficult than the guerrilla struggle against the previous Somoza regime. Jaime Wheelock Román, minister of agrarian reform and one of the top Sandinista leaders, said: "This is a learning process and each day presents its major challenge."

The problems of getting the country back together following the 18-month civil war of 1978–79 and the even longer guerrilla struggle against the entrenched Somoza family dynasty had been immense. But considerable progress was made in 1980. By the July 19 anniversary of liberation, the Sandinistas had restored agriculture from a low of 40 percent of normal to 70 percent. Unemployment, running at 60 percent in 1979, was down to 40 percent, due largely to public works projects. This good report continued through the year.

The Sandinistas faced their first major government crisis in April, when the two most conservative members of the ruling government junta stepped down—Violeta Barrios de Chamorro for legitimate health reasons, and Alfonso Robelo Callejas in protest over the growing domination of the government by former guerrillas. Robelo, a businessman who had been a leader in the moderate noncombatant opposition to Gen. Anastasio Somoza Debayle, argued that the ouster of the longtime dictator was the result of his role and that of fellow businessmen just as much as it was the result of the Sandinista guerrilla activity.

The junta countered fears of an unraveling political coalition by naming two well-known and respected moderates as replacements. The new junta members, Rafael Córdova Rivas, a Conservative Party politician and a member of the Supreme Court, and Arturo Cruz Porras, president of the Central Bank, openly expressed their desire to continue the pluralistic arrangement and preserve the private sector. But in November several prominent businessmen were arrested, one was killed, and censorship was imposed on independent newspapers.

The presence of some 2000 Cuban teachers and medical personnel in Nicaragua caused concern in Washington, as did the announcement by junta member Daniel Ortega Saavedra that free elections would not take place until at least 1985. To counter the Sandinista Cuban connection—Cuban President Fidel Castro also attended the first anniversary celebration—the United States provided a variety of aid to help in reconstructing the shattered economy. After heated debate, the U.S. Congress approved a $75,000,000 package aimed at aiding agriculture and light industry, with the intent to provide assistance to the country's private sector. Tomás Borge Martínez, one of the top Sandinista leaders and minister of the interior, said the U.S. help "is needed, wanted, and appreciated."

The assassination of Gen. Somoza on Sept. 17 in Asunción, Paraguay, where he was in exile, was greeted warmly in Managua, the Nicaraguan capital, although the Sandinista-led government denied culpability. But the government continued to press informally for the return to Nicaragua of other Somoza family members and the repatriation of the family wealth.

*See* STATISTICS OF THE WORLD. *See also* PARAGUAY.                                            J.N.G.

**NIGER.** *See* STATISTICS OF THE WORLD.

**NIGERIA.** In 1980 President Shehu Shagari completed his first year as the first civilian ruler of Nigeria in 13 years. Political feuding increased during 1980, as did Nigeria's economic power.

Shagari had secured a working legislative majority through an alliance of his National Party of Nigeria and the Nigerian People's Party (NPP), led by Nnamdi Azikiwe. In February Shagari appointed 16 special assistants for liaison with the state governments and deported a popular opposition leader in the state of Bornu. Both measures were taken without consultation with the NPP. Joining the opposition, Azikiwe denounced the actions as capricious. Amid accusations of plots and secessionist moves, Azikiwe and Shagari met in March and patched over their differences.

While political opponents continued to criticize Shagari's policies, the president maintained the firm support of the civil service and the military. This was due, in part, to his handling of the economy. In 1978–79 the economy had suffered from decreased oil income and rising imports. Public expenditures were cut and many imports banned. Recognizing the importance of oil income, the government raised its price for crude oil to $37 a barrel by April, 1980, and oil revenues in 1980 were expected to reach $30 billion. Foreign exchange reserves, which had fallen to $2 billion in 1978, reached a record $8.68 billion in mid-1980. Shagari was able to provide Nigeria's 150,000-man army, the third largest in Africa, with more and better equipment and facilities. Restrictions on wage increases and imports were partially lifted. Recognizing the need to improve agriculture, as well as education and housing for the poor, Shagari gave these areas budgetary priority.

Although the second largest exporter of oil to the United States, Nigeria was receiving only a fraction of its imports from the U.S. Thus, by late 1980, Nigeria had built up an annual trade surplus with the U.S. of some $13 billion. To redress this imbalance, in July Vice-President Walter F. Mondale visited Lagos, where agreements were signed to improve trade and investment. In October, when Shagari visited the U.S., he insisted that Washington use its power to oppose South African policies and implied that Nigeria's "oil weapon" would be used if necessary. President Jimmy Carter responded with a pledge to continue U.S. efforts to end South African rule in Namibia (South-West Africa).

*See* STATISTICS OF THE WORLD.                    J.T.S.

**NORTH ATLANTIC TREATY ORGANIZATION,** abbreviated NATO. In 1980 the Western political and military alliance entered its fourth decade. Under the leadership of Secretary-General Joseph Luns of the Netherlands and U.S. Army Gen. Bernard W. Rogers, the supreme military commander, NATO concentrated on upgrading its military strength to keep pace with forces of the Warsaw Treaty Organization. But disagreements between the United States and its allies over the Soviet invasion of Afghanistan and the seizure of

Above: Joseph Luns, secretary-general of NATO, meets the press after a conference of foreign and defense ministers of NATO countries in Brussels on May 14.

Above, left: NATO maneuvers in the Mediterranean, held in June, had the participation of U.S., British, West German, Dutch, Italian, and Canadian ships.

Below, left: Large-scale NATO maneuvers in northern Norway, March 14–19, involved more than 18,000 soldiers from seven countries. Western concern had mounted over increasing Soviet activity in the western Arctic Ocean.

American hostages in Iran, as well as American insistence that European nations share more of the burden of common defense, generated considerable strain within the alliance.

**Friction.** Relations between the U.S. and its European allies were severely strained throughout the year by major differences on how to respond to the seizure of American hostages by Iran and the Soviet invasion of Afghanistan. As diplomatic negotiations to free the hostages in Iran remained fruitless, the U.S. stepped up pressure on its European allies to impose stringent economic and political sanctions against the Iranians. The Europeans, however, were noticeably cool to the idea, preferring diplomacy to punitive sanctions. After public criticism from President Jimmy Carter of European foot-dragging, the allies finally began moving toward concrete reprisals against Iran. In a meeting of foreign ministers in Luxembourg in April, the allies agreed to reduce their diplomatic staffs in Tehran and cut off arms sales to Iran.

The alliance split even more sharply over the Soviet invasion of Afghanistan. Carter termed the invasion the most serious threat to world peace since World War II and urged strong reprisals against the Soviets. Many European leaders, however, considered Afghanistan a regional problem and feared that retaliatory steps against the Soviets would jeopardize East-West détente. Some sanctions were ultimately approved, including a partial boycott of the Moscow Olympic Games, and NATO foreign ministers condemned the Afghan invasion at their annual meeting in June. But the Americans were privately critical of European timidity in the matter, further straining relations on both sides of the Atlantic.

The U.S. also pushed the Europeans to assume more of the military burden of defending the alliance, proposing that critically low European stocks of ammunition be built up and various other readiness improvements be considered. The U.S. was also annoyed that some smaller NATO members were failing to abide by the 1978 agreement to increase defense spending by 3 percent annually above inflation. In private communications to government officials in Denmark and the Netherlands, U.S. defense officials hinted in October that those nations might not be able to count on U.S. support in time of crisis unless they lived up to their NATO defense commitments. The hint must have been lost on the West Germans, because in late October they too decided to restrain military spending and drop their 3 percent pledge.

**Nuclear Modernization.** A controversial modernization program for NATO's defensive nuclear umbrella was reaffirmed by NATO defense ministers on June 4 at a meeting of the alliance's nuclear planning group in Norway. Under the new defense plan, originally approved in December, 1979, 464 ground-launched cruise missiles would be deployed by the mid-1980's at U.S. bases in Great Britain, West Germany, Italy, Belgium, and the Netherlands, and 108 Pershing II missiles would replace older Pershings based in West Germany. Both weapons would have a range of more than 1000 mi. and could reach targets in the Soviet Union. U.S. officials reported that the first cruise missiles would be deployed in Great Britain and Italy beginning in late 1983. The defense ministers also urged the Soviet Union to consider participating in arms control talks to limit deployment of nuclear weapons in Europe, but the Russians insisted that the NATO modernization plan be scrapped before any talks could begin. Despite the decision to proceed, the basing proposal continued to generate intense political debate within the alliance, with Belgium remaining uneasy about going along and the Dutch deferring a decision on final approval until 1981.

In July the Soviet Union changed its mind and agreed to begin talks on limiting medium-range nuclear weapons in Europe. Preliminary talks opened in Geneva in October but soon hit a snag when the Soviet Union insisted on including certain U.S. aircraft which, according to U.S. sources, were assigned mainly to conventional rather than nuclear missions.

**Turkey and Greece.** Economic problems and political violence in Turkey raised anxieties throughout the alliance about a possible takeover of the country by political forces sympathetic to the Soviet Union. Those fears were eased in September, however, when the pro-Western Turkish military overthrew the civilian government in a bloodless coup and immediately announced that Turkey would remain a member of the alliance and honor all its NATO commitments. The continuing failure of Turkey and Greece to resolve their disagreements over Cyprus and the Aegean Sea, however, seriously threatened the security of NATO's southeastern flank. Greece offered to rejoin NATO's military command, which it had left in 1974, provided NATO agreed to Greek control of air and sea lanes in the Aegean. That proposal was blocked by Turkey until a compromise was reached that would defer decisions on operational rights. Greece returned to the military wing of NATO on Oct. 20, and the gap in the southeastern flank was closed.

**War Games.** Thousands of soldiers from NATO and the Warsaw Pact participated in annual military exercises in September. More than 40,000 Soviet and East bloc troops took part in "Brotherhood in Arms '80," the largest such maneuvers staged in East Germany since 1970. The Warsaw Pact war games coincided with the start of NATO's fall maneuvers, code-named "Autumn Forge." More than 180,000 Western troops took part in the NATO exercises, which included operations in several Western European nations and the Mediterranean Sea. As part of the maneuvers, more than 17,000 U.S.-based soldiers and airmen were airlifted to bases in Europe to simulate a rapid reinforcement of NATO forces in Europe in the event of an attack by Warsaw Pact forces.

See also COMMUNISM; MILITARY AND NAVAL AFFAIRS; and articles on NATO member nations. T.D.

**NORTH CAROLINA.** See STATISTICS OF THE WORLD.
**NORTH DAKOTA.** See STATISTICS OF THE WORLD.
**NORTHWEST TERRITORIES.** See STATISTICS OF THE WORLD.

**NORWAY.** Inflation, labor discontent, and an unfavorable balance of trade troubled the Norwegian economy during 1980, despite the country's relative economic strength and the promise of a bright future as the exploitation of North Sea oil and natural gas fields expanded.

The economy had compiled a growth rate of 3 percent in 1979 despite burdensome foreign debts and a $1 billion deficit in the balance of payments. A report by the Organization for Economic Cooperation and Development on Feb. 5 predicted that both growth rate and foreign-debt burden would improve, because of higher prices and increased production of oil and gas from the North Sea oilfields, provided that the government tightened up on fiscal policy and reduced support for industry. A major economic problem was inflation, which raised consumer prices by 4.75 percent in 1979 and accelerated in 1980.

A dispute with Iceland was settled on May 10, with Norway making concessions to Iceland over fishing rights within the 200-mi. economic zone around Jan Mayen Island, a Norwegian possession in the Arctic.

A strike of 2000 Norwegian oil and gas workers on July 3 halted production in Norway's offshore oilfields. The government submitted the issue to the National Arbitration Board on July 16. This action made continuation of the strike illegal, and workers began returning to the drilling rigs on July 17, but others had meantime walked out. Agreement to end the second strike was reached on Aug. 13.

The government of Prime Minister Odvar Nordli deferred decision on a proposal to stockpile weapons and equipment in the north for possible use by U.S. Marines. The proposal was a response to increased Soviet military and naval activity on the Kola Peninsula and in the North Atlantic, but some Norwegians feared that such a buildup would only spur the Soviets to greater activity. Some favored a revised plan to "pre-position" the supplies farther south, but support for any stockpiling plan was at best only lukewarm even in Nordli's own Labor Party. The pre-positioning controversy did not interfere with North Atlantic Treaty Organization exercises held in Norway in September. The objective of the training operation was to rehearse means of reinforcing and resupplying Norway in case of war.

*See* STATISTICS OF THE WORLD.                    L.A.S.

**NOVA SCOTIA.** *See* STATISTICS OF THE WORLD.

**NUCLEAR POWER.** The March, 1979, Three Mile Island (TMI) accident near Harrisburg, Pa., was "most definitely not a disaster from a public health standpoint," according to a report by the U.S. House of Representatives Committee on Science and Technology in March, 1980. Virtually all health experts had agreed that the radiation leaked from the damaged Number 2 reactor would result in only one or two more deaths from cancer than would have naturally occurred in the area. But the accident, which was the worst in the history of commercial nuclear power in the United States, dealt the industry a staggering blow from which it continued to reel throughout 1980.

As the year began, 120 reactors stood on order awaiting construction permits or work authorizations. By Sept. 18 nearly 25 percent had been canceled, postponed, or shelved indefinitely. Economics, regulatory problems, and uncertainty

*While many U.S. utilities shelved plans to build new nuclear power plants, France continued its ambitious construction program in 1980. Cooling towers of one of France's 19 operating nuclear power plants are shown.*

over the long-term public acceptance of nuclear power were most frequently cited as reasons for revising the reactors' prospects. Only three start-up licenses and two operating licenses for nuclear power plants were granted by the Nuclear Regulatory Commission (NRC) in 1980. In April, 67 nuclear power plants were in operation.

Symptomatic of the utilities' growing disenchantment with nuclear generation was the Nov. 25 announcement by the Virginia Electric Power Co. (Vepco) that it would abandon its partially completed North Anna 4 generating station. Although Vepco was one of the nation's first utilities to make a major commitment to nuclear power, company president William W. Berry explained that continued financial problems and the cost of adopting new post-TMI nuclear safety features made cost estimates for the 10 percent completed plant too shaky. Berry added that although projected demand for electricity among Vepco's customers had declined, "When a new generating unit does become necessary, it will be coal-fired rather than nuclear."

General Public Utilities, a holding company and owner of the crippled TMI plant, spent the year teetering on the brink of bankruptcy as it continued work toward decontaminating and replacing its Number 2 reactor. By mid-November, work crews had completed four surveys into the damaged plant, learning enough to conclude that previous estimates of what it would take to bring the generating unit back into service—roughly $500,000,000 and two years' time—were too low by as much as $500,000,000 and five years.

According to one congressional study, the estimated cost of implementing safety-related changes in other nuclear plants as a result of the TMI accident would probably range between $37,000,000 and $204,000,000 per reactor. These changes would also add an additional $1,000,000 to $7,000,000 onto the annual cost of operating each plant.

**Fusion.** Congress passed a bill in September to speed development of fusion power. The goal of the Magnetic Fusion Energy Engineering Act of 1980 was to foster development of an operational fusion power reactor by the year 2000, nearly 20 years earlier than had previously been scheduled. The U.S. Department of Energy estimated that the direct cost of this accelerated fusion-development schedule would actually reduce by $2 billion the $14.3 billion price tag associated with the former research timetable. The goal of magnetic-confinement fusion research was to "bottle" a hot, fully ionized gas of light atomic nuclei within magnetic fields until the nuclei collide and fuse to liberate enormous stores of energy. Soviet and British researchers also reported progress toward that goal in 1980.

**International Developments.** A report by nuclear experts from 46 nations offered no suggestions for a way to prevent the spread of nuclear materials usable for making weapons as a result of the growth of civilian nuclear power programs. The report examined the economics of what it considered to be the three major fuel cycle options—fast breeder cycles, thorium-uranium fuel cycles, and other advanced reactor systems—and concluded that no one fuel cycle had an economic advantage in all cases. The report considered President Jimmy Carter's contention that the best way to curb the spread of nuclear weapons was to ban the manufacture and use of plutonium, which is a fuel for fast breeder reactors, but concluded it was too late to stop a country from building a bomb merely by outlawing plutonium-based technology.

In 1980 Argentina, Brazil, Iraq, and Pakistan were among countries that were importing European nuclear technology, equipment, or fuel that could enhance the ability of these countries to develop nuclear weapons. The Carter administration, overruling the NRC, approved the sale of 38 tons of enriched uranium fuel to India, although India rejected full international inspections and refused to say it would not produce nuclear weapons. (India exploded an atomic device in 1974.)

The Soviet Union announced on April 8 that it had put the world's biggest fast breeder reactor into operation. Fast breeder reactors are intended to produce more nuclear fuel than they consume. It was the second Soviet commercial reactor of this kind to go into operation. A fast breeder reactor was being built in France with West German and Italian help, and the French government said it would build two more. Great Britain had a fast breeder demonstration reactor in operation. Because President Carter feared that the plutonium-producing reactors would lead to nuclear proliferation, the U.S. earlier halted work on building an experimental fast breeder at Clinch River, Tenn.

As of August, 1980, France had 19 nuclear power plants in operation and 32 under construction; by 1985 half of France's electricity was scheduled to be provided by nuclear power. Soviet plans called for five new nuclear power plants each year. West Germany had 14 nuclear power plants in operation in 1980, but further development had been practically stopped by court action. Swedish voters endorsed a plan to expand the number of reactors there from 6 to 12 during the 1980's. J.A.R.

# O

**OBITUARIES.** Each entry below contains the name of a notable person who died in 1980. It also contains a brief description of the accomplishments and events that contributed to making the person listed notable.

**Adamson, Joy,** Austrian-born author, with her husband George, of *Born Free* (1959), the best-selling story of Elsa, a lion cub the couple raised and returned to the African wild. Two sequels and several other books followed. Investigators in Kenya, where she died, first said she was killed by an animal, probably a lion, but an employee of hers was later charged with murder. Died Jan. 3, age 69.

**Agar, Herbert Sebastian,** American journalist and historian. He received the 1934 Pulitzer Prize in history for *The People's Choice,* a study of U.S. Presidents. Died Nov. 24, age 83.

**Allon, Yigal,** Israeli statesman. Allon gained prominence as leader of a commando force that fought the Arabs in the war for independence. He joined the cabinet in 1961 and rose to become deputy prime minister and foreign minister in the Labor government. Died Feb. 29, age 61.

**Amalrik, Andrei A.,** Soviet dissident exile. He was twice sent to Siberia for opposition to Soviet policies and wrote two books published abroad before he left the Soviet Union in 1976. Died Nov. 11, age 42.

**Ardrey, Robert,** American author of works on anthropology and human behavior, including *The Territorial Imperative* and *African Genesis.* All his works advanced his controversial thesis that man's aggressive and territorial drives, rather than his environment, lead to war. Died Jan. 14, age 71.

**Aronson, Boris,** Russian-born American stage designer. He designed more than 100 productions for the Broadway stage and won six Tony Awards. Died Nov. 16, age 81.

**Barthes, Roland,** French writer and literary critic whose special target was the stereotyped ideas that to him characterized the bourgeoisie. Died March 25, age 64.

**Bates, L(ucius) C(hristopher),** American newspaper publisher. He and his wife Daisy played a key role as black leaders in the historic 1957 desegregation of Central High School in Little Rock, Ark. Died Aug. 22, age 79.

**Bateson, Gregory,** British anthropologist and philosopher. His wide-ranging interests included studies of Bali, cybernetics, and mammalian communications, especially with dolphins. Died July 4, age 76.

*Joy Adamson's love of wild animals found expression in her widely read books.*

*Sir Cecil Beaton's versatile artistry was expressed in several fields and made him a favorite in society.*

**Beaton, Sir Cecil,** British portrait photographer, painter, designer of costumes and stage sets, and writer. For more than 35 years he was the favored photographer of royalty, entertainment figures, and other celebrities. As a stage designer he conceived the sets and costumes for some dozen shows, and he won Academy Awards in 1959 and 1965 for his work on the musical films *Gigi* and *My Fair Lady.* He also designed hotel lobbies and clubs and wrote several volumes of lively memoirs. Died Jan. 18, age 76.

*Liberal Supreme Court Justice William O. Douglas set a record for tenure on the High Court bench.*

**Borg Olivier, George,** Maltese statesman. He was prime minister of Malta between 1962 and 1971 and steered the island to independence from Great Britain in 1964. Died Oct. 29, age 69.

**Boussac, Marcel,** French industrialist whose textile empire at one time included 65 factories. Died March 21, age 91.

**Brown, Rachel Fuller,** American chemist who, with Elizabeth L. Hazen, discovered the first antifungal antibiotic for humans in 1950. Forgoing monetary reward, the two women turned over all financial rights to the discovery to research. Died Jan. 14, age 81.

**Bullard, Sir Edward,** British geophysicist who pioneered the theory that the continents were once joined as a single supercontinent. Died April 3, age 72.

**Burpee, David,** American businessman. He developed hundreds of varieties of flowers and vegetables during his 55 years as head of the W. Atlee Burpee Co., the largest mail-order seed company in the world. Died June 24, age 87.

**Byrd, Henry,** American singer and pianist, known as Professor Longhair. He was regarded as one of the musicians who transformed rhythm-and-blues into rock 'n' roll. Died Jan. 30, age 61.

**Caetano, Marcello,** Portuguese leader. Under his rule as premier (1968–74), Portugal remained an authoritarian one-party state. In 1974 the government was overthrown and Caetano went into exile. Died Oct. 26, age 74.

**Champion, Gower,** American dancer and choreographer. He first reached prominence on television and in movies with his dance partner and first wife, Marge. Later he received two Tony Awards as a stage musical director and choreographer. His death came hours before the Broadway premiere of *42nd Street,* for which he was the choreographer. Died Aug. 25, age 60.

**Clurman, Harold,** American theater director and critic. In 1931 he founded the influential Group Theatre, which introduced the Method technique for actors to the American stage. Since 1953 he had written criticism for *The Nation.* Died Sept. 9, age 78.

**Cochran, Jacqueline,** American aviator who, in 1953, became the first woman to fly faster than the speed of sound. In all, she set more than 200 flying records. During World War II she was director of the Women's Air Force Service Pilots. Died Aug. 9, age early 70's.

**Connelly, Marc,** American playwright. He received the 1930 Pulitzer Prize in drama for *The Green Pastures.* Died Dec. 21, age 90.

**Day, Dorothy,** American Roman Catholic activist who was a founder of the Catholic Worker Movement in 1933. Pacifism, black rights, day-care centers, and farm unions were among the causes she embraced. Died Nov. 29, age 83.

**Dodds, Harold W.,** American educator. As president of Princeton University (1933–57), he presided over a period of great expansion and fostered the values of liberal education. Died Oct. 25, age 91.

**Doenitz, Karl,** German naval officer. He directed submarine warfare during World War II, becoming the navy's commander in chief in 1943. Adolf Hitler, before killing himself, appointed Doenitz his successor as leader of Nazi Germany, but Doenitz surrendered shortly thereafter. He served ten years in prison for war crimes. Died Dec. 24, age 89.

**Douglas, Helen Gahagan,** American actress, singer, and politician. After success on Broadway, in films, and on the opera stage, she served in the U.S. House of Representatives as a liberal Democrat from California (1945–51). In 1950 she ran for the Senate but was defeated by Richard M. Nixon. Died June 28, age 79.

**Douglas, William O(rville),** American jurist who was a U.S. Supreme Court justice for 36 years—1939 to 1975—the longest such tenure ever. A liberal, he considered the First Amendment a virtually absolute curb on government interference of any sort with free speech, press, or assembly. He was also an outspoken supporter of the rights of minorities. An inveterate globe-trotter, Douglas was a conservationist, naturalist, and writer of more than a score of books. Died Jan. 19, age 81.

**Dragonette, Jessica,** Indian-born American singer who was one of radio's most popular performers. A soprano, she was heard on radio by millions in operettas and semiclassical music. In 1935 listeners voted her radio's most popular performer. Died March 18, age middle or late 70's.

**Drew, Richard G.,** American chemical engineer who invented Scotch tape in 1930. Died Dec. 14, age 81.

**Durante, Jimmy,** one of America's most popular comedians in vaudeville and nightclubs, on the stage and in films, and on radio and television. His fractured English and assaults on the piano were his trademarks. In Durante's brand of good-natured humor, he was the butt of his own jokes, drawing attention to his battered hat and the prominent nose that earned him the nickname "Schnozzola." Died Jan. 29, age 86.

**Evans, Bill,** American jazz pianist celebrated for his lyricism and probing harmonic structures. Died Sept. 15, age 51.

**Ewing, Oscar R.,** American politician who was administrator of the Federal Security Agency—precursor of the Social Security Administration—from 1947 to 1952, preparing the agency for elevation to cabinet status as the Department of Health, Education, and Welfare in 1953. Died Jan. 8, age 90.

**Farago, Ladislas,** Hungarian-American author. He wrote more than a dozen books on contemporary history, war, and espionage. Died Oct. 15, age 74.

Jazz pianist Bill Evans was celebrated for his inventiveness and lyricism.

Jimmy Durante was one of the most beloved entertainers in the U.S.

**Farb, Peter,** American naturalist, linguist, and anthropologist. Among his books were those on the natural history of North America, the history of North American Indians, and an inquiry into spoken language; Humankind was a survey of recent scientific findings about the human species. Died April 8, age 50.

**Finletter, Thomas Knight,** American lawyer and politician. He held several foreign policy posts before serving as secretary of the U.S. Air Force (1950–53). Died April 24, age 86.

**Fischetti, John,** American newspaper editorial cartoonist. He received a Pulitzer Prize for his cartoons in 1969. Died Nov. 18, age 64.

**Fogarty, Anne,** American fashion designer whose romantic, feminine fashions of the 1950's were full-skirted, tiny-waisted, and propped with as many as a dozen petticoats. Died Jan. 15, age 60.

**Fouché, Jacobus Johannes,** South African statesman. He served as administrator of the Orange Free State and minister of defense before becoming president of South Africa (1968-75). Died Sept. 23, age 82.

**Fox, Virgil Keen,** American musician. During a 55-year career he established the organ as a concert instrument, performing before an estimated 6,000,000 people around the world. Died Oct. 25, age 68.

**Froman, Jane,** American singer and actress who appeared in several Broadway musicals before being seriously injured while on a tour to entertain servicemen during World War II. Died April 23, age 72.

**Fromm, Erich,** German-born American psycho-analyst and social philosopher. Among his 20 books, many of them hailed as major works, were *Escape from Freedom* (1941) and *The Art of Loving* (1956). Died March 18, age 79.

**Gandhi, Sanjay,** Indian politician and son of Prime Minister Indira Gandhi; *see also* INDIA. In the mid-1970's while Indira Gandhi ruled under emergency powers, he carried out some of her more controversial policies, such as population control—including mass sterilizations. His many enemies accused him of using family influence for personal gain. Died in a plane crash June 23, age 33.

**Gary, Romain,** Lithuanian-born French novelist. Among his works was *The Roots of Heaven* (1956), for which he received the Prix Goncourt. Died Dec. 2, age 66.

**Giri, V(arahagiri) V(enkata),** Indian statesman. A trade-union leader and advocate of independence from Great Britain, he later held political office and served as president (1969–74). Died June 24, age 85.

**Gorman, Patrick Emmet,** American labor leader. He was head of the Amalgamated Meat Cutters and Butcher Workmen of North America from 1923 to 1976. The union merged with the Retail Clerks International Union in 1979. Died Sept. 3, age 87.

**Gregg, Peter,** American racing driver who was the dominant driver on the International Motor Sports Association's Grand Touring circuit. Died Dec. 15, age 40.

**Guston, Philip,** American artist who was a painter of the abstract expressionist school. Died June 7, age 66.

**Hall, Paul,** American labor leader who had been president of the Seafarers International Union since 1957. Died June 22, age 65.

**Haskell, Arnold Lionel,** English writer who popularized ballet through his writings and helped form what became the Royal Ballet School, which he directed from 1947 to 1965. Died Nov. 14, age 77.

**Hayden, Robert E.,** American poet whose work was largely based on Afro-American themes. He taught English first at Fisk University and later at the University of Michigan. Died Feb. 25, age 66.

**Haymes, Dick,** Argentine-born American singer who was a leading soloist with big bands of the World War II era. He also appeared in 35 movies. But six failed marriages and alcoholism led to bankruptcy. Died March 28, age 63.

**Hays, H(offman) R(eynolds),** American author, translator, and critic. Among his works were *From*

*Film director Alfred Hitchcock was a master of suspense and the macabre.*

*Ape to Angel* (1958), one of the first general histories of anthropology, and *The Dangerous Sex* (1964), an examination of cultural attitudes toward women. Died Oct. 17, age 76.

**Hitchcock, Alfred Joseph,** British-born American film director. He was a master of suspense who often exploited childhood anxieties, such as fear of heights, enclosed places, and open space. Often the main character in his films would be unjustly accused of a crime and hunted by both villains and police. His distinctive style stressed imagery over dialogue. After making such classic British thrillers as *The 39 Steps* and *The Lady Vanishes,* he moved in 1939 to Hollywood, where his films included *Rebecca, Lifeboat, Notorious, Strangers on a Train, Rear Window, Vertigo, North by Northwest, Psycho, The Birds,* and *Frenzy.* He also produced two television series for which he served as host. Died April 29, age 80.

**Hollander, Louis,** Polish-born American union leader who helped found the Amalgamated Clothing Workers of America in 1914 and was a vice-president of the union from 1932 to 1976. Died Jan. 3, age 86 or 87.

**Howard, Elston,** American baseball player. Howard was the first black to play for the New York Yankees. A catcher, he played in ten World Series and was named the American League's most valuable player in 1963. Died Dec. 14, age 51.

**Ingelfinger, Franz J.,** German-born American physician who was considered the dean of American specialists on disorders of the bowel. In 1967 he began a ten-year career as editor of *The*

*New England Journal of Medicine,* whose scope he broadened to include social and ethical problems of medicine. Died March 26, age 69.

**Iturbi, José,** Spanish-born American pianist and conductor. Millions of people, however, knew him best as a film actor. He generally appeared as himself, playing classical, popular, and jazz compositions. Died June 28, age 84.

**Janssen, David,** American actor who achieved his greatest fame in the title role of the television series *The Fugitive.* He also appeared in many films. Died Feb. 13, age 49.

**Johnson, Gerald White,** American author, reporter, historian, and educator. An editorial writer and columnist for the Baltimore *Sun* (1926–43) and columnist for *The New Republic* (after 1954), Johnson advocated civil rights and progress in race relations. He published more than 30 books on American life and history and also wrote mystery novels under a pen name. Died March 23, age 89.

*José Iturbi delighted millions of filmgoers with his virtuoso piano playing.*

**Jones, Howard Mumford,** American cultural historian who wrote more than 30 books, many of them dealing with American literature as related to national development. In 1965 he received a Pulitzer Prize for *O Strange New World,* on the early formative years of American culture. Died May 11, age 88.

**Joseph, (Bernard) Dov,** Canadian-born Israeli statesman. In 1948 he served the fledgling state as military governor of besieged Jerusalem, which successfully held out against Arab attack. Died Jan. 6, age 80.

*Oskar Kokoschka's expressionist paintings were characterized by psychological and emotional penetration.*

**Kaminska, Ida,** Polish actress who reigned for decades as the queen of classical Yiddish theater. In 1968 she immigrated to the United States, citing an anti-Semitic campaign by the Polish government. Died May 21, age 80.

**Kendrick, Pearl Luella,** American microbiologist. She developed a vaccine that led to the virtual elimination of whooping cough, and the standard DPT shot, which protects against diphtheria and tetanus as well. Died Oct. 8, age 90.

**Kintner, Robert E.,** American broadcast executive. As president of the American Broadcasting Co. (1949–56) and the National Broadcasting Co. (1956–65), he presided over steady growth in earnings and ratings. He served as a special White House assistant and cabinet secretary (1966–67) in the administration of President Lyndon B. Johnson. Died Dec. 20, age 71.

**Kokoschka, Oskar,** Austrian-born British painter whose expressionist works were hailed for psychological and emotional penetration. He also wrote "decadent" plays that brought him under attack, ultimately forcing him to flee from Nazi-dominated Central Europe. Died Feb. 22, age 93.

**Kostelanetz, André,** Russian-born American musical conductor whose arrangements were credited with having sold 52,000,000 records. Died Jan. 13, age 78.

**Kosygin, Aleksei Nikolayevich,** Soviet statesman who was premier of the U.S.S.R. from 1964 until October, 1980. Noted for his administrative skills, Kosygin advocated reducing centralized state control over factory managers and encouraging them to reward productive workers with benefits from profits. Under his guidance, Soviet industry received stimulus from Western technology and managerial methods. Died Dec. 18, age 76.

*John Lennon, one of the four Beatles and, with Paul Mc-Cartney, creator of most of the group's hit songs.*

**Léger, Jules,** governor-general of Canada, 1974–79. A career diplomat, he was previously ambassador to several countries. Died Nov. 22, age 67.

**Lennon, John,** British musician who was one of the four members of the Beatles, the most popular and influential of rock 'n' roll groups. With fellow Beatle Paul McCartney, Lennon wrote more hit songs than any popular composer in modern history. They were also the band's lead singers. After the Beatles broke up in 1970, Lennon continued to write songs and to record music, but for several years he and his second wife, Yoko Ono, lived in seclusion. Lennon was slain outside his New York City apartment house. Died Dec. 8, age 40.

**Lesage, Jean,** Canadian politician. He became head of Québec's Liberal Party in 1958 and was premier of the province from 1960 to 1966. Died Dec. 11, age 68.

**Levene, Sam,** American actor. He appeared in more than 100 motion pictures and Broadway plays, often playing characters who were kind and loving beneath a gruff exterior. Died Dec. 28, age 75.

**Levenson, Sam,** American comedian and humorist. His monologues on his experiences growing up and teaching school in New York City were popular on television, where he had his own show. He also wrote several books drawing on personal and family experiences. Died Aug. 27, age 68.

**Libby, Willard Frank,** American chemist. He received the 1960 Nobel Prize in chemistry for developing a method employing carbon-14 to date archeological artifacts. During World War II he helped create the gaseous-diffusion process for separating isotopes of uranium in the manufacture of the atom bomb. As a member of the Atomic Energy Commission (1954–59), he led President Dwight D. Eisenhower's "Atoms for Peace" program. Died Sept. 8, age 71.

**Loden, Barbara,** American actress and director. She won a Tony Award for her performance in the play *After the Fall* (1964) and was one of the first women to write, direct, and star in a feature film, *Wanda,* which won an award at the Venice Film Festival in 1970. Died Sept. 5, age 48.

**Longley, James B.,** American businessman and politician. After making a fortune in insurance, he served (1975–78) as governor of Maine—the nation's only independent (nonparty) governor. Died Aug. 16, age 56.

**Longo, Luigi,** Italian politician who was secretary-general of the Communist Party (1964–72). Died Oct. 16, age 80.

**Longworth, Alice Roosevelt,** American social figure in the nation's capital who was the daughter of President Theodore Roosevelt and wife of Nicholas Longworth, Speaker of the House of Representatives in the 1920's. Noted for her caustic wit and influential political connections, she was sometimes called "Washington's other monument." Died Feb. 20, age 96.

**Lowenstein, Allard K.,** American politician who was active in the civil rights and antiwar movements of the 1960's and who organized the effort to deny President Lyndon Johnson the 1968 Democratic Party Presidential nomination. Later he briefly served as a congressman from New York. He was murdered by a former associate. Died March 14, age 51.

**Malik, Yakov A.,** Soviet diplomat who was his country's delegate to the United Nations from 1948 to 1952 and 1968 to 1976. Died Feb. 12, age 73.

**Mandelstam, Nadezhda,** Russian writer and widow of poet Osip Mandelstam. Her memoirs fostered appreciation of the works of her husband, who perished in a Siberian labor camp in 1938. Died Dec. 29, age 81.

**Mantovani, Annunzio Paolo,** Italian-born British musician whose arrangements became popular for canned music and "easy listening" radio stations. Between 1951 and 1966, 18 recordings by his orchestra sold at least 500,000 copies each in the U.S. Died March 29, age 74.

**Marquard, Richard (Rube),** American baseball player whose 19 consecutive wins in 1912 were still a major-league record in 1980. He won 205 big-league games and was elected to baseball's Hall of Fame. Died June 1, age 90.

**Martinez, Maria Povara,** American Indian potter known for her black-on-black pottery and for shaping perfectly balanced pots without a potter's wheel. Museums throughout the world display her work. Died July 20, age 94.

**Mauchly, John W.,** American physicist. He was co-inventor, with J. Presper Eckert, Jr., in 1942 of the world's first electronic computer, dubbed ENIAC. In later years they developed smaller, more powerful models and directed the development of UNIVAC. Died Jan. 8, age 72.

**McCormack, John W.,** American politician. A Boston Democrat, he served in the U.S. House of Representatives (1929–70) and was Speaker of the House (1962–70). Died Nov. 22, age 88.

**McDonnell, James Smith, Jr.,** American industrialist. He founded the McDonnell Aircraft Corp. in 1939. In 1946 he delivered the world's first carrier-based jet fighter, and later his company was the prime contractor for the Mercury and Gemini manned spacecraft. In 1967 the company merged with Douglas Aircraft Corp. to become McDonnell Douglas Corp., the second largest military manufacturing company in the nation. Died Aug. 22, age 81.

**McEwen, Sir John,** Australian politician. As leader of the Country Party (1958–71), he championed his country's farmers and ranchers, serving in several cabinet posts and briefly as prime minister (1967–68). Died Nov. 20, age 80.

**McLuhan, Marshall,** Canadian communications theorist who declared that "the medium is the message." He believed that electronic media affect perceptions in ways hardly suspected and are creating a "global village." Died Dec. 31, age 69.

*Rugged Steve McQueen was one of the most popular film stars.*

**McQueen, Steve,** American actor. He was one of the most popular film stars of the 1960's and 1970's, playing adventurous characters in such pictures as *The Great Escape* (1963), *Bullitt* (1968), and *Papillon* (1973). Died Nov. 7, age 50.

**McWilliams, Carey,** American journalist who was editor of the liberal weekly *The Nation* from 1955 to 1975. He championed the interests of economically deprived and minority groups. Died June 27, age 74.

**Meany, George,** American labor leader. He became first president of the multimillion-member American Federation of Labor–Congress of Industrial Organizations (AFL-CIO) in 1955 and held the job until he retired in 1979. He sought the best possible cash and fringe benefits for the members of his federation of more than 100 unions. Born in New York City, Meany quit school

*James S. McDonnell was an aerospace pioneer.*

*George Meany ruled American labor for more than 30 years.*

to become a plumber's helper at the age of 16 and gradually rose in union affairs to become president of the AFL in 1952. A strong foe of corruption, Meany backed the expulsion of the Teamsters from the AFL-CIO in 1957. In the 1960's he was branded as a member of the old guard for his inflexible anti-Communism and hawkish line on the Vietnam war. He broke with the more liberal Walter Reuther—who led the United Automobile Workers out of the federation in 1967—and denied AFL-CIO support for Democratic Party Presidential nominee George McGovern in 1972. Later, however, he began associating labor with the rebels of the 1960's, including farm workers, blacks, and women. Died Jan. 10, age 85.

**Milestone, Lewis,** Russian-born American film director. Among his pictures were *All Quiet on the Western Front* (1930), *The Front Page* (1931), and *Of Mice and Men* (1939). He received two Academy Awards. Died Sept. 25, age 84.

**Miller, Henry,** American writer whose books established him as a literary sexual pioneer. *Tropic of Cancer* (1934) was banned as obscene in the U.S. until 1964 but, nevertheless, millions of copies were sold. Other novels and nonfiction works also advanced his outlook of bawdy anarchism. Miller insisted his aim was to teach "joy and acceptance of life." Born in Brooklyn, Miller moved to Paris in 1930 and established his reputation there. Later he settled at Big Sur on the California coast. Died June 7, age 88.

**Monroney, A. S. ("Mike"),** American politician who served in the U.S. House of Representatives and Senate for 30 years as a Democrat from Oklahoma. In 1946 he cosponsored the only major re-

organization of congressional procedures in half a century. Died Feb. 13, age 77.

**Moscovitz, Shalom,** Israeli primitive painter and designer of stained-glass windows who was known as Shalom of Safed. Died Jan. 3, age about 85.

**Mosley, Sir Oswald,** British politician who was a fascist leader in the 1930's. Died Dec. 2, age 84.

**Muñoz Marín, Luis,** the first elected governor of Puerto Rico (1949–65). He did much to foster the island's development under "Operation Bootstrap," which granted tax exemptions to U.S. companies willing to open branch factories in Puerto Rico. In 1952, as a result of his urging, Congress granted the island a measure of self-government as a commonwealth with its own constitution. Died April 30, age 82.

**Nenni, Pietro,** Italian statesman who led his nation's Socialist Party from 1949 to 1969. He first allied his party with the Communists, but later broke with them and in 1957 joined the governing Christian Democrats in a coalition that ruled Italy until 1976. He served as deputy premier in three cabinets. Died Jan. 1, age 88.

**Nielsen, Arthur Charles,** American businessman who in 1923 founded the A. C. Nielsen Co., which

*Henry Miller's bawdy works changed the course of American literature.*

grew to become the largest marketing research organization in the world. Nielsen ratings chart what the average family watches on television and radio by sampling each week 1170 of the nation's households. Died June 1, age 83.

**O'Brien, John A.,** American Roman Catholic priest who was a prominent educator and scholar. Among his many books was *The Faith of Millions* (1938). A progressive in church matters, he urged Pope Paul VI to rescind his decision condemning all artificial methods of birth control. Died April 18, age 87.

**Ohira, Masayoshi,** prime minister of Japan from December, 1978. He served in several cabinet posts and as secretary-general of the ruling Liberal-Democratic Party before becoming prime minister. Ohira died on the eve of new elections he had called after foes within his party deserted the government; *see* JAPAN. Died June 12, age 70.

**Owens, Jesse,** American athlete who was one of the greatest track-and-field stars of all time. At the 1936 Olympic Games in Berlin, he won four gold medals, embarrassing Adolf Hitler and the Nazis, who regarded blacks as an inferior race. A year earlier, Owens had broken five world records and equaled a sixth within an hour. No lucrative contracts awaited Owens after the Olympics—not even a visit to the White House—but he barnstormed the country and later opened his own public-relations and marketing firm. Died March 31, age 66.

*Jesse Owens was one of the greatest track-and-field athletes of all time.*

*Pomp and pageantry were essential ingredients of Mohammed Riza Pahlavi's 38-year reign as shah of Iran.*

*Masayoshi Ohira was prime minister of Japan.*

**Pahlavi, Mohammed Riza,** shah of Iran from 1941 to 1979. He acceded to the throne during World War II, when the Allies forced his father, Riza Shah Pahlavi, to abdicate. With American help, he survived an attempt to overthrow him in 1953 and sponsored an ambitious economic development program. His despotic rule, however, alienated many, including the influential Muslim clergy. In early 1979 he fled into exile. Ill from cancer, he was admitted to the U.S. for medical treatment. Iranians responded by storming the U.S. embassy and seizing Americans there as hostages. After a brief stay in Panama, the shah found refuge in Egypt. *See also* EGYPT; PANAMA. Died July 27, age 60.

**Pal, George,** Hungarian-born American film producer and director. He was regarded by many as the father of the contemporary science-fiction film, with special effects and camera work earning him eight Academy Awards. Died May 2, age 72.

**Patrick, Lynn,** Canadian hockey player who was an all-star with the New York Rangers and later a coach and general manager. Died Jan. 27, age 67.

**Patterson, William Allan,** American business executive who was a pioneer in the commercial aviation industry. In 1931 he became general manager of the newly formed United Airlines and built it into the largest commercial air carrier in the world, serving as president from 1934 to 1963. Died June 13, age 80.

**Piaget, Jean,** Swiss psychologist. He won acclaim for his studies of how biology and environment interact in child development. He argued that children, starting with primitive notions of nature, replace them with more mature concepts in four major stages. Died Sept. 16, age 84.

**Porter, Katherine Anne,** American writer. Her short stories were highly regarded; in 1966 her collected stories received both the Pulitzer Prize and National Book Award for fiction. *Ship of Fools* (1962) was her only full-length novel. Died Sept. 18, age 90.

**Powers, John A. ("Shorty"),** American Air Force officer who described the early U.S. manned spaceflights over radio and television. He coined the phrase "A-OK." Died Jan. 1, age 57.

**Raft, George,** American actor who played an elegant hoodlum in at least 60 films but was most famous for a role in *Scarface* (1932), in which he flipped a coin as he was shot down. Died Nov. 24, age 85.

**Ravitz, Shlomo,** Israeli musician whose compositions for cantors and choirs made him a pioneer of Jewish music. He founded and directed a seminary for cantors in Tel Aviv. Died Dec. 28, age 95.

**Reed, Stanley Forman,** American jurist who was a justice of the U.S. Supreme Court from 1938 to 1957, writing more than 300 opinions that often defied prediction or categorization. Died April 3, age 95.

**Renaldo, Duncan,** Rumanian-born American actor best known for his television role as the Cisco Kid in the 1950's series. Died Sept. 3, age 76.

Katherine Anne Porter was a master of the short story.

**Rhine, J(oseph) B(anks),** American psychologist who contended that extrasensory perception exists and made "ESP" a household word. Rhine's first book on the subject was published in 1934, after some 90,000 experiments were carried out testing the ability to identify distinctive symbols on cards not visible to the subject. He joined Duke University in 1930 and became director of the parapsychology laboratory there in 1940. Died Feb. 20, age 84.

**Roberts, Rachel,** Welsh actress. She won awards for her performances in the British films *Saturday Night and Sunday Morning* (1960) and *This Sporting Life* (1963). Died Nov. 26, age 53.

**Romero, Oscar Arnulfo,** Roman Catholic archbishop of San Salvador. In the late 1970's he emerged as his country's most outspoken advocate of human rights and social change and also as its most popular figure, particularly among poor workers and peasants. He was murdered while officiating at a Mass; *see* EL SALVADOR. Died March 24, age 62.

**Ronne, Finn,** Norwegian-born American polar explorer who traveled some 3600 mi. by ski and dogsled—more than any other such explorer in history—to chart the vast frozen wastes of the Antarctic, which he visited on nine different expeditions. Died Jan. 12, age 80.

**Rukeyser, Muriel,** American poet. Her work was marked by social and political commitment and protest. Died Feb. 12, age 66.

**Sá Carneiro, Francisco,** Portuguese politician. In 1974 he founded what became the Social Democratic Party. In 1979 the rightist coalition he headed won a parliamentary majority and he became premier. *See also* PORTUGAL. Died Dec. 4 in a plane crash, age 46.

**Sanders, Harland,** American businessman who was founder of the Kentucky Fried Chicken Corp. The honorary Kentucky colonel, with white hair, white suit, and black string tie, was a walking advertisement for his fast-food chain. Died Dec. 16, age 90.

**Sartre, Jean-Paul,** French writer and philosopher. In works such as *Being and Nothingness* (1943), he suggested that "man makes himself" despite living in an "absurd world" without God—a philosophy called existentialism that was highly influential in the 1940's and 1950's. Among works reflecting this theme were the novel *Nausea* and the play *No Exit.* Sartre supported a wide range of left-wing causes, despite his break with the Communist Party in the 1950's. He rejected the 1964 Nobel Prize in literature, arguing that acceptance would compromise his integrity as a writer. Died April 15, age 74.

**Schary, Dore,** American playwright, screenwriter, director, and producer. He was production head of Metro-Goldwyn-Mayer (1948–56). Died July 7, age 74.

Peter Sellers, a film comedy immortal. Perhaps his funniest role was that of the bumbling Inspector Clouseau.

**Sellers, Peter,** British comedian, best known as the bumbling Inspector Clouseau in the popular "Pink Panther" film series. A highly versatile actor, his next-to-last film performance in *Being There* (1979) was one of his finest. Died July 24, age 54.

**Sherrill, Henry Knox,** American clergyman who was presiding bishop of the Episcopal Church in the U.S. from 1946 to 1958. He became first president of the National Council of Churches of Christ in 1950 and was a president of the World Council of Churches from 1954 to 1961. Died May 11, age 89.

**Silverheels, Jay,** Canadian-born actor who played the faithful Indian sidekick, Tonto, in the popular television series *The Lone Ranger* from 1949 to 1957. Silverheels, who also appeared in many films—mostly Westerns—was himself a Mohawk Indian. Died March 5, age 62.

**Smith, Tony,** American sculptor known for monochromatic minimalist structures on a monumental scale. Died Dec. 26, age 68.

**Smythe, Constantine Falkland ("Conn"),** Canadian owner of hockey's Toronto Maple Leafs. He was inducted into the league's hall of fame in 1958. Died Nov. 18, age 85.

**Snow, C(harles) P(ercy),** British author and scientist. His *Strangers and Brothers,* a series of 11 novels that began appearing in 1940, is a panorama of middle- and upper-middle-class society since 1920. Originally a physicist, he became a civil servant as well as a writer. He stirred controversy in 1959 with a celebrated lecture arguing

*Existentialism was the term used to describe the philosophy of French writer and activist Jean-Paul Sartre.*

*Tito led the fight against the Axis in Yugoslavia during World War II, then ruled his country for 35 years.*

that literary culture had become antisocial. Snow was knighted in 1957 and made a life peer in 1964. Died July 1, age 74.

**Somoza Debayle, Anastasio,** Nicaraguan dictator who ruled the Central American country from 1967 until his overthrow in 1979. He fled to Paraguay in August, 1979, where he was assassinated; *see* PARAGUAY. Died Sept. 17, age 54.

**Stein, William H.,** American biochemist. He and two Rockefeller University colleagues shared the 1972 Nobel Prize in chemistry for deciphering the molecular structure of the enzyme ribonuclease and identifying that part of the molecule that performs its vital role. Died Feb. 2, age 68.

**Still, Clyfford,** American artist ranked among the founders of abstract expressionism. Died June 23, age 75.

**Summerskill, Edith Clara,** British stateswoman who fought for women's rights and social welfare. Originally a physician, she developed a large general practice among the London poor and in 1938 was elected to the House of Commons as a Labour Party member, eventually serving 23 years. She was minister of insurance (1950–51) and became a life peer in 1961. Died Feb. 4, age 78.

**Sutherland, Graham,** British artist whose specialty was portraits of the famous and wealthy, including Somerset Maugham, Lord Beaverbrook, and Helena Rubenstein. But his portrait of Winston Churchill found little favor with the statesman, whose wife eventually destroyed it. Sutherland also undertook two major religious paintings and was eminent as a landscapist. Died Feb. 17, age 76.

**Sutton, Willie,** American bank robber. He estimated that he stole more than $2,000,000 from

banks because, as he said, that was "where the money was." He escaped from prison three times but nevertheless spent 33 years in jail. Died Nov. 2, age 79.

**Teale, Edwin Way,** American naturalist, photographer, and writer. He received the 1966 Pulitzer Prize in general nonfiction for *Wandering through Winter,* the last of four volumes on the four seasons in America. Died Oct. 18, age 81.

**Tito,** assumed name of JOSIP BROZ, leader of Yugoslavia from the 1940's. During World War I he was taken prisoner in Russia and returned a dedicated Communist. After Germany invaded Yugoslavia and the Soviet Union in 1941, Tito became leader of the most effective guerrilla force fighting the Axis. After the war he assumed power but broke with Moscow in 1948. While political opposition was not tolerated under his Communist regime, elements of a market economy, with worker self-management, were adopted. *See also* YUGOSLAVIA. Died May 4, age 87.

**Tolbert, William Richard, Jr.,** president of Liberia from 1971. He was the son of a South Carolinian who immigrated to Africa and became a prosperous planter. Tolbert was chosen vice-president in 1951. As president, he freed political prisoners and dismissed cabinet ministers for corruption, but his limited reforms only emboldened those who opposed the one-party rule of his True Whig Party. *See also* LIBERIA. Assassinated April 12, age 66.

**Travers, Ben,** British playwright who was a master of stage farce but was never successfully produced in the U.S. Died Dec. 18, age 94.

**Tynan, Kenneth,** British drama critic who championed such playwrights as Arnold Wesker and

John Osborne and "devised" the play *Oh! Calcutta!* He was literary manager of the National Theatre from 1963 to 1973. Died July 26, age 53.

**Vagnozzi, Egidio Cardinal,** papal envoy to the Roman Catholic Church in the U.S., 1959–67. The Roman-born cardinal was widely regarded by liberal American Catholics as opposed to the spirit of the reforms adopted by Vatican Council II. Died Dec. 26, age 74.

**Van, Bobby,** American actor, comedian, and dancer. He appeared in a dozen Broadway musicals and nine films, and was the host of two television game shows. Died July 31, age 47.

**Vance, Nina,** American theatrical producer and director. In 1947 she founded Houston's Alley Theater, one of the nation's leading resident repertory theaters. Died Feb. 18, age 65.

**Van Vleck, John Hasbrouck,** American physicist. He shared the 1977 Nobel Prize in physics for work describing the magnetic properties of solids. Died Oct. 27, age 81.

**Vysotsky, Vladimir,** Soviet balladeer and actor. He often satirized officials and the Soviet elite, becoming as popular as a rock star in the West. Thousands of people flocked to his Moscow gravesite in a rare spontaneous assembly. Died July 24, age 46.

*William Richard Tolbert, Jr., met a violent death after nine years as president of Liberia.*

*Mae West and W. C. Fields in the film comedy classic* My Little Chickadee *(1940).*

293

# OBITUARIES

**Walsh, Raoul,** American film director. Among the more than 100 motion pictures he directed were many for Warner Bros., including *The Roaring Twenties* (1939), *High Sierra* (1941), *Gentleman Jim* (1942), and *White Heat* (1949). Died Dec. 31, age 93.

**Walsh, Stella,** Polish-born American track star. Born Stanislawa Walasiewicz, she was brought to the U.S. in infancy but won a 1932 gold medal and a 1936 silver medal as a sprinter for Poland in Olympic competition. Died Dec. 4, age 69.

**West, Mae,** American actress. On stage and screen, the buxom actress burlesqued sex. In *Diamond Lil* (1928) she was a bad girl with a heart of gold; on screen the play became *She Done Him Wrong* (1933), with Cary Grant. Another screen success of hers was *My Little Chickadee* (1940), with W. C. Fields. Died Nov. 22, age 87 or 88.

**Wharton, Hunter P.,** American labor leader. As president of the International Union of Operating Engineers (1962–75), he helped dispel the union's reputation for corruption and was credited with a major role in passage of federal occupational safety legislation. Died Nov. 14, age 80.

*The nearly 6-ft. model Wilhelmina appeared on the covers of more than 300 issues of major magazines.*

**Wilder, Alec,** American composer. He wrote several hundred popular songs and also a variety of classical works, including operas. Died Dec. 24, age 73.

**Wilhelmina,** in full, WILHELMINA BEHMEN-BURG COOPER, Dutch-born American model. When she retired in 1967 to open her own model agency, the nearly 6-ft. model had appeared on the covers of more than 300 issues of major American and European magazines. Died March 1, age 40.

**Wright, James,** American poet who won the Pulitzer Prize in poetry in 1972. Some of his work was accounted among the finest lyric poetry written since World War II. Died March 25, age 52.

**Yahya Khan, Agha Mohammed,** Pakistan's president from 1969 to 1971. As commander in chief of the armed forces, he assumed power when riots overthrew his predecessor, Mohammed Ayub Khan. Yahya Khan organized the first nationwide free elections in Pakistan's history, but victory for an autonomy movement in East Pakistan led him to send troops there. East Pakistan, backed by India, won the war, and Yahya was ousted. Died Aug. 8, age 63.

**OHIO.** See STATISTICS OF THE WORLD.

**OKLAHOMA.** See STATISTICS OF THE WORLD.

**OMAN.** See STATISTICS OF THE WORLD. See also PERSIAN GULF STATES.

**ONTARIO.** See STATISTICS OF THE WORLD.

**OREGON.** See STATISTICS OF THE WORLD.

**ORGANIZATION OF AMERICAN STATES,** abbreviated OAS. Human rights was the main subject of the tenth General Assembly of the OAS, which concluded its meeting in Washington, D.C., on Nov. 27, 1980. A compromise resolution named Argentina, Chile, El Salvador, Haiti, Paraguay, and Uruguay as countries of special concern for violations of human rights but did not specifically condemn them. In a 16–5 vote on another resolution, the OAS "deplored" the July seizure of power in Bolivia by military officers and asked its Inter-American Human Rights Commission to prepare a report on violations in Bolivia "as soon as possible."

On April 18 the commission issued its long-awaited report on human rights in Argentina, charging that the Argentine military government, in office since 1976, had killed and tortured hundreds of people held in detention. The commission expressed concern that thousands who were missing "can be presumed to be dead." The commission's report was a strong indictment of Lt. Gen. Jorge Rafael Videla's government, which, it claimed, had engaged in "systematic torture and cruel, inhuman, and degrading practices."

Guerrillas in both El Salvador and Honduras

seized regional offices of the OAS in protest against those two governments' efforts to round up guerrillas, on Aug. 15 in Honduras and on Sept. 17 in El Salvador. In both cases the guerrillas held OAS officials hostage and did material damage to the facilities. The office of OAS Secretary-General Alejandro Orfila condemned the occupations.

See articles on most of the individual countries mentioned. J.N.G.

**ORGANIZATION OF PETROLEUM EXPORTING COUNTRIES,** abbreviated OPEC. The struggle between OPEC "moderates" and "radicals" over prices and rates of production continued during 1980. Tentative agreements reached by the organization's 13 members were jeopardized by political clashes and by the outbreak of war between Iraq and Iran.

**Unified Price Structure.** The committee on long-term strategy developed a plan for a unified price structure in which the price of OPEC oil would be based on world economic conditions. Inflation, rates of economic growth, and currency fluctuations would be taken into account. But three members of the organization, Algeria, Iran, and Libya, opposed these "indexing" proposals when they were introduced in the oil ministers' conference at Taif, Saudi Arabia, during May.

After failing to reach an agreement in Algiers in June, members reached a partial compromise at the meeting in OPEC headquarters in Vienna during September. Saudi Arabia, the world's largest oil exporter, agreed to raise its price from $28 to $30 a barrel and other members agreed to freeze prices until the end of the year. If satisfied with the moderation of other members, Saudi Arabia agreed to cut back production by 1,000,000 bbl during 1981 from the 1980 level of 9,500,000 bbl. Most of the other OPEC nations continued to charge at least $32 a barrel, and, with various surcharges, some members charged as much as $37.

In June total OPEC production was 27,300,000 bbl a day, the lowest it had been since 1976. Prices had increased by 130 percent over an 18-month period, causing a decrease in demand; production cuts were the response, in order to keep an oil glut from growing. Even so, prices on the open or "spot" market were dropping before the Iran-Iraq war brought about a massive disruption of supply.

**Disruptions.** Plans for future action were thrown awry by the outbreak of war between Iran and Iraq in September. With escalation of the fighting, exports from the two countries were cut off. When the war began, Iraq had been exporting 2,800,000 bbl a day, and Iran, 700,000. Saudi Arabia agreed to raise its production by 500,000 bbl to make up some of the loss, and smaller Gulf states

OPEC oil ministers, shown meeting in Algeria in June, sought to unify their pricing system. Tentative agreements reached by the 13 members in 1980 were jeopardized by the outbreak of fighting between Iran and Iraq.

increased exports slightly. Western oil companies were drawing on their record stocks, totaling 5.5 billion bbl, for the rest. Although some experts estimated that it would take a year after the war began before world inventories would be depleted, there was fear that supplies from other Gulf countries would also be imperiled if the fighting spread. The war caused the cancellation of OPEC's 20th anniversary meeting, which was to have been held in Baghdad, Iraq, in November.

In December OPEC oil ministers met again in Indonesia. They agreed on Dec. 16 to allow oil prices to rise as high as $41 a barrel. Saudi Arabia raised its price to $32 a barrel.

*See* PETROLEUM AND NATURAL GAS. D.P.

# P

**PACIFIC ISLANDS.** The former British-French condominium of the New Hebrides in the South Pacific became independent on July 30, 1980, as the new nation of Vanuatu. The Reverend Walter Lini, an Anglican priest, became first prime minister of the 72-island group, which had a population of about 120,000 and is located more than 1000 mi. off northeastern Australia. Lini's party, consisting mostly of British-educated persons, was elected to power in 1979 on a platform calling for wide-ranging land redistribution.

The prospect of independence led to a secessionist movement on Espiritu Santo, the largest of the islands. Backed by French and mixed-race

planters, about 600 plantation workers, armed with bows and arrows, rose in rebellion on May 28, seizing the police station. They were reported to have received aid from Nevada businessmen seeking a tax haven. A joint force of about 200 British and French troops landed on the island on July 24, but the rebels had melted into the jungle. On Aug. 31, about 150 troops from Papua New Guinea occupied the last rebel stronghold and arrested their leader, Jimmy Stevens.

**Micronesia.** Washington pursued its goal of giving semi-independence to the Trust Territory of the Pacific Islands, or Micronesia, a United Nations trusteeship consisting of islands seized from

*Warriors of Espiritu Santo, wielding bows and arrows, sought to secede from the British-French condominium of the New Hebrides as it prepared to become the independent nation of Vanuatu. Outside forces stamped out the revolt.*

*Afghan refugees are shown in neighboring Pakistan after fleeing the Soviet occupation of their country. It was estimated that more than 1,000,000 Afghans had crossed the border in 1980 to settle in camps and villages in Pakistan.*

Japan during World War II. One group, the Northern Mariana Islands, functioned as a U.S. commonwealth like Puerto Rico. Two other Micronesian units, the Marshall Islands and the Federated States of Micronesia, initialed a pact on Oct. 31 enabling them to act independently in all areas except defense, which would remain under exclusive U.S. control. Another group, the Palau Islands of Micronesia, initialed the pact on Nov. 19. In return for their signing the 15-year pact, the United States promised the three units a combined annual financial contribution of $90,000,-000, in addition to about $30,000,000 a year in various federal programs.

See STATISTICS OF THE WORLD.          R.H.

**PACIFIC ISLANDS, TRUST TERRITORY OF THE.** See PACIFIC ISLANDS.

**PAKISTAN.** Pakistan was the center of considerable international attention in 1980 because of its proximity to war-torn Afghanistan, with which it shares a 1200-mi. border. President Muhammad Zia ul-Haq, Pakistan's military ruler, condemned the Soviet invasion of Afghanistan in December, 1979, and opened Pakistan's border to those who fled the fighting. In August the government estimated that more than 1,000,000 Afghans were in camps and villages in Pakistan.

In January the Carter administration, anxious to strengthen Pakistan as a buffer against further Soviet expansionism in the region, offered Pakistan a two-year package of $200,000,000 in economic aid and $200,000,000 in military assistance. Gen. Zia termed the offer "peanuts," and in March his government rejected it on the grounds that it would give Pakistan enough arms to antagonize the Soviet Union but not nearly enough to deter it. Ties with the United States were also strained by the oft-expressed suspicion in Washington that Pakistan secretly was developing its own nuclear weapons.

**Politics.** Zia and his military supporters retained tight control over the country. In March Zia strengthened his grip on the army, extending his own term as chief of staff and placing his most loyal followers in key posts. Two of the country's top generals, Faiz al Chishti and Ghulam Hasan, resigned in protest.

Zia had trouble with other military men as well, including Air Marshal Asgah Khan, president of the centrist Tehricke Istiqlal Party, who was released from six months of detention in April and promptly defied the martial law ban on political activity. In May Asgah Khan presided over a meeting of his party's central committee that demanded that general elections—called off by Zia the previous October—be held without delay. Zia placed his critic under house arrest.

Civilian opposition also began to be heard. In March a group of political leaders who formerly backed Zia called for a restoration of democracy

*PLO fighters keep watch from their headquarters in southern Lebanon, a castle built by Crusaders. Israeli attacks and inter-Arab tensions hampered the group's operations in 1980.*

and a return of the military to their barracks. In June a convention of lawyers in Lahore turned into a noisy anti-Zia street demonstration that was broken up by troops with tear gas and batons.

Even more threatening to Zia was the shadow of Zulfikar Ali Bhutto, the former prime minister who was hanged by the military regime in April, 1979. On the anniversary of Bhutto's death, huge crowds gathered at the gravesite near the family home at Larkana. The event was peaceful, and a few days later Zia released from detention Bhutto's widow, Begum Nusrat Bhutto, and his daughter, Benazir. For a time the two women kept a low profile. But in August they went to Lahore, capital of the Punjab, for talks with the leaders of Bhut-

to's party, the Pakistan People's Party (PPP). So nervous was the Zia regime about the PPP, which observers believed would sweep a general election, that it banned the Bhutto women from the Punjab for a period of three months.

**Islamicization.** President Zia continued his efforts to bring Pakistan into conformity with the teachings of Islam. Koranic punishments for drinking alcohol, theft, and adultery were in effect and were sometimes carried out. In September the government decreed that female college students and teachers must wear full head coverings. A system of interest-free banking was under study, in line with the Koran's condemnation of usury.

Parts of the Islamicization program were opposed not only by westernized Pakistanis but by the Muslims of the minority Shi'ite sect. In July, 25,000 Shi'ites demonstrated in Islamabad against the imposition of the Koranic *zakat*—a tax on wealth, with the distribution of the proceeds to the poor. The Shi'ites claimed that Zia's proposal would not be handled properly, and fearing trouble, Zia promised to restudy the tax.

**The Economy.** Pakistan remained grindingly poor, with an average per capita income of little more than $200 a year. A good harvest generated healthy exports of rice, cotton, and textiles, however, and domestic belt-tightening cleared the way for a whopping $1.7 billion loan from the International Monetary Fund in November. It was the largest ever given to a developing country, but Pakistan's foreign debt was at least $8 billion. Another important asset was the money produced by the 150,000 Pakistanis who left their country in 1979 to work in the oil-producing states of the Middle East. They, and those who preceded them, sent home $1.7 billion in 1979.

**Foreign Affairs.** In rebuffing the U.S. aid offer, Zia stressed that the foundations of Pakistan's foreign policy were nonalignment between East and West and solidarity with the Muslim world. Zia clearly hoped to finance a modernization of his army with money from oil-rich fellow Muslims. Indeed, widespread rumors surfaced in September that Saudi Arabia had given Pakistan a large sum for military purchases in Europe.

See STATISTICS OF THE WORLD.                R.J.C.

**PALESTINE LIBERATION ORGANIZATION,** abbreviated PLO. While the PLO continued to extend its diplomatic activities, it also kept up terrorist attacks inside Israel and confrontations with Israeli troops in southern Lebanon during 1980.

**Diplomatic Progress.** In March Austria announced that it was granting the PLO official status described as "a new form of diplomatic recognition." India also announced that it was extending full diplomatic recognition. France moved closer to the PLO when President Valéry Giscard d'Estaing called for Palestinian "self-determination" and PLO participation in Middle East peace talks, during his visit to the Persian Gulf region in March.

The Council of Europe and the European Community (EC) both passed resolutions calling for Palestinian self-determination, the council at its April meeting in Strasbourg, France (with 10 abstentions out of 21 votes), and the EC at a summit meeting of seven chiefs of state in Venice during June. The Venice declaration stated that the PLO should be "associated with" the negotiations for a peace settlement.

During July the United Nations General Assembly passed a resolution reaffirming the Palestinian right to establish an "independent sovereign state." The vote was 112 in favor, 24 abstentions, 9 not voting, and 7 against (including the United States). On April 30 a U.S. veto in the Security Council had prevented passage of a similar resolution.

**Inter-Arab Relations.** Deteriorating relations among Arab states and the war between Iraq and Iran created serious problems for the PLO. In January Libya severed ties with Al Fatah, the largest PLO faction, charging that it had moved away from guerrilla warfare as a means to redeem Palestine. The links with Libya, including financial aid, were restored in April when Fatah leader Yasir Arafat endorsed a hard-line policy against Israel.

In November Arafat tried to persuade the Arab nations to postpone an Arab League summit conference scheduled to open in Amman, Jordan, on Nov. 25. Some Arab leaders felt that the meeting would only increase the strains between radical and moderate Arab states that had already been aggravated by the Iran-Iraq war. The PLO had hoped to avoid an open breach and retain the support of all Arab states, but finally decided to join Syria, Libya, South Yemen, Algeria, and Lebanon in boycotting the conference. According to observers, the PLO thus ended up in apparent alliance with the radical minority sympathetic to Iran and in danger of losing ground to Jordan as spokesman for the Palestinians.

See also ARAB LEAGUE; MIDDLE EAST; and articles on individual countries mentioned.              D.P.

**PANAMA.** The government scored a victory of sorts in balloting for seats in the upper house of Panama's legislature on Sept. 28, 1980. It won 12 of the 19 seats, but at least 40 percent of the eligible voters did not cast ballots. Moreover, the opposition polled almost as many votes as the government party, although divisions within the opposition gave government candidates the edge. The largest opposition grouping, the Panameñista Party, led by former President Arnulfo Arias Madrid, shunned the voting and, when the results were in, claimed credit for having kept many voters away from the polls.

Working behind the scenes, Gen. Omar Torrijos Herrera and his Democratic Revolutionary Party had left little to chance. Occupants of 38 seats in the upper house had already been appointed from the national assembly, which was elected in 1978. Parties were not allowed to field candidates in that election, and most of those chosen were progovernment.

The operation of the Panama Canal under joint Panama-U.S. control celebrated its first anniversary on Oct. 1 with evidence that the arrange-

Panamanian security officers patrol the island hideaway of Mohammed Riza Pahlavi, the former shah of Iran, in early 1980 to guard against intruders. He spent only three months in Panama before moving to Egypt.

ment, called for under terms of the new Panama Canal treaties, was working "exceedingly well," as a spokesman said on the occasion. Talk of building a new, sea-level Panama Canal was revived during the year as a Japanese consortium expressed interest. A feasibility study was undertaken on the massive project, which carried an estimated price tag of about $20 billion.

On March 23, Mohammed Riza Pahlavi, the deposed shah of Iran, left Panama and flew to Egypt, just 24 hours before Iran was due to make a formal request for his extradition. He had arrived in Panama from the U.S. in late 1979.

The annual inflation rate in 1980 was estimated at 14 percent and the unemployment rate at 17 percent.

See STATISTICS OF THE WORLD. J.N.G.

**PAPUA NEW GUINEA.** See PACIFIC ISLANDS.

**PARAGUAY.** The assassination in Paraguay in 1980 of exiled former Nicaraguan dictator Anastasio Somoza Debayle was followed by a new crackdown on dissidents opposed to the government of Paraguayan President Alfredo Stroessner. A roundup of suspected leftists began soon after

the incident on Sept. 17. At least 500 were jailed, including Domingo Laíno, vice-president of the opposition Radical Liberal Party and an economist and university professor. He had been arrested and detained by Paraguayan authorities on at least five previous occasions in the past decade. Paraguayan opponents of Gen. Stroessner's rule said, in the wake of the Somoza assassination, that his days were numbered.

Earlier, Paraguayan government forces were blamed for killing 20 peasants during repressive raids in several parts of the country in March. Amnesty International, the London-based human rights organization, said the incidents took place in Villarrica and Paraguarí. The group also charged that 300 peasants had been jailed in Asunción, the capital. Peasants in the countryside had become increasingly restive in recent years, complaining of poor living conditions, unemployment, and malnutrition. Several children reportedly died of malnutrition in Villarrica in January, sparking the complaints.

See STATISTICS OF THE WORLD. J.N.G.

**PENNSYLVANIA.** See STATISTICS OF THE WORLD.

# PEOPLE IN THE NEWS

In 1980 it seemed as if everyone was on the move: politicians running for office, athletes running for glory, and fitness freaks just plain running. One man crossed the Atlantic Ocean on the wing of a plane, another went around the world solo in a boat, and two more crossed North America in a balloon. Still another spent 205 straight hours on a roller coaster.

Bold-faced names command our attention in newspapers, in magazines, in celebrity-soaked memoirs, and on the lips of television gossips. We are treated to an endless stream of personalities, many of whom are forgotten by tomorrow's coffee break, but some of whom remain to color and define our world. What follows is a scrapbook of the names, faces, and general goings-on that caught the public's attention in 1980—some sublime and some just plain silly. Profiles of significant figures of the year appear after the gambler places his $777,000 bet.

Neatly stepping around the curbside garbage on East 65th Street, former President **Richard M. Nixon** became a resident of New York City in February. His four-story town house, bought for a reported $750,000, was located next door to the home of a longtime associate, the president of the Chase Manhattan Bank, **David Rockefeller.**

*A number of fugitive radicals surfaced in 1980. One was Abbie Hoffman, who, under an assumed name, had been leading environmental protests in upstate New York.*

*Richard and Pat Nixon arrive at their new residence on Manhattan's East Side, a four-story town house bought for a reported $750,000.*

Also returning to New York was **Abbie Hoffman,** the counterculture media king of the 1960's, who had been in hiding since he jumped bail in 1974 to avoid charges of selling cocaine. Hoffman, using the name Barry Freed, had been living for the last four years on a St. Lawrence River island in upstate New York. There he led successful environmental protests against a plan to alter the river's course for winter navigation.

One of Hoffman's Yippie pals, **Jerry Rubin,** officially joined the establishment in July as a research analyst for a Wall Street investment and securities firm. And **Cathlyn Platt Wilkerson** received a three-year jail sentence for her role in the 1970 bomb factory explosion that killed three people. The blast occurred in the basement of her father's Greenwich Village town house in New York City. Wilkerson, active in the radical

Bert Lance, President Jimmy Carter's former budget director, beat charges of bank fraud in early 1980.

Weather Underground group, vanished after the incident, but surrendered on July 8, 1980.

Yet another 1960's revolutionary, **Bernardine Dohrn,** reputed leader of the Weather Underground, surrendered to authorities in Chicago, ten years after going into hiding to avoid arrest on charges arising from the violent 1969 "Days of Rage" demonstrations there. Dohrn, 38, and a longtime associate, **William Ayers,** had been living in New York City with their two children.

Legendary airline hijacker **"D. B. Cooper"** didn't turn himself in, but February picnickers gathering firewood along the Columbia River near Vancouver, Wash., found part of his $200,000 ransom. The Federal Bureau of Investigation (FBI) confirmed that the loot was part of the money the hijacker collected after commandeering a Northwest Airlines flight from Portland, Oreg., to Seattle on Nov. 24, 1971. After he parachuted from the plane with the marked $20's strapped to his belly, "D. B." vanished and became a regional legend.

Another plane trip cost $325,000. **Jaromir Wagner,** a 41-year-old West German ski instructor–airplane wing walker–used car dealer, strapped himself on top of a small private plane and made a chilly crossing of the Atlantic Ocean. The 12-day, 7-stop flight from his homeland to a small airfield in New Jersey was undertaken "for the risk."

The New York *Times* reported that during the first three-and-a-half years of Jimmy Carter's Presidency, his brother, **Billy Carter,** had spent the equivalent of more than 500 working days under questioning by federal investigators, lawyers, and grand juries. This estimate predated the U.S. Senate investigation of Billy's ties with Libya. On July 14 Billy registered with the Justice Department as an agent of the government of Libya. Still, the Senate investigators were interested in a personal loan of $220,000 from Libya to Billy. When asked if Billy's position may have influenced U.S. foreign policy, the answer was "No." The man who brought the world Billy Beer told the Senators that none of this fuss would have happened if he had not been the President's brother. The highly publicized incidents proved embarrassing to the Carter reelection campaign.

President Jimmy Carter's chief of staff, Hamilton Jordan, could breathe more easily after a grand jury declined to pursue charges that he had used cocaine during a visit to a New York City disco.

Billy also testified in the bank fraud case against **Bert Lance,** President Carter's former federal budget director. After an Atlanta jury cleared Lance of nine charges, the Justice Department dropped action on the remaining three. **Tim Kraft,** the President's national campaign manager, left his post following disclosures that he was under investigation for alleged use of cocaine. The charges echoed those made earlier in the year against Carter's chief of staff, **Hamilton Jordan.** A grand jury declined to pursue that case.

If one were looking for an embarrassed politician, the television news of Oct. 15 fit the bill.

It's all in the family as Ronald Reagan's clan joins him in acknowledging cheers from the Republican Party National Convention, which nominated him to be their Presidential candidate. Left to right: Son Ronald and daughter Patricia; wife Nancy; Reagan; grandson Cameron with son Michael and daughter-in-law Colleen; daughter Maureen.

Millions saw excerpts of the FBI's Abscam videotapes that had been viewed by the jury in the bribery-conspiracy trial of Rep. **Michael O. Myers** (D, Pa.). Myers, who had been convicted in August, was expelled from Congress on Oct. 2.

The family of President-elect **Ronald Reagan** also came under the media's scrutiny in 1980. A varied brood was revealed—**Maureen,** Reagan's daughter by his first wife, **Jane Wyman,** was both an ardent Republican and a committed feminist, and his adopted son, **Michael,** was trying to establish his own business selling gasohol equipment to farmers. Reagan's children by his second wife, **Nancy,** are **Patricia Davis,** a songwriter and actress who signed an exclusive six-figure contract with NBC after her father's election, and **Ronald,** a dancer with New York City's Joffrey Ballet.

"Did you win?" asked **Bill Rodgers,** winner of the 1980 Boston Marathon. "Yes," said the woman wearing the winner's laurel wreath. "Who are you?" asked Rodgers. He was not alone in his perplexity, because soon after, **Rosie Ruiz** of New York City lost her title. The judges and race observers could find no evidence that she had in fact run the entire race, so **Jacqueline Gareau,** the "second" finisher among the women, was eventually awarded the prize.

Among people who did finish races in 1980 were **Maxie L. Anderson** and his son **Kris,** who completed a grueling four-day voyage in May and thus became the first to negotiate a trans-North American balloon trip. On the seas, **David Scott Cowper,** a 38-year-old Briton, guided his 40-ft. yacht around the world in a record sailing time of 225 days.

Another yachtsman, **Philip Weld,** a retired newspaper publisher from Gloucester, Mass., set a record for the single-handed transatlantic race from Plymouth, England, to Newport, R.I. His time: 17 days 23 hr. 12 min. **Richard Rodriguez**'s time of 205 hr. took him nowhere except into the *Guinness Book of World Records* for continuous time spent on a roller coaster. Rodriguez traveled from his Brooklyn, N.Y., home to Blackpool, England, to tame the Big Dipper.

The world's first solar-powered aircraft, the *Gossamer Penguin,* flew a total of 2.1 mi. on Aug. 7. Invented by **Paul MacCready** and piloted by **Janice Brown,** the craft stayed aloft for 14 min. 21 sec. In December another MacCready solar-powered craft, again piloted by Brown, flew for 6 mi.

*Maxie L. Anderson (left) and son Kris became in May the first to cross North America nonstop in a balloon.*

Mary Marvich, 107 years old, cast her first vote in November. Although she came to the U.S. in 1894 from what is now Yugoslavia, she was not naturalized until June.

and 22 min. In contrast, fitness maven **Jack LaLanne** took slightly over an hour to swim a mile across Lake Ashinoko at the foot of Japan's Mt. Fuji. His slow pace could be excused, however. He was handcuffed and shackled, and he towed 65 rowboats loaded with 6500 lb. of wood pulp. That was one rowboat for each of his 65 years.

Celebrating his 18th birthday, Boy Scout **John G. Gelinas, Jr.,** heaved a sigh of relief—he had met the deadline and become one of a handful of scouts to earn every possible merit badge, 121 in all. The superscout traveled from Scarsdale, N.Y., to Florida to earn his final merit badge, in waterskiing. It took **Mary Marvich** until her 107th birthday to prod West Virginia officials into action on her request for American citizenship. It seems Mrs. Marvich, who came to the United States from what is now Yugoslavia in 1894, could not be naturalized because she was unable to recall the name of the ship that brought her to the U.S. The immigration office decided it did not matter.

Comedian **Richard Pryor** was severely burned over almost half his body on June 9. Pryor's lawyers said the accident occurred when a glass of rum was accidentally ignited, but police at first expressed the belief that the explosion was caused by a flammable drug mixture used to make free base, a cocaine derivative. Despite the doctors' doubts of his surviving the accident, an articulate but subdued Pryor appeared on the *Tonight* show in September.

That late-night show's host, **Johnny Carson,** signed a new three-year contract in 1980 for a streamlined 60-min. program at a salary reported to far exceed $5,000,000 a year. Sweetening the pot for Carson, whose show was reported to pro-

vide NBC with at least 20 percent of its pretax profits, was an additional contract to develop and produce new projects for the network.

A successor for **Walter Cronkite,** the sage of CBS News who would reach the network's mandatory retirement age of 65 in November, 1981, was found in **Dan Rather.** The choice prompted **Roger Mudd,** a 19-year veteran mentioned for the slot, to jump to NBC as the network's chief Washington correspondent. Finally, **Charles Kuralt,** whose amiable "On the Road" segments enlivened Cronkite's broadcasts beginning in 1967, parked his van, after traveling more than 750,000 mi., to take over anchor duties on the *CBS Morning News.*

Pop sociologists say marriage is on the rise, and 1980 produced a bumper crop of celebrity ceremonies: actress **Candice Bergen** to French film director **Louis Malle,** *Today* regular **Jane Pauley** to "Doonesbury" cartoonist **Garry Trudeau,** tennis ace **Björn Borg** to fellow player **Mariana Simionescu,** actress **Raquel Welch** to French film writer and producer **André Weinfeld,** television host **Phil Donahue** to "That Girl" **Marlo Thomas,** octogenarian **Fred Astaire** to 37-year-old jockey **Robyn Smith,** and Communist Party Vice-Presidential candidate **Angela Davis** to photographer **Hilton Braithwaite.** Honors for a newsworthy ceremony were earned by Haiti's President-for-life **Jean-Claude** ("Baby Doc") **Duvalier** and **Michèle Bennett,** whose $3,000,000 wedding was capped by a 101-gun salute and $100,000 worth of fireworks, and by the marriage of *The New York-*

Doctors gave comedian Richard Pryor only a one-in-three chance to survive the burns he incurred in June, but six weeks later he was almost ready to leave the hospital.

er's ghoulishly stylish cartoonist **Charles Addams** to **Marilyn Mathews Miller** in a pet cemetery. President-elect Ronald Reagan became a father-in-law again on Nov. 24, when his son Ron married **Doria Palmieri** in a civil ceremony in New York City.

*Jean Harris was the defendant in 1980's most sensational murder trial. She was accused of killing Herman Tarnower, an author of the best-selling* Complete Scarsdale Medical Diet.

*Under an arch of tennis rackets, five-time Wimbledon champion Björn Borg was wed to Mariana Simionescu.*

If marriage was on the rise, however, divorce could not be far behind. Among the unions that ended in 1980 was that of **Chip Carter** and his wife, **Caron,** and **Lee** (*Six Million Dollar Man*) **Majors** and **Farrah** (*Charlie's Angels*) **Fawcett. Christina Onassis** was divorced from her third husband, **Sergei Kauzov,** and **Anita Bryant,** the singer known for promoting Florida orange juice and the American family, was divorced from her husband of 20 years, **Bob Greene.** Finally, **Princess Caroline** of Monaco was granted a lightning-quick divorce from **Philippe Junot,** her husband of two years.

The battle between the sexes took a violent turn, resulting in one of the year's most publicized trials, in the killing of **Dr. Herman Tarnower,** coauthor of the phenomenally successful best-seller *The Complete Scarsdale Medical Diet.* Accused of the murder was his longtime companion, **Jean Harris,** headmistress of the socially prestigious Madeira School in a suburb of Washington, D.C. The presumed motive lay in the doctor's increased personal involvement with other women.

Another of the year's tonier criminal cases involved **John Buettner-Janusch** of New York University's anthropology department. He was found guilty of operating an illegal laboratory that produced methaqualone, a depressant often known by the trade name Quaalude, and LSD.

Eyebrows were raised at the Bendix Corp. when **Mary E. Cunningham** was appointed vice-president for strategic planning. The post made her, at 29, one of the highest-ranking women in American industry. Several quick promotions by Bendix's chairman, **William M. Agee,** had prompted growing rumors of favoritism, and Cunningham eventually resigned to quell the controversy.

*Princess Caroline of Monaco was divorced in 1980. Here she is seen with Ingrid Bergman's son, Roberto Rossellini, after her separation from Philippe Junot.*

*One of hockey's greatest players, Gordie Howe, 52, retired in 1980 after a 32-year professional career.*

On a positive note, the Reverend **Marjorie S. Matthews** of Traverse City, Mich., became the first woman appointed bishop of the United Methodist Church. Among the graduates of the nation's military academies were the first women to be so commissioned: **Andrea Hollen** from West Point, **Elizabeth Belzer** from the Naval Academy, and **Kathleen Conley** from the Air Force Academy.

A landmark in the legal status of homosexuals was established in November when the Air Force agreed to a $160,000 back-pay settlement for **Leonard Matlovich,** five years after he was dismissed for admitting his homosexuality. And another landmark of sorts was reached at the Cumberland (R.I.) High School senior prom when, under the orders of a federal judge, **Aaron Fricke** was permitted to attend the dance with a male date.

**Gordie Howe,** whose professional hockey career spanned 32 seasons in five decades, announced his retirement in 1980. Howe had retired once before but had reneged to play professional hockey with his two sons, **Mark** and **Marty,** with the Houston Aeros.

For the Beatles, 1980 began badly and ended tragically. **Paul McCartney** was held in a Japanese jail for ten days after bringing 7.7 oz. of marijuana into the country, thus forcing the cancellation of 11 concerts in Japan. On Dec. 8 **John Lennon,** who had celebrated his 40th birthday by recording his first album in five years, was shot to death outside his New York City apartment house. **Rich-**

**ard Queen,** the 29-year-old consular affairs officer at the U.S. embassy in Iran, returned home after becoming seriously ill while held hostage in Tehran. Examinations following his July 11 release indicated that Queen was suffering from multiple sclerosis. His rapid improvement upon returning home enabled him to share with the nation his accounts of the events in Iran.

Two incidents of grace under pressure deserve a final nod. **Wallace Edwards,** a Canadian printer, after not being paid by the Soviet government for a $26,000 job ordered by its embassy, pressed his case for 13 years. The courts finally ordered seized as hostage a Soviet ship. At this point the Soviets relented, paying the debt and $10,000 to cover accumulated interest and, at Edwards's insistence, a case of vodka and enough Russian caviar to celebrate the settlement. Equally unflappable, a mysterious gambler wearing cowboy boots walked into a Las Vegas, Nev., casino carrying two identical cases, opened one, and placed $777,000 in neatly stacked bills on a single bet of craps. He won, and walked away with the two bags filled with more than $1,500,000.

*Canadian businessman Wallace Edwards displays the $36,000 in $1 bills he received from the Soviet government after pressing payment for a debt for 13 years. At Edwards's insistence, he also received enough vodka and caviar for a victory celebration.*

### BANI-SADR, ABOLHASSAN

President of Iran, born 1933 in Hamadan. Bani-Sadr was installed on Feb. 4 as the first president of the Iranian republic following a January election in which he received about 75 percent of the vote. Considered by U.S. diplomats to be a moderate among Iranian leaders, the new president was believed anxious to resolve the hostage crisis, but these hopes were dashed continually in 1980. The bickering between Bani-Sadr and more militant Islamic hard-liners also kept the president from dealing effectively with Iran's troubled economy.

Under the impact of an Iraqi attack, however, the Iranian government mobilized for the war effort. With the support of Ayatollah Ruhollah Khomeini, Bani-Sadr became the nation's key authority during the autumn battle.

*An independent candidate for President, John Anderson did well in public opinion polls during the summer but won only 7 percent of the vote in Nov. 4 balloting.*

### ANDERSON, JOHN B(AYARD)

Independent candidate for President, born Feb. 15, 1922, in Rockford, Ill. After failing in his primary bid for the Republican Presidential nomination, John B. Anderson, a ten-term U.S. Representative from Illinois, announced in early May that he would run for President as an independent. During his early congressional years, Anderson rarely strayed from the conservative Republican ranks, but the riots of the late 1960's swung Anderson's sentiments to the Left. He had come to characterize his political transformation as a maturing process.

Anderson was on the ballot in all 50 states by summer's end and found himself with a 15 percent rating in public opinion polls. Choosing as a running mate former Wisconsin Gov. Patrick J. Lucey, a Democrat, Anderson pledged that he was in the campaign for the duration and denied charges that he was a "spoiler." Although quite conservative on many economic issues, he endorsed a number of liberal social positions. Soon after, Anderson faced Republican candidate Reagan in a televised debate. (President Carter did not participate, insisting instead on a one-on-one encounter with Reagan.) As the campaign closed, Anderson's ratings in the polls began to decline, and he managed to win only about 7 percent of the total popular vote.

*Iranian President Abolhassan Bani-Sadr survived sniping from the clerical faction in 1980. He was considered a moderate among Iranian leaders, anxious to resolve the hostage crisis.*

### BEGIN, MENACHEM

Prime Minister of Israel, born July 31, 1913, in Brest Litovsk (now Brest), Russia. It was a difficult year for Begin, as his governing coalition barely survived efforts in the parliament to overturn it. His popularity fell to new lows under the impact of triple-digit inflation. Talks with Egypt on Palestinian autonomy were suspended by Cairo in August following Israel's declaration of all Jerusalem as its unified capital. Begin defended Israel's policy on Jerusalem and denounced the U.S. for abstaining on an Aug. 20 United Nations Security Council resolution censuring the move.

Begin's government continued to permit the

establishment of Israeli settlements in lands occupied after the 1967 war. On March 6 the Security Council voted to demand an Israeli withdrawal from settlements in occupied Arab territories and challenged its rule in Jerusalem. Although President Carter termed the U.S. affirmative vote a communication error, Begin rejected the explanation.

## BREZHNEV, LEONID I(LYICH)

President of the Presidium of the Supreme Soviet and General Secretary of the Soviet Communist Party, born Dec. 19, 1906, in Kamanskoye. Brezhnev had hoped that 1980 would bring U.S. Senate ratification of the strategic arms limitation treaty (SALT II) with the U.S. and a propaganda boost in hosting the first Olympic Games to be held in a Communist country. Negative worldwide reaction to the Soviet invasion of Afghanistan was cited for the failure of both efforts. The Soviet leader made no apologies for the Afghan intervention, declaring that internal unrest in the neighboring country created a "seat of serious danger to the security of the Soviet state." Hostile reaction to the Soviet moves prompted a number of nations—including such leading competitors as the U.S., Japan, and West Germany—to boycott the Summer Olympics in Moscow. A challenge to the authority of the Communist Party in neighboring Poland bedeviled Brezhnev and his colleagues, who were anxious to avoid another mili-

George Bush lost his battle for the Republican Presidential nomination, but he won a place on the winning ticket as Vice-Presidential running mate for Ronald Reagan.

In 1980 Soviet President Leonid I. Brezhnev presided over the first Olympic Games to be held in a Communist country, but relations with the West, and particularly with the U.S., deteriorated in the wake of the Soviet invasion of Afghanistan.

tary intervention but determined to maintain Soviet control over Eastern Europe. In December he paid a visit to India and offered a plan to keep the Persian Gulf region free from military bases by outside powers.

## BUSH, GEORGE H(ERBERT) W(ALKER)

Vice-President-elect of the U.S., born June 12, 1924, in Milton, Mass. After waging a two-year battle to win the Republican nomination for President, Bush accepted the second spot on the Reagan ticket and immediately began "emphasizing common ground." Although Bush almost lost the Vice-Presidential slot to former President Gerald Ford in a last-minute attempt at a "Republican dream ticket," political observers considered Bush a shrewd choice, citing both his appeal in the northern industrial states and his politically moderate image.

After serving as a U.S. Navy pilot in World War II, Bush earned an economics degree from Yale University and moved his family (he has five children) to Texas, where he entered the oil business. In 1966 he followed the path of his father, who had served as a Senator from Connecticut, by winning a seat in the House of Representatives. Before and after his two terms in the House were two unsuccessful bids for the Senate. In the 1970's Bush served as U.S. ambassador to the U.N., Republican Party national chairman, head of the U.S. liaison office in Peking, and director of the Central Intelligence Agency.

### CARTER, JAMES EARL, JR.
*See* PRESIDENT OF THE UNITED STATES.

### CASTRO (RUZ), FIDEL
President of Cuba, born Aug. 13, 1927, in Biran, Oriente Province. More than 125,000 Cubans fled that Caribbean island for the U.S. from mid-April to October with the tacit approval of Castro. Many suspected Castro of using the exodus to rid his country of criminals and political agitators and to lessen the burden on an already troubled economy. The exodus took place aboard private boats hired by Cuban exiles in southern Florida that were dubbed the "freedom flotilla." Although it was a clear embarrassment to Castro, the migration created an economic burden for Florida and the U.S. government—an estimate put the cost of processing and resettling the refugees at $1 billion. Later in the year Castro suffered two setbacks: a friendly Jamaican government was overturned at the polls, and Ronald Reagan defeated Jimmy Carter in the U.S. The new President was expected to take a more hard-line posture than Carter toward Cuba's efforts to expand its influence in Latin America and Africa.

*Indira Gandhi returned to power as prime minister of India in early 1980 following an overwhelming victory for her party in parliamentary elections. She suffered personal tragedy when her son Sanjay was killed in a plane crash in June.*

*More than 125,000 people fled Fidel Castro's Cuba in 1980. Although the exodus was an embarrassment to the Cuban president, it enabled him to rid the country of malcontents and reduce the burden on the economy.*

### CHUN DOO HWAN
President of South Korea, born Dec. 6, 1932, near Taegu. The son of a farmer, he pursued a military career and also became a judo expert before assuming control of the army in December, 1979, shortly after the Oct. 26, 1979, assassination of Korean President Park Chung Hee. Chun expanded his control in April, when he was named head of the Korean Central Intelligence Agency.

Martial law was imposed on May 18 in an operation that quelled widespread antigovernment demonstrations by students and others in Seoul and five other cities. On Aug. 27 Chun was elected president, replacing Choi Kyu Hah, who had resigned under pressure on Aug. 16. Chun, who resigned from the army to accept the presidency, was the sole candidate for the post. U.S. officials were not pleased. The Carter administration informed the new leader that future relations with Seoul would be conducted on the assumption that the Korean government would carry out plans for constitutional revision and the election of a broadly based government.

### GANDHI, INDIRA NEHRU
Prime Minister of India, born Nov. 19, 1917, in Allahabad. Indira Gandhi's Congress-I Party regained its plurality in January elections, thus culminating her drive from defeat in 1977 and from subsequent charges of misconduct lodged against her following her removal from office. Once again in power, Gandhi criticized Soviet intervention in Afghanistan but refused to publicly condemn the move. She also spoke against other world powers active in the region, a reference to the Carter ad-

ministration's later-aborted plans to supply India's foe, Pakistan, with additional arms. Later in the year she moved closer to Moscow again and concluded a major arms deal with the Soviets.

Domestically, Gandhi faced particularly serious problems in the northeastern state of Assam, where violence erupted in a student-led campaign to deport several million settlers, mostly Bengalis, who had entered the area during the past 20 years. When protesters stopped the shipment of oil from Assam, the government had to send in troops.

Gandhi suffered personal tragedy when her son Sanjay, considered one of the most powerful figures in Indian politics, died in the crash of the light plane he was piloting over New Delhi on June 23.

### GISCARD D'ESTAING, VALÉRY

President of France, born Feb. 2, 1926, in Koblenz in the then French-occupied Rhineland. Speaking in West Germany, President Giscard d'Estaing said that France and West Germany "must undertake common action to restore to Europe its influence in the world." Accordingly, the French president was active in foreign affairs during 1980. Following a joint French-German pronouncement objecting to the Soviet invasion of Afghanistan, Giscard held a five-hour meeting with Soviet President Brezhnev in Warsaw on May 19. Although the meeting predictably revealed differing views, the French president said that the dialogue was worthwhile, ignoring U.S. complaints that he had failed to brief his Western allies before the meeting. In early March Giscard visited the Persian Gulf states and Jordan and called for Palestinian self-determination as well as participation by the Palestine Liberation Organization in Mideast peace talks. In return, Giscard received what was described as "moral guarantees" of steady oil supplies from the oil-producing Arab states. At home, Giscard was preparing for the 1981 presidential election campaign; despite economic problems in France, he was favored to win reelection.

### HUSSEIN, SADDAM

President of Iraq, born 1937, in Tikrit. A veteran of behind-the-scenes intrigue, Hussein dealt ruthlessly with political rivals. His brother was Iraq's intelligence chief and his brother-in-law headed the military.

Saddam Hussein led his country into a border war against Iran in late September. Although relations between the two countries had long been sour, Hussein reached an accord in 1975 with the shah of Iran that eased tensions. The rise to power of Ayatollah Ruhollah Khomeini, however, reactivated old animosities. As relations between

*French President Valéry Giscard d'Estaing was active in foreign affairs during 1980. At home, he prepared to seek a second presidential term in 1981.*

the two countries worsened, Hussein, a Sunni Muslim, rounded up thousands of people believed to be of Iranian origin and deported them to Iran. For their part, Iran's Shi'ite Muslims had been encouraging their Iraqi brethren toward revolution. The outbreak of fighting and Iraq's drive to establish control of the Shatt-al-Arab waterway by capturing the oil-producing region of southern Iran emphasized that Hussein saw the undeclared Persian Gulf war as more than a mere border skirmish. He was widely believed to be seeking to make Iraq the leader of the Arab world and the prime power in the Middle East.

### JOHN PAUL II

Pope of the Roman Catholic Church, born Karol Wojtyła on May 18, 1920, in Wadowice, Poland. John Paul II made four international pilgrimages during 1980, visiting Africa, Brazil, France, and West Germany. On May 2 the pope set out on an 11-day trip to Africa. Visiting six countries, the pope spoke of Christianity's social role in Africa. He responded to the "Africanization" of church liturgy and sacraments by reminding African Catholics that, while they are privy to special social and religious traditions, they are still part of a universal church.

On June 30 the pope began a 12-day pilgrimage through Brazil. It was both the longest papal journey outside Italy in modern times and the first visit by a pope to Brazil, the nation with the world's largest number of Catholics. In regard to his views on the local clergy's political and social activities, the pope reaffirmed the church's commitment to seek nonviolent social change, to fight the denial of human rights by dictatorships of both the Right and the Left, and to denounce political and economic injustice. He warned, however, that activist clergy working for the poor must proceed without encouraging class violence and in accordance with Christian—not Marxist—ideology.

### KANIA, STANISLAW

First Secretary of the Polish Communist Party, born March 8, 1927, in Wrocanka. Kania replaced Edward Gierek following the Polish workers' strike in August. After joining the party in 1945, Kania held a series of administrative posts in the Warsaw organization beginning in 1958. In June, 1971, he was chosen supervisor of the police, army, and security. When government and Communist Party officials were replaced as a result of the strikes, Kania added to his positions that of supervising the trade union federation. Diplomats assumed that Kania's background in the security forces made him the party's choice for the post. He was faced with the difficult task of dealing with the rise of independent trade unions and the promises of change that resulted from the strikes, as well as the economic disarray that was left in their aftermath. Failure to resolve the crisis, it was thought, would mean Soviet military intervention.

*Speaking before a portrait of Lenin, Polish Communist leader Stanislaw Kania addresses a party session. Kania succeeded to national leadership at a time when Polish workers were demanding rights never before tolerated in a Soviet-bloc nation.*

*Vice-President Walter F. Mondale campaigned tirelessly, but in the end, futilely, for the reelection of President Jimmy Carter. After the debacle, in which Mondale succeeded in carrying his native Minnesota for the ticket, he appeared to be a prime possibility for the 1984 Democratic Party Presidential nomination.*

### KENNEDY, EDWARD M(OORE)

Democratic Senator from Massachusetts, born Feb. 22, 1932, in Boston. Edward Kennedy took his campaign for the Democratic Presidential nomination to the floor of the August convention. There his forces lost a last-ditch rules fight that would have freed the delegates to "vote their conscience." President Carter's supporters argued that the delegates' first vote must adhere to the candidates to whom they were pledged in the state primaries. Kennedy's early campaign lagged, although he gained momentum later, with major primary victories in New York, Connecticut, Pennsylvania, and Massachusetts. Despite his loss of the rules fight, he delivered a convention speech on Aug. 12 that was cheered by the crowd for 35 min. Although he appeared less than enthusiastic after President Carter accepted his renomination, Kennedy campaigned actively in behalf of the President in the fall and kept alive his Presidential hopes, perhaps for 1984.

### MONDALE, WALTER F(REDERICK)

Vice-President of the U.S., born Jan. 5, 1928, in Ceylon, Minn. After assuming office in 1976, Walter Mondale was advised by two of his predecessors, Hubert Humphrey and Nelson Rockefeller, that an effective Vice-President maintains a good relationship with the President. Mondale did this with vigor. Between September, 1979, and the August, 1980, renomination of President Carter, Mondale visited 36 states, traveled 125,000 mi., gave 210 speeches, attended 150 receptions and meetings, and held more than 225 news conferences, interviews, and sessions with editors. He was equally active in the fall, chiefly as Carter's emissary to labor unions and minority groups. One of the few states carried by the ticket was Mondale's own, Minnesota.

Having served two terms as Senator from Minnesota, Mondale brought liberal credentials to the administration that at times conflicted with Carter's own views. His role in selling the President's policies to often unenthusiastic Democrats, as well as his access to Carter, gave him, in the view of many legislators, perhaps more influence than any other Vice-President in recent memory.

Edmund S. Muskie, who left his U.S. Senate seat in April to become secretary of state, prepared to pack at the end of 1980 along with other high officials of the outgoing Carter administration. Like his predecessor, Cyrus R. Vance, Muskie sometimes clashed with Carter's national security adviser, Zbigniew Brzezinski.

Robert Mugabe became prime minister of the newly independent nation of Zimbabwe in 1980. Although a Marxist, he sought Western private capital in order to foster economic development.

### MUGABE, ROBERT G(ABRIEL)

Prime Minister of Zimbabwe, born Feb. 21, 1924, in Kutama, Southern Rhodesia (now Zimbabwe). When his Zimbabwe African National Union Party won control of the House of Assembly in February elections, Mugabe ended 20 years of political struggle by becoming prime minister. During the mid-1970's, Mugabe, a twice-jailed Marxist, built up a revolutionary force that conducted raids against minority-ruled Rhodesia from Socialist Mozambique. After a settlement was reached

in 1979 that paved the way for the elections, Mugabe emerged as a black nationalist leader untainted by compromise.

Although Mugabe's campaign pointed "towards the socialist transformation of Zimbabwean society," the future prime minister added that "the capitalist system cannot be transformed overnight," and conceded that "private enterprise will have to continue until circumstances are ripe for socialist change." In August Mugabe traveled to the U.S. to speak before the U.N. on the eve of Zimbabwe's joining the General Assembly and to meet with President Carter and members of Congress in Washington.

### MUSKIE, EDMUND S(IXTUS)

Secretary of State, born March 28, 1914, in Rumford, Maine. When Cyrus Vance resigned on April 26 as secretary of state in protest over the Carter administration's military approach to freeing the U.S. hostages in Iran, President Carter turned to Edmund Muskie. Muskie brought a seasoned diplomacy derived from 22 years in the Senate and two terms as governor of Maine. Although known for his hair-trigger temper, he was a man with few enemies. In his new post, diplomatic observers saw Muskie's major challenge as establishing himself as the Administration's architect of foreign policy, a role that brought him into occasional conflict with national security adviser Zbigniew Brzezinski. In August Muskie expressed dismay that the State Department had not been consulted on the Administration's new nuclear strategy that called for more flexible determination of Soviet targets. Reassured by President Carter, Muskie told reporters that "my role will be enhanced from now on," but rifts between the secretary of state and the national security adviser ended only with Carter's defeat at the polls.

## QADDAFI, MUAMMAR EL-

Ruler of Libya, born 1943 in Syrte. Celebrating his eleventh year in power, Col. Qaddafi still had not realized the objectives he had set for himself since the late Egyptian leader Gamal Abdel Nasser called him "the guardian of Arab nationalism and of Arab unity." He maintained no diplomatic contact with his Arab neighbors, Egypt, the Sudan, and Tunisia, and a significant portion of his army was stationed on Libya's eastern border with Egypt. Furthermore, even militant states such as Algeria, Iran, and Syria and the Palestine Liberation Organization kept their distance from the Libyan revolutionary, who had disseminated his

*Ronald Reagan ended his 12-year quest for the White House with his Nov. 4 election as President of the U.S. The former screen actor's conservative views were likely to be heeded by the new, more conservative Congress.*

*In 1980 Libyan leader Muammar el-Qaddafi continued his efforts to transform the Arab world. Using a variety of means, including subversion and assassination, he sought to overturn his rivals in both Africa and the Middle East.*

"Third International Theory" as a blueprint for world revolution. On Sept. 2 Libya and Syria agreed to merge their countries, but this action was considered only a union on paper.

Qaddafi's Libya remained a haven for the extremist fringe. Diplomats reported that Libya, aided by Cuban, East German, and Soviet instructors, was training Egyptians, Palestinians, Tunisians, and other Arabs and Africans in subversion and guerrilla war techniques. Domestically, Qaddafi's authoritarian and often confusing application of socialist theories, applied harshly, fostered growing discontent.

## REAGAN, RONALD W(ILSON)

Republican President-elect of the U.S., born Feb. 6, 1911, in Tampico, Ill. On July 16 Reagan achieved what he had vigorously sought for 12 years—the Republican nomination for President. Although Reagan lost similar campaigns in 1968 and 1976, the current political season saw his conservative style and ideals sweep him to the nomination over a number of other Republican hopefuls and subsequently into the White House.

Raised in Dixon, Ill., the President-elect remained sentimentally attached to his small-town childhood. Reagan graduated from Eureka College in 1932 with a business degree. After five

313

*President Anwar el-Sadat tightened his control of Egypt in 1980. The outspoken leader defied his Arab rivals and also suspended peace talks with Israel.*

manent resident (the shah died of cancer on July 27). Sadat suspended talks with Israel as a result of Israel's assertion that all Jerusalem was its capital, including East Jerusalem with its Muslim shrines.

Domestically, Sadat reshuffled his cabinet on May 15 and named himself prime minister as well as president in order to tighten his control of Egypt's internal affairs. The change consolidated efforts to combat inflation, unemployment, and an acute housing shortage. He immediately announced a reduction in the price of basic goods and a 25 percent increase in the minimum wage. A change in Egypt's constitution was intended to underline its Islamic heritage.

*Helmut Schmidt won another term as chancellor of West Germany when his governing coalition won parliamentary elections held in October. International events, however, undercut his hopes for continued détente between the U.S. and U.S.S.R.*

years as a radio sports announcer, he became a motion picture actor, achieving a measure of prominence in the 1940's. From 1947 to 1952 he served as president of the Screen Actors Guild. Later, he took to the lecture circuit as a representative of the General Electric Co. The public appearances enabled Reagan to hone the comfortable speaking style and conservative rhetoric—although he was originally a liberal Democrat—that would, in 1966, easily elect him to the first of two terms as governor of California.

Reagan was opposed to abortion and the Equal Rights Amendment, wanted to scrap SALT II, which he felt was advantageous to the U.S.S.R., and believed that the federal bureaucracy had grown too large and powerful. He favored transferring to the states the responsibility for programs such as welfare and mass transit, and returning educational policies to local control by abolishing the Department of Education. The President-elect believed that U.S. military superiority was the best way to maintain peace.

### SADAT, ANWAR EL-
President of Egypt, born Dec. 25, 1918, in Talah Moniufiya. Sadat, who had alienated his Arab neighbors by entering into peace talks with Israel, further demonstrated his independence on March 24 when he welcomed Iran's deposed Shah Mohammed Riza Pahlavi to Cairo as a per-

### SCHMIDT, HELMUT H(EINRICH) W(ALDEMAR)
Chancellor of the Federal Republic of Germany, born Dec. 23, 1918, in Hamburg. On Oct. 5, 1980, Chancellor Schmidt's coalition government of Social Democrats and Free Democrats was returned to power with a strengthened majority in the lower house of parliament. It was unlikely, however, that Schmidt's decisive victory over the Christian Democrats' Franz Josef Strauss would alleviate West Germany's present problems.

Events outside West Germany hindered Schmidt's stated goal of establishing a rapport among European countries capable of withstanding the vagaries of U.S.-Soviet relations. Strikes in Poland unseated Communist leader Edward Gierek, Schmidt's friend, and frightened East Germany, which decided to curtail its ties with West Germany. The Iran-Iraq war emphasized West Germany's dependence on that area's oil. The conflict also undermined attempts by the European Community countries to push forward new peace proposals in the Middle East. Economically, West Germany had its first foreign trade deficit in 15 years, and one government-commissioned report predicted that the unemployment rate of 3.7 percent would double by the end of Schmidt's new term.

### SUZUKI, ZENKO

Premier of Japan, born 1911 in Yamada. Suzuki was elected prime minister of Japan on July 17, succeeding the late Masayoshi Ohira, a longtime associate. A politician astute in the art of compromise, Suzuki's main challenge was to reconcile the frequently hostile factions in the governing Liberal-Democratic Party.

Entering politics after World War II as a member of the Socialist Party, Suzuki subsequently ran for the parliament as a member of the Liberal Party, a conservative group that united with the Democratic Party in 1955 to form the Liberal-

Teng Hsiao-ping (Deng Xiaoping), though officially the number-two man in both China's government and Communist Party, continued in 1980 to be the country's actual leader.

Zenko Suzuki became prime minister of Japan in July. His chief challenge was to reconcile the warring factions in the ruling Liberal-Democratic Party.

Democratic Party. Suzuki held both cabinet and party posts, seemingly satisfied with his behind-the-scenes role as "the fixer." Following Ohira's death on June 12, however, a deadlock between two other party leaders for the top office led to Suzuki as a compromise choice. Observers expected little shift under Suzuki in Japan's policy of steady economic growth in a free market system and the maintenance of strong ties with the U.S.

### TENG HSIAO-PING (DENG XIAOPING)

Vice-Chairman of the Chinese Communist Party and First Deputy Premier of the People's Republic of China, born Aug. 22, 1904, in Kuang-an (Guangan), Szechwan (Sichuan) Province. Deputy Premier Teng orchestrated a political switch in September that could have profound effects on the future of China. At the National People's Congress, Hua Kuo-feng (Hua Guofeng) tendered his resignation as prime minister and asked to be replaced by Chao Chi-yang (Zhao Ziyang). (Hua retained his post as chairman of the Communist Party.) Chao, a longtime associate of Teng, earned his reputation by dramatically expanding the economy of Szechwan Province during his five years as first secretary. With Teng's support, he was expected to bring his methods into play nationally, including the relatively revolutionary

British Prime Minister Margaret Thatcher failed to lift her nation out of the economic doldrums in 1980; indeed, conditions became worse. She continued to maintain, however, that only the tough measures she advocated could restore Great Britain to economic health.

After nearly a year out of office, Pierre Elliott Trudeau returned to power once again in early 1980 as prime minister of Canada. In the face of fierce resistance, he unveiled a proposed constitution that would strengthen federal authority over Canada's natural resources.

ideas of individual enterprise and incentives for workers. Foreign observers believed that Teng, despite his nominal number-two ranking, remained China's top leader. The "Gang of Four" trial in late 1980 enabled him to settle scores with old rivals who had purged him from power in the past.

### THATCHER, MARGARET (HILDA ROBERTS)

Prime Minister of Great Britain, born Oct. 13, 1925, in Grantham. In July, the fifteenth month of Conservative Party rule in Britain, the opposition Labour Party mounted an offensive in response to Prime Minister Thatcher's economic policies. During her first year in office, inflation had doubled to 20 percent, unemployment had risen to 6 percent, and interest rates had reached an all-time high of 20 percent for the average borrower. In her defense, Thatcher replied that the difficult road to economic health could only come through spending cuts, increased productivity, and industrial incentives.

In foreign affairs, Thatcher secured economic concessions from the European Community. A diplomatic coup came with the peaceful and surprisingly fair elections that brought majority rule to Zimbabwe, ending the seven-year-old civil war in the former British colony of Rhodesia. The prime minister supported the U.S. call for an Olympic boycott to protest the Soviet invasion of Afghanistan and economic sanctions against Iran in response to the holding of American hostages.

### TRUDEAU, PIERRE ELLIOTT

Prime Minister of Canada, born Oct. 18, 1919, in Montréal. On Feb. 18 Trudeau and his Liberal Party were swept back into power. The victory came only four months after Trudeau had announced his retirement from politics, a decision abandoned after the Dec. 13, 1979, vote of no confidence against the minority Conservative government of Joe Clark. Clark had beaten Trudeau in national elections the previous May, but the Liberal Party had ruled Canada for 38 of the previous 45 years, and Trudeau had been its party chief from 1968.

Trudeau announced plans to retire after perhaps three years of his party's term in office, and political observers saw his efforts toward establishing a Canadian constitution as his political swan song. A strong federalist, he continued to warn of the dangers of Québec's separatist movement. A constitutional convention in September, however, failed to find harmony among Canada's ten provinces. The most heated debates centered on Trudeau's desire to create a U.S.-style bill of rights and to strengthen the country's economic unity, which meant, in effect, increased federal control of natural resources.                      J.M.

**PERSIAN GULF STATES.** The small Gulf states of Bahrain, Oman, and Qatar, and the United Arab Emirates, a loose federation of seven small Gulf states, found themselves uncomfortably close to the fighting between Iran and Iraq that developed in 1980. Oman had aligned itself closely with the United States. The other states, like Oman, were ruled by Sunni Arabs who were sympathetic to Arab Iraq. Each, however, harbored considerable numbers of ethnic Iranian Shi'ite Muslims, Arab Shi'ites, and Palestinians, all of whom were suspected of being sympathetic to Iran. The Palestinians reportedly had been put under tight restrictions, including a ban on political meetings, in several Persian Gulf states.

Oman, long pro-Western, concluded an agreement with the U.S. on April 9. It gave American warplanes and warships the right to use its airfields and ports, in return for $100,000,000 in military and economic aid over the next two years. The U.S. was expected to begin constructing supply facilities for fuel and ammunition and repair depots at several existing port and air bases. Oman's northern tip juts into the Strait of Hormuz, the gateway to the Persian Gulf, which is the sea route for much of the oil received by Western nations. Oman also had close military ties with Great Britain, which provided about 650 soldiers for its armed forces.

The U.S. urged the small Gulf states to remain neutral in the war. These states, though anxious not to alienate any of the larger Gulf countries, were primarily worried about the capacity of Iranian leader Ayatollah Ruhollah Khomeini to stir trouble by his constant calls for an Islamic revolution. Bahrain, which provided docking and refueling services for U.S. ships, was particularly nervous because Iran had revived former claims to its territory.

*See* STATISTICS OF THE WORLD. *See also* KUWAIT; MIDDLE EAST. R.H.

**PERU.** In winning Peru's presidential election on May 18, 1980, Fernando Belaúnde Terry enjoyed a sense of sweet vindication. He had been ousted from the presidency by Peru's military 12 years earlier, and with the military having decided to go back to the barracks, Belaúnde, along with 14 others, sought the presidency. When the votes were counted, Belaúnde had outdistanced his rivals with 43 percent of the vote.

Elections were held simultaneously for Peru's congress. Belaúnde's Popular Action Party failed to gain a majority in these elections, which were contested by 18 parties. The Popular Action Party did better in provincial elections Nov. 23–24, winning control of about half of Peru's 23 provinces. Leftists were victorious in six provinces.

In the 12 years between Belaúnde's two presidencies, Peru's population soared from 11,000,000 to more than 17,000,000. Moreover, Peru's basic economic and social foundations underwent a restructuring during the decade. Oil, mining, fish meal, and banking were nationalized, a sweeping agrarian reform program began, and the traditional landowning elite lost much of its economic and political power.

Some of these changes were expected to be modified by Belaúnde. On Aug. 1 he returned the newspapers seized by the country's military rulers to their original owners and voided decrees that restricted press freedom. Civilians were appointed to run a variety of state enterprises formerly run by military men. A return to emphasis on private investment, including foreign investment, was promised.

Economically, the new government faced a severe crisis, with unemployment running at more than 20 percent in the urban centers and much higher in rural areas. An agricultural slump, industrial strikes, and high inflation added to the problems. Belaúnde said in a Sept. 1 speech that the nation should not expect "an economic miracle" overnight, but he promised to "take the steps to bring the economy around to a manageable situation."

*See* STATISTICS OF THE WORLD. J.N.G.

**PETROLEUM AND NATURAL GAS.** In sharp contrast to the situation in 1979, there was a surplus of oil available on world markets during much of 1980. A certain nervousness about the future, however, proved justified when war broke out between Iraq and Iran in September, halting the export of close to 4,000,000 bbl of oil a day.

For the first eight months of 1980, U.S. oil imports were down 19 percent from the same period in 1979. The drop was the result of higher prices, increased supplies from Alaska, the recession, and conservation efforts, including better gasoline mileage by new car models.

**World Oil Supplies.** The year started with an oil glut, partly because of a mild winter, and partly because Western industrial countries had been stockpiling oil supplies at record rates. The price of oil on world spot markets (and of oil produced in the United States) was cut several times. Gasoline prices in the U.S. fell by as much as 6¢ a gallon during the summer.

Some oil-exporting nations responded by cutting production. The prices imposed by the Organization of Petroleum Exporting Countries (OPEC) continued to rise, notwithstanding the glut, but some countries offered discounts. Plans by OPEC to support its prices by imposing new production cuts were halted by the Iran-Iraq war,

As federal price controls on domestic oil and natural gas continued to be phased out in 1980, drillers began exploiting reserves in areas long ago abandoned as uneconomic. Here a gas well is being drilled on a farm in north-central Pennsylvania.

which stopped the export of well over 10 percent of OPEC's daily oil production. Because of the large stockpiled oil surplus, the shortfall was only felt immediately by countries heavily dependent on Iran and Iraq for their oil supplies. Moreover, Iraq was able to resume some oil exports late in the year, and Saudi Arabia was reported to have stepped up its oil production. With no end to the fighting in sight, however, 1981 appeared likely to be a year of diminishing oil supplies and sharply higher prices.

**U.S. Congressional Actions.** On March 27 Congress passed a windfall profits tax to capture roughly half the proceeds that U.S. oil producers would receive from the phased decontrol of oil prices that would be completed in September, 1981. The tax would yield the federal government $227.3 billion before being phased out, probably in 1988. It was a major victory for the Carter administration's proposed energy program.

President Jimmy Carter's proposed standby gasoline-rationing program narrowly survived attempts to reject it by Congress and became law on July 31. It empowered the President to impose rationing in the case of a gasoline shortage of 20 percent or greater. Gasoline would be rationed by coupons collected at service stations at the time of gasoline purchase. Coupons would be distributed on the basis of vehicle registration, but businesses could get additional allotments based on historical gasoline consumption.

On March 14 President Carter imposed a fee on imported oil of $4.62 a barrel with the direction that it be passed on to consumers as a 10¢-a-gallon surcharge at the gasoline pump. A federal district court judge ruled on May 13 that the President did not have the legal authority to apply the fee to gasoline prices. On June 4 Congress voted to block the oil-import fee; when Carter vetoed the resolutions, Congress overrode the veto.

**U.S. Oil Production.** Domestic oil production declined in 1979 by an estimated 2.2 percent from 1978, but the American Petroleum Institute reported on Aug. 1 that there were signs production was rising in 1980. During the first six months of the year, 35 percent more oil wells were completed than in the same period of 1979. The *Oil & Gas Journal* predicted that U.S. drillers would complete 59,107 wells in 1980, surpassing the record set in 1956. Industry sources credited the increased activity to the decontrol of prices for newly discovered oil.

**Natural Gas.** Increased oil-drilling activity was also stimulating natural gas production, with additions to natural gas reserves reported growing by 35 percent in 1979, the largest jump in 12 years. And, on Dec. 1, Secretary of the Interior Cecil D. Andrus issued a right-of-way grant enabling a gas pipeline to cross 430 mi. of federally owned land in Alaska. The pipeline from Prudhoe Bay to the lower 48 states was intended to deliver 26 trillion cu.ft. of gas over 25 years, starting in 1985, at a cost of more than $25 billion.

The Canadian government gave its approval for the pipeline to cross Canada on July 21. Canadian interests would construct and operate the pipeline along Canada's 2000 mi. of the 4700-mi. route. Canada's approval immediately authorized construction of 527 mi. of this pipeline to connect with two segments in the lower U.S. This section was to be in service in 1981, delivering part of 2.3 trillion cu.ft. of gas that had been authorized for sale to the U.S. from Canadian fields over seven years. Canada, however, was faced with slumping U.S. demand for its gas because the price of U.S.-produced gas was lower.

**Strategic Petroleum Reserve.** In August plans were announced to resume filling the U.S. strategic petroleum reserve after a year of inactivity. A frustrated Congress passed legislation in June ordering the Carter administration to pump 100,000 bbl of crude oil a day into the reserve for a year, beginning on Oct. 1, 1980. The oil would be added to 92,000,000 bbl previously stored in Louisiana salt caverns along the coast of the Gulf of Mexico. A delay in filling the reserve had been announced in March, following objections from Saudi Arabia.

*See also* ENERGY; ORGANIZATION OF PETROLEUM EXPORTING COUNTRIES. J.A.R.

**PETS.** Pets in the United States during 1980 continued their great popularity and economic importance, as billions of dollars were spent on their purchase, feeding, and health needs. The relative popularity of the different types of pets, however, continued the shift that had been evident over the last five years. Dogs and cats remained by far the leading pets in monetary terms, but birds continued their rise in popularity, spurred by the sale of parrots. Some types of parrots were being sold for more than $6000 per bird.

The hobby of owning birds, however, remained threatened by new restrictions. During the year some types of birds imported in quantity were proposed for inclusion on lists of threatened or

U.S. imports of oil declined 19 percent during the first eight months of 1980 from the same period in 1979. One reason was better gasoline mileage from newer, smaller cars. A public service advertisement bearing the face of Iranian leader Ayatollah Ruhollah Khomeini employed patriotism to urge conservation.

*His face was almost hidden from view, but Stonybrooks' Lord Alfred, a 5½-month-old bearded collie pup, was a winner at the Mid Island Kennel Club dog show on Long Island (N.Y.) in February. He won first place and best of breed.*

endangered species. Outbreaks of infectious Newcastle disease gave rise to demands for stricter quarantine procedures.

Outbreaks of parvo virus canine infection, a viral disease that was especially lethal among puppies less than five months old, frightened dog owners, because no drug was yet available to kill the virus in affected dogs. A shortage of vaccine for immunization against this recently recognized disease compounded the problem.

Figures released by the American Kennel Club in early 1980 showed that only four of the top ten breeds had scored increases in the number of puppies registered over the last year for which figures were available. The most significant numerical increases within the top ten breeds were recorded for cocker spaniels and golden retrievers, whereas the most notable decrease in registration occurred among Irish setters.

The number of rabbit fanciers continued to grow as pet shops offered a wider selection of purebred rabbits. Gerbil, hamster, and guinea pig sales remained static despite the introduction of new color varieties.

Snakes—especially boas and pythons—and iguanid lizards dominated interest among ama-

teur herpetologists, and snake owners competed with one another to see who could come up with the cleverest name for a pet snake. Unofficially but reliably acknowledged as winner was the California owner of a boa constrictor named Julius Squeezer.

The animal that made the most headway as a new pet during 1980 was the ferret. Sales of ferrets reached a popularity level never before achieved, especially among urban apartment dwellers looking for a small, furry pet.

The tropical fish hobby's continued decline in popularity was attributed in part to energy conservation consciousness. The trend toward the replacement of heat-loving tropical species with cool-water species made no progress during the year, however, and no great increase in interest in native fishes was apparent.　　　　N.P.

---

### Age Before Beauty

Snuffy had to wait to the ripe old age of 11—that's 77 in human terms—until he finally won honors and a kind of fame in his own hometown. On Aug. 9, in Petaluma, Calif., the part-Chihuahua mutt defeated 44 opponents to be named winner of the fifth annual Ugly Dog Contest. His closest competitor was the Florida state champion, a purebred bulldog. But how could Snuffy lose? His qualifications: He weighed in at approximately 3 lb., his front feet were splayed like Charlie Chaplin's, one back paw didn't even reach the ground, and he had only a few tufts of multicolored fur to his name.

---

**PHILIPPINES.** In his eighth year of one-man rule and his fifteenth as president of the Philippines, strongman Ferdinand E. Marcos came under a steady drumbeat of attack in 1980.

**Politics.** The first local elections in nine years were held in January. Two of the main opposition parties, the Liberals and the coalition Laban, boycotted the voting, and so it came as no surprise that Marcos's New Society Movement won an overwhelming number of the contested offices. Afterward Marcos rejected appeals for an end to martial law but said he would consider that step in March, 1981, if the economy was reasonably stable and if the Muslim insurgency in the south was tamed.

In May Marcos unexpectedly released his old political enemy, Benigno Aquino, from jail after seven years of detention. Aquino, who had a heart condition, immediately left the country, underwent successful heart surgery in Texas, and then accepted a fellowship at Harvard University. In August Aquino began to speak out, warning American audiences that Marcos, reportedly in bad health, would have to accept a peaceful transition to democracy or face a rising tide of political violence.

During the year the Marcos government uncovered a number of alleged plots involving middle-level officers and old-line politicians. In September eight major political blocs, in a show of unity rare in the Philippines, united in a demand for an end to martial law and a return to democracy. In the United States, Aquino and other exiles announced their support for the political alliance.

A potentially more disturbing problem for Marcos was an outbreak of urban terrorism. From August through October a series of bombs were exploded in Manila. Stores, government buildings, and—most embarrassing to Marcos—the annual convention of the American Society of Travel Agents were bombed. A group called the April 6 Liberation Movement took credit for the explosions, which wounded dozens of Filipinos and killed one American woman. The Marcos government rounded up many suspects and alleged that Aquino and other exiles were implicated.

In November the government claimed that the seemingly endless Muslim insurgency in the southern islands was under control. After consultations with major Islamic nations, the Manila government took a conciliatory tone with the Muslims, offering them a substantial degree of autonomy in their traditional areas. Another insurgency, that of the Maoist New People's Army, continued to sputter on in the jungles of the north and the south.

**Economy and Foreign Affairs.** Escalating oil prices rocked the Philippine economy, which depended heavily on imported oil. Real income plummeted while inflation soared to an annual rate of around 17 percent. U.S. investors, however, expressed confidence in the immediate future of the Philippine economy.

Over the year, President Marcos supported the anti-Communist stance of the other members of the Association of Southeast Asian Nations. His major problem was with the U.S., the former colonial power that, still acting somewhat like a big brother, did not approve of his refusal to end martial law and give democracy another try.

*See* STATISTICS OF THE WORLD.        R.J.C.

*Philippine opposition groups grew restive in 1980, the fifteenth year of the rule of President Ferdinand E. Marcos. Gerardo Roxas (left), president of the Liberal Party, and José Laurel, Jr., a Nationalist Party leader, announce on Aug. 29 the launching of a movement working toward the lifting of martial law.*

# PHOTOGRAPHY.

**PHOTOGRAPHY.** Events in the world of photography during 1980 included some noteworthy shows, major publications, disruption at a major museum, and honors for photographers.

**Major Shows.** An exhibition of 220 prints by Lewis Hine, the documentary photographer whose depiction of child labor practices and other social ills spurred the passage of labor laws in the early 1900's, opened in Peking on Feb. 25. The show, entitled "America and Lewis Hine," was the first major photographic exhibition sent by the United States to China as part of a cultural exchange program. The Hine exhibition was first shown at the Brooklyn Museum in 1977. In return, the Chinese government sent a show of Huxian peasant paintings to the Brooklyn Museum. Stops in Jinan, Shanghai, and Canton were scheduled for the Hine show after its appearance in Peking.

Among a number of outstanding shows in the U.S. during 1980 was that of August Sander's vivid portraits of the German people. The photographs, taken between 1910 and 1935, were exhibited at the Philadelphia Museum of Art in the spring.

**Publications.** A number of large-format books of photographs were released in 1980. *Flowers* by Irving Penn, *Allure* by Diana Vreeland, and *Photographs for the Tsar: The Pioneering Color Photography of Sergei Mikhailovich Prokudin-Gorskii,* edited by Robert H. Allshouse, were well received. *Diana and Nikon: Essays on the Esthetics of Photography* contained a collection of Janet Malcolm's writings on the philosophies and works of major photographers.

In October the first issue of *Camera Arts* magazine appeared on the newsstands. Dedicated to the aesthetics of photography, *Camera Arts* presented portfolios of photographs along with critical, historical, and technical articles on the medium.

**The Eastman Museum.** In November, 1979, Robert J. Doherty, director of the International Museum of Photography since 1973, resigned in a dispute

*An exhibit on the American West that opened at the Smithsonian Institution's National Museum of History and Technology in Washington, D.C., in July included 170 nineteenth-century photographs. The camera was included in this 1872 scene of what became Zion National Park, Utah, for size reference and perspective—and also personal pride in apparatus.*

*A photograph of Lev Tolstoi, taken on his 80th birthday, is reproduced in a 1980 book,* Photographs for the Tsar: The Pioneering Color Photography of Sergei Mikhailovich Prokudin-Gorskii.

over growing financial problems. The Rochester, N.Y., institution, also known as the Eastman Museum, has long been considered the foremost photography museum in the world. Included in its archives are collections of historical and contemporary photographs unmatched in their importance. The museum's film collections are among the most notable in the country, featuring many examples of early silent movies.

In April the board of the financially strapped institution voted to keep the museum's collections in Rochester and to add six new board members to reflect a broader range of interests. At the same time the board agreed to begin a major fund-raising drive and elected Robert Taub as its chairman. In October Robert Mayer was named the new director of the museum.

**Photographic Equipment.** Silver price increases were reflected in the soaring cost of photographic film in early 1980. Producers then turned to the development of nonsilver substitutes such as photopolymers, or light-sensitive plastics. The drop in the price of silver was later reflected in lowered film prices.

**People.** In June the renowned landscape photographer Ansel Adams was among 14 winners of the Medal of Freedom, the highest civilian honor awarded by the U.S. government. The winner of the Pulitzer Prize for spot news photography chose to remain anonymous for his own safety. The award-winning photograph was of a firing squad in Iran executing Kurdish rebels.      C.H.

**PHYSICS.** Physics research in 1980 was dominated by developments in the field of particle physics. Controversy arose over the possible existence of oscillating neutrinos, which, if confirmed, would be of major significance not only in particle physics but in cosmological theory as well. Extensive research was also done in quantum chromodynamics, the relativistic quantum field theory that deals with quarks and gluons, which are the theoretical basic building blocks of subatomic particles. Physicists using the electron accelerator at Cornell University confirmed the existence of a fifth kind of quark, called "beauty" or "bottom." This finding left one more kind of quark, called "truth" or "top," to be discovered, according to current theory.

**Oscillating Neutrinos.** In April physicists Frederick Reines, Henry Sobel, and Elaine Pasierb of the University of California at Irvine announced that they had found indirect evidence that neutrinos may be unstable. According to theory, neutrinos are particles that have effective mass only when in motion; they have no mass at rest and hence do not exist in that state. Three forms of neutrinos, called electron neutrinos, muon neutrinos, and tau neutrinos (and their antiparticles), are supposed to exist, although tau neutrinos had not yet been detected. According to the California scientists, the three forms may in fact oscillate, changing from electron neutrinos to muon neutrinos and so forth. Such oscillations would explain

Above: Technicians at Cornell University's electron accelerator construct a special chamber for detecting and identifying high-energy particles. In 1980 the gas-filled chamber, which contains about 20,000 fine wires for tracking the particles, provided data whose interpretation went far toward confirming the existence of a fifth kind of quark, called "beauty," "bottom," or simply "b." Current particle theory requires six kinds of these fundamental constituents of matter; the sixth is not yet confirmed.

Below: A cross section of the special chamber used at Cornell's electron accelerator in 1980 to help confirm the existence of a fifth kind of quark. The tracks of particles produced by the collision of electrons and positrons entering the chamber from opposite directions are curved by the detector's magnetic field. Surrounding the central gas-filled chamber are other detecting devices.

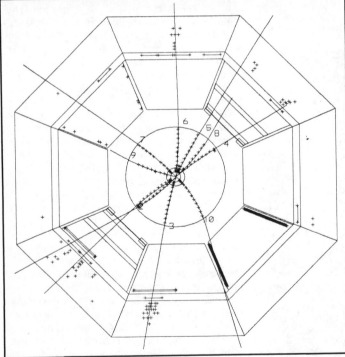

some unusual experimental results that the scientists found and could help to account for the unexplained low number of observed neutrinos from the sun, but they would also be profoundly significant to basic theory. According to quantum mechanics, if neutrinos can oscillate they must have some rest mass. And if they do, a significantly large fraction of the mass of the universe could be tied up in neutrinos.

According to astrophysicists, clusters of relatively massive neutrinos, perhaps distributed in halos around galaxies, might furnish enough mass to explain why clusters of galaxies remain together even though they do not now seem to have enough mass to remain gravitationally linked. If neutrinos have a rest mass of more than a few electron volts, they might even provide enough mass to keep the universe closed, rather than open and forever expanding as many cosmologists believe.

Soviet scientists announced in the summer of 1980 that they had indeed found experimental evidence more directly indicating that neutrinos do have rest mass. The scientists, who had been studying a form of radioactivity known as beta decay of nuclei, stated that the electron antineutrinos formed in the process were found to have a rest mass somewhere between 14 and 46 EV (electron volts). Much more work remained to be done in order to verify or refute these results, however, which were doubted by many physicists.

**Time-Standard Studies.** Another entry in the open-universe debate came from V. M. Canuto and S. H. Hsieh of the Goddard Institute for Space Studies. They reported in March that they had found evidence for believing that the universe is open by taking a new look at the comparison between gravitational and atomic time. Gravitational time is based on measurements of periodic motions of astronomical objects, whereas atomic time depends on regular, gravity-independent processes that take place inside atoms. The general assumption was that the two times can be compared directly, and that they are now and have always been the same. Canuto and Hsieh said, however, that the two can only be compared as they are right now, and that the relationship might have been different in the past and may also vary in the future.

As evidence, the scientists cited the record of changes in the moon's orbital motion (due to tidal action with the earth) and compared the results using gravitational and atomic time. They felt that the difference in results using these two different means of measuring time was significant, and that this supported their conclusion that the universe is open.

**New Look at Cosmic Rays.** University of Utah particle physicists began taking a new look at cosmic rays in 1980, in an attempt to study high-energy subatomic particles at energies not available in particle accelerators. The investigations at the Dugway Proving Grounds in Utah make use of the so-called Fly's Eye, a group of 67 mirrors arranged like the lenses in the compound eye of a fly. Photomultiplier tubes are placed at the foci of the mirrors. As high-energy cosmic rays strike nitrogen atoms in the earth's atmosphere, the atoms

emit electronic radiation very faintly and quickly. The system picks up these scintillations, recording about 30 to 50 such events each night, and allows the scientists to watch the progress of cosmic-ray showers. By using the Fly's Eye, the scientists hoped to be able to learn more not only about cosmic rays themselves but also about the behavior of the theoretical particles called quarks and gluons.

**Project Dumand.** Tests were also conducted in 1980 of a quite different device for detecting particles from space. The tests took place off Hawaii, under 4800 m (15,800 ft.) of water, to screen out radiation other than the neutrinos and muons that scientists wished to observe. Sea-bottom detectors, attached to recording instruments on the surface by long buoy lines, observed the light flashes produced when such particles travel through water at speeds faster than the speed of light in water. First results were encouraging, especially as the water proved so clear that fewer detectors were needed than was first thought necessary. The full-scale project—Dumand, for Deep Underwater Muon and Neutrino Detection—would involve setting up a detector array for a huge volume of water, but U.S. scientists were first proposing a smaller test version.     J.S.

**POLAND.** Poland was shaken by a workers' revolt in 1980. The event was the most dramatic and far-reaching political development in Eastern Europe since the Soviet invasion that ended liberalization in Czechoslovakia in 1968.

**Economic Crisis.** Poland began the year in a state of economic crisis. To modernize the economy, the regime led by Communist Party First Secretary Edward Gierek had borrowed $20 billion in the West in recent years. Repayment of interest took so much of the budget that the regime could scarcely make ends meet; in the meantime, the national income had begun to decline rather than grow. Following a Communist Party Congress in February, Prime Minister Piotr Jaroszewicz, 70, was dismissed from office because of the economic morass; he was replaced by Edward Babiuch, a 53-year-old administrator and economist.

As a first step toward fiscal soundness, Babiuch decided to cut back on subsidies paid to keep food prices low. Although he declared his general intent in advance, an unannounced hike in meat costs, when it took effect on July 1, set off a wave of strikes across the country. The government refused to roll back the price increase; instead, it granted wage raises on a case-by-case basis.

**Workers' Demands.** On Aug. 14, 17,000 workers at the Lenin shipyard in Gdańsk went on strike. Under the leadership of Lech Walesa, a 38-year-old

*Polish workers, receiving Communion during the August strike, won for the Roman Catholic Church the right to broadcast services regularly. The church, which considers itself the guardian of Polish sovereignty, remained neutral during the strike but later expressed sympathy for the workers. In December, however, it condemned those it termed political extremists for bringing on the possibility of a Soviet invasion.*

electrician, they broadened their demands from the purely economic to issues affecting the very heart of Communist Party rule. Among their demands were new trade unions independent of party control.

Workers' committees in other cities made common cause with the Gdańsk group, and soon more than 300,000 workers were on strike. On Aug. 23 the government agreed to recognize Walesa's committee as the workers' bargaining agent. The following day, in a gesture of conciliation to the workers, Babiuch and several other top officials were relieved of their jobs; Jozef Pinkowski became prime minister.

After a week's hard bargaining, the government on Aug. 31 agreed to terms unique in Communist history. Among other concessions, it agreed to permit the formation of independent self-governing unions and to recognize the right to strike. On Sept. 6 Gierek, 67, who reportedly suffered a heart attack, was dismissed as party leader and replaced by Stanislaw Kania, 53, a Politburo member who had been in charge of the military and security police. In a further shake-up many low-level officials were fired in early October.

Workers returned to their jobs, but when authorities proved slow to carry out pledges of widespread reform, a test of wills ensued. Walesa called a 1-hr. strike on Oct. 3 to force the government to register formally a new nationwide union, which was called Solidarity. Its membership was estimated at 5,000,000. Walesa and other

militants said they would carefully monitor the government to see that it fulfilled promises to loosen control of the press, deal more openly with the public, and adopt more rational economic management. They successfully resisted a government effort to extract recognition of the primacy of the Communist Party from Solidarity.

By mid-September industrial production had fallen by 20 percent. Shortages had developed not only of meat, but also of sugar, potatoes, and grain. U.S. President Jimmy Carter announced on Sept. 12 that $670,000,000 in credits would be extended to Poland for the purchase of U.S. grain. The Soviet Union on Dec. 2 promised $1.3 billion in emergency aid to Poland, but also maintained a steady drumbeat of harsh warnings against "antisocialist elements" who were undermining Communist control of Poland—an accusation that threatened to lead to armed intervention.

**Crisis Deepens.** By late November many more party leaders had been dismissed in a bid by Kania to consolidate his power. On Dec. 2 four longtime members of the Politburo were dismissed and two new members appointed, one of them Gen. Mieczyslaw Moczar, a strong nationalist with a reputation for ruthlessness toward rivals. On Dec. 4 the Communist Party's Central Committee declared "continuing unrest is leading our homeland to the brink of economic and moral destruction." A day later the Warsaw Treaty Organization unexpectedly held a summit conference in Moscow. Although Kania reportedly

## Hero of Poland's Workers

Thin, 5'7" tall, with a bulbous nose, a mop of brown hair and a walrus mustache, Lech Walesa (pronounced Vah-*wen*-sah) does not look like the folk hero he became in the summer and fall of 1980. But on Aug. 14, only hours after shipyard workers in Gdańsk walked off the job, he took charge of the movement for independent trade unions and the right to strike. The unemployed electrician, a devout Roman Catholic, married and the father of six children, achieved international fame during the next few weeks, as he made dozens of speeches before thousands of singing, chanting, and flower-throwing Polish workers. The 60-day revolt by Polish workers ended with an agreement, upheld by the Polish Supreme Court on Nov. 9, establishing an independent trade union movement in that Communist country.

*Lech Walesa.*

persuaded the leaders of the other Soviet bloc countries gathered there that he was in control of events, during the following two weeks Soviet troops were mobilized and appeared ready to invade Poland.

Poland's Roman Catholic Church leaders warned on Dec. 12 that political dissidents were endangering the nation. But Solidarity said it would defend jailed dissidents, and farmers were demanding the right to form an independent union.

*See* STATISTICS OF THE WORLD.          F.W.

**PORTUGAL.** Two important elections in 1980 and the death of Prime Minister Francisco Sá Carneiro in an airplane crash left President António Ramalho Eanes apparently the sole force for stability in Portugal.

**Movement to the Right.** Sá Carneiro was sworn in as prime minister on Jan. 3 at the head of a government of the center-right Democratic Alliance, a coalition of three parties. It was the first government with an elected majority and the first with no military officials in the cabinet since the 1974 coup. Sá Carneiro's commitment to conservative social and economic policies and to the primacy of his office put him on a collision course with Eanes and the military-led Council of the Revolution (CR). The disputes focused on the degree to which the socialist spirit of the 1976 constitution should be retained and on what role the armed forces should continue to play in Portuguese politics.

The Sá Carneiro government accelerated the program to return farmland that had been seized

by Communist militants during the 1975 revolutionary upheavals to the original owners. Nevertheless, about 1,170,000 acres remained under the control of cooperatives or Communist-dominated collectives in the Baixo Alentejo region in the south. Sá Carneiro also secured the passage of bills allowing private banks and insurance companies to compete with their nationalized counterparts, but the action was ruled unconstitutional by the president in April and by the CR in May. Thus blocked, Sá Carneiro aimed for another victory in upcoming parliamentary elections and for the defeat of Eanes in the subsequent presidential one.

**Fall Elections.** In the Oct. 5 parliamentary elections the Democratic Alliance increased its margin in the 250-seat parliament from 128 seats to 136, capturing 47 percent of the vote. The Socialist Party came in second with 28 percent of the vote and 73 seats, a showing roughly similar to its performance a year earlier but one that induced much internal debate and led to the resignation on Oct. 19 of Mário Soares as the party's secretary-general. The Communists dropped from 19 percent to 16.7 percent in the popular vote.

With the presidential election scheduled for Dec. 7, Sá Carneiro said he would resign the prime ministership if the conservative candidate, Gen. António Soares Carneiro, failed to defeat Eanes. Sá Carneiro, however, was killed in a plane crash on Dec. 4, and three days later Eanes won reelection with about 57 percent of the vote. On Dec. 13 the Social Democratic Party, senior partner in the Democratic Alliance, chose Francisco

Pinto Balsemão to be the next prime minister.

**The Economy.** In April the government targeted a growth rate of 3.6 percent for 1980. Inflation was then running at an annual rate of about 22 percent.

**Foreign Affairs.** The Sá Carneiro government reaffirmed the Portuguese commitment to the North Atlantic Treaty Organization and pressed for rapid entry into the European Community. It also took a strong stand against the Soviet intervention in Afghanistan and supported the United States on other issues. For example, on April 17 Portugal banned all trade with Iran until the release of the American hostages, sacrificing about a fifth of its imported oil to do so.

*See* STATISTICS OF THE WORLD.                    E.M.L.

**PRESIDENT OF THE UNITED STATES.** Jimmy Carter, thirty-ninth President of the United States, was born Oct. 1, 1924, near Plains, Ga. Carter's four years as President came to an end with his overwhelming defeat by Republican Party candidate Ronald Reagan on Nov. 4, 1980. Carter thus became the first Democratic Party incumbent since Grover Cleveland in 1888 to be denied reelection. His defeat reflected widespread dissatisfaction with the country's economic problems, a general perception of ineffective and vacillating leadership during his term in office, and frustrations over the continued holding of American hostages in Iran. The election also seemingly closed a remarkable political career that had seen the former peanut farmer and Georgia governor rise from obscurity to capture the Democratic Party's nomination for President and then defeat incumbent President Gerald R. Ford in the 1976 general election.

**Iranian Crisis.** The continuing crisis regarding the seizure of Americans by the Iranian government in late 1979 overshadowed all else for Carter in 1980 and kept the President's fortunes on an emotional roller coaster. His handling of the crisis rallied the nation behind him for the first few months, sent his anemic political popularity ratings soaring, and almost single-handedly destroyed the challenge of Sen. Edward M. Kennedy in the Democratic primaries. As the crisis dragged on, however, public sentiment began to turn against Carter. The failure of a military rescue mission in April not only prompted Secretary of State Cyrus R. Vance to resign in protest but also resurrected questions about Carter's leadership. The hostages were in their second year of captivity as Carter prepared to leave office.

**Other Foreign Policy Events.** Détente turned sour as a result of the Soviet invasion of Afghanistan. Terming the invasion the gravest threat to world peace since the end of World War II, Carter ordered retaliatory sanctions against the Soviets, including an embargo on U.S. grain sales, the suspension of sales of high-technology equipment, and a boycott of the Moscow Olympics by U.S. athletes. Carter also encouraged other nations to join the Olympic boycott, with mixed success, and pushed the European allies to impose their own sanctions to protest the Soviet action.

With the strategic arms limitation treaty in limbo because of Afghanistan, Carter declared that increased U.S. military preparedness was his main foreign policy priority for 1980. He asked for increased defense spending, particularly for U.S. forces in Western Europe, ordered a significant buildup of American forces in the Persian Gulf region, and asked for draft registration to enable the military to mobilize rapidly in time of crisis. Carter made two foreign trips during the year, attending a June Western economic summit conference in Italy, followed by visits to Yugoslavia, Spain, and Portugal, and appearing at the memorial services for the late Japanese Premier Masayoshi Ohira in Tokyo in July.

**Domestic Policy.** Halting the nation's continued economic decline was Carter's top domestic priority. He unveiled a five-point anti-inflation program in March that included $13 billion in spending cuts, credit restraints, and a fee on oil imports to reduce domestic energy consumption. He also announced an economic revitalization program in August that called for almost $27 billion in individual and business tax cuts in 1981. The plan was his fifth major economic initiative since taking office, but unemployment, inflation, and interest rates were all at high levels in 1980.

Carter had more success in implementing his national energy policy to reverse the country's massive reliance on foreign oil. Congress passed two of his major energy proposals, establishing an Energy Security Corporation to develop and produce synthetic fuels, and imposing a windfall profits tax to recover some of the profits the oil companies would reap from the forthcoming full decontrol of oil prices.

Besides the energy victories, Carter's legislative achievements in 1980 included draft registration, trucking deregulation, and a landmark lands bill protecting more than 104,000,000 acres of Alaskan wilderness from commercial development. But Congress blocked action on two key elements of Carter's energy plan, the Energy Mobilization Board to expedite construction of energy projects and the oil import fee.

**Reelection Campaign.** Despite his impressive victory over Kennedy in the Democratic primaries, Carter's reelection prospects seemed doomed as the campaign approached in midsummer. With

*In August the President and First Lady Rosalynn Carter attend White House ceremonies observing the 60th anniversary of the Nineteenth Amendment, which gave women the vote. The President attacked the Republican Party platform for not endorsing the equal rights amendment, the proposed Twenty-Seventh Amendment to the Constitution, which would ban discrimination on account of sex.*

both Harris and Gallup polls showing his popularity ratings the lowest ever recorded for any President, Carter sought to make Reagan's fitness for the job the central issue of the campaign, repeatedly suggesting in his speeches that Reagan's hawkish views were dangerous and might lead the U.S. into a catastrophic nuclear confrontation with the Russians. Despite these efforts to focus voter attention on his opponent, however, the campaign developed into a referendum on his own leadership, and a summertime Senate investigation concerning his brother Billy's dealings with the radical government of Libya did not help matters. Although a special subcommittee concluded that Billy Carter's actions were "irresponsible but not illegal," revelations that the President's brother had accepted a $220,000 loan from the Libyans and that Attorney General Benjamin

R. Civiletti was less than swift in his handling of the Justice Department's investigation of the matter were clear embarrassments to the Administration.

The election results reflected a resounding rejection of Carter's stewardship. Carter managed to carry only six states and the District of Columbia, one of the worst trouncings ever inflicted upon an incumbent President. Reagan won the popular vote by ten percentage points and the electoral vote by an overwhelming 489-to-49 margin. The results were so lopsided that Carter conceded his defeat before all the polls had closed.

**Transition Period.** After the shock of his loss wore off, Carter was said to have reconciled himself quickly to the verdict of the voters, concluding that his loss was less a personal repudiation than a reflection of public frustration over the country's

329

economic problems and the Iranian crisis. He pledged full cooperation with the President-elect in order to effect a smooth transition and met Reagan at the White House on Nov. 20. Carter said that after January, 1981, he would make plans for a library devoted to his Presidency and would "write more than one book."

Carter left the White House persuaded that history would judge him far more kindly than the voters had done at the polls. He believed that his legacy would include his fervent commitment to arms control and human rights, his spectacular triumph in securing a peace treaty between Egypt and Israel, the successful negotiation of the Panama Canal treaties, the establishment of a national energy policy, and a willingness to address politically unpopular problems. "I've not achieved all I set out to do," Carter observed in his concession speech, "but we have faced the tough issues," an assertion that might well prove to be the epitaph to Carter's bittersweet Presidency.         T.D.

**PRINCE EDWARD ISLAND.** *See* STATISTICS OF THE WORLD.

**PRIZES AND AWARDS.** The following is a selected listing of prizes awarded during 1980 and the names of the persons who received them. For awards given in specific fields, see the appropriate subject entry, such as MOTION PICTURES.

### NOBEL PRIZES

Eight Americans were among the winners of the 1980 Nobel prizes, announced in October. Among the winners was a little-known human rights activist from Argentina and a chemist who earned his second Nobel Prize. All the winners are listed below.

**Chemistry.** Two Americans and an Englishman shared the 1980 Nobel Prize in chemistry for the development of methods that make it possible to map the structure and function of deoxyribonucleic acid (DNA), the substance that governs the machinery of the living cell:

*Paul Berg* (1926–   ), professor of biochemistry at Stanford University since 1959, received half the prize and was cited "for his fundamental studies of the biochemistry of nucleic acids, with particular regard to recombinant DNA."

*Walter Gilbert* (1932–   ), professor of molecular biology at Harvard University since 1968, and *Frederick Sanger* (1918–   ), professor of molecular biology at Cambridge University since 1961, split the other half of the prize. The two men were cited "for their contributions concerning the determination of base sequences in nu-

After receiving their awards from King Carl XVI Gustaf of Sweden, ten 1980 Nobel laureates congratulate one another at the Dec. 10 ceremonies in Stockholm.

cleic acids." The award was Sanger's second Nobel Prize in chemistry; his first award was in 1958.

**Economics.** For "the leading research worker within the field of the economic science which deals with the construction and analysis of empirical models of business fluctuations":

*Lawrence R. Klein* (1920–    ), professor of economics at the University of Pennsylvania, noted as a developer of models for forecasting economic trends and developing policies to deal with them. The citation noted: "Few, if any, research workers in the empirical field of economic science have had so many successors and such a large impact as Lawrence Klein."

**Literature.** For writing that, "with uncompromising clearsightedness, voices man's exposed condition in a world of severe conflicts":

*Czeslaw Milosz* (1911–    ), Polish émigré poet and novelist who became an American citizen and taught at the University of California at Berkeley. Active in the Polish resistance movement in German-occupied Warsaw during World War II, he defected to Paris in 1951 after serving the postwar Communist government as a diplomat. The citation noted: "The world that Milosz depicts in his poetry, prose, and essays is the world in which man lives after having been driven out of paradise."

**Medicine.** For discoveries that helped to explain how the structure of cells relates to diseases and organ transplants. The honored work was performed over several decades and helped provide the theoretical basis for tissue transplants and explain why some people are more susceptible than others to particular diseases. Three researchers in immunology, two Americans and a Frenchman, shared the prize:

*Baruj Benacerraf* (1921–    ), chairman of the pathology department of the Harvard University Medical School, born in Caracas, Venezuela, and naturalized as an American citizen in 1943.

*George D. Snell* (1904–    ), a staff scientist at the Jackson Laboratory in Bar Harbor, Maine, where he had been working since 1935.

*Jean Dausset* (1917–    ), head of the department of immunology at the University of Paris, whose contribution was to "dramatically blaze the trail" toward transplantation in human beings as well as animals.

**Peace Prize.** For representing views that "carry a vital message to many other countries, not least in Latin America, where social and political problems, as yet unsolved, have resulted in an escalation of the use of violence":

*Adolfo Pérez Esquivel* (1932–    ), Argentine Roman Catholic lay leader and human rights activist. As head of the Service for Peace and Justice in Latin America, he coordinated ecumenical human rights efforts throughout Latin America. Pérez had been jailed and tortured by the Argentine regime because of his human rights activities.

**Physics.** For work that demonstrated an asymmetry in the behavior of particles and thereby contributed to an explanation of how matter in the universe could exist, despite grounds for believing that it should have been annihilated at the birth of the universe:

*Val L. Fitch* (1923–    ), chairman of the physics department at Princeton University, where he had served on the faculty since 1954. The Nobel citation was for work done at Princeton in 1964 in collaboration with James W. Cronin, who was also teaching at the university.

*James W. Cronin* (1931–    ), professor of physics at the University of Chicago. His 16-year-old research with Val Fitch was cited as support for proposals that similar asymmetries in the production of particles during the fiery birth of the universe could explain why it became composed primarily of matter.

### PULITZER PRIZES

The 1980 Pulitzer prizes were announced on April 14. In journalism the Gannett News Service won the public service gold medal for exposing mismanagement of gifts and contributions to the Pauline Fathers, a Roman Catholic religious community. The Boston *Globe* collected three prizes, the second time this had happened in the 64-year history of the awards. Norman Mailer won his second Pulitzer for the novelistic story of the life and execution of Utah murderer Gary Gilmore.

**Biography.** Edmund Morris, *The Rise of Theodore Roosevelt.*

**Commentary.** Ellen H. Goodman of the Boston *Globe.*

**Criticism.** William A. Henry 3rd, television critic for the Boston *Globe.*

**Drama.** Lanford Wilson, *Talley's Folly.*

**Editorial Cartooning.** Don Wright of the Miami *News.*

**Editorial Writing.** Robert L. Bartley of the *Wall Street Journal.*

**Feature Writing.** Madeleine Blais of the Miami *Herald.*

**Fiction.** Norman Mailer for *The Executioner's Song.*

**General Nonfiction.** Douglas R. Hofstadter for *Gödel, Escher, Bach: An Eternal Golden Braid.*

**History.** Leon F. Litwack for *Been in the Storm So Long: The Aftermath of Slavery.*

**Music.** David Del Tredici for *In Memory of a Summer Day.*

**Photography, Feature.** Erwin H. Hagler of the Dallas *Times-Herald.*

**Photography, Spot News.** "Firing Squad in Iran," a photograph submitted by United Press International on behalf of an unidentified free-lancer whose name was withheld because "present unrest in Iran" could endanger him.

**Poetry.** Donald R. Justice for *Selected Poems.*

**Reporting, General Local.** The staff of the Philadelphia *Inquirer* for stories about the Three Mile Island nuclear accident.

**Reporting, International.** Joel Brinkley, reporter and son of NBC newsman David Brinkley, and Jay Mather, photographer, both of the Louisville (Ky.) *Courier-Journal,* on "the Cambodian nightmare."

**Reporting, National.** Betty Swenson Orsini and Charles Stafford of the St. Petersburg (Fla.) *Times* for an investigation of the Church of Scientology.

**Reporting, Special Local.** The Boston *Globe* for a reporting team's description of mismanagement in the transit system.

### OTHER PRIZES AND AWARDS

Among the many other prizes and awards distributed during 1980, the following were notable.

**Academy of American Poets.** $10,000 fellowship to Mark Strand.

**Albert Einstein Peace Prize.** $10,000 to Alva Myrdal.

**Albert Lasker Awards.** $15,000 each for medical research and public health. Basic research award (shared) to Paul Berg, Stanley N. Cohen, and A. Dale Kaiser of Stanford University and Herbert W. Boyer of the University of California at San Francisco. Clinical research award (shared) to Vincent J. Freda and John Gorman of Columbia University's College of Physicians and Surgeons, William Pollack of Columbia and Ortho Diagnostics, Inc., Cyril A. Clarke of the University of Liverpool, and Ronald Finn of Royal Liverpool Hospital. Public health award to National Heart, Lung and Blood Institute.

**American Academy and Institute of Arts and Letters.** Awards of $4000 each to Ann Beattie, William Dickey, Paul Fussell, Maxine Kumin, George Open, Robert Pinsky, Lewis Thomas, Larry Woiwode; $4000 awards in art to Richard Anuszkiewicz, Edward Dugmore, Marion Lerner Levine, and Charmion von Wiegand; $4000 awards in music to Donald Grantham, Eugene O'Brien, Malcolm C. Peyton, and Lawrence L. Widdoes; $5000 Harold D. Vursell Memorial Award to Tom Wolfe; $3000 Richard and Hinda Rosenthal Foundation Awards to Stanley Elkin for *The Living End;* in art to Dolores Milmoe; gold medal for drama to Edward Albee.

**Association of American Publishers, American Book Awards.** National Medal for Literature ($15,000) to Eudora Welty. Hardcover awards: general fiction, William Styron; first novel, William Wharton; general nonfiction, Tom Wolfe; biography, Edmund Morris; autobiography, Lauren Bacall; history, Henry Kissinger; science, Doug Hofstadter; current interest, Julia Child; children's book, Joan W. Blos. Paperbacks: general paperback fiction, John Irving; general paperback nonfiction, Peter Matthiessen; paperback biography, A. Scott Berg; paperback autobiography, Malcolm Cowley; paperback history, Barbara W. Tuchman; paperback science, Gary Zukav; current interest, Christopher Lasch; children's book, Madeleine L'Engle; poetry, Philip Levine.

**Avery Fisher Prize.** Award of $5000 to Richard Goode for achievement by an American instrumentalist.

**Capezio Award in Dance.** Prize of $1000 to Walter Terry.

**National Endowment for the Humanities.** Jefferson Lecturer ($10,000), Barbara Tuchman.

**National Teacher of the Year Award.** Beverly Bimes of St. Louis.

**Templeton Prize for Progress in Religion.** John M. Templeton Foundation Award of $206,000 to Ralph Wendell Burhoe, former chairman of the department of theology at Meadville Theological School in Chicago.

**Wolf Foundation.** Awards of $100,000 each in science: agriculture, Karl Maramorosch of Rutgers University; mathematics (shared), Andrei N. Kolomogorov of Moscow State University and Henri Cartan of the University of Paris; chemistry, Henry Eyring of the University of Utah; physics (shared), Michael E. Fisher and Kenneth G. Wilson of Cornell University and Leo P. Kadanoff of the University of Chicago; medicine (shared), Leo Sachs of the Weizmann Institute and James L. Gowans and Cesar Mistein of the Medical Research Council (England).                                          L.A.S.

**PUBLISHING.** Three of the oldest and most prestigious magazines in the United States, *Harper's, Atlantic Monthly,* and *Saturday Review,* changed hands in 1980. Random House, a major book publisher, was bought by the expanding Newhouse newspaper chain. And the *Wall Street Journal* became the country's largest-circulation daily newspaper.

**Books.** Newhouse Publications, the nation's third largest newspaper chain, agreed in principle on Feb. 6 to buy Random House, a subsidiary of the RCA Corp., for between $65,000,000 and $70,000,000 in cash. RCA bought Random House in 1966 for $40,000,000. Random House's divisions included Alfred A. Knopf, Inc., Ballantine Books, Vintage Books, Pantheon Books, and Modern Library. The family-owned Newhouse chain controlled 29 daily newspapers, several radio and cable television stations, and the Condé Nast group of magazines, including *Vogue, Mademoiselle, Glamour,* and *House and Garden.* Because of Newhouse's reputation for allowing its properties to operate independently, the change in ownership was welcomed by many publishing industry observers.

In what was termed an "economy move," Harper & Row on March 27 absorbed its Lippincott and Crowell lines into the Harper imprint. Harper had acquired the J. B. Lippincott Co. in 1978 and combined its trade operation with that of Thomas Y. Crowell, which had been acquired a year earlier. Under the consolidation, the Lippincott-Crowell operation was moved to Harper & Row headquarters, the editorial staff was trimmed, and the overall list was eventually to be cut in half.

Houghton Mifflin continued its recent expansion by purchasing Rand McNally's elementary, high school, and college text lines for $11,600,000. The transaction ended Rand McNally's role as an educational books publisher after more than 100 years. Rand McNally retained its map, atlas, trade book publishing, book manufacturing, and specialty-forms businesses.

Encyclopaedia Britannica, Inc., signed an agreement with the People's Republic of China for a Chinese-language edition of the set in ten volumes. It was to have an initial run of 50,000 copies and would be available for the equivalent of $100.

Sponsors of The American Book Awards (TABA), which replaced the National Book Awards in 1979, announced on Oct. 20 that they would overhaul the controversial awards program

*Joining the growing ranks of science periodicals, Time Inc.'s monthly newsmagazine,* Discover, *offered a variety of science-related stories in its premier issue.*

to meet objections of authors and publishers who boycotted the first annual TABA ceremonies in 1980. TABA reduced the number of prize categories from 33 to 18 and abolished the original system of choosing winners by polling members of the publishing industry. In the future, nominees and winners would be chosen by jury panels made up of authors, critics, booksellers, librarians, and publishers.

On Oct. 5 it was reported that a February ruling of the Internal Revenue Service had adversely affected the publishing industry. The ruling, which prohibited publishers from depreciating the value of unsold inventories of books to lessen their tax burden, would reportedly cause publishers to remainder quickly some slow-moving but meritorious titles, publish smaller first printings, and let titles go out of print faster. Fewer noncommercial books would be published, it was predicted. Some publishers said they would shred poor sellers to pulp.

In its annual statistical roundup, the Association of American Publishers reported that book sales at retail reached a total of $7.2 billion in 1979, an increase of 10 percent over the year before. The number of new titles published rose to 45,182, an increase of 9.6 percent over the previous year.

---

### With the Law Firm of Savage and Green?

What is green, incredibly savage, strong, tall, and voluptuous, has a flowing mane of wild dark hair and almond-shaped eyes, and wears carefully shredded short-shorts? It's the Savage She-Hulk, the cousin of the Incredible Hulk and Marvel Comics' highly successful new superperson. Because almost half of all comic-book readers are girls, publishers have moved quickly to add to the thin ranks of female superheroes. (Spider Woman and Wonder Woman were the only continuing stars until the Savage She-Hulk came along.) Advocates of women's liberation can be proud of the She-Hulk. When not destroying bad guys, she is Jennifer Walters, a brilliant criminal lawyer.

Two new monthlies directed to the interests of women in management appeared with first issues dated January, 1980: Savvy, subtitled "The Magazine for Executive Women," and Enterprising Women, aimed at entrepreneurs.

**Periodicals.** Harper's magazine was saved from oblivion after 130 years of publication on July 9 when it was bought by two wealthy foundations that would operate the literary and political monthly as a nonprofit enterprise. The Minneapolis Star and Tribune Co., which acquired Harper's in 1965, announced in June that efforts to sell the magazine had failed and publication would cease with the August issue. Harper's had lost $1,500,000 in 1979, and its circulation had dropped to 325,000. The magazine was rescued at the last minute by the John D. and Catherine T. MacArthur Foundation of Chicago and the Atlantic Richfield Foundation, which joined to purchase it. The reported price was only $250,000, since the magazine had few assets beyond its reputation, subscription list, and paper stocks. The two foundations agreed, however, to commit some $3,000,-000 toward future operations.

The Atlantic Monthly Co., parent of the 123-year-old Atlantic Monthly magazine and the 63-year-old Atlantic Monthly Press, was purchased for an undisclosed sum by Boston real-estate developer Mortimer Zuckerman, it was reported on March 1. While the Atlantic Monthly had a circulation of about 340,000, it had suffered from increased mailing rates and production costs. Robert Manning, editor in chief, said that the takeover would provide new resources for both the magazine and the book publishing operation.

The Saturday Review, which had changed hands several times in the past decade, was purchased on May 20 by Macro Communications Inc., publisher of Financial World, a small investment magazine. Macro bought Saturday Review for "several million" dollars. Founded in 1924, Saturday Review flourished as a journal of politics and literature under longtime editor Norman Cousins. The magazine reportedly had not been profitable since the 1960's and was declared bankrupt in 1973. It had recently been losing as much as $1,000,000 a year, and its circulation had fallen to 500,000. Carll Tucker was to stay on as editor of the Review, which would become a monthly and shift to a greater emphasis on literature and the arts, with more news and reviews of books; it would also return to the newsstands.

After losing some $10,000,000 on Us magazine (circulation 950,000), the New York Times Co. sold the fortnightly to the Macfadden Group Inc., publisher of True Confessions, True Story, and Photoplay, it was reported on March 7. The Times Co. had launched Us in 1977 as a rival of Time Inc.'s flourishing celebrity weekly People (circulation 2,300,000). Macfadden assumed Us's subscription liabilities of about $4,000,000 and was to pay the Times Co. more than $5,000,000 out of the magazine's future profits, if any.

Reader's Digest started its first new magazine in 58 years with the introduction of Families, designed to fill the readership gap between Parents magazine and the big women's service magazines. Time Inc. came out in September with its seventh magazine, Discover, subtitled "The Newsmagazine of Science." And the Washington Post Co. started testing its new magazine, Focus, a six-times-a-year publication devoted to a single topic per issue, such as "Mysteries of the Cosmos." The company's Inside Sports, a monthly magazine, first appeared in April.

The increasing availability of cable television had meant more viewer options, and four new magazines devoted to television made their debuts in 1980. Dial, a slick monthly put out by the nation's four largest public television stations in September for their 650,000 paying members, immediately ran into controversy for accepting advertising. A rival for-profit publisher filed charges of unfair competition, and the Postal Service ruled that Dial could not use the cheaper nonprofit second-class rates for mailing. The magazine's right to promote itself on public television was also under review. Of the 35,000 periodicals regularly sent through the mails, about 10,000—including some of the nation's best-known publications—had some form of nonprofit subsidy in 1980, to the occasional complaint of for-profit competitors. Some, such as *Harper's*, converted to nonprofit status in order to stay in business. Similarly, the *National Review* and *New Republic*, though ideological opposites, joined forces in 1980 to establish a nonprofit foundation that would channel funds to the periodicals. The intention was to reduce postal costs.

Magazine advertising revenues continued to increase in 1980. The Publishers Information Bureau reported that ad revenues for the first ten months of the year totaled nearly $2.3 billion, a jump of 9 percent over the same period in 1979. **Newspapers.** Afternoon dailies in large metropolitan areas lost readers to their morning competitors during the 1970's. In 1980 this trend affected the fortunes of afternoon newspapers in Philadelphia, Denver, Cleveland, and New Orleans.

The Philadelphia *Bulletin*, once the nation's largest afternoon daily, was sold on April 10 to the Charter Media Co., a newly formed communications firm. Founded in 1847, the *Bulletin* had seen its circulation drop steadily in the 1970's, and industry observers believed the paper was losing substantial amounts of money. On Sept. 30 Charter Media was dissolved and Phoenix entrepreneur Karl Eller assumed sole proprietorship of the *Bulletin.*

The Times Mirror Co. of Los Angeles agreed in principle on Oct. 22 to buy the 88-year-old Denver *Post* for about $95,000,000. The new owner was expected to introduce a morning edition of the *Post* to compete with the Scripps-Howard-owned *Rocky Mountain News*, which surpassed the *Post* in circulation for the first time in 1980. The Times Mirror Co. owned seven other newspapers in 1980, including the Los Angeles *Times,* the Dallas *Times Herald,* and the Long Island (N.Y.) *Newsday.*

The Cleveland *Press* was purchased in November for a reported $20,000,000 by industrialist Joseph E. Cole, a former chairman of the Democratic Party's National Committee. Cole concluded the sale with the F. W. Scripps Co. two days before the paper's 102nd anniversary. He announced plans to publish a Sunday edition that would compete directly with the morning *Plain Dealer*, which in recent years had outsold the *Post.*

New Orleans became a one-newspaper town when the morning *Times-Picayune* and the afternoon *States-Item,* both owned by the Newhouse chain, merged into a single all-day newspaper with a combined editorial staff. The *States-Item* had declined in recent years, while the *Times-Picayune* had grown.

The *Wall Street Journal* sprinted past the New York *Daily News* in 1980 to become the nation's largest-circulation daily newspaper. As circulation climbed to an average daily sale of 1,800,000 copies, the prosperous financial journal announced it would cut back on its growth since rapid expansion was straining its printing and delivering capacities. The *Journal* raised its newsstand price from 30¢ to 35¢, eased its radio and television promotion, and split into two sections, raising the maximum number of pages from 48 to 56 a day so that it could accept more ads.

In late August the morning New York *Daily News* started a new evening tabloid, *Tonight,* with an anticipated circulation of 300,000. It thus entered direct competition with the financially troubled New York *Post,* circulation 654,000.

In its annual statistical roundup, the 1980 edition of *Editor & Publisher International Yearbook* reported that daily newspaper circulation in the U.S. increased in 1979 for the fourth successive year. Total daily circulation reached 62,223,040, an increase of 233,000 over 1978. The number of daily newspapers increased from 1756 in 1978 to 1763 in 1979.                                                R.F.

**PUERTO RICO.** In a gubernatorial election that was too close to call for more than a month after Nov. 4, 1980, balloting, Puerto Ricans decisively rejected both statehood and independence as immediate future courses for the island. Incumbent Gov. Carlos Romero Barceló and former Gov. Rafael Hernández Colón each received about 46.9 percent of the total vote, with Romero holding a 700-vote margin as a recount continued into December. The final margin was about 3500 votes. Legislative elections also ended in a standoff, with Hernández's Popular Democratic Party winning control of the island's senate and Romero's New Progressive Party apparently retaining control of the house of representatives by two seats.

Regardless of the outcome, which some observers predicted would not be clear until inauguration day in early January, the voting indicated that Puerto Ricans were a long way from supporting statehood. Romero, an advocate of statehood, said on Nov. 5 that he would not press for it "during my second term." Hernández supported Puerto Rico's current commonwealth status, which gives islanders U.S. citizenship and federal funds but no vote in federal elections.

Also of importance was the growing terrorism carried on by pro-independence groups operating both on the island and the mainland. The December, 1979, ambush of a U.S. Navy bus, in which two sailors were killed, sparked an antiter-

335

The coffin of Puerto Rican statesman Luis Muñoz Marín is escorted from San Juan Cathedral on May 2. The day was declared a national holiday to honor the man who attained commonwealth status for the island and became its first elected governor, serving from 1948 to 1964.

rorist training program for police on the island. On March 12, terrorists ambushed an automobile carrying uniformed U.S. Army personnel, one of whom was slightly wounded in the machine-gun attack. On the mainland, police in the Chicago area on April 4 rounded up elements of the Armed Forces of National Liberation (FALN), a longtime Puerto Rican terrorist group, claiming they were the "hard core of Chicago elements of the FALN." *See* CRIME AND LAW ENFORCEMENT.

The death on April 30 of former Gov. Luis Muñoz Marín, the architect of the commonwealth system and of Operation Bootstrap, the island's economic development program, marked the end of an era in island politics and symbolized the passing of leadership to new hands.

Puerto Rico continued to suffer a variety of economic problems. Unemployment held at 19 percent, according to a July report, but unofficial statistics suggested it was much higher. Inflation ran at a projected 16 percent for the year, with high-priced foreign oil and food imports blamed in part for the cost-of-living spiral.

*See* STATISTICS OF THE WORLD. J.N.G.

# Q

**QATAR.** *See* STATISTICS OF THE WORLD. *See also* PERSIAN GULF STATES.

**QUÉBEC.** *See* STATISTICS OF THE WORLD. *See also* CANADA.

# R

**RADIO.** *See* TELEVISION AND RADIO BROADCASTING.

**RECORDINGS.** *See* MUSIC.

# RELIGION

The world's age-old religious concerns yearly become more visible. The drama of television and the speed of international travel create a wide interest in swiftly reported events that would once have affected only small bodies of believers over long stretches of time.

In 1980 Americans continued to react to international religious events. Pope John Paul II traveled to Africa, Brazil, France, and West Germany, revealing himself in frequent statements as a conservator of Catholic tradition. The motives of Islamic revolutionaries in Iran puzzled U.S. officials who were attempting to free Americans held hostage. An internationally publicized anti-Semitic incident in France drew worldwide condemnation.

### CHRISTIAN ECUMENISM

The most important religious events of 1980 were most likely not spectacular papal tours, acts of Muslim militants, or church-state conflicts, but several milestones on the long road toward reunion between the Roman Catholic Church and Christianity's other three largest communions, involving nearly a billion believers.

**Orthodoxy.** Official delegates of the Catholic and Eastern Orthodox churches met to negotiate for the first time since the 15th-century Council of Florence. The meeting, from May 29 to June 4, of 30 hierarchs and theologians from each side opened symbolically with joint worship in a venerable monastery on the Greek island of Patmos, where St. John is thought to have written the Book of Revelations. The actual talks occurred on the island of Rhodes.

The Orthodox delegates, particularly the Greeks, took offense because the Catholics included representatives of Eastern Rite churches that follow most Orthodox practices but recognize the pope's universal jurisdiction. The Orthodox declared that they did not recognize the Eastern Rite churches; this question would be an item for future talks. Some Orthodox were also incensed by a statement from Pope John Paul II reaffirming papal infallibility, one of the most divisive issues.

The meeting elected an ongoing secretariat under the Vatican's Cardinal Jan Willebrands and Archbishop Stylianos of Australia, representing Ecumenical Patriarch Demetrios I. Although the huge Orthodox Church of Russia participated, it protested the noninclusion of churches in the United States and Japan whose independence it recognizes. Such intra-Orthodox tensions might produce as many difficulties as Orthodox-Catholic differences.

Before the next plenary meeting, within two years, three subcommittees were to work on the agreed first topic for negotiation, the Eucharist, on which substantial agreement already existed. The official communiqué concluded: "We hope that the re-establishment of full communion . . . will contribute to the reconciliation of mankind and to the peace of the world."

Meanwhile, the Vatican held its fifth bilateral talks with the Orthodox Church of Russia. The two sides declared they saw no way to "change a universal and uninterrupted tradition, begun by the Lord and the apostles, of not allowing the ordination of women" as priests.

**Lutheranism.** A 450th anniversary statement from the joint negotiating commission between the Vatican and the Lutheran World Federation emphasized common ground with regard to the 1530 Augsburg Confession, the central creed for Lutherans. In a statement reminiscent of Martin Luther's doctrine of "justification by grace through

---

### "Our Parent, Which Art in Heaven . . ."

The National Council of Churches of Christ in the United States received a report from one of its special task forces in June, recommending that God no longer be referred to in terms of gender—that pronouns such as "He" and "His" and terms such as "Father" should be eliminated. The report also suggested that Jesus Christ be called the "Child," rather than the "Son," of God, and that the word "patriarch" be replaced with the word "ancestor." Members of denominations across the country, who were to vote on whether or not these changes should be adopted, reputedly began engaging in hot debate as soon as the report was released.

Canterbury Cathedral is crowded with world church figures, royalty, and statesmen on March 25 for the enthronement of Robert Runcie (not seen) as archbishop of Canterbury, head of the Church of England and titular head of world Anglicanism. He had been active in ecumenical efforts, and among the guests at the ceremony was a Greek Orthodox prelate (seated, left).

faith alone," the commission declared: "It is solely by grace and by faith in Christ's saving work and not because of any merit in us that we are accepted by God and receive the Holy Spirit who renews our hearts and equips us for and calls us to good works." The Reverend George Lindbeck of Yale University, the Lutheran co-president, said Luther "would have been overjoyed" at this section. More broadly, the group said its work had shown that the confession "can be regarded as an expression of the common faith" and had found "broad consensus" even on the alleged abuses cited by the confession. The commission listed these "unresolved problems": the number of the sacraments, the papacy, aspects of the office of bishops and teaching authority, and dogmas that Rome had promulgated since 1530 (papal infallibility and primal jurisdiction, and Mary's Immaculate Conception and bodily assumption into heaven). The actual June Augsburg anniversary was marked by an ecumenical conference in West Germany and a warm statement from the pope in Rome. During his November tour of West Germany, however, the pope told a meeting of Lutheran leaders that full doctrinal agreement must precede sharing in the Eucharist.

**Anglicanism.** The newly enthroned archbishop of Canterbury, Robert Runcie, titular head of world Anglicanism, had his first meeting with Pope John Paul on May 9 in Accra, Ghana, while both were touring Africa. They declared jointly: "Time is too short and the need too pressing to waste Christian energy pursuing old rivalries. . . . The talents and resources of all churches must be shared if Christ is to be seen and heard effectively." At an audience for the joint Anglican-Catholic theological negotiators, on Sept. 4, the pope listed four "practical problems" regarding unity: "questions of orders, of mixed marriages, of shared sacramental life, of Christian morality."

With Vatican approval, the U.S. Catholic hierarchy made special arrangements in August to receive into the priesthood several dozen priests who left the Episcopal Church in 1977 over the decision to ordain women and other liberal trends. Although many were married, technically this was no innovation; in recent decades Catholicism had admitted a few married converts into the priesthood. But the Vatican also agreed to let them keep a "common identity," apparently including some liturgies. Many Episcopalians objected to the action as "sheep stealing" or as an offense against Episcopal women priests. Others considered the requirement that the Anglicans be reordained a new attack on the validity of Anglican orders.

**Other Ecumenical Events.** During his installation, in March, noteworthy for its Catholic participation, Archbishop Runcie chose to delete the clause "and the son" (Latin: *filioque*) from the Nicene Creed. This action reverted from Western and Catholic to Orthodox wording, and a spokesman for the Ecumenical Patriarchate praised the gesture. (Runcie was chairman of the group considering world Anglican-Orthodox relations before his elevation.) The Church of England synod, with Runcie's support, proposed official talks with Catholic and Orthodox churches on the dispute over women priests. The English church found no theological objections but had not ordained women, partly for ecumenical reasons.

The World Council of Churches (WCC), which claims a nominal constituency of most of the world's Protestants and Orthodox and the Vatican dissolved their only permanent joint agency, a social issues committee formed in 1968. The official explanation was that this action was not a retreat from ecumenism but that the two sides had become "less symmetrical in their relationship" on social issues. Observers felt that this might be a reference to the WCC move toward controversial activism.

The WCC appeared to settle the dispute over its unconditional grants to African liberation parties and armies, which are intended for nonmilitary purposes. Critics have held that these grants give moral endorsement to political violence. However, a WCC consultation called because of the criticisms gave strong endorsement to the antiracism grants, urged new efforts against white minority regimes in South Africa and Namibia (South-West Africa), and assailed the world's "dominant economic systems," which "promote the self-interest, greed, and values of the 'white world.'" In August the Programme to Combat Racism announced a record $775,500 in new grants to organizations for the oppressed.

The All Africa Conference of Churches chose as its new general secretary the Reverend Maxime Rafransoa of Madagascar, thus ending a pro-

*Pope John Paul II celebrates High Mass as he takes part in the ordination of nine bishops in Zaire on May 4, part of his extensive tour of Africa in 1980.*

Sponsors of the large "Washington for Jesus" rally staged in the U.S. capital on April 29 said that the sole intent was to "return the nation to God." Other religious leaders, however, saw such rallies as intended to exert political pressure in opposition to the proposed Equal Rights Amendment, legalized abortion, and homosexual rights.

in the U.S., issued a new policy statement in November, calling the Palestine Liberation Organization (PLO) "the only organized voice of the Palestinian people" and the only body that appears able to negotiate on their behalf. It demanded that the PLO recognize Israel's right to exist as a Jewish state and urged all sides to shun violence. Jewish organizations protested the statement because the changes in PLO policy had not been made a precondition to PLO participation in Middle East peace talks.

The education division of the NCC rejected task force recommendations for language changes to meet feminist objections to the Revised Standard Version of the Bible (RSV), currently being reedited. The RSV translators were eliminating many male nouns and pronouns in cases where the Hebrew and Greek texts do not require them, but they refused to alter the texts or the customary ways of referring to God. The NCC division did, however, authorize a more radical lectionary translation, which could be the first step toward an ecumenical Bible acceptable to strong feminists.

### RELATIONS BETWEEN CHURCH AND STATE

Religion was unusually conspicuous in the 1980 U.S. Presidential and congressional campaigns. The new element was the rise of evangelical and fundamentalist Protestant activists who insisted on conservatism not only on traditional moral issues (abortion, homosexuality, pornography, public-school prayer) but in foreign and other domestic policies. Most prominent was the group called the Moral Majority, led by Jerry Falwell, a

tracted ecumenical leadership crisis in the only continent where Protestantism is growing rapidly. Rafransoa had been Africa secretary for the WCC relief commission.

The National Council of Churches (NCC), speaking for 32 Protestant and Orthodox bodies

**His Next Project: To Reform Television**

The Reverend Jerry Falwell, pastor of the Thomas Road Baptist Church in Lynchburg, Va., founded Moral Majority, Inc., in 1979. In 1980 the organization reportedly spent more than $3,000,000 in its effort against the reelection of several liberal U.S. Senators. Among the supporters of Moral Majority are the estimated 18,000,000 who watch and listen to Falwell's weekly *Old-Time Gospel Hour*—carried by almost 700 TV and radio stations. They are urged to work for candidates who hold the organization's views against the Equal Rights Amendment, abortion, pornography, and homosexuality. The 47-year-old Falwell, who preaches a return to what he calls "family values," is married and has three children. He met his wife when she was an organist in the church in which Falwell, then 19, first accepted Jesus Christ.

*The Reverend Jerry Falwell.*

television evangelist and pastor of a huge independent Baptist church in Lynchburg, Va.

The electoral victories of Ronald Reagan and other conservative Republicans appeared to result, in part, from an appeal on "family" and "morality" issues to the nation's two largest religious communities, the Roman Catholics and the more diffuse evangelicals, a conservative element that exists within most Protestant denominations. The Gallup organization estimated the evangelicals at 30,000,000 persons of voting age.

The Republican Party platform pleased both Protestant and Catholic activists by urging a constitutional amendment to "restore protection of the right to life for unborn children," appointment of judges who "respect traditional family values and the sanctity of innocent human life," and tax credits to aid parents of students at religious day schools.

An election year pastoral letter from the Roman Catholic bishops of the U.S. opposed "single-issue" voting and asked Catholics to examine candidates' views not only on abortion but also on disarmament, race relations, housing, and other serious questions. Cardinal Humberto Medeiros of Boston, however, took the single-issue approach in a pastoral letter prior to a Massachusetts primary. He declared that legislators and those who vote for them could share guilt for the "horrendous crime" of abortion. The two implicitly targeted Democratic Party candidates won anyway. No outcries were heard when another Catholic bishop opposed a Ku Klux Klan candidate, or when a leader of Reform Judaism endorsed Sen. Edward M. Kennedy in the Presidential primaries.

Examples of international church and state relations included the position of the Catholic hierarchy on the political tensions in Poland in the fall. There, Lech Walesa's shipyard workers in Gdańsk sparked wide labor strikes, resulting in unprecedented recognition of new independent unions. Catholic primate Cardinal Stefan Wyszynski preached a sermon read by many as a criticism of the strikes, but the hierarchy as a whole issued a strong endorsement of workers' rights to form independent unions; see also POLAND.

In South Africa, as Christian protests against racial apartheid continued, police arrested 35 prominent members of the clergy during a demonstration march in late May, including Secretary-General Desmond Tutu of the South African Council of Churches. The clerics were later fined and released.

The government-approved Patriotic Catholic Association in the People's Republic of China was allowed to hold its first national synod since 1962,

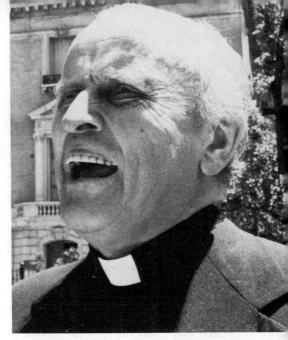

Rep. Robert Drinan (D, Mass.), a Roman Catholic priest, canceled his reelection plans in 1980 when Pope John Paul II enforced Article 139 of the church's canon law, which forbids members of the clergy to hold elective (but not appointive) office.

in Peking, in May. It was attended by 30 bishops and 100 priests. Bishop Zong Huaide was elected chairman of the group, which complied with their government's insistence that they maintain no ties with the Vatican. (Bishop Deng Yiming of Canton, who favored Vatican links, was freed from prison in June after 22 years.) The similar "Three-Self" Patriotic Movement of Protestants was able to hold its first national congress in 20 years, in Shanghai at the end of February. It was attended by 200 persons.

In Taiwan, in early 1980, the regime arrested Kao Chun-ming, general secretary of the Presbyterian Church, on charges of fomenting revolution. He headed the country's biggest Protestant group, made up mostly of Taiwanese, rather than mainland Chinese. In June he was sentenced to a seven-year prison term.

In South Korea the new government continued the long-standing repression of Christians who seek democracy. Catholic layman Kim Dae Jung was sentenced to death in September, and five prominent Protestant colleagues were given prison terms ranging from 3 to 20 years.

In the Soviet Union, Gleb Yakunin, an Orthodox priest and human rights activist, was sentenced in August to five years in prison and five of internal exile for publicly protesting religious repression. Another well-known activist Orthodox priest, Dmitri Dudko, publicly confessed sup-

*Swiss-born Roman Catholic theologian Hans Küng, who had been banned from teaching Catholic theology at West Germany's Tübingen University, rouses students on Jan. 10 with his protest against the action. He remained head of the Institute for Ecumenical Research at Tübingen.*

Throughout 1980, John Paul enhanced his reputation as a shrewd, popular conservative. In January he held an unusual synod of Dutch bishops at the Vatican to treat tensions, decline, and dissent from papal policy. Although Dutch liberals won some points, the Vatican obtained major commitments from the bishops to stop treating celibacy as an "open" question, gradually remove married former priests from seminary faculties, prevent laity from performing priestly functions, end unauthorized Mass revisions, revive individual confession—nearly extinct in the Netherlands—and stop Protestants from receiving Catholic Communion.

John Paul offered his personal explanation of the late 1979 Vatican declaration that West Germany's Father Hans Küng is no longer considered a "Catholic" theologian. In a letter to Germany's bishops, the pope defended limits to theological speculation and said "we should be profoundly fearful lest our belief in the gift of Christ which guarantees that faith, namely infallibility, be cast in doubt." Küng's status was settled on April 10. In a compromise, he left the Catholic faculty of the University of Tübingen but retained a university professorship and remained director of the Institute for Ecumenical Research.

To heighten the distinctiveness of priests, in May John Paul enforced (without a decree) his policy against clergy in elective office. The Reverend Robert F. Drinan (D, Mass.) obeyed his Jesuit superiors and did not seek reelection as a U.S. Representative.

The Vatican issued new rules in the fall that

posed crimes against the state in June after months in prison. The Soviets also arrested Viktor Brailovsky, a cybernetics expert and editor of an underground journal, and other prominent Jewish activists during the year.

### INTERNAL CHURCH AFFAIRS

Events within the Christian churches followed familiar lines.

**Roman Catholic Church.** Pope John Paul II presided over his first international—the fifth—Synod of Bishops in September, with controversial family issues as the topic. John R. Quinn, archbishop of San Francisco and president of the National Council of Bishops, and other Western bishops stated frankly that numerous Catholics neither understand nor obey the church ban on artificial birth control, but the synod's public message reaffirmed the ban. The Vatican did not make public any of the synod's dozens of proposals to the pope, but reportedly the bishops asked for a study of possible slight liberalization of the ban on Communion for divorced Catholics who remarry, such as the Eastern Rite Catholic policy of permitting this action if a spouse is unjustly abandoned. The pope's closing statement made it clear that any person who leaves a spouse and has sexual relations with another person cannot receive Communion. A divorced person who remarries must abstain from all sexual relations with the second spouse in order to receive the Host.

**Dial-an-Atheist**

In many U.S. cities it is possible to dial a specified telephone number and receive a short message of spiritual uplift—Dial-a-Prayer, this service is called. In Chicago during 1980, the loyal opposition took advantage of the constitutional guarantee of free speech and instituted its own service. A message recorded by Troy Soos, a 22-year-old disciple of atheist activist Madalyn Murray O'Hair, stated, among other things, that the Bible was a "fictitious novel." In spite of violent vilification from some of the callers who replied to his message, Soos claimed that during Dial-an-Atheist's first six weeks his organization added the names of 70 new supporters to its mailing list.

In West Germany, the Bavarian village of Oberammergau's 1980 production of the Passion Play, staged every ten years, again aroused Jewish and even local protests over what critics described as the play's strident assertion of collective Jewish guilt for the death of Jesus.

basically limited dispensations from priestly vows to men who had long since deserted priestly life, to those proven not to have taken vows freely, and to those proven to have been ordained without sufficient scrutiny of their fitness for the priesthood.

The pope conducted long, triumphant tours across Africa in May and Brazil in July. To Brazilians, the largest nominal Catholic population of any nation, he spoke strongly for socioeconomic justice, tending in his remarks to support the activist hierarchy; see BRAZIL. In his second encyclical, *Dives in Misericordia* ("On the Mercy of God"), issued in December, he expanded his discussion of justice, which "constitutes . . . the goal of forgiveness" and is founded in "that kindly love that we call mercy."

In January, John Paul named William W. Baum, archbishop of Washington, D.C., as prefect of the Congregation for Catholic Education, making him the ranking American in the Vatican and only the third person from the U.S. to head a major Vatican agency. In June the pope named Archbishop James A. Hickey to the Washington see. Hickey had served as bishop of Cleveland since 1974. During the year, Vatican offices also issued decrees opposing widespread abuses in the Mass; reaffirming opposition to euthanasia, but repeating that extraordinary and burdensome means are not morally required to prolong life when death is inevitable; and formally reopening the case of Galileo, condemned for heresy in the 17th century for maintaining that the earth revolves around the sun.

**Protestant Churches.** In July the United Methodist Church became the first major U.S. denomination to elect a woman bishop. Marjorie S. Matthews, a former district superintendent in Michigan, was assigned as bishop for Wisconsin. The Methodists' General Conference in April retained its official policy against homosexual practice but rejected conservative appeals to ban ordination or appointment of practicing homosexuals in the clergy, apparently leaving this an option for local units.

The United Presbyterian Church suffered a small schism of conservatives after its annual General Assembly (at the end of May) tightened control over congregations' property, and repeated that local churches must elect women as well as men to their boards. Dissidents felt this action violated the injunction of Saint Paul in 1 Timothy 2:12 ("I permit no woman to teach or to have authority over men; she is to keep silent") and denied the congregations' historic right to choose their own officers.

The annual Southern Baptist Convention in June chose Oklahoma pastor Bailey Smith, an outspoken advocate of total Bible inerrancy, as president and exhorted seminary boards to employ only teachers with a conservative view of the Bible. Concerning abortion, the nation's largest Protestant denomination dropped its moderate stand and called for laws or a constitutional amendment to forbid abortion except "to save the life of the mother." A new abortion policy was also passed by another large U.S. Protestant group, the American Lutheran Church.

## JUDAISM

Israel's declaration of united Jerusalem as its "eternal" capital produced a call for a *jihad* (holy war) from 43 foreign ministers of Muslim nations and criticism from the Central Committee of the WCC and the Vatican daily *L'Osservatore Romano*. The Vatican preferred an "international statute" to govern the holy city.

During the summer, Jewish organizations disagreed over how vehemently to oppose the 1980 rendition of West Germany's Oberammergau Passion Play. The townspeople who perform in the folk pageant once again revised it to meet accusations of anti-Semitism. Fears that anti-Semitism in France might be growing were stirred by a bombing outside a Paris synagogue in October that left four dead; *see* FRANCE.

In intra-Jewish affairs, the convention of rabbis in the Conservative branch endorsed the ordination of women rabbis and insisted that New York City's Jewish Theological Seminary act quickly on a tabled proposal to train and ordain women. The seminary later announced an $18,000,000 building program, in which quarters for its 200,000-volume library of Judaica were to be consolidated.

*See also* ISRAEL.

## ISLAM

The Islamic world was torn by conflict in 1980. In Iran the clergy under Ayatollah Ruhollah Kho-

meini consolidated control of state and society, winning out against religious and secular moderates and leftists. The Shi'ite Islamic regime apparently permitted harassment of Bahais and Christians, but it tried to placate Sunni Muslim opposition to the new constitution, which established Shi'ite Islam as the official religion of Iran. Although the ayatollah's movement justified the holding of the U.S. diplomatic hostages as Muslim justice, scholars of the Sunni branch, predominant in most nations, said this action violated the Prophet Muhammad's teachings. So—privately—did some Shi'ite scholars within Iran.

Two conferences of the world's Islamic foreign ministers met in Islamabad, Pakistan, to denounce the Soviet military occupation of Afghanistan and demand the immediate withdrawal of troops. Resistance to the Soviets persisted within Afghanistan, on both religious and nationalistic grounds.

Iraq, Iran's western neighbor, contains the major Shi'ite shrines and has a Shi'ite majority under a Sunni-dominated regime. When Iraq invaded Iran in September, Khomeini termed Iraqi President Saddam Hussein an "infidel" and called on his people to topple the government. Libya's Muammar el-Qaddafi sided with Iran and called for a *jihad* to "liberate the House of God in Mecca"—that is, overthrow the Saudi Arabian monarchy, which backed Iraq. Hussein, too, referred to

*At a world Islamic conference held in Islamabad, Pakistan, in January, Afghanistan's empty seat underscores the rift between Muslim nations and the Marxist regime installed in Afghanistan following the December, 1979, invasion of that country by the Soviet Union.*

Japanese Buddhist monks head a seven-nation gathering in September as they inaugurate a peace pagoda that they constructed at Milton Keynes, a town recently developed in Berkshire, not far from London.

the Iraqi campaign in religious terms, reminding his people that the Arabs had brought Islam to Persia (now Iran).

In Syria the regime crushed violent subversion by Sunni militants against the government, which was dominated by heterodox Alawites. In May, Egyptian voters ratified a constitutional amendment making *shari'a* (religious law) "the" rather than "a" principal source of law. In March leaders of the Coptic Christian minority in Egypt charged that the community was being subjected to growing Muslim harassment and called upon Copts to abstain from customary Easter celebrations in protest. In India, Muslims in Uttar Pradesh state rioted in August upon rumors that police had desecrated a mosque. Clashes between majority Hindus and the Muslims left more than 150 dead, most of them Muslims.

### BUDDHISM
In its move to restore limited religious liberty, China permitted some temples to reopen and some Chinese to start training as monks. In Tibet the Dalai Lama's home monastery, which once housed 10,000 monks and currently had 170, took its first novices since 1959. China made overtures to the Dalai Lama, exiled former spiritual and temporal ruler of independent Tibet, indicating a wish that he return but serve only in his religious role. The Dalai Lama said he would return if it were the Tibetans' will, praising Chinese national policies but criticizing local Tibetan conditions. In October in Montréal, however, he said that he saw little chance of an early return. The Panchen Lama, who had cooperated with Peking's occupation but was later jailed anyway, was restored as a member of an advisory state council.

In a report from Indochina, *Time* magazine stated that after the Communist takeover of Cambodia (Kampuchea), 50,000 of the 80,000 monks were assassinated and most temples ravaged but the current regime was following the more tolerant line of its ally Vietnam. It was estimated during the year that one fourth of the Laotian populace had fled into Thailand during five years under Communism, in part to escape religious persecution.                                                                R.N.O.

**REPUBLICAN PARTY.** In a political renaissance unequaled since Dwight D. Eisenhower's landslide in 1952, the Republican Party erased the bitter memories of the Watergate scandal and regained control of the White House. Former California Gov. Ronald Reagan trounced incumbent President Jimmy Carter in the November election, winning 44 states and an electoral landslide. Riding the Reagan juggernaut and a rising conservative tide in the country, the party scored resounding triumphs in the congressional elections, wresting control of the U.S. Senate from the Democrats for the first time in 28 years and gaining 33 seats in the U.S. House of Representatives.

The party's main themes in 1980 were lower taxes, a balanced budget, fiscal restraint, and increased military expenditures. With a conservative majority in both houses of Congress, the Re-

The Republican Party's national convention adopted a party platform that called for a constitutional amendment limiting abortion. Here antiabortion convention delegates applaud the party's Presidential nominee, Ronald Reagan, who supported their stand.

publicans were poised to convert their campaign rhetoric into political reality during the Reagan administration.

**Campaign for the Nomination.** As the primary season approached in January, Reagan was considered the front-runner in a crowded field of aspirants including Senate minority leader Howard Baker, former Texas governor and Nixon administration official John B. Connally, former Central Intelligence Agency director and emissary to China George Bush, and U.S. Representatives John B. Anderson and Philip M. Crane of Illinois. But Bush shocked Reagan in the Jan. 21 precinct caucuses in Iowa, benefiting from superior organization and Reagan's decision not to debate there. Reagan rebounded in the Feb. 26 New Hampshire primary, swamping Bush by better than 2-to-1 after a strong showing in a debate with the major competitors.

After dismal showings in the early going, Connally and Baker withdrew, while Anderson decided to run as an independent, narrowing the contest to a Reagan-Bush race. Reagan continued to win easily in several Southern and Midwestern primaries, although Bush doggedly hung in with wins in Connecticut on March 25 and Pennsylvania on April 22. Reagan delivered the clincher in Bush's own state by winning the May 3 Texas pri-

mary, but Bush remained in the race, winning in Michigan on May 20. With the situation all but hopeless, Bush conceded to Reagan on May 26. In all, Reagan won 28 primaries to Bush's 7 and assured himself of a first-ballot nomination.

**The Convention.** With Reagan's nomination on ice, the Republican National Convention, held from July 14 to 17 in Detroit, was expected to be little more than a coronation. Instead, it was the backdrop for one of the most exciting dramas in modern U.S. political history—Reagan's attempt to draft former President Gerald R. Ford as his running mate.

Ford and Reagan had been bitter political enemies, with Ford believing that Reagan's challenge to him in the 1976 primaries had contributed to his defeat by Carter. But Reagan was persuaded that having Ford as his running mate would form a "dream ticket." Reagan privately broached the idea to Ford on the second day of the convention and enlisted the help of such former Ford aides as Henry Kissinger and Alan Greenspan to convince Ford to agree. Ford remained skeptical but refused to close the door, and for 24 hours it appeared that political history was about to be made. According to news reports, however, Ford's aides demanded extraordinary powers for Ford that would have made him virtually a co-President. Reagan began having second thoughts, and shortly before midnight on July 16, Ford visited Reagan's suite to say that he had concluded the concept was unworkable. Reagan dashed to the convention hall and announced that his choice as running mate was Bush, the clear favorite before the flirtation with Ford.

In their nearly 40,000-word party platform, the longest in U.S. political history, the Republicans mentioned tax cuts 46 times. They also promised to increase arms spending sharply and balance the budget. The platform took no position on the ratification of the proposed Equal Rights Amendment. It called for a constitutional amendment against elective abortion and for the appointment of judges who, in effect, opposed abortion.

**Presidential Campaign.** Reagan's strategy was to make what he repeatedly termed Carter's "failed Presidency" the central campaign issue, with particular emphasis on tarring Carter for the country's economic miseries. He hammered away at Carter's inability to control inflation, unemployment, and soaring interest rates, and he also charged that a foreign policy of weakness and vacillation had tarnished U.S. prestige in the world.

But the strategy went awry in the first two weeks of the campaign when a series of Reagan gaffes focused press attention on his own fitness to be President rather than Carter's alleged failures. When Reagan suggested he might restore official relations with the Nationalist Chinese government on Taiwan, the People's Republic of China suggested relations with the United States would be harmed if Reagan were elected. Carter officials gleefully asserted that Reagan's grasp of foreign policy was naive and simplistic. Reagan was also damaged politically by an inaccurate assertion that Carter had begun his campaign in Alabama at the birthplace of the Ku Klux Klan. Reagan eventually recovered from these mistakes and began scoring with his critique of Carter's economic policies, but not before Carter had pulled even in the polls.

Many political analysts concluded that the decisive moment in the campaign was the televised

*Some of the Republican Party congressional members who supported Ronald Reagan early in his campaign and who also served as advisers are seen with the victorious Reagan in December.*

Rumanian President Nicolae Ceaușescu and his wife Elena are flanked by Sweden's King Carl XVI Gustaf and Queen Silvia in November. Ceaușescu made numerous foreign contacts during a busy year in which he also promoted his wife to the post of first deputy prime minister.

debate between Reagan and Carter on Oct. 28 in Cleveland. Reagan had ducked a two-way debate for weeks, holding out for a formula that included Republican-turned-independent Anderson, whose candidacy clearly was siphoning more votes away from Carter than Reagan. But, with his lead dwindling or gone, Reagan finally agreed to debate Carter alone, and the postmortems seemed to indicate that Reagan's genial, conversational performance had devastated Carter's strategy of persuading voters that Reagan was a dangerous lightweight whose views on arms control and military preparedness might lead the nation into a nuclear confrontation with the Soviet Union.

**Election Results.** In defeating Carter by a comfortable 8,300,000 votes in the popular balloting and by a 489-to-49 margin in electoral votes, Reagan made sizable inroads into traditional Democratic constituencies, gaining strong support among blue-collar voters in the industrial states and doing surprisingly well among Southern Democrats and Jewish voters. Reagan's landslide also helped revitalize the Republican Party and served notice that superior organization and more aggressive fund raising could offset the Democrats' numerical edge in party membership and would make the GOP a force even more to be reckoned with in the 1982 congressional elections.

See ELECTIONS. See also biographies of John B. Anderson, George Bush, and Ronald Reagan in the biography section of PEOPLE IN THE NEWS. T.D.

**RHODE ISLAND.** See STATISTICS OF THE WORLD.
**RHODESIA.** See ZIMBABWE.
**RUMANIA.** In 1980 Rumanian President Nicolae Ceaușescu continued to pursue policies that would ensure him firm domestic control and a greater degree of independence from Soviet dictates than was enjoyed by other Warsaw Pact nations.

**Domestic Affairs.** The cult of personality surrounding Ceaușescu and his family, many members of which held high office, bloomed during the year. On the occasion of the president's 62nd birthday, he was referred to in a sycophantic poem as "our lay god." In March, when he reshuffled the cabinet, Ceaușescu promoted his wife, Elena, to the post of first deputy prime minister.

Rumanians tendered Ceaușescu respect, but there was growing discontent over the quality of life he provided for them. In terms of personal freedom and consumer goods, Rumanians were worse off than any of their Warsaw Pact neighbors. Western newsmen visiting the country reported a climate of fear and passivity. Along with the worldwide energy crisis, exacerbated by the fact that Rumania, once one of the leading oil producers in the world, had found it necessary to import difficult-to-obtain foreign oil for its industry and petrochemical plants, this mood contributed to a slowing of the growth rate. While national income reportedly rose 7.6 percent as recently as 1978, the 1980 estimate was 3 or 3.5 percent.

Despite public grumbling, Ceauşescu made no real reforms. After strikes broke out in Poland during the summer, the Rumanian Communist Party newspaper *Scinteia* sternly warned Rumanians that such actions "cannot resolve but only complicate economic problems." In August Ceauşescu postponed a trip to Jordan to keep a close eye on the domestic scene. He attempted to placate the public by promising to cut defense spending and improve living standards.

**Foreign Affairs.** Rumania withheld approval of the Soviet invasion of Afghanistan. At the United Nations in January, 1980, the Rumanians abstained on a resolution calling for withdrawal of foreign troops from Afghanistan; other Soviet allies voted against the resolution. When Soviet Foreign Minister Andrei Gromyko called on him in February, Ceauşescu again refused to follow the Kremlin line on Afghan policy.

The Rumanian president maintained a wide network of foreign contacts to enlarge his room for international maneuver. During 1980 he met with the heads of state of France, Jordan, Zaire, Guinea, and North Korea and with British Prime Minister Margaret Thatcher, U.S. Vice-President Walter F. Mondale, and Chinese Communist Party Chairman Hua Kuo-feng (Hua Guofeng).

*See* STATISTICS OF THE WORLD. F.W.

**RUSSIA.** *See* UNION OF SOVIET SOCIALIST REPUBLICS.

**RWANDA.** *See* STATISTICS OF THE WORLD.

# S

**SAHARA, WESTERN.** *See* AFRICA; MOROCCO.

**ST. LUCIA.** *See* STATISTICS OF THE WORLD.

**ST. VINCENT AND THE GRENADINES.** *See* STATISTICS OF THE WORLD.

**SAMOA, AMERICAN.** *See* STATISTICS OF THE WORLD.

**SAMOA, WESTERN.** *See* WESTERN SAMOA.

**SAN MARINO.** *See* STATISTICS OF THE WORLD.

**SÃO TOMÉ AND PRÍNCIPE.** *See* STATISTICS OF THE WORLD.

**SASKATCHEWAN.** *See* STATISTICS OF THE WORLD.

**SAUDI ARABIA.** In 1980 the Saudi monarchy sought to strengthen itself both domestically and regionally against attempts by revolutionaries to undermine the regime.

**Internal Developments.** In early January, 63 Muslim fundamentalists, including their leader, Juselman bin Seif al-Oteibi, were publicly beheaded for their participation in the two-week seizure of the Grand Mosque in Mecca in November, 1979. It was the largest mass execution in Saudi history.

To counteract the charges of this group that the Saudi monarchy had betrayed Islam, Islamic law was more strictly enforced than before. Shopkeepers had to close for observance of the five times of daily prayer, more religious programs were scheduled on radio and television, the employment of women was restricted, and photographs of women were not allowed to appear in newspapers. In addition, members of the royal family made more public appearances and continued to lavish gifts on tribal leaders.

Major changes in senior civil and military personnel also occurred in early January, reportedly because of the mosque seizure and Shi'ite Muslim unrest in the oil-rich Eastern Province in late 1979 that left scores dead and wounded. Shi'ite Muslims, who reportedly felt they were second-class citizens in a country in which the majority are Sunni Muslims, had been targets of broadcasts from Shi'ite Iran, which was trying to export its Islamic revolution.

In May, Saudi Arabia began an ambitious third five-year plan (1980–85) of industrial and agricultural development that would cost an estimated $290 billion. The plan included an overhaul of the education system.

***Death of a Princess.*** Saudi relations with Great Britain and the United States became strained in the spring after television networks in both countries ignored Saudi requests to cancel telecasts of the British-made film *Death of a Princess*, a fictionalized account of the 1977 execution of a married Saudi princess, who was the grandniece of King Khalid, and her lover on charges of adultery. The Saudis denounced the film as an "unprincipled attack" on Islam and as a distortion of the values of their society. After its British telecast in April, Saudi Arabia suspended normal relations with Great Britain and barred British business from lucrative construction contracts. Relations were resumed in July.

**Oil.** Saudi Arabia, the world's leading oil exporter, kept production at 9,500,000 bbl a day as a means of fostering an oil glut that would force a return to uniform pricing by other members of the Organization of Petroleum Exporting Countries (OPEC). The Saudis did not raise their oil prices as high as other OPEC members. Because the Iran-Iraq war caused a sharp decline in oil exports from those countries, Saudi Arabia in October increased production to 10,300,000 bbl a day.

Saudi Arabia signed joint venture deals that would give it the capacity to produce large quantities of refined oil products and basic petrochemical commodities by 1985. It sold an increased amount of its oil to companies involved in Saudi industrial projects. And in September the government completed its takeover of the Arabian-American Oil Co. (Aramco) by purchasing the 40 percent owned by four U.S. companies.

**Other International Developments.** In 1980 the Saudis pressed in vain their long-standing request for bomb racks and refueling equipment for 60 U.S.-made F-15 fighter jets that were to begin arriving in 1981. Because this equipment would give the Saudis the capability of attacking Israel, there was considerable U.S. opposition. Saudi Arabia was also unhappy about U.S. plans to build up its strategic petroleum reserve, since a large stock-pile of oil would reduce Saudi leverage on Washington's policies.

After the outbreak of the Iran-Iraq war, Saudi Arabia remained officially neutral but gave tacit support to Iraq, reportedly agreeing to make the port of Jidda available to Iraqi-bound cargo ships if the Jordanian port of 'Aqaba became overburdened. According to a Nov. 20 report, military supplies were being unloaded at three Saudi ports and sent to Iraq by truck.

The Saudis requested and received in October four U.S. Air Force radar and command planes (AWACS—Airborne Warning and Control Systems) and 300 U.S. personnel to man them because they were afraid their eastern oilfields were vulnerable to Iranian air attacks. Later in October the U.S. sent a mobile ground radar station and another 96 airmen to eventually replace the AWACS, and two aerial refueling tanker planes that would meanwhile enable the AWACS to stay in the air longer. After Libya demanded the removal of the AWACS and threatened to strike at

*Saudi Arabia's royal family was infuriated in 1980 when U.S. and British television networks aired* Death of a Princess, *a dramatization of the 1977 execution of King Khalid's grandniece and her lover on charges of adultery. In this scene, the princess lies dead, in black, as her lover is beheaded.*

*In 1980, construction was under way on a terminal for Muslim pilgrims going to Mecca, Saudi Arabia. The terminal at the Jidda airport was to be a structure of 210 fiberglass tent units, forming, it was believed, the largest covered area in the world—105 acres. It was designed to accommodate as many as 80,000 pilgrims.*

them, Saudi Arabia severed diplomatic relations with Libya on Oct. 28. The Iran-Iraq war also caused the Saudis to subject Saudi Shi'ites and Palestinians to new restrictions because of suspected ties with Iran.

The Saudis continued to support the Arab cause against Israel. In August, Crown Prince Fahd called for a holy war against Israel because of its recent reaffirmation of its annexation of East Jerusalem.

*See* STATISTICS OF THE WORLD. *See also* MIDDLE EAST; ORGANIZATION OF PETROLEUM EXPORTING COUNTRIES. C.G.

**SENEGAL.** *See* STATISTICS OF THE WORLD.

**SEYCHELLES.** *See* STATISTICS OF THE WORLD.

**SIERRA LEONE.** *See* STATISTICS OF THE WORLD.

**SINGAPORE.** Singapore's durable Prime Minister Lee Kuan Yew continued in 1980 to govern the booming city-state with a firm and innovative hand.

On Dec. 23 Lee's People's Action Party (PAP) won a resounding electoral victory, retaining every single seat in the parliament for the fourth straight time. The government continued to control the press, and about 30 political prisoners remained in jail indefinitely without trial.

The election results gave Lee a mandate to carry out his stated objective of looking beyond the successes of the past and planning the future of the country's leadership and economy. At a 25th anniversary rally of the PAP in January, Lee identified seven younger party leaders as the country's

wave of the future. In June he advanced two of them: Tony Dan to be education minister and Suppiah Dhanabalan to be foreign minister.

In 1980 Singapore enjoyed Asia's highest standard of living after Japan, with a per capita annual gross national product of more than $3000. Inflation was running at 9 percent; unemployment was negligible. The growth rate was more than 10 percent. Lee, however, was convinced that Singapore would retain its competitive edge in foreign trade only by switching from labor-intensive industries to high-technology fields such as computer software.

In Lee's view, the Soviet threat to the region, in the form of Vietnamese aggression, outweighed the danger of China. Lee strongly condemned the Soviet intervention in Afghanistan, and in November he visited Peking for talks with top Chinese leaders. Although Singapore did not have diplomatic relations with China, the visit may have portended friendlier ties.

*See* STATISTICS OF THE WORLD. R.J.C.

**SOCIAL SECURITY.** Under the Social Security Disability Amendments of 1980, the total amount of family benefits payable to a disabled worker with dependents was limited to the lesser of 85 percent of average indexed monthly earnings or 150 percent of the primary insurance amount (but no less than 100 percent of that amount).

The number of years of low or no earnings excludable in computing disability benefits was also reduced. Dropout years could in future range from none for disabled workers under age 27 to five for those age 47 and over. For benefits payable after June, 1981, a disabled worker was allowed to drop additional years from the computation period if, for such years, the worker had a child under age 3 living with him or her and had no earnings. When child-care dropout years were used, the total number of child-care and regular dropout years could not exceed three.

**Work Incentive Provisions.** Generally effective December, 1980, these provisions included: (1) Social security disability benefits and supplemental security income (SSI) disability payments might be reinstated without a new disability application if, during the 15-month period following a trial work period, a person who had not recovered medically no longer engaged in substantial gainful activity; (2) Medicare protection would be provided during the automatic reentitlement period and for 24 additional months; (3) the nine-month trial work period would be extended to disabled widows and widowers; (4) certain impairment-related work expenses would be deducted from a disabled beneficiary's earnings in determining substantial gainful activity (SGA).

The following provisions were made effective January, 1981, for a three-year period only, pending a study of their effectiveness: (1) Disabled persons receiving SSI payments whose earnings equaled or exceeded the SGA level, and who continued to have a disabling condition, would be entitled to special benefits until their countable income reached the federal "break-even" point (at least $561 monthly for individuals, effective July, 1980) and would continue to be eligible for Medicaid and social services on the same basis as regular SSI recipients; (2) a blind or disabled SSI recipient would continue to be eligible for Medicaid and social services despite income above the break-even point as long as the person continued to have a disabling condition and met certain other criteria.

**OASDI Benefits and Changes.** Under the old-age, survivors, and disability insurance (OASDI) program, cash benefits of $9.1 billion were being paid in May, 1980, to 35,300,000 persons.

A 14.3 percent cost-of-living increase in social security benefits became effective in June, 1980, and was reflected in the July checks of all beneficiaries. As a result of the increase, the average monthly amount payable to a retired-worker couple, both members of which were receiving benefits, was $563. Monthly benefits for retired workers alone averaged $330.

**Medicare.** During the period October, 1978–September, 1979, $19.9 billion was disbursed from the hospital insurance trust fund for hospital and re-

lated benefits. A total of 27,459,000 aged or disabled persons were enrolled for these benefits as of July 1, 1979. In January, 1981, the amount the beneficiary pays before reimbursement occurs was to rise from $180 to $204 for the first 60 days and to $51 a day for the 61st to 90th days. For each of the 60-day nonrenewable lifetime reserve days after 90 days are used, all but $102 a day of expenses would be paid by the program. For care in a skilled nursing facility after the first 20 days, the beneficiary would pay $25.50 a day up to the 100th day.

Under Medicare's supplementary medical insurance program, about 26,757,000 aged or disabled persons were enrolled as of July 1, 1979, and were voluntarily paying premiums ($9.60 monthly from July, 1980) for medical care coverage. From July, 1979, through June, 1980, 141,998,000 bills were approved. For federal fiscal year 1980 (October, 1979, through September, 1980) payments of $9.17 billion were recorded in the central office file as an interim reimbursement amount.

**Other Programs.** Under SSI, payments totaling $614,700,000 went to 4,164,500 aged, blind, and disabled individuals in May, 1980. The 14.3 percent cost-of-living increase, effective in July, 1980, raised the maximum federal monthly payment levels to $238 for individuals and to $357 for couples.

Under the program of aid to families with dependent children, a total of $975,600,000 was paid in January, 1980. Payments averaged about $272 per family.

**SOLOMON ISLANDS.** *See* STATISTICS OF THE WORLD.

**SOMALIA.** The ongoing guerrilla war in Ethiopia's Ogaden region and the threat of starvation among ethnic Somalis fleeing the war dominated Somali affairs in 1980. Guerrillas, reportedly led by regular Somali troops, appeared firmly in control of the Ogaden countryside, while Ethiopian forces remained isolated in garrisons situated in the major towns.

Ethiopian air attacks, together with a severe drought, forced large numbers of nomadic Somali refugees to flee the Ogaden for safety in Somalia. By late 1980, United Nations sources estimated that more than 700,000 refugees were housed in about 30 camps, with an additional 700,000 to 1,500,000 scattered throughout the country. The government was unable to provide adequate help. International relief agencies provided $132,000,000 in food and other aid, with the United States supplying more than $70,000,000 in aid. Health and nutrition conditions among the refugees appeared to be gradually improving until, with the outbreak of the Iraq-Iran war, Soma-

*Above: Refugees fleeing into Somalia from the war-racked Ogaden region of Ethiopia receive food. Relief efforts were hampered, however, by bureaucratic inefficiency as well as the sheer size of the influx.*

*Below: The use of naval and air facilities at Berbera, a Somali port on the Gulf of Aden, was granted to the U.S. in August in exchange for military aid.*

lia's source of fuel was cut. Deprived of Iraqi oil and diesel fuel, Somalia found it increasingly difficult to transport supplies to the refugees, and within the camps diesel-powered water pumps and generators were crippled. Appeals to Arab oil producers and stopgap measures averted starvation, but conditions remained critical.

In August U.S. officials and Somali representatives had reached an agreement whereby American forces were granted the use of naval and air facilities. In exchange the U.S. promised to provide $25,000,000 in military aid in 1981, mostly for defensive arms, and additional sums in later years. Fearful that American equipment would be used in the Ogaden or ignite another war between Ethiopia and Somalia, Congress hesitated to approve the appropriations. The war between Iraq

and Iran heightened American concerns over security in the region, and, as a consequence, the U.S. House Appropriations Subcommittee approved the arms sale on Sept. 30. Approval was conditional, however, on verification that all of the regular Somali forces were removed from the Ogaden.

In other news, the People's Assembly (parliament) was convened on Jan. 24 for the first session in more than ten years. President Muhammad Siad Barre was reconfirmed as head of state on Jan. 26 for a six-year term. On Oct. 20, however, Siad Barre declared a state of emergency because of tribal dissidents and revived the Supreme Revolutionary Council, an organ of military rule that had held sway from 1969 to 1976.

*See* STATISTICS OF THE WORLD.                J.T.S.

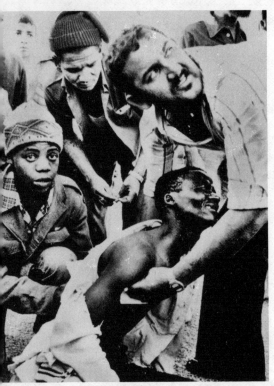

*A South African receives medical aid after being injured during rioting in July at Elsie's River, a mixed-race area near Cape Town. Street violence in such areas occurred during ongoing protests against inequities in the nation's segregated educational system.*

**SOUTH AFRICA.** Black militancy increased dramatically in South Africa in 1980. While the government responded, for the most part, by clamping down on activists, measures were introduced to ease restrictions on urban blacks.

**New Black Militancy.** A wave of major industrial strikes by black workers began in Port Elizabeth in November, 1979. By May the wildcat strikes had spread to Durban, Boksburg, and Cape Town. Labor unrest accelerated in July, with thousands of black workers protesting low wages and demanding recognition of black unions and the rehiring of dismissed workers. While most strikes against private firms ended in compromise settlements, strikes against government agencies were less effective. In July some 10,000 black municipal workers in Johannesburg walked off their jobs. The strike was broken on Aug. 1 after the city council forcibly deported some 1200 strikers to the Bantustan homelands of Transkei and Venda. Also in July more than 18,000 black construction workers struck and rioted at a government oil-from-coal complex. After a four-day layoff, the workers, who complained of military harassment, were back at work.

School boycotts began in April in the Coloured areas of the Cape peninsula. Focusing on the poor quality of schooling given Coloured, black, and Asian students and the disproportionate moneys spent on white education, the boycotts spread throughout the country and occurred at all levels of education. For the most part, provincial governments responded by arresting boycott organizers and closing the affected schools. In late September, 77 Coloured schools in Cape of Good Hope Province were closed after months of intermittent boycotts. Fort Hare University, the oldest black institution in South Africa, was closed indefinitely. On Nov. 11 the government announced that compulsory education for all black children would be phased in over several years.

A well-organized national campaign by black leaders was initiated in early 1980 with the objective of freeing Nelson Mandela, the president of the banned African National Congress. Imprisoned since 1964 under a life sentence without parole, Mandela was regarded by most black South Africans as the leader of the country's black nationalist movement. Although the campaign won widespread support among the black populace, the government gave no sign in 1980 that it would free Mandela.

Throughout the year the government stepped up its campaign against black, Coloured, and Asian militants, banning a number of prominent activists and arresting or detaining others. On June 13 the government banned all political meetings; this ban continued through August.

White South Africa received a severe shock on June 1, when black nationalists succeeded in sabotaging three major oil refining complexes. More than $1,900,000 in equipment and $5,400,000 in fuel were destroyed in coordinated attacks. Isolated attacks on police facilities also occurred during the year.

**New Government Initiatives.** Throughout 1980 Prime Minister Pieter W. Botha publicly stressed the need to relax restrictions on nonwhites. He reshuffled his cabinet in late August to weaken the conservatives within his government. At the end of October, draft legislation was circulated giving the descendants of blacks who resided legally in the country's urban areas the right to reside there. This proposal, if adopted, would in effect mark the end to the contention that blacks were only temporary residents in white areas. Officials also said that legislation would soon be introduced to eliminate a kind of internal passport that all blacks must carry when in areas designated as white.

The government was promoting a new multiracial President's Council, intended to replace the upper house of the parliament, as a major step forward in race relations, but critics derided the advisory body as insignificant. Of the 54 members nominated on Oct. 2, 39 were white, and none of the 15 Coloureds and Asians represented any political party. Plans for a separate black council were dropped because of opposition by black leaders.

**The Economy.** South Africa's economy remained strong and dominant in southern Africa. Increases in the price of gold, a major export, made it possible for the government to cut income taxes drastically in March.

See STATISTICS OF THE WORLD. See also AFRICA; SOUTH-WEST AFRICA.                                    J.T.S.

**SOUTH CAROLINA.** See STATISTICS OF THE WORLD.
**SOUTH DAKOTA.** See STATISTICS OF THE WORLD.
**SOUTH-WEST AFRICA,** also known as NAMIBIA. Throughout 1980 negotiations to bring independence to South-West Africa continued to be stalemated. In December, 1979, South Africa had indicated that it would agree to United Nations-supervised elections in the territory, which it had administered since 1915, if it could maintain troops on the South-West African side of a proposed 62-mi.-wide demilitarized zone on both sides of the border with Angola and Zambia. The entire zone would also be policed by U.N. forces instructed to prevent armed groups passing in either direction. South Africa also stipulated that the movement fighting for independence, the South-West Africa People's Organization (SWAPO), must be disarmed after the elections. After

A South African soldier guards Soviet-made weapons captured during a June raid on South-West African (Namibian) guerrilla bases in neighboring Angola. Angola was supporting the guerrillas in their efforts to gain independence for South-West Africa from South Africa.

Members of a political group in South-West Africa (Namibia) demonstrate in Windhoek, the territory's capital, in July. The demonstrators were demanding that South Africa grant South-West Africa its long-delayed independence.

*Vietnamese cosmonaut Pham Tuan (left) and Soviet space veteran Viktor V. Gorbatko were launched toward the earth-orbiting laboratory Salyut 6 on July 23. The flight was part of the Soviet Union's Intercosmos program for sharing the experience of space exploration with nations that are members of the program. They boarded the space station and conducted research, returning to earth on July 31.*

protracted negotiations, it was proposed in June that South Africa could maintain 20 bases in its half of the zone, while Zambian and Angolan troops would have 7 bases in their half. South Africa then questioned the impartiality of U.N. officials because a U.N. Security Council resolution had described SWAPO as the sole and authentic representative of the territory's people. South African officials refused to meet with a U.N. mission until late October; discussions in Pretoria then ended after four days in apparent failure.

On Nov. 24 the U.N. announced that South Africa had agreed to a cease-fire in March, 1981, on the condition that "trust and confidence" could be established among all the parties, including SWAPO, at a January, 1981, conference. Election of a constitutional assembly would be held before the end of 1981. Observers were not sure whether this agreement was a true breakthrough or merely another South African holding action.

The guerrilla war passed through its fifteenth year in 1980. SWAPO continued its hit-and-run attacks on isolated white farms, vehicles, and power lines, while South African forces made periodic sweeps through southern Angola to destroy SWAPO bases and supplies. In June, for example, South African forces struck deep into Angola, claiming to have killed about 360 guerrillas and seizing 100 tons of equipment, but at a cost of 17 of their own soldiers killed. The raid was strongly criticized at the U.N.

*See* STATISTICS OF THE WORLD. J.T.S.

**SOVIET UNION.** *See* UNION OF SOVIET SOCIALIST REPUBLICS.

**SPACE SCIENCE AND EXPLORATION.** In 1980 two Soviet cosmonauts established a new endurance record for humans in space. The United States was again forced to delay the first orbital flight of its space shuttle, but the National Aeronautics and Space Administration (NASA) achieved a spectacular success in space science as Voyager I photographed Saturn and its moons and Pioneer-Venus radar-mapped Venus's hidden surface. And India became the seventh nation to launch its own satellite into orbit.

**Soviet Missions.** The Soviet Union vigorously pursued its manned space program, with the apparent goal of a permanent space station in the 1980's. The focus of the 1980 missions was the Salyut 6 earth-orbiting laboratory, launched on Sept. 29, 1977, and home for two cosmonauts for a record-breaking 175 days in 1979. On April 9 one of those cosmonauts, Valery V. Ryumin, was launched with Leonid I. Popov in Soyuz 35 for an even longer occupation of Salyut. A prime goal of the mission was a photographic survey of Soviet agriculture. The cosmonauts also conducted medical, biological, and physical studies, made astronomical observations, and ran materials-pro-

cessing experiments using a variety of metals.

During their sojourn, the men were visited by four other crews for a few days at a time. Three missions were entries in the Soviet Intercosmos program, in which cosmonauts from the program's member nations formed part of the mission crews. On May 26 Hungarian Bertalan Farkas was sent aloft with Valery Kubasov; on July 23, Vietnamese Pham Tuan and Viktor V. Gorbatko were orbited; and on Sept. 18, Cuban Arnaldo Tamayo Méndez and Yuri Romananko sped toward Salyut 6. (Rumanian and Mongolian cosmonauts were yet to have their turn.) Such flights were mainly of propaganda value to the Soviet Union, demonstrating its willingness to share spaceflight with other countries.

The fourth mission to join Ryumin and Popov was more important technologically because cosmonauts Yuri V. Malyshev and Vladimir V. Akse-

*Working on the U.S. space shuttle* Columbia, *a technician uses a non-metallic scraper to clean one of the cavities on the fuselage and wings. Nearly 31,000 thermal tiles had to be bonded on the surface of the craft in order to protect its crew from the heat of atmospheric reentry. The need to strengthen the fragile tiles was one reason for the years-long delay in the program.*

*The Solar Maximum Mission earth satellite was launched by NASA on Feb. 14 to observe solar flares during a period of heightened activity on the sun's surface. Equipped with seven telescopes that operate at wavelengths ranging from visible light to gamma rays, it weighs 5100 lb.*

nov, who were launched on June 5, flew an advanced craft called Soyuz T2 that gave them greater independent control over navigation than on previous Soyuz flights. A further advance came on Nov. 27, when Leonid Kizim, Gennady Strekalov, and Oleg Makarov were sent in Soyuz T3 for a short stay on Salyut. This was the first three-man Soviet crew in space since the deaths of three cosmonauts in 1971.

Prior to the arrival of Soyuz T3, Ryumin and Popov had returned to earth on Oct. 11 after a record 185 days in orbit. Both men appeared in excellent health and had even gained weight.

**Space Shuttle Woes.** The U.S. space program, which had chosen the different tack of developing a reusable shuttle that could service spacecraft and serve as a launch platform, was experiencing difficulties. Many thousands of the delicate tiles that were to serve as thermal protec-

tion during atmospheric reentry had to be replaced on the shuttle, a slow and costly process. In November the shuttle, *Columbia,* at last was moved from its hangar and prepared for a manned launch in early 1981, more than two years behind schedule. Another hurdle remained: the final testing of the orbiter's main rocket engines, which had performed poorly on several occasions. One reason for these setbacks, said NASA, was that the program had been underfunded from the start, so that NASA had been unable to explore several different technological routes at the same time.

Payload bookings for the shuttle were filled through 1984, but some slated participants were growing nervous. A few took the precaution of reserving launch times with Arianespace, a newly formed and mainly French-owned corporation. (The Ariane rocket, Arianespace's launch vehicle, exploded during a test in May, however, and further tests were not scheduled until 1981.) Nevertheless, NASA selected 19 more astronauts for its shuttle program, including two women, one black man, and one Hispanic man, for a total of 62 astronauts for the space shuttle program.

**Other NASA Activities.** NASA achieved remarkable successes in 1980 with its Voyager I and Pioneer-Venus probes and the Solar Maximum Mission Satellite; see ASTRONOMY. However, as budget cutbacks forced the cancellation of some major projects, and budget and shuttle problems caused the delay of others, the space agency seemed to be coming to the end of an era of program development in space research.

To some observers, NASA's future role in space appeared likely to be reduced to the servicing and launching of spacecraft for other agencies, organizations, and nations. For example, Geostationary Operational Environmental Satellite 4 (GOES 4), launched by NASA in September to photograph weather and measure atmospheric temperatures and moisture at various altitudes, was in fact supervised by the National Oceanic and Atmospheric Administration. NASA's own shuttle would carry primarily non-NASA payloads. And of the next 17 satellites to be launched by the space agency in 1981, only two of them were developed by NASA.

**Communications Satellites.** In 1980 the first of three communications satellites was orbited by NASA for Satellite Business Systems Co. (SBS).

---

**Blast Off with the Sundance Kid**

A story published in *Parade* magazine during the year brought an unexpected (and unappreciated) $7000 windfall to the National Aeronautics and Space Administration. It arrived in the form of fourteen $500 checks from individuals who wanted to make reservations to ride on the space shuttle. The magazine article, which first listed the names of several celebrities who had expressed interest in riding the shuttle, went on to state that scientists could reserve space for experimental (nonhuman) payloads on forthcoming flights, at $500 per experiment. Confused readers thought the celebrities as well as the scientists were booking space. So some 200 of them sent letters, including one couple who requested seats next to screen actor Robert Redford, one of those mentioned.

---

Owned by International Business Machines Corp. (IBM), Aetna Life & Casualty Co., and Communications Satellite Corp. (COMSAT), SBS was to provide high-volume data transmission services. The satellite had ten channels, each able to provide nearly 200,000 words or items of information per second. NASA also launched two satellites that completed the U.S. Navy's global communications network. In December the Federal Communications Commission approved the building of 20 new communications satellites for eight different companies by 1983.

In 1980 Honduras and Niger joined the International Telecommunications Satellite Organization (Intelsat), increasing its membership to 104 nations, and in December Intelsat 5 was launched. The first of Intelsat's new series of communications satellites, it was able to handle 12,000 two-way telephone circuits and two-color television transmissions. In addition, an agreement was reached to establish an Arabsat regional satellite communications system that would use two satellites to provide communications and television service to 16 Middle Eastern countries.

**Other Space Developments.** In January Landsat 2, one of two NASA satellites for scientific observation of the earth's resources, was deactivated because of a malfunction. In June, however, NASA technicians managed to restore the spacecraft to operational status.

India became the seventh nation to launch its own satellites when it sent a 35-kg (77-lb.) test satellite into orbit in July. (The Soviet Union had launched India's two previous satellites.) The other members of the space-launch club, in addition to the U.S. and the Soviet Union, were China, France, Great Britain, and Japan.          F.C.D. III

**SPAIN.** In 1980 Spain completed more than three years of parliamentary democracy under Premier Adolfo Suárez González and his party, the Union of the Democratic Center (UCD), but the country was troubled by persistent economic and political problems.

**Politics.** Head of government since July, 1976, and a key figure along with King Juan Carlos I in the Spanish transition to democracy, Suárez had to deal with important challenges to his stewardship in 1980, especially the demand for devolution of tax and police powers to the regions. The government was caught in a withering cross fire between conservative groups that opposed most concessions to regional demands and left-wing terrorist groups such as ETA, which demanded outright independence for the Basque provinces. By early December the ETA had taken 84 lives in 1980.

The continued rise of regional sentiment found

RREFUXIATUAK EUSKADIN
AMNISTIA TOTAL
E.... .. H. P.T.E. E.E. L.K.I.

*A measure of regional autonomy was granted to the Basque provinces in 1980, but for some Basques nothing short of separation from Spain was acceptable. Assemblies such as this gathering of about 150,000 people in San Sebastián underscored the region's dissatisfaction with its political status.*

clear expression in March, 1980, elections in the Basque country and Catalonia, where parties committed to home rule won pluralities. The regional governments established after the elections demanded more powers, including control over education, taxes, and police powers, than the national government was ready to yield. Suárez postponed devolution of these powers until 1983. UCD candidates fared poorly in both regional votes. The party's principal national challenger, the Socialist Workers' Party (PSOE), also fared poorly, however. In Andalusia, a majority of voters also backed regional autonomy, against Suárez's wishes. The proposal lost because it did not gain enough backing in one of the region's eight provinces. On Oct. 23 Suárez promised a new vote on Andalusian autonomy in 1981. Galicia voted for home rule on Dec. 22.

The poor UCD showing, bickering within the party, and a deepening economic crisis led to a ministerial shuffle in early May. On May 30 the government narrowly defeated a motion of censure presented by the PSOE. In September Suárez again reshuffled the cabinet. He promised new concessions on the autonomy question and won a new vote of confidence from the lower house of the parliament, 180–164, on Sept. 17.

**The Economy.** Economic problems proved difficult to resolve. Unemployment was in excess of 11 percent in 1980, and the gross national product was expected to rise only 0.5 percent during the year. The government presented a new economic program in early 1980 designed to reactivate the economy. It included reform of banking laws, liberalization of credit, subsidies for housing construction, and an effort to conclude a national wage agreement between business and labor. But the key problem remained to find ways of increasing exports to meet the growing cost of importing oil.

**Foreign Affairs.** The priority goal of Spanish foreign policy in 1980 remained entry into the European Community. Because of increasingly evident French opposition, however, the government came to realize that its hopes for full membership by 1983 were overly optimistic. Renegotiation of the military base agreement with the United States and possible Spanish entry into the North Atlantic Treaty Organization (NATO) were also issues. U.S. President Jimmy Carter visited Madrid on June 25 and urged Spain to apply for NATO membership, but the Socialist and Communist parties expressed their opposition.

On April 10 Spain announced it was ready to lift the land blockade of Gibraltar that it had imposed in 1969. Spain has called for the return of the 276-year-old British colony to its sovereignty, and Spanish officials said NATO entry was unthinkable before the question was settled.

*See* STATISTICS OF THE WORLD. E.M.L.

# SPORTS

Among the sports stars of 1980 were names both familiar and new. These included, to list just a few, George Brett, Earl Campbell, Earvin ("Magic") Johnson, Sugar Ray Leonard, Jack Nicklaus, Wayne Gretzky, and Björn Borg.

## AUTO RACING

Johnny Rutherford of Fort Worth, Texas, was the most productive American driver in 1980. He won the world's richest race ever, the $1,502,425 Indianapolis 500, on May 25 and finished second to Bobby Unser of Albuquerque, N.Mex., in the Pocono 500 on June 22 in Long Pond, Pa., and the California 500 on Aug. 31 in Ontario, Calif.

Because of a long-standing dispute between administrators and car owners, the more affluent Indy-car teams could not take full advantage of their turbochargers, and their cars never reached their potential speed. As a result, the Indianapolis 500 was the slowest in 18 years.

With regard to the Formula One Grand Prix races for the world driving championship, most car owners wanted more speed than the administrators of the races were willing to sanction. A ban was imposed for 1981 on lateral "skirts" that hold cars to the ground and thus permit higher and sometimes dangerous speeds on turns. The owners who opposed the ban responded by announcing their own championship series of races for 1981, but they later backed down.

There were 15 Grand Prix races, including one in Spain that lost its sanction because of the struggle between car owners and administrators. Alan Jones of Australia won six races, including the one in Spain, in a Williams-Ford, and Nelson Piquet of Brazil won three in a Brabham-Ford. Jones became the world champion.

The National Association for Stock Car Auto Racing ran a 31-race, $6,000,000 series for late-model sedans. Buddy Baker of Charlotte, N.C., driving an Oldsmobile, won the most celebrated race, the $663,250 Daytona 500, on Feb. 17 in Daytona Beach, Fla. Dale Earnhardt of Kannapolis, N.C., took the series title, usually driving a Chevrolet but sometimes an Oldsmobile.

## BASEBALL

The Philadelphia Phillies won the World Series by defeating the Kansas City Royals, 4 games to 2. The presence of these two teams was a new twist. The Phillies had won only two National League pennants in their previous 97 years and had never won a World Series. The Royals had never won a pennant in their 11 previous years, though, like the Phillies, they had just won their fourth division title in 5 years.

The biggest winners during the major-league season were the New York Yankees with 103 victories, the Baltimore Orioles with 100, and the Royals with 97. The Yankees, with starting pitchers aged 42, 39, 37, and 36, finished three games ahead of the Orioles in the American League East,

**NATIONAL LEAGUE**

| Eastern Division | W | L | Pct. | GB |
|---|---|---|---|---|
| Philadelphia Phillies | 91 | 71 | .562 | — |
| Montréal Expos | 90 | 72 | .556 | 1 |
| Pittsburgh Pirates | 83 | 79 | .512 | 8 |
| St Louis Cardinals | 74 | 88 | .457 | 17 |
| New York Mets | 67 | 95 | .414 | 24 |
| Chicago Cubs | 64 | 98 | .395 | 27 |

| Western Division | W | L | Pct. | GB |
|---|---|---|---|---|
| *Houston Astros | 93 | 70 | .571 | — |
| Los Angeles Dodgers | 92 | 71 | .564 | 1 |
| Cincinnati Reds | 89 | 73 | .549 | 3½ |
| Atlanta Braves | 81 | 80 | .503 | 11 |
| San Francisco Giants | 75 | 86 | .466 | 17 |
| San Diego Padres | 73 | 89 | .451 | 19½ |

* Won division in one-game playoff

**AMERICAN LEAGUE**

| Eastern Division | W | L | Pct. | GB |
|---|---|---|---|---|
| New York Yankees | 103 | 59 | .636 | — |
| Baltimore Orioles | 100 | 62 | .617 | 3 |
| Milwaukee Brewers | 86 | 76 | .531 | 17 |
| Boston Red Sox | 83 | 77 | .519 | 19 |
| Detroit Tigers | 84 | 78 | .519 | 19 |
| Cleveland Indians | 79 | 81 | .494 | 23 |
| Toronto Blue Jays | 67 | 95 | .414 | 36 |

| Western Division | W | L | Pct. | GB |
|---|---|---|---|---|
| Kansas City Royals | 97 | 65 | .599 | — |
| Oakland A's | 83 | 79 | .512 | 14 |
| Minnesota Twins | 77 | 84 | .478 | 19½ |
| Texas Rangers | 76 | 85 | .472 | 20½ |
| Chicago White Sox | 70 | 90 | .438 | 26 |
| California Angels | 65 | 95 | .406 | 31 |
| Seattle Mariners | 59 | 103 | .364 | 38 |

**PENNANT PLAYOFFS**
**National League**—Philadelphia defeated Houston, 3 games to 2
**American League**—Kansas City defeated New York, 3 games to 0

**WORLD SERIES**—Philadelphia defeated Kansas City, 4 games to 2

*Mike Schmidt, the Philadelphia Phillies slugger, leads his team to victory over the Kansas City Royals in the World Series. He was named most valuable player in both the Series and the National League.*

though they did not clinch the division title until the next-to-last day of the season. The Royals won the Western Division by 14 games, the only runaway victory in either major league. The Royals then won the pennant by beating the Yankees in three straight games.

The National League races were harrowing. In the East the Phillies and Montréal Expos, tied for first place, met in the last three games of the season. The Phillies won the first two games and the pennant.

In the West the Houston Astros started the final weekend three games ahead of the Los Angeles Dodgers, but when the Dodgers won all three games between them, they ended the season tied for first place. The next day, in a one-game playoff in Los Angeles, Houston won, 7–1. Philadelphia then beat Houston in the pennant playoff, 3 games to 2, with each game more exciting than the previous one. In the World Series, Oct. 14–21, the first played entirely on artificial turf, Philadelphia won in six games. Tug McGraw, the Philadelphia reliever, pitched in 9 of the club's 11 World Series and playoff games.

Mike Schmidt, the Philadelphia third baseman, was voted most valuable player in the World Series. The most valuable players during the regular season were Schmidt in the National League and George Brett, the Kansas City third baseman who batted .390 and was above .400 for weeks late in the season, in the American League. Steve Carlton of the Phillies won the Cy Young award as the best pitcher in the National League; Steve Stone of the Orioles won the award in the American League. J. R. Richard of Houston, perhaps the best pitcher in the sport, suffered a stroke on July 30, and his baseball future was uncertain.

Brett's effort to become the major leagues' first .400 hitter since Ted Williams in 1941 was hampered by injuries and ailments that sidelined him for 44 games. Between aches, he hit safely in 30 consecutive games, but the pressure to bat .400 was overwhelming.

Even so, there were rewards for Brett. The Royals increased his salary for the next two years and signed him for the years following that at $1,000,-000 a year. Houston signed pitcher Nolan Ryan in the free-agent draft for $1,167,000 a year. Relief pitcher Bruce Sutter of the Chicago Cubs received a $700,000 salary in arbitration. To keep their stars from declaring free agency, Philadelphia signed outfielder Garry Maddox for $700,000 a year, the St. Louis Cardinals gave first baseman Keith Hernandez $700,000 a year, and the New York Mets retained pitcher Craig Swan for $600,000 a year. In December outfielder Dave Winfield of the San Diego Padres, who had become a free agent, signed a ten-year contract with the Yankees that could bring him as much as $25,000,000, the richest pact in sports history.

On one hand, many club owners seemed willing to pay high salaries to free agents who had spent at least six years in the major leagues and whose contracts had expired. On the other hand, they wanted to discourage huge free-agent contracts. So the owners proposed that compensation for free agents consist of major-league players rather than college and high-school players.

The players rejected this idea, saying it would wreck free agency, and when negotiations with club owners for a new four-year contract proved unfruitful, the players voted on April 1 by 971 to 1 to cancel the remaining week of the exhibition season. They threatened a strike during the regular season if a new contract was not completed by May 22. Agreement was reached hours before that deadline, with the compensation issue put off until January, 1981.

The Mets and the Oakland A's acquired new owners. The Mets were sold for $21,000,000 to a group headed by Nelson Doubleday, a great-grandnephew of Abner Doubleday, who supposedly invented baseball. Charles O. Finley sold the A's for $12,700,000. Earlier, he hired the equally controversial Billy Martin as manager; Martin led the team through a surprisingly successful 1980 season.

Baseball writers voted Al Kaline and Duke Snider, outfielders who became baseball broadcasters, into the Baseball Hall of Fame in Cooperstown, N.Y. The veterans committee voted in posthumously Chuck Klein, an outfielder, and Tom Yawkey, who owned the Boston Red Sox.

## BASEBALL

Although other teams were more glamorous and attracted more attention, the Los Angeles Lakers and the University of Louisville won the major titles of the 1979–80 basketball season. The Lakers won the championship of the 22-team National Basketball Association (NBA), and Louisville captured the 48-team championship tournament of the National Collegiate Athletic Association (NCAA).

The Boston Celtics, with a 29–53 record the previous season, improved to 61–21, the best in the professional league. They had the rookie of the year in Larry Bird and the coach of the year in Bill Fitch. The Philadelphia 76ers had Julius Erving and other stars and a 6-ft.-11½-in. center in Darryl Dawkins, whose fierce slam dunks shattered glass backboards twice within a month.

The Lakers had new people, too—Earvin ("Magic") Johnson as a rookie guard, Jerry Buss as owner, and Jack McKinney as head coach. Early in the season, McKinney fell off a bicycle and suffered severe head injuries. Paul Westhead, his assistant coach, took over and led the Lakers to the championship. At season's end, Westhead was named head coach and McKinney moved to the Indiana Pacers.

The Lakers beat the 76ers, 4 games to 2 in the playoff finals. In the last game, played on May 16 in Philadelphia, Johnson moved to center because Kareem Abdul-Jabbar had badly sprained his left ankle in the previous game. Johnson responded with 42 points and 15 rebounds and was named most valuable player in the playoffs. Abdul-Jabbar, the NBA's regular-season most valu-

---

**NATIONAL BASKETBALL ASSOCIATION**
**1979–80 Regular Season**

**EASTERN CONFERENCE**

| Atlantic Division | W | L | Pct. | GB |
|---|---|---|---|---|
| Boston Celtics | 61 | 21 | .744 | — |
| Philadelphia 76ers | 59 | 23 | .720 | 2 |
| Washington Bullets | 39 | 43 | .476 | 22 |
| New York Knickerbockers | 39 | 43 | .476 | 22 |
| New Jersey Nets | 34 | 48 | .415 | 27 |

| Central Division | W | L | Pct. | GB |
|---|---|---|---|---|
| Atlanta Hawks | 50 | 32 | .610 | — |
| Houston Rockets | 41 | 41 | .500 | 9 |
| San Antonio Spurs | 41 | 41 | .500 | 9 |
| Cleveland Cavaliers | 37 | 45 | .451 | 13 |
| Indiana Pacers | 37 | 45 | .451 | 13 |
| Detroit Pistons | 16 | 66 | .195 | 34 |

**WESTERN CONFERENCE**

| Midwest Division | W | L | Pct. | GB |
|---|---|---|---|---|
| Milwaukee Bucks | 49 | 33 | .598 | — |
| Kansas City Kings | 47 | 35 | .573 | 2 |
| Chicago Bulls | 30 | 52 | .366 | 19 |
| Denver Nuggets | 30 | 52 | .366 | 19 |
| Utah Jazz | 24 | 58 | .293 | 25 |

| Pacific Division | W | L | Pct. | GB |
|---|---|---|---|---|
| Los Angeles Lakers | 60 | 22 | .732 | — |
| Seattle SuperSonics | 56 | 26 | .683 | 4 |
| Phoenix Suns | 55 | 27 | .671 | 5 |
| Portland Trail Blazers | 38 | 44 | .463 | 22 |
| San Diego Clippers | 35 | 47 | .427 | 25 |
| Golden State Warriors | 24 | 58 | .293 | 36 |

**PLAYOFFS**

**First Round**
Philadelphia defeated Washington, 2 games to 0
Houston defeated San Antonio, 2 games to 1
Seattle defeated Portland, 2 games to 1
Phoenix defeated Kansas City, 2 games to 1

**Conference Semifinals**
Boston defeated Houston, 4 games to 0
Philadelphia defeated Atlanta, 4 games to 1
Los Angeles defeated Phoenix, 4 games to 1
Seattle defeated Milwaukee, 4 games to 3

**Conference Finals**
Philadelphia defeated Boston, 4 games to 1
Los Angeles defeated Seattle, 4 games to 1

**Championship Finals**
Los Angeles defeated Philadelphia, 4 games to 2

*The NBA's most valuable player, Kareem Abdul-Jabbar of the Los Angeles Lakers, soars high above Darryl Dawkins of the Philadelphia 76ers to score in pro basketball's championship series. The Lakers won the series despite Abdul-Jabbar missing the final game because of injury.*

able player, watched the playoff finals on television at home.

De Paul University of Chicago was the outstanding team of the college season, winning 26 straight games before a 76-74 loss to Notre Dame on Feb. 27. But in the NCAA championships, favored De Paul was eliminated in the second round by the University of California, Los Angeles (UCLA).

The last four teams in the NCAA tournament were a strange mixture—Louisville, champion of the Metro Conference; Purdue, third in the Big Ten; Iowa, tied for fourth in the Big Ten; and UCLA, fourth in the Pacific 10. In the final, March 24 at Indianapolis, Louisville rallied in the last five minutes and beat UCLA, 59-54. Darrell Griffith, a senior guard, led Louisville's comeback, scored 23 points, and was named the tournament's most valuable player.

## BOATING

The United States, which had won all 23 previous challenges in 110 years, won again in 1980 in America's Cup yachting.

The winning sloop was *Freedom,* built in 1979 and skippered by Dennis Conner of San Diego, twice the Star Class world champion. First, *Freedom* eliminated *Courageous* (the 1974 and 1977 victor) and *Independence* in trials to select the American defender. Then it defeated the Australian sloop *Australia* in the cup races Sept. 16-25 off Newport, R.I., losing only one of the five races. *Australia,* also the challenger in 1977, had won an elimination series involving the three other potential challengers—*France 3, Lionheart* of Great Britain, and *Sverige* of Sweden.

In powerboating, Dean Chenoweth of Tallahassee, Fla., won the national unlimited hydroplane title in *Miss Budweiser* despite a midseason acci-

The 12-m yacht Freedom, the successful defender of the America's Cup, breezes home a victor over Australia, the challenger representing the nation whose name it bore.

dent that resulted in seven broken ribs. Bill Elswick of Fort Lauderdale, Fla., became national offshore champion in the 39-ft. Cigarette.

## BOWLING

Wayne Webb of Rehoboth, Mass., won the $150,000 Tournament of Champions; Steve Martin of Kingsport, Tenn., the United States Open; and Johnny Petraglia of Staten Island, N.Y., the Professional Bowlers Association (PBA) championship. Those were the most important of the 34 tournaments on the 1980 PBA tour, which carried prize money of $3,300,000. Webb won three tournaments and led in earnings with $115,080. Mark Roth of Little Silver, N.J., the leading money win-

ner the three previous years, won one tournament, took second four times, and finished second in earnings with $101,660.

On the women's tour, Pat Costello of Union City, Calif., won the United States Open and Donna Adamek of Duarte, Calif., the Women's International Bowling Congress Queens tournament. Adamek led in earnings with $26,232.

The most spectacular feat came on Aug. 25 in the first qualifying rounds of a Women's PBA tournament in Rochester, Minn. Pam Buckner of Reno, Nev., rolled 30 consecutive strikes, a women's record that produced two successive 300 games. On the 31st, she left the 10 pin standing.

*Roberto Durán (left) follows through on a left hook on his way to winning the welterweight title from Sugar Ray Leonard in Montréal on June 20. Leonard regained the title from Durán in New Orleans on Nov. 25.*

## BOXING

Sugar Ray Leonard of Palmer Park, Md., and Roberto Durán of Panama provided the major boxing excitement of 1980. Muhammad Ali provided the major disappointment.

Durán had renounced the world lightweight championship in 1979 after a seven-year reign. On June 20 in Montréal, with a punishing body attack, he took the World Boxing Council (WBC) welterweight title from the previously unbeaten Leonard on a unanimous decision. In a return bout on Nov. 25 in New Orleans, Leonard regained the title when Durán quit in the eighth round, saying he had stomach cramps. Leonard earned $9,500,000 for the first fight and $7,000,000 for the second. Durán earned $1,900,000 for the first fight and $9,500,000 for the second.

The outspoken Ali had not fought since September, 1978, and had not fought impressively for five years. At age 38, lured by $8,000,000, he ended his retirement and tried to become the first four-time winner of the heavyweight title. His opponent was Larry Holmes of Easton, Pa., who had knocked out Lorenzo Zanon, Leroy Jones, and Scott LeDoux earlier in the year in defenses of his WBC title (Mike Weaver of Pomona, Calif., held the World Boxing Association title). Holmes battered Ali badly and won on an 11th-round technical knockout. It was the first knockout defeat ever for Ali, who had held the heavyweight title most of the time since 1964.

## FOOTBALL

A bitter struggle over the future home of the Oakland Raiders almost overshadowed the National Football League's (NFL) exciting regular season and playoffs. Among the colleges, Ohio State, Alabama, and Notre Dame were ranked number one nationally before the University of Georgia took over and became unofficial national champion.

**College.** Of the 138 major college football teams, only Georgia finished the regular season undefeated and untied, with 11 victories in 11 games. But the Bulldogs did not assure themselves of the unofficial national championship until they defeated favored Notre Dame, 17–10, in the Sugar Bowl game on Jan. 1, 1981, in New Orleans.

Two days later, in their final polls of the season, the Associated Press and United Press International ranked Georgia number one. Each poll ranked Pittsburgh second, Oklahoma third, Michigan fourth, Florida State fifth, Alabama sixth, Nebraska seventh, and Penn State eighth.

Georgia's star was running back Herschel Walker, an 18-year-old freshman from Wrightsville, Ga. During the regular season, his 1616 yd. rushing broke the freshman record of 1586 by Tony Dorsett of Pittsburgh in 1973. In the Sugar Bowl, Walker gained 150 yd. on 36 carries and scored both Georgia touchdowns after Notre Dame fumbles.

George Rogers, a South Carolina senior, was the nation's leading runner with 1781 yd. and received the Heisman Trophy as the year's outstanding player. Hugh Green, a Pittsburgh defensive end, placed second in the Heisman voting. Walker was third, the highest finish ever by a freshman.

*Running back George Rogers of South Carolina, college football's leading rusher in 1980, with the Heisman Trophy he won as the outstanding college player of the year.*

No defensive player had ever won the Heisman Trophy, but Green did win the Maxwell and Walter Camp trophies as player of the year and the Vince Lombardi Award as the outstanding lineman. All-time passing records were broken by Neil Lomax of Portland (Oreg.) State, Jim McMahon of Brigham Young, Dave Wilson of Illi-

## NATIONAL FOOTBALL LEAGUE

### AMERICAN CONFERENCE

**Eastern Division**

| | W | L | T |
|---|---|---|---|
| Buffalo Bills | 11 | 5 | 0 |
| New England Patriots | 10 | 6 | 0 |
| Miami Dolphins | 8 | 8 | 0 |
| Baltimore Colts | 7 | 9 | 0 |
| New York Jets | 4 | 12 | 0 |

**Central Division**

| | W | L | T |
|---|---|---|---|
| Cleveland Browns | 11 | 5 | 0 |
| *Houston Oilers | 11 | 5 | 0 |
| Pittsburgh Steelers | 9 | 7 | 0 |
| Cincinnati Bengals | 6 | 10 | 0 |

**Western Division**

| | W | L | T |
|---|---|---|---|
| San Diego Chargers | 11 | 5 | 0 |
| *Oakland Raiders | 11 | 5 | 0 |
| Kansas City Chiefs | 8 | 8 | 0 |
| Denver Broncos | 8 | 8 | 0 |
| Seattle Seahawks | 4 | 12 | 0 |

### NATIONAL CONFERENCE

**Eastern Division**

| | W | L | T |
|---|---|---|---|
| Philadelphia Eagles | 12 | 4 | 0 |
| *Dallas Cowboys | 12 | 4 | 0 |
| Washington Redskins | 6 | 10 | 0 |
| St. Louis Cardinals | 5 | 11 | 0 |
| New York Giants | 4 | 12 | 0 |

**Central Division**

| | W | L | T |
|---|---|---|---|
| Minnesota Vikings | 9 | 7 | 0 |
| Detroit Lions | 9 | 7 | 0 |
| Chicago Bears | 7 | 9 | 0 |
| Tampa Bay Buccaneers | 5 | 10 | 1 |
| Green Bay Packers | 5 | 10 | 1 |

**Western Division**

| | W | L | T |
|---|---|---|---|
| Atlanta Falcons | 12 | 4 | 0 |
| *Los Angeles Rams | 11 | 5 | 0 |
| San Francisco 49ers | 6 | 10 | 0 |
| New Orleans Saints | 1 | 15 | 0 |

**AMERICAN CONFERENCE PLAYOFFS**
*Wild-Card Round
Oakland 27, Houston 7

**First Round**
Oakland 14, Cleveland 12
San Diego 20, Buffalo 14

**Championship**
Oakland 34, San Diego 27

**NATIONAL CONFERENCE PLAYOFFS**
*Wild-Card Round
Dallas 34, Los Angeles 13

**First Round**
Philadelphia, 31, Minnesota 16
Dallas 30, Atlanta 27

**Championship**
Philadelphia, 20, Dallas 7

**SUPER BOWL**
Oakland 27, Philadelphia 10

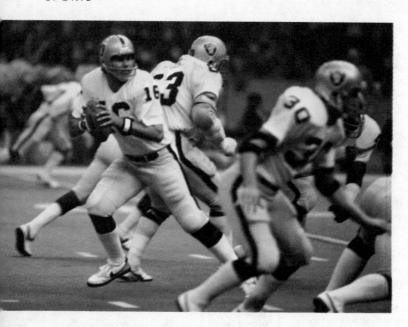

*Well protected by his team-mates, Oakland Raiders quar-terback Jim Plunkett threw three touchdown passes to lead his team to victory over the Philadelphia Eagles, 27-10, in professional football's Super Bowl XV.*

nois, Rich Campbell of California, and Mark Herr-mann of Purdue.

Several colleges were cited for recruiting viola-tions and tampering with the academic grades and credits of athletes, mostly football players. The hardest hit was the Pacific 10 Conference, which on Aug. 11 placed 5 of its 10 members, including Southern California and UCLA, on pro-bation for grade tampering.

**Professional.** The Oakland Raiders, a wild-card team, and the Philadelphia Eagles, a division champion, won the conference playoffs and met on Jan. 25, 1981, in Super Bowl XV in New Or-leans. Oakland won, 27-10.

The following is a sampling of regular-season performances:

Oakland—Surprisingly strong because of a sound defense. The offense was limited, although the Raiders won 9 of 11 games after Jim Plunkett, signed in 1979 as a free agent, replaced the in-jured Dan Pastorini at quarterback.

San Diego Chargers—Best offense and passing of the NFL's 28 teams. Dan Fouts passed for 4407 yd., breaking his year-old record of 4082. Kellen Winslow, John Jefferson, and Charlie Joiner led their conference in receptions and gained more than 1100 yd. each.

Cleveland Browns—Exciting because of Brian Sipe's passing and last-minute heroics.

Buffalo Bills—A young but good defense and reliable running.

Houston Oilers—Solid running from Earl Camp-bell, again the league leader. Steady short passing

from Ken Stabler, obtained in a trade for Pasto-rini. But when the Oilers lost their playoff opener, Coach O. A. ("Bum") Phillips was fired.

Philadelphia—Best defense in the league. Of-fense combined Ron Jaworski's passing and Wil-bert Montgomery's running.

Dallas Cowboys—Productive offense led by Danny White, who replaced the retired Roger Staubach at quarterback.

Atlanta Falcons—Exceptional front seven on defense helped win first division title in the team's 15-year history. Improved from 6-10 record in 1979 to 12-4.

Los Angeles Rams—Veteran team with an out-standing offensive line. Widespread dissension as many players, including quarterback Vince Ferra-gamo, attempted to renegotiate contracts.

Minnesota Vikings—Improving quarterback in Tommy Kramer. Made playoffs with 9-7 record by winning 6 of last 8 games.

Pittsburgh Steelers—The 1979 and 1980 Super Bowl winners failed to make the playoffs for the first time in nine years. Age caught up with Franco Harris, Rocky Bleier, and Mean Joe Greene.

Oakland had to win three playoff games to reach the Super Bowl. Its defense sacked Stabler seven times in a 27-7 victory over Houston on Dec. 28 in Oakland. An end-zone interception by Mike Davis with 41 sec. to play preserved a 14-12 upset of Cleveland on Jan. 4, 1981, in Cleveland. Then, in the American Football Conference final on Jan. 11 in San Diego, Oakland upset the Char-gers, 34-27, with opportunistic defensive plays.

Philadelphia won its playoff opener from Minnesota, 31–16, on Jan. 3 in Philadelphia by forcing the Vikings to make eight turnovers. In the National Football Conference final on Jan. 11 in Philadelphia, the Eagles stopped Dallas, 20–7, with Montgomery running for 194 yd.

Before the season the Rams moved from Los Angeles to Anaheim, a half-hour drive to the southeast. Al Davis, the managing general partner of the Raiders, then tried to move his team 400 mi. from Oakland to Los Angeles to take advantage of prospective profits from cable television.

Commissioner Pete Rozelle said NFL bylaws required a three-quarters vote from club owners before any move. Davis said no vote was needed. Shortly after the club owners voted by 22–0 on March 10 against the move, Davis decided to keep the team in Oakland in 1980, but he sued the NFL in federal court. Trial was scheduled for February, 1981.

**Canadian.** The Edmonton Eskimos won the Canadian Football League championship for the third consecutive year. In the Grey Cup game on Nov. 23 in Toronto, Edmonton overwhelmed the Hamilton Tiger-Cats, 48–10, the most lopsided Canadian final in 57 years.

## GOLF

Tom Watson of Kansas City, Mo., enjoyed the most lucrative season of any golfer in history and was named player of the year for the fourth consecutive year by the Professional Golfers' Association (PGA). Yet a strong case could have been made for Jack Nicklaus.

At age 40, playing in fewer than half of the tournaments, Nicklaus won two of the four major championships—the United States Open, June 12–15 in Springfield, N.J., and the PGA title, Aug. 7–10 in Rochester, N.Y. His 72-hole score of 272 was the lowest in Open history, and his winning margin of seven strokes was the largest in PGA history. Nicklaus thus extended his career record to 19 major titles.

In the other major tournaments, Watson won the British Open, July 17–20 in Muirfield, Scotland, and Severiano Ballesteros of Spain captured the Masters, April 10–13 in Augusta, Ga.

In 23 tournaments, Watson won seven times and placed in the first 10 nine other times. His victories included the World Series of Golf and the Tournament of Champions, both with small but elite fields. At year's end, Watson's $530,808 in earnings had broken his 1979 record of $462,636.

The leading money winners on the Ladies PGA tour were Beth Daniel, with $231,000, and Donna Caponi Young, with $220,619. Of the 38 tournaments, Young won six, JoAnne Carner five, and Daniel four. Daniel was named player of the year.

*Still a champ at age 40, Jack Nicklaus reacts gleefully as his final putt drops to clinch his victory in the PGA championship tournament on Aug. 10.*

Young's victories included the richest tournament, the $305,000 Colgate-Dinah Shore Winners Circle, April 3–6 in Rancho Mirage, Calif. Amy Alcott won the United States Women's Open, July 10–13 in Nashville.

## GYMNASTICS

Soviet gymnasts swept the major honors in 1980. The Olympic boycott, injuries, and Kurt Thomas's retirement ended American hopes for a strong international showing.

In the Olympics, the Soviet men were led by Aleksandr Ditiatin with eight medals (the maximum) and Nikolai Andrianov with five. Yelena Davidova, a late addition to the Soviet team, won the Olympic women's all-around title. She barely defeated Nadia Comaneci of Rumania and Maxi Gnauck of East Germany, who tied for second.

Bogdan Makuts and Stella Zakharova of the Soviet Union became World Cup all-around

### Girl Talk

Until just two weeks before the Kentucky Derby, trainer LeRoy Jolley had resisted entering his filly Genuine Risk. But he finally gave in to the wishes of her owners, Bert and Diana Firestone, and on May 3 Genuine Risk became the first filly to win the derby since Regret in 1915. Her overall time was not outstanding, but her time for the final quarter mile was an astonishing 24⅖ sec. Talk of a possible female Triple Crown winner was rampant. The filly and her jockey, Jacinto Vasquez, tried valiantly: On May 17 she was second in the Preakness; on June 7 on a sloppy track at the Belmont she finished second again. She was the first filly to compete—let alone place—in all three events of the Triple Crown.

*Genuine Risk.*

champions Oct. 24–26 in Toronto. Ditiatin, Davidova, Comaneci, and many other leading gymnasts bypassed this competition, as did Thomas of Mesa, Ariz., and Bart Conner of Morton Grove, Ill., 1979 world champions. Thomas had retired in June and Conner had a torn bicep. Jim Hartung of Omaha, the only American in the World Cup competition, finished 13th in the men's all-around.

### HARNESS RACING

The 3-year-old pacer Niatross broke almost every possible earnings and speed record in 1980 and again was voted harness horse of the year.

He won 25 of his 27 races, the last 18 in a row. He swept the triple-crown races—the Cane Pace, Little Brown Jug, and Messenger Stakes. His earnings for the year were $1,414,313, the most of any horse in any type of racing. His career earnings of $2,019,212 broke the all-time harness record of $1,964,573 established by the retired French trotter Bellino II.

Niatross broke the world one-mile records for a half-mile and one-mile track. His records included the fastest mile ever in a time trial (1 min. 49⅕ sec., Oct. 1 in Lexington, Ky.) and the fastest ever in a race (1 min. 52⅕ sec., Nov. 16 in Inglewood, Calif.).

Other outstanding horses included the 2-year-old pacer French Chef and the 3-year-old trotter Final Score. Land Grant won the richest horse race in history, the $2,011,000 Woodrow Wilson Memorial for 2-year-old pacers on Aug. 6 at the Meadowlands track in East Rutherford, N.J.

### HORSE RACING

The 4-year-old Spectacular Bid and the 3-year-olds Temperence Hill and Genuine Risk were thoroughbred racing's biggest winners in 1980.

Spectacular Bid won the Eclipse award as horse of the year. Temperence Hill was named 3-year-old colt of the year, and Genuine Risk was picked as the best 3-year-old filly.

Spectacular Bid won his nine races, including the $146,660 Woodward Stakes on Sept. 20 at Belmont Park, Elmont, N.Y., when no other horse opposed him. His career earnings of $2,781,607 broke Affirmed's all-time record of $2,393,818.

Spectacular Bid was syndicated for $22,000,000, a record for thoroughbreds, and retired to stud. The only higher syndication price for a horse was announced Oct. 28, a $30,000,000 package for Easy Jet, a 13-year-old quarter-horse sire.

Temperence Hill, named for a Methodist church near Fordyce, Ark., won 8 of 17 races and $1,130,452. He took the year's two richest races—the $549,000 Jockey Club Gold Cup on Oct. 4 at Belmont Park and the $500,000 Super Derby on Oct. 18 at Bossier City, La., each by 5½ lengths.

Genuine Risk captured the $339,300 Kentucky Derby on May 3 at Churchill Downs, Louisville, Ky., the first filly to win America's classic race since Regret in 1915. In the other Triple Crown races, Genuine Risk finished second to Codex in the $250,600 Preakness on May 17 at Pimlico in Baltimore and second to Temperence Hill in the $293,700 Belmont Stakes on June 7 at Belmont Park.

Chris McCarron, who won the most races and the most money, was chosen as jockey of the year. Bud Delp, the trainer of Spectacular Bid, was named trainer of the year.

### ICE HOCKEY

The Philadelphia Flyers started as if they would never lose a game. After a shaky beginning, the Montréal Canadiens played as if they would never

*The New York Islanders (white jerseys) swarm to defend their goal against the Philadelphia Flyers during the Stanley Cup finals of the National Hockey League. The Islanders won the championship series, 4 games to 2.*

lose a game. But in the end, the New York Islanders won the Stanley Cup and became National Hockey League (NHL) champions.

From Oct. 10, 1979, to Jan. 6, 1980, the Flyers won 25 games, tied 10, and lost none. The 35-game unbeaten streak, the longest in NHL history, ended Jan. 7 with a 7–1 loss to the Minnesota North Stars. The Flyers finished the regular season with the best record in the league.

The Canadiens, who had won the Stanley Cup the four previous seasons, had trouble acclimating to their new coach, Bernie ("Boom Boom") Geoffrion, and on Dec. 12, 1979, Geoffrion quit and was replaced by Claude Ruel.

The 21 NHL teams included Hartford, Edmonton, Winnipeg, and Québec, all absorbed when the World Hockey Association (WHA) dissolved after the previous season. Hartford and Edmon-

**NATIONAL HOCKEY LEAGUE**
**1979–80 Regular Season**

### PRINCE OF WALES CONFERENCE

| Norris Division | W | L | T | Pts. | Adams Division | W | L | T | Pts. |
|---|---|---|---|---|---|---|---|---|---|
| Montréal Canadiens | 47 | 20 | 13 | 107 | Buffalo Sabres | 47 | 17 | 16 | 110 |
| Los Angeles Kings | 30 | 36 | 14 | 74 | Boston Bruins | 46 | 21 | 13 | 105 |
| Pittsburgh Penguins | 30 | 37 | 13 | 73 | Minnesota North Stars | 36 | 28 | 16 | 88 |
| Hartford Whalers | 27 | 34 | 19 | 73 | Toronto Maple Leafs | 35 | 40 | 5 | 75 |
| Detroit Red Wings | 26 | 43 | 11 | 63 | Québec Nordiques | 25 | 44 | 11 | 61 |

### CLARENCE CAMPBELL CONFERENCE

| Patrick Division | W | L | T | Pts. | Smythe Division | W | L | T | Pts. |
|---|---|---|---|---|---|---|---|---|---|
| Philadelphia Flyers | 48 | 12 | 20 | 116 | Chicago Black Hawks | 34 | 27 | 19 | 87 |
| New York Islanders | 39 | 28 | 13 | 91 | St. Louis Blues | 34 | 34 | 12 | 80 |
| New York Rangers | 38 | 32 | 10 | 86 | Vancouver Canucks | 27 | 37 | 16 | 70 |
| Atlanta Flames | 35 | 32 | 13 | 83 | Edmonton Oilers | 28 | 39 | 13 | 69 |
| Washington Capitals | 27 | 40 | 13 | 67 | Colorado Rockies | 19 | 48 | 13 | 51 |
| | | | | | Winnipeg Jets | 20 | 49 | 11 | 51 |

### STANLEY CUP PLAYOFFS

**First Round**
New York Islanders defeated Los Angeles, 3 games to 1
Philadelphia defeated Edmonton, 3 games to 0
Buffalo defeated Vancouver, 3 games to 1
Minnesota defeated Toronto, 3 games to 0
Boston defeated Pittsburgh, 3 games to 2
New York Rangers defeated Atlanta, 3 games to 1
Montréal defeated Hartford, 3 games to 0
Chicago defeated St. Louis, 3 games to 0

**Second Round**
New York Islanders defeated Boston, 4 games to 1
Philadelphia defeated New York Rangers, 4 games to 1
Buffalo defeated Chicago, 4 games to 0
Minnesota defeated Montréal, 4 games to 3

**Semifinal Round**
New York Islanders defeated Buffalo, 4 games to 2
Philadelphia defeated Minnesota, 4 games to 1

**Championship Finals**
New York Islanders defeated Philadelphia, 4 games to 2

ton, among the 16 teams that gained the Stanley Cup playoffs, were eliminated quickly. Minnesota upset Montréal in seven games in the quarterfinals. The Islanders, with the most explosive attack in the league, beat Philadelphia in six games in the finals, which ended May 24.

The season also marked the NHL debut of 19-year-old Wayne Gretzky of Edmonton, a prodigy from the WHA. Gretzky became the youngest winner ever of an NHL individual award, gaining the Hart Trophy as the most valuable player and the Lady Byng Trophy for sportsmanship. He lost the Art Ross Trophy as scoring champion to Marcel Dionne of Los Angeles, though both scored 137 points, because Dionne had more goals, 53 to 51.

Dionne finished second to Gretzky in the voting for most valuable player, but Gretzky finished second to Dionne in the voting for all-star center. The other all-stars were Charlie Simmer of Los Angeles and Guy Lafleur of Montréal at the wings, Larry Robinson of Montréal and rookie Ray Bourque of Boston as defensemen, and Tony Esposito of Chicago as goalie.

### ICE SKATING

Eric Heiden of Madison, Wis., the world's best speed skater since 1977, reached the peak of his career in 1980 by winning all five men's events in the Winter Olympics.

The 21-year-old Heiden also gained his fourth straight world sprint championship, but Hilbert van der Duim of the Netherlands foiled his bid for a fourth straight world overall championship (Heiden finished second). The women's world champions were Natalia Petruseva of the Soviet Union (overall) and Karin Enke of East Germany (sprint).

In figure skating, Robin Cousins of Great Britain and Anett Poetzsch of East Germany won the Olympic titles, and Jan Hoffmann of East Germany and Poetzsch, the world titles. Charles Tickner of Littleton, Colo., and Linda Fratianne of Northridge, Calif., the American champions for the fourth straight year, won Olympic and world medals.

### ROWING

East Germany and the Soviet Union, as expected, gained the major rowing honors. In the Olympic Games, the East Germans won seven gold medals and one bronze in the eight men's events and four gold, one silver, and one bronze in the six women's events. The Soviets took seven men's and five women's medals.

Because of the Olympics, there were no world senior championships. Eastern Europeans dominated the world junior and lightweight championships Aug. 13–17 in Willebroek, Belgium. U.S.

*Andreas Wenzel, from the tiny country of Liechtenstein, won the World Cup for men's skiing.*

lightweights won silver medals in single sculls (Bill Belden of Paoli, Pa.) and double sculls (Scott Roop of New Rochelle, N.Y., and Dr. Larry Klecatsky of Pelham Manor, N.Y.). No American juniors qualified for a final.

The U.S. Olympic eight, representing the Charles River Rowing Association of Boston, won the Grand Challenge Cup in the Henley Royal Regatta July 3–6 in Henley, England. The U.S. Olympic women's eight upset East Germany on June 14 in the final of the Lucerne regatta in Switzerland.

### SKIING

Hanni Wenzel, 23, and her brother Andreas, 22, won the World Cup overall championships in 1980. They came from the tiny European principality of Liechtenstein, which has only 25,000 residents and seven ski lifts.

Hanni Wenzel was the most successful Alpine skier in the Winter Olympics, with two gold medals and one silver in the three women's events. Ingemar Stenmark, 23, of Sweden won the Olympic men's slalom and giant slalom, events he had dominated for five years. Stenmark placed second in the World Cup men's standing, scoring the maximum points in his two specialties but never skiing in a downhill race.

The best American was Phil Mahre of White Pass, Wash., third in the World Cup final standing and second in the Olympic slalom. Eleven months before the Olympics, he had suffered such a badly broken left ankle that his career seemed ended.

Nordic skiing (cross-country and jumping) produced an exciting newcomer in Steve Collins, a 15-year-old Ojibwa Indian from Thunder Bay, Ontario. Collins set a world record by leaping 421 ft. from a 90-m hill. He also won the world junior jumping championship and a World Cup senior competition and finished ninth in the Olympic 90-m jump, large accomplishments for a youth of 5 ft. 3 in. and 100 lb.

## SOCCER

The Cosmos, who played in a New York City suburb, had a new coach in Hennes Weisweiler of West Germany and 15 new players on their 30-man roster. Still, they won the Soccer Bowl, emblematic of the North American Soccer League (NASL) championship, for the third time in four years. League-leading scorer Giorgio Chinaglia made two goals as the Cosmos defeated the Fort Lauderdale Strikers, 3–0, in 97° F. heat in the title game Sept. 21 in Washington, D.C.

The 24 teams each played 32 games during the regular season. A players' poll named Roger Davies, a Seattle Sounders striker from England, as the league's most valuable player. Soccer writers voted that honor to Jack Brand, Seattle's Canadian goalie. Many fans thought that Chinaglia deserved the award.

The NASL also held a 1979–80 indoor season, with ten teams playing the six-man game for the first time. The Major Indoor Soccer League, which began the year before, played a similar season, also with ten teams.

The foreign winners included West Germany in the European Nations championship and Nottingham Forest of England, the defender, in the European Cup competition. Italian soccer was shaken by a scandal in which 19 major-league players were suspended, two for life, on charges of fixing games.

*The scoring star of the Cosmos, Giorgio Chinaglia, exults after kicking a goal. Chinaglia led his team to the North American Soccer League title.*

*Greg Louganis displays winning form in a platform diving competition. He won NCAA titles in 1980 in both men's diving events.*

## SWIMMING

In the Olympic Games, the major competition of the year, Soviets won 7 of the 13 gold medals for men and East Germans 11 of the 13 for women.

Had the U.S. not boycotted the Moscow competition, its men probably would have won most of the gold medals and its women probably would have cut into the East German total. The Americans received minor consolation when gold medals were won by Par Arvidsson of Sweden, a University of California junior, in the men's 100-m butterfly, and Duncan Goodhew of Britain, a 1979 graduate of North Carolina State University, in the men's 100-m breast stroke.

During the year, men's world records were broken by three American collegians—Ambrose ("Rowdy") Gaines 4th of Winter Haven, Fla., in the 200-m freestyle (1 min. 49.16 sec.); Craig Beardsley of Harrington Park, N.J., in the 200-m butterfly (1 min. 58.21 sec.), and Bill Barrett of Cincinnati in the 200-m individual medley (2 min. 3.20 sec.).

Fifteen-year-old Mary T. Meagher of Louisville lowered both women's world records for the butterfly, with times of 59.26 sec. for 100 m and 2:06.37 for 200 m. Earlier, her training had been interrupted by a collapsed lung.

Vladimir Salnikov of the Soviet Union set a men's world record of 14 min. 58.27 sec. for the 1500-m freestyle in the Olympics, a milestone performance. Outstanding Americans included Mike Bruner, Brian Goodell, Steve Lundquist, and the diver Greg Louganis among the men, and Tracy Caulkins, Cynthia ("Sippy") Woodhead, and Kim Linehan among the women. Caulkins won 3 national titles indoors and 4 outdoors, giving her 27 national titles by age 17.

## TENNIS

Björn Borg's pursuit of the Grand Slam—winning the Wimbledon, United States, French, and Australian Opens in one year—provided tennis excitement in 1980.

The 24-year-old Swede, without losing a set, won his fifth French Open by beating Vitas Gerulaitis of Kings Point, N.Y., 6-4, 6-1, 6-2, in the final June 8 in Paris. Next, Borg won his fifth straight Wimbledon title in England, defeating John McEnroe of Douglaston, N.Y., 1-6, 7-5, 6-3, 6-7, 8-6, in a spectacular final July 6. The fourth-set tie breaker, which McEnroe won, 18–16, was one of the memorable moments in tennis history.

Borg's streak ended in the United States Open final when McEnroe, the defender, outlasted him, 7-6, 6-1, 6-7, 5-7, 6-4, Sept. 7 in Flushing, N.Y. Because his Grand Slam had been foiled, Borg passed up the Australian Open in December.

The leading money winners were Borg and McEnroe with $523,000 each, and Jimmy Connors of Belleville, Ill., with $409,000. Among the women, Martina Navratilova of Dallas won $611,000, Tracy Austin of Rolling Hills, Calif., $536,000, and Chris Evert Lloyd of Fort Lauderdale, Fla., $343,000.

Lloyd, whose dominance ended in 1979 after her marriage, took three months off in early 1980 to be with her husband. When she returned, she won her fourth French title and her fifth United States Open in six years, and she reached the Wimbledon final in England before losing to

Evonne Goolagong Cawley of Hilton Head, S.C., 6-1, 7-6, on July 4.

The outstanding women included three teenagers—the 17-year-old Austin; 18-year-old Hana Mandlikova of Czechoslovakia, a United States Open finalist; and 15-year-old Andrea Jaeger of Lincolnshire, Ill., a quarterfinalist and youngest seeded player ever at Wimbledon, and the youngest semifinalist ever in the United States Open.

### TRACK AND FIELD

Year in and year out, American male athletes are the best in the world or close to it. In 1980, perhaps because of the U.S. boycott of the Moscow Olympics, Americans yielded most of the honors to Soviets, East Germans, and Britons.

The only Americans who dominated their events during the year were Edwin Moses of Mission Viejo, Calif., in the 400-m hurdles; Renaldo Nehemiah of Scotch Plains, N.J., in the 110-m hurdles; and Stanley Floyd of Albany, Ga., in the 100-m dash. The only Americans who broke world records were Moses in the 400-m hurdles (47.13

sec. on July 3 in Milan, Italy) and Mary Decker of Eugene, Oreg., in the women's mile (4 min. 21.7 sec. on Jan. 26 in Auckland, New Zealand).

The Soviets and East Germans won most of the Olympic gold medals—14 of the 24 for men and 12 of the 14 for women. One Soviet winner was Tatyana Kazankina in the women's 1500 m. Two weeks after the Olympics, she lowered her world record to 3 min. 52.47 sec. Decker finished second in 3 min. 59.43 sec., her fourth American record of the year at the distance.

The most prolific record-breaker was Steve Ovett of England. He broke the world record for the mile with 3 min. 48.8 sec. on July 1 in Oslo. He equaled the 1500-m record of 3 min. 32.1 sec. on July 15 in Oslo, then broke it with 3 min. 31.4 sec. on Aug. 27 in Koblenz, West Germany. Sebastian Coe of England, who had held both records, ran his first 1000 m July 1 in Oslo and set a world record of 2 min. 13.40 sec. In the Olympics, Ovett finished first and Coe second in the 800 m, Coe first and Ovett third in the 1500 m.     F.L.

# SPORTS: THE OLYMPIC GAMES

With the United States and many other nations not present at the Moscow Olympics, the Soviet Union and East Germany dominated competition. The same two countries led the standings at Lake Placid, but Americans took pride in the victories of Eric Heiden and the U.S. hockey team.

In ancient times, wars were stopped and politics put aside every four years for the Olympic Games. In 1980 military action and international politics diminished the quality of the first Olympic Games ever staged in a Soviet bloc nation.

The Games of the XXII Olympiad were held on schedule from July 19 to Aug. 3 in the Soviet capital of Moscow despite efforts by the U.S. to have them postponed, canceled, or moved. In December, 1979, Soviet troops invaded neighboring Afghanistan, and the U.S. organized a retaliatory boycott of the Olympics.

In all, 81 nations competed in the Olympics and 66 did not. Those 66 included such powers as the U.S., West Germany, Japan, China, and Canada. It also included small nations that were absent for reasons other than the boycott.

**The Boycott.** President Jimmy Carter told the Soviets Jan. 20 that unless their troops left Afghanistan in 30 days, the U.S. would boycott the Moscow Olympics. The decision was not really his, however. The United States Olympic Committee (USOC) ultimately had to decide whether to accept or decline the Soviet invitation to compete, but the Carter administration put fierce pressure on the USOC to vote against attending. On April 12 the USOC, with athletes casting 20 percent of the vote, decided by a 2-1 margin to boycott.

Many athletes were bitter about losing their only chance for glory, even though an Olympic team was picked and did compete in scattered alternative competitions. The entire Olympic team was honored in Washington July 26-30 and given special congressional gold medals. When

*Straining at the tape, Sebastian Coe of Great Britain wins the Olympic 1500-m race. Steve Ovett (279), who finished third, had earlier defeated Coe in the 800-m race.*

President Carter spoke the athletes did not applaud.

The USOC is the only national Olympic committee in the world without government funding, and some athletes thought it ironic that the USOC should yield to government pressure while Olympic committees in many other nations, though dependent on government funds, did not.

As an American boycott appeared likely, the State Department tried to convince other nations to bypass the Moscow Olympics. The governments of Australia, New Zealand, and most Western European nations supported the boycott, but in most cases their national Olympic committees dissented.

Australia and New Zealand competed in Moscow with scaled-down teams. Of the Western European nations, only West Germany, Norway, Liechtenstein, and Monaco did not attend. The others devised their own protests, such as barring their national anthems and flags from the Olympics and substituting the Olympic hymn and flag.

Had the U.S. and the other boycotting nations competed, they would have affected the results materially in such sports as men's track and field, swimming, basketball, boxing, gymnastics, and field hockey, and women's basketball, volleyball, and field hockey. Nevertheless, the reasons for the boycott were often distorted or misunderstood by Soviet bloc nations. "In most European countries, no one could understand the boycott," said Horst Baacke, head of East Germany's volleyball program. "We thought the United States was afraid they would lose because they ranked third in Montréal and Lake Placid."

**Summer Games.** Indeed, as in Montréal in the 1976 Olympics, the Soviet Union and East Germany were the big winners in Moscow. Soviet athletes won 18 of a possible total of 42 medals in women's track and field, 18 of 60 in wrestling, 17 of 36 in men's swimming, 14 of 24 in men's gymnastics, 12 of 42 in rowing, 8 of 30 in weight lifting, 8 of 44 in boxing, 8 of 19 in equestrian sports, 8 of 24 in fencing, 6 of 12 in diving, and 3 of 6 in modern pentathlon. East Germans won 11 of the 13 gold medals in women's swimming and 11 of the 14 in men's and women's rowing.

The Soviet Union gained 80 gold medals, East Germany 47, and no other nation more than 8. In total medals, the Soviet Union took 197, East Germany 126, and third-place Bulgaria 40. If the U.S. had competed, it probably would have ranked third in gold and total medals.

Boycott or not, much competition was first rate, especially in men's track and field. World records fell to Wladyslaw Kozakiewicz of Poland, with a pole vault of 18 ft. 11½ in., and Gerd Wessig of

*Gerd Wessig of East Germany flops over the bar to set a new world record in the high jump and win the gold medal in the Moscow Olympic Games.*

East Germany, with a high jump of 7 ft. 8¾ in. Britain, long dormant in track, won the 100 m with Allan Wells (10.25 sec.), the 800 m with Steve Ovett (1 min. 45.4 sec.), the 1500 m with Sebastian Coe (3 min. 38.4 sec.), and the decathlon with Daley Thompson (8495 points). Lasse Viren of Finland, who won two distance races in 1972 and two in 1976, was shut out this time and watched Miruts Yifter of Ethiopia win two gold medals instead.

Gymnastics produced the usual arguments about scoring. Nadia Comaneci of Rumania, the star of 1976 Olympic gymnastics, won two gold medals, but she narrowly lost the gold in the all-around after the judges had debated for a half-hour over her score.

In the men's competition Aleksandr Ditiatin, a Soviet gymnast, won eight medals (including the gold in the all-around), the most by any athlete in any sport in any Olympics. Teofilo Stevenson of Cuba won the gold medal in heavyweight boxing for the third straight Olympics, a record for any weight class.

Mark Johnson rejoices after scoring the goal that clinched the victory of the U.S. team over Finland in the final game of the Olympic hockey series, giving the U.S. the gold medal.

**Winter Games.** The Winter Olympics were held Feb. 12-24 in Lake Placid, N.Y., a village of 2700 in a remote Adirondacks Mountain area. Lake Placid is 300 mi. north of New York City and a two-hour drive south from Montréal. Although the village also staged the 1932 Winter Olympics, it is basically a resort with insufficient in-town housing for Olympic spectators.

Many came by buses and had no problems, but spectators who commuted by auto had to park 10 mi. or so from downtown and take shuttle buses. The problem was too few buses, drivers, and dispatchers, and for almost a week people often waited for hours in the cold for transportation to the events. Eventually, the state of New York stepped in, hired more buses, drivers, and supervisors, and ended the problem.

The state and federal governments furnished most of the $150,000,000 cost of the Winter Olympics. Still, there was a $4,300,000 deficit; the orga-

### Fame? "It Stinks," Said the Hero

In February, 21-year-old Eric Heiden did something that had never been done before: He won five gold medals at the Olympic Winter Games. And, in winning five events, he set three world records. The handsome, articulate speed skater from Madison, Wis., seemed destined for the total media exposure that greeted previous Olympic stars like Mark Spitz and Bruce Jenner. But Heiden, who said he "never went into skating to be rich or famous," preferred to go his own way. He spent the month after the Olympics sailing. Then he began a grueling schedule of bicycle races. The best he did was fifth place, but wherever he raced he was the reluctant center of attention. Finally, insisting that he wanted to be known as "just a kid who skated well," Heiden enrolled at the University of California at San Diego as a premedical student.

*Eric Heiden.*

*Sweden's Ingemar Stenmark won gold medals in the men's Olympic slalom and giant slalom events at Lake Placid.*

nizers, fighting bankruptcy, held a tag sale (which netted $300,000) and appealed for public contributions. When the Games were over and the arenas, ski jumps, and bobsled and luge runs remained, no governmental unit wanted to assume financial responsibility for maintaining them.

The competition was excellent. The Soviets won more gold medals than the East Germans (10 to 9) but the East Germans won more total medals (23 to 22). The U.S. ranked third among the 37 nations in each category, with 6 gold and 12 total medals.

The most exciting achievement for the Americans came in hockey. The Soviets had been perennial world and Olympic champions, and some of their players were in their third Olympics. The American team of collegians and minor-league professionals was the product of a six-month crash program. Its coach, Herb Brooks of the University of Minnesota, introduced passing and checking concepts familiar to Europeans but new to Americans.

The American team played seven games. It tied its first against Sweden and won its last six. The emotional game was the next to last, against a Soviet team that had crushed the Americans, 10-3, in an exhibition three days before the Olympics began. This time, on Feb. 22, the Americans won, 4-3, with people across the nation watching on television.

In the final game, the U.S. played Finland and, with the Olympic scoring system, the Americans, by losing, could have finished fourth in the final standing. Instead, they won, 4-2, and with the vic-tory came the gold medal. In a memorable scene, Jim Craig, the American goalie, stood on the victory stand, an American flag draped over him, and joined spectators in singing the national anthem.

Eric Heiden of Madison, Wis., swept the five gold medals in men's speed skating, the most medals of any kind in any Winter Olympics. Of the other American medals, three came in women's speed skating, two in figure skating, and one (by Phil Mahre of White Pass, Wash.) in men's slalom skiing. Hanni Wenzel of Liechtenstein and Ingemar Stenmark of Sweden won two gold medals each in Alpine skiing, and Wenzel added a silver. F.L.

**SRI LANKA,** formerly CEYLON. The moderate Sri Lankan government of President Junius R. Jayawardene wielded its power with unexpected determination in 1980.

In January former Prime Minister Sirimavo Bandaranaike was buoyed by the return to office of her friend Indira Gandhi in India. But Bandaranaike was to have no such good fortune. In October the Supreme Court of Sri Lanka upheld a special government commission's report that she had abused her power during her 12 years as prime minister. A day later, on Oct. 16, the parliament, dominated by Jayawardene's United National Party, voted to expel her from the legislative body and prohibit her from voting or participating in elections for seven years.

After his overwhelming victory over Bandaranaike in the 1977 elections, Jayawardene had reversed the country's socialist trend and achieved considerable economic gains for Sri Lanka

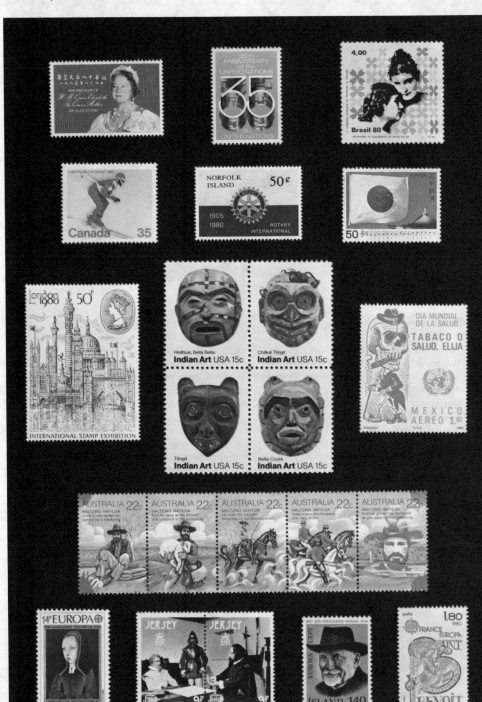

through an emphasis on the private sector. In 1980, however, an inflation rate of almost 40 percent induced by rising world oil prices began to make a serious impact on wage earners. In July Communist-led unions, allied with opposition parties, used the issue of falling real wages to call a general strike. Jayawardene reacted decisively, calling in troops to prevent violence and threatening to have strikers in public service fired. The show of force worked; the strike subsided and the government claimed an important victory.

See STATISTICS OF THE WORLD. R.J.C.

**STAMPS, POSTAGE.** International politics, special anniversaries, and concern with problems of health, economy, and ecology were illustrated on many postage stamps issued during 1980.

**U.S. Issues.** Thirty-two new stamps of the 15¢ denomination were issued to commemorate notable people and outstanding events. Individuals honored were W. C. Fields, Benjamin Banneker, Frances Perkins, Emily Bissell, Helen Keller and Anne Sullivan, Gen. Bernardo de Gálvez, and Edith Wharton. Stamps issued for special events and continuing series themes were the 1980 Winter Olympics, National Letter Writing Week, the 50th Anniversary of the Veterans Administration, Coral Reefs, Organized Labor, Education in America, Northwest Indian Masks, and the second group in the American Architecture Series.

Additional postal issues were a booklet of 20 small-format 15¢ stamps depicting five different windmill designs, a 15¢ issue portraying Dolley Madison, a 19¢ issue for the new international postcard rate, a 3.5¢ coil stamp for nonprofit organizational mailings, a single 1¢ definitive coil in the Americana series, and two 15¢ Christmas stamps. New airmail issues were released in anticipation of international rate increases effective in January, 1981. These were in 28¢, 35¢, and 40¢ denominations.

In a controversial decision, the U.S. Postal Service removed from sale all Summer Olympic stamps and postal stationery in March to support the U.S. government's boycott of the event. After the close of the Games, these items were again made available to collectors.

**Worldwide Issues.** An ever-increasing number of new postal issues continued to be released by members of the Universal Postal Union. Some of the major events that were commemorated in 1980 were the 75th anniversary of Rotary International, the 80th birthday of Queen Mother Elizabeth, the London 80 National Stamp Exhibition, the 26th Commonwealth Parliamentary Conference, the 25th annual Europa issues, and the Summer Olympic Games.

**United Nations.** The U.N. Postal Administration released five commemorative issues in recognition of the New International Economic Order, the Decade for Women, Peacekeeping Operations, the 35th anniversary of the U.N., and the Economic and Social Council. These were released simultaneously at the U.N. post offices in New York City, Geneva, and Vienna in the currency of the issuing country. A new 2.50 schilling stamp was released in Vienna to meet the Austrian postcard rate.

The long-awaited U.N. Flag Stamp series was launched in September with the issuance of four miniature sheets, each containing 16 stamps. The first 16 countries whose flags were so honored were Yugoslavia, France, Venezuela, El Salvador, Cameroon, Fiji, Bangladesh, Guinea, Hungary, Luxembourg, Madagascar, Mali, Rwanda, Suriname, Turkey, and Vietnam.

**Rare Stamp Auctions.** The famous British Guiana 1856 one-cent magenta established a record price paid for any postage stamp when it sold for $850,000 at a public auction held in New York City on April 5. The stamp originally sold for about $1.50 in 1873 and is the only known copy in existence.

A record price of $230,000 was paid for a single U.S. stamp in November. The 2¢ Hawaiian Missionary stamp was one of two copies auctioned in New York City. J.W.K.

*Opposite page:* Outstanding Stamps of 1980. *Top row (left to right): Hong Kong celebrates the 80th birthday of the Queen Mother Elizabeth; the U.N. commemorates its 35th anniversary; Brazil honors Helen Keller. Second row (left to right): Canada's issue for the 1980 Winter Olympic Games; Norfolk Island recognizes the 75th anniversary of Rotary International; Japan stresses music in its continuing Song Series. Third row (left to right): The United Kingdom publicizes its international stamp exhibition held in London; the U.S. features Indian art in its continuing American Folk Art series; Mexico warns against the hazards of smoking. Fourth row: Australia relates the story of "Waltzing Matilda" on this folklore issue. Fifth row (left to right): 1980 Europa issues from Belgium, Jersey (Channel Islands), Iceland, and France.*

*Following the June 3 defeat of Proposition 9 by California's voters, sponsor Howard Jarvis announces to reporters that he will soon resume his efforts to halve the state income tax. Jarvis, a retired business executive, was the cosponsor of the 1978 Jarvis-Gann initiative, which drastically cut California's property taxes.*

**STATE GOVERNMENT REVIEW.** The much talked about taxpayers' revolt fizzled in 1980, apparently headed off by legislative tax-cutting during 1978 and 1979 and by indications that politicians were growing more responsive to demands that government be more frugal.

**Taxes.** In California, which launched the so-called taxpayers' revolt with passage of Proposition 13 in 1978, voters turned down an initiative to halve income taxes that was placed on the June ballot by Howard Jarvis, Proposition 13 coauthor.

On Nov. 4, measures patterned after Proposition 13 to roll back property taxes failed in five states. Three other tax-cut proposals were defeated in Michigan, and a measure to reduce the taxes of the lower and middle classes and increase the taxes of businesses and the upper classes lost in Ohio. The major tax reduction initiative approved was Proposition 2½ in Massachusetts, aimed at gradually reducing property taxes, which were above the national average.

The November balloting also emphasized the shift in the tax revolt from extreme Proposition 13-style measures to more moderate ones as

means of containing government taxing and spending. In 1980 Delaware, Hawaii, Missouri, and South Carolina joined the list of states with spending lids. On June 3, Arizona voters set spending limits on localities and schools, an action that cleared the way for implementation of a new law to exempt food from the sales tax, and approved a constitutional amendment setting a 7 percent limit on state spending increases. On Nov. 4, Montana became the ninth state to adopt indexing the state income tax rate to inflation so that inflation did not put taxpayers in higher tax brackets.

Arkansas voted to allow a mill levy rollback when assessments rose more than 10 percent annually because of court-ordered statewide property reassessment. Ohio approved two assessment categories, allowing different levies for residential-farm property than for commercial-industrial property. Increased homestead-tax exemptions or other relief measures for the elderly were approved on Nov. 4 in Georgia, Louisiana, New Jersey, Virginia, and West Virginia. Homestead relief was expanded in Florida, and property-tax exemptions for the elderly and disabled were increased in Arizona.

Tax action was relatively limited in legislative sessions during 1980, perhaps because of the widespread tax cuts made during 1978 and 1979. For the first time in three years, however, tax increases totaled more than tax decreases. Most of the tax hikes were in motor-fuel levies to pay for road improvements. Gasoline taxes were raised in 11 states (Alabama, Indiana, Kentucky, Massachusetts, Minnesota, Nebraska, New Mexico, South Carolina, South Dakota, Virginia, and Wisconsin). In an attempt to deal with the problem of declining road revenues as motorists bought less gasoline, some states switched to percentage taxes tied to the price of gasoline, on the assumption that gas prices would continue to rise.

The major legislative tax-relief measure was repeal of the Alaska income tax, made possible by the state's oil wealth. The U.S. Supreme Court was to rule on the constitutionality of a legislative plan cleared by the Alaska Supreme Court to distribute shares of the state's oil wealth to its residents, based on the numbers of years they had lived in the state.

Major tax relief was also granted in Colorado (income taxes), Louisiana (income taxes), and Illinois (reduction of the sales tax on food). General sales taxes were hiked in Connecticut and South Dakota. Cigarette taxes were increased in Alabama and Maryland.

Attempts to prevent oil companies from passing on to consumers new taxes on gross earnings levied by Connecticut and New York ran into trouble in the courts. On Nov. 4, North Dakota voted to hike the oil-production tax, and Oregon earmarked future oil and natural gas taxes for schools. Severance taxes were hiked in New Mexico. The trend toward encouraging the use of gasohol—a blend of alcohol and gasoline—continued, with more than half the states granting tax or other breaks by the end of 1980. Illinois ran its state automobile fleet on gasohol in 1980.

**Business.** Skyrocketing interest rates in March and April led many states to lift ceilings on various types of loans. Arkansas, however, voted down lifting its 10 percent lid. New York lifted its ceilings, but apparently acted too late to prevent the Citibank Corp. from moving its credit-card operations to South Dakota, which had passed legislation to facilitate the relocation of the huge consumer lender.

The slump in auto sales hurt Michigan badly. Gov. William Milliken had proposed nearly $1 billion in budget cuts by November. However, Michigan, as well as three other states, authorized state loans to help the Chrysler Corp. qualify for federal aid. Michigan and Ohio also cut the sales tax for a limited time on new-car sales. New Jersey banned state purchase of imported cars.

The U.S. Supreme Court ruled in cases involving Vermont and Wisconsin that a state can tax the entire income of a multistate or multinational corporation, not just its earnings in a particular state or locality.

**Health.** A number of decisions affecting states were handed down by the U.S. Supreme Court. Most significantly, the Court ruled on June 30 that neither the federal nor state governments were required to finance abortions for poor women in most cases. Antiabortion laws requiring women to "give informed consent" before having abortions were passed in Louisiana, Rhode Island, and South Dakota, but the Louisiana law was struck down by a federal court. A similar 1979 North Dakota provision was voided by another federal court. In Alabama a federal court placed state mental health facilities in the receivership of Gov. Forrest H. James, Jr.

Massachusetts voters approved a constitutional amendment guaranteeing rights for the handicapped.

More states permitted supervised use of marijuana by cancer or glaucoma patients. In Georgia the law was supported by Rep. Virlyn Smith, a sufferer from lung cancer.

In Connecticut, Gov. Ella T. Grasso continued her duties while undergoing cancer treatment, but her worsening condition forced her to resign at the end of 1980.

**Education.** Religion and schools continued to be a controversial mix, as the U.S. Supreme Court struck down Kentucky's requirement for posting the Ten Commandments in every public-school classroom in the state. A similar North Dakota law was voided by a federal court as well. Voluntary prayer in classrooms was ruled out by the Massachusetts Supreme Judicial Court.

Texas protested a court ruling that it provide free public education to children of illegal aliens. Ohio was told by a federal court to help pay for Cleveland school desegregation. Illinois created an authority to issue $500,000,000 in bonds to help rescue Chicago schools.

**Environment.** In the wake of the Love Canal situation (see ENVIRONMENT), some 20 states passed laws dealing with hazardous substances and wastes. Washington, one of only three states with commercial nuclear waste dumps, voted to ban nonmedical radioactive waste originating in another state. At least nine other states passed laws on radioactive waste. The voters of three states rejected restrictions on new nuclear power plants, but Oregon voted to ban the construction of new plants until adequate waste facilities were provided. Nevada's call for state takeover of federal public lands was joined by five other western states.

**Elections.** Republican gubernatorial candidates won 7 of the 13 statehouses contested on Nov. 4, giving the party a total of 23. Incumbent governors lost in primaries in Montana and Washington, and on Nov. 4 in Arkansas, Missouri, and North Dakota. Democrats generally kept their grip on state legislatures, although Republicans made some gains, winning a majority in the Illinois, Montana, and Washington houses and the Ohio and Pennsylvania senates. Nationwide, Republicans picked up more than 200 legislative seats.

In addition to tax referendums, many other issues were on state ballots. Government-run lotteries were authorized in Arizona, Colorado, and the District of Columbia. (Fourteen states already had lotteries.) Bingo was cleared by voters in Missouri, Texas, and West Virginia. Illinois approved cutting the size of its House of Representatives by one third. Iowa defeated a state equal rights amendment. Discontented with approval by only nine state legislatures of the proposed amendment to give the District of Columbia voting rights in Congress, District voters approved an initiative to hold a convention that would draft a state constitution. Meanwhile, Alaska voted to reexamine its statehood.

**Crime.** The U.S. Supreme Court voided Alabama's capital punishment law. State supreme courts upheld death penalty laws in California and Tennessee but struck down a Massachusetts law. Drug paraphernalia were the target of bans in a number of states, but most of the laws were contested in court. New York cracked down on handguns.

Some prominent state officials were indicted or were found guilty of crimes. Former Maryland Gov. Marvin Mandel began serving a three-year prison term for mail fraud and racketeering. Former Gov. Ray Blanton of Tennessee was indicted for bid-rigging. However, Texas House Speaker Billy Clayton was acquitted of charges of fraud, conspiracy, and racketeering resulting from a major undercover operation by the Federal Bureau of Investigation.                                    E.S.K.

**SUDAN.** As the Sudan tried to step up production for export during 1980, it continued to be plagued by increases in the price of oil, staggering debts, threats of reduction in foreign aid, and an influx of refugees.

After a warning from the International Monetary Fund to restrict imports of consumer goods and increase exports of its major cash crops, cotton and groundnuts, President Gaafar Mohammed al-Nimeiry invited foreign technicians and agricultural experts to the Sudan to make recommendations on agricultural projects. The International Bank for Reconstruction and Development began work on a program to double the amount of land under cultivation. New oil discoveries in the Upper Nile region led to the hope that within three years the Sudan would not only be self-sufficient in oil but might also be able to export small amounts. The nation's 1980 oil bill of $360,000,000 was devouring 60 percent of its 1980 export earnings.

Prior Sudanese development projects had left the country with a $3.5 billion debt. Many of these projects were subsidized by Saudi Arabia, Kuwait, and Abu Dhabi, which continued to assist the Sudan. The United States increased its financial assistance in 1980 to $130,000,000 a year.

Refugees from Chad, Zaire, Uganda, and Eritrea continued to be a major problem. Although some had been resettled as farmers, most remained in ill-maintained refugee camps that strained the resources of the Sudan.

The Sudan's relations with other North African nations were as complex as its mixed Arab and black population. On Feb. 26, Sudanese students marched on the Egyptian and U.S. embassies in Khartoum to protest the exchange of ambassadors between Egypt and Israel. On Oct. 10, Uganda protested that forces loyal to former Ugandan dictator Idi Amin were entering Uganda from Zaire and the Sudan. Both countries denied the charge. In December Nimeiry offered to mediate

in the 19-year-old hostilities between Ethiopia and the Eritrean guerrilla groups fighting for independence from Ethiopia. A settlement would mean the repatriation of about 400,000 Eritrean refugees in the Sudan.

*See* STATISTICS OF THE WORLD.                       R.M.

**SUPREME COURT OF THE UNITED STATES, THE.** The Supreme Court made a number of significant rulings in 1980, particularly in the areas of civil rights, freedom of the press, and government secrecy. In two key decisions, the Court upheld the power of Congress to impose affirmative action quotas to alleviate past racial discrimination, and it upheld the right of the press and public to attend criminal trials.

**Membership.** No changes occurred in the membership of the Court in 1980, and the Court continued to resist ideological characterization because of its idiosyncratic voting patterns. To some observers, the Court's case-by-case approach to decision making prevented it from articulating general principles for the guidance of lower courts.

Associate Justice William H. Rehnquist was still the most conservative member of the Court, often joined by Chief Justice Warren E. Burger, and Associate Justices William J. Brennan, Jr., and Thurgood Marshall were still the most liberal members. Remaining in the middle and determining the result in an important number of cases were Associate Justices Potter Stewart, Byron R. White, Harry A. Blackmun, Lewis F. Powell, Jr., and John Paul Stevens.

**Civil Rights.** For the third consecutive term the Court considered a claim of "reverse discrimination" directed by whites against a program designed to enhance opportunities for minorities. On July 2, by a 6–3 vote, the Court upheld the constitutionality of a provision attached to a federal public works act mandating that, where possible, 10 percent of the allocated funds be distributed to minority contractors. The majority ruled that the provision was an appropriate exercise of Congress's power to alleviate past discrimination in the construction industry.

But civil rights proponents suffered a potentially severe setback on April 22. A 6–3 majority of the Court upheld the constitutionality of the at-large system of electing the Mobile, Ala., three-member governing commission, even though no black had been elected in the 68-year history of the system.

In a 5–4 ruling on April 16, the Court held that local officials accused of committing civil rights violations cannot escape liability by claiming that they acted in "good faith." And on June 25 the Court ruled, 6–3, that an 1871 civil rights act al-

*This cartoon envisions the creation of a laboratory monster as a result of the U.S. Supreme Court's ruling on genetic engineering. In June the justices ruled that new life forms created in a laboratory could be patented and could thus be protected from unlawful duplication or use.*

lows private citizens to sue state officials whenever a state policy violates a federal law.

**Women's Rights.** The Court broke no new ground in the area of sex discrimination, but in a June 30 ruling, a 5–4 majority upheld the constitutionality of a congressional ban on the use of federal funds for Medicaid abortions except when the mother's life is endangered or in cases of rape or incest. The decision reaffirmed previous Court pronouncements that, while a woman has a constitutional right to obtain an abortion, she has no comparable right to have the government pay for it. *See also* WOMEN.

**Free Press and Free Speech Rights.** On July 2 the Court upheld the right of the press and public to attend criminal trials. The 7–1 decision blunted the impact of a 1979 ruling that the press and public could be excluded from pretrial criminal hearings.

In the area of free speech, the Court on June 9 unanimously upheld a state's right to require private owners to allow citizens to circulate petitions in their shopping centers. It ruled on June 20 that states could not bar utility companies from expressing views on public issues or from promoting their products. But on Jan. 21 a 5–3 major-

ity rejected First Amendment challenges to Air Force, Navy, and Marine Corps regulations requiring servicemen to obtain the approval of their commanding officers before circulating petitions on military bases.

On Feb. 19, by a 6–3 vote, the Court required former Central Intelligence Agency (CIA) agent Frank Snepp to surrender all profits from a book that he failed to submit to the agency for prepublication review, as specified in his CIA contract. In a March 31 ruling the Court held, 6–3, that the First Amendment protects public employees from being fired solely on the basis of their political affiliation.

**Law Enforcement.** The Court continued to require strict procedural standards for the imposition of the death penalty. On May 19 the High Court in a 6–3 vote overturned the death sentence of a convicted Georgia murderer, and on June 20, by a 7–2 vote, it struck down Alabama's death penalty law as unconstitutional because it did not allow jurors to convict a defendant charged with first-degree murder of a lesser offense instead. An 8–0 vote on June 30 indefinitely stayed the scheduled July 1 execution of another convicted Georgia murderer, Jack Potts, allowing a federal appeals court to review his challenge to the death sentence.

Civil libertarians and privacy proponents hailed the Court's April 15 holding that, except in emergency cases, police must obtain a warrant before making an arrest in a suspect's home. The 6–3 decision overturned laws in 23 states allowing police to make routine home arrests without warrants.

In a number of Fourth Amendment rulings, the Court eased the introduction of illegally seized evidence into criminal trials. A 6–3 decision on May 12, for example, held that casual questioning by police which led to incriminating statements by a suspect did not amount to illegal interrogation. And by a 5–4 vote on March 18 the Court upheld Texas's habitual-offender statute, under which a person convicted of three nonviolent felonies that netted less than $230 was mandatorily sentenced to life in prison. On Dec. 9 the Supreme Court ruled 5–4 that the constitutional protection against double jeopardy is no bar to the prosecution appealing a sentence it considers too lenient.

**Other Cases.** In a 5–4 decision on Feb. 20 the Court made it more difficult for faculty members at private colleges and universities to unionize, ruling that professors at Yeshiva University in New York City were "managerial employees" who were not entitled to protection under the federal labor laws. The Court ruled unanimously on Feb. 28 that workers have the right, under certain circumstances, to refuse to perform certain tasks they believe to be hazardous.

On June 16 the Court held, 5–4, that scientifically manufactured forms of life can be patented. The decision was considered a boon for the burgeoning genetic engineering industry.

The High Court on June 30, in an 8–1 decision, ordered the federal government to pay $122,500,-000 to eight tribes of Sioux Indians in compensation for the illegal seizure of land in the Black Hills of South Dakota in 1877. *See also* INDIANS, AMERICAN.

On June 10 the Court ruled unanimously that a zoning ordinance limiting land development in the name of conservation does not necessarily violate the constitutional rights of property owners.

The Supreme Court ruled unanimously on June 16 that farmers in California's Imperial Valley were entitled to federally subsidized irrigation water regardless of the size of their farms. The Reclamation Act of 1902 limited the availability of cheap federal water to family farms of 160 acres or less, but state laws exempted the Imperial Valley from the acreage limit.

The Court faced another challenge to the "wall of separation between church and state" in 1980.

On Nov. 17, by a 5–4 margin, it struck down a Kentucky law that required the posting of the Ten Commandments in every public-school classroom in the state.

*See also* CIVIL RIGHTS AND CIVIL LIBERTIES; CRIME AND LAW ENFORCEMENT; STATE GOVERNMENT REVIEW. D.C.

**SURINAME.** *See* STATISTICS OF THE WORLD.

**SWAZILAND.** *See* STATISTICS OF THE WORLD.

**SWEDEN.** Mounting inflation, the controversy over nuclear-power development, and labor discontent were major issues that Sweden contended with during 1980.

**Government Spending and Politics.** The $49 billion budget for fiscal 1981, made public on Jan. 11, projected a deficit of $13.4 billion. Cuts of $1.5 billion in government spending were announced by the government on Sept. 16 in an effort to reduce the deficit. About 40 percent of the cuts were to come from subsidies for food, housing, and household items. In an earlier move to reduce domestic demand for goods and the growing deficit in international payments, the government on Aug. 19 had announced an increase of

*An almost unprecedented general strike brought most of Sweden's industries and services, including most rail transit, to a halt in early May. After nine days, the labor unions settled their disputes with management and authorized a return to work on May 11.*

*For months prior to Sweden's March 23 referendum on nuclear energy development, proponents of each of the three options engaged in heated national debates. The proposal preferred by the voters called for operating a maximum of 12 nuclear power plants and phasing out nuclear power after 25 years.*

2.83 percentage points in the value-added tax (VAT), a kind of sales tax, thus raising Sweden's VAT to 23.46 percent, the highest in the world.

On Oct. 22, for the first time in Swedish history, the government faced a no-confidence vote. The three-party, center-right coalition of Prime Minister Thorbjörn Fälldin survived by one vote, 175–174, and remained committed to reductions in public spending. The opposition Social Democrats, led by former Prime Minister Olof Palme, had challenged Fälldin's economic policies.

**Nuclear Power.** In a referendum on nuclear-energy development, the Swedish electorate on March 23 voted to continue the use of this controversial energy source for at least 25 years. Although the referendum was not binding, Fälldin said the government would accept the decision of the voters. Fälldin's Center Party and the Communists had opposed nuclear power, and an earlier Fälldin government had been forced out of office over the issue in 1978.

The referendum gave voters a choice of three options. Two proposals for continued use of nuclear power received, jointly, 58 percent of the vote. They provided for operating a maximum of 12 nuclear plants for 25 years. The third option, supported by 38.6 percent, advocated the dismantling of Sweden's six existing reactors in ten years, with no new ones to be built. The six nuclear plants were providing 25 percent of the country's electricity in 1980.

**Labor Trouble.** A series of strikes and lockouts that began on April 25 had shut down much of the country's industry and transportation by early May. Ultimately, about 25 percent of the nation's workers were involved, including about 900,000 in the private sector and 26,000 in the public sector. It was Sweden's first nationwide strike in 70 years. The shutdowns were ended by agreement on May 11 to a wage compromise proposed by government-appointed mediators. Although the Swedish Employers' Confederation had originally rejected the proposal, which provided for raises of about 7 percent, the employers later yielded to cabinet requests that they accept. The Employers' Confederation said that the settlement would add 2 or 3 percent to the 13 percent annual inflation rate, further damaging Sweden's competitiveness in international markets.

*See* STATISTICS OF THE WORLD.                L.A.S.

**SWITZERLAND.** The healthy Swiss economy made continued advances during 1980. The gross national product was expected to increase by 2.5 percent in 1980, after adjustment for inflation. The inflation rate for the year was expected to be relatively low, about 5 percent.

**National Affairs.** Swiss voters endorsed the government's continued support of Protestant and

*The world's longest vehicular tunnel was opened on Sept. 5. Starting in Göschenen, a procession of antique automobiles traveled 10 mi. through the Swiss Alps to Airolo to inaugurate the new road.*

Roman Catholic churches. In a national referendum on March 2, a proposal to prohibit all church-state ties was defeated.

Switzerland on Sept. 5 opened a 10.1-mi. Alpine road tunnel linking Göschenen and Airolo. The longest vehicular tunnel in the world, it was bored through the St. Gotthard Massif at a cost of $420,000,000 and 19 lives.

**Youth Discontent.** A rash of youth demonstrations and public violence broke out with a protest by about 8000 young people in Zürich on May 30 and continued sporadically through much of the year, occurring also in Basel, Bern, Geneva, and Lausanne. The initial outbreak came after Zürich officials decided to spend about $38,000,000 to renovate the city's opera house. Young people demanded that the money be used for "alternative cultural activities." They had been demanding another youth center to replace centers closed by the authorities in 1970 and 1977 for attracting drug users, drug pushers, and runaways. An unused downtown factory was provided in early June to serve as a youth center, but the po-

lice closed it in early September, again because it had become a hangout for drug dealers and runaways. The shutdown provoked new rioting for several days. City officials decided against reopening the center on Nov. 13.

**Economic Espionage.** Two French customs officials were arrested in Basel on April 15 on what the Swiss government said on May 7 were charges of "economic espionage." Bernard Rui and Pierre Schultz, the French agents, had scheduled a meeting with an employee of the Swiss Bank Corp., the country's biggest bank. The bank worker reportedly had agreed to give them information about depositors. The French government, protesting the arrests, said on May 8 that the French officials were on a "routine mission" to obtain data about French citizens using Swiss bank accounts for tax evasion and currency smuggling. French customs closed the Swiss border briefly in protest against the arrests. After both men were released, one of them after admitting the charges, their conviction in absentia was reported on June 18.

*See* STATISTICS OF THE WORLD.     L.A.S.

**SYRIA.** The ten-year-old government of President Hafez al-Assad used both the army and security forces to deal with mounting opposition from the Muslim Brotherhood and other critics during 1980. New links were forged with Libya and the Soviet Union, while tensions rose between Syria and Iraq and Syria and Jordan.

**Internal Unrest.** The Muslim Brotherhood, long opposed to the government, was blamed for assassinations and bombings that reportedly had killed more than 150 persons by mid-August. This underground group usually perpetrated violence against Muslims of Assad's own sect, the Alawites, who dominated the government and army although comprising only about 12 percent of Syria's population. Membership, or even suspicion of membership, in the brotherhood was made a capital crime. The government offered an exemption from the death sentence to any member who turned himself in; by late August, 900 members supposedly had accepted.

In March, demonstrations and strikes broke out in every major city and town except the capital, Damascus. Ten thousand troops were sent to Aleppo and Hama. Some diplomats estimated the death toll in restoring order at 180. The government's response was increased repression, including the creation of civilian militias with the right to mete out summary punishment.

The government also attempted to disarm opposition by redressing grievances. In March a half dozen unpopular governors were replaced, about 25 heads of state enterprises were dismissed on charges of incompetence or corruption, 200 political prisoners were released, and the jurisdiction of state security courts was curtailed. Earlier, in January, a new cabinet was formed under a new Sunni Muslim prime minister, Abdel-Raouf al-Kassem, but Alawites remained in the key security posts.

**Economic Problems.** Inflation, shortages of food and other basic items, and pervasive corruption in government offices were cited as the chief reasons for the growing unrest. It was believed that the March strikes and demonstrations were touched off by a government decision to freeze prices after granting a salary increase of about 70 percent to all state employees. Shopkeepers and professionals felt threatened by this action.

**Arab Relations.** Syria continued to maintain its sizable peacekeeping army in Lebanon. Old hatreds between Syria and Iraq were inflamed by incidents in both countries that resulted in a mutual closing of embassies in August. Iraq broke diplomatic relations on Oct. 10, charging that Syria was aiding Iran in the Iran-Iraq war. On Sept. 10, Syria and Libya proclaimed the unification of their countries, but exactly how the merger would work was not made clear.

A new enmity developed between Syria and Jordan, which was supporting Iraq in its war with Iran. Syria charged that Jordan was aiding the Muslim Brotherhood and massed more than 35,000 troops near their common border in late November, when an Arab League conference was being held in Amman. Jordan sent 24,000 of its troops to the same area and refused any concessions. Both sides withdrew by mid-December.

**Other Foreign Relations.** In 1980 the Assad government continued its earlier allegations of U.S. involvement in terrorism and strikes within Syria. On Oct. 8, Assad signed a 20-year friendship treaty with the Soviet Union in Moscow. The treaty, similar to ones that Moscow had signed with Iraq and South Yemen, obliged the signers to consult with each other in any national emergency but was not a mutual defense treaty. Almost all of Syria's arms came from the U.S.S.R.

*See* STATISTICS OF THE WORLD. *See also* ARAB LEAGUE; JORDAN; LEBANON; MIDDLE EAST.     R.M.

# T

**TAIWAN,** *or* **FORMOSA,** seat of the Republic of China. In 1980 the Kuomintang regime ruling Taiwan eased its control of the political process. Trade increased with the People's Republic of China, and a longtime friend of Taiwan, Ronald Reagan, was elected President of the United States.

**Politics.** Candidates of the Kuomintang, or Nationalist Party, won 57 of the 70 seats at stake on Dec. 6 in parliamentary elections. Party candidates also won 63 of the 76 seats contested in the National Assembly, whose main function is to elect a president every six years. Both bodies continued to be dominated by life members chosen from mainland constituencies before the Nationalist government fled to Taiwan from mainland China in 1949. The winning opposition candidates, including two wives of jailed politicians, said they considered their showing a moral victory.

On April 18 the government sentenced eight opposition leaders to long prison terms after an open trial before a military tribunal. They were accused of plotting to overthrow the government and of promoting Taiwanese independence, or permanent separation from mainland China. (The Nationalists profess to continue to seek reunification of China under their rule.) The trial was unusual in that it was open to the press and reported in the newspapers. The defendants, native Taiwanese, denied challenging the government by any other than democratic means, but opposition political parties were not legal.

**The Economy and Foreign Affairs.** In 1979 the mainland Chinese government in Peking waived duties on imports from Taiwan. Taiwan continued to forbid trade with the mainland officially, but such trade was growing and in 1980 was estimated at $200,000,000 through third parties in Japan, Hong Kong, and elsewhere—a threefold increase over 1979.

Despite the U.S.-Taiwan break in diplomatic relations on Jan. 1, 1979, when formal ties were established between Washington and Peking, the U.S. continued to facilitate trade with and investment in Taiwan through the American Institute in Taiwan (which replaced the U.S. embassy) and the American Trade Center. Both were funded by the U.S. government, although they were technically private foundations. But on Oct. 9 Peking protested a pact that gave Taiwan's representatives in the U.S. and U.S. representatives in Taiwan privileges and immunities traditionally enjoyed by diplomats.

Peking apparently grew touchy about the Taiwan issue because U.S. Presidential candidate Ronald Reagan had called for elevating U.S. ties with Taiwan to an official level, although in establishing diplomatic relations with the People's Republic of China the Carter administration had agreed to terminate such ties. On Aug. 25 Reagan backtracked, saying he would abide by the Taiwan Relations Act of 1979, which ruled out official relations between the U.S. and Taiwan, and would not try to change the status of the U.S. liaison office in Taiwan.

The Taiwanese economy continued strong in 1980. Per capita income was topped in Asia only by Japan and Singapore. Trade with the U.S. was expected to reach a volume of nearly $11 billion in 1980. The real gross national product was expected to increase by 6.5 percent during the year. Unemployment was less than 2 percent in early 1980, and inflation was at an annual rate of less than 10 percent. A trade deficit, however, was re-

ported for the first half of 1980 because of rising costs for imported oil.

Although the mutual defense treaty with Washington lapsed in 1979, on Jan. 3, 1980, the Carter administration approved the sale of $291,700,000 worth of weapons termed defensive. Taiwan's request for advanced U.S. fighter planes was rejected.

*See* STATISTICS OF THE WORLD.                    T.L.K.

**TANZANIA.** Drought and growing discontent plagued the government headed by Tanzanian President Julius K. Nyerere throughout 1980. The second year of drought in east Africa severely reduced Tanzania's food crops. With the country able to produce less than one quarter of its corn (maize) requirements, more than 210,000 tons of corn had to be purchased. Emergency shipments from the United States, Japan, Canada, and Western Europe helped avert famine. With its foreign exchange reserves depleted by the 1979 war in Uganda, the government was forced to reduce expenditures and imports. Both measures sparked protests, which led to arrests.

Tanzanian involvement in Uganda continued during 1980. When a military coup overthrew Ugandan President Godfrey L. Binaisa in May, the coup leaders immediately flew to Tanzania, where they won Nyerere's recognition. In October some of the 10,000 Tanzanian troops in Uganda were reported to have expelled invaders loyal to deposed dictator Idi Amin.

Zanzibar, which had been under martial law since joining with Tanganyika to form Tanzania in 1964, elected a House of Representatives for the first time in January. On Oct. 26 Aboud Jumbe, running unopposed, was elected the first president of semiautonomous Zanzibar. On the same day, Nyerere, also running unopposed, was reelected president of Tanzania for five years. Voters, however, rejected more than half of the 111 incumbent members of parliament in protest against the chronic shortage of food and consumer goods.

*See* STATISTICS OF THE WORLD.                    J.T.S.

**TECHNOLOGY.** In 1980 the so-called high technologies of robotics, computers, and semiconductors were emphasized by industry in the United States as it sought to check declining productivity and to meet soaring fuel costs through more efficient processes and products. Of particular significance was the mass production of very-large-scale integrated circuits.

According to many business and government leaders in 1980, American industry was in a stagnant condition because it had failed to be sufficiently innovative since World War II. Production machinery in U.S. factories was estimated to be

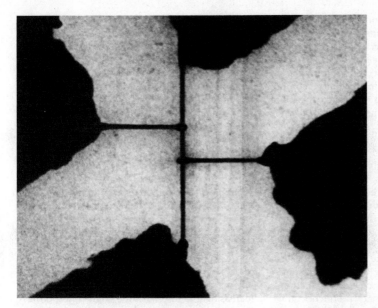

*Nearly 20 years after its discovery, the principle of superconducting circuits was being used by International Business Machines Corp. in 1980 to design a computer that could by far surpass all existing models in speed and power. It would use circuits made of niobium wires (the straight lines in the illustration) only 1/500,000 in. in width.*

nearly 25 years old on the average—a major reason that factory productivity increased at a rate of less than 1 percent per year from 1973 through 1979. At the same time, productivity in other industrialized nations such as Japan had climbed at a significantly faster rate, and the relative lag in U.S. productivity contributed to inflation.

**Robot Factories.** The situation led to a call for the "reindustrialization" of American industry through the sweeping modernization of production facilities. Factories of the future were expected to rely increasingly heavily on "smart" machine tools and on robots.

The characteristics of the new machine tools were discussed in a 1980 report from the Machine Tool Task Force, a group organized by the Lawrence Livermore National Laboratory under a government contract. Lathes, borers, grinders, and milling machines of the future were to incorporate electronic control systems, most of them built around tiny microprocessors that would improve machine performance and raise operating speeds. Microprocessors, which have already been used in a number of industrial processes and products, can serve many functions. For example, programmable automatic control systems enable one machine to produce many different kinds of parts without the intervention of a human operator. Sensors can monitor the condition of the cutting tools within a machine and automatically adjust cutting speeds and other factors to compensate for wear. They can also monitor the product to determine if it meets specifications, adjust a machine automatically if errors are

detected, and keep track of the machine's record of performance.

As for the proposed robots, which had already been used on some assembly lines for several years, they bore little resemblance to the humanized robots of much science fiction. Instead they were designed solely to perform a range of specific tasks, particularly repetitive chores, transfer operations (moving of manufactured parts from one factory site to another), and operations in dangerous or unpleasant environments such as radioactive or high-temperature areas. A good example of a repetitive chore was the spot welding of automobile bodies. At the Chrysler Corp. assembly plant in Newark, Del., 98 percent of all spot welds were already being done by robots in 1980.

Microprocessor advances had greatly reduced the cost of robots, which offer the advantage of turning out goods with great precision and at rates faster than humans can perform. They also make possible the production of high-quality standardized goods on a smaller scale than has previously been economically feasible. On the other hand, because one multiprogrammed robot can take the place of several human workers, some analysts saw robots as a threat to the labor force in the future. Advocates of robots stated that the jobs robots perform are not desirable anyway and that the expanding robot industry is itself providing many new jobs, as would any future general increase in productivity. In any case, manufacturers in 1980 were ordering robots in record numbers.

**VLSI Circuits.** The revolution in electronics that spawned robots, as well as mammoth digital computers, was based on integrated-circuit technology: the manufacture of electric circuits, each containing many interconnected solid-state components, on tiny silicon chips. The more components that can be crowded on a chip, the more sophisticated such circuits become. In 1980 interest focused on very-large-scale integrated (VLSI) circuits, which are usually defined as being able to handle at least 64,000 bits of information. Several semiconductor manufacturers began mass production of VLSI circuits, with a battle for supremacy being waged between U.S. and Japanese firms. One U.S. manufacturer, Intel Corp., surprised the competition by using a design concept known as fault tolerance, in which a circuit is designed so that defective components can be replaced during testing of the chip. The Intel VLSI circuit, planned for production in 1981, actually had about 67,700 memory cells, necessitating a slightly larger chip and longer production time, but Intel said that the higher number of good chips produced outweighed these disadvantages.

Japanese scientists indicated, however, that by 1983 they might have a chip on the market that would be able to handle more than 256,000 bits of information. And, according to some predictions, a 1,000,000-component chip would not be impossible by the end of the decade. Current technology placed some limitations on this trend, however. Squeezing thousands of components on a chip not much larger than the letter O meant that each component must measure less than 0.00025 cm (0.0001 in.) long, and scientists estimated that the limit on reducing component size might be only about five times smaller than currently possible. Circuit designers could simply make the chips larger, but this would require extensive changes in the equipment that manufacturers use to process integrated circuits. On the other hand, a 1,000,000-component chip would offer the computing power of today's large computers.

**Superconducting Circuits.** Silicon chips are not the only route for progress in the computer field. In 1980 technologists of International Business Machines Corp. (IBM) announced the assembly of a computer switch based on the principle of superconductivity. An electron beam was used to deposit a microscopic electric circuit of niobium wires. When cooled by liquid helium to a temperature near absolute zero, the circuit became superconducting—that is, the supercooled niobium lost practically all resistance to electricity, and the circuit could be switched off or on by the application or removal, respectively, of a magnetic field.

Switching on such a circuit can take place at speeds 10 to 100 times faster than are possible with semiconductor chips. Superconducting circuits can also be packed together more closely in a computer without overheating. Thus larger assemblies can be placed in a smaller space, and operating time is further reduced because interconnecting wires can be much shorter. The principle of superconducting circuits had been known since 1962, but not the technology to build a computer using such circuits. IBM predicted that it would produce a computer with superconducting circuits by 1984.

**Technology and Government.** Interest in applied technology was emphasized by the National Science Foundation in 1980. Since its founding in 1950, the agency, which was distributing about $1 billion in government grants each year, had primarily supported so-called pure scientific research, with only about 10 percent going to engineering and applied sciences. In 1980, however, increasing pressure from the engineering profession, industry, and Congress, as well as from the incoming administration of Ronald Reagan, led the agency to rethink its policies. A great need was seen for basic engineering research in the high-technology areas mentioned above, in order to spur industrial growth and provide the groundwork for major innovations in the future.

A 1980 report prepared by the agency and the Department of Defense indicated a further area for government concern: engineering education. Potential future educators in the field had been drained away from pursuing higher degrees in recent years by the lure of high-paying jobs in industry. Thus the report saw a need for increased graduate-study stipends and funds to update facilities in engineering schools.

**A Technological Nonevent.** In 1979 several journals in the U.S. and Western Europe created a furor by publishing a story about a great mathematical breakthrough in linear computer programming by an obscure Soviet scientist, L. G. Khachian. His work appeared to have profound implications in many areas, including the breaking of secret codes. Further pursuit of the story in 1980, however, revealed that Khachian's work, while of theoretical interest, had no such major implications. The whole affair turned out to be a matter of garbled science reporting by a few journalists.                                                                R.B.

**TELEVISION AND RADIO BROADCASTING.** A three-month strike by about 60,000 film and television actors delayed the beginning of the 1980–81 television season until mid-November and left many feature films stalled at mid-production. A major part of the negotiations concerned

Posing outside the Ewing family home at the start of the new television season were the dramatis personae of Dallas: (back row, left to right) Bobby, Pam, Miss Ellie, J. R.; (front row, left to right) Lucy, Jock, Sue Ellen. The prime-time soap opera drew large audiences and nurtured a spin-off, Knots Landing, during its first season.

the method of payment for acting in projects to be distributed over new technologies such as cable television and video disk. In 1980 every part of the communications industry was speculating on the changes that new distribution systems would bring. Besides a 32.25 percent increase in the minimum wage over the life of the three-year contract, the actors agreed to a 4.5 percent share of the producers' gross revenues for original programming on video cassettes and video disks. Royalties were to be paid, however, only after a specified amount of sales or exposure. Because of this qualification as well as other points of dispute (including the royalty rate itself), opposition was raised about the proposed contract, but it was eventually ratified on Oct. 23.

The Federal Communications Commission (FCC) issued rulings in 1980 that helped to define the technological future facing the entertainers. On June 22 the commission ruled that cable systems could carry an unlimited number of stations from outside their franchise area. The FCC also scrapped rules that allowed broadcasters to block cable-aired programs already available on local outlets. The two decisions almost completely deregulated the cable industry, which, by its own estimate, served 17,000,000 subscribers in the United States. On Sept. 18 the FCC gave preliminary approval to the addition of more than 140 new television stations on the very high frequency (VHF) band.

**Prime-Time Programming.** CBS narrowly surpassed ABC as the most watched network during the prime evening hours of the 1979–80 season. CBS, which began the season in third place, relied on the long-term success of many of its shows and kept them in regular time slots to develop a loyal following while ABC juggled its schedule of established situation comedies to attract audiences for new programs. By season's end, NBC, after quickly capturing a large share of the audience in the fall, dropped to third place among the major networks.

CBS had major hits, including Lou Grant and

*CBS received acclaim for its presentation of* Playing for Time, *starring Vanessa Redgrave (center), with Robin Bartlett (left) and Marisa Berenson as concentration camp inmates. Jewish groups criticized the casting of Redgrave as a Jew because of her outspoken opposition to Zionism.*

*Archie Bunker's Place.* Its most unexpected success, however, was *Dallas,* a prime-time soap opera. The last episode of the 1979–80 season, during which lead character J. R. Ewing was shot, drew the highest rating of the year's regularly scheduled programs. After the audience had the summer and early fall to speculate on the attempted murderer's identity, CBS televised the

revelatory episode on Nov. 21. According to the A. C. Nielsen rating service, a record (for a single entertainment program) 53.3 percent of U.S. households with television sets, or about 83,000,-000 people, watched to learn that Ewing's sister-in-law and former mistress had pulled the trigger.

Much of the credit for CBS's victory was given to its use of strategically placed miniseries, made-

**Tarzan Swings Again**

In January a furor arose in some quarters with the announcement that Bert Parks, 65, was being dropped after 25 years as host of the Miss America pageant. In March, after, as Parks said, they had gone "up into the trees to get someone," the new host was introduced: Ron Ely, 41, a former TV Tarzan. Apparently it worked well for the pageant: The 1980 program had higher viewer ratings than the 1979 program. In November there was a third announcement: Ely had been rehired for the 1981 Labor Day extravaganza.

*Ron Ely (left) and Bert Parks.*

for-television movies, and entertainment specials. CBS scored high ratings with a country-music vehicle, *Kenny Rogers as the Gambler,* a miniseries based on Judith Krantz's novel *Scruples,* and a two-part dramatization of the career of the late Reverend Jim Jones called *Guyana Tragedy.*

NBC had a disappointing year. The network agreed to forgo its planned 152 hr. of Summer Olympics broadcasts, adhering to President Jimmy Carter's request for nonparticipation in the Games. Despite an insurance policy with Lloyd's of London, the network was expected to lose as much as $70,000,000.

The actors' strike clouded the official beginning of the 1980–81 season, but NBC asserted that the new television year began with the broadcast of its 12-hr. miniseries, *Shogun,* which became the second most popular short series of all time, after *Roots.* Because the program's commercials were sold for NBC's average audience size, the network did not immediately realize a profit on the $22,000,000 production. CBS received impressive ratings from its showing of *Playing for Time,* a made-for-television movie dealing with a World War II German concentration camp. Jewish groups criticized the casting of Vanessa Redgrave, a supporter of the Palestine Liberation Organiza-

tion, as Fania Fenelon, a survivor of the Nazis' Auschwitz death camp. While critics praised Redgrave's performance, the woman she portrayed threatened to sue CBS.

Another of 1980's controversial offerings, shown on the Public Broadcasting System (PBS), was *Death of a Princess,* a fictionalized account of the 1977 execution of a Saudi Arabian princess and her lover on charges of adultery. The film, which had caused a temporary break in diplomatic relations between the United Kingdom and Saudi Arabia after it was broadcast on British television, stirred little reaction when it was shown in the U.S. In an effort to mollify the Saudi complaints of unfairness, PBS followed the showing with a 30-min. panel discussion on the work.

The television scandal of 1980 involved ABC and the production company headed by Aaron Spelling and Leonard Goldberg, which had given the network such highly rated programs as *Charlie's Angels.* A number of inquiries were initiated. The Securities and Exchange Commission investigated the business practices of ABC with relation to the production company; the Los Angeles district attorney looked into possible fraud between the producers and various investors in their company; and the Justice Department filed suit charg-

*In the first episode of the 1980–81 television season for CBS's* Archie Bunker's Place, *Archie, portrayed by Carroll O'Connor, brooded beside the empty chair formerly occupied by his television wife, Edith, who passed away during the summer, leaving Archie to face the new season alone.*

## A Hill Erupts and a Joke Backfires

The Great Blue Hill is a peaceful mound that rises 635 ft. above the Boston suburb of Milton. On the April 1 edition of the early news on Boston's Channel 7, viewers were told that the little hill was spewing lava and ash, as part of a chain reaction begun by the eruption of Mount St. Helens in Washington the previous week. As reporter Jan Harrison ended her disaster bulletin she held up a sign reading "April Fool!" But many viewers had already started fleeing the Milton area. Telephone calls deluged the station; they continued even after a lengthy apology was offered on the late news. The following day, Homer Cilley, the executive producer who thought up the joke, was fired.

ing, among other things, that ABC-TV sought to stifle competition by giving unfair advantage to companies such as Spelling-Goldberg.

Because of the actors' strike, most of the Emmy winners did not attend the Sept. 7 ceremony. The thirty-second annual presentation included the award of a seventh Emmy to Ed Asner (best actor in a dramatic series, *Lou Grant*). Other winners included Barbara Bel Geddes (best actress in a dramatic series, *Dallas*), Richard Mulligan and Cathryn Damon (best actor and actress in a com-

edy series, *Soap*), Harry Morgan and Loretta Swit (best supporting actor and actress in a comedy series, *M*A*S*H*), and *Taxi* (best comedy series).

**Television News.** Reporting the results of Presidential elections has become a major function of network news staffs. Many viewers in 1980 chose to watch CBS for Walter Cronkite's last election night broadcast before his retirement (Dan Rather was to replace the veteran anchorman). Ronald Reagan's early victory on Nov. 4 left the networks without the predicted cliff-hanger to carry the audience through the evening. The year's broadcast news event was the third night (July 16) of the Republican National Convention, or the night of the "dream ticket." When former President Gerald R. Ford was interviewed by Cronkite on the *CBS Evening News* that evening, he admitted involvement in serious talks with the former California governor and did not deny Cronkite's speculation about a "co-Presidency." Two hours later, immediately before Vice-Presidential hopeful George Bush was preparing to speak to the convention delegates, the networks reported that Bush was not Reagan's choice. By 10:10 Eastern Daylight Time, CBS made the rumor semiofficial, announcing that negotiations were under way for a Reagan-Ford ticket and that the two men would appear together at the podium that night. Within a half hour, the networks were reporting a change in their prediction, and by 11:54 it was official: George Bush was Ronald Reagan's running mate. This bizarre chain of televised events prompted criticism that questioned television's influence on the workings of the convention. Although the in-

### Dan Rather Replaces Walter Cronkite

For two years Walter Cronkite had been requesting release from his job as anchorman for the *CBS Evening News*. On Feb. 13 his plea was honored. William A. Leonard, president of CBS News, announced that early in 1981 Dan Rather would take over the job. It was the culmination of a 20-year rise for Rather. In 1961 he had attracted national attention with his on-the-spot reporting of hurricane Carla from his native Texas. Appointed Dallas bureau chief, he covered the assassination of President John F. Kennedy. In early 1964 he was named CBS White House correspondent. In 1974 he joined *CBS Reports* and one year later accepted an assignment as an editor of *60 Minutes*. His ambition in his new job: "To be an honest broker of information."

*Dan Rather.*

Six satellite earth stations near the Atlanta headquarters of the Turner Broadcasting System began beaming the Cable News Network to millions of viewers on June 1. The system broadcasts continuous news programs to much of the country via local cable facilities.

cident was the talk of the press, television newscasters quickly defended their medium by pointing to the July 17 first edition headline of the Chicago *Sun-Times:* "It's Reagan and Ford."

Television had an impact on the postconvention Presidential campaign. On Sept. 21 Reagan and independent candidate John Anderson debated the issues in Baltimore before the cameras of all three major networks; President Jimmy Carter, the Democratic Party candidate, declined to appear. On Oct. 28 Carter and Reagan met in Cleveland in a nationally televised debate that some observers believed decided the election; *see also* ELECTIONS. Anderson, in Washington, D.C., responded to the same questions put to Carter and Reagan on several cable-television stations.

Much speculation was also raised in 1980 as to the possible influence on political races of religious political action groups whose views were frequently expressed on both television and radio. The Reverend Jerry Falwell, for example, founder and president of Moral Majority, Inc.—

largest of the evangelical Christian political action organizations—headed the *Old-Time Gospel Hour,* carried weekly over about 700 radio and television stations.

The continued success of CBS's *60 Minutes* had prompted other networks to introduce their own newsmagazines, and ABC's *20/20* fared well during the 1979–80 season. NBC's *Prime Time,* with *Tomorrow* show host Tom Snyder, did not succeed, however, and was eventually replaced by a newsmagazine hosted by David Brinkley.

A major television trend in 1980 was to shows that emphasized real-life subjects, an approach directly linked to the popularity of the news-documentary shows. Following the success of *Real People,* an NBC show that featured unusual interviews and reports from America's heartland, a number of other "reality shows" were added to the programming schedules. ABC offered *That's Incredible,* a series that focused on daredevils, both amateur and professional. Television critics and performers alike scoffed at these programs as being in poor taste, but the networks saw the reality shows as a much less expensive alternative to the average situation comedy.

**Expanding Options.** Beyond the access to out-of-town broadcasts that cable systems offered to subscribers (including superstations such as Ted Turner's WTBS and his Atlanta-based all-news channel), pay television also became a major viewer option. For the first time the services offered by outlets such as Home Box Office (HBO) and Showtime made a significant dent in the major networks' prime-time audiences. An example of the growing influence of pay television was the election night showing of the Academy Award-winning 1978 film *The Deer Hunter*. Although CBS originally held the television option for the movie, the network decided against showing it, citing the film's excessive violence and rough language. Meanwhile, *The Deer Hunter* had already enjoyed a popular and unexpurgated run on HBO and other pay television outlets. Consequently, a number of local stations ran the movie on Nov. 4, some with light editing and others with the film intact.

The dependence of pay television outlets on uncut feature films prompted some moviemakers to reexamine their relationship with such outlets. Pay television offers movie producers supplementary income after a film's exhibition in theaters, and a film that fails at the box office can be quickly sold to pay television. In 1980 a major example of how the pay television option can work against filmmakers was *The Great Santini,* a small-scale drama that was sold to HBO and an airline movie service after it failed in numerous test markets. Taking matters into their own hands, the movie's producers opened the film in New York City, garnered rave reviews from influential national critics, and found themselves with a hit movie that was already on television, competing with itself.

In December a new cable network, RCTV, announced that it had acquired exclusive ten-year rights to thousands of hours of programming from the British Broadcasting Corporation (BBC). The BBC offerings had long been a staple of public broadcasting outlets.

The Justice Department on Aug. 14 filed an antitrust suit against a plan announced on April 22 by four major film companies and Getty Oil Co. (which already maintained ESPN, the national sports network) to establish a pay television network. The government charged that antitrust laws were threatened because the plan would limit the availability of feature films to both existing pay and commercial networks. Analysts doubted that it would be the movie industry's last attempt at increasing its involvement in pay television.

The most far-reaching telecommunications network was being pursued by the Communications Satellite Corp., better known as COMSAT. By 1982, COMSAT hoped to have three of its powerful satellites beaming special programming to subscribers in the continental U.S. But the estimated $200 cost for installing the special rooftop aerial might inhibit some customers, who would also pay a $15–$20 monthly fee comparable to cable costs.

The wide variety of entertainment options to be offered in the 1980's led to both intense speculation and major contractual agreements in the broadcast field. Alliances were being struck between major corporations to gain a foothold in the lucrative field (Warner Brothers and American Express Co. and the American Telephone and Telegraph Co. and Western Union Corp. were two such alliances). Industry analysts expected many similar partnerships to form in the 1980's as rival technologies were abandoned (three incompatible video disk systems were on the market), and the public's acceptance of the new hardware was gauged.

**Radio.** Although radio often appeared to be a minor element in broadcasting when compared with the television/video field, the industry was thriving economically in 1980 and looking toward its own technological advances. Stereo AM still awaited final approval by the FCC; however, the commission opened up frequencies formerly dominated by long-distance outlets known as "clear channel" stations, paving the way for an additional 125 stations. More than 8600 radio stations were operating in 1980 in the U.S., compared with 3688 in 1960.

Radio programming had become diversified during recent years, with talk and all-news formats becoming increasingly popular on the AM band and adult contemporary music a favorite on FM. Programs produced by radio networks for distribution to affiliates were also increasing in number. They included rock concerts on shows such as the *King Biscuit Flower Hour* and nationwide radio talk shows such as Mutual's *Larry King Show*. News programs were also being tailored for specific demographics, such as NBC's *Source,* which reached 146 outlets with lighthearted news and features tailored to the 18-to-34-year age group. National Public Radio continued to break ground with programming such as *Earplay,* a drama series with counterparts on commercial stations, and *All Things Considered,* which was thought by many to be radio's finest newscast.                                                   J.M.

**TENNESSEE.** *See* STATISTICS OF THE WORLD.

**TEXAS.** *See* STATISTICS OF THE WORLD.

**THAILAND.** In 1980 governmental power in Thailand was transferred without the use of military force—a rare occurrence.

**Politics.** A sharp hike in gasoline prices, double-digit inflation, and a wave of labor unrest led to January rumors of a military coup to replace Prime Minister Kriangsak Chamanand. A major cabinet shake-up in February failed to placate Kriangsak's critics. Faced with a no-confidence vote in parliament, Kriangsak, who came to power through a military coup in 1977, quietly handed in his resignation on Feb. 19.

On March 3 the parliament chose the popular defense minister, Gen. Prem Tinsulanonda, to replace Kriangsak. In an effort to build a wide political base, Prem named a largely civilian cabinet from the ranks of the major political parties. During the latter part of the year, however, persisting inflation and a severe sugar shortage caused grumbling in the parliament and a waning of public enthusiasm for Prem.

**Insurgents.** Ideological squabbling within the pro-Chinese Communist Party of Thailand and the loss of its bases in pro-Soviet Laos and Cambodia resulted in a sharp drop in guerrilla incidents in the northern provinces. Moreover, China, anxious to strengthen Thailand as a buffer against the Vietnamese, began to withdraw direct aid to the guerrillas. The Muslim-dominated southern provinces became a major trouble spot, however. Throughout the year, Muslim separatists attacked government buildings and terrorized the Buddhist population. The most active of the separatist groups, the Pattani United Liberation Organization, acknowledged that it received support from Libya.

**The Economy.** The country's economy retained its basic strengths, including self-sufficiency in food. But a severe drought damaged the rice crop, the most important source of foreign exchange. The rice shortage, in addition to the soaring price of imported oil, sent Thailand's balance of payments deep into the red. The inflation rate hovered around 20 percent.

**Refugees.** Hundreds of thousands of refugees from the Communist-ruled countries of Vietnam,

The international relief effort to provide food for famine-stricken Cambodia was partially suspended in February following reports that the supplies were being expropriated by Vietnamese troops. Here participants in a "March for Survival" are stopped by Thai troops from crossing the border into Cambodia to deliver food supplies.

*Circus pageantry came to the Broadway stage in* Barnum, *a musical tribute to the great showman. Jim Dale, star of the extravaganza, won a Tony Award as the best actor in a musical for his performance.*

Laos, and Cambodia continued to fill camps in Thailand. Despite the considerable burden, Thailand continued its policy of offering haven to Indochinese refugees. Some refugee camps became sanctuaries for guerrillas fighting against the Vietnamese-backed regime in Cambodia. As a consequence, Vietnamese troops crossed the Thai border in June and raided several camps. After sharp exchanges with Thai troops, the Vietnamese returned to Cambodia.

**Foreign Policy.** Vietnamese Foreign Minister Nguyen Co Thach visited Bangkok in May, but Vietnam's military annexation of Cambodia remained an implacable issue. Relations grew even colder after the Vietnamese incursion into Thailand in June. United Nations Secretary-General Kurt Waldheim visited Bangkok and Hanoi in August but failed to smooth relations between the two countries. Along with the other members of the Association of Southeast Asian Nations—Malaysia, Singapore, Indonesia, and the Philippines—Thailand retained its strong anti-Vietnamese and anti-Soviet foreign policy stance.

*See* STATISTICS OF THE WORLD. *See also* CAMBODIA; LAOS.

R.J.C.

**THEATER.** In 1980 the American theater displayed all of the lively activity that had characterized its recent history. According to *Variety,* the show business weekly, Broadway box-office receipts for the 1979–80 season totaled $143,400,000, topping all previous records. The increase was due both to rising ticket costs and larger audiences; attendance rose to 9,300,000. Attendance and box-office business also boomed nationally, reported *Variety,* which rated Los Angeles, Chicago, San Francisco, Washington, Philadelphia, and Boston as the nation's six leading road cities. In New York City, Off Broadway and Off Off Broadway continued to offer performances for a wide variety of audiences. Off Off Broadway, however, was hampered by a long-standing dispute with Actors' Equity Association that affected playwrights as well as players. Professional nonprofit playhouses around the nation made a steady contribution to the health of the theater in the United States.

**Musicals.** As usual, musical comedies made the biggest splash on Broadway. David Merrick's *42nd Street,* fetching a record box-office ticket price of $35, harked back to the musicals of the 1930's, with a score by Harry Warren and Al Dubin. Tri-

Lee Roy Reams shares the dancing spotlight with Wanda Richert in 42nd Street. The theater maxim "the show must go on," on which the story was based, was tested by the death of the show's director-choreographer, Gower Champion, on the day of the Broadway opening.

umph and tragedy coincided on opening night, Aug. 25, when Merrick announced that Gower Champion, the show's director-choreographer, had died earlier that day; see OBITUARIES.

Nostalgia characterized most of the year's popular musicals. Returning to Broadway were such memorable successes as *Camelot*, with Richard Burton recreating his 1960 role of King Arthur; *West Side Story*; and *Brigadoon*. *Barnum* celebrates the career of the 19th-century showman. *A Day in Hollywood/A Night in the Ukraine* combines Hollywood song and dance with an Anton Chekhov farce adapted as if intended for the Marx Brothers. The year's musicals included a pair of exceptional black shows. Vinnette Carroll's gospel-inspired *Your Arms Too Short to Box with God* returned to the Broadway stage, and *Black Broadway* presented young talent sharing the stage with grand old stars.

Three of the year's more intimate musicals also paid tribute to the past. *Billy Bishop Goes to War*, a two-man show, commemorates the adventures of Canada's World War I flying ace. *Tintypes* provides nostalgia through a medley of American songs, mostly from the late 19th and early 20th centuries. *Hijinks!* turns Clyde Fitch's 1901 comedy *Captain Jinks of the Horse Marines* into a period musical.

Radio City Music Hall reveled in its new lease on life with such shows as *A Rockette Spectacular*, starring Ginger Rogers. The art of prestidigitation returned to Broadway as Harry Blackstone, Jr., revived some of his father's famed illusions in a spectacle entitled *Blackstone!*

**Comedies and Dramas.** In the field of straight plays, a major event of the year was Nikolai Erdman's *The Suicide*, the story of a 1920's Russian Everyman who threatens to kill himself as a protest against the oppressive evils of the Stalin era. Current South African history and the specter of apartheid are reflected in Athol Fugard's *A Lesson from Aloes*. Among the year's final arrivals was *Amadeus*, Peter Shaffer's London hit about a rival of Wolfgang Amadeus Mozart. The Broadway

401

Opposite page, above: Richard Burton and Christine Ebersole as King Arthur and Queen Guinevere watch, with their subjects, a jousting match in the 1980 revival of Camelot. Burton recreated the role he introduced on Broadway in 1960. Below: The Marx Brothers' outrageous comedy style was recalled in the second act of A Day in Hollywood/A Night in the Ukraine. Recreating the brothers in their quintessential roles were (left to right) David Garrison as Groucho, Priscilla Lopez as Harpo, and Frank Lazarus as Chico.

Left: Neil Simon's new comedy offering in 1980 was I Ought to Be in Pictures, starring (left to right) Ron Liebman, Dinah Manoff, and Joyce Van Patten. A Tony Award for best featured actress in a play went to Manoff for her performance.

production starred Ian McKellen as Antonio Salieri, Tim Curry as Mozart, and Jane Seymour as Mozart's wife.

*Whose Life Is It Anyway?* reopened on Broadway with a new setting and cast. The paralyzed English accident victim originally played by Tom Conti became a U.S. paralytic in the person of Mary Tyler Moore, who was generally acclaimed for her performance in Brian Clark's revised version.

New works by three of America's major playwrights opened and closed in short order. Tennessee Williams's *Clothes for a Summer Hotel,* Edward Albee's *The Lady from Dubuque,* and Arthur Miller's *The American Clock* failed to capture the excitement that usually accompanied offerings by such noted playwrights.

Comedy fared better than serious drama. Neil Simon's *I Ought to Be in Pictures* is a funny and touching account of a father-daughter reunion. In *Home,* Samm-Art Williams traces the adventures of a black North Carolina farm boy who takes the route of the prodigal son. Lanford Wilson continued the story of the Talley family in *Fifth of July,* a later segment in Wilson's contemplated five-play cycle. *A Life* gave British actor Roy Dotrice an opportunity to exhibit one of his finely etched performances, as a character expanded by Hugh Leonard from his award-winning *Da.* Jean Kerr's *Lunch Hour,* which is a frothy domestic trifle, co-

British playwright Harold Pinter (seated) appears with actors (left to right) Roy Scheider, Blythe Danner, and Raul Julia, who performed in his drama Betrayal. The New York Drama Critics' Circle voted it best foreign play of the 1979–80 season.

starred Gilda Radner as a kooky young woman who startles a straitlaced marriage counselor (Sam Waterston) with the news that their respective spouses are having an affair. Infidelity in the British manner is treated in Harold Pinter's Betrayal, a subtly ironic and complex triangle that featured Blythe Danner, Raul Julia, and Roy Scheider in the principal roles.

Revivals made a conspicuous contribution to theater fare in the lighter vein. At Lincoln Center the Vivian Beaumont Theater, dark for more than three years, reopened with Philip Barry's 1939 comedy, The Philadelphia Story, starring Blythe Danner. Other notable revivals included George Bernard Shaw's Major Barbara, George S. Kaufman and Moss Hart's The Man Who Came to Dinner, Paul Osborn's Morning's at Seven, and Henrik Ibsen's John Gabriel Borkman.

Off Broadway presented, among other plays, well-received revivals of Terence Rattigan's The Winslow Boy and John Osborne's Look Back in Anger, the latter starring England's Malcolm McDowell. The Public Theater revived Bertolt Brecht's Mother Courage and Her Children, Chekhov's The Sea Gull, and Gilbert and Sullivan's The Pirates of Penzance with Linda Ronstadt. The Brooklyn Academy of Music Theater Company under David Jones launched a promising first season with a repertory that included Shakespeare (The Winter's Tale), Maksim Gorki (Barbarians), Charles MacArthur (Johnny on a Spot), and Rachel Crothers (He and She). Director Peter Brook and his Paris-based company, Le Centre International de Creations Théâtrales, brought four works drawn from ancient and modern sources to New York City's La Mama Experimental Theater Club. One of the most ambitious projects by any group was a repertory season of Sophocles' Oedipus Rex, Oedipus at Colonus, and Antigone by the Classic Stage Company.

Among the more successful new works presented Off Broadway were John Ford Noonan's A

*Coupla White Chicks Sitting Around Talking,* William Hamilton's *Save Grand Central,* and William Mastrosimone's *The Woolgatherer.* Maurice Sendak and Carole King adapted some of Sendak's storybook characters to the musical stage for *Really Rosie.*

**The National Stage.** Although hampered by economic pressures, the nation's nonprofit professional theaters continued to flourish. At the end of 1980, the Theater Communications Group (TCG), a nonprofit service organization, numbered 196 member theaters, an increase of 17 over 1979.

Two developments on the national scene were the opening of the $13,000,000 Helen G. Bonfils Theater complex in Denver and the launching of the Virginia Stage Company, a resident professional troupe, at the historic Wells Theater in Norfolk, Va. Special events of the year included the five-week Black Theater Festival International at Lincoln Center, New York City, with performances by U.S., British, and Nigerian troupes, and a week-long TCG conference at Princeton University that brought together 250 theater professionals with experts in the social and natural sciences.

**Tony Awards.** The 1979–80 Antoinette Perry Awards were presented on June 8 at the Mark Hellinger Theatre. *Children of a Lesser God* received the award for best play, and its stars, John Rubinstein and Phyllis Frelich, won Tonys for best actor and actress. Jim Dale of *Barnum* was chosen best actor in a musical, and Patti LuPone captured the award for best actress. *Evita,* the show in which she portrayed the title character, won the Tony for best musical. Harold Prince was chosen best director of a musical for the same show. For *Morning's at Seven* Vivian Matalon received the award for best director of a play.            J.B.

**TOGO.** *See* STATISTICS OF THE WORLD.

**TONGA.** *See* STATISTICS OF THE WORLD.

*Appropriately staged in the state where the characters live, Hoagy, Bix and Wolfgang Beethoven Bunkhaus, by Adrian Mitchell, premiered in the U.S. at the recently restored Indiana Repertory Theatre in Indianapolis. Jamey Sheridan (left) portrayed Hoagy Carmichael and Gregory Salata played the songwriter's friend William Moenkhaus.*

*The Talley family of Missouri returned to Broadway in Lanford Wilson's play,* Fifth of July. *Set a generation after* Talley's Folly, *which won a Pulitzer Prize for Wilson,* Fifth of July *starred (left to right) Christopher Reeve, Swoosie Kurtz, and Amy Wright.*

The latest DC-9 model to begin regular passenger service was the fuel-efficient Super 80. Largest of the DC-9 series, the Super 80 made its first scheduled flight on Oct. 5. As many as 172 passengers can be accommodated in the short-to-medium-range jetliner.

**TRANSPORTATION.** Deregulation picked up momentum in 1980 with the enactment of major trucking and railroad decontrol legislation. The recession generally had a severe effect on transport industries. Airlines had stormy flying during their second year under deregulation; service cutbacks continued and fare increases were substantial. While the trucking industry waged a largely unsuccessful fight to prevent deregulation, railroads experienced adoption of another important decontrol measure. Ocean shipping showed some signs of a modest pickup from a long maritime slump. Mass transit and Amtrak ridership leveled off but held the gains achieved during 1979.

## AVIATION

The U.S. airline industry suffered a drop in ridership in 1980, carrying about 300,000,000 passengers, about 17,000,000 fewer than in 1979. Scheduled airlines received revenues of more than $32 billion, up from $26.5 billion the previous year, as fares soared. There was a loss of more than $150,000,000, however, after a profit of $409,000,000 in 1979. Statistics were equally glum for the world's carriers. At the October general meeting in Montréal of the International Air Transport Association, Knut Hammarskjöld, director general, said 1980 was "expected to be the bleakest year in international aviation history" in terms of profits. On Dec. 22 he said that the international airlines had lost an estimated $2.53 billion, the "worst year in their history."

Carriers continued to pick and choose their routes, seeking to limit new service to the higher-volume markets. While regional airlines prospered, larger carriers were forced to trim operations and staff during the recession. Air fare bargains narrowed and basic fares were raised sharply, in part to take advantage of new fare flexibility given by the Civil Aeronautics Board (CAB).

A National Academy of Sciences (NAS) panel said in June that the aircraft certification program of the Federal Aviation Administration (FAA) should be reviewed and the safety overview bolstered. FAA engineers fell behind the aviation industry in competence, the panel said. The NAS group was formed after the May, 1979, crash of a DC-10 at Chicago that killed 273 persons. Only one U.S. airline fatality occurred during 1980.

**Fares Head Upward.** Airlines sought to make up for declining traffic and rising expenses by boosting fares. The average "yield," or price per mile to the passenger, went up by nearly 35 percent. Discounts on fares were less generous; the popular "Super Saver" was narrowed from 45 percent to 25 percent during midweek and from 35 percent to 15 percent on weekends. The CAB allowed basic fare increases of more than 11 percent and permitted airlines to raise fares up to 30 percent for flights of more than 400 mi. and by unlimited amounts for flights of up to 200 mi., in addition to a $15 surcharge on top of that level. Price cutting occurred on transcontinental flights, with summer fares as low as $99 offered on New York–California trips. Later in the year, however, these bargains disappeared.

Internationally, the CAB allowed fare increases of more than 20 percent, and also gave airlines the freedom to raise fares up to 15 percent above the basic level, or by unlimited amounts in some instances.

**Pulling in Their Horns.** Some airlines were forced to retrench after expansion during 1979, deregulation's first full year, or to cut back flights because of the travel slump. Climbing fuel expenses were blamed for the end of supersonic Concorde flights by Braniff International Corp. between Washington, D.C., and Dallas.

**New Aviation Agreements.** A U.S.-China pact signed in September opened the way for the first scheduled airline service between the two countries since 1949. It allowed each country to name one carrier for flights during the first two years, with additional airlines possible thereafter. Pan American World Airways and the Civil Aviation Administration of China, the Chinese national carrier, planned service for January, 1981. Pan Am, chosen from five applicants by the CAB, intended to link New York City, San Francisco, and Los Angeles with Peking and Shanghai, stopping at Tokyo en route.

A separate U.S.-British agreement allowed more service between the United States and London, possibly adding 13 U.S. cities and permitting more service for Boston and either Baltimore or New York. The CAB began adding routes to and from London and granting rights to more airlines.

## MASS TRANSIT

Steady patronage during the first nine months of 1980 resulted in a 1.8 percent increase in ridership over the equivalent 1979 figure of 6.03 billion. But transit's 32 months of consecutive increases in ridership were ended in April by a New York City transit strike.

**Rising Commuting Costs.** As the deficits of transit systems surpassed $3 billion for the first time, government subsidies failed to keep pace. Fares increased at a much faster rate than before, signaling an end to the policy of expanding the ridership by keeping fares low. In Portland, Oreg., for instance, a fare rise was necessary to avert reduced service. The transit board hoped to have the riders pay for at least 40 percent of the system's cost by 1985. The Philadelphia area's Southeastern Pennsylvania Transportation Authority instituted a 15¢ fare increase, to 65¢, in July after the courts had invalidated the first increase attempt. Transit officials in Atlanta and Los Angeles had to overcome similar court battles before boosting their fares.

The nation's largest mass transit system, in New York City, was shut down April 1-11 by striking subway and bus workers. Soon after the wage settlement, the transit fare rose from 50¢ to 60¢.

An 11-week strike of the Port Authority Trans-Hudson railroad forced 80,000 daily commuters to find other means of transportation between New Jersey and New York City. Service resumed on Sept. 2.

Boston's Massachusetts Bay Transportation Authority was briefly forced to shut down the metropolitan area's subway, bus, rail, and trolley lines when the system's finances ran out. The state failed to reach a solution to the transit network's monetary problems by the Dec. 6 deadline. The following day the legislature approved a $41,000,-000 plan to keep the nation's oldest mass transit system alive.

Bus fares went from 75¢ to $1 in Miami, Fla., and another tentative rise was set for Jan. 1, 1981, if Dade County did not get enough monetary aid from the state. Ridership increased in cities such as York, Pa., despite climbing fares. Intercity bus ridership also showed a gain of about 5 percent in 1980, an increase attributed to higher gasoline prices and rising air fares.

Problems with local service arose after undercarriage cracks were found on new Grumman "Flxible" buses in several cities, including Los Angeles and New York. The buses were purchased to meet the requirement of the Urban Mass Transportation Administration (UMTA) that vehicles purchased with funds from UMTA be domestically manufactured.

**Rail Transit Plans.** San Diego worked to complete a 16-mi. light-rail, or trolley, line to Tijuana on the Mexican border. The U.S. Department of Transportation authorized funding for final engineering of a 15-mi. light-rail system in greater Portland, Oreg. Sacramento, Calif., and Detroit had their own trolley plans, and Denver officials discussed building an initial light-rail segment of up to 15 mi. by mid-1985. Pittsburgh's first planned light-rail subway could be in operation by the end of 1984. Subways were also planned for Los Angeles and Houston, Texas. Miami and Baltimore proceeded with construction of their new subway systems, while Washington, D.C., continued to expand its rapid transit network.

The New York State Metropolitan Transportation Authority (MTA) challenged a 1979 federal requirement that transit systems modify many subway stations and all regular-route buses to accommodate the handicapped. The MTA considered the requirement excessively costly. After announcing in September that it would forgo $375,000,000 in annual federal aid by refusing to

Commuters in New York City showed their resilience when faced with a transit strike in April. Warnings of dreaded "gridlock"—traffic congestion so severe that movement in any direction is impossible—kept many motorists out of Manhattan.

comply with the mandate, the authority relented in October.

### MOTOR TRANSPORT

Motor carriers in the U.S. fell upon hard times in 1980. The recession decreased the transport volume of automobiles, auto parts, and other goods. Truckers tried to prevent major deregulation but finally went along with the decontrol measure that Congress passed.

**Deregulating Road Firms.** ICC monitoring of the trucking industry was substantially rolled back by a law signed on July 1. The law made it easier for truck concerns to initiate or expand service. Existing firms could no longer block applications easily, greater emphasis was placed on competition rather than on protecting existing carriers, and a range of commodity and route restrictions was lifted. Independent owner-operator truckers were provided substantial opportunity to move pro-

cessed foods without regulation in addition to the raw farm goods that were already exempt from ICC control.

The new law, reluctantly endorsed by the American Trucking Association Inc. (ATA), the industry's trade group, also encouraged more rate competition. It allowed truckers to adjust freight rates by 10 percent or more to reflect changes in the government's producer price index of finished goods. Big trucking firms applauded those provisions but showed less enthusiasm for others that limited joint rate-setting by regional groups. That provision would take effect in 1984.

A law signed on Oct. 15 encouraged household goods movers to give binding rate estimates to customers and gave more freedom in rate-setting. Some of the paperwork and other regulatory burdens imposed by the ICC were removed. The ICC also advocated wide deregulation of intercity bus routes and fares. The plan was generally endorsed by the Transportation Association of America.

**Business Ebbs.** The nation's recession depressed truck operations until late in the year. The ATA said that the freight movements of about 825,000,-000 tons were 18 percent below 1979 figures. The ICC-backed rate increases helped revenues rise about 5 percent, to $43.3 billion. Profits fell sharply, from $820,000,000 in 1979 to about $150,000,000 before write-offs, and they declined further after write-offs of operating-rights licenses, the ATA calculated.

**Highways.** In 1980 the interstate highway system was reported to be so battered by trucks of increasingly heavy weight that vast stretches were in need of rebuilding. Daniel Hanson, president of the American Road and Transportation Builders Association, estimated that the nation's road system was wearing out twice as fast as necessary repairs were being made. The question of raising taxes to finance road repairs faced almost every state legislature during the year.

### RAILROADS

The nation's railroad industry did well in 1980, with heavy coal and grain hauling compensating for a recessionary slump. Congress enacted a deregulation law and the Interstate Commerce Commission (ICC) moved ahead to remove shackles from railroad rate-setting.

**Decontrolling the Industry.** A significant deregulation bill became law on Oct. 14, culminating a long, tedious legislative struggle. The measure's backers partly acceded to customer concerns about unbridled rate freedom for railroads in order to get the legislation approved. The law still gave railroads considerable freedom to raise or lower freight rates, sign contracts with individual shippers, and abandon money-losing lines.

The ICC acted quickly to carry out the deregulation plan. The commission issued a proposal late in the year to modify the calculation of rates for carrying coal by assigning more system-wide costs to these heavy, long-haul movements, thus justifying greater increases. The agency also proposed a plan permitting railroads to use their own cost index to calculate quick, quarterly, and automatic rate increases for all freight. Such increases were to supplant the old method by which regional railroad groups agreed on general rate boosts and submitted them for approval by the ICC.

The ICC also approved railroad freight rate increases of about 11 percent through September, with an additional 5 percent request pending. These higher rates helped boost earnings in the first nine months of 1980 to $613,100,000, 10 percent higher than that of the same 1979 span. Operating revenues for the period rose to $20.7 billion, or 12 percent above the first nine months of 1979.

**Mergers Quicken.** The ICC was generally more receptive to rail mergers than it had been in the past. Railroads proceeded with consolidation agreements to strengthen their hold on competitive rail service markets.

Union Pacific Corp. moved to acquire the Missouri Pacific Corp. and Western Pacific Railroad lines. Santa Fe Industries Inc. announced on May 15 that it would seek to take over the Southern Pacific Co., but the deal later fell through. The Southern Railway System and the Norfolk & Western Railway Co. revived, on June 2, plans to merge. The ICC on April 17 approved merger plans of Burlington Northern Inc. and the St. Louis–San Francisco Railway and on Sept. 24 sanctioned consolidation of Seaboard Coast Line Industries Inc. with the Chessie System Inc. Officials of the government-funded Consolidated Rail Corp. (Conrail) requested a minimum of $900,000,000 in additional federal aid to remain in operation through 1985. The federally financed National Railroad Passenger Corp. (Amtrak) re-

*The Advanced Passenger Train being developed for British Rail was tested for intercity passenger use in the near future. The train can attain speeds of 155 mph.*

ported little change in ridership from the brisk 1979 pace.

### SHIPPING

Merchant marine operations increased slightly in 1980 as fewer ships were laid up.

**Maritime Commercial Gains.** The longtime overcapacity in oil tankers eased worldwide, and U.S. fleets were busily transporting oil from Alaska to other parts of the nation. The accelerated ordering of tankers was highlighted by a contract valued at more than $500,000,000 for General Dynamics Corp. to supply a unit of Zapata Corp. with three liquefied natural gas tankers.

Some shipping rates for cargo moving from Europe to the Persian Gulf fell sharply in late 1980 because of the Iran-Iraq war and the collapse of the Iranian market. A total of 3111 merchant vessels were on order worldwide as of June 30, a 5 percent increase over 1979. Tonnage of ships on order rose by 28 percent to 32,500,000 gross tons. The value of merchant vessel orders for U.S. shipbuilders declined to $2.7 billion on Sept. 1, however, from $3.1 billion for the same period of 1979, according to the Federal Maritime Administration. A $1.2 billion U.S. Navy order for an aircraft carrier to be built by Newport News Shipbuilding put the year-end Navy backlog at $8.95 billion, off slightly from $9.08 billion at the close of 1979, the Shipbuilders Council estimated.

**China Pact.** The U.S. and China signed a formal merchant marine agreement on Sept. 17. The pact made possible full-scale resumption of Sino-American ocean trade after a lapse of more than 30 years. It guaranteed that each country's vessels would transport at least a third of the U.S.-China ocean trade. U.S. ships were granted access to 20 Chinese ports after giving 7 days' notice, and Chinese vessels gained entry to 55 U.S. ports on 4 days' notice, with 7 days' notice required for many other ports.

**Disasters.** Twenty-three crewmen of a U.S. Coast Guard ship died on Jan. 28 in the collision of their vessel and an oil tanker near the Sunshine Skyway Bridge at the mouth of Tampa Bay. It was the worst peacetime disaster in Coast Guard history. On May 9 a Liberian-flag freighter rammed into the Sunshine Skyway Bridge, sending part of the bridge into the bay and killing 35 persons in vehicles that plunged into the water.

The U.S. grain-carrying vessel *Poet*, with 34 crew members aboard, vanished in the Atlantic Ocean after sailing from Philadelphia on Oct. 24, bound for Port Said, Egypt. An intensive nine-day air and sea search was halted on Nov. 17.

*See also* AUTOMOBILES. A.R.K.

**TRINIDAD AND TOBAGO.** See STATISTICS OF THE WORLD.

**TUNISIA.** The moderate and fairly prosperous North African nation of Tunisia was rocked by a devastating guerrilla raid in 1980. Labor unrest continued while students clashed in disagreement over the country's future.

Gafsa, in central Tunisia, was the scene of a large-scale guerrilla attack on an army barracks on Jan. 27. Soldiers, gendarmes, and recruits were slaughtered by raiders who tortured some of their victims before killing them. Forty-four people were killed, 111 wounded. The Tunisian government blamed Libya. The two countries had been hostile to each other since the mid-1970's, after Tunisia backed out of a 1974 agreement to merge with Libya. After the raid, a Libyan-based radio station calling itself Radio Free Gafsa broadcast insults against the Tunisian leadership. The Tunisian government accused 57 individuals of taking part in the raid. On April 17, 13 were hanged; others were sentenced to hard labor or lesser punishments or acquitted. Trial evidence pointed to Algerian and Libyan involvement. The United States airlifted 10 armored personnel carriers to Tunisia on Feb. 29.

Habib Bourguiba, Tunisia's ailing president for life, seemed to rally in 1980. When his stand-in as head of government and would-be successor, Prime Minister Hedi Nouira, was paralyzed by a stroke at the end of February, Bourguiba quickly named Mohammed Mzali, the minister of education, as new prime minister and also as his successor. Mzali eliminated from important positions those who took a hard line against labor. Official repression of the 500,000-member General Union of Tunisian Workers and attempts to replace its leaders with progovernment officers in 1978 had led to nationwide strikes.

Tunisia's relatively liberal atmosphere allowed for some expression of ideological differences, which sometimes erupted into violent clashes between fundamentalist Muslim students and leftists influenced by Albanian Marxists. Tunisia's intellectuals as well as its opposition politicians urged a political liberalization. The Destour Socialist Party remained the only legal party.

*See* STATISTICS OF THE WORLD. R.M.

**TURKEY.** Although the government headed by Süleyman Demirel managed to secure desperately needed international financial assistance in early 1980, it was unable to deal effectively with Turkey's beleaguered economy or its violently opposed political and religious factions. Strikes, riots, and assassinations led to a military coup in September.

**Terrorism.** Left-wing and right-wing Turkish groups inflicted violence on each other in 1980. Before the September coup, the number of armed leftists was estimated at 10,000 to 15,000 and the number of armed rightists at 10,000. About 3000 people had died in terrorist violence during the past two years. Within a single week in July, three well-known Turkish leaders were killed. Neither of Turkey's two major political parties held a parliamentary majority, and the national assembly was unable to pass urgent legislation.

**Military Coup.** On Sept. 11, Turkish armed forces seized control of the country and established a six-man ruling military junta with Gen. Kenan Evren as chairman. The parliament was dissolved and all political activity banned, although the junta promised to restore democratic rule when conditions allowed. Retired Adm. Bülent Ulusu was named prime minister on Sept. 20; he appointed a 27-member cabinet that included 7 other retired officers. Major political leaders were taken into custody. A Sept. 26 decree dismissed 1700 elected mayors and their city councils.

About 60 legislators were freed on Oct. 11, including Demirel and his chief rival, Bülent Ecevit, but Alpaslan Turkes, leader of the right-wing Nationalist Action Party, was formally arraigned Oct. 15 and 11,500 people, according to official count, were still being held on Oct. 28, most of them reportedly belonging to extremist groups. Two convicted terrorists were hanged on Oct. 8 in the first executions in Turkey since 1972. Martial law was in effect throughout the country. On Oct. 27 the junta promulgated a decree that in effect superseded the country's constitution. The decree also said that Evren would exercise the powers of the presidency.

**The Economy.** Turkey began the year with an unemployment rate of at least 20 percent, an annual inflation rate of close to 100 percent, and its industrial base seriously damaged by sabotage and labor unrest. In January the International Monetary Fund (IMF) approved its largest credit ever, a three-year, $1.6 billion loan to Turkey. The United States, West Germany, and Saudi Arabia also extended new loans. In return for the IMF credit, however, Turkey had to agree to austerity measures, including slashing subsidies for state enterprises, curtailing public spending and bank lending to the private sector, imposing annual limits on foreign borrowing, lifting price controls, and devaluing the Turkish currency, the lira. Following these measures, prices soared, increasing fourfold for some commodities.

In December, Turkey's economic problems were still immense. Unemployment and inflation had not eased in 1980, the foreign debt exceeded $16 billion, and the nation's oil bill shot up because the government had to enter the high-priced spot market after its two major suppliers, Iran and Iraq, went to war. The inflation rate for 1980 was 118 percent.

**Foreign Relations.** The U.S. and Turkey signed an agreement on March 29 enabling the U.S. to continue using an air base, four intelligence-gathering installations, and seven communications stations in Turkey in return for about $450,000,000 in American economic and military aid in 1980. Turkey abrogated a military treaty with the U.S. in 1975 in retaliation for a U.S. arms embargo after Turkey's 1974 invasion of Cyprus. After the embargo was lifted in 1978, Turkey allowed the U.S. to use the bases pending a new agreement.

Turkey welcomed Greece's return to the North Atlantic Treaty Organization military command on Oct. 20. The two countries did not settle their conflicting claims over the Aegean Sea's continental shelf, territorial waters, and airspace in 1980, but Turkey made several small gestures to improve its relations with Greece. R.M.

**TUVALU.** See STATISTICS OF THE WORLD.

# U

**UGANDA.** Amid continued economic chaos and widespread lawlessness, in 1980 political power in Uganda gradually shifted back to former President Milton Obote and his supporters.

**Obote's Restoration.** After his overthrow by Idi Amin in 1971, Obote fled to neighboring Tanzania. There, under the protection of his close friend, Tanzania's President Julius K. Nyerere, Obote attempted to form a resistance movement to the regime of dictator Idi Amin. (Obote himself suspended the constitution and jailed thousands while in power from 1962 to 1971.) After the Tanzanian-Ugandan war of 1979, Obote's supporters returned to Uganda, and some took prominent positions in the loose political coalition that ruled following Amin's overthrow. Torn by religious, ethnic, and personality differences, the government was extremely weak. A Tanzanian occupation army of some 10,000 provided much of the country's fragile order.

Godfrey L. Binaisa had been installed as president in mid-1979; supported by southern, Bagandan factions, he worked to ease pro-Obote people out of positions of power. In April Binaisa announced that parliamentary elections would be held by the end of 1980. In early May he formally banned all political parties, requiring that all candidates run under a single banner. Several days later, Binaisa dismissed army chief of staff Brig. David Oyite Ojok, an Obote supporter. Ojok's troops ousted Binaisa and installed an Obote supporter, Paulo Muwanga, in power on May 14. The ban on political parties was lifted and, on May 27, Obote returned to Uganda to a tumultuous welcome. In mid-September Muwanga announced that only members of Obote's party, the Uganda People's Congress (UPC), would be allowed to remain in the ruling commission.

Obote's political machinations fed widespread discontent, and supporters of Amin invaded northern Uganda from Zaire and the Sudan in early October. Government forces, supported by the Tanzanian garrison, quickly counterattacked, driving them out of Uganda by mid-October.

Parliamentary elections were held Dec. 9–10. It first appeared that the opposition Democratic Party had won, but Muwanga took the vote counting into his own hands. When rural returns came in Obote's UPC gained the lead. Amid charges of fraud and gun battles in the streets of Kampala, the UPC was awarded a clear majority in the 126-seat parliament. Obote was inaugurated president on Dec. 16.

**Anarchy and Famine.** In 1980 Uganda had yet to recover from the wreckage left by Amin. In the barren northeast, tens of thousands of people had starved to death. It was difficult for international relief workers to transport food because of widespread lawlessness and corruption. Throughout the country, including Kampala, killings, many of them over food, were a nightly occurrence. The coffee trade, once the basis of the economy, was mostly run by smugglers. Prices rose so high that it was virtually impossible for an ordinary citizen to support a family without cheating or stealing. Some residents of the cities returned to the bush to subsist. Even foreign aid was in short supply. The United States and Great Britain, fearful for the safety of aid personnel, suspended assistance.

*See* STATISTICS OF THE WORLD. *See also* AFRICA.   J.T.S.

**UNION OF SOVIET SOCIALIST REPUBLICS.** The Soviet Union had little to celebrate as 1980 closed. The retirement of longtime Premier Aleksei N. Kosygin pointed up the advanced age of most of the remaining Kremlin leaders. The economy was performing badly, and the Moscow

Summer Olympic Games had been marred by a foreign boycott. Soviet forces were fighting a war in Afghanistan, and U.S.-Soviet relations were strained. Meantime, worker unrest threatened stability in neighboring Poland.

**Politics.** On Oct. 23, Premier Kosygin, 76, retired from office on account of ill health; he died on Dec. 18. Observers noted that although the premier served for 16 years, the other Soviet leaders made no move to praise his record. Kosygin was succeeded by Nikolai A. Tikhonov, a 75-year-old Ukrainian economic planner who had been serving as first deputy premier. No policy changes were expected to result from the shift.

In October two other significant political developments occurred. Sixty-two-year-old Pyotr Masherov, head of the Communist Party in the White Russian S.S.R. and a nonvoting member of the Communist Party Politburo, was killed in a car accident. Mikhail Gorbachev, a 49-year-old agricultural specialist, was appointed a full member of the Politburo, thus becoming the youngest member of that body.

**The Economy.** The economy gravely concerned Kremlin leaders in 1980. They were attempting to increase both military spending and consumer goods supplies but with limited means at their disposal. Manpower was short, and workers had little incentive to step up their efforts because of a shortage of quality consumer goods to buy with their pay. Bad weather produced a disappointing 1980 harvest. In addition, an American partial grain embargo instituted after the 1979 Soviet invasion of Afghanistan forced Moscow to pay higher prices for often lower quality grain from other suppliers. Some foreign observers believed Soviet meat production would eventually fall because of low feed supplies for livestock.

At October meetings of the Communist Party Central Committee and the Supreme Soviet (parliament), leaders acknowledged economic shortcomings. State Planning Commission Chairman Nikolai Baibakov announced that the industrial growth rate for 1980 would be 4 percent, lower than the 4.5 percent planned.

Figures disclosed on Dec. 1 for the next five-year plan, covering 1981–85, called for industrial production to rise 26 to 28 percent over that period, and for national income to rise 18 to 20 percent. The grain crop in 1980 was only 189,000,000 metric tons, 46,000,000 below the target.

The Soviet Union became the world's leading oil producer in 1974, but oil production growth seemed to be slowing. The 1985 production goal was set at 640,000,000 metric tons; this figure was originally intended to be reached in 1980, but actual production in 1980 only reached 603,000,000.

Foreign analysts expected oil exports to Western Europe, the principal earner of foreign currency for the Soviet Union, gradually to be replaced by natural gas. The new five-year plan called for a sharp rise in natural gas production.

**Olympic Games.** After three years of elaborate planning and the outlay of $500,000,000 to $1 billion, the Soviet Union played host to the 1980 Summer Olympic Games. Opened on July 19 by President Leonid I. Brezhnev, the Games, which concluded on Aug. 3, were neither the unalloyed triumph Kremlin officials had hoped for nor the joyless affair envisioned by U.S. President Jimmy Carter and other Western leaders who backed the idea of an Olympic boycott to protest the Soviet invasion of Afghanistan. *See also* SPORTS: THE OLYMPIC GAMES.

Soviet preparations for the Games included a gigantic beautification effort and a massive security campaign. In Moscow thousands of buildings were repainted, miles of roads were repaved, trees and flower beds were planted, and new facilities built. Security men forced potential political dissidents to leave the city, and authorities repeatedly warned citizens against unauthorized contacts with Westerners. Political observers believed that the boycott had failed to make any impression on the average Soviet citizen.

**Dissent and Emigration.** The Soviet government continued its campaign to stamp out dissent to its policies. The year's most prominent victim was Andrei Sakharov, the father of the Soviet hydrogen bomb and winner of the 1975 Nobel Peace Prize for his efforts to force the Kremlin to respect human rights. In the past, Soviet authorities had

*Welcoming visitors to the Olympic Games in Moscow was Misha, the mascot of the 1980 Summer Olympics. The Olympic Village behind the display included housing for the athletes who participated in the events.*

hesitated to move decisively against Sakharov because of his worldwide eminence and the possible repercussions of such a move in international relations. On Jan. 22, however, shortly after Sakharov signed a plea for withdrawal of Soviet troops from Afghanistan, he was seized by police and exiled to Gor'kiy, a city closed to foreigners.

---

### Who Else but Me?

Although he became a full-time human rights activist in 1968, Andrei Sakharov had never been formally arrested until Jan. 22, 1980. On that day the 58-year-old physicist, elected to the Soviet Academy of Sciences at age 32 for his work on atomic fusion, was banished to Gor'kiy. It was negative official reaction to his 1968 manifesto, known in the West as *Progress, Peaceful Coexistence and Intellectual Freedom,* that prompted the end of Sakharov's scientific career. Thenceforth he dedicated himself to transmitting to the outside world news of rights violations within the U.S.S.R. Although awarded the Nobel Peace Prize in 1975, he was barred from attending the awards ceremony. In spite of such harassment, he continued to press his campaign. "Who else is going to do it," he once asked, "but me?"

*Andrei Sakharov.*

Sakharov refused to be silenced by the action; in July he sent an open letter to Brezhnev, again criticizing Soviet intervention in Afghanistan.

Vasily P. Aksyonov, a prominent writer whose recent works had been banned, emigrated to the West with his family on July 22. Lev Kopelev, a writer who had been attacked in the press as a traitor, left for West Germany with his wife on Nov. 12. Vladimir Voinovich, a popular satiric novelist, departed for West Germany with his family on Dec. 21.

The Soviet government sharply reduced the number of Jews allowed to emigrate during 1980. Western observers regarded the action as a reflection of the chill in East-West relations following the Afghan crisis. In contrast to 1979, when 50,000 Jews were permitted to leave the U.S.S.R., only an estimated 20,000 Jews received exit papers in 1980.

On Aug. 21 the Soviet Union began jamming Voice of America broadcasts in seven languages, possibly to keep information about worker unrest in Poland from reaching the Soviet people. Jamming had been discontinued in 1973 with the advent of détente.

**Space Exploration.** Two Soviet cosmonauts, Leonid I. Popov and Valery V. Ryumin, returned to earth in October after a record 185 days in spaceflight aboard the orbiting station Salyut 6. This mission was the highlight of an active year for the Soviets in space; *see also* SPACE SCIENCE AND EXPLORATION.

**Foreign Relations.** Soviet leaders faced three very troublesome international problems in 1980: the war in Afghanistan, worsening relations with Washington, and unrest in Poland.

The Soviets invaded Afghanistan in December, 1979, and installed a puppet government under Afghan Communist Babrak Karmal. Some Western observers believed the Soviet action was aimed merely at establishing a secure buffer state; others saw it as a first move toward the strategic waters of the Indian Ocean and Persian Gulf. Afghanistan was reportedly also rich in high-grade iron ore as well as oil and gas, which may have spurred Soviet action. Whatever their long-term goal, the Soviets committed 85,000 troops to Afghanistan to fight Muslim rebels. In the process, they brought down worldwide condemnation on their own heads. In January, 104 members of the United Nations General Assembly deplored the Soviet move. That same month, foreign ministers of the Islamic states condemned the Kremlin intervention. On Nov. 20 the U.N. General Assembly approved 111-22 a resolution to renew its appeal to the Soviet Union to withdraw its forces from Afghanistan.

---

**No More Rasputins**

Yevgeniya Davitashvili, a waitress from Tbilisi, capital of the Georgian S.S.R., became a Soviet VIP during the year. She was a "sensitive" reported to have cured thousands of people—including President Leonid Brezhnev—of a multitude of illnesses by means of her "biological force field." Top Soviet philosophers, the official labor union daily, and the official Communist youth daily all trumpeted her successes. But the cult of personality growing around Dzhuna, as she was known throughout the U.S.S.R., began to worry some officials. On Aug. 27 the Ministry of Health issued a statement that her activities had been examined by a panel of scientists; they refuted the possibility of cures by "biological field." In the U.S.S.R., after all, medical care is free—and Dzhuna charged 250 rubles ($375) for each séance.

---

The Afghan crisis strained Soviet-American ties. President Carter called for an international boycott of the Moscow Olympics. He ordered an embargo that limited American grain sales to the U.S.S.R., tightened controls on technology transfers, and delayed indefinitely the consideration of the strategic arms limitation treaty (SALT II), which was up for ratification in the U.S. Senate. In addition, the President stepped up plans for increased American military spending and for new U.S. bases on the fringe of southwest Asia, and he prodded other North Atlantic Treaty Organization countries to limit their own trade and contacts with the Soviets. By October the United States had fallen from first to sixth in ranking among Western countries exporting goods to the U.S.S.R.

Moscow responded with a campaign to woo the Western allies away from the U.S. It met with partial success. In May French President Valéry Giscard d'Estaing met in Warsaw with Soviet President Brezhnev to discuss East-West relations. West German Chancellor Helmut Schmidt made a two-day visit to Moscow at the end of June and agreed to a long-term economic treaty. Both countries increased their exports to the U.S.S.R. in 1980.

Strikes in Poland, which began during July, posed an additional challenge to the Kremlin. Worker demands for free trade unions threatened to undermine Polish Communist Party control. Soviet leaders extended economic aid to Poland

This five-member mission was sent to Iran by U.N. Secretary-General Kurt Waldheim in February to investigate Iran's grievances against the deposed shah—and, unofficially, to seek ways of resolving the crisis arising from the seizure of American hostages at the U.S. embassy in Tehran. The mission was fruitless, as Iran continued to ignore a 1979 Security Council resolution demanding the release of the hostages.

but issued warnings against "undermining socialism" in that country. In December Soviet troops were mobilized along the border with Poland, evidently ready to enter the country rapidly if ordered to do so; see also POLAND.

One area where the Soviet Union appeared to make some diplomatic headway in 1980 was the Middle East. Although its ties with Iraq were not as close in 1980 as in recent years, the U.S.S.R. remained that nation's principal arms supplier. At the same time, it was seeking closer ties with Iran. And on Oct. 8, two weeks after Iraq attacked Iran, Moscow signed a 20-year cooperation treaty with Syria.

Relations between the Soviet Union and China remained chilly in 1980. Elsewhere in Asia, Moscow maintained close links with Vietnam, whose 1978 invasion of Cambodia the Soviets had backed. Top Vietnamese leaders visited the Soviet capital for consultations in July. In December Brezhnev visited India, signed new Soviet-Indian trade and technology agreements, and called for an agreement to keep the Persian Gulf region free from foreign military bases.

See STATISTICS OF THE WORLD. See also AFGHANISTAN; COMMUNISM; MIDDLE EAST; MILITARY AND NAVAL AFFAIRS.                                F.W.

**UNITED ARAB EMIRATES.** See PERSIAN GULF STATES. See also STATISTICS OF THE WORLD.

**UNITED NATIONS, THE,** abbreviated U.N. The year 1980 was a busy one for the world organization, beginning with the reaction to the Soviet invasion of Afghanistan in December, 1979, and ending with concern over the fate of Poland. Interspersed were other major problems, such as the continued detention of American hostages in Iran, the war between Iran and Iraq in the Persian Gulf area, continued hostilities in Indochina, and continued tensions in the Middle East and southern Africa.

**The Afghanistan Invasion.** Soviet troops entered Afghanistan in late December, 1979. The Security Council on Jan. 7 voted 13-2 to demand the "immediate and unconditional withdrawal" of foreign forces. The two votes against the resolution were cast by the Soviet Union and East Germany, and the Soviet vote vetoed it. After this Soviet veto, the council called for an emergency special session of the General Assembly. On Jan. 14 the General Assembly supported the call for withdrawal, 104-18, with 18 abstentions. The regular assembly session on Nov. 20 voted again for immediate withdrawal, 111-22, with 12 abstentions. But as the year ended, Soviet occupation of Afghanistan continued; see also AFGHANISTAN.

**The Hostages.** U.N. Secretary-General Kurt Waldheim paid a visit to Tehran at the outset of 1980, but reported that the Iranians were not prepared to observe the Security Council's December, 1979, call for the release of the American hostages taken captive at the U.S. embassy in Tehran on Nov. 4, 1979. On Jan. 13 the council voted 10-2, with 2 abstentions and China not participating, to impose sanctions against Iran, but the Soviet veto prevented passage.

On Feb. 17 Waldheim announced the establish-

Voting in favor of a Jan. 7 U.N. Security Council resolution calling for the withdrawal of foreign troops from Afghanistan are ambassadors Sir Anthony Parsons of Great Britain and Donald McHenry of the U.S. Oleg Troyanovsky (left) of the U.S.S.R. cast a vote against the resolution, thus vetoing it.

ment of a five-member inquiry commission in an attempt to break the deadlock. This commission visited Tehran at the end of February, but, having been denied a meeting with the hostages, it left on March 11 with its task undone.

On May 24 the International Court of Justice in The Hague, the Netherlands, unanimously demanded that Iran "immediately release each and every one of the hostages." Iran boycotted the court hearings and ignored the decision; see also IRAN.

**Iran-Iraq War.** When war broke out between Iran and Iraq on Sept. 22, the secretary-general appealed to the parties to desist and the following day called for urgent Security Council consultations. The council immediately issued a request that the parties settle their dispute by peaceful means. On Sept. 28 it adopted a unanimous resolution asking the parties "to refrain from any further use of force." Iraqi President Saddam Hussein responded that he was ready to comply if Iran stopped fighting, but Iranian President Abolhassan Bani-Sadr declared on Oct. 1 that Iran would not agree to any cease-fire as long as Iraqi troops were on Iranian soil.

On Oct. 10 Secretary-General Waldheim asked for a local cease-fire in the Shatt-al-Arab waterway so that 63 foreign ships trapped at the head of the Persian Gulf could depart. Iran agreed but Iraq refused, unwilling to "internationalize" the waterway, which it claimed as its own, by the ships' use of the protective U.N. flag.

On Nov. 5 the council welcomed Waldheim's decision to send a special envoy to the area, and on Nov. 11 the secretary-general was able to report that both parties had agreed to his selection of former Swedish Prime Minister Olof Palme for the task. Palme visited first Tehran and then Baghdad, Iraq. Returning to New York City at the end of November, he reported that "principal agreement" on the release of the ships, under Red Cross flags, had been achieved. But, though fighting abated, the year ended without peace. See also IRAN; IRAQ; MIDDLE EAST; MILITARY AND NAVAL AFFAIRS.

**Indochina.** Thailand complained to the Security Council on June 24 that Vietnamese forces had invaded its territory from Cambodia. On June 25 Waldheim expressed his concern over the new crisis. On June 27 Vietnam countercharged that "remnants of the Pol Pot clique" were being smuggled back from Thailand into Cambodian border territory.

The secretary-general visited Hanoi on Aug. 2 and Bangkok on Aug. 4, and he was able to arrange for the meeting of the two foreign ministers under his auspices in New York. On Oct. 2 he reported that the meeting had taken place with agreement for another meeting at a later date. He also remarked that while international humanitarian efforts at alleviating the plight of the Cambodian people were bearing fruit, renewed attempts were needed for a political settlement.

On Oct. 22 the General Assembly voted 92–23, with 22 abstentions, for the withdrawal of foreign forces from Cambodia and the convening of an international conference, as demanded by the five members of the Association of Southeast Asian Nations, in early 1981. Vietnam and its Soviet bloc allies, however, voted against the resolution, and thus the project appeared to be moribund.

Meanwhile, in another diplomatic defeat for Vietnam, on Oct. 13 the assembly voted, 74 in favor, 35 against, and 32 abstaining, to confirm the validity of the credentials of the delegation sent by the Pol Pot resistance forces to the U.N. *See also* CAMBODIA.

**Arab-Israeli Disputes.** Dealing with the issue of Israeli settlements in occupied Arab territories, the Security Council on March 1 unanimously demanded the dismantling of such settlements, "including [those in] Jerusalem." Reacting to Israeli protests, U.S. President Jimmy Carter renounced the supporting U.S. vote as a mistake. On June 30, when the Security Council voted to protest Israeli measures altering the character of Jerusalem, the United States abstained. On Aug. 20 the council condemned the passage of a new law by Israel's parliament declaring Jerusalem the eternal capital of Israel, and it called on countries with embassies there to withdraw them. By Sept. 7 all 13 countries represented in Jerusalem had announced their intention to move their missions to Tel Aviv.

The U.S. vetoed on April 30 a council resolution that would have established the right of the Palestinians to set up their independent state on the West Bank and Gaza Strip, areas occupied by Israel. On July 22 an emergency special session of the General Assembly repeated this call by 112-7, with 24 abstentions, setting a Nov. 15 deadline for Israeli compliance, which Israel ignored. During the first two weeks of December, after lengthy debates, the regular assembly session passed six more resolutions on the subject, although with less impressive voting majorities.

On still another issue concerning Israel, the Security Council demanded on May 8 that Israel readmit to the West Bank the mayors of Hebron and Halhul and the Muslim judge in Hebron, who had been expelled after the May 2 murder of six Jews returning from worship in Hebron. The U.S. abstained in the otherwise unanimous vote, as it did again on May 20, when the council repeated its request. On Dec. 19, after Israel once again refused to readmit the mayors, the U.S. also voted in favor of a resolution asking that they be permitted to return. The mayors then staged a six-day hunger strike on U.N. premises, quitting the day before Christmas.

On April 24, with both the U.S. and U.S.S.R. abstaining, the Security Council by 12-0 rebuked

Israel for a recent armed incursion into southern Lebanon that followed an Arab raid on an Israeli kibbutz.

*See also* ISRAEL; LEBANON; MIDDLE EAST.

**Southern Africa.** The former British colony of Rhodesia achieved its independence as the black-ruled nation of Zimbabwe on April 18. Negotiations for the independence of Namibia, ruled by South Africa as South-West Africa, were not completed by year's end. A "preimplementation meeting" of external and internal parties was agreed upon to take place Jan. 7-14, 1981. South Africa was censured by the Security Council on June 13 for its treatment of nonwhites and on June 27 for aggression against Angola in a resolution that called on it to withdraw its troops from South-West Africa. *See also* SOUTH AFRICA; SOUTH-WEST AFRICA.

**Other Events and Activities.** The greatest disappointment of the year for most U.N. member nations was the failure to agree on the holding of global negotiations aimed at worldwide economic cooperation between rich and poor nations. On Sept. 15 a special General Assembly session called for this purpose ended in failure. During the regular assembly session, its president, Baron Ruediger von Wechmar of West Germany, attempted to reach agreement for such talks in 1981, but at the end of the session he also had to report failure.

The seven-year-long negotiations for a new Law of the Sea treaty seemed more promising at year's end. By the end of the summer a "breakthrough" was reported, but the untimely death of the president of the Law of the Sea Conference, Hamilton Shirley Amerasinghe of Sri Lanka, on Dec. 4, cast doubt on success in 1981. He had been regarded as instrumental in directing the complex negotiations.

Among the many other conferences held under U.N. aegis in 1980, the World Conference of the U.N. Decade for Women, which was held in Copenhagen in July, was one of the most important; *see* WOMEN.

A conference of the U.N. Educational, Scientific, and Cultural Organization adopted a resolution on Oct. 25 in Belgrade, Yugoslavia, setting forth some basic principles of a new world information order demanded by Third World countries. Western nations expressed strong reservations, fearing the resolution could be used to justify restrictions on freedom of the press.

The new state of Zimbabwe became the 153rd member of the U.N. on Aug. 25, and a small new Caribbean nation, St. Vincent and the Grenadines, was admitted on Sept. 16, making the U.N. membership total 154 as 1980 ended.     L.H.

# UNITED STATES OF AMERICA

In 1980 the United States elected a new President and a new Congress but faced familiar economic problems and increasing cold war tensions. Volcanic eruptions and a heat wave, a flood of refugees, draft registration, and the Winter Olympic Games were also part of the scene.

A year of economic difficulties, cold war tensions, and inability to resolve the hostage crisis with Iran culminated in a landslide victory for Ronald W. Reagan in the 1980 Presidential election. Republicans won a majority in the Senate for the first time since the 1952 elections as a conservative tide seemingly swept the nation. They promised to enact a tax cut, slash government spending, and adopt a tougher line in foreign policy.

## DOMESTIC AFFAIRS

**Politics.** Jimmy Carter survived a determined challenge from Sen. Edward M. Kennedy to win the Democratic Party nomination to run for a second term as President. The going was easier for Reagan. Although he lost several primaries to George Bush, he handily secured the Republican Party nomination in July; Reagan then chose Bush as his running mate. Widespread dissatisfaction with the major party nominees presented an opportunity for Rep. John Anderson (R, Ill.), who unsuccessfully sought the Republican nomination in early primaries before dropping out to wage an independent candidacy.

A lackluster campaign ensued in which Reagan sought to make Carter's handling of the economy the issue and Carter characterized Reagan as a danger to peace and a foe of the working class. Polls indicated that the election would be close and that a large number of prospective voters were finding it difficult to make a choice. But on Election Day, Reagan won in every section of the country, garnering 51 percent of the vote to 41 percent for Carter and 7 percent for Anderson in a light turnout. Carter thus became the first elected President to lose his bid for reelection since Herbert Hoover in 1932.

The electorate indicated that it was holding the Democratic Party in general, and not only the President in particular, responsible for the nation's difficulties. Republicans gained a net increase of 12 Senate seats and 33 seats in the new House of Representatives. Republicans also registered a net gain of 4 governorships and more than 200 legislative seats. *See also* DEMOCRATIC PARTY; ELECTIONS; REPUBLICAN PARTY.

**The Economy.** The U.S. economy was racked by double-digit inflation and recession during 1980. The unemployment rate increased. The hardest-hit sector of the economy was automobile manufacturing; sales of U.S.-made cars during the 1980 model year slumped by almost 2,000,000 from the previous year. The four domestic automakers were expected to lose $4 billion during the year, and Chrysler Corp. needed federal loan guarantees to forestall bankruptcy. The U.S. was overtaken by Japan as the world's leading producer of automobiles.

Steelmakers reported lower profits, primarily because of the recession-caused slump in automotive, appliance, and consumer goods production. The steel and apparel industries continued to seek relief from foreign imports. New housing starts dropped as a result of high mortgage interest rates. Federal regulation of interstate trucking and railroads was eased. *See also* AUTOMOBILES; BANKING AND FINANCE; ECONOMY AND BUSINESS; MANUFACTURING INDUSTRIES; TRANSPORTATION.

**Public Finance.** The deficit for fiscal 1980 was $59 billion, the second highest in history and far above the $12.9 billion that President Carter had estimated in January. Spending totaled $579 billion, while revenues, which were diminished by the recession, totaled $520 billion. For fiscal 1981, which began on Oct. 1, 1980, the Office of Management and Budget initially projected a deficit of $15.8 billion, but by January, 1981, the estimated deficit had grown to an estimated $55 billion, not considering passage of a tax cut advocated by President-elect Reagan.

**Agriculture.** Although wheat production increased slightly, a severe drought and heat wave in the nation's midsection significantly reduced the corn and soybean crops. Net farm income dropped by 25 percent because of reduced crop yield, high interest rates, and sharply higher production costs, including the cost of fuel. But U.S. agricultural exports climbed to a record $40 billion. *See also* AGRICULTURE.

**Energy.** Congress enacted President Carter's proposed windfall profits tax on the oil industry, de-

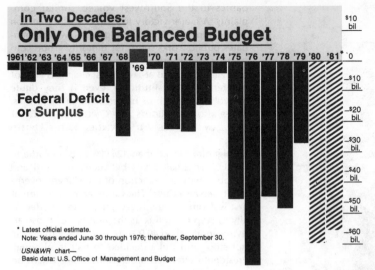

**In Two Decades:**
# Only One Balanced Budget

1961 '62 '63 '64 '65 '66 '67 '68   '70 '71 '72 '73 '74 '75 '76 '77 '78 '79 '80 '81* 0

'69

**Federal Deficit
or Surplus**

$10 bil
0
—$10 bil.
—$20 bil.
—$30 bil.
—$40 bil.
—$50 bil.
—$60 bil.

*A bar graph of federal budgets since fiscal year 1961 shows only one year with a surplus, despite almost annual promises to control government spending.*

\* Latest official estimate.
Note: Years ended June 30 through 1976; thereafter, September 30.

*USN&WR* chart—
Basic data: U.S. Office of Management and Budget

Reprinted from "U.S. News & World Report." © 1980.

signed to raise $227.3 billion in revenue over ten years in return for a gradual lifting of price controls on domestic oil production. It also adopted the President's proposal to create a federal program to speed the production of synthetic fuels. But it rejected his proposal to place a fee on imported oil or to create an Energy Mobilization Board.

Supplies of petroleum were plentiful in 1980. Net oil imports were down about 18 percent, partly because of the recession and partly because of conservation efforts, as the cost of imported oil continued to climb. Electricity consumption failed to increase at all, again in part because of cost increases. Nuclear power did not make significant gains; only two new plants had been licensed since the Three Mile Island incident of March, 1979, in which a reactor became dangerously overheated.

*See also* ENERGY; NUCLEAR POWER; PETROLEUM AND NATURAL GAS.

**Environment.** Mount St. Helens erupted in the state of Washington on May 18, killing at least 34 persons and virtually obliterating 150 sq.mi. of land. The first active volcano in the continental U.S. since 1915, it continued to spew forth ashes and steam at intervals throughout the year. A fearsome heat wave and drought left 1265 dead and caused nearly $20 billion in damages in 26 states.

There was increased concern over toxic wastes as a pollution problem. More than 2000 people had left the Love Canal section of Niagara Falls, N.Y., where chemicals leaking from a toxic dump caused concern over health problems. The Environmental Protection Agency announced new regulations that would cost industry an estimated $1 billion a year to curb future damage. But officials warned that a cleanup of existing chemical waste dumps would cost from $28 billion to $55 billion.

A report said that occupational exposure to cancer-causing substances was believed to be a factor in more than 20 percent of all cases of cancer. A Presidential commission found the quality of the nation's air and water to have improved since 1975, but experts voiced concern over acid rainfall in the Northeast, warning that the problem, already severe, would intensify as the nation's electric power plants converted from burning oil to burning coal. *See also* ENVIRONMENT.

---

**Tax Court Disrupts Unwedded Bliss**

A Maryland couple who gained national attention by divorcing and marrying twice to save money on taxes was ordered on Aug. 6 to pay the Internal Revenue Service $3135.34 in back taxes. Angela and David Boyter, both government workers, had discovered that as a married couple they were paying more than as singles. They divorced in Haiti, remarried, divorced in the Dominican Republic, and then decided not to remarry but to live together. The U.S. Tax Court, however, ruled the Boyters "never intended to and never did physically separate from each other prior to or subsequent to either of the divorces," making the divorces invalid in the eyes of the court.

The summer-long 350th birthday celebration of Boston was inaugurated on May 30 when a parade of tall ships sailed into the city's harbor. Among the vessels arriving in port was Colombia's bark, Gloria of Cartagena.

**Defense.** The Soviet invasion of Afghanistan and the failure to resolve the hostage crisis—including an abortive U.S. rescue attempt in April—were perceived as signs of U.S. military weakness. President Carter responded by building up U.S. naval strength in the Indian Ocean. Draft registration was adopted for young men 19 and 20 years of age. There was talk of building a new strategic bomber and a new land-based missile system. A new counterforce nuclear strategy to deter a possible Soviet first strike called for shifting priority to strikes on military installations and command centers instead of population centers. But military spending was reported still far lower than that of the Soviet Union as a percentage of gross national product. And there were frequent reports that U.S. military personnel were unfit for their tasks, with all three services claiming a severe shortage of skilled people, particularly in the enlisted ranks, and shortages of equipment, including spare parts. See also MILITARY AND NAVAL AFFAIRS.

**Minorities.** Blacks were beset by growing unemployment as the economy sagged. Competition for jobs between blacks and Cuban immigrants appeared to be an important factor in a Miami ghetto riot in which 18 persons were killed and at least $100,000,000 of damage was sustained. Another reason for ghetto unrest was alleged police abuses and brutality in a number of cities; His-

panics in the Southwest voiced similar complaints. A major victory for blacks was a decision by the Supreme Court upholding a law that mandates public works funds for minority group contractors. However, the High Court ruled in a Mobile, Ala., case, that at-large local elections are not inherently unconstitutional, even if they dilute the voting strength of blacks or other minorities.

See also CIVIL RIGHTS AND CIVIL LIBERTIES; CRIME AND LAW ENFORCEMENT; NEGROES IN THE UNITED STATES.

**Immigration.** More than 125,000 Cubans came to the U.S. in small boats between mid-April and October, with the sanction of the Cuban government; see also CUBA. The Carter administration at first welcomed the refugees, then tried ineffectually to stop the influx as the number of those arriving approached 40,000. The exodus actually did not stop until Cuba decided to halt it, although President Carter had ordered the Coast Guard on May 14 to begin seizing vessels making the voyages.

Most of the refugees eventually found haven with relatives or sponsors after they were processed at military bases, but thousands had still not been settled in late 1980. The city of Miami, home to many Cuban-Americans, bore the brunt of the influx; overcrowding in city schools led many of them to hold double sessions, and the crime rate soared. In all, officials said that accommodating the Cuban refugees would cost the U.S. $1 billion.

The Cubans were admitted to the U.S. under the President's parole power in order to give Congress time to enact special legislation, as requested by the Administration. A refugee act passed shortly before the influx would have increased the number of refugees who could be admitted annually to 50,000 a year, but this legislation was inadequate to meet the situation.

The parole power was also extended to refugees from Haiti in response to charges that these "boat people" were being made victims of racial discrimination. About 25,000 to 30,000 Haitians were believed to be in Florida illegally, and, as of June 20, an additional 15,000 were being held in deportation or exclusion proceedings. Before parole power was extended, the State Department maintained that Haitians were not eligible for admission as refugees because they were coming to the U.S. for economic rather than political reasons. Representatives of the Haitian community argued that political persecution was common on the island and that people who had been deported back to Haiti were being arrested or otherwise mistreated. See also CARIBBEAN COUNTRIES.

The Immigration and Naturalization Service reported on Sept. 21 that, of more than 58,000 Iranian students in the U.S., 12,000 were in the country illegally. (Restrictions on Iranian aliens had been imposed in late 1979 after the seizure of Americans at the U.S. embassy in Tehran.) As a result of the new regulations, about 2000 Iranians had been ordered to leave after formal deportation hearings, and 10,000 were awaiting hearings after having been accused of violating immigration laws, the terms of their visas, or special reporting requirements. Approximately 430 had been deported, and about 5000 had left the U.S. voluntarily. About 2000 had filed applications for asylum, claiming they would face persecution if they returned to Iran. About 9000 Iranians immigrated to the U.S. between November, 1979, and March, 1980.

The number of illegal aliens in the U.S. continued to be a subject of controversy. A U.S. study released in February concluded that the number was far lower than the Carter administration's earlier estimate of 3,000,000 to 6,000,000—almost certainly fewer than 3,000,000 and possibly only 1,500,000 to 2,000,000. Most of this total was believed to be from Mexico. A three-year Mexican government study of migration calculated the number of illegal aliens in the U.S. from Mexico at any particular time as ranging from only 480,000 to 1,220,000.

**The Census.** Vincent P. Barabba, director of the U.S. Census Bureau, said on Nov. 17 that his bureau had counted 226,000,000 people in the U.S., 4,000,000 more people than it had estimated in April, shortly after the nation's households received questionnaires to be filled out. In 1970 the Census Bureau recorded a population of 203,235,298 in the U.S.

Virtually all the additional 4,000,000 people were found in the South and West, Barabba stated. He said the underestimate occurred because it had been more difficult to estimate populations in areas of new growth and because some of the bureau's methods of estimating population had been flawed. Barabba's finding meant a probable shift of at least 17 seats in the U.S. House of Representatives in 1982 from northern and eastern states to southern and western states. Population figures were also a factor in the apportionment of some $50 billion in federal aid and grants to states, cities, and municipalities.

On Sept. 25 a federal district court judge, Horace W. Gilmore of Detroit, invalidated the 1980 census on the ground that it had undercounted blacks and Hispanic Americans. He ordered the federal government to adjust the figures upward for those groups throughout the country. The decision was appealed.

## Preliminary Census Figures

| State | 1980 pop. | 1970 pop. | Percent change |
|-------|-----------|-----------|----------------|
| ALA. | 3,863,698 | 3,444,354 | +12.2 |
| ALASKA | 400,331 | 302,583 | +32.3 |
| ARIZ. | 2,714,013 | 1,775,399 | +52.9 |
| ARK. | 2,280,687 | 1,923,322 | +18.6 |
| CALIF. | 23,510,372 | 19,975,069 | +17.7 |
| COLO. | 2,877,726 | 2,209,596 | +30.2 |
| CONN. | 3,096,951 | 3,032,217 | +2.1 |
| DEL. | 594,779 | 548,104 | +8.5 |
| D.C. | 635,233 | 756,668 | −16.0 |
| FLA. | 9,579,495 | 6,791,418 | +41.1 |
| GA. | 5,396,425 | 4,587,930 | +17.6 |
| HAWAII | 964,624 | 769,913 | +25.3 |
| IDAHO | 943,629 | 713,015 | +32.3 |
| ILL. | 11,321,350 | 11,110,258 | +1.9 |
| IND. | 5,454,154 | 5,195,392 | +5.0 |
| IOWA | 2,908,797 | 2,825,368 | +3.0 |
| KANS. | 2,355,536 | 2,249,071 | +4.7 |
| KY. | 3,642,143 | 3,220,711 | +13.1 |
| LA. | 4,194,299 | 3,644,637 | +15.1 |
| MAINE | 1,123,560 | 993,722 | +13.1 |
| MD. | 4,193,378 | 3,923,897 | +6.9 |
| MASS. | 5,728,288 | 5,689,170 | +0.7 |
| MICH. | 9,236,891 | 8,881,826 | +4.0 |
| MINN. | 4,068,856 | 3,806,103 | +6.9 |
| MISS. | 2,503,250 | 2,216,994 | +12.9 |
| MO. | 4,901,678 | 4,677,623 | +4.8 |
| MONT. | 783,674 | 694,409 | +12.9 |
| NEBR. | 1,564,727 | 1,485,333 | +5.3 |
| NEV. | 800,312 | 488,738 | +63.8 |
| N.H. | 919,114 | 737,681 | +24.6 |
| N.J. | 7,335,808 | 7,171,112 | +2.3 |
| N.MEX. | 1,290,551 | 1,017,055 | +26.9 |
| N.C. | 5,846,159 | 5,084,411 | +15.0 |
| N.DAK. | 652,437 | 617,792 | +5.6 |
| N.Y. | 17,476,798 | 18,241,391 | −4.2 |
| OHIO | 10,758,421 | 10,657,423 | +0.9 |
| OKLA. | 2,998,124 | 2,559,463 | +17.2 |
| OREG. | 2,617,444 | 2,091,533 | +25.1 |
| PA. | 11,824,561 | 11,800,766 | +0.2 |
| R.I. | 945,761 | 949,723 | −0.4 |
| S.C. | 3,067,061 | 2,590,713 | +18.4 |
| S.DAK. | 687,643 | 662,257 | +3.8 |
| TENN. | 4,539,834 | 3,926,018 | +15.6 |
| TEXAS | 14,152,339 | 11,198,655 | +26.4 |
| UTAH | 1,454,630 | 1,059,273 | +37.3 |
| VT. | 511,299 | 444,732 | +15.0 |
| VA. | 5,321,521 | 4,651,448 | +14.4 |
| WASH. | 4,109,634 | 3,413,244 | +20.4 |
| W.VA. | 1,928,524 | 1,744,237 | +10.6 |
| WIS. | 4,689,055 | 4,417,821 | +6.1 |
| WYO. | 468,909 | 332,416 | +41.1 |
| P.R. | 3,187,570 | 2,712,033 | +17.5 |

*Source: Bureau of the Census*

The Census Bureau conceded that it had missed some Americans in the past—2.5 percent, or 10,200,000 people in 1970, for example. It also conceded that it undercounted whites by only 1.9 percent but blacks by 7.7 percent in 1970. The bureau added 4,900,000 people to its final 1970 figures to partly correct for the undercount and allocated them among the 50 states. One factor in the undercount was that some groups, including illegal aliens who fear being deported, avoid being counted. Enumerators were also said to be reluctant to make a thorough survey of residents of high-crime big-city areas.

Although census figures were not available until mid-December, the older big cities and their older suburbs were reported to have lost population. New York City alone lost nearly 1,000,000 residents from the 1970 total. Smaller cities, outer suburbs, and rural areas all showed substantial population increases. Early in the 1970's, industry increasingly began moving into the suburbs, allowing a growing number of people to take up residence in formerly rural areas and to commute to work in the suburbs.

*To show their opposition to military draft registration, proposed by President Jimmy Carter, demonstrators at Saint Olaf College in Northfield, Minn., gather on Feb. 14 to greet Vice-President Walter F. Mondale with signs reminiscent of the 1960's. Despite opposition on many college campuses, Congress approved draft registration for young men 19 and 20 years of age.*

On Dec. 31 the Census Bureau released the final population count of 226,504,825 for 1980, 11.4 percent higher than in 1970. New York remained the nation's largest city, with 7,015,608 people.

**Religion.** The influence of religious groups on politics was a subject of discussion during the election campaign. A number of evangelical Christian groups advocated bloc voting by Christians for candidates who had stated firm opposition to abortion, homosexual rights, the proposed Equal Rights Amendment to the Constitution, pornography, and other social phenomena that they regarded as threatening to the family or to the moral foundation of the nation. These groups also advocated allowing prayer in public schools. One group, Christian Voice, issued a "morality rating" of legislators that considered matters such as a balanced budget, the status of Taiwan, the existence of the Department of Education, and sanctions against the former white-minority government of Rhodesia relevant to whether a candidate was or was not pro-family or pro-God. In addition, the so-called electronic church of television preachers was believed to be a potent political and cultural force. *See also* RELIGION.

**Science.** Although a report claimed that American education was producing a generation less well versed in science and technology than its Soviet counterpart, continued U.S. scientific dominance was indicated in the awarding of seven scientific Nobel Prizes to U.S. citizens. The Voyager I scrutiny of the planet Saturn in November was perhaps the chief U.S. scientific accomplishment of the year. But there were also major advances in gene splicing to produce drugs that could be highly useful in the treatment of various diseases. In June the Supreme Court ruled that biological organisms could be patented under federal law, clearing the way for major new investments in gene splicing by pharmaceutical companies. *See also* ASTRONOMY; LIFE SCIENCES; SPACE SCIENCE AND EXPLORATION.

### FOREIGN AFFAIRS

The Carter administration responded to the Soviet invasion of Afghanistan by, in effect, shelving détente. It chose not to seek ratification of the strategic arms limitation treaty (SALT II), curtailed trade, and boycotted the Moscow Olympics. The President's attempts to win similar actions from U.S. allies were not successful, however. Western European countries were also reluctant to follow Washington's lead in seeking to punish Iran for its seizure of American hostages.

After a period of progress, the Camp David settlement between Israel and Egypt stalled over the question of Palestinian autonomy. Washington, however, was preoccupied with other Mid-

Robert Mugabe (left), the first prime minister of independent Zimbabwe, is welcomed to the White House by President Jimmy Carter on Aug. 27. Mugabe had come to the U.S. to ask for aid in rebuilding his strife-torn African nation.

dle East matters—Afghanistan, Iran, and the war that broke out between Iran and Iraq, threatening the Western world's oil supplies. The U.S. reaction was to shore up its relations with other oil producers in the area, particularly Saudi Arabia.

**U.S.-Soviet Relations.** President Carter's reaction to the invasion of Afghanistan was to recall the U.S. ambassador to Moscow, delay Senate consideration of SALT II, boycott the Moscow Olympics, impose a grain embargo, curtail Soviet fishing in American waters, stop delivery of computers and oil-drilling equipment, tighten curbs on other high-technology exports, and defer new cultural and economic exchanges. Carter asked for, and received, authority to impose draft registration. Trade between the U.S. and the U.S.S.R. declined by 50 percent during the first half of 1980 as compared to the same period in 1979.

The Carter administration chose not to step up the arms race, however. It was also careful not to provoke Moscow by infiltrating significant armaments to the Afghan rebels, and its bid to strengthen the military position of neighboring Pakistan was dismissed as "peanuts" by President Zia ul-Haq.

**Iran.** Frustrated in earlier efforts to secure the release of 53 American hostages seized in Tehran, Carter severed diplomatic relations on April 7, banned exports to Iran, and ousted its diplomats in the U.S. An airborne attempt to free the hos-

tages failed on April 24, and Secretary of State Cyrus R. Vance resigned in protest against the action. In the fall, Iran postulated four conditions for the release of the hostages: a promise not to intervene in Iranian affairs, the release of frozen Iranian assets in the U.S., the turning over of the late shah's property in the U.S. to Iran, and cancellation of financial claims by U.S. companies and private citizens. The U.S. accepted these conditions "in principle," but pointed out that under U.S. laws it would have problems carrying out the last two conditions.

**Persian Gulf.** The invasion of Afghanistan was seen as a clear threat to oil supplies passing to the West by sea via the Persian Gulf, and in his State of the Union address on Jan. 23, Carter warned that the U.S. was prepared to go to war if necessary to protect oil supplies. Yet a week later he admitted that the U.S. alone could not protect the region from a Soviet takeover. U.S. naval strength in the neighboring Indian Ocean was reinforced; basing agreements were signed with Kenya, Oman, and Somalia; and a Rapid Deployment Force was established. The force existed primarily on paper, however, with military authorities conceding it would take weeks to deploy any significant number of troops in the area.

The Iran-Iraq conflict found the U.S. on the sidelines, without formal relations with either country. However, it voiced determination to

423

keep the Strait of Hormuz open, and thus keep oil flowing from Saudi Arabia, Kuwait, and other oil-producing Gulf states. In October the U.S. sent radar surveillance planes to Saudi Arabia and said it was willing to supply similar aid to other Gulf states if they stayed out of the conflict. *See also* MIDDLE EAST.

**Western Europe.** U.S. allies rejected Washington's call for meaningful trade sanctions against Moscow and imposed only limited sanctions against Iran. West Germany signed a long-term economic pact with the U.S.S.R. The European Community, in opposition to Washington, advocated a role for the Palestine Liberation Organization in the Arab-Israeli dispute. But U.S. diplomacy helped bring about the return of Greece to military participation in the North Atlantic Treaty Organization and thus the continued presence of U.S. troops there. And Turkey agreed to let the U.S. keep military bases. *See also* EUROPEAN COMMUNITIES; NORTH ATLANTIC TREATY ORGANIZATION.

**Eastern Europe.** Washington's response to labor unrest in Poland was cautious, designed to give Moscow no pretext to intervene. On Dec. 2 the White House warned that Soviet intervention would severely affect East-West relations. Earlier, after the death of President Tito of Yugoslavia, Carter visited Belgrade and voiced support for "continued development of an independent Yugoslavia."

**Israel and Egypt.** Although the border between Israel and Egypt was opened, ambassadors exchanged, and direct air flights begun, talks were suspended in August because of the impasse over Palestinian autonomy. Washington angered Israel and American Jews by supporting a United Nations Security Council resolution calling on Israel to dismantle settlements on occupied Arab territory; Carter then disavowed the vote. The U.S. vetoed a resolution calling for the establishment of a Palestinian state and abstained from a resolution condemning Israel's affirmation of all Jerusalem as its capital. *See also* MIDDLE EAST; UNITED NATIONS.

**South Asia.** Although Pakistan rejected stepped-up U.S. military aid, Washington assured the country it could depend on U.S. forces in the event of any large-scale Soviet attack. The U.S. also courted India, with Carter agreeing to the sale of enriched U.S. uranium despite India's refusal to allow inspection of all its nuclear facilities. Nevertheless, India made a major purchase of Soviet arms and became the first non-Communist country to recognize the Vietnamese-imposed Cambodian government.

**Far East.** With détente scrapped, Washington announced in January that it was willing to sell Pe-

king military equipment but not weapons. A trade pact was ratified, other agreements were signed, and in October China agreed to a major long-range purchase of U.S. grain. Peking, however, continued to regard U.S. ties with Taiwan as too close.

U.S. and Japanese leaders exchanged visits, and Japan was receptive to Washington's anti-Soviet actions. But Tokyo resisted U.S. pressure to increase its armed force significantly. U.S. relations with South Korea continued to be poor. The State Department unsuccessfully urged the military government to broaden its base and stop repressing its political opponents. With regard to Indochina, the U.S. stepped up delivery of arms to Thailand to help it cope with incursions by Vietnamese troops.

**Latin America.** The U.S. continued to support the beleaguered El Salvador government, opposing both left- and right-wing violence. Despite the Marxist orientation of Nicaragua, U.S. aid was extended, and U.S. banks rescheduled the country's debts. Carter allowed Cuba to send its disaffected to the U.S., with more than 125,000 arriving in Florida before Cuba stopped the flow in October. The U.S. condemned the July military takeover in Bolivia, recalling its ambassador and cutting off virtually all aid.

**Black Africa.** It was a quiet year in regard to U.S. relations with Africa south of the Sahara. In August Robert Mugabe, prime minister of the new nation of Zimbabwe (formerly Rhodesia), came to the U.S. and praised President Carter for refusing to support the former white minority government there. Mugabe sought U.S. private investment despite his government's Marxist convictions.

In October Nigerian President Shehu Shagari paid his first visit to the U.S. He warned that his country would use "all means at our disposal, including oil" to convince the U.S. to oppose more forcefully South Africa's system of racial segregation. Carter assured Shagari of a continuing U.S. commitment to majority rule in South-West Africa, currently governed by South Africa.

*See* STATISTICS OF THE WORLD.                    R.H.

**UPPER VOLTA.** *See* STATISTICS OF THE WORLD.

**URUGUAY.** The ruling military government was jolted as Uruguayans handily rejected continued military rule in a plebiscite on Nov. 30, 1980. The vote on a proposed constitution that would have given the armed forces final authority on almost all government policies was roughly 58 percent to 42 percent. Nevertheless, Lt. Gen. Luis V. Queirolo, head of the ruling junta of 28 generals and admirals, said on Dec. 4 that after seven years of military rule, Uruguay was still not ready for a return to democracy.

The proposed constitution would have established a military-controlled national security council firmly in power. The military would also have appointed the judges of a proposed political-control tribunal with power to impeach any civilian official, including the president. Free elections for a congress would have been held in 1981 and the first presidential election in 1986. Moreover, there would be only one presidential candidate, proposed jointly by the political parties and approved by the military.

Almost all the country's former civilian political leaders had long been prohibited by the junta from engaging in political activity. Political prisoners were said to number 1250 in late 1980, and

Amnesty International reported that secret detention, unfair trials, some torture, and arrests on vague charges persisted. The military had seized control of Uruguay in 1973 after a five-year wave of terrorism by urban guerrillas and an intensifying economic crisis.

Uruguay's economy showed some signs of improvement as its traditional exports—beef, grains, and citrus products—brought a 40 percent increase in export earnings between mid-1979 and mid-1980. But inflation soared to 40 percent during 1980, and unemployment rose to 13 percent, an increase of 2 percent.

*See* STATISTICS OF THE WORLD.                              J.N.G.

**UTAH.** *See* STATISTICS OF THE WORLD.

# V

**VANUATU.** *See* STATISTICS OF THE WORLD. *See also* PACIFIC ISLANDS.

**VENEZUELA.** A Watergate-like scandal in Venezuela arose, subsided, and then continued to fester throughout 1980. At its center was former President Carlos Andrés Pérez, whose Democratic Action Party government was ousted from power in late 1978, and his administration's 1977 purchase of the Norwegian refrigerated freighter, the *Sierra Nevada,* for $11,900,000. A congressional committee, investigating the fact that the government paid $20,000,000 to acquire the ship, found that an $8,100,000 overcharge was made with the full knowledge of the government, that the money went to a number of Venezuelans, and that the administration sought to cover up the payments. Pérez was censured by the Venezuelan congress on May 8, and he faced both the possibility of legal action and the loss of his immunity as a member of the Senate, an office he acquired because he is a former president. Pérez denied culpability in the incident, blaming "multinational interests" and the desire of the governing Social Christian Party, headed by President Luis Herrera Campins, to discredit him.

The government faced major economic problems through the year. After years of being on a spending spree fueled by oil revenues, Venezuela underwent a minor recession in 1980. Tight credit measures cut sharply into new construction, spawning a wave of unemployment that reached almost 20 percent of the labor force. Much private capital left the country, perhaps $300,000,000, to seek higher interest rates abroad, and new foreign investment was less than $100,000,000.

Compounding the problem, and the result of loose immigration policies of the past, was the continued influx of illegal aliens. The government admitted that there were between 3,000,000 and 4,000,000 illegal aliens in Venezuela. Most of them were from Colombia, but efforts by the government to reach an agreement with Colombia to slow the tide and perhaps send some of them home were unsuccessful—just like similar efforts by earlier governments.

*See* STATISTICS OF THE WORLD.                              J.N.G.

**VERMONT.** *See* STATISTICS OF THE WORLD.

**VIETNAM.** Faced with severe economic and social problems in 1980, Vietnam undertook a major shake-up of its leadership.

**Politics.** On the 50th anniversary of the Vietnamese Communist Party, Feb. 2, party leader Le Duan hinted that there would soon be changes at the top. A week later, Hanoi announced that Gen. Vo Nguyen Giap—the military strategist given credit for the victories over the French and the U.S.-backed South Vietnamese—had been replaced as defense minister by the younger Gen. Van Tien Dung. Giap continued to hold his post as vice premier, however, and some analysts believed that he would eventually succeed Pham Van Dong as premier.

Other changes included the replacement of aging foreign minister Nguyen Duy Trinh by the urbane Nguyen Co Thach. The shuffle also brought new leaders to the ministries of foreign trade, transportation and communications, and interior. In the critical area of economic policy, Le Thanh Nghi was replaced as chairman of the State Planning Commission by Nguyen Lam.

*During a year marked by poor harvests in Vietnam, this enterprising young couple in Ho Chi Minh City could anticipate a profitable end to their trip to market with a cargo of live chickens.*

**Resistance and Flight.** The cabinet changes did not seem to portend any relaxation of the Communist grip on power. But five years after the fall of South Vietnam, there were signs of a small but growing anti-Communist resistance in the south. The National Restoration Front, a group of former South Vietnamese officers and civil servants, launched occasional guerrilla strikes, particularly in the Mekong Delta. The Montagnards, a racial minority in the central highlands, stepped up a campaign of raids and ambushes under the banner of the United Front for the Struggle of the Oppressed Races.

Some 50,000 veterans of the defeated South Vietnamese army and former Saigon government officials languished in "reeducation" camps, while 250,000 southerners labored with inadequate tools and supplies in "new economic zones," underdeveloped rural areas that the government hoped could be cultivated. For the city dweller, 1980 was a year of food shortages and rationing.

The flight from Vietnam's Spartan life-style continued. The number of "boat people" declined from the peak year of 1979, but each month of 1980 thousands braved the open seas in flimsy boats in search of new lives abroad.

**The Economy.** Vietnam was dogged by another poor harvest in 1980, chiefly the result of drought or flood. Moreover, a devastating typhoon hit the central provinces in mid-September, wiping out almost 1000 sq.mi. of freshly planted rice at the critical flowering stage. Natural disasters apart, the country's rice fields failed to produce as much as expected due to a shortage of labor and resistance by the farmers to socialist controls.

The overall economy grew at less than 2 percent, leaving consumer goods in short supply. The country was kept afloat by $3,000,000 to $5,000,000 a day in Soviet aid. The biggest drain on Vietnam's economy was military spending. The country mounted a massive mobilization effort in 1980 that beefed up its army to about 60 divisions totaling 1,000,000 men. With more than 2,600,000 men under arms, Vietnam in 1980 had the third largest military force in the world (after China and the Soviet Union). About 200,000 troops were stationed in Cambodia and 40,000 in Laos.

**Foreign Affairs.** The military buildup was required for two major reasons: fear of China and Hanoi's own continued domination of the Indochinese region. Over the year, Vietnam became even more firmly pro-Soviet and anti-Chinese. Almost 300,000 Vietnamese troops were massed along the Chinese border, and the two countries engaged in an almost continual war of words.

*See* STATISTICS OF THE WORLD. *See also* CAMBODIA; LAOS. R.J.C.

**VIRGINIA.** *See* STATISTICS OF THE WORLD.

**VIRGIN ISLANDS.** *See* STATISTICS OF THE WORLD.

# W

**WARSAW TREATY ORGANIZATION.** *See* COMMU-
NISM.

**WASHINGTON.** *See* STATISTICS OF THE WORLD.

**WESTERN SAMOA.** *See* STATISTICS OF THE WORLD.

**WEST INDIES.** *See* STATISTICS OF THE WORLD.

**WEST VIRGINIA.** *See* STATISTICS OF THE WORLD.

**WISCONSIN.** *See* STATISTICS OF THE WORLD.

**WOMEN.** In the United States during 1980 the
drive for ratification of the Equal Rights Amendment (ERA) stalled and the controversy surrounding abortion continued, but successes were
achieved in legal battles against sex discrimination. Events inaugurating the World Decade for
Women often proved controversial.

**The ERA.** The drive for ratification of the ERA
halted in 1980; approval by three more states was
still needed. The Illinois House of Representatives
failed to ratify the amendment for the seventh
time in eight years. The deadline for ratification
by 38 states was June 30, 1982.

Reversing 40 years of support for the ERA, the
Republican Party National Convention did not
endorse the amendment in its platform. Republican Presidential candidate Ronald Reagan opposed the amendment; President Jimmy Carter
continued to support it. The Democratic Party
platform included a plank endorsing the with-
holding of financing and campaign assistance
from party candidates opposed to the ERA.

**Abortion.** On Oct. 1 Congress voted to allow
Medicaid funding of abortions only if the mother's life was at stake, or in cases of incest, or rape
if reported within 72 hr. Then Congress voted to
leave to the discretion of each state whether to
permit Medicaid-funded abortions.

The 1976 Hyde amendment congressional restrictions limited Medicaid-funded abortions to
those necessary to save the life of the mother. In
1977 the Senate added cases of incest or rape if
reported within 60 days. On June 30 the U.S. Supreme Court upheld the Hyde amendment, reversing a January ruling that labeled the amendment a violation of the rights of poor women.

The Republican Party National Convention affirmed support of a constitutional amendment "to
restore protection of the right to life for unborn
children." It also supported "the congressional efforts to restrict the use of taxpayers' dollars for
abortion" and pledged to work for the appointment of judges "who respect . . . the sanctity of
innocent human life." At the Democratic National Convention, delegates pushed through a
plank endorsing federal financing of abortions for
poor women despite President Carter's opposition.

**Job Discrimination.** A $100,000 out-of-court cash
settlement was made in a seven-year-old sex discrimination suit against the University of Minne-

**Woman at the Top**
In July, 2000 delegates assembled in Copenhagen for
the 1980 United Nations World Conference on
Women. Occupying the secretary-general's chair was
a Jamaican diplomat, Lucille Mathurin Mair. In spite
of the hectic 15-month preparation period, she welcomed the opportunity because, as she stated:
"Third World women are acutely conscious of their
condition. There comes a time when we need to put
the problem in a global context. This is it." Born in
Jamaica, she was graduated from the University of
London and earned advanced degrees from the University of the West Indies, where she also taught,
even though widowed with three small children. She
represented Jamaica at the U.N. from 1975 until 1978,
when she was named Jamaica's ambassador to Cuba.
Tall and dignified, articulate and elegant, Lucille Mair
cuts an impressive figure on the diplomatic stages of
the world.

*Lucille Mathurin Mair.*

One participant in the Aug. 26 rally in New York City marking the 60th anniversary of women's suffrage in the U.S. expresses an opinion that offers little room for compromise. The rally was organized to draw attention to the drive for ratification of the equal rights amendment.

sota. Shyamala Rajender had sued the university after she was denied a tenure-track post in the chemistry department. Simultaneously, the university was made subject by a federal court to hiring quotas, with a court appointee ensuring compliance until 1989. Similar discrimination suits were pending at other academic institutions.

Private luncheon clubs for businessmen were challenged to open their doors to women. These all-male "refuges" were seen by many women as arenas in which important business decisions were made in their absence, thereby limiting their career advancement. In 1980 the U.S. Department of Labor prepared regulations to withhold government business from any federal contractor paying fees to a club discriminating because of race, gender, or creed.

Resistance to female membership in fraternal societies and service clubs remained strong. Kiwanis International opposed any new regulations, the Junior Chamber of Commerce threatened to decertify the 100 chapters that had admitted women, and U.S. Rotary rejected a proposal to enroll women members.

In class action litigation, waitresses at Detroit's International Airport sued their employer, Michigan Hosts, Inc., contending that they were expected to wear revealing uniforms that resulted in sexual harassment. In April the Equal Employment Opportunity Commission set new regulations prohibiting the sexual harassment of employees in business or government.

**Women in the Military.** Among the 1980 graduates of the four service academies were 227 women, who joined about 20,000 previously commissioned women trained at officer candidate schools or in the Reserve Officers Training Corps.

On Feb. 8 President Carter asked that his proposal for Selective Service registration of 19- and 20-year-olds include women, as well as men.

Most women's organizations backed the principle of equal liability if draft registration were enacted. In April the U.S. House of Representatives rejected the proposal for registering women, and on June 10 the Senate rejected an amendment by Sen. Nancy Kassebaum (R, Kans.) to include women in the registration.

**Milestones.** On Aug. 21 Joyce Dannen Miller became the first woman elected to the 35-seat executive council of the American Federation of Labor and Congress of Industrial Organizations; *see also* LABOR. A woman entered the religious hierarchy of a U.S. church body for the first time when the Reverend Marjorie S. Matthews was elected bishop of the United Methodist Church on July 17.

Marguerite Yourcenar became the first woman elected to the 345-year-old French Academy, which preserves French intellectual and cultural life; *see also* FRANCE. In June Vigdis Finnbogadóttir, a leftist political leader, became the world's first popularly elected female head of state after winning a closely contested race for the presidency of Iceland.

**Copenhagen Conference.** At the July 31 conclusion of the United Nations World Conference on Women in Copenhagen, delegates from 94 of the 120 countries represented approved a controversial five-year plan of action. Along with adopting educational and antipoverty programs, the plan equated Zionism with racism and supported the Palestine Liberation Organization. Delegates from Western nations, including the U.S., felt that women's issues were slighted at the conference, while Third World, Soviet bloc, and Arab delegates argued that politics was a women's issue. U.S. participation in any future U.N. activities that referred to the document was in doubt.

The conference drew attention to the U.N. Convention on the Elimination of All Forms of Discrimination Against Women. The convention's 30 articles were aimed at obtaining equal rights for women. Delegates from 53 nations including the U.S. signed the convention on July 17. It was to take effect when 20 nations had ratified it; only Sweden and East Germany had ratified it by mid-July.

**U.S. Elections.** Postelection polls indicated that Ronald Reagan's landslide victory was achieved entirely with the support of male voters, since women's votes were believed to have been evenly divided between the two major party candidates. A massive conservative shift in the Senate indicated a possible renewed effort to enact a constitutional ban on abortion.

The 15 women incumbents in Congress who sought reelection all won their races. Four women, all Republicans, were elected to the House for the first time. Paula Hawkins, a conservative Republican, was elected to the Senate from Florida.                                    R.M.

**WYOMING.** *See* STATISTICS OF THE WORLD.

# Y

**YEMEN, PEOPLE'S DEMOCRATIC REPUBLIC OF.** The only declared Marxist state among the Arab nations, the People's Democratic Republic of Yemen (South Yemen) continued to solicit aid and arms to bolster its military might and deficient economy during 1980. Its head of state and party leader, Abdel Fattah Ismail, resigned on April 21 in an apparent power struggle over the country's future. Ali Nasser Mohammed al-Hassani took power as prime minister and head of the Yemeni Socialist Party. Although both men were Marxists, Mohammed looked for closer relations with his country's Arab neighbors, whereas Ismail had favored exclusive ties with the Soviet Union. In addition, Ismail was born in the Yemen Arab Republic (North Yemen), and Mohammed was born in the South. Ismail had urged an early union between the two Yemens, but Mohammed and his government slowed such efforts. In June Ismail was reported to be under house arrest.

Some fighting occurred between the army of North Yemen and guerrillas from the South in May after Ismail was removed from office. Ismail had supported South Yemeni guerrilla groups in their activities against Oman and North Yemen. When Mohammed attempted to increase government control over the guerrillas, they moved into the North and fought with the tribes there.

After the Soviet invasion of Afghanistan in December, 1979, the Soviet military presence in South Yemen increased, especially on the Oman and North Yemen borders. Soviet planes, naval arms, T-72 tanks, and surface-to-air missiles were reported to be in South Yemen in 1980. The number of Soviet military advisers reached 1000. More than 4000 Cuban military instructors were reported. Advisers from East Germany ran the country's intelligence and security operations. South Yemen's 50,000-man army was, in effect, commanded by Soviet officers. Soviet warships were based on South Yemen's Socotra Island, 600 mi. to the east of Aden in the Arabian Sea.

Mohammed visited Syria and sent representatives to other Arab nations in an attempt to end his country's isolation within the Arab world. Efforts were made to secure foreign aid and economic ties with both Arab nations and the West.

On Jan. 8 South Yemen announced support of the Soviet invasion of Afghanistan. It boycotted the Jan. 27-29 conference of Islamic nations where the Soviet action and Iran's holding of American hostages were condemned. At an Arab summit meeting in Tripoli, Libya, April 14-15, South Yemen agreed with Syria, Libya, Algeria, and the Palestine Liberation Organization to challenge the United States over the Egyptian-Israeli peace treaty and to strengthen ties with the Soviet Union. Along with the other four, South Yemen boycotted the Arab League summit conference held in Amman, Jordan, Nov. 25-27.

See STATISTICS OF THE WORLD. See also MIDDLE EAST.                                            R.M.

**YEMEN ARAB REPUBLIC.** The strategic location of the Yemen Arab Republic (North Yemen) allowed its president, Ali Abdullah Saleh, to maneuver between Saudi Arabian influence and rival offers of Soviet military assistance in 1980. Efforts to unite North Yemen with the People's Democratic Republic of Yemen (South Yemen) slowed with the change of leaders in South Yemen.

Relations between North Yemen and neighboring Saudi Arabia were strained as border incidents occurred in 1980, although such incidents were played down in an effort by both countries to remain on good terms. Six Yemenis were known to have been killed in early February by a Saudi border patrol searching out smugglers. Another skirmish involving Saudi aircraft was reported in mid-February, and some others were hinted at.

North Yemen continued to serve as a buffer between royalist and conservative Saudi Arabia and the Marxist states of South Yemen and Ethiopia. Except for Saudi Arabia, North Yemen is the most populous of the Arabian Peninsula states. Its people provided Saudi Arabia with a work force of 600,000 in 1980.

In late 1979, in the wake of a border war with South Yemen, North Yemen sought and obtained increased Soviet military aid. Its supplies of arms from the United States, including a $400,000,000 emergency shipment paid for by the Saudis, had seemed insufficient, and the arms were slow in arriving because they came by way of Saudi Arabia. In reprisal, Saudi Arabia stopped its considerable military assistance and budget subsidies ($700,000,000 annually) for December, 1979, and

January, 1980. As a result, Yemeni government employees were not paid. In late January North Yemen's prime minister, Abdel-Aziz Abdel-Ghani, went to the Saudi capital. On March 18 it was reported that the Yemenis had agreed to invite no further Soviet advisers to North Yemen and eventually to remove those already in the country.

The Saudis insisted on and obtained a lessening of Soviet presence, but Soviet influence remained. Most North Yemeni soldiers in 1980 were using Soviet arms. The country's official policy, however, remained one of nonalignment, and there appeared to be little sympathy with Communist ideology.

In the war between Iraq and Iran, North Yemen gave Iraq verbal backing and reportedly also allowed the stationing of Iraqi planes in North Yemen.

See STATISTICS OF THE WORLD. See also MIDDLE EAST.                                            R.M.

*Tribal loyalties often overshadow nationalistic fervor in North Yemen. Guerrilla fighters such as these defended their territory in 1980 from a threatened invasion by mercenaries from South Yemen.*

The coffin containing the body of Yugoslavia's President Tito begins its final journey from the parliament building to its interment site on Dedinje Hill outside Belgrade on May 8. The president died on May 4 after a long illness.

**YUGOSLAVIA.** President Tito, founder of Communist Yugoslavia and its leader since World War II, died on May 4, 1980, at the age of 87. As Tito had hoped, his nation weathered his passing well, and its new leaders pledged to continue his policies.

**Domestic Affairs.** Tito was hospitalized in Ljubljana on Jan. 3. He had been staying at his hunting lodge in northern Yugoslavia when a circulatory problem began to cause him discomfort. On Jan. 20 his left leg was amputated. His condition remained satisfactory for a time, and he began physiotherapy. But within a few weeks, his heart and kidneys began to fail.

Tito continued to take an active interest in world affairs, receiving top Yugoslav officials in his hospital room and even firing off personal notes, in late February, to U.S. President Jimmy Carter and Soviet President Leonid I. Brezhnev, appealing to them to renew their efforts to develop détente. Finally, on May 4, the Yugoslav leader died.

Tito's body was brought from Ljubljana to Belgrade by train. Hundreds of thousands of Yugoslavs paid homage to their fallen president as the train made its slow progress. Burial took place on May 8, and it was attended by scores of world leaders, among them Soviet President Brezhnev, Chinese Premier Hua Kuo-feng (Hua Guofeng), Indian Prime Minister Indira Gandhi, Japanese Prime Minister Masayoshi Ohira, British Prime Minister Margaret Thatcher, and West German Chancellor Helmut Schmidt.

The elaborate plan for political succession that had been engineered by Tito took effect with relative ease. Twin leadership bodies divided responsibilities between state affairs and those of the ruling Communist Party, and each was designed to distribute political power among the country's numerous ethnic groups.

At the top of the state hierarchy, a collective state presidency consisted of eight members selected on a regional basis, with the post of president rotating. The first post-Tito president was Lazar Kolisevski, a native of Yugoslav Macedonia; he was succeeded in mid-May, a scheduled rotation time, by Cvijetin Mijatovic, a native of Bosnia and Hercegovina. At the top of the party hierarchy was a presidium of 23 members. Stevan Doronjski, a Serb, became its president on Tito's death; his term ended in October, and he was succeeded on Oct. 20 by Lazar Mojsov, a native of Yugoslav Macedonia and former president of the United Nations General Assembly.

**The Economy.** The foremost domestic problem facing Yugoslavia's new leaders was the state of the economy. The country was suffering a severe balance of payments deficit (about $4 billion in 1979) and inflation of 25 percent annually. On June 6 the government decided on a drastic, 30 percent devaluation of the dinar to stimulate exports and boost foreign tourism. At the same time, investment in social projects was cut, and priority was given to investment in domestic energy and raw materials sources and in agriculture.

Miran Potro, the Yugoslav trade union chief, said in December that unrest in Poland had made him and his associates more attentive to workers' demands than in the past. More than 3000 strikes had occurred since 1958 in Yugoslavia, where they were tolerated in practice though not recognized by law.

**Foreign Relations.** Yugoslav officials appeared determined to follow Tito's chosen foreign policy path. They gave primary emphasis to independence from the Soviet Union and to nonalignment between the United States and the U.S.S.R.

Relations with the Soviet Union remained correct, but the Belgrade government was wary of Soviet intentions; it feared that the Russians would attempt to assert control over Yugoslavia. During his attendance at Tito's funeral, Brezhnev stated that he would respect Yugoslav sovereignty. Throughout the year, however, the Soviet press kept up a drumbeat of criticism of Yugoslavia on a variety of issues, among them Belgrade's firm opposition to the Soviet invasion of Afghanistan and its refusal to attend a Soviet-sponsored

conference of European Communist parties in April.

To help stave off Soviet pressure, Yugoslavia cultivated ties with Western as well as Third World nations. While Tito lay ill, officials negotiated a closer relationship with the European Community (EC). In an agreement signed on April 2, the EC removed many of the barriers that had blocked Yugoslav exports and had caused an annual trade imbalance of nearly $3 billion with the Common Market countries.

To the distress of the Yugoslav government, U.S. President Jimmy Carter did not attend Tito's funeral. In June, however, Carter journeyed to Belgrade to give assurances of American backing for Yugoslavia's independence. He received the warmest public welcome any visiting leader had won in many years.

*See* STATISTICS OF THE WORLD.                  F.W.

**YUKON TERRITORY.** *See* STATISTICS OF THE WORLD.

# Z

**ZAIRE.** In 1980 political and economic malaise continued in Zaire. In mid-January President Mobutu Sese Seko reshuffled his cabinet. Thirteen of 22 ministers were required to resign; among the replacements was a prominent opposition leader. Dismissals of corrupt officials and an effort to enlist Jean Tshombe, exiled son of Moise Tshombe, the leader of the former secessionist movement in Shaba (Katanga) Province, as a Mobutu ally were seen as attempts to make Zaire more democratic and Mobutu's rule more acceptable to political dissidents.

These overtures were ignored by Mobutu's opponents, and in February Mobutu declared that no political opposition would be allowed during his rule. Following student strikes in March and April that protested government policies, Kinshasa University was closed until October, and hundreds of students, teachers, and others were arrested. In June five opposition groups banded together to form the Council for the Liberation of the Congo. Declaring the Mobutu government a corrupt dictatorship, they pledged to continue armed struggle until Mobutu was overthrown. In an August cabinet shuffle, Nguza Karl-i-Bond was reinstated as prime minister.

While 1980 marked a continuation of the president's low political standing, steps taken by the government improved Zaire's position in the world economic community. In late February the national currency was devalued 30 percent in an

action designed to meet loan conditions set by the International Monetary Fund. In April a portion of Zaire's foreign debt of nearly $4 billion was rescheduled by international agreement, and backing was given to a plan to invest more than $1 billion in new mining, industrial, and agricultural projects. Nevertheless, inflation was said to be running at about 200 percent annually, and unemployment was around 50 percent.

*See* STATISTICS OF THE WORLD.                  J.T.S.

**ZAMBIA.** In 1980 President Kenneth D. Kaunda's insistence upon bolstering defense and preparing for the eventual liberation of white-dominated southern Africa appeared to hurt his popularity and political position within Zambia. In February Zambia ordered some $85,400,000 in Soviet arms, including 16 MiG-21's. Seen as a reaction to heavy Rhodesian bombings and incursions in 1979, the purchase ran into strong domestic criticism because of the country's balance-of-payments and external-debt problems. The purchase also perhaps influenced the decision of the U.S. Congress in June to trim $6,700,000 from aid to Zambia, reducing the sum to $20,300,000.

In April Kaunda hosted a meeting of ministers from nine southern African nations to devise plans to lessen their economic dependency on South Africa. Plans were formulated to develop alternative transportation routes, sources of consumer goods and fuel, and new markets for their goods. Opponents of Kaunda's rule questioned whether Zambia's weakened economy could support these policies.

Critics of Kaunda suffered a severe loss in late January, when Simon Kapwepwe, his chief political rival, died of a stroke. In April Kaunda tightened government controls over the local press, and in June he clamped down on strikers, who were responsible for some 120 work stoppages in a year. As Kaunda increased the pressure on his opponents, some began to plan for a violent counterattack. In late October the government announced that dissidents, allegedly aided by South Africa, had been plotting to overthrow the government. Some 40 were captured, and others had been killed. On Dec. 4 Kaunda reshuffled the cabinet, announcing seven changes.

In other news, in May Kaunda launched "Operation Food Production," a ten-year plan financed by some $460,000,000 in foreign aid. The plan focused on establishing a number of large state farms and state-run enterprises and was designed to stimulate national self-sufficiency. In early September it was reported that China had agreed to help Zambia and Tanzania to improve the troubled Tanzam Railroad, an 1160-mi. line built by the Chinese in the mid-1970's. Some of the railroad's problems had been caused by past Rhodesian raids.

*See* STATISTICS OF THE WORLD. J.T.S.

**ZIMBABWE,** formerly RHODESIA. The 15-year struggle for black African control of Zimbabwe came to an end in 1980. Despite the installation of the most radical of the black nationalist groups as Zimbabwe's rulers, the transition to black control was peaceful for the most part.

**Transition.** Great Britain resumed administrative control of the territory in mid-December, 1979, after a 14-week constitutional conference in London and immediately ended military raids into neighboring countries and the execution of captured guerrillas. Food shipments to neighboring Zambia, on the verge of famine, also were resumed. At the end of December, a cease-fire was arranged between the Patriotic Front, comprising guerrilla forces loyal to Robert Mugabe's Zimbabwe African National Union (ZANU) and Joshua Nkomo's Zimbabwe African People's Union (ZAPU), and the white settler-backed government of Bishop Abel T. Muzorewa. According to plans for independence accepted by the Patriotic Front, Britain, and the Muzorewa government, British administrators were to govern the territory until elections could be held, some four to six weeks after the start of 1980. The stage was set for, first, a voter registration drive and, then, a strongly contested election campaign. The two-month campaign pitted ZANU and ZAPU candidates against one another and against Bishop Muzorewa's supporters.

Regarded as the least of the possible evils, Muzorewa was widely supported by the white community, including former Prime Minister Ian D. Smith and his Rhodesian Front. Intimidation of voters and assassination attempts against party candidates, including two attempts against Mugabe's life, marred the campaign.

Elections were held Feb. 27–29, with some 150 official observers from the Commonwealth and the European Community watching to examine the fairness of the procedures. Much to the amazement of many political commentators, Robert Mugabe's ZANU won 57 of the 80 parliamentary seats available to blacks. (The 20 seats reserved for whites had all been won by Smith's Rhodesian Front earlier in February.) The voting was heavily tribal in nature. Mugabe's party had overwhelming support from the Mashona people, who make up 80 percent of the country's blacks; Nkomo's party was backed by the Matabele.

On April 18 Mugabe officially became prime minister of an independent Zimbabwe. Nkomo, whose ZAPU supporters secured only 20 parliamentary seats, was persuaded to serve as minister for home affairs, after the post was stripped of some of its major responsibilities. The cabinet also included three other ZAPU members, two whites, and two women. The figurehead post of president went to the Reverend Canaan Banana, a Mugabe supporter. Mugabe, a self-proclaimed Marxist and the most radical of the candidates, quickly announced a series of programs aimed at smoothing over differences and preserving peace.

**Security.** The new government's first priority was security. At independence, Mugabe controlled some 23,000 seasoned troops, while 13,000 men were under Nkomo's ZAPU commanders; the regular Rhodesian army was loyal to Lt. Gen. Peter Walls, their commander. Walls was appointed by Mugabe to head the joint command and supervise the integration of the ZANU and ZAPU forces into the standing army. In June a plan was adopted to integrate 9500 guerrillas into the army, with the rest assigned to community and agricultural projects. Few, however, even began training. Walls, already on leave in Europe pending retirement, was dismissed in mid-September, after he said that he had earlier urged the British not to recognize the Mugabe election victory. He was later barred from returning to the country.

The rivalry between ZANU and ZAPU forces remained a serious problem. Occasionally the two groups battled or raided farms or settlements near their bases. In one of the worst clashes, in November, 58 persons were killed and 300 wounded,

The British Union Jack was lowered for the last time in all of Africa with the independence of Rhodesia, now Zimbabwe. Great Britain's Prince Charles (left) stood beside the governor, Lord Soames, to witness the historic event.

most of them black civilians caught in the cross fire.

**Black-White Relations.** Mugabe's second priority was to balance the expectations of the country's black population for radical economic and social changes against white fears that their position would deteriorate rapidly. More than 100 wildcat strikes occurred soon after independence. While Mugabe spoke of satisfying the aspirations of the black workers, minimum wages were raised only moderately, and workers were urged to maintain order and discipline.

The government instituted a policy of accelerating the advancement of blacks in the civil service. It also began to redistribute abandoned farms to landless black farmers or returning refugees. Many whites left Zimbabwe immediately after Mugabe's victory, the bulk of them military personnel or police and their families. It was estimated that some 18,000 of the country's 200,000 whites would leave in 1980.

White fears increased in early December, when Edgar Z. Tekere, a minister in the Mugabe cabinet, was freed by a court even though it had found that he and a bodyguard had killed a white farmer in August. Ironically, Tekere was freed under a law passed in 1975 by the Smith regime (and still on the books in August) that protected ministers from criminal prosecution if they acted "in good faith" to suppress terrorism. A white judge

ruled that Tekere had not acted in good faith, but he was outvoted by two nonwhite judges.

**The Economy.** The new government's third priority was to stimulate foreign aid and investment. The government welcomed foreign investment and promised a beneficial climate for investors, including easy profit repatriation. Prospective investors, however, for the most part took a wait-and-see attitude. In 1980 some $100,000,000 in Western government aid was received, with more pledged. Although far below the government's expectations, it helped offset some of the costs of the land redistribution program. Mugabe warned on Nov. 2, however, that his government might seize white-owned farms without compensation if more aid was not forthcoming.

In late 1980 economic growth for the year was estimated at 6 percent after declining through much of the 1970's. Inflation was running at an annual rate of about 7 percent.

**Foreign Policy.** The Mugabe government worked to realign the country's foreign policies. Diplomatic relations with South Africa were severed in early September; trade, however, was maintained. Zimbabwe declared itself eager to work with other southern African states to reduce their dependence on South African exports and transportation systems.

See STATISTICS OF THE WORLD. See also AFRICA.

J.T.S.

# STATISTICS
# OF THE WORLD

*in the tables on the following pages will
be found the latest available statistics on*

# THE COUNTRIES OF THE WORLD

| Nation Capital | Population | Area of Country (sq mi/ sq km) | Type of Government | Heads of State and Government | Currency; Value in U.S. Dollars | GNP (000,000); GNP per capita |
|---|---|---|---|---|---|---|
| **AFGHANISTAN** . . . . . . . Kabul | 21,452,000 . . . . 377,700 | 250,000 . . . . 647,497 | . Republic . . . . . . | . President: . . . . . . . . . . . . . . . . . . . . Babrak Karmal | . Afghani . . . . . . $ 0.02 | 3,530 240 |
| **ALBANIA** . . . . . . . . . . . . Tiranë | 2,670,000 . . . . 192,300 | 11,100 . . . . 28,748 | . People's . . . . . socialist republic | . Presidium President: . . . . . . . . . . Haxhi Lleshi Chairman, Council of Ministers (Prime Minister): Mehmet Shehu | . Lek . . . . . . . . . 0.14¹ | 1,920 740 |
| **ALGERIA** . . . . . . . . . . . . Algiers | 19,130,000 . . . . 1,800,000 | 919,595 . . . . 2,381,741 | . Republic . . . . . . | . President: . . . . . . . . . . . . . . . . . . . . Col. Chadli Benjedid Premier: Col. Mohamed Ben Ahmed Abdelghani | . Dinar . . . . . . . . 0.26 | 22,290 1,260 |
| **ANGOLA** . . . . . . . . . . . . Luanda | 6,900,000 . . . . 480,600² | 481,353 . . . . 1,246,700 | . People's . . . . . republic | . President: . . . . . . . . . . . . . . . . . . . . José Eduardo dos Santos | . Kwanza . . . . . . 0.02 | 2,000 300 |
| **ARGENTINA** . . . . . . . . . . Buenos Aires | 26,730,000 . . . . 2,982,000 | 1,068,301 . . . . 2,766,889 | . Federal . . . . . . republic | . President: . . . . . . . . . . . . . . . . . . . . Lt. Gen. Jorge Rafael Videla | . Peso . . . . . . . . 0.0005 | 50,250 1,910 |
| **AUSTRALIA** . . . . . . . . . Canberra | 14,420,000 . . . . 234,700² | 2,967,907 . . . . 7,686,848 | . Federal . . . . . . parliamentary state (C) | . Governor-General: . . . . . . . . . . . . Sir Zelman Cowen Prime Minister: Malcolm Fraser | . Dollar . . . . . . . . 1.17 | 113,830 7,920 |
| **AUSTRIA** . . . . . . . . . . . . Vienna | 7,510,000 . . . . 1,580,600 | 32,374 . . . . 83,849 | . Federal . . . . . . republic | . President: . . . . . . . . . . . . . . . . . . . . Rudolf Kirchschläger Chancellor: Bruno Kreisky | . Schilling . . . . . . 0.08 | 52,720 7,030 |
| **BAHAMAS** . . . . . . . . . . . Nassau | 220,000 . . . . 133,300² | 5,380 . . . . 13,935 | . Parliamentary . state (C) | . Governor-General: . . . . . . . . . . . . Sir Gerald Cash Prime Minister: Lynden O. Pindling | . Dollar . . . . . . . . 1.00 | 570 2,620 |
| **BAHRAIN** . . . . . . . . . . . Manama | 290,000 . . . . 114,000 | 240 . . . . 622 | . Emirate . . . . . . . | . Emir: . . . . . . . . . . . . . . . . . . . . . . . Isa bin Sulman al-Khalifah Prime Minister: Khalifah bin Sulman al-Khalifah | . Dinar . . . . . . . 2.66 | 1,510 4,100 |
| **BANGLADESH** . . . . . . . . Dacca | 86,640,000 . . . . 2,000,000² | 55,598 . . . . 143,998 | . Republic . . . . . . (C) | . President: . . . . . . . . . . . . . . . . . . . . Maj. Gen. Ziaur Rahman Prime Minister: Shah Mohammad Azizur Rahman | . Taka . . . . . . . . 0.07 | 7,630 90 |
| **BARBADOS** . . . . . . . . . Bridgetown | 250,000 . . . . 8,800 | 166 . . . . 431 | . Parliamentary . state (C) | . Governor-General: . . . . . . . . . . . . Sir Deighton Ward Prime Minister: Tom Adams | . Dollar . . . . . . . . 0.50 | 490 1,940 |
| **BELGIUM** . . . . . . . . . . . Brussels | 9,850,000 . . . . 1,015,700² | 11,781 . . . . 30,513 | . Constitutional . monarchy | . King: . . . . . . . . . . . . . . . . . . . . . . . Baudouin Premier: Wilfried Martens | . Franc . . . . . . . . 0.035 | 89,520 9,070 |
| **BENIN** . . . . . . . . . . . . . Porto-Novo | 3,470,000 . . . . 104,000 | 43,484 . . . . 112,622 | . People's . . . . . . republic | . President: . . . . . . . . . . . . . . . . . . . . Lt. Col. Mathieu Kérékou | . CFA franc . . . . 0.0049 | 770 230 |

The section on countries presents the latest information available. All monetary figures are expressed in United States dollars. The symbol (C) signifies that the country belongs to the Commonwealth of Nations. NA means that the data were not available. * indicates that the category does not apply to the country under discussion. Footnotes at the end of the section contain more specialized information.

| Imports Exports | Revenue Expenditure | Elementary Schools: Teachers Students | Secondary Schools: Teachers Students | Colleges and Universities: Teachers Students |
|---|---|---|---|---|
| $ 328,000,000 ............$ | 357,000,000 ............. | 29,789 ............. | 5,798......... | 1,062 |
| 431,000,000 | 381,000,000 | 942,817 | 111,148 | 12,480 |
| NA............. | 1,114,000,000 ............. | 22,686 | 3,990......... | 1,153 |
| NA | 1,107,000,000 | 569,600 | 102,600 | 28,668 |
| 8,682,000,000 ............. | 9,826,000,000 ............. | 80,853 ............. | 32,621......... | 6,421 |
| 6,322,000,000 | 9,821,000,000 | 2,972,242 | 844,291 | 51,510 |
| NA............. | NA ............. | 25,000 ............. | NA......... | NA |
| NA | NA | 1,026,291 | 105,868 | 1,109 |
| 3,834,000,000 ............. | 6,913,000,000 ............. | 221,050 ............. | 175,080......... | 39,970 |
| 6,400,000,000 | 6,913,000,000 | 3,818,250 | 1,325,515 | 619,950 |
| 16,432,000,000 ............. | 26,493,000,000 ............. | 85,273 ............. | 80,485......... | 19,087 |
| 18,473,000,000 | 30,949,000,000 | 1,894,654 | 1,161,514 | 263,821 |
| 20,254,000,000 ............. | 19,000,000,000 ............. | 31,897 ............. | 37,937......... | 10,996 |
| 15,483,000,000 | 21,046,000,000 | 502,389 | 961,895 | 94,386 |
| 3,053,000,000 ............. | 204,000,000 ............. | NA ............. | NA......... | NA |
| 1,989,000,000 | 202,000,000 | 23,348 | 23,719 | 3,000 |
| 2,046,000,000 ............. | 743,000,000 ............. | 2,550 ............. | 910......... | 86 |
| 1,893,000,000 | 743,000,000 | 46,326 | 20,776 | 763 |
| 1,294,000,000 ............. | 1,158,000,000 ............. | 172,448 ............. | NA......... | NA |
| 576,000,000 | 763,000,000 | 9,483,090 | 2,317,119 | 121,155 |
| 424,000,000 ............. | 132,000,000 ............. | 3,175 ............. | 1,432......... | NA |
| 151,000,000 | 150,000,000 | 33,989 | 28,677 | 2,032 |
| 60,410,000,000[3] ............. | 30,892,000,000 ............. | 48,041 ............. | NA......... | NA |
| 56,258,000,000[3] | 37,240,000,000 | 923,677 | 849,937 | 159,660 |
| 267,000,000 ............. | 111,000,000 ............. | 6,326 ............. | 1,198......... | 153 |
| 26,000,000 | 111,000,000 | 293,648 | 55,075 | 2,118 |

| Nation<br>Capital | Population | Area of<br>Country<br>(sq mi/<br>sq km) | Type of<br>Government | Heads of State and<br>Government | Currency;<br>Value in<br>U.S. Dollars | GNP<br>(000,000);<br>GNP<br>per capita |
|---|---|---|---|---|---|---|
| **BHUTAN**<br>Thimphu | 1,269,000<br>8,900 | 18,147<br>47,000 | Monarchy | King:<br>Jigme Singye<br>Wangchuk | Ngultrum<br>0.12 | $ 120<br>100 |
| **BOLIVIA**<br>Sucre<br>La Paz | 5,430,000<br>63,600<br>654,700 | 424,164<br>1,098,581 | Republic | President:<br>Gen. Luis García<br>Meza Tejada | Peso<br>0.04 | 2,690<br>510 |
| **BOTSWANA**<br>Gaborone | 790,000<br>36,900 | 231,805<br>600,372 | Republic<br>(C) | President:<br>Quett Masire | Pula<br>1.28 | 460<br>620 |
| **BRAZIL**<br>Brasília | 118,650,000<br>763,300[2] | 3,286,487<br>8,511,965 | Federal<br>republic | President:<br>Gen. João Baptista<br>de Figueiredo | Cruzeiro<br>0.02 | 187,190<br>1,570 |
| **BULGARIA**<br>Sofia | 8,950,000<br>1,059,200 | 42,823<br>110,912 | People's<br>republic | Chairman, Council of State:<br>Todor Zhivkov<br>Chairman, Council of Ministers<br>(Prime Minister):<br>Stanko Todorov | Lev<br>1.18[1] | 28,450<br>3,200 |
| **BURMA**<br>Rangoon | 32,910,000<br>2,276,000 | 261,218<br>676,552 | Socialist<br>republic | President:<br>U Ne Win<br>Prime Minister:<br>U Maung Maung Kha | Kyat<br>0.15 | 4,900<br>150 |
| **BURUNDI**<br>Bujumbura | 4,380,000<br>172,400[2] | 10,747<br>27,834 | Republic | President:<br>Col. Jean-Baptiste Bagaza | Franc<br>0.01 | 610<br>140 |
| **CAMBODIA**<br>**(PEOPLE'S REPUBLIC**<br>**OF KAMPUCHEA)**<br>Phnom Penh | 4,800,000<br><br><br>500,000 | 69,898<br>181,035 | People's<br>republic | President, People's<br>Revolutionary Council:<br>Heng Samrin | Vietnamese<br>dong<br>0.49 | [4]<br>[4] |
| **CAMEROON**<br>Yaoundé | 8,250,000<br>313,700[2] | 183,569<br>475,442 | Republic | President:<br>Ahmadou Ahidjo<br>Prime Minister:<br>Paul Biya | CFA franc<br>0.0049 | 3,700<br>460 |
| **CANADA**<br>Ottawa | 23,690,000<br>726,400[2] | 3,851,807<br>9,976,139 | Federal<br>parliamentary<br>state<br>(C) | Governor-General:<br>Edward R. Schreyer<br>Prime Minister:<br>Pierre Elliott Trudeau | Dollar<br>0.86 | 216,090<br>9,170 |
| **CAPE VERDE**<br>Praia | 320,000<br>21,500[2] | 1,557<br>4,033 | Republic | President:<br>Aristides M. Pereira<br>Premier:<br>Maj. Pedro Rodrigues Pires | Escudo<br>0.03 | 50<br>160 |
| **CENTRAL AFRICAN**<br>**REPUBLIC**<br>Bangui | 2,305,000<br><br>350,000[2] | 240,535<br>622,984 | Republic | President:<br>David Dacko<br>Premier:<br>Bernard Ayandho | CFA franc<br>0.0049 | 480<br>250 |
| **CHAD**<br>N'Djamena | 4,420,000<br>303,000[2] | 495,755<br>1,284,000 | Republic | President:<br>Goukouni Oueddei | CFA franc<br>0.0049 | 620<br>140 |
| **CHILE**<br>Santiago | 10,920,000<br>3,448,700[2] | 292,258<br>756,945 | Republic | President:<br>Gen. Augusto Pinochet Ugarte | Peso<br>0.026 | 15,180<br>1,410 |
| **CHINA, PEOPLE'S**<br>**REPUBLIC OF**<br>Peking | 970,920,000<br><br>8,487,000[2] | 3,705,406<br>9,596,961 | People's<br>republic | Chairman, Standing<br>Committee of the<br>National People's Congress:<br>Marshal Ye Jianying (Yeh Chien-<br>ying)<br>Prime Minister:<br>Zhao Ziyang<br>(Chao Chi-yang) | Yuan<br>0.67[1] | 424,620<br>460 |
| **COLOMBIA**<br>Bogotá | 26,360,000<br>4,055,900[2] | 439,737<br>1,138,914 | Republic | President:<br>Julio César Turbay Ayala | Peso<br>0.02 | 21,790<br>870 |
| **COMOROS**<br>Moroni | 330,000<br>18,300[2] | 838<br>2,171 | Republic | President:<br>Ahmed Abdallah<br>Premier:<br>Salim Ben Ali | CFA franc<br>0.0049 | 70<br>180 |

| Imports<br>Exports | Revenue<br>Expenditure | Elementary<br>Schools:<br>Teachers<br>Students | Secondary<br>Schools:<br>Teachers<br>Students | Colleges and<br>Universities:<br>Teachers<br>Students |
|---|---|---|---|---|
| $ NA ........ $ | 11,000,000 ......... | 488 ......... | 334 ......... | 45 |
| NA | 23,000,000 | 18,821 | 1,536 | 304 |
| 1,001,000,000 ......... | 582,000,000 ......... | NA ......... | NA ......... | NA |
| 777,000,000 | 582,000,000 | 945,733 | 150,493 | 51,585 |
| 370,000,000 ......... | 156,000,000 ......... | 4,653 ......... | 1,126 ......... | 85 |
| 233,000,000 | 154,000,000 | 145,459 | 18,977 | 762 |
| 19,804,000,000 ......... | 11,071,000,000 ......... | 994,031 ......... | 168,451 ......... | 95,758 |
| 15,250,000,000 | 11,071,000,000 | 20,340,577 | 2,391,465 | 1,159,046 |
| 8,514,000,000 ......... | 12,356,000,000 ......... | 49,345 ......... | 27,236 ......... | 11,619 |
| 8,869,000,000 | 12,333,000,000 | 980,857 | 336,802 | 103,662 |
| 319,000,000 ......... | 2,705,000,000 ......... | 84,593 ......... | 32,586 ......... | 3,922 |
| 363,000,000 | 2,947,000,000 | 3,731,160 | 939,478 | 112,671 |
| 153,000,000 ......... | 82,000,000 ......... | NA ......... | NA ......... | NA |
| 105,000,000 | 67,000,000 | 142,763 | 13,863 | 1,447 |
| [4] ......... | [4] ......... | NA ......... | NA ......... | NA |
| [4] | [4] | NA | NA | NA |
| 1,271,000,000 ......... | 925,000,000 ......... | NA ......... | NA ......... | NA |
| 1,129,000,000 | 925,000,000 | 1,202,841 | 175,894 | 10,001 |
| 43,434,000,000 ......... | 36,720,000,000 ......... | 266,057[5] ......... | [5] ......... | 52,373 |
| 46,065,000,000 | 43,044,000,000 | 5,158,406[5] | [5] | 611,520 |
| 29,000,000 ......... | NA ......... | 1,269 ......... | 331 ......... | * |
| 1,500,000 | 19,000,000 | 55,406 | 7,025 | * |
| 57,000,000[6] ......... | 93,000,000 ......... | 3,329 ......... | 562 ......... | 85 |
| 72,000,000[6] | 93,000,000 | 221,412 | 23,895 | 555 |
| 118,000,000 ......... | 82,000,000 ......... | 2,610[7] ......... | NA ......... | NA |
| 59,000,000 | 82,000,000 | 210,882 | 19,580 | 547 |
| 4,218,000,000 ......... | 5,398,000,000 ......... | NA ......... | NA ......... | NA |
| 3,766,000,000 | 4,279,000,000 | 2,333,601 | 609,567 | 130,208 |
| 11,100,000,000 ......... | 74,172,000,000 ......... | NA ......... | NA ......... | NA |
| 10,000,000,000 | 74,172,000,000 | 146,240,000 | 65,480,000 | 850,000 |
| 4,437,000,000 ......... | 2,050,000,000 ......... | 128,494 ......... | 79,742 ......... | 27,384 |
| 3,381,000,000 | 1,904,000,000 | 4,160,527 | 1,616,111 | 290,624 |
| 17,000,000 ......... | 16,000,000 ......... | 849[8] ......... | 118[8] ......... | * |
| 9,000,000 | NA | 34,181[8] | 2,586[8] | * |

| Nation Capital | Population | Area of Country (sq mi/ sq km) | Type of Government | Heads of State and Government | Currency; Value in U.S. Dollars | GNP (000,000); GNP per capita |
|---|---|---|---|---|---|---|
| **CONGO** Brazzaville | 1,500,000 310,000[2] | 132,047 342,000 | People's republic | President: Col. Denis Sassou-Nguesso Premier: Col. Louis Sylvain Goma | CFA franc 0.0049 | $ 780 540 |
| **COSTA RICA** San José | 2,190,000 242,700 | 19,575 50,700 | Republic | President: Rodrigo Carazo Odio | Colón 0.12 | 3,250 1,540 |
| **CUBA** Havana | 9,850,000 1,986,500 | 44,218 114,524 | Socialist republic | President and Premier: Fidel Castro | Peso 1.39[1] | 7,860 810 |
| **CYPRUS** Nicosia | 620,000 160,000[2] | 3,572 9,251 | Republic (C) | President: Spyros Kyprianou | Pound 2.88 | 1,370 2,110 |
| **CZECHOSLOVAKIA** Prague | 15,250,000 1,188,600 | 49,370 127,869 | Federal socialist republic | President: Gustáv Husák Premier: Lubomír Štrougal | Koruna 0.10[1] | 71,320 4,720 |
| **DENMARK** Copenhagen | 5,120,000 662,500 | 16,629 43,069 | Constitutional monarchy | Queen: Margrethe II Prime Minister: Anker Jørgensen | Krone 0.18 | 50,410 9,920 |
| **DJIBOUTI** Djibouti | 242,000 160,000[2] | 8,494 22,000 | Republic | President: Hassan Gouled Aptidon Premier: Barkad Gourad Hamadou | Djibouti franc 0.0056 | 140 450 |
| **DOMINICA** Roseau | 80,000 16,800 | 290 751 | Republic (C) | President: Aurelius Marie Prime Minister: Mary Eugenia Charles | East Caribbean dollar 0.37 | 30 440 |
| **DOMINICAN REPUBLIC** Santo Domingo | 5,280,000 1,170,500[2] | 18,816 48,734 | Republic | President: Silvestre Antonio Guzmán Fernández | Peso 1.00 | 4,680 910 |
| **ECUADOR** Quito | 8,150,000 742,900 | 109,483 283,561 | Republic | President: Jaime Roldós Aguilera | Sucre 0.04 | 6,890 910 |
| **EGYPT** Cairo | 40,980,000 5,084,500 | 386,661 1,001,449 | Republic | President and Prime Minister: Anwar el-Sadat | Pound 1.45 | 15,520 400 |
| **EL SALVADOR** San Salvador | 4,660,000 408,800 | 8,124 21,041 | Republic | President and head, National Revolutionary Movement: José Napoleón Duarte | Colón 0.40 | 2,810 600 |
| **EQUATORIAL GUINEA** Malabo | 360,000 19,300 | 10,831 28,051 | Republic | President, Supreme Military Council: Lt. Col. Teodoro Obiang Nguema Mbasogo | Ekuele 0.015 | NA NA |
| **ETHIOPIA** Addis Ababa | 30,420,000 1,196,300 | 471,778 1,221,900 | Socialist state | Head of State, Chairman of the Provisional Military Administrative Council, and Chairman of the Council of Ministers: Lt. Col. Mengistu Haile Mariam | Birr 0.48 | 3,640 120 |
| **FIJI** Suva | 610,000 63,600 | 7,056 18,274 | Parliamentary state (C) | Governor-General: Ratu Sir George K. Cakobau Prime Minister: Ratu Sir Kamisese Mara | Dollar 1.24 | 860 1,440 |
| **FINLAND** Helsinki | 4,760,000 484,900 | 130,120 337,009 | Republic | President: Urho K. Kekkonen Prime Minister: Mauno Koivisto | Markka 0.27 | 32,380 6,820 |
| **FRANCE** Paris | 53,480,000 2,299,800 | 211,208 547,026 | Republic | President: Valéry Giscard d'Estaing Premier: Raymond Barre | Franc 0.24 | 439,970 8,270 |
| **GABON** Libreville | 1,300,200 225,200[2] | 103,347 267,667 | Republic | President: Omar Bongo Premier: Léon Mébiame | CFA franc 0.0049 | 1,930 3,580 |

| Imports<br>Exports | Revenue<br>Expenditure | Elementary<br>Schools:<br>Teachers<br>Students | Secondary<br>Schools:<br>Teachers<br>Students | Colleges and<br>Universities:<br>Teachers<br>Students |
|---|---|---|---|---|
| $ 261,000,000[6] | $ 288,000,000 | 6,675 | 3,489 | NA |
| 139,000,000[6] | 288,000,000 | 345,736 | 138,333 | 3,642 |
| 1,409,000,000 | 480,000,000 | 13,108 | 5,195 | NA |
| 923,000,000 | 691,000,000 | 393,361 | 150,659 | 38,629 |
| 4,687,000,000 | NA | 86,300 | 50,700 | 10,200 |
| 4,456,000,000 | NA | 1,693,900 | 645,500 | 122,500 |
| 1,001,000,000 | 333,000,000 | 2,703 | 3,245 | 90 |
| 456,000,000 | 286,000,000 | 72,813 | 62,113 | 782 |
| 14,262,000,000 | 22,613,000,000 | 91,876 | NA | 17,738 |
| 13,198,000,000 | 22,603,000,000 | 1,878,000 | 811,382 | 183,632 |
| 18,450,000,000 | 17,385,000,000 | 58,954[5] | [5] | NA |
| 14,506,000,000 | 20,335,000,000 | 561,132 | 293,310 | 110,271 |
| 104,000,000 | NA | NA | NA | * |
| 19,000,000 | 61,000,000 | 13,011 | 3,408 | * |
| 28,000,000 | 10,600,000 | 423 | 320 | 8 |
| 16,000,000 | 11,500,000 | 15,220 | 10,214 | 154 |
| 1,055,000,000 | 628,000,000 | 17,932 | 4,765 | 429 |
| 869,000,000 | 690,000,000 | 903,521 | 143,249 | 42,395 |
| 1,627,000,000 | 762,000,000 | 33,567 | 26,107 | NA |
| 1,494,000,000 | 919,000,000 | 1,278,402 | 431,315 | 170,173 |
| 3,837,000,000[6] | 14,641,000,000 | 126,397 | 80,745 | 24,969 |
| 1,840,000,000 | 18,470,000,000 | 4,151,956 | 2,269,374 | 717,053 |
| 1,028,000,000 | 472,000,000 | NA | NA | NA |
| 848,000,000 | 438,000,000 | 858,811 | 72,898 | 31,351 |
| NA | NA | NA | 165 | * |
| NA | NA | NA | 1,523 | * |
| 576,000,000 | 676,000,000 | 33,252[5] | [5] | NA |
| 423,000,000 | 773,000,000 | 1,176,636 | 281,450 | NA |
| 470,000,000 | 229,000,000 | 4,209 | 1,904 | 150 |
| 249,000,000 | 234,000,000 | 132,440 | 35,416 | 1,448 |
| 11,400,000,000[6] | 10,372,000,000 | 27,414 | 30,799 | 5,780 |
| 11,175,000,000 | 11,394,000,000 | 438,804 | 431,090 | 119,274 |
| 106,994,000,000 | 113,763,000,000 | 214,795 | 306,593 | NA |
| 98,059,000,000 | 118,898,000,000 | 5,014,682 | 5,193,688 | 1,041,916 |
| 589,000,000[6] | 1,535,000,000 | 2,866 | 1,585 | 231 |
| 1,307,000,000[6] | 1,535,000,000 | 140,632 | 26,342 | 1,284 |

| Nation Capital | Population | Area of Country (sq mi/ sq km) | Type of Government | Heads of State and Government | Currency; Value in U.S. Dollars | GNP (000,000); GNP per capita |
|---|---|---|---|---|---|---|
| **GAMBIA, THE**........<br>Banjul | 580,000....<br>45,600 | 4,361....<br>11,295 | Republic....<br>(C) | President:................<br>Sir Dawda K. Jawara | Dalasi........$<br>0.59 | 130<br>230 |
| **GERMAN**............<br>**DEMOCRATIC**<br>**REPUBLIC**<br>East Berlin | 16,740,000....<br><br><br>1,129,000 | 41,768....<br>108,178 | Socialist......<br>republic | Chairman, Council of State:....<br>Erich Honecker<br>Chairman, Council of Ministers<br>(Prime Minister):<br>Willi Stoph | Mark........<br>0.56[1] | 95,490<br>5,660 |
| **GERMANY, FEDERAL**<br>**REPUBLIC OF**<br>Bonn | 61,340,000....<br><br>285,100 | 95,976....<br>248,577 | Federal........<br>republic | President:................<br>Karl Carstens<br>Chancellor:<br>Helmut Schmidt | Deutsche Mark<br>0.56 | 587,700<br>9,600 |
| **GHANA**............<br>Accra | 11,320,000....<br>716,600 | 92,100....<br>238,537 | Republic....<br>(C) | President:................<br>Hilla Limann | Cedi........<br>0.36 | 4,250<br>390 |
| **GREAT BRITAIN**......<br>London | 55,880,000....<br>6,918,000[2] | 94,227....<br>244,046 | Limited........<br>monarchy (C) | Queen:..................<br>Elizabeth II<br>Prime Minister:<br>Margaret Thatcher | Pound........<br>2.40 | 281,090<br>5,030 |
| **GREECE**............<br>Athens | 9,440,000....<br>867,000 | 50,944....<br>131,944 | Republic....<br>| President:................<br>Constantine Karamanlis<br>Prime Minister:<br>George J. Rallis | Drachma......<br>0.02 | 30,530<br>3,270 |
| **GRENADA**..........<br>St. George's | 100,000....<br>6,600 | 133....<br>344 | Parliamentary..<br>state (C) | Governor-General:........<br>Sir Paul Scoon<br>Prime Minister:<br>Maurice Bishop | East.........<br>Caribbean<br>dollar<br>0.37 | 60<br>530 |
| **GUATEMALA**........<br>Guatemala City | 7,050,000....<br>814,800 | 42,042....<br>108,889 | Republic....<br>| President:................<br>Gen. Fernando Romeo Lucas<br>García | Quetzal.......<br>1.00 | 6,040<br>910 |
| **GUINEA**............<br>Conakry | 4,890,000....<br>412,000[2] | 94,926....<br>245,857 | Republic....<br>| President:................<br>Sékou Touré<br>Premier:<br>Louis Lansana Beavogui | Syli.........<br>0.05 | 1,070<br>210 |
| **GUINEA-BISSAU**......<br>Bissau | 777,200....<br>109,500[2] | 13,948....<br>36,125 | Republic....<br>| Head, Council of.............<br>the Revolution:<br>Commdt. João Bernardo Vieira | Peso.........<br>0.03 | 160<br>200 |
| **GUYANA**............<br>Georgetown | 860,000....<br>72,000 | 83,000....<br>214,969 | Republic......<br>(C) | President:................<br>Forbes Burnham<br>Prime Minister:<br>Ptolemy Reid | Dollar.......<br>0.39 | 460<br>550 |
| **HAITI**...............<br>Port-au-Prince | 4,920,000....<br>745,700 | 10,714....<br>27,750 | Republic....<br>| President:................<br>Jean-Claude Duvalier | Gourde.......<br>0.20 | 1,240<br>260 |
| **HONDURAS**.........<br>Tegucigalpa | 3,560,000....<br>371,700[2] | 43,277....<br>112,088 | Republic....<br>| President:................<br>Gen. Policarpo Paz García | Lempira......<br>0.50 | 1,650<br>480 |
| **HUNGARY**...........<br>Budapest | 10,700,000....<br>2,093,200 | 35,919....<br>93,030 | People's......<br>republic | Chairman, Presidential Council:...<br>Pál Losonczi<br>Chairman, Council of Ministers<br>(Prime Minister):<br>György Lázár | Forint........<br>0.0491[1] | 36,860<br>3,450 |
| **ICELAND**............<br>Reykjavík | 230,000....<br>83,400 | 39,769....<br>103,000 | Republic....<br>| President:................<br>Vigdís Finnbogadóttir<br>Prime Minister:<br>Gunnar Thoroddsen | Króna........<br>0.002 | 1,880<br>8,320 |
| **INDIA**...............<br>New Delhi | 650,980,000....<br>301,800 | 1,269,345....<br>3,287,590 | Federal........<br>republic<br>(C) | President:................<br>N. Sanjiva Reddy<br>Prime Minister:<br>Indira Gandhi | Rupee........<br>0.13 | 112,660<br>180 |
| **INDONESIA**..........<br>Djakarta | 148,470,000....<br>6,178,500 | 735,271....<br>1,904,345 | Republic....<br>| President and Prime Minister:.....<br>Suharto | Rupiah.......<br>0.0016 | 48,820<br>360 |

| Imports<br>Exports | Revenue<br>Expenditure | Elementary<br>Schools:<br>Teachers<br>Students | Secondary<br>Schools:<br>Teachers<br>Students | Colleges and<br>Universities:<br>Teachers<br>Students |
|---|---|---|---|---|
| $ 141,000,000<br>58,000,000 | $ 42,550,000<br>40,306,000 | 1,249<br>32,220 | 490<br>8,101 | *<br>* |
| 16,214,000,000<br>15,063,000,000 | 68,789,000,000<br>68,737,000,000 | NA<br>2,420,494[9] | NA<br>673,764 | NA<br>127,473 |
| 157,747,000,000<br>171,540,000,000 | 99,461,000,000<br>117,771,000,000 | 281,198<br>6,417,143 | 243,105<br>5,822,204 | 91,036<br>905,897 |
| 1,398,000,000<br>965,000,000 | 1,164,000,000<br>1,055,000,000 | 41,407[7]<br>1,213,291[7] | 27,054[7]<br>576,979[7] | 1,103<br>9,079 |
| 102,969,000,000<br>91,030,000,000 | 113,453,000,000<br>132,041,000,000 | 237,699<br>5,572,523 | 285,106<br>4,844,165 | 33,100<br>753,800 |
| 9,640,000,000<br>3,855,000,000 | 10,253,000,000<br>10,253,000,000 | 33,816<br>931,560 | 24,252<br>729,035 | 5,750<br>100,000 |
| 36,000,000<br>17,000,000 | 21,000,000<br>26,000,000 | NA<br>NA | NA<br>NA | *<br>* |
| 1,286,000,000<br>1,089,000,000 | 838,000,000<br>799,000,000 | 21,060<br>709,018 | 8,604<br>145,770 | 1,934<br>25,978 |
| 279,000,000<br>327,000,000 | 363,000,000<br>363,000,000 | NA<br>NA | NA<br>NA | NA<br>NA |
| 51,000,000<br>13,000,000 | 27,000,000<br>44,000,000 | 2,620<br>93,256 | 540<br>4,972 | *<br>* |
| 279,000,000<br>289,000,000 | 190,000,000<br>223,000,000 | 6,172<br>166,239 | 2,675<br>79,890 | NA<br>1,536 |
| 212,000,000<br>155,000,000 | 78,000,000<br>78,000,000 | 12,140<br>608,348 | NA<br>NA | 697<br>5,195 |
| 693,000,000<br>606,000,000 | 500,000,000<br>500,000,000 | 14,369<br>528,138 | 2,899<br>110,683 | 931<br>18,933 |
| 8,674,000,000<br>7,938,000,000 | 20,049,000,000<br>20,226,000,000 | 71,925<br>1,106,744 | 14,954<br>351,854 | 13,450<br>105,926 |
| 824,000,000<br>781,000,000 | 439,000,000<br>435,000,000 | 2,716<br>38,576 | 4,091<br>13,945 | 335<br>3,092 |
| 8,150,000,000<br>6,440,000,000 | 15,464,000,000<br>22,513,000,000 | 2,064,923<br>76,236,375 | 641,734<br>16,338,219 | 153,368<br>3,965,875 |
| 7,225,000,000<br>15,578,000,000 | 8,677,000,000<br>11,059,000,000 | 709,511<br>22,389,796 | 290,897<br>4,469,918 | 21,802<br>304,025 |

| Nation<br>Capital | Population | Area of<br>Country<br>(sq mi/<br>sq km) | Type of<br>Government | Heads of State and<br>Government | Currency;<br>Value in<br>U.S. Dollars | GNP<br>(000,000);<br>GNP<br>per capita |
|---|---|---|---|---|---|---|
| **IRAN**<br>Tehran | 36,940,000<br>4,496,200 | 636,296<br>1,648,000 | Islamic<br>republic | Faqih:<br>Ayatollah Ruhollah Khomeini<br>President, Revolutionary Council:<br>Abolhassan Bani-Sadr<br>Prime Minister:<br>Mohammed Ali Rajai | Rial<br>0.01 | $ NA<br>NA |
| **IRAQ**<br>Baghdad | 12,770,000<br>3,205,700 | 167,925<br>434,924 | Republic | President and Prime Minister:<br>Saddam Hussein | Dinar<br>3.39 | 22,720<br>1,860 |
| **IRELAND,<br>REPUBLIC OF**<br>Dublin | 3,364,000<br>543,600 | 27,136<br>70,283 | Republic | President:<br>Patrick J. Hillery<br>Prime Minister:<br>Charles J. Haughey | Pound<br>2.09 | 11,210<br>3,470 |
| **ISRAEL**<br>Jerusalem | 3,780,000<br>386,600 | 8,019<br>20,770 | Republic | President:<br>Itzhak Navon<br>Prime Minister:<br>Menachem Begin | Shekel<br>0.18 | 15,300<br>4,120 |
| **ITALY**<br>Rome | 56,910,000<br>2,914,700 | 116,304<br>301,225 | Republic | President:<br>Alessandro Pertini<br>Premier:<br>Arnaldo Forlani | Lira<br>0.0012 | 218,320<br>3,840 |
| **IVORY COAST**<br>Abidjan | 7,920,000<br>900,000[2] | 124,503<br>322,462 | Republic | President:<br>Félix Houphouët-Boigny | CFA franc<br>0.0049 | 6,580<br>840 |
| **JAMAICA**<br>Kingston | 2,160,000<br>169,800 | 4,244<br>10,991 | Parliamentary<br>state (C) | Governor-General:<br>Florizel A. Glasspole<br>Prime Minister:<br>Edward P. G. Seaga | Dollar<br>0.56 | 2,350<br>1,110 |
| **JAPAN**<br>Tokyo | 115,870,000<br>8,543,800 | 143,751<br>372,313 | Constitutional<br>monarchy | Emperor:<br>Hirohito<br>Prime Minister:<br>Zenko Suzuki | Yen<br>0.0046 | 836,160<br>7,330 |
| **JORDAN**<br>Amman | 3,090,000<br>711,850 | 37,738<br>97,740 | Constitutional<br>monarchy | King:<br>Hussein I<br>Prime Minister:<br>Mudar Badran | Dinar<br>3.43 | 2,270<br>1,050[10] |
| **KENYA**<br>Nairobi | 15,320,000<br>818,000[2] | 224,961<br>582,646 | Republic<br>(C) | President:<br>Daniel arap Moi | Shilling<br>0.14 | 4,830<br>320 |
| **KIRIBATI (GILBERT<br>ISLANDS)**<br>Tarawa | 56,000<br>17,200[2] | 332<br>861 | Republic<br>(C) | President:<br>Ieremia T. Tabai | Dollar<br>1.17 | 40<br>690 |
| **KOREA,<br>DEMOCRATIC<br>PEOPLE'S<br>REPUBLIC OF**<br>P'yŏngyang | 17,490,000<br>1,500,000 | 46,540<br>120,538 | People's<br>republic | President:<br>Marshal Kim Il Sung<br>Premier:<br>Li Jong Ok | Won<br>0.64 | 12,530<br>730 |
| **KOREA, REPUBLIC OF**<br>Seoul | 37,600,000<br>7,823,000 | 38,025<br>98,484 | Republic | President:<br>Chun Doo Hwan<br>Prime Minister:<br>Nam Duck Woo | Won<br>0.0017 | 42,460<br>1,160 |
| **KUWAIT**<br>Al Kuwait | 1,270,000<br>78,100 | 6,880<br>17,818 | Constitutional<br>emirate | Emir:<br>Sheikh Jaber al-Ahmad al-Sabah<br>Prime Minister:<br>Sheikh Saad al-Abdullah al-Salem<br>al-Sabah | Dinar<br>3.74 | 18,040<br>14,890 |
| **LAOS**<br>Vientiane | 3,630,000<br>200,000 | 91,429<br>236,800 | People's<br>republic | President:<br>Prince Souphanouvong<br>Premier:<br>Kaysone Phomvihan | New Kip<br>0.10 | 300<br>90 |
| **LEBANON**<br>Beirut | 3,090,000<br>702,000 | 4,015<br>10,400 | Republic | President:<br>Elias Sarkis<br>Prime Minister:<br>Shafiq al-Wazan | Pound<br>0.29 | NA<br>NA |

| Imports Exports | Revenue Expenditure | Elementary Schools: Teachers Students | Secondary Schools: Teachers Students | Colleges and Universities: Teachers Students |
|---|---|---|---|---|
| $  7,261,000,000 | $ 39,674,000,000 | 167,457 | 96,395 | 13,952 |
| 19,000,000,000 | 41,659,000,000 | 4,768,588 | 2,356,878 | 154,215 |
| 4,213,000,000 | 12,359,000,000 | 87,148 | 29,466 | 5,207 |
| 11,064,000,000 | 12,359,000,000 | 2,459,870 | 850,440 | 89,197 |
| 9,837,000,000 | 4,117,000,000 | 17,803 | 17,953 | 1,373 |
| 7,180,000,000 | 4,924,000,000 | 541,687 | 292,616 | 22,776 |
| 7,471,000,000 | 10,689,000,000 | 32,225 | 13,712 | NA |
| 4,553,000,000 | 10,689,000,000 | 602,535 | 154,259 | 83,910 |
| 77,970,000,000 | 62,307,000,000 | 271,747 | 481,698 | 43,120 |
| 72,242,000,000 | 95,027,000,000 | 4,584,300 | 5,267,381 | 1,001,012 |
| 2,488,000,000 | 1,380,000,000 | NA | NA | NA |
| 2,516,000,000 | 1,380,000,000 | 894.184 | 167.042 | 20.087 |
| 874,000,000 | 395,000,000 | 9,889 | 10,368 | NA |
| 744,000,000 | 724,000,000 | 367,625 | 225,741 | 10,305 |
| 110,670,000,000 | 146,721,000,000 | 445,719 | 481,668 | 216,069 |
| 103,045,000,000 | 193,821,000,000 | 11,146,859 | 9,463,367 | 2,289,197 |
| 1,949,000,000 | 1,218,000,000 | 13,351 | 10,936 | 996 |
| 402,000,000 | 1,269,000,000 | 431,107 | 231,088 | 20,317 |
| 1,535,000,000 | 76,000,000 | 89,773 | 13,368 | 892 |
| 1,062,000,000 | 96,000,000 | 2,974,849 | 329,296 | 5,837 |
| 13,000,000 | 13,000,000 | 435 | 117 | * |
| 21,000,000 | 11,000,000 | 13,679 | 1,256 | * |
| 1,538,000,000 | 19,012,000,000 | 100,000[5] | [5] | NA |
| 1,319,000,000 | 19,012,000,000 | 2,561,674 | 2,000,000 | 100,000 |
| 20,339,000,000 | 9,367,000,000 | 115,245 | 100,600 | 25,603 |
| 15,055,000,000 | 8,328,000,000 | 5,604,365 | 3,871,756 | 406,087 |
| 5,359,000,000 | 11,867,000,000 | 6,923[7] | 11,443[7] | 606 |
| 17,499,000,000 | 8,238,000,000 | 113,509[7] | 123,602[7] | 9,318 |
| NA | 116,000,000 | NA | NA | NA |
| 18,000,000 | 124,000,000 | 487,000 | 72,000 | 1,684 |
| 1,740,000,000 | 1,048,000,000 | NA | NA | NA |
| 546,000,000 | 1,448,000,000 | NA | NA | NA |

| Nation Capital | Population | Area of Country (sq mi/ sq km) | Type of Government | Heads of State and Government | Currency; Value in U.S. Dollars | GNP (000,000); GNP per capita |
|---|---|---|---|---|---|---|
| **LESOTHO** Maseru | 1,310,000 14,700 | 11,720 30,355 | Constitutional monarchy (C) | King: Moshoeshoe II Prime Minister: Chief Leabua Jonathan | South African. $ rand 1.33 | 360 280 |
| **LIBERIA** Monrovia | 1,800,000 208,600 | 43,000 111,369 | Republic | Chairman, People's Redemption Council: Master Sgt. Samuel K. Doe | Dollar 1.00 | 820 460 |
| **LIBYA** Tripoli | 2,860,000 800,000 | 679,362 1,759,540 | Socialist republic | Revolutionary leader: Col. Muammar el-Qaddafi Secretary-General, General People's Congress: Abdul Ali al-Obeidi | Dinar 3.38 | 18,960 6,910 |
| **LIECHTENSTEIN** Vaduz | 25,000 4,900 | 61 157 | Constitutional monarchy | Sovereign: Prince Francis Joseph II Chief of Government: Hans Brunhart | Swiss franc 0.61 | NA NA |
| **LUXEMBOURG** Luxembourg | 360,000 76,500 | 998 2,586 | Constitutional monarchy | Grand Duke: Jean Prime Minister: Pierre Werner | Franc 0.04 | 3,730 10,410 |
| **MADAGASCAR** Antananarivo | 8,510,000 468,000 | 226,658 587,041 | Socialist republic | President: Lt. Comdr. Didier Ratsiraka Prime Minister: Lt. Col. Désiré Rakotoarijaona | Franc 0.0049 | 2,050 250 |
| **MALAWI** Lilongwe | 5,820,000 102,900[2] | 45,747 118,484 | Republic (C) | President: Hastings Kamuzu Banda | Kwacha 1.25 | 1,010 180 |
| **MALAYSIA** Kuala Lumpur | 13,300,000 557,000 | 127,317 329,749 | Federal constitutional monarchy (C) | Supreme Head of State: Sultan Haji Ahmad Shah al-Musta'in Billah ibni al-Marhum Prime Minister: Datuk Hussein bin Onn | Ringgit 0.47 | 14,540 1,090 |
| **MALDIVES** Male | 150,000 29,600 | 115 298 | Republic | President: Maumoon Abdul Gayoom | Rupee 0.13 | 20 150 |
| **MALI** Bamako | 6,470,000 404,000[2] | 478,766 1,240,000 | Republic | President: Brig. Gen. Moussa Traoré | Franc 0.0024 | 760 120 |
| **MALTA** Valletta | 350,000 14,000 | 122 316 | Republic (C) | President: Anton Buttigieg Prime Minister: Dom Mintoff | Pound 2.95 | 730 2,160 |
| **MAURITANIA** Nouakchott | 1,590,000 135,000[2] | 397,955 1,030,700 | Islamic republic | President, Chairman of the Military Committee for National Salvation, and Prime Minister: Lt. Col. Mohammed Khouna Ould Haidala | Ouguiya 0.02 | 420 270 |
| **MAURITIUS** Port Louis | 910,000 142,900 | 790 2,045 | Parliamentary state (C) | Governor-General: Dayendranath Burrenchobay Prime Minister: Sir Seewoosagur Ramgoolam | Rupee 0.13 | 760 830 |
| **MEXICO** Mexico City | 69,380,000 8,988,200 | 761,604 1,972,547 | Federal republic | President: José López Portillo | Peso 0.04 | 84,150 1,290 |
| **MONACO** Monaco-Ville | 25,000 1,700 | 0.58 1.49 | Constitutional monarchy | Prince: Rainier III Minister of State: André Saint-Mleux | French franc 0.24 | NA NA |
| **MONGOLIAN PEOPLE'S REPUBLIC** Ulan Bator | 1,620,000 402,900 | 604,250 1,565,000 | People's republic | Presidium Chairman: Yumzhagiyen Tsedenbal Chairman, Council of Ministers (Prime Minister): Zhambyn Batmunkh | Tugrik 0.35[1] | 1,470 940 |

| Imports<br>Exports | Revenue<br>Expenditure | Elementary Schools:<br>Teachers<br>Students | Secondary Schools:<br>Teachers<br>Students | Colleges and Universities:<br>Teachers<br>Students |
|---|---|---|---|---|
| $  229,000,000 ............$<br>14,000,000 | 89,000,000 .............<br>58,000,000 | NA .............<br>228,523 | NA............<br>19,512 | NA<br>847 |
| 481,000,000 ............<br>486,000,000 | 206,000,000 .............<br>194,000,000 | 7,360[5] ...........<br>129,776 | [5]...........<br>108,077 | NA<br>3,089 |
| 4,602,000,000 .............<br>9,907,000,000 | NA .............<br>6,029,000,000 | 26,182 ............<br>574,770 | 15,247............<br>225,286 | 1,922<br>17,174 |
| NA .............<br>420,000,000 | 128,000,000 .............<br>127,000,000 | 91 .............<br>2,008 | 83............<br>1,720 | 60<br>1,599 |
| [11] ............<br>[11] | 1,613,000,000 .............<br>1,620,000,000 | 1,821 ............<br>33,638 | NA............<br>23,920 | NA<br>NA |
| 443,000,000 ............<br>386,000,000 | 484,000,000 .............<br>595,000,000 | NA .............<br>1,100,000 | NA............<br>122,000 | NA<br>11,000 |
| 400,000,000 ............<br>233,000,000 | 215,000,000 .............<br>315,000,000 | 11,115 ............<br>675,740 | 900............<br>17,665 | 122<br>1,155 |
| 6,489,000,000[12] .............<br>8,042,000,000[12] | 4,134,000,000 .............<br>3,979,000,000 | 61,267 ............<br>1,929,914 | NA<br>NA | NA<br>40,755 |
| 4,000,000 ............<br>1,500,000 | 2,700,000 .............<br>3,360,000 | 179 ............<br>8,749 | 113............<br>3,684 | *<br>* |
| 219,000,000 ............<br>107,000,000 | 190,000,000 .............<br>190,000,000 | 8,280 ............<br>291,966 | NA<br>NA | 435<br>2,920 |
| 759,000,000 ............<br>424,000,000 | 303,000,000 .............<br>296,000,000 | 1,529 .............<br>30,863 | 2,461............<br>30,285 | 285<br>1,757 |
| 259,000,000 ............<br>148,000,000 | 234,000,000 .............<br>234,000,000 | 1,775 .............<br>72,932 | NA............<br>10,097 | *<br>* |
| 501,000,000 .............<br>326,000,000 | 216,000,000 .............<br>238,000,000 | NA .............<br>133,432 | NA............<br>81,901 | NA<br>802 |
| 12,004,000,000 .............<br>8,768,000,000 | 17,911,000,000 .............<br>22,311,000,000 | 274,717 .............<br>12,148,221 | 192,970............<br>3,241,421 | 40,980<br>539,372 |
| NA .............<br>NA | 161,000,000 .............<br>124,000,000 | NA .............<br>4,904[5] | NA............<br>[5] | *<br>* |
| 346,000,000 .............<br>266,000,000 | 1,428,000,000 .............<br>1,428,000,000 | NA .............<br>386,500[5] | NA............<br>[5] | NA<br>19,700 |

| Nation<br>Capital | Population | Area of<br>Country<br>(sq mi/<br>sq km) | Type of<br>Government | Heads of State and<br>Government | Currency;<br>Value in<br>U.S. Dollars | GNP<br>(000,000);<br>GNP<br>per capita |
|---|---|---|---|---|---|---|
| **MOROCCO**<br>Rabat | 19,470,000<br>704,100[2] | 172,414<br>446,550 | Constitutional<br>monarchy | King:<br>Hassan II<br>Prime Minister:<br>Maati Bouabid | Dirham<br>0.26 | $ 12,610<br>670 |
| **MOZAMBIQUE**<br>Maputo | 10,200,000<br>354,700[2] | 302,329<br>783,030 | People's<br>republic | President:<br>Samora M. Machel | Metical<br>0.02 | 1,360<br>140 |
| **NAURU**<br>Yaren | 7,250<br>NA | 8<br>21 | Republic<br>(C) | President:<br>Hammer DeRoburt | Australian<br>dollar<br>1.17 | NA<br>NA |
| **NEPAL**<br>Kathmandu | 13,710,000<br>171,400 | 54,362<br>140,797 | Constitutional<br>monarchy | King:<br>Birenda Bir Bikram Shah Dev<br>Prime Minister:<br>Surya Bahadur Thapa | Rupee<br>0.08 | 1,580<br>120 |
| **NETHERLANDS, THE**<br>Amsterdam | 14,030,000<br>718,600 | 15,770<br>40,844 | Constitutional<br>monarchy | Queen:<br>Beatrix<br>Prime Minister:<br>Andreas van Agt | Guilder<br>0.51 | 117,190<br>8,390 |
| **NEW ZEALAND**<br>Wellington | 3,100,000<br>139,200 | 103,736<br>268,676 | Parliamentary<br>state (C) | Governor-General:<br>David Stuart Beattie<br>Prime Minister:<br>Robert D. Muldoon | Dollar<br>0.98 | 15,270<br>4,790 |
| **NICARAGUA**<br>Managua | 2,640,000<br>517,700 | 50,193<br>130,000 | Republic | Government of National<br>Reconstruction | Córdoba<br>0.10 | 2,100<br>840 |
| **NIGER**<br>Niamey | 5,150,000<br>225,300 | 489,191<br>1,267,000 | Republic | President:<br>Col. Seyni Kountché | CFA franc<br>0.0049 | 1,110<br>220 |
| **NIGERIA**<br>Lagos | 74,600,000<br>1,060,800 | 356,669<br>923,768 | Federal<br>republic<br>(C) | President:<br>Shehu Shagari | Naira<br>1.84 | 45,720<br>560 |
| **NORWAY**<br>Oslo | 4,070,000<br>457,400 | 125,182<br>324,219 | Constitutional<br>monarchy | King:<br>Olav V<br>Prime Minister:<br>Odvar Nordli | Krone<br>0.21 | 38,500<br>9,510 |
| **OMAN**<br>Muscat | 860,000<br>15,000 | 82,030<br>212,457 | Sultanate | Sultan:<br>Qabus bin Said | Rial<br>2.90 | 2,160<br>2,570 |
| **PAKISTAN**<br>Islamabad | 79,840,000<br>77,300 | 310,404<br>803,943 | Federal<br>republic | President:<br>Muhammad Zia ul-Haq | Rupee<br>0.10 | 17,530<br>230 |
| **PANAMA**<br>Panamá | 1,880,000[13]<br>439,900 | 29,762<br>77,082 | Republic | President:<br>Arístides Royo Sanchez | Balboa<br>1.00 | 2,350<br>1,290 |
| **PAPUA NEW GUINEA**<br>Port Moresby | 3,080,000<br>121,600[2] | 178,260<br>461,691 | Parliamentary<br>state (C) | Governor-General:<br>Sir Tore Lokoloko<br>Prime Minister:<br>Sir Julius Chan | Kina<br>1.52 | 1,640<br>560 |
| **PARAGUAY**<br>Asunción | 2,970,000<br>463,700 | 157,048<br>406,752 | Republic | President:<br>Gen. Alfredo Stroessner | Guaraní<br>0.0079 | 2,450<br>850 |
| **PERU**<br>Lima | 17,290,000<br>4,376,100[2] | 496,224<br>1,285,216 | Republic | President:<br>Fernando Belaúnde<br>Terry<br>Prime Minister:<br>Manuel Ulloa | Sol<br>0.0034 | 12,440<br>740 |
| **PHILIPPINES**<br>Manila | 47,720,000<br>1,438,300 | 115,831<br>300,000 | Republic | President and Prime Minister:<br>Ferdinand E. Marcos | Peso<br>0.13 | 23,250<br>510 |
| **POLAND**<br>Warsaw | 35,230,000<br>1,552,300 | 120,725<br>312,677 | People's<br>republic | Chairman, Council of State:<br>Henryk Jabłoński<br>Chairman, Council of Ministers<br>(Prime Minister):<br>Jozef Pinkowski | Złoty<br>0.031[1] | 128,330<br>3,660 |
| **PORTUGAL**<br>Lisbon | 9,870,000<br>859,200 | 35,553<br>92,082 | Republic | President:<br>Gen. António Ramalho Eanes<br>Prime Minister:<br>Francisco Pinto Balsemão | Escudo<br>0.02 | 19,540<br>2,020 |

| Imports<br>Exports | Revenue<br>Expenditure | Elementary<br>Schools:<br>Teachers<br>Students | Secondary<br>Schools:<br>Teachers<br>Students | Colleges and<br>Universities:<br>Teachers<br>Students |
|---|---|---|---|---|
| $  3,807,000,000 | $  5,242,000,000 | 50,829 | NA | NA |
| 1,872,000,000 | 5,777,000,000 | 1,925,187 | 677,019 | 76,054 |
| 278,000,000 | 203,000,000 | NA | NA | NA |
| 129,000,000 | 252,000,000 | NA | NA | NA |
| 15,000,000 | 47,000,000 | 129[5] | [5] | * |
| 1,000,000 | 39,000,000 | 2,200[5] | [5] | * |
| 240,000,000 | 144,000,000 | NA | NA | NA |
| 100,000,000 | 257,000,000 | 921,000 | 445,000 | 31,000 |
| 67,284,000,000 | 50,686,000,000 | 62,956 | 97,216 | 28,000 |
| 63,667,000,000 | 53,530,000,000 | 1,521,037 | 1,361,333 | 261,188 |
| 4,542,000,000 | 4,241,000,000 | 21,100 | 16,168 | 2,907 |
| 4,694,000,000 | 3,839,000,000 | 519,431 | 382,709 | 48,511 |
| 848,000,000 | 231,000,000 | 9,729 | 2,954 | 1,204 |
| 774,000,000 | 453,000,000 | 368,895 | 105,429 | 23,171 |
| 127,000,000 | 283,000,000 | 4,215 | 865 | 34 |
| 134,000,000 | 283,000,000 | 177,620 | 22,277 | 782 |
| 12,857,000,000 | 15,709,000,000 | NA | NA | 5,019 |
| 9,483,000,000 | 16,967,000,000 | NA | NA | 32,971 |
| 13,818,000,000 | 14,946,000,000 | 20,543 | NA | 6,679 |
| 13,271,000,000 | 18,985,000,000 | 397,700 | 348,007 | 66,710 |
| 1,387,000,000 | 3,287,000,000 | NA | NA | * |
| 2,284,000,000 | 2,878,000,000 | 77,974 | 8,424 | * |
| 4,061,000,000 | 3,356,000,000 | 148,059 | 120,186 | 18,129 |
| 2,036,000,000 | 3,452,000,000 | 6,170,000 | 1,856,000 | 376,000 |
| 942,000,000 | 466,000,000 | 15,559 | 6,491 | 2,520 |
| 244,000,000 | 519,000,000 | 380,621 | 142,938 | 37,031 |
| 810,000,000 | 853,000,000 | 8,590 | 2,445 | 1,235 |
| 963,000,000 | 871,000,000 | 268,136 | 43,513 | 9,804 |
| 432,000,000 | 198,000,000 | 17,525 | 9,663 | 1,945 |
| 305,000,000 | 279,000,000 | 493,231 | 101,126 | 20,496 |
| 2,022,000,000 | 1,344,000,000 | 75,491 | 35,183 | 13,468 |
| 3,533,000,000 | 1,766,000,000 | 3,019,624 | 969,129 | 233,420 |
| 6,142,000,000 | 3,283,000,000 | 270,764 | 82,191 | 26,003 |
| 4,601,000,000 | 4,131,000,000 | 7,861,641 | 2,878,656 | 946,860 |
| 17,488,000,000 | 34,982,000,000 | 190,000 | 98,100 | 52,300 |
| 16,233,000,000 | 32,060,000,000 | 4,216,500 | 2,489,300 | 485,200 |
| 6,085,000,000 | 5,693,000,000 | 40,011 | 30,911 | 7,419 |
| 3,468,000,000 | 5,693,000,000 | 925,857 | 497,464 | 81,955 |

| Nation Capital | Population | Area of Country (sq mi/ sq km) | Type of Government | Heads of State and Government | Currency; Value in U.S. Dollars | GNP (000,000); GNP per capita |
|---|---|---|---|---|---|---|
| **QATAR** | 210,000 | 4,247 | Constitutional emirate | Emir and Prime Minister: Sheikh Khalifa bin Hamad al-Thani | Riyal 0.27 | $ 2,840 |
| Doha | 180,000 | 11,000 | | | | 12,740 |
| **RUMANIA** | 22,070,000 | 91,699 | Socialist republic | President: Nicolae Ceauşescu Chairman, Council of Ministers (Prime Minister): Ilie Verdet | Leu 0.22 | 38,170 |
| Bucharest | 1,807,000 | 237,500 | | | | 1,750 |
| **RWANDA** | 4,650,000 | 10,169 | Republic | President: Maj. Gen. Juvénal Habyarimana | Franc 0.01 | 830 |
| Kigali | 117,700[2] | 26,338 | | | | 180 |
| **ST. LUCIA** | 110,000 | 238 | Parliamentary state (C) | Governor-General: Boswell Williams Prime Minister: Allan Louisy | East Caribbean dollar 0.37 | 80 630 |
| Castries | 45,000 | 616 | | | | |
| **ST. VINCENT AND THE GRENADINES** | 100,000 | 150 388 | Parliamentary state (C) | Governor-General: Sir Sydney Gun-Munro Prime Minister: R. Milton Cato | East Caribbean dollar 0.37 | 40 380 |
| Kingstown | 25,000 | | | | | |
| **SAN MARINO** | 21,000 | 24 | Republic | Co-Regents: NA Secretary of State for Foreign Affairs: Giordano Bruno Reffi | Italian lira 0.0012 | NA |
| San Marino | 4,600 | 61 | | | | NA |
| **SÃO TOMÉ AND PRÍNCIPE** | 80,000 | 372 964 | Republic | President: Manuel Pinto da Costa | Dobra 0.03 | 40 490 |
| São Tomé | 20,000 | | | | | |
| **SAUDI ARABIA** | 8,110,000 | 830,000 | Monarchy | King and Prime Minister: Khalid ibn Abdul-Aziz | Riyal 0.30 | 63,310 |
| Riyadh | 666,800 | 2,149,690 | | | | 8,040 |
| **SENEGAL** | 5,520,000 | 75,750 | Republic | President: Léopold Sédar Senghor Premier: Abdou Diouf | CFA franc 0.0049 | 1,830 |
| Dakar | 798,800 | 196,192 | | | | 340 |
| **SEYCHELLES** | 60,000 | 108 | Republic (C) | President: F. Albert René | Rupee 0.16 | 70 1,060 |
| Victoria | 23,000[2] | 280 | | | | |
| **SIERRA LEONE** | 3,380,000 | 27,699 | Republic (C) | President: Siaka P. Stevens | Leone 0.97 | 690 210 |
| Freetown | 274,000 | 71,740 | | | | |
| **SINGAPORE** | 2,360,000 | 224 | Republic (C) | President: Benjamin Henry Sheares Prime Minister: Lee Kuan Yew | Dollar 0.47 | 7,690 3,260 |
| Singapore | 2,334,400[2] | 581 | | | | |
| **SOLOMON ISLANDS** | 210,000 | 10,983 | Parliamentary state (C) | Governor-General: Baddeley Devesi Prime Minister: Peter Kenilorea | Dollar 1.22 | 90 430 |
| Honiara | 16,500 | 28,446 | | | | |
| **SOMALIA** | 3,540,000 | 246,201 | Republic | President, Supreme Revolutionary Council: Maj. Gen. Muhammad Siad Barre | Shilling 0.16 | 470 130 |
| Mogadishu | 286,000 | 637,657 | | | | |
| **SOUTH AFRICA, REPUBLIC OF** | 28,480,000 | 471,445 1,221,037 | Republic | President: Marais Viljoen Prime Minister: P. W. Botha | Rand 1.33 | 40,940 1,480 |
| Cape Town | 892,200 | | | | | |
| Pretoria | 650,600 | | | | | |
| **SPAIN** | 37,180,000 | 194,897 | Constitutional monarchy | King: Juan Carlos I President, Council of Ministers (Prime Minister): Adolfo Suárez González | Peseta 0.01 | 128,920 3,520 |
| Madrid | 4,120,900 | 504,782 | | | | |
| **SRI LANKA (CEYLON)** | 14,740,000 | 25,332 | Republic (C) | President: Junius R. Jayawardene Prime Minister: Ranasinghe Premadasa | Rupee 0.06 | 2,720 190 |
| Colombo | 616,000 | 65,610 | | | | |
| **SUDAN** | 17,890,000 | 967,499 | Republic | President and Prime Minister: Maj. Gen. Gaafar Mohammed al-Nimeiry | Pound 2.00 | 5,540 320 |
| Khartoum | 1,089,300 | 2,505,813 | | | | |

450

| Imports<br>Exports | Revenue<br>Expenditure | Elementary<br>Schools:<br>Teachers<br>Students | Secondary<br>Schools:<br>Teachers<br>Students | Colleges and<br>Universities:<br>Teachers<br>Students |
|---|---|---|---|---|
| $  1,425,000,000 | $  2,267,000,000 | 1,377 | 925 | 118 |
| 3,731,000,000 | 1,693,000,000 | 25,266 | 10,347 | 910 |
| 10,916,000,000 | 70,674,000,000 | 150,415 | 57,811 | 14,227 |
| 9,724,000,000 | 70,674,000,000 | 3,423,135 | 1,236,307 | 190,560 |
| 179,000,000 | 116,000,000 | NA | NA | NA |
| 70,000,000 | 99,000,000 | 515,712 | 13,799 | 975 |
| 83,000,000 | 18,700,000 | 863 | 208 | * |
| 27,000,000 | 18,900,000 | 30,295 | 4,878 | * |
| 36,000,000 | 14,600,000 | 1,087 | 319 | * |
| 16,000,000 | 16,000,000 | 25,181 | 5,581 | * |
| NA | 55,000,000 | 132 | NA | * |
| NA | 55,000,000 | 1,623 | 1,209 | * |
| 10,500,000 | 5,000,000 | 527 | 111 | * |
| 6,600,000 | 12,000,000 | 14,162 | 3,167 | * |
| 20,424,000,000 | 48,000,000,000 | 35,139 | 15,728 | 2,133 |
| 40,716,000,000 | 48,000,000,000 | 686,108 | 222,797 | 26,437 |
| 762,000,000 | 643,000,000 | 9,496 | 2,578 | NA |
| 623,000,000 | 643,000,000 | 345,198 | 92,474 | NA |
| 50,000,000 | 19,000,000 | 424 | 235 | 16 |
| 11,000,000 | 21,000,000 | 10,001 | 4,694 | 142 |
| 278,000,000 | 165,000,000 | 6,700 | 2,572 | 327 |
| 161,000,000 | 204,000,000 | 218,379 | 53,801 | 2,077 |
| 17,635,000,000[14] | 1,799,000,000 | 11,112 | 8,482 | 1,685 |
| 14,233,000,000[14] | 1,799,000,000 | 300,398 | 189,641 | 20,377 |
| 57,000,000 | 13,350,000 | NA | NA | * |
| 67,000,000 | 11,760,000 | 26,790 | 3,204 | * |
| 241,000,000 | 187,000,000 | 6,540 | 959 | 324 |
| 107,000,000 | 176,000,000 | 229,030 | 12,389 | 2,040 |
| 7,193,000,000 | 8,818,000,000 | 145,132[5] | [5] | 10,597 |
| 7,182,000,000 | 11,283,000,000 | 4,112,079 | 999,966 | 136,293 |
| 25,432,000,000 | 14,028,000,000 | 211,037 | 79,541 | 31,160 |
| 17,903,000,000 | 13,548,000,000 | 6,640,246 | 1,191,776 | 647,298 |
| 1,441,000,000 | 740,000,000 | 50,665[7] | NA | 1,860 |
| 890,000,000 | 1,184,000,000 | 1,492,141[7] | 1,088,089[7] | 14,568 |
| 1,198,000,000 | 1,817,000,000 | 33,783 | NA | 1,420 |
| 533,000,000 | 1,633,000,000 | 1,217,510 | 327,043 | 21,342 |

| Nation Capital | Population | Area of Country (sq mi/ sq km) | Type of Government | Heads of State and Government | Currency; Value in U.S. Dollars | GNP (000,000); GNP per capita |
|---|---|---|---|---|---|---|
| **SURINAME** . . . . . . . . . . Paramaribo | 380,000 102,300 | 63,037 . . . 163,265 | Republic . . . . . . | President and Prime Minister: Chin A. Sen | Guilder . . . . . . . 0.56 | $ 820 2,110 |
| **SWAZILAND** . . . . . . . . . Mbabane | 540,000 22,300 | 6,704 . . . 17,363 | Monarchy . . . . (C) | King: Sobhuza II Prime Minister: Maj. Gen. Maphevu Dlamini | Lilangeni . . . . . . 1.30 | 310 590 |
| **SWEDEN** . . . . . . . . . . . Stockholm | 8,290,000 653,900 | 173,732 . . . 449,964 | Constitutional monarchy | King: Carl XVI Gustaf Prime Minister: Thorbjörn Fälldin | Krona 0.24 | 84,750 10,210 |
| **SWITZERLAND** . . . . . . . Bern | 6,330,000 142,900 | 15,941 . . . 41,288 | Federal republic | President: Georges-André Chevallaz | Franc 0.61 | 76,050 12,100 |
| **SYRIA** . . . . . . . . . . . . . Damascus | 8,350,000 1,142,000 | 71,498 . . . 185,180 | Socialist . . . . republic | President: Lt. Gen. Hafez al-Assad Prime Minister: Abdel-Raouf al-Kassem | Pound . . . . . . . 0.25 | 7,490 930 |
| **TAIWAN** or **FORMOSA** . (REPUBLIC OF CHINA) Taipei | 17,375,100 . . . . 2,163,600 | 13,892 . . . . 35,981 | Republic . . . . | President: Chiang Ching-kuo Premier: Sun Yun-suan | New Taiwan . . . dollar 0.03 | 23,930 1,400 |
| **TANZANIA** . . . . . . . . . . Dar es Salaam | 17,980,000 517,000 | 364,900 . . . . 945,087 | Republic . . . . (C) | President: Julius K. Nyerere Prime Minister: Edward M. Sokoine | Shilling . . . . . . 0.12 | 3,880[15] 230[15] |
| **THAILAND** . . . . . . . . . . Bangkok | 46,140,000 4,870,500 | 198,456 . . . . 514,000 | Constitutional . monarchy | King: Bhumibol Adulyadej Prime Minister: Gen. Prem Tinsulanonda | Baht 0.05 | 21,790 490 |
| **TOGO** . . . . . . . . . . . . . Lomé | 2,470,000 229,400 | 21,925 . . . . 56,785 | Republic . . . . | President: Gen. Gnassingbe Eyadéma | CFA franc . . . . 0.0049 | 770 320 |
| **TONGA** . . . . . . . . . . . . Nuku'alofa | 100,000 . . . . 18,400[2] | 270 . . . . 699 | Constitutional . monarchy (C) | King: Taufa'ahau Tupou IV Prime Minister: Prince Fatafehi Tu'ipelehake | Pa'anga . . . . 1.19 | 40 430 |
| **TRINIDAD AND TOBAGO** Port-of-Spain | 1,130,000 120,000[2] | 1,980 . . . . 5,128 | Republic . . . . (C) | President: Sir Ellis Clarke Prime Minister: Eric Williams | Dollar . . . . . . 0.42 | 3,310 2,910 |
| **TUNISIA** . . . . . . . . . . . Tunis | 6,200,000 550,400 | 63,170 . . . . 163,610 | Republic . . . . | President: Habib Bourguiba Prime Minister: Mohammed Mzali | Dinar . . . . . . . 2.50 | 5,760 950 |
| **TURKEY** . . . . . . . . . . . . Ankara | 45,218,000 2,106,000 | 301,382 . . . 780,576 | Republic . . . . . | President, National Security Council, Chief of State, and head of General Staff: Gen. Kenan Evren Prime Minister: Adm. Bülent Ulusu | Lira . . . . . . . . . 0.01 | 51,750 1,210 |
| **TUVALU** . . . . . . . . . . . (ELLICE ISLANDS) Funafuti | 7,500 . . . . . 2,200 | 10 . . . . 26 | Parliamentary . . state (C) | Governor-General: Penitala Fiatau Teo Prime Minister: Toalipi Lauti | Dollar . . . . . . 1.17 | NA NA |
| **UGANDA** . . . . . . . . . . . Kampala | 13,220,000 . . . . 540,000[2] | 91,134 . . . 236,036 | Republic . . . . (C) | President: Milton Obote Prime Minister: Otema Alimadi | Shilling . . . . . . 0.14 | NA NA |
| **UNION OF SOVIET SOCIALIST REPUBLICS** Moscow | 262,436,000 . . . . 8,011,000[2] | 8,649,534 . . 22,402,200 | Federal . . . . . . socialist state | Chairman, Presidium of the Supreme Soviet (President): Leonid I. Brezhnev Chairman, Council of Ministers (Prime Minister): Nikolai A. Tikhonov | Ruble . . . . . . . 1.56[1] | 965,520 3,700 |

| Imports<br>Exports | Revenue<br>Expenditure | Elementary<br>Schools:<br>Teachers<br>Students | Secondary<br>Schools:<br>Teachers<br>Students | Colleges and<br>Universities:<br>Teachers<br>Students |
|---|---|---|---|---|
| $ 396,000,000<br>308,000,000 | $ 349,000,000<br>364,000,000 | 3,077<br>85,250 | 1,704<br>34,088 | 113<br>938 |
| 224,000,000<br>168,000,000 | 139,000,000<br>204,000,000 | 2,672<br>96,835 | 1,073<br>20,331 | 136<br>1,150 |
| 28,488,000,000<br>27,240,000,000 | 27,904,000,000<br>38,445,000,000 | NA<br>686,811 | NA<br>575,190 | NA<br>198,798 |
| 29,354,000,000<br>26,507,000,000 | 9,590,000,000<br>10,439,000,000 | NA<br>524,500 | NA<br>639,700 | 5,414<br>71,500 |
| 3,307,000,000<br>1,637,000,000 | 5,768,000,000<br>5,768,000,000 | 41,550<br>1,326,414 | 33,542<br>395,638 | NA<br>85,474 |
| 11,037,000,000<br>12,662,000,000 | 5,394,000,000<br>5,394,000,000 | 68,413<br>2,278,726 | 66,320<br>1,572,687 | 15,452<br>317,188 |
| 1,117,000,000<br>457,000,000 | 751,000,000[15]<br>1,321,000,000[15] | 38,199<br>1,956,320 | 3,731<br>67,859 | 434<br>3,064 |
| 7,156,000,000<br>5,308,000,000 | 3,015,000,000<br>3,766,000,000 | 270,567<br>6,810,747 | 49,500<br>1,259,082 | 9,070<br>130,965 |
| 448,000,000<br>241,000,000 | 311,000,000<br>311,000,000 | 6,528<br>395,381 | 2,161<br>81,374 | 177<br>2,186 |
| 29,000,000<br>7,000,000 | 11,280,000<br>11,730,000 | 761<br>19,730 | 687<br>12,795 | *<br>* |
| 1,946,000,000<br>2,476,000,000 | 2,108,000,000<br>2,108,000,000 | 6,474<br>190,200 | NA<br>86,788 | NA<br>2,830 |
| 2,830,000,000<br>1,766,000,000 | 1,579,000,000<br>1,216,000,000 | 25,149<br>991,908 | 11,874<br>230,868 | 3,089<br>23,137 |
| 4,946,000,000<br>2,261,000,000 | 10,532,000,000<br>11,582,000,000 | 184,512<br>5,548,000 | 88,825<br>2,028,000 | 17,465<br>346,476 |
| NA<br>NA | 1,730,000<br>1,730,000 | 48<br>1,600 | 12<br>260 | *<br>* |
| 187,000,000<br>591,000,000 | 643,000,000<br>529,000,000 | 32,554<br>1,139,420 | 3,309<br>70,111 | 283<br>3,338 |
| 57,773,000,000<br>64,762,000,000 | 444,950,000,000<br>444,548,000,000 | 2,868,000[5]<br>34,300,000 | [5]<br>15,062,000 | 336,000<br>5,109,600 |

453

| Nation<br>Capital | Population | Area of<br>Country<br>(sq mi/<br>sq km) | Type of<br>Government | Heads of State and<br>Government | Currency;<br>Value in<br>U.S. Dollars | GNP<br>(000,000);<br>GNP<br>per capita |
|---|---|---|---|---|---|---|
| UNITED ARAB<br>EMIRATES<br>Abu Dhabi | 750,000<br><br>250,000[2] | 32,278<br>83,600 | Federal<br>state | President:<br>Sheikh Zaid bin<br>Sultan al-Nahayan<br>Prime Minister:<br>Rashid bin Said<br>al-Maktum | Dirham<br>0.27 | $  11,440<br>14,230 |
| UNITED STATES<br>Washington, D.C. | 226,504,825<br>637,651 | 3,618,467<br>9,371,786 | Federal<br>republic | President:<br>Jimmy Carter | Dollar | 2,117,890<br>9,700 |
| UPPER VOLTA<br>Ouagadougou | 6,730,000<br>168,600 | 105,869<br>274,200 | Republic | Head, Military<br>Committee of<br>Recovery for<br>National Progress:<br>Col. Saye Zerbo | CFA franc<br>0.0049 | 870<br>160 |
| URUGUAY<br>Montevideo | 2,880,000<br>1,229,700 | 68,037<br>176,215 | Republic | President:<br>Aparicio Méndez | Peso<br>0.11 | 4,660<br>1,610 |
| VANUATU (NEW<br>HEBRIDES)<br>Port Vila | 112,600<br><br>17,400[2] | 5,700<br>14,763 | Republic (C) | President:<br>George Kalkoa<br>Prime Minister:<br>Rev. Walter Lini | Franc[16]<br>0.015 | 60<br>540 |
| VENEZUELA<br>Caracas | 13,520,000<br>2,850,000[2] | 352,144<br>912,050 | Federal<br>republic | President:<br>Luis Herrera Campins | Bolivar<br>0.23 | 40,710<br>2,910 |
| VIETNAM<br>Hanoi | 51,080,000<br>1,521,200 | 127,242<br>329,556 | Socialist<br>republic | President:<br>Nguyen Huu Tho<br>Premier:<br>Pham Van Dong | Dong<br>0.49 | 8,870<br>170 |
| WESTERN SAMOA<br>Apia | 150,000<br>32,100[2] | 1,097<br>2,842 | Constitutional<br>monarchy<br>(C) | Head of State:<br>Malietoa Tanumafili II<br>Prime Minister:<br>Tupuola Taisi Efi | Tala<br>1.10 | NA<br>NA |
| YEMEN, PEOPLE'S<br>DEMOCRATIC<br>REPUBLIC OF<br>Aden | 1,840,000<br><br><br>271,600 | 128,560<br>332,968 | People's<br>republic | Chairman, Presidential<br>Council, and Prime Minister:<br>Ali Nasser Mohammed | Dinar<br>2.90 | 740<br>420 |
| YEMEN ARAB<br>REPUBLIC<br>San'a | 5,790,000<br><br>134,600 | 75,290<br>195,000 | Republic | President:<br>Col. Ali Abdullah Saleh<br>Prime Minister:<br>Abdel-Aziz Abdel-Ghani | Rial<br>0.22 | 2,960<br>580 |
| YUGOSLAVIA<br>Belgrade | 22,160,000<br>870,000 | 98,766<br>255,804 | Federal<br>socialist<br>republic | President:<br>Cvijetin Mijatovic<br>President, Federal Executive<br>Council (Prime Minister):<br>Veselin Djuranović | Dinar<br>0.04 | 52,340<br>2,390 |
| ZAIRE<br>Kinshasa | 27,940,000<br>2,710,300 | 905,567<br>2,345,409 | Republic | President:<br>Gen. Mobutu Sese Seko<br>First State Commissioner (Prime<br>Minister):<br>Nguza Karl-i-Bond | Zaire<br>0.34 | 5,510<br>210 |
| ZAMBIA<br>Lusaka | 5,650,000<br>559,000 | 290,586<br>752,614 | Republic<br>(C) | President:<br>Kenneth D. Kaunda<br>Prime Minister:<br>Daniel M. Lisulo | Kwacha<br>1.29 | 2,530<br>480 |
| ZIMBABWE<br>(RHODESIA)<br>Salisbury | 7,140,000<br><br>616,000[2] | 150,804<br>390,580 | Republic (C) | President:<br>Rev. Canaan S. Banana<br>Prime Minister:<br>Robert G. Mugabe | Dollar<br>1.44 | 3,320<br>480 |

1. Noncommercial exchange rates applied to tourism and remittances from outside the ruble-yuan area.
2. Population of metropolitan area.
3. Combined figure with Luxembourg.
4. Money was abolished in Kampuchea from 1978 to March 1980.
5. Combined figure for elementary and secondary education.
6. Excluding trade with other members of the Customs and Economic Union of Central Africa (Cameroon, Central African Republic, Congo, Gabon).
7. Figure for public schools.
8. Including figures for Mayotte, a major island of the Comoro archipelago which is a dependency of France.

| Imports<br>Exports | Revenue<br>Expenditure | Elementary<br>Schools:<br>Teachers<br>Students | Secondary<br>Schools:<br>Teachers<br>Students | Colleges and<br>Universities:<br>Teachers<br>Students |
|---|---|---|---|---|
| $ 6,960,000,000<br>13,574,000,000 | $ 2,975,000,000<br>2,975,000,000 | 3,876<br>60,742 | NA<br>15,225 | *<br>* |
| 217,664,000,000<br>178,578,000,000 | 520,000,000,000<br>579,000,000,000 | 1,169,000[7]<br>25,052,000[7] | 1,007,000[7]<br>17,559,000[7] | 562,000<br>11,391,950 |
| 191,000,000<br>42,000,000 | 196,000,000<br>196,000,000 | 3,204<br>159,948 | 1,025<br>17,618 | 124<br>1,673 |
| 1,172,000,000<br>789,000,000 | 617,000,000<br>673,000,000 | 15,679<br>382,759 | 18,180<br>188,000 | 2,149<br>39,927 |
| 63,000,000<br>43,000,000 | 22,000,000<br>39,000,000 | NA<br>10,987 | NA<br>1,021 | *<br>* |
| 10,614,000,000<br>9,126,000,000 | 9,307,000,000<br>10,797,000,000 | 94,218<br>2,204,074 | 54,176<br>906,929 | 19,787<br>247,518 |
| 1,500,000,000<br>416,000,000 | 5,198,000,000<br>5,198,000,000 | 217,064<br>7,722,524 | 127,635<br>3,200,912 | 10,475<br>100,027 |
| 73,000,000<br>18,000,000 | 31,000,000<br>27,000,000 | 1,471<br>41,453 | 562<br>9,534 | 38<br>207 |
| 544,000,000<br>181,000,000 | 101,000,000<br>137,000,000 | 6,467<br>196,466 | NA<br>39,696 | 92<br>934 |
| 1,283,000,000<br>7,000,000 | 660,000,000<br>961,000,000 | 6,604<br>255,301 | 1,345<br>24,240 | NA<br>2,408 |
| 12,862,000,000<br>6,491,000,000 | 9,291,000,000<br>9,947,000,000 | 131,547<br>2,831,480 | 53,460<br>913,969 | 23,269<br>439,608 |
| 589,000,000<br>925,000,000 | 1,200,000,000<br>1,315,000,000 | NA<br>3,429,076 | NA<br>446,067 | NA<br>21,021 |
| 630,000,000<br>853,000,000 | 712,000,000<br>1,007,000,000 | 19,300<br>907,867 | 4,248<br>86,977 | 412<br>3,447 |
| 937,000,000<br>1,154,000,000 | 888,000,000<br>1,404,000,000 | 23,768<br>838,205 | 4,381<br>80,500 | 230<br>1,798 |

9. Figure for ten-year polytechnical high schools.
10. Figure for East Bank of Jordan.
11. Included in figure for Belgium.
12. Including trade among the states of Malaysia.
13. Excluding population of the former Canal Zone.
14. Excluding trade with Malaysia.
15. Excluding Zanzibar.
16. Before independence, the Australian dollar was also legal tender. Its use is being phased out.

# THE STATES AND OUTLYING AREAS OF THE UNITED STATES

| State / Capital | Population | Area (sq mi/ sq km) | Per Capita Personal Income | Governor / Lieutenant-Governor | Revenue / Expenditure | Roads (Miles) |
|---|---|---|---|---|---|---|
| **ALABAMA** | 3,890,061 | 51,609 | $ 6,962 | Forrest H. James, Jr. (D) | $ 3,293,000,000 | 87,013 |
| Montgomery | 156,333 | 133,667 | | George D. H. McMillan (D) | 3,216,000,000 | |
| **ALASKA** | 400,481 | 589,757 | 11,219 | Jay S. Hammond (R) | 1,508,000,000 | 9,403 |
| Juneau | 19,093 | 1,527,470 | | Terry Miller (R) | 1,348,000,000 | |
| **ARIZONA** | 2,717,866 | 113,909 | 8,423 | Bruce Babbitt (D) | 2,274,000,000 | 56,342 |
| Phoenix | 684,516 | 295,024 | | * | 2,133,000,000 | |
| **ARKANSAS** | 2,285,513 | 53,104 | 6,933 | Bill Clinton (D) | 1,798,000,000 | 74,209 |
| Little Rock | 153,494 | 137,539 | | Joe Purcell (D) | 1,773,000,000 | |
| **CALIFORNIA** | 23,668,562 | 158,693 | 10,047 | Edmund G. Brown, Jr. (D) | 25,068,000,000 | 176,309 |
| Sacramento | 264,511 | 411,015 | | Mike Curb (R) | 25,279,000,000 | |
| **COLORADO** | 2,888,834 | 104,247 | 9,122 | Richard D. Lamm (D) | 2,554,000,000 | 87,133 |
| Denver | 475,098 | 270,000 | | Nancy Dick (D) | 2,320,000,000 | |
| **CONNECTICUT** | 3,107,576 | 5,009 | 10,129 | Ella T. Grasso (D) | 2,828,000,000 | 19,205 |
| Hartford | 130,015 | 12,973 | | William A. O'Neill (D) | 2,621,000,000 | |
| **DELAWARE** | 595,225 | 2,057 | 9,327 | Pierre S. du Pont 4th (R) | 807,000,000 | 5,227 |
| Dover | 23,021 | 5,328 | | James D. McGinnis (D) | 703,000,000 | |
| **DISTRICT OF COLUMBIA** | 637,651 | 67 | 10,570 | Mayor: | * | 1,101 |
| * | * | 174 | | Marion S. Barry, Jr. (D) | * | |
| **FLORIDA** | 9,739,992 | 58,560 | 8,546 | D. Robert Graham (D) | 6,298,000,000 | 97,119 |
| Tallahassee | 85,856 | 151,670 | | Wayne Mixson (D) | 6,133,000,000 | |
| **GEORGIA** | 5,464,265 | 58,876 | 7,630 | George Busbee (D) | 4,101,000,000 | 103,151 |
| Atlanta | 416,715 | 152,489 | | Zell Miller (D) | 4,074,000,000 | |
| **HAWAII** | 965,000 | 6,450 | 9,223 | George R. Ariyoshi (D) | 1,447,000,000 | 3,795 |
| Honolulu | 324,871 | 16,706 | | Jean Sadako King (D) | 1,407,000,000 | |
| **IDAHO** | 943,935 | 83,557 | 7,571 | John V. Evans (D) | 831,000,000 | 64,603 |
| Boise | 107,687 | 216,413 | | Philip E. Batt (R) | 787,000,000 | |
| **ILLINOIS** | 11,418,461 | 56,400 | 9,799 | James R. Thompson, Jr. (R) | 9,656,000,000 | 133,954 |
| Springfield | 87,520 | 146,076 | | Dave O'Neal (R) | 9,340,000,000 | |
| **INDIANA** | 5,490,179 | 36,291 | 8,570 | Otis R. Bowen (R) | 4,230,000,000 | 91,074 |
| Indianapolis | 704,556 | 93,994 | | Robert D. Orr (R) | 3,840,000,000 | |
| **IOWA** | 2,913,387 | 56,290 | 8,772 | Robert D. Ray (R) | 2,576,000,000 | 112,146 |
| Des Moines | 193,772 | 145,791 | | Terry E. Branstad (R) | 2,737,000,000 | |
| **KANSAS** | 2,363,208 | 82,264 | 9,233 | John Carlin (D) | 1,961,000,000 | 134,855 |
| Topeka | 122,065 | 213,064 | | Paul V. Dugan (D) | 1,900,000,000 | |

The material in the following tables is the latest available. As before, it should be noted that the symbol * indicates that the category is not applicable to the area mentioned, and that NA means that the data were not available. The Office of Territorial Affairs was helpful in supplying some data for the table on Outlying Areas.

| Railways (Miles) | Radio and Television Stations | English-language Daily Newspapers | Public Elementary Schools: Teachers Students | Public Secondary Schools: Teachers Students | Colleges & Universities: Institutions Students |
|---|---|---|---|---|---|
| 4,214 | 225 26 | 27 | 18,000 382,562 | 19,000 379,104 | 58 161,579 |
| 542 | 41 10 | 8 | 2,600 49,895 | 2,400 40,833 | 16 26,351 |
| 1,847 | 102 15 | 19 | 16,900 349,695 | 7,300 160,135 | 23 176,612 |
| 3,171 | 151 13 | 33 | 10,900 241,178 | 11,600 215,520 | 34 72,318 |
| 6,693 | 507 71 | 122 | 109,100 2,728,637 | 72,600 1,459,330 | 262 1,650,155 |
| 3,078 | 137 14 | 28 | 15,500 307,001 | 14,500 251,284 | 41 152,359 |
| 296 | 82 10 | 25 | 21,500 396,975 | 14,900 196,782 | 47 152,431 |
| 207 | 20 1 | 3 | 2,500 53,041 | 3,500 57,993 | 10 30,918 |
| 27 | 20 8 | 2 | 3,600 61,361 | 2,400 52,497 | 16 81,807 |
| 3,740 | 341 41 | 52 | 38,100 776,607 | 36,400 737,212 | 77 377,100 |
| 5,141 | 289 29 | 36 | 33,100 NA | 20,400 NA | 72 174,867 |
| 0 | 36 12 | 5 | 4,400 89,630 | 3,500 81,131 | 12 47,535 |
| 2,384 | 72 11 | 15 | 4,900 108,744 | 4,700 94,278 | 9 39,255 |
| 11,198 | 309 32 | 86 | 54,900 1,395,192 | 52,400 704,965 | 154 611,412 |
| 5,458 | 222 27 | 78 | 26,200 720,671 | 27,100 392,660 | 66 222,791 |
| 6,966 | 174 21 | 41 | 15,900 295,748 | 17,500 272,792 | 62 129,181 |
| 7,405 | 118 14 | 50 | 13,800 227,325 | 11,900 206,222 | 52 127,323 |

| State Capital | Population | Area (sq mi/ sq km) | Per Capita Personal Income | Governor Lieutenant-Governor | Revenue Expenditure | Roads (Miles) |
|---|---|---|---|---|---|---|
| **KENTUCKY** Frankfort | 3,661,433 23,506 | 40,395 104,623 | $ 7,390 | John Y. Brown, Jr. (D) $ Martha Layne Collins (D) | 3,466,000,000 3,611,000,000 | 69,229 |
| **LOUISIANA** Baton Rouge | 4,203,972 308,178 | 48,523 125,675 | 7,583 | David C. Treen (R) Robert L. Freeman (D) | 4,063,000,000 3,773,000,000 | 55,397 |
| **MAINE** Augusta | 1,124,660 21,164 | 33,215 86,027 | 7,039 | Joseph E. Brennan (D) * | 1,071,000,000 1,020,000,000 | 21,797 |
| **MARYLAND** Annapolis | 4,216,446 33,124 | 10,577 27,394 | 9,331 | Harry Hughes (D) Samuel W. Bogley 3rd (D) | 4,419,000,000 4,264,000,000 | 26,422 |
| **MASSACHUSETTS** Boston | 5,737,037 618,493 | 8,257 21,386 | 8,893 | Edward J. King (D) Thomas P. O'Neill 3rd (D) | 6,166,000,000 5,832,000,000 | 33,586 |
| **MICHIGAN** Lansing | 9,258,344 127,128 | 58,216 150,779 | 9,403 | William G. Milliken (R) James H. Brickley (R) | 9,747,000,000 9,356,000,000 | 119,359 |
| **MINNESOTA** St. Paul | 4,077,148 265,971 | 84,068 217,736 | 8,865 | Albert H. Quie (R) Lou Wangberg (IR) | 4,803,000,000 4,483,000,000 | 127,933 |
| **MISSISSIPPI** Jackson | 2,520,638 190,542 | 47,716 123,584 | 6,178 | William F. Winter (D) Brad Dye (D) | 2,217,000,000 2,171,000,000 | 68,983 |
| **MISSOURI** Jefferson City | 4,917,444 36,511 | 69,686 180,487 | 8,251 | Joseph P. Teasdale (D) William C. Phelps (R) | 3,293,000,000 3,086,000,000 | 117,548 |
| **MONTANA** Helena | 786,690 28,142 | 147,138 381,087 | 7,684 | Thomas L. Judge (D) Ted Schwinden (D) | 811,000,000 769,000,000 | 77,829 |
| **NEBRASKA** Lincoln | 1,570,006 163,937 | 77,227 200,018 | 8,684 | Charles Thone (R) Roland E. Luedtke (R) | 1,264,000,000 1,215,000,000 | 96,657 |
| **NEVADA** Carson City | 799,184 27,674 | 110,540 286,299 | 10,521 | Robert F. List (R) Myron E. Leavitt (D) | 727,000,000 649,000,000 | 49,901 |
| **NEW HAMPSHIRE** Concord | 920,610 28,980 | 9,304 24,097 | 8,351 | Hugh Gallen (D) * | 614,000,000 631,000,000 | 15,577 |
| **NEW JERSEY** Trenton | 7,364,158 96,951 | 7,836 20,295 | 9,747 | Brendan T. Byrne (D) * | 6,377,000,000 6,540,000,000 | 33,249 |
| **NEW MEXICO** Santa Fe | 1,299,968 46,855 | 121,666 315,115 | 7,560 | Bruce King (D) Roberto A. Mondragón (D) | 1,678,000,000 1,510,000,000 | 72,617 |
| **NEW YORK** Albany | 17,557,288 107,798 | 49,576 128,402 | 9,104 | Hugh L. Carey (D) Mario M. Cuomo (D) | 20,426,000,000 19,255,000,000 | 109,064 |
| **NORTH CAROLINA** Raleigh | 5,874,429 138,005 | 52,586 136,198 | 7,385 | James B. Hunt, Jr. (D) James C. Green (D) | 4,812,000,000 4,962,000,000 | 91,949 |
| **NORTH DAKOTA** Bismarck | 652,695 40,911 | 70,665 183,022 | 8,231 | Arthur A. Link (D) Wayne G. Sanstead (D) | 742,000,000 727,000,000 | 106,641 |
| **OHIO** Columbus | 10,797,419 532,339 | 41,222 106,765 | 8,715 | James A. Rhodes (R) * | 7,880,000,000 7,937,000,000 | 109,957 |
| **OKLAHOMA** Oklahoma City | 3,025,266 371,802 | 69,919 181,090 | 8,509 | George Nigh (D) Spencer Bernard (D) | 2,675,000,000 2,435,000,000 | 109,723 |
| **OREGON** Salem | 2,632,663 83,738 | 96,981 251,181 | 8,938 | Victor Atiyeh (R) * | 2,683,000,000 2,518,000,000 | 112,371 |
| **PENNSYLVANIA** Harrisburg | 11,866,728 56,105 | 45,333 117,412 | 8,558 | Dick Thornburgh (R) William W. Scranton 3rd (R) | 10,446,000,000 9,610,000,000 | 118,495 |
| **RHODE ISLAND** Providence | 947,154 160,982 | 1,214 3,144 | 8,510 | J. Joseph Garrahy (D) Thomas R. DiLuglio (D) | 1,038,000,000 1,014,000,000 | 6,043 |
| **SOUTH CAROLINA** Columbia | 3,119,208 110,851 | 31,055 80,432 | 7,057 | Richard W. Riley (D) Nancy Stevenson (D) | 2,644,000,000 2,518,000,000 | 61,648 |

| Railways (Miles) | Radio and Television Stations | English-language Daily Newspapers | Public Elementary Schools: Teachers Students | Public Secondary Schools: Teachers Students | Colleges & Universities: Institutions Students |
|---|---|---|---|---|---|
| 3,582 | 221 26 | 27 | 20,500 441,712 | 12,000 251,287 | 42 132,706 |
| 3,359 | 170 19 | 27 | 23,300 565,844 | 18,100 250,825 | 32 152,207 |
| 1,690 | 83 12 | 9 | 7,400 161,797 | 4,900 78,219 | 27 41,460 |
| 826 | 95 10 | 13 | 20,700 402,609 | 22,500 407,324 | 54 214,734 |
| 857 | 155 16 | 48 | 30,700 544,746 | 34,500 536,718 | 119 384,500 |
| 4,208 | 283 34 | 52 | 45,500 961,821 | 41,200 949,524 | 96 485,292 |
| 6713 | 192 18 | 30 | 20,100 390,437 | 24,500 417,279 | 65 189,087 |
| 3,226 | 186 18 | 25 | 13,800 274,173 | 11,000 219,537 | 46 97,569 |
| 6,049 | 223 27 | 52 | 24,400 489,283 | 23,900 410,719 | 84 221,281 |
| 4,659 | 76 13 | 11 | 5,500 109,463 | 4,000 54,863 | 13 31,103 |
| 5,021 | 92 23 | 19 | 9,400 156,662 | 8,400 141,134 | 31 81,691 |
| 1,412 | 40 8 | 9 | 3,000 74,644 | 3,000 71,637 | 6 33,539 |
| 570 | 51 7 | 9 | 4,800 117,241 | 4,400 55,148 | 24 41,549 |
| 1,250 | 93 10 | 28 | 47,500 827,978 | 29,000 509,349 | 63 308,304 |
| 2,057 | 96 12 | 20 | 6,900 143,927 | 6,900 135,322 | 19 55,717 |
| 4,032 | 349 41 | 79 | 77,200 1,520,552 | 87,100 1,573,333 | 286 955,547 |
| 3,598 | 328 28 | 53 | 37,300 800,807 | 17,900 362,003 | 126 262,757 |
| 5,041 | 44 13 | 10 | 4,400 57,902 | 3,100 64,119 | 16 32,325 |
| 6,517 | 325 36 | 96 | 54,000 1,246,513 | 51,300 855,927 | 133 450,633 |
| 4,585 | 126 15 | 55 | 15,600 321,187 | 15,300 267,683 | 43 149,397 |
| 2,755 | 130 17 | 22 | 13,100 276,905 | 10,700 194,469 | 43 146,349 |
| 6,497 | 361 35 | 104 | 54,800 1,008,664 | 57,600 1,038,082 | 178 472,577 |
| 92 | 27 4 | 7 | 5,000 85,771 | 4,100 74,885 | 13 63,553 |
| 2,797 | 172 19 | 20 | 17,500 428,682 | 11,800 196,249 | 61 130,076 |

459

| State Capital | Population | Area (sq mi/ sq km) | Per Capita Personal Income | Governor Lieutenant-Governor | Revenue Expenditure | Roads (Miles) |
|---|---|---|---|---|---|---|
| **SOUTH DAKOTA** ...... | 690,178 .... | 77,047 ..... | $ 7,455 .... | William J. Janklow (R) ......... $ | 604,000,000 .... | 82,519 |
| Pierre | 11,939 | 199,552 | | Lowell C. Hansen 2nd (R) | 618,000,000 | |
| **TENNESSEE** .......... | 4,590,750 .... | 42,244 .... | 7,343 .... | Lamar Alexander (R) ......... | 3,226,000,000 .... | 82,052 |
| Nashville | 428,957 | 109,412 | | John S. Wilder (D) | 3,107,000,000 | |
| **TEXAS** ..............| 14,228,383 .... | 267,338 .... | 8,788 .... | William P. Clements, Jr. | 10,101,000,000 ....| 261,627 |
| Austin | 323,250 | 692,405 | | (R) | 9,100,000,000 | |
| | | | | William P. Hobby (D) | | |
| **UTAH** .............. | 1,461,037 .... | 84,916 .... | 7,197 .... | Scott M. Matheson (D) ......... | 1,314,000,000 .... | 46,326 |
| Salt Lake City | 167,404 | 219,932 | | David S. Monson (R) | 1,332,000,000 | |
| **VERMONT** ............ | 511,456 .... | 9,609 .... | 7,329 .... | Richard A. Snelling (R) ....... | 557,000,000 .... | 13,996 |
| Montpelier | 7,953 | 24,887 | | Madeleine M. Kunin (D) | 552,000,000 | |
| **VIRGINIA** ............ | 5,346,279 .... | 40,817 .... | 8,587 .... | John N. Dalton (R) ............. | 4,573,000,000 .... | 64,797 |
| Richmond | 223,212 | 105,716 | | Charles S. Robb (D) | 4,463,000,000 | |
| **WASHINGTON** ........ | 4,130,163 .... | 68,192 .... | 9,565 .... | Dixy Lee Ray (D) ............. | 4,445,000,000 .... | 83,924 |
| Olympia | 28,697 | 176,617 | | John A. Cherberg (D) | 4,176,000,000 | |
| **WEST VIRGINIA** ....... | 1,949,644 .... | 24,181 .... | 7,372 .... | John D. Rockefeller 4th (D) ..... | 1,982,000,000 .... | 36,253 |
| Charleston | 66,965 | 62,629 | | * | 2,079,000,000 | |
| **WISCONSIN** .......... | 4,705,335 .... | 56,154 .... | 8,484 .... | Lee S. Dreyfus (R) ............. | 5,232,000,000 ....| 106,547 |
| Madison | 168,932 | 145,439 | | Russell A. Olson (R) | 5,032,000,000 | |
| **WYOMING** ............ | 470,816 .... | 97,914 .... | 9,922 .... | Ed Herschler (D) ............. | 670,000,000 .... | 34,511 |
| Cheyenne | 48,274 | 253,597 | | * | 568,000,000 | |

# OUTLYING AREAS OF THE U.S.

| Area Capital | Population | Area (sq mi/ sq km) | Status | Governor Lieutenant-Governor | Revenue Expenditure | Roads (Miles) |
|---|---|---|---|---|---|---|
| **AMERICAN SAMOA** ...... | 32,395 .... | 76 ........ | Unorganized, .......... | Peter T. Coleman ........ $ | 59,002,746 .... | 94 |
| Pago Pago | 4,700 | 197 | unincorporated territory | Tufele Li'A | 59,002,746 | |
| **GUAM** ................. | 106,000 .... | 212 ........ | Unincorporated ....... | Paul M. Calvo | 155,576,000 .... | 230 . |
| Agaña | 2,500 | 549 | territory | Joe F. Ada | 151,951,000 | |
| **PUERTO RICO** .......... | 3,187,570 .... | 3,435 ........ | Commonwealth ....... | Carlos Romero Barceló ... | 3,074,900,000 .... | 10,456 . |
| San Juan | 514,500 | 8,897 | | * | 2,797,200,000 | |
| **TRUST TERRITORY** | 132,350 .... | 8,489 ........ | U.N. Trust ............ | High Commissioner: ...... | 114,738,000 .... | 64 . |
| **OF THE PACIFIC** | | 21,987 | Territory | Adrian P. Winkel | 117,230,800 | |
| **ISLANDS**[1] | | | | | | |
| Capitol Hill, on Saipan Island | NA | | | | | |
| **VIRGIN ISLANDS** ........ | 95,650 .... | 133 ........ | Unincorporated ........ | Juan Luis ........ | 180,200,000 .... | 621 . |
| Charlotte Amalie | 12,220 | 344 | territory | Henry Millin | 176,900,000 | |

1. The Northern Mariana Islands in 1980 were an internally self-governing part of the Trust Territory of the Pacific Islands. The government of the Northern Marianas was headed by Gov. Carlos S. Camacho and Lt.-Gov. Francisco C. Ada. The capital was Susupe, on Saipan Island.

| Railways (Miles) | Radio and Television Stations | English-language Daily Newspapers | Public Elementary Schools: Teachers Students | Public Secondary Schools: Teachers Students | Colleges & Universities: Institutions Students |
|---|---|---|---|---|---|
| 3,017 | 63 / 19 | 13 | 5,300 / 90,437 | 3,000 / 47,791 | 18 / 30,931 |
| 3,059 | 259 / 24 | 32 | 24,600 / 616,060 | 15,800 / 256,976 | 76 / 194,667 |
| 12,924 | 513 / 69 | 118 | 79,400 / 1,999,905 | 72,100 / 867,349 | 147 / 656,004 |
| 1,654 | 75 / 5 | 6 | 6,600 / 182,924 | 6,400 / 142,102 | 14 / 88,989 |
| 330 | 47 / 6 | 8 | 3,300 / 57,625 | 2,900 / 43,667 | 21 / 29,577 |
| 3,361 | 226 / 22 | 33 | 33,800 / 642,590 | 25,000 / 412,648 | 71 / 258,368 |
| 4,681 | 167 / 20 | 26 | 17,900 / 395,560 | 15,800 / 373,686 | 49 / 275,299 |
| 2,994 | 111 / 12 | 25 | 11,200 / 269,979 | 9,600 / 125,743 | 28 / 79,007 |
| 5,515 | 228 / 27 | 37 | 30,000 / 486,599 | 25,400 / 399,820 | 62 / 241,384 |
| 1,760 | 46 / 5 | 10 | 2,700 / 51,300 | 2,700 / 43,028 | 8 / 19,933 |

| Railways (Miles) | Radio and Television Stations | Daily Newspapers | Public Elementary and Secondary School Teachers | Public School Students: Elementary Secondary | Higher Education: Institutions Students |
|---|---|---|---|---|---|
| 0 | 1 / 1 | 2 | 395 | 6,464 / 2,777 | 1 / 777 |
| 0 | 7 / 2 | 1 | 1,328 | 15,850 / 10,211 | 2 / 5,572 |
| 60 | 94 / 11 | 4 | 24,761 | 475,979 / 212,613 | 23 / 100,885 |
| 0 | 8 / 3 | 0 | 1,701 | 28,014 / 6,471 | 1 / 573 |
| 0 | 8 / 2 | 3 | 1,540 | 15,894 / 9,677 | 1 / 2,122 |

461

# THE PROVINCES AND TERRITORIES OF CANADA

| Province<br>Capital | Population | Area<br>(sq mi/<br>sq km) | Per Capita<br>Personal<br>Income | Premier<br>Lieutenant-Governor |
|---|---|---|---|---|
| **ALBERTA**<br>Edmonton | 2,086,400<br>594,900[1] | 255,285<br>661,185 | $9,717 | Peter Lougheed<br>Frank Lynch-Staunton |
| **BRITISH COLUMBIA**<br>Victoria | 2,642,400<br>224,800[1] | 366,255<br>948,596 | 9,821 | William Bennett<br>Henry Bell-Irving |
| **MANITOBA**<br>Winnipeg | 1,028,700<br>590,300[1] | 251,000<br>650,087 | 8,198 | Sterling Lyon<br>Francis L. Jobin |
| **NEW BRUNSWICK**<br>Fredericton | 707,600<br>45,248 | 28,354<br>73,436 | 6,472 | Richard B. Hatfield<br>Hédard J. Robichaud |
| **NEWFOUNDLAND**<br>St. John's | 580,900<br>147,900[1] | 156,185<br>404,517 | 5,862 | Brian Peckford<br>Gordon A. Winter |
| **NORTHWEST TERRITORIES**<br>Yellowknife | 43,000<br>8,256 | 1,304,903<br>3,379,684 | 8,569[2] | Commissioner:<br>John H. Parker |
| **NOVA SCOTIA**<br>Halifax | 853,100<br>273,200[1] | 21,425<br>55,491 | 7,088 | John Buchanan<br>John Elvin Shaffner |
| **ONTARIO**<br>Toronto | 8,576,000<br>2,864,700[1] | 412,582<br>1,068,582 | 9,608 | William G. Davis<br>John Black Aird |
| **PRINCE EDWARD ISLAND**<br>Charlottetown | 124,500<br>17,063 | 2,184<br>5,657 | 6,057 | J. Angus MacLean<br>Dr. Joseph Aubin-Dorion |
| **QUÉBEC**<br>Québec | 6,306,500<br>559,100[1] | 594,860<br>1,540,680 | 8,341 | René Lévesque<br>Jean-Pierre Coté |
| **SASKATCHEWAN**<br>Regina | 970,100<br>163,700[1] | 251,700<br>651,900 | 8,335 | Allan Blakeney<br>C. Irwin McIntosh |
| **YUKON TERRITORY**<br>Whitehorse | 21,400<br>13,311 | 186,300<br>482,515 | 8,569[2] | Commissioner:<br>Douglas Bell |

1. The population given is that of the Census Metropolitan Area of the capital and represents latest estimates available.
2. Figure is the combined average for the Northwest Territories and Yukon Territory.

The material in this table has been prepared with the kind assistance of Statistics Canada, Ottawa. It should be noted that all dollar figures are in Canadian dollars.

| Revenue Expenditure | Motor Vehicle Registrations | Railways (Miles) | Radio and Television Stations | Daily Newspapers | Elementary and Secondary Schools: Teachers Enrollment | Post-secondary Education: Institutions Enrollment |
|---|---|---|---|---|---|---|
| $7,522,008,000 | 1,413,173 | 5,868 | 47 | 9 | 22,608 | 23 |
| 6,668,677,000 | | | 11 | | 446,300 | 48,195 |
| 5,182,277,000 | 1,633,739 | 4,685 | 69 | 20 | 28,001 | 26 |
| 5,147,738,000 | | | 10 | | 539,351 | 48,095 |
| 1,952,577,000 | 628,427 | 4,126 | 27 | 8 | 12,190 | 14 |
| 2,065,980,000 | | | 6 | | 225,441 | 19,115 |
| 1,460,911,000 | 340,777 | 1,635 | 22 | 6 | 7,782 | 13 |
| 1,501,610,000 | | | 5 | | 157,621 | 12,690 |
| 1,322,633,000 | 188,357 | 906 | 28 | 3 | 7,846 | 7 |
| 1,414,604,000 | | | 7 | | 150,784 | 8,615 |
| 293,180,000 | 15,342 | 129 | 15 | 0 | 665 | 0 |
| 292,409,000 | | | 0 | | 12,828 | 0 |
| 1,620,003,000 | 413,034 | 1,223 | 29 | 6 | 10,975 | 24 |
| 1,701,625,000 | | | 5 | | 192,000 | 20,355 |
| 14,601,943,000 | 4,496,105 | 9,756 | 174 | 48 | 96,903 | 51 |
| 16,190,351,000 | | | 29 | | 1,935,086 | 221,935 |
| 288,269,000 | 65,501 | 253 | 4 | 2 | 1,396 | 3 |
| 289,751,000 | | | 1 | | 27,342 | 2,110 |
| 15,517,513,000 | 3,042,726 | 5,230 | 113 | 13 | 66,108 | 80 |
| 16,713,593,000 | | | 20 | | 1,249,445 | 213,810 |
| 2,229,175,000 | 722,643 | 7,978 | 28 | 4 | 11,318 | 6 |
| 2,161,087,000 | | | 7 | | 217,086 | 16,600 |
| 101,090,000 | 15,625 | 58 | 2 | 0 | 265 | 0 |
| 109,827,000 | | | 1 | | 5,122 | 0 |

# KEY TO SIGNED ARTICLES

Here is a list of contributors to this Yearbook. The initials at the end of an article are those of the author, or authors, of that article.

We would like to thank the following organization for its kind assistance: Social Security Administration, U.S. Department of Health and Human Services.

**A.E.,** AGNES ERDELYI, B.A., M.L.S. Reference Librarian, Sachem Public Library.

**A.J.R.,** ALLAN J. RISTORI, B.A. Member, Board of Directors, American League of Anglers. New Jersey Coordinator, American Sportfishing Federation.

**A.R.K.,** ALBERT R. KARR, B.S., M.S. Staff Reporter, *The Wall Street Journal*.

**B.M.P.,** B. M. PARKER, B.A., M.A., PH.D. Instructor of English, John Abbott College, Québec.

**B.Q.,** BENJAMIN QUARLES, B.A., M.A., PH.D. Emeritus Professor of History, Morgan State University. Author of *Black Abolitionists* and other books.

**B.R.,** BEA RIEMSCHNEIDER, B.A., M.A. Managing Editor, *Archaeology*. Associate Trustee, American Schools of Oriental Research.

**C.G.,** CHARLOTTE GROSS, B.A., M.A. Freelance Editor and Writer.

**C.H.,** CHARLES HAGEN, A.B., M.F.A. Consulting Editor, *Afterimage*.

**C.P.,** CARL PROUJAN, B.S. Independent Writer, Editor, A/V Producer. Former Editorial Director, Science Department, Scholastic Magazines, Inc. Author of *Secrets of the Sea*.

**D.Ca.,** DIANE CAMPER, A.B., M.S.L. Washington Bureau Correspondent, *Newsweek*.

**D.D.,** DAVE DOOLING. Science Editor, The Huntsville *Times*. Member, Board of Directors, AIAA local section. Author of *Shuttle to the Next Space Age*.

**D.H.,** DAVID HALL, B.A. Curator, Rodgers and Hammerstein Archives of Recorded Sound, Performing Arts Research Center, New York Public Library.

**D.H.D.,** DONALD H. DUNN, B.J. Editor, *Business Week*.

**D.J.H.,** DONALD J. HARVEY, B.A., M.A., PH.D. Professor of History at Hunter College, City University of New York. Consultant, Rockefeller Foundation Humanities Fellowships. Associate Editor, *Reviews in European History*. Author of *France Since the Revolution*.

**D.M.,** DERWENT MAY, M.A. Literary Editor, *The Listener*. Author of *Dear Parson, The Professionals,* and *A Revenger's Comedy*.

**D.Mac.,** DONNARAE MacCANN, B.A., M.L.S. Associate Professor of English, Virginia Polytechnic University. Coauthor of *The Black American in Books for Children* and other books.

**D.P.,** DON PERETZ, B.A., M.A., PH.D. Professor of Political Science and Director of the Southwest Asia-North Africa Program, State University of New York at Binghamton. Author of *Middle East Reader* and other books and articles.

**D.S.,** DAVID STERRITT, B.A.
Film Critic, *The Christian Science Monitor* and National Public Radio.

**E.M.L.,** EUSEBIO MUJAL-LEON, B.A., M.A., J.D., PH.D.
Assistant Professor of Government, Georgetown University.

**E.S.K.,** ELAINE STUART KNAPP, B.A.
Senior Editor, *Council of State Governments.*

**F.C.D. III,** FREDERICK C. DURANT III, B.S.
Former Assistant Director for Astronautics, National Air and Space Museum, Smithsonian Institution.

**F.L.,** FRANK LITSKY, B.S.
Assistant Sports Editor, New York *Times,* and President, Track Writers Association.

**F.W.,** FAY WILLEY, A.B., M.A.
General Editor, *Newsweek.*

**G.S.,** GIL SEWALL, A.B., A.M., M.S.
Associate Editor, *Newsweek.* Author of *After Hiroshima: America Since 1945.*

**H.H.,** HARVEY HINDIN, B.S., M.S.
Communications Editor, *Electronics Magazine.*

**H.T.H.,** HENRY T. HOPKINS, B.A.E., M.A.E.
Director, San Francisco Museum of Modern Art.

**I.K.,** I. KEPARS, B.A., A.L.A.A.
Chief Reference Librarian, Australian Reference, National Library of Australia. Editor, *Australian Books.*

**I.S.,** IVAN SANDERS, B.A., M.A., PH.D.
Professor of English, Suffolk County Community College.

**J.A.R.,** JANET A. RALOFF, B.S.J., M.S.J.
Policy/Technology Editor, *Science News.*

**J.B.,** JOHN BEAUFORT
Contributing Drama Critic, *The Christian Science Monitor.* Treasurer, New York Drama Critics' Circle.

**J.Bo.,** JEAN BOWEN, A.B., A.M., M.S.
Assistant Chief, Music Division, The New York Public Library.

**J.M.,** JOHN MILWARD, B.S.
Supervising Editor, Funk & Wagnalls Yearbook. Freelance Writer and Editor. Former pop music critic, Chicago *Daily News.*

**J.N.,** JOHN NORMAN, B.A., M.A., PH.D.
Chairman, Department of History and Government, Pace University. State Factfinder, Connecticut Board of Mediation and Arbitration.

**J.N.G.,** JAMES NELSON GOODSELL, B.A., M.A., PH.D.
Latin American Editor, *The Christian Science Monitor.* Author of *The Quest for Change in Latin America.*

**J.O.,** JEANNE O'NEILL, B.A.
Associate Editor, *Science World.*

**J.S.,** JANE SAMZ, A.B., M.A.
Editor, *Science World,* Scholastic Magazines, Inc.

**J.T.S.,** JAMES T. SABIN, B.S., M.A., PH.D.
Vice-President, Editorial, Greenwood Press.

**J.W.K.,** JOHN W. KAMPA, B.S.
Publishing Consultant. Former Executive Vice-President, Oxford Book Company.

**K.B.H.,** KENNETH B. HIGBIE, B.S.
Deputy Director, Research Center Operations, Bureau of Mines, U.S. Department of the Interior.

**L.A.S.,** LESTER A. SOBEL, B.B.A.
Editor, Vice-President, Facts On File, Inc. Author of *Russia's Rulers: The Khrushchev Period* and other books.

**L.H.,** LOUIS HALASZ, J.D.
United Nations Correspondent, International Feature Service. Lecturer on International Affairs.

**L.W.W.,** LARRY W. WATERFIELD, B.S.J.
Washington Editor, Food & Agriculture Group, Vance Publishing Corp. Freelance Writer, Editor, and Consultant on food and agriculture.

**M.H.,** MARION HENDELSON
Merchandising and Fashion Consultant to retail stores and manufacturers. Former Lecturer, Merchandising, Laboratory Institute of Merchandising.

**M.M.,** MAGGIE MALONE, B.A., M.L.S.
Researcher/Reporter with the Art Section, *Newsweek.*

**M.S.O.,** M. SHELDON OSBORN
Business Writer.

**N.P.,** NEAL PRONEK, B.B.A.
Managing Editor, T.F.H. Publications, Inc. Former Managing Editor, *Tropical Fish Hobbyist.*

**N.T.G.,** NANCY TRILLING GOLDNER, B.A.
Dance Critic, *The Christian Science Monitor, Soho News.*

**O.U.,** OWEN ULLMANN, B.A., M.A.
National Labor Correspondent for the Associated Press.

**R.B.,** RONALD BENREY, B.S., M.S.
Science Writer. Author of *How to Get the Most from an Electronic Calculator* and other books.

**R.F.,** RUSSELL FREEDMAN, B.A.
Freelance Writer and Faculty Member, The New School for Social Research. Author of *Immigrant Kids* and other books.

**R.H.,** ROBERT HALASZ, A.B., M.A.
Editor, Funk & Wagnalls Yearbook. Former Editor, *World Progress.*

**R.J.C.,** RAYMOND J. CARROLL, B.A.
General Editor and United Nations Bureau Chief, *Newsweek.* Author of *Dwellers in an Icy World* and *Finding a New World.*

**R.J.S.,** ROBERT J. SHAW, B.S., B.A., M.S.
Freelance Writer. Author of *Libraries: Building for the Future.*

**R.M.,** ROSEMARY MAYER, A.B.
Art Critic for *Arts, Art in America,* and other publications. Cofounder of the first women artists' gallery.

**R.N.O.,** RICHARD N. OSTLING, A.B., M.S.J., M.A.
Religion Editor, *Time.* Former President, Religion Newswriters Association. Author of *Secrecy in the Church.*

**R.P.P.,** RAYMOND P. POINCELOT, B.A., PH.D.
Associate Professor of Botany; Chairman, Biology Department, Fairfield University.

**R.W.S.,** RUTH W. STIDGER, B.A.
Editorial Director, International Group, Technical Publishing Company. Author of *The Competence Game: How to Find, Use, and Keep Competent Employees* and other books.

**S.C.L.,** STEPHEN C. LEWIS, B.A., M.A., PH.D.
Chairman, Humanities Division, Suffolk County Community College. Coauthor of *Focus on the Written Word* and *Student Critic.*

**S.M.,** STEVEN MOLL, B.A.
Supervising Editor, Funk & Wagnalls Yearbook. Freelance Science Writer and Editor.

**S.P.W.,** SUSAN P. WALTON, B.A., M.A.
Features and News Editor/Writer, *Bioscience.* Former Science Writer Intern for *Science News* and National Cancer Institute.

**S.W.,** SUSAN WEST, B.A., M.A.
Earth Sciences Editor, *Science News.*

**T.D.,** THOMAS DEFRANK, B.A., M.A.
Correspondent, *Newsweek.*

**T.L.K.,** THOMAS L. KENNEDY, A.B., M.A., PH.D.
Acting Dean, College of Sciences and Arts, Washington State University. Author of articles on China.

**V.L.,** VINCE LOVETT
Public Information Specialist, Bureau of Indian Affairs, U.S. Department of the Interior. Writer of *Indian News Notes,* for Indian tribal and organizational publications.

**W.A.C.,** WILLIAM A. CHECK, B.S., PH.D.
Associate Editor, *JAMA Medical News.*

**W.E.M.,** WILLIAM E. METCALF, A.B., A.M., PH.D.
Chief Curator and Curator of Roman and Byzantine Coins, The American Numismatic Society. Adjunct Associate Professor, Department of Art History and Archaeology, Columbia University.

**W.M.,** WEBSTER MARTIN, B.A., C.E.P.
Managing Editor, *Europe Magazine.* Financial desk, *International Herald Tribune.*

# PICTURE CREDITS

110 Ponomareff/Gamma-Liaison
111 Canadian Consulate
113 Wide World
114 Lawrence Livermore Laboratory
116 Gamma-Pekin/Liaison
117 Wide World
118 Xinhua News Agency
119 UPI
120 Wilmer White/Gamma-Liaison
121 U.S. Department of the Treasury
123 Gamma Paris/Liaison
124 S. Basak/Gamma-Liaison
125 Bell Labs
126 Bell Labs
127 Alain Dejean/Sygma
130 Wide World
131 Howard J. Rubenstein Associates, Inc.
134 UPI
135 Owen Franken/Sygma
138 *Clockwise from Upper Left:* Herbert Migdall; UPI; Lois Greenfield
140 Philippot-Goldberg/Sygma
141 UPI
143 Wide World
144 Al Giddings/Sea Films, Inc./© 1980 National Geographic Society
146 UPI
147 UPI
149 Atlanta Chamber of Commerce
150 Wide World
152 UPI
153 UPI
154 Wide World
155 Wally MacNamee/Newsweek
157 UPI
158 *Top, Right:* Wide World
159 UPI
161 Chauvel/Sygma
162 Tenneco photo by B. J. Nixon
165 Philippot/Sygma
166 Wide World
169 Michael Norcia-Atelier/Photoreporters, Inc.
170 *Top, Left:* Malden Luxury Fabrics, Inc.; *Top, Right:* Sterns; *Bottom:* Sterns
172 *Top:* Saludi/Gamma-Liaison; *Bottom:* Sterns
173 Chauvel/Sygma
174 French Embassy Press and Information Division
175 UPI
177 Sven Simon/Katherine Young
178 German Information Center
179 UPI
181 *Top:* Wide World; *Bottom:* British Information Services
182 Marlow/Sygma
183 Keystone
184 *Both Pictures:* Greek Press and Information Services
185 Keystone
188 Tom Kelly
189 Tom Kelly
190 Tom Monaster/New York *Daily News*
191 Tony Jerome/New York *Times*
192 Tom Kelly
193 Ames Research Center/NASA
194 National Institute of Dental Research
196 *Top:* Robert Halasz; *Bottom:* Time Street-Porter/AIA
198 *Top:* Santosh Basak/Gamma-Liaison; *Bottom:* Keystone
200 Kateri Foundation
201 Bettmann Archive
203 Kalarsi/Sygma
204 Wide World
205 UPI
206 Jacques Pavlovsky/Sygma
207 Claude Salhani/Gamma-Liaison
208 David Rubinger/© Time, Inc.
209 Benami Neumann/Gamma-Liaison
210 Wide World
211 Vezio Sabatini/Photoreporters, Inc.
212 Giansanti/Sygma
213 Japan Information Center
214 Sekai Bunka
217 François Lochon/Gamma-Liaison
218 UPI

220 Amalgamated Clothing and Textile Workers Union
221 UPI
222 Zimberoff/Sygma
223 Henri Bureau/Sygma
225 Robert Halasz
226 Mario Leanza/Gamma-Liaison
228 *Left:* University of Illinois; *Right:* Yale University
229 Jim Pozarik/Liaison
231 Goodyear Tire and Rubber Co.
232 *Top:* © 1980 National Geographic Society; *Bottom:* TASS from Sovfoto
233 Jerry Bauer
234 *Top:* © Thomas Victor; *Center:* © Paul Davis; *Bottom:* © Thomas Victor-New Directions Publishing Corp.
235 The White House
238 Harcourt Brace Jovanovich
239 *Clockwise from Upper Left:* Saxon Donnelly/University of California at Berkeley; © Vera Kundera; Sophe Bassouls-Rush/Katherine Young; Wide World; Sven Simon/Katherine Young
240 Charles Scribner's Sons
243 Inland Steel Co.
244 Tom Walters/Business Week
245 UPI
246 Wide World
248 The New York *Times*
249 UPI
250 Wide World
251 UPI
252 U.S. Navy
255 *Top:* UPI; *Bottom:* Tom Kelly
258 Cindy Charles/Gamma-Liaison
259 Wide World
260 Christine Spengler/Sygma
261 20th Century-Fox
262 20th Century-Fox
263 *Top:* S. Kong/Sygma; *Bottom:* S. Tretick/Sygma
264 *Top:* Photo Trends; *Bottom:* 20th Century-Fox
265 New World Pictures
266 David Strick/Pictorial Parade
268 Colbert Artists Management, Inc.
269 Abramson/Liaison
271 Mark Sherman/Pictorial Parade
272 K. Jewell
273 *Top:* UPI; *Bottom:* Wide World
274 Netherlands Consulate
277 *Top, Left:* Diego Goldberg/Sygma; *Top, Right:* UPI; *Bottom:* Lehtikuva/Pentti Koskinen/Photoreporters, Inc.
279 Alain Nogues/Sygma
281 *Top:* Nation Newspapers/Sygma; *Bottom:* The Times, London/Pictorial Parade
282 Katherine Young
283 *Top:* Pictorial Parade; *Bottom:* Wide World
284 Phil Burchman/Pictorial Parade
285 *Top:* UPI; *Bottom:* The Times, London/Pictorial Parade
286 UPI
287 *Top:* UPI; *Bottom:* UPI
288 *Top:* Pictorial Parade; *Bottom:* Katherine Young
289 *Clockwise from Upper Right:* Paris Match/Pictorial Parade; Culver Pictures; Arthur Grace/Sygma
290 UPI
291 *Top:* Keystone; *Bottom:* Keystone
292 Keystone
293 *Top:* Keystone; *Bottom:* Culver
294 UPI
295 Ledru/Sygma
296 Dejean/Sygma
297 Maureen Lembray/Gamma-Liaison
298 Saddeh/Gamma-Liaison
300 John T. Barr/Gamma-Liaison
301 *Top:* UPI; *Bottom:* New York *Daily News*
302 *Top:* UPI; *Bottom:* Fred Conrad/Sygma
303 *Top:* UPI; *Bottom:* UPI
304 *Top:* UPI; *Bottom:* UPI
305 *Clockwise from Upper Left:* Sipa Press/Black Star; New York *Daily News*; Angeli/Gamma-Liaison
306 *Top:* Wide World; *Bottom:* UPI
307 *Top:* UPI; *Bottom:* UPI
308 *Top:* UPI; *Bottom:* Sven Simon/Katherine Young
309 *Top:* Sven Simon/Katherine Young; *Bottom:* Sven Simon/Katherine Young

# INDEX
# TO THE
# 1981 YEARBOOK
## EVENTS OF 1980

## INTRODUCTION

This Index is a comprehensive listing of persons, organizations, and events that are discussed in the 1981 Yearbook. Entries in **boldface** letters indicate subjects on which the Yearbook has an individual article. Entries in lightface type are to individual references within articles. In either type of entry, the letters a and b refer, respectively, to the left and right column of the page cited. If no letter follows a page number, the reference is to text that is printed across the full width of a page. Only the first significant mention of a subject in a given article has been included in the Index.

In a main entry such as **Australia:** 91a, the first number refers to the page on which the article begins. The succeeding lightface page numbers refer to other text discussions in the volume. The first number in lightface entries, when not in numerical order, will similarly provide the most extensive information on the subject. If, as in **Congress of the United States:** 129a; Elections, 153b, another title precedes the second page reference, the discussion is located in the titled subentry in the page location mentioned. In the case of comprehensive articles such as the **United States of America,** reference is made to the page location of the beginning of the article. The discussion of foreign relations of the United States in that article may be augmented by reference to separate articles on the countries and international organizations concerned.

When an entry is followed by the abbreviation **illus.,** the reference is to a caption and picture on the page mentioned. When a text mention and an illustration of a specific subject fall within the same article, only the text location is included in the index.

### LIST OF ABBREVIATIONS USED IN THE INDEX

FALN   Armed Forces of National
  Liberation
NATO   North Atlantic Treaty Or-
  ganization

OPEC   Organization of Petroleum
  Exporting Countries
PLO   Palestine Liberation Organi-
  zation
SALT   strategic arms limitation
  talks

U.N.   United Nations
U.S.   United States
U.S.S.R.   Union of Soviet Socialist
  Republics

Brezhnev, Leonid I.: 308a, 69a, 106a, 179b, 413a, 431a
Brezhnev Doctrine: 127a
Brilab probe: 134a
Brinkley, David: 397b
Brinkley, Joel: 332a
British Columbia: 462
Brooks, Edwin B., Jr.: 195a
Brooks, Herb: 379a
Brown, Harold: 107b
Brown, Janice: 303b
Brown, Rachel Fuller: 282a
Bruner, Mike: 374b
Bryant, Anita: 305a
Brzezinski, Zbigniew: 106a
Bucaram, Assad: 148b
Buckner, Pam: 365b
Buddhism: 345a
budget, U.S.: 130a; **illus.** 419a
Buettner-Janusch, John: 305b
**Bulgaria:** 105b, 438
Bullard, Edward: 282a
Bumpers, Dale: 160b
Burger, Warren E.: 384b
Burhoe, Ralph Wendell: 332b
**Burma:** 106a, 438
Burnham, Forbes: 186b
Burpee, David: 282a
burros: **illus.** 166a
Burton, Richard: **illus.** 402
Burundi: 438
Bush, George H.W.: 308b, 154a, 346a, 396b; **illus.** 59
business. *See* ECONOMY AND BUSINESS
Buss, Jerry: 363b
Byrd, Henry: 282a

# C

**Cabinet, United States:** 106a
cable television: 393a
Cabral, Luis de Almeida: 72a
Caetano, Marcello: 282a
California: 142b, 382a, 421b, 456
Callaghan, James: 182a
Calvin, Melvin: 115a
Calvino, Italo: **illus.** 238a
**Cambodia (Kampuchea):** 108a, 124a, 127a, 345b, 399b, 438; U.N., 416b
*Camelot:* 401a
Cameroon: 438
Campbell, Earl: 368a
Campbell, Rich: 368a
**Canada:** 109b, 167b, 204a, 438, 462; Fisheries, 174b; Literature, 236b; Petroleum, 319a; Sports, 369a
canals: 79b, 97a, 299b
cancer: 188a, 228a, 383a, 419b
Canterbury Cathedral: **illus.** 338
Cape Verde: 438
capital punishment: 349b, 383b, 385b
Carazo Odio, Rodrigo: 133a
**Caribbean Countries:** 112b, 417b, 420b
Carl XVI Gustaf: **illus.** 348
Carlton, Steve: 362b
Carner, JoAnne: 369a
Caroline, Princess: 305a
Carreira, Henrique ("Iko"): 76b
Carson, Johnny: 304a
Cartan, Henri: 332b
Carter, Amy: **illus.** 235
Carter, Billy: 107a, 302a, 329a; **illus.** 226a

Carter, Caron: 305a
Carter, Chip: 305a
Carter, Jimmy (James Earl, Jr.): 328a, 8, 94a, 106a, 120b, 136a, 145a, 179a, 213b, 248a, 273a, 280b, 318a, 345b, 397a, 427a, 431a; **illus.** 52a, 101; Congress, 129a; Democratic Party, 139b; Elections, 153b; Energy, 163a; Labor, 219b; Military and Naval Affairs, 251b; U.N., 417a; U.S., 418a; U.S.S.R., 413a
Carter, Rosalynn: **illus.** 235, 329
Castro (Ruz), Fidel: 309a, 135b
Catholicism: 337a
Caulkins, Tracy: 374b
Cawley, Evonne Goolagong: 375a
Ceaușescu, Elena: **illus.** 348
Ceaușescu, Nicolae: 348b
census: 274a, 421a
Central African Republic: 438
Ceylon. *See* SRI LANKA
Cézanne, Paul: **illus.** 85a
Chad: 70b, 227a, 438
Chakrabarty, Ananda Mohan: 228a
Chamorro, Violeta Barrios de: 276a
Chamoun, Dany: 223a
Champion, Gower: 282a, 401a
Chao Chi-yang: **illus.** 61b
Charles, Prince: **illus.** 183, 434
Charter 77: 136b
**Chemistry:** 114b, 330b
Chenoweth, Dean: 364b
Chiang Ch'ing: 117a
Child, Julia: 332b
children's literature: 240a
**Chile:** 115b, 438
**China, People's Republic of:** 116a, 19, 175b, 243b, 347b, 351b, 399b, 407a, 426b, 433a, 438; Agriculture, 75a; Art, 87a; Communism, 127a; Literature, 240a; Military and Naval Affairs, 254b; Religion, 341a; Taiwan, 389a; U.S., 424b; U.S.S.R., 415a
China, Republic of. *See* TAIWAN
Chinaglia, Giorgio: 373b
Chňoupek, Bohuslav: 137b
Choi Kyu Hah: 216b
Christianity: 24, 337a, 422b
**Chronology for 1980:** 52a
Chrysler Corp.: 93b, 100b, 391b, 418b
Chun Doo Hwan: 309a, 216b, 257a
Church, Frank: 157a
circuits, electric: 392a
city planning. *See* ARCHITECTURE AND CITY PLANNING
Civil Aeronautics Board: 406b
Civiletti, Benjamin R.: 107a, 329b
**Civil Rights and Civil Liberties:** 119a, 92a, 133b, 272a, 354b, 384b
Clark, Ed: 154a
Clark, Joe: 109b
Clarke, Cyril A.: 332a
Clarke, Everett: 135a
Clarke, John Cooper: 235b
classical music: 266a
Clausen, A. W.: 101a
Clayton, Billy: 384a
climatology: 144b, 359a
Cline, Martin: 192b, 229b
Clinton, Bill: 160a
cloning: 192a

Clurman, Harold: 282b
coal: 163b, 200b
cobalt: 257b
Cochran, Jacqueline: 282b
Codex: 370b
Coe, Sebastian: 375b
Cohen, Geula: 208a
Cohen, Stanley N.: 332a
**Coin Collecting:** 122a
Collins, Cardiss: 274a
Collins, Steve: 373a
**Colombia:** 123a, 425b, 438
Colombo, Emilio: **illus.** 169
Colorado: 382b, 421b, 456
*Columbia* (spacecraft): 358b
Comaneci, Nadia: 369b
Comecon. *See* COUNCIL FOR MUTUAL ECONOMIC ASSISTANCE
comets: 89b
Common Market. *See* EUROPEAN COMMUNITIES
**Commonwealth of Nations:** 124a
**Communications:** 125a, 102b, 152b, 359a, 392b
**Communism:** 127a, 13, 176a, 202b, 326a, 327b
Comoros: 438
computers: 125b, 254a, 390b
Conference of Islamic States: 202a, 247a
Congo: 440
Congress, Library of: **illus.** 225
**Congress of the United States:** 129a, 253a, 353a, 384b, 418a, 432b; Crime, 133b; Democrats, 139b; Elections, 153b; Nuclear Power, 279b; Petroleum, 318a; President, 328b; Republicans, 345b; Transportation, 408a; Women, 427b
Congressional Black Caucus: 274a
Conley, Kathleen: 306a
Connally, John B.: 346a
Connecticut: 382b, 421b, 456
Connelly, Marc: 282b
Conner, Bart: 370a
Conner, Dennis: 364b
Connors, Jimmy: 374b
conservation: 131a, 162a, 164b, 231b, 386a, 419a
constitution, Canadian: 111b
**Construction:** 131a, 407b; **illus.** 351; Housing, 195a
Contreras Véliz, Alvaro: 186a
conventions, political: 140a, 346b, 396b, 427b; **illus.** 60a
Converse, Richard: 231a
cookery: 36
"Cooper, D. B.": 302a
cooperatives, apartment: 195a
Copts: 151b, 345a
Córdova Rivas, Rafael: 276a
Corman, James: 159a
Corso, Gregory: 235b
cosmic rays: 325a
Cossiga, Francesco: 210b; **illus.** 169
**Costa Rica:** 132b, 440
Costello, Pat: 365b
Costle, Douglas M.: 166b
Council for Mutual Economic Assistance: 128b, 147b
Cousins, Robin: 372a
Cowley, Malcolm: 332b
Cowper, David Scott: 303a
Cox, Robert: 84a
Craig, Jim: 379b
Crane, Philip M.: 346a
Cranston, Alan: 160b

472

National Council of Churches: 340a
National Science Foundation: 392b
natural gas. See PETROLEUM AND NATURAL GAS
Nauru: 448
Navon, Yitzhak: 152b, 208b
Navratilova, Martina: 374b
Nebraska: 382b, 421b, 458
**Negroes in the United States:** 272a, 151a, 159b, 194a, 219b, 384b; Civil Rights, 119a; Crime, 134a; U.S., 420a
Nehemiah, Renaldo: 375a
Nelson, Charles M.: 78a
Nelson, Gaylord: 157a
Nenni, Pietro: 288b
Nepal: 448
**Netherlands:** 274b, 168b, 448
neutrinos: 90b, 323b
Nevada: 383b, 421b, 458
New Brunswick: 462
Newfoundland: 110b, 462
New Hampshire: 421b, 458
New Hebrides. See VANUATU
Ne Win: 106a
New Jersey: 382b, 421b, 458
New Mexico: 382b, 421b, 458
newspapers: 121b, 126a, 331b, 335a
New York: 200a, 383a, 421b, 458
New York Islanders: 371a
**New Zealand:** 275a, 448
Nguyen Co Thach: 425b
Nguyen Duy Trinh: 425b
Nguyen Lam: 425b
Nguza Karl-i-Bond: 432a
Niatross: 370a
**Nicaragua:** 275b, 448
Nicklaus, Jack: 369a
Nickles, Don: 157b
Nielsen, Arthur Charles: 288b
Niger: 448
**Nigeria:** 276a, 448
Nimeiry, Gaafar al-: 72a, 384a
nitrites: 74a, 189a
Nixon, Richard M.: 301a
Nkomo, Joshua: 433a
Nobel Prizes: 330b
Nordli, Odvar: 279a
**North Atlantic Treaty Organization:** 276b, 128a, 182b, 185b, 279b, 360b
North Carolina: 421b, 458
North Dakota: 383a, 421b, 458
Northern Ireland: 183a, 207a
North Korea. See KOREA, DEMOCRATIC PEOPLE'S REPUBLIC OF
Northwest Territories: 110b, 462
North Yemen. See YEMEN ARAB REPUBLIC
**Norway:** 278b, 197a, 448
Nouira, Hedi: 410b
Nova Scotia: 462
**Nuclear Power:** 279b, 130b, 141b, 175a, 199a, 419b; Construction, 132b; Military and Naval Affairs, 254a; NATO, 278a; Sweden, 387a
numismatics. See COIN COLLECTING
Nureyev, Rudolf: 139a
Nyerere, Julius K.: 390b, 411a

# O

Oates, Joyce Carol: **illus.** 233b
**Obituaries:** 281a

Obote, Milton: 411a
O'Brien, Eugene: 332a
O'Brien, John A.: 289a
oceanography: 144a
O'Connor, Carroll: **illus.** 395
Off Broadway: 404a
Off Off Broadway: 400b
Ogaden: 70b, 168b, 352b
Ohio: 382a, 421b, 458
Ohira, Masayoshi: 212a, 289a
oil. See PETROLEUM AND NATURAL GAS
Ojok, David Oyite: 412a
Oklahoma: 421b, 458
Olson, Allen: 160b
Olympic Games: 376a, 369b, 413a
Oman: 317a, 448
Omega 7: 135a
Onassis, Christina: 305a
Ontario: 462
Open, George: 332a
opera: 266a
orchestras: 266a
Oregon: 383a, 421b, 458
Organization of African Unity: 71a, 259b
**Organization of American States:** 294b, 104a, 113b, 195a
**Organization of Petroleum Exporting Countries:** 295a, 148a, 317b, 349b
Orr, Robert: 160b
Orsini, Betty Swenson: 332a
Osserman, E. F.: 229a
Ovett, Steve: 375b
Owens, Jesse: 289a

# P

"Pablo Picasso: A Retrospective": 85b
**Pacific Islands:** 296a, 184a
Packwood, Robert: 160b
Pahlavi, Mohammed Riza: 153a, 289b, 300a; **illus.** 54a
**Pakistan:** 297a, 199b, 423a, 448
Pal, George: 290a
paleontology: 232a
**Palestine Liberation Organization:** 299a, 78b, 224a, 247a, 340b
Palme, Olof: 247b, 387a, 416b
Palmieri, Doria: 305a
**Panama:** 299b, 448
Panchen Lama: 116b, 345b
pandas: 231b
paper: 243a
Papua New Guinea: 448
**Paraguay:** 300a, 448
Parks, Bert: 394a
Parsons, Anthony: **illus.** 416
Passion Play: **illus.** 343
Pastorini, Dan: 368a
Patrick, Lynn: 290a
Patterson, William Allan: 290a
Pauley, Jane: 304b
Pavarotti, Luciano: **illus.** 269
"Paysan en Blouse Bleue": **illus.** 85a
pay television: 398a
Paz García, Policarpo: 195a
Peace Prize, Nobel: 331a
Pennsylvania: 383b, 421b, 458
**People in the News:** 301a
Pérez, Carlos Andrés: 290a
Pérez Esquivel, Adolfo: 331a
periodicals: 334a
**Persian Gulf States:** 317a

**Peru:** 317a, 80a, 448
pest control: 231a
pesticides: 114b
Petraglia, Johnny: 365a
**Petroleum and Natural Gas:** 317b, 15, 76a, 109b, 117b, 180b, 200b, 202a, 204b, 205b, 210b, 219b, 242a, 247a, 276b, 278b, 328b, 382b, 384a; Congress, 129a; Economy, 148a; Energy, 162a; Mexico, 245a; OPEC, 295a; Saudi Arabia, 349b; U.S., 418b; U.S.S.R., 412b
Petruseva, Natalia: 372a
**Pets:** 319b
Peyton, Malcolm C.: 332a
Pham Tuan: **illus.** 356b
Pham Van Dong: 425b
Philadelphia Phillies: 361a
philately. See STAMPS, POSTAGE
**Philippines:** 320b, 448
Phillips, O. A. ("Bum"): 368b
**Photography:** 322a, 331b
photosynthesis: 114b
**Physics:** 323b, 331b
Piaget, Jean: 290a
Picasso, Pablo: 85b; **illus.** 322
Pinkowski, Josef: 326a
Pinochet Ugarte, Augusto: 115b
Pinsky, Robert: 332a
Pinter, Harold: **illus.** 404b
Pinto Balsemão, Francisco: 328a
pipelines: 319a
Piquet, Nelson: 361a
planets: 87a
plate tectonics: 143a
*Playing for Time:* 395a
Plunkett, Jim: 368a
plutonium: 280b
Poetzsch, Anett: 372a
**Poland:** 325b, 73a, 127a, 238b, 341a, 424a, 448; **illus.** 61; East Germany, 176a; U.S.S.R., 414a
Polisario: 71a, 259a
Pollack, William: 332a
pollution: 165a, 419b
Pol Pot: 108a, 127a
Poniatowski, Michel: 175a
Popov, Leonid I.: 357a, 414a
popular music: 270a
pornography: 102a, 134a, 261a, 340a, 422b
Porter, Katherine Anne: 290a
**Portugal:** 327a, 448
Potro, Miran: 431b
Potts, Jack: 385b
Powell, Lewis F., Jr.: 384b
Powers, John A. ("Shorty"): 290a
Prem Tinsulanonda: 399a
**President of the United States:** 328a, 8
Preyer, Richardson: 159a
Prince, Harold: 405a
Prince Edward Island: 462
prisons: 135a
**Prizes and Awards:** 330a, 83b, 236b, 265b, 323b, 333a, 396a, 405a
Prokudin-Gorskii, S. M.: 322b
*Propliopithecus:* 77a
Protestantism: 337b
Pryor, Richard: 304a
psychiatry: 194a
psychology. See BEHAVIORAL SCIENCES
public utilities: 163b, 279b
**Publishing:** 332b, 68a, 121b, 317b, 322b, 331a, 385a, 392b, 397a
**Puerto Rico:** 335b, 421b, 460
Pulitzer Prizes: 331b, 323b

478

479